THE LAW OF INVESTMENT MANAGEMENT

By

Harvey E. Bines

Member of the
Massachusetts and Virginia Bars

WARREN, GORHAM & LAMONT

Boston

For Joan

and for

Jonathan, Joel and Susanne

FOREWORD

Investment managers today are subject to a multitude of legal responsibilities which are sometimes cumulative, but also, not infrequently, duplicative or inconsistent. It is a formidable task to analyze the substance of and the interrelationships between established and evolving common-law principles of agency, trust and torts, federal and state securities laws, federal regulation of the investment management services of foundations and banks, and federal regulation of pension fund investment managers under the Employee Retirement Income Security Act of 1974 (ERISA). This treatise affords an overview of this environment and, in a very real sense, a path through the complex maze of legal restrictions and obligations governing investment managers today. In so doing, it provides an understanding and a perspective for an assessment of the law of investment management.

Publication of this treatise is particularly welcome at this time. In 1971, the Securities and Exchange Commission, in its *Institutional Investor Study Report*, reviewed the growing institutionalization of the securities markets up through the 1960s. To a limited extent, the *Report* also highlighted some of the legal problems arising from this institutional activity and the accompanying institutional competition for performance and asset management. It also brought into focus the conflicts of interest arising from financial integration and the multiple roles of many institutional investment managers. The institutionalization trend has continued, accompanied by Commission enforcement activities and private litigation which have done much to spell out new legal limits for institutional investment managers.

Congress also has not been inactive. ERISA, enacted in 1974, spells out a complex set of obligations and restrictions applicable to investment managers and other pension plan fiduciaries. The Securities Reform Act of 1975 made several changes in the federal regulation of investment management, including provision for a limited form of separation of brokerage and investment management; authorization for the Commission to require institutional-sized investment managers to report their securities holdings and transactions; special protection to enable investment managers executing portfolio transactions for accounts under their management to pay more than the lowest commission costs under limited circumstances; and amendment of the Investment Company Act of 1940 to make clear that investment advisers to investment companies might benefit, under specified circumstances, in connection with the transfer of their advisory office.

v

Furthermore, as an expression of focused congressional interest in the securities activities of banks, Section 11A(e) was added to the Exchange Act to formally authorize and direct the Commission to study the extent to which banks maintain accounts for public customers for buying and selling publicly held securities and whether the exclusion of banks from the statutory definition of "brokers" and "dealers" should be continued. The Commission has just completed that effort, which includes a study of bank investment management and advisory services. Congressional hearings on legislation to implement the report is in the offing. As another example of congressional interest in investment management, in 1976, Congress considered at some length—and the Senate passed—a bill amending the Investment Advisers Act of 1940 to provide the Commission with significant added authority under that statute.

While all this activity has been going on, the SEC itself has been attempting to come to grips with the changing pattern of investment management. Thus, in August 1972, as part of a major reorganization of the Commission, the Division of Investment Management Regulation was formed with responsibility to administer the Commission's programs under the Investment Company and Investment Advisers Acts. The Division was also charged, as the Commission's budget presentation made clear, with developing "a uniform and coordinated approach to the entire area of investment management and [determining] if amendments to statutes or rules are required." Mr. Bines, as a visiting professor, worked with me and other members of the Division's staff in formulating a program intended to meet that objective. It may well be that this treatise is a product, in part, of the spadework Mr. Bines participated in then.

More recently, the newly named Division of Investment Management has undertaken a broad comprehensive review of the regulation of investment management. As Chairman Hills has described it, the study "will have two main thrusts"—". . . a 'spring cleaning' of the Investment Company Act" and an examination ". . . whether a statute which relates only to 'investment companies' as presently defined, is adequate to protect today's investor." The goal of these efforts is, in the Chairman's words, ". . . to put all investment funds, whether under the jurisdiction of ERISA, Bank Regulatory Agencies or the SEC on the same regulatory standard. . . ."

In the long run, while this treatise will be of great service to practicing attorneys, businessmen, scholars, and students, perhaps its most significant value lies in the legal foundation it will provide for the conclusions and recommendations of the policy makers at the Commission and in the Congress who are engaged in these regulatory review efforts. Some may agree with Mr. Bines' observations and conclusions; others may disagree. But there should be no dispute over the value and quality of this comprehensive, carefully considered, well-presented, and well-documented treatise on the law of investment management. It is a remarkable and imaginative work and an important reference for all the diverse entities and individuals involved in investment management or in counseling those who are.

ALLAN S. MOSTOFF

Washington, D.C.
July 1977

PREFACE

The emergence of investment management as a recognized and distinct profession necessarily has had as a cost expanding governance of its activities by the law. Consequently, it seemed to me to be timely and useful to gather and discuss the principal legal developments currently affecting investment managers. This book, however, is not written merely for the purpose of collating, organizing, and indexing investment management law. Rather, I have tried to present existing law in a fashion emphasizing the process by which general principles have become rules of conduct, the better to aid understanding of sources of future growth in the law.

Limits on a project of this nature are necessarily arbitrary. For the most part, the emphasis has been on federal law, state common law, and uniform acts. Local regulation, even for states where regulation is comprehensive, is discussed only in this context and generally for the purpose of illustration.

I am grateful to many for the help they gave me. Allan S. Mostoff generously furnished teaching materials and advice as I began my study of investment management, and he made a summer at the Securities and Exchange Commission instructive and interesting. John L. Casey somehow found time to review the entire manuscript and offer many suggestions for improvement. Many others have seen portions of the manuscript in earlier draft, and their criticisms have been important aids to me. I especially want to thank Thomas F. Bergin, Norman A. Bikales, Charles J. Goetz, and Roy A. Schotland.

Equally important to completion of this project has been the research, editorial, and administrative support I have received. Carol Launer has combined her marvelous talent as editor with the right blend of tolerance, good humor, and flattery to sharpen and refine the manuscript. The efforts of Stephen R. Kruft and Margaret Reamy Ancarrow far exceeded that which reasonably may be asked of student assistants. The editorial boards of the *Columbia Law Review* and the *Boston College Industrial and Commercial Law Review* were very helpful with earlier drafts of portions of the manuscript which were published as articles. The staff of the Law Library at the University of Virginia were an invaluable asset in finding and obtaining documents and publications promptly. Susan Mentser has been diligent and tenacious in checking citations for form and accuracy. Finally, I have had careful and accurate typing of the various drafts of the manuscript. Sandy

Harris and Debbie Dodson in Charlottesville and Barbara DePesa and Ernestine Potter in Boston deserve special thanks for their close attention to organization and to form which freed me to attend to other things.

HARVEY E. BINES

Boston
October 1977

TABLE OF CONTENTS

PART II ESTABLISHING THE CLIENT-MANAGER RELATIONSHIP

Chapter 3

DEVELOPING NEW BUSINESS

Chapter 5

SPECIAL PROBLEMS IN STRUCTURING THE INVESTMENT MANAGEMENT AGREEMENT

PART III STRUCTURING THE PORTFOLIO

Chapter 6

PROFESSIONAL COMPETENCE IN PORTFOLIO SELECTION

Chapter 7

THE APPLICATION OF MODERN PORTFOLIO THEORY TO LEGAL STANDARDS OF PROFESSIONAL COMPETENCE

PART IV ONGOING MANAGEMENT: EXECUTIONS

Chapter 8

EXECUTING INVESTMENT DECISIONS AS A LEGAL DUTY

Chapter 9

USE OF COMMISSIONS TO PURCHASE SUPPLEMENTARY SERVICES

Part I

PRINCIPLES OF INVESTMENT MANAGEMENT LAW

Chapter 1

THE FUNDAMENTAL PRINCIPLES OF INVESTMENT MANAGEMENT LAW

¶ 1.01. EVOLUTION OF THE FUNDAMENTAL PRINCIPLES

To warrant separate study of the law pertaining to any one area of human activity, two conditions must be satisfied. The activity must be sufficiently varied and detailed to have produced a complex set of rules requiring organized analysis. And the rules must be sufficiently related to be rationalized on the basis of easily understood principles. Both these conditions characterize the law of investment management.

In contemporary America, individual and charitable trusts, endowment funds, pension funds, investment companies, personal agency accounts, and other investment vehicles require extensive investment management to protect savings and provide public services. The very size and variety of these holdings has produced a large body of case law, legislation, and regulations imposing obligations on investment managers and circumscribing their discretion. Complementing the common law of trusts and of agency are diverse federal and state statutes regulating the securities activities of investment managers and the treatment to be afforded different classes of clients. It would be impossible to manage the assets of these investors without taking the obligations thus created into account.

Disparate as these sources of legal duty may appear, however, they are doctrinally related. Historical inquiry reveals that the body of law pertaining to investment management has arrived at its current state on the basis of three identifiable, if unspoken, principles:

(1) The first, a product of the law of negligence, establishes the standard that investment management responsibilities undertaken voluntarily must be carried out with reasonable care.

(2) The second, a fundamental postulate of the law of trusts and the law of agency, maintains that one managing another's wealth must act with undivided loyalty toward the other's interests.

(3) The third, of more recent origin, is an outgrowth of the expanded importance of the securities markets and holds that the

interest of all investors in a properly functioning marketplace obliges each investor to deal openly and fairly with everyone else.

This chapter examines the origin of these principles and tests some of the theory which supports them.

Often, doctrinal origins are traced to a case or a statute as if spontaneous generation were the explanation for the creation of a legal principle. A case decision or a statute represents the crystallized recognition of a principle which has received widespread enough acceptance to be taken as fundamental. The doctrinal origins of other principles are less spectacular. The fundamental principle becomes articulated only after a common theme is recognized as the explanation for a set of events previously only loosely associated. Investment management law has experienced both these phenomena.

[1] The Duty of Reasonable Care and the Duty of Loyalty

The duty of reasonable care is an expression of a principle traceable to a single event, after which virtually all ensuing related legal developments reflected the testing of that principle in different factual contexts. The watershed case expressing the principle that one entrusted with investment management responsibility owes a duty of reasonable care is *Harvard College v. Amory*, decided in 1830.[1] The narrow question was whether a trustee might invest in the stock of manufacturing companies, but the actual holding approving a trustee's discretion to do so—which became a matter of contention for over a century afterwards—is less important than the court's statement of principle justifying its holding:

> "All that can be required of a trustee to invest, is, that he shall conduct himself faithfully and exercise a sound discretion. He is to observe how men of prudence, discretion and intelligence manage their own affairs, not in regard to speculation, but in regard to the permanent disposition of their funds, considering the probable income, as well as the probable safety of the capital to be invested." [2]

After *Harvard College*, this principle, often called the prudent-man rule, became the inescapable starting point for analysis of an investment manager's duty of care. While cases differed in result and statutes varied in the scope of investment discretion they authorized, the question was always whether a particular type of commitment was prudent. The fun-

---

[1] 26 Mass. 446, 9 Pick. 454 (1830) (parallel pagination citations to Pickering omitted hereinafter).

[2] *Id.* at 461.

damental assumption that absent affirmative justification to the contrary, prudence is the proper standard was never again questioned.

Unlike the prudent-man rule, the principle that undivided loyalty is fundamental to an investment management relationship developed more as an expression of distilled wisdom than as the product of a single event. From the early cases came separate rules concerning a trustee's power to purchase assets of a trust,[3] a beneficiary's remedies in the event of such a purchase,[4] a trustee's power to sell trust assets to an organization in which he has an interest,[5] a trustee's power to sell his own property to the trust,[6] a trustee's power to use trust assets for his own interests,[7] a trustee's right to commissions for performing related services,[8] and so forth. The holdings of these cases eventually were perceived as an expression of a prohibition against self-dealing, which in turn became refined into an affirmative duty in the first *Restatement of Trusts* and *Restatement of Agency*. According to the *Restatements*, it is a fundamental principle that a fiduciary act solely in the interests of his beneficiary or principal.[9]

[a]   The emergence of investment management as a profession

Although investment management has been a recognized activity at least since the New Testament told the parable of the talents,[10] its rise as a professional occupation of significance is of more recent origin. In the nineteenth century, the parallel rapid growth of investment opportunity and of personal and charitable trusts with funds to invest led to a need for experienced and competent investment management.[11] To provide such services, individuals became professional trustees and corporations sought and acquired trust powers.[12]

---

[3] E.g., Davoue v. Fanning, 2 Johns. Ch. 252 (N.Y. 1816).

[4] E.g., Hayward v. Ellis, 30 Mass. (13 Pick.) 272 (1832).

[5] E.g., Fulton v. Whitney, 66 N.Y. 548 (1876).

[6] E.g., Smith v. Howlett, 29 App. Div. 182, 51 N.Y.S. 910 (1898).

[7] E.g., Boston & Colo. Smelting Co. v. Reed, 23 Colo. 523, 48 P. 515 (1897).

[8] E.g., Sherman v. Lanier, 39 N.J. Eq. 249 (1884).

[9] *Restatement of Trusts* § 170(1) (1935); *Restatement of Agency* § 387 (1933).

[10] Matt. 25:14-30.

[11] Friedman, "The Dynastic Trust," 73 Yale L.J. 547 (1964).

[12] Compare White v. South Parish, 54 Mass. (13 Met.) 506 (1847) (corporation authorized to exercise trust powers), with Phillips Academy v. King, 12 Mass. 546 (1815) (corporation may not exercise trust powers). See generally 2 A. Scott, *Law of Trusts* § 96.5 (3d ed. 1967) (hereinafter cited as Scott).

But the emergence of the professional trustee and the extension of trust powers to corporations created problems for the law of trusts. Previously, trust law had concerned itself essentially with arrangements arising out of personal commitment rather than business purpose. The new engagements raised questions about the nature of trustee obligations, the investment acumen a trustee should possess, the limits of trustee discretion, and the effects of overlapping interests of trustees and beneficiaries. The birth of the prudent-man rule, the debate over its meaning, and the expansion of the duty of loyalty to cope with subtler situations than blatant self-dealing are all developments largely attributable to the changing character of investment management as trust administration became a business.

Furthermore, even while the law of trusts was adapting to the conceptual nuances resulting from the professionalization of trust management, two structural developments that would ultimately have a profound impact on investment management law occurred. Early in the twentieth century, trustees lost their monopoly over the provision of investment management services as agency arrangements began to evolve. At about the same time, trustees began to manage common trust vehicles in which the assets of many participants would be combined into a single entity. The importance of these two developments was not simply the parallel pressures they put on the law of trusts and the law of agency as separate areas of jurisprudence to respond to new problems. On the contrary, the success of each bred imitation in the other so that in short order investment pools were being managed on an agency basis and trust arrangements were being created which were trusts in name only. The important point is that together these developments created conditions which intensified the pressure on traditional trust principles until they could not adequately respond.

[b] The expanding influence of the contract approach

The immediate effect of the spread of agency relationships and the rise of common trust arrangements was to make the philosophy of contract a much more important element in investment management relationships than had been the case when professional investment management meant professional trusteeship on a personal basis. Unlike a trustee, who has legal title and therefore independent control over the assets placed in his care, an agent is subject to the control of his principal and must act to carry out the instructions expressed or implied in the agency contract. On first impression, this shift in emphasis can be subtle, since the common-law rules governing agency management are ostensibly close to the rules governing trust management. Like the obligation of prudence imposed on trustees,[13] the law of agency imposes its own duty of prudence.[14] Similarly, the duty of loyalty is common to both trust law and agency law.[15] But the scope of an agency derives from the agency contract, and to the courts of the early twentieth century, the philosophy of freedom of contract diverged critically from the philosophy inherent in acceptance of trust. Whereas a whole tradition of equitable duty protected a beneficiary of a trust from overreaching by a trustee, the power of an agent-manager to contract with his principal in derogation of his common-law fiduciary duties enabled such a manager, as a practical matter, to place his client at the mercy of caveat emptor.

But if, with respect to investment management, the conceptual distinction between trust and agency was real, it rapidly became subverted by the rise of common trust arrangements. Of necessity, common trust arrangements require extensive verbal structuring to state the purposes, rights, and obligations of the parties. Since, by its very nature, a common trust can only serve those interests which are common to the participants and cannot be adapted to any one participant's changing needs or desires, the range and scope of its activities must be sharply defined. Furthermore, the fact of widespread participation tends to complicate administration, supervision, and enforcement. Consequently, mechanisms for those functions must be created. In any event, the end result was that as extensive documentation became a dominant characteristic of common trust arrangements, the documentation insidiously took on its own life to the point that trust documents took on independent authority as the source of trustee duties. In effect, it became possible for trustee managers to determine their duties by contract instead of being forced to adhere to traditional fiduciary principles.

By the time of the Great Crash in 1929, pooled investment vehicles had become a significant phenomenon in the financial world. Banks were operating common trust funds, placing mortgage participations, and acting as indenture trustees. Stockbrokers, investment bankers, and investment counselors were also operating pooled investment vehicles, often organized as investment trusts, but also in corporate form as investment companies. Furthermore, whether these pooled accounts took a trust or corporate form, they were contractual creations of the or-

---

[13] *Restatement (Second) of Trusts* §§ 174, 227 (1959).
[14] *Restatement (Second) of Agency* §§ 379, 425 (1958).
[15] *Restatement (Second) of Trusts* § 170 (1959); *Restatement (Second) of Agency* § 387 (1958).

ganizers. No one representing the investors participated in the drafting of the controlling documents, and consequently those responsible for administering these investment vehicles gave themselves extensive contractual protection from the obligations they would have assumed at common law.

The contract approach made itself felt on both the duty of reasonable care and the duty of loyalty. In derogation of the prudent-man rule, contractual provisions in both agency agreements and trust documents exculpating investment managers for their negligence became common. Although there was no question of the validity of such provisions,[16] their purpose was to protect nonprofessional trustees serving as an accommodation to a friend or relative. Nonetheless, despite the irony of relieving a professional investment manager from responsibility for providing competent management services, the very reason he was hired in the first place, the popularity of exculpatory provisions for negligence spread rapidly throughout the investment management community. Indeed, the legitimacy of exculpatory provisions for professional negligence became so well established that they received the apparent endorsement of Congress in the Investment Company Act of 1940.[17] Although ostensibly acting against exculpatory provisions in the organic documents of an investment company, Congress made unlawful only those provisions offering protection from liability to an investment adviser or principal underwriter "by reason of willful misfeasance, bad faith, or gross negligence, in the performance of his duties, or by reason of reckless disregard of his obligations and duties. . . ." [18]

In derogation of the duty of loyalty, contractual provisions authorized investment managers to act while serving conflicting interests. Though the courts agreed that these provisions did not protect against conduct in bad faith, they gave effect to these provisions in ways which largely rendered duty-of-loyalty considerations nugatory. For one thing, because of its moral overtones, bad faith was regarded as a specific intent offense, meaning a complainant would virtually have to prove a design to defraud. More important as a practical matter, however, these contractual provisions were treated as a sufficient basis for shifting the burden of proof from the fiduciary to justify his conduct in a conflict-of-interest situation to the beneficiary or client to show that

---

16 See, e.g., Warren v. Pazolt, 203 Mass. 328, 89 N.E. 381 (1909) (expenditure of $470,000 to improve land valued at $375,000 in estate of $920,000 held negligent, but trustee saved from surcharge by trust provision excusing "neglect").

17 Pub. L. 76-768, 54 Stat. 789 (Aug. 22, 1940).

18 *Id.* § 17(i).

the manager's conduct had in fact caused him injury *as a consequence of the conflict of interest.*

Consider, for example, the case of *Spiegel v. Beacon Participations, Inc.*,[19] decided by one of the country's leading common-law courts. The facts are complex, but in essence, the record shows that the Beacon Trust Co., a bank, formed an investment company affiliate, a practice which was common in the twenties. Beacon Trust kept all the common stock and a subordinated issue of preferred stock in Beacon Participations, and the boards of directors of the two organizations were virtually identical. Beacon Trust operated banking outlets at two locations in facilities owned by another wholly owned affiliate, Beacon Building Trust Co. Shortly after the incorporation of Beacon Participations, the company bought without recourse a demand note from Beacon Trust made by Beacon Building Trust. The transaction was promoted by Beacon Trust's president and it was approved without dissent by Beacon Participations' board of directors. The evidence showed that the note could not have been paid on demand at the time it was purchased, and Beacon Participations ultimately sold it at a large loss.

On this claim,[20] the plaintiff offered two theories for recovery. First,

---

[19] 297 Mass. 398, 8 N.E.2d 895 (1937).

[20] There were three other claims made by plaintiff, each of which, if true, involved conduct by defendant-directors preferring the interests of Beacon Trust (and its successor) or the interests of a stock brokerage firm owned by two of the directors to the interests of the shareholders of Beacon Participations. Plaintiff also alleged that defendant-directors had caused the company unlawfully to use its funds by participating in a joint trading account with a stockbroker, had caused dividends to be paid out of capital when there were no earnings or surplus, and had caused the company to buy its own stock at excessive prices when the capital was impaired. The stockbrokerage firm was owned by two directors of Beacon Participations, and the agreement was that Beacon Participations would finance a trading account for which it and the firm would split profits and losses. The court held this culpably negligent but not a bad-faith transaction. The purpose behind the issuing of dividends from capital was to avoid turning voting control over to the holders of Class A preferred shares, the class of securities owned by plaintiff and issued to the public. Nonetheless, since no creditors of Beacon Participations were affected and since plaintiff and his class received the dividends, this claim was dismissed. Finally, the claim based on the repurchase of Class A preferred stock was also rejected because the repurchase was expressly authorized by the articles of incorporation and there was no injury. Actually, the purpose of the repurchase was to maintain control over the assets in the common stock. See 3 SEC, *Report on Investment Trusts and Investment Companies*, H.R. Doc. No. 136, 77th Cong., 1st Sess. 2593-2595 (1942).

he argued that because of the defendant directors' fiduciary duty to Beacon Participations, the burden was on them to justify the fairness of the transaction. Second, he argued that the directors were culpably negligent in purchasing the note. Because the trial judge had found culpable negligence and his findings were not clearly erroneous, the court affirmed the judgment against the defendant directors on those grounds. But the court also specifically rejected the fiduciary-duty theory, and it did so on grounds of contract. The articles of incorporation of Beacon Participations expressly authorized interlocking directorships and the articles further authorized the directors to engage in transactions on behalf of Beacon Participations with other corporations and associations in which they were interested.

[c] The expanded opportunities for abuse of duty in connection with common investment vehicles

The rise of common trust and agency arrangements also expanded the opportunities for, if not the incidence of, self-dealing on the part of investment managers.[21] In principle, the hazards facing a common investment vehicle need not differ from the hazards facing a set of individual accounts, since an investment manager exercising control over individual accounts could have them act as a unit. But in practice, common investment vehicles are far more exposed to abuse for at least four reasons:

(1) The sheer effort in organizing a number of different accounts to act as a unit and the possibility that participants or co-trustees of at least some of the accounts will object to proposed actions by the investment manager makes common investment vehicles easier to manipulate.

(2) Common investment vehicles are faceless, and compromises

---

[21] For modest trust accounts, the advantages for both trustee and beneficiary in common investment vehicles were substantial, but common-law doctrine made the institution of such vehicles problematic. Even though the terms of the several trusts under management might authorize common investment, rules against commingling, problems of earmarking, self-dealing, valuation, and so forth acted to make administration difficult and to undercut the contractual protection trustees might obtain in the trust instruments. To effect changes in the law necessary to permit trustees to offer common trusts and mortgage participations without excessive exposure, corporate trustees obtained enabling legislation, two of the most notable examples of which concerned commingled trust accounts and mortgage participations. See generally 3 Scott, note 12 *supra*, § 227.9.

which a manager of individual accounts, knowing personally the beneficiaries, settlors and testators, co-trustees, or principals of those accounts, is unwilling to make are much easier to rationalize when the client is an anonymous corporate undertaking.

(3) Common investment vehicles tend to increase the exposure of investment manager trustees to the competing demands of serving as both adviser and promoter in the same transaction. It is a subtle shift, for example, for a trustee using mortgage participations in order to obtain advantageous real estate interests for trust accounts to begin using mortgage participations as a means of floating a mortgage among trust accounts; or to go from placing common trust funds or investment companies into profitable securities commitments to using a common fund or investment company to support an issue in which the manager has other interests; or, as an indenture trustee, to go from protecting holders of corporate debt to accommodating issuers in order to attract additional business or to protect the trustee's own commercial loans.

(4) Perhaps most important, the governing documents for common investment vehicles are the investment manager's own product. The opportunities for the manager to enhance his own discretion while protecting himself from the consequences of exercising his authority to the detriment of beneficiaries are much greater when the trustee drafts the details of his undertakings, as is the case with respect to common investment vehicles, than when the manager must operate within the corners of trust documents or agency contracts drafted by the trustor's or principal's representative, as is generally the case with respect to individual trusts, though less often so with respect to individual agency accounts.

This is not to say that all common investment vehicles are necessarily less secure from overreaching than are individual accounts. On the contrary, the economic power of common investment vehicles makes them potentially safer from abuse and better managed than individual accounts, and, on a one-to-one basis, an individual account is much more at hazard from an incompetent or unethical investment manager. As a practical matter, however, without strong independent oversight for common investment vehicles, their strategic opportunities can easily be transformed into vulnerabilities having much greater collective impact than the negligent or intentional mismanagement of a set of individual accounts. These vulnerabilities were exposed in the Great Crash.

[d] Legislative reinforcement of fiduciary principles

The Great Crash focused attention on and galvanized action against the many ways which a number of the nation's financial institutions had found to serve competing interests, their own included, and it marked the ebb of the law's accommodation of fiduciary duty to contract. Since the courts, either by excessive deference to contract or by an inability to develop remedies adequate to deal with contemporary management practices, had failed to extend to investment management the principles that had developed under trust and agency law, the primary vindication of those principles had to shift to a different forum. In less than a decade, Congress passed seven major statutes[22] to correct securities practices thought to have exacerbated the general economic collapse. One of the primary accomplishments of this legislation was to restore the commitment of investment management law to observance of the traditional fiduciary principles of reasonable care and loyalty.

The new legislation and its implementing regulations brought about the shift in perspective from the contract approach to the fiduciary-duty approach in two ways. One, the more straightforward, was to reshape, redirect, or even, in the extreme, terminate structural relationships through prescription and proscription. For example, one of the purposes of the Glass-Steagall Act's separation of investment banking and commercial and trust banking was to eliminate the debasement of the fiduciary obligations of banks toward their customers possible when underwriting and advisory services are combined.[23] Similarly, in the Investment Company Act of 1940, to prevent self-dealing and to provide independent supervision over the management of investment com-

---

[22] Securities Act of 1933, Ch. 38, Tit. I, 48 Stat. 74; Banking Act of 1933, Ch. 89, 48 Stat. 162; Securities Exchange Act of 1934, Ch. 404, 48 Stat. 881; Public Utility Holding Company Act of 1935, Ch. 687, Tit. I, 49 Stat. 803; Trust Indenture Act of 1939, Ch. 411, 53 Stat. 1149; Investment Company Act of 1940, Ch. 686, Tit. I, 54 Stat. 789; Investment Advisers Act of 1940, Ch. 686, Tit. II, 54 Stat. 847.

[23] The congressional hearings are replete with criticism of the practice of a bank's selling customers' securities in an issue underwritten by the bank. Hearings Pursuant to S. Res. 71 Before a Subcomm. of the Senate Comm. on Banking and Currency, 71st Cong., 3d Sess. (1931). The importance of this factor to application of the statute cannot be overemphasized. For example, in Investment Co. Inst. v. Camp, 401 U.S. 617, 633 (1971), the Court, in disapproving the management of pooled agency accounts by banks

panies, Congress prohibited transactions between and joint transactions with such companies and their affiliates, and it established controls over the structure and operation of statutory companies, including, among other things, the composition of the board of directors, as well as approval and assignment of the advisory contract.

The second change wrought by the spate of new legislation was less immediate in impact, but ultimately more far-reaching. To achieve its purpose of substituting "a philosophy of full disclosure for the philosophy of *caveat emptor*," [24] Congress enacted a number of open-ended antifraud provisions. This method of combating the contract approach had two important consequences : (1) It created a set of federal remedies, thereby evading the restrictions of common-law precedent; and (2) it enabled the federal courts and regulatory authorities to adapt to devices and arrangements which were not conceived of at the time the legislation was passed, and which, though perhaps complying with the letter of the law, circumvented its intent.

[2] The Public-Duty Principle

The disclosure philosophy, as the common theme of federal securities legislation, had both a private and a public aspect. A principal undertaking of Congress was to return some balance to private relationships between investors and those providing them with investment services. In this respect, disclosure was to serve the same function as the fiduciary principle requiring the informed consent of a beneficiary for a trustee, and of a principal for an agent, to act in his own interest or in the interest of another.[25] This principle had suffered extensively under the contract approach (discussed in ¶ 1.01[1][b]); which had accepted contractual authorization as an adequate surrogate for informed consent.

But in addition to redressing the imbalance in private relationships, the disclosure philosophy also formed the foundation of an emerging concept of public duty. One of the ideas implicit in these legislative efforts was that the securities markets are affected with the public inter-

---

as a prohibited underwriting, pointed to the legislative history of the Act in which Congress expressed its concern over "the plain conflict between the promotional interest of the investment banks and the obligation of the commercial banker to render disinterested investment advice."

[24] SEC v. Capital Gains Research Bureau, Inc., 375 U.S. 180, 186 (1963).

[25] *Restatement (Second) of Trusts* § 216 (1959); *Restatement (Second) of Agency* §§ 389-392 (1958).

est and that activities deleterious to a properly functioning market system ought to be prohibited or controlled. This is precisely the mission the regulatory authorities, with the support of the courts, have taken upon themselves. They have extended the jurisdiction of the organic statutes they administer and expanded the definitions of statutory fraud to respond to a variety of activities perceived as harmful to the public interest. While these developments affect everyone in the securities business, they have also had special consequences for investment managers, including the placing of restrictions on their access to and use of investment information and the disclosure of their securities holdings. In short, the notion that there is a general duty to protect the integrity of the marketplace introduced a third principle into the law of investment management. Under the public-duty rationale, investment managers must take into account the effects of their practices on the securities markets as well as on their clients.

[3] The Establishment of Operative Rules: Post-1940 Developments

Adoption of the federal securities laws signaled the entry of investment management law into its period of most creative reform. The nineteenth century had seen the evolution and early development of the principles of reasonable care and of loyalty. The early part of the twentieth century had provided a serious test of the validity of these principles in a head-on contest with the philosophy of contract. The federal securities laws gave these principles renewed legitimacy and vitality and introduced a new principle of public duty. What remained was to translate all three into operative rules and standards.

[a] Rules of conduct evidencing reasonable care

In 1940, the reasonable-care principle affected trustee managers differently from agent managers. Most trustees were subject to restrictive "legal lists" of permissible investments and to vague investment rules, such as the duty to diversify, unless the beneficiaries specified otherwise.[26] Agent managers, on the other hand, had total investment discretion in choosing among investment opportunities, subject only to limiting directions by the client. By and large, the new federal securities laws had done little to affect that situation. Outside of restrictions on capital structure[27] and prescriptions for disclosure of investment policy in the

---

[26] See ¶ 6.02.

[27] Investment Company Act § 18, 15 U.S.C. § 80a-18. One of the purposes of this section was to eliminate speculation through leveraging either

Investment Company Act of 1940,[28] and the imposition in the Trust Indenture Act of 1939 of a general prudent-man standard on indenture trustees[29] with respect to investment management, the federal securities laws had concentrated far more effort on rules to shore up observance of the duty of loyalty than on rules expanding the reasonable-care principle.

But over the next thirty-five years, refinement of the abstract principle of reasonable care into rules of conduct of discernible dimension progressed rapidly. This process manifested itself at the professional, regulatory, and legislative levels in a number of different ways:

(1) An expanding role for professional societies through their rules for membership and their procedures for enforcing professional standards[30];

(2) An increasing emphasis on regulatory doctrine—the suitability and reasonable-basis doctrines, for example—with roots in a reasonable-care standard[31];

---

individual securities or an entire portfolio. See Investment Company Act § 1(b)(7), 15 U.S.C. § 80a-1(b)(7).

[28] Investment Company Act §§ 8(b), 13(a), 15 U.S.C. §§ 80a-8(b), 80a-13(a).

[29] Trust Indenture Act § 315(c), 15 U.S.C. § 77ooo(c).

[30] With respect to securities analysis, the Financial Analysts Federation, the New York Society of Securities Analysts, and the Institute of Chartered Financial Analysts (the latter administering a rigorous multilevel set of examinations which has come to be recognized in many quarters as setting the minimum standards of competence for entry in the absence of state or federal regulation) constitute the principal professional associations concerned primarily with investment selection. Other professional associations —principally the American Bankers Association, the Investment Counsel Association of America, and, to a lesser extent, the securities exchanges and the National Association of Securities Dealers—set standards of care in investment management for securities analysis also, but their scope extends to general financial counseling, suitability, custodianship, and related activities of investment managers. Although the efforts of this latter group of organizations have emphasized ethical considerations much more than standards of professional competence, there is no question that attention to such standards is a matter of growing concern. See, e.g., Testimony of Chairman of the Investment Counsel Association of America, in Hearings on S. 2849 Before the Subcomm. on Securities of the Senate Comm. on Banking, Housing and Urban Affairs, 94th Cong., 2d Sess. 274 (1976).

[31] The suitability doctrine is discussed more fully in ¶ 4.01[2], and the reasonable-basis doctrine in ¶ 7.07[1]. Both developed in connection with the selling practices of broker-dealers, and the enabling authorities through which they are applied are refinements of the statutory fraud provisions of

(3) Reliance on a reasonable-care standard in investment management to determine qualifications for tax-preferred status and the imposition of tax sanctions for imprudent investment[32];

(4) Adoption of federal legislation explicitly imposing the prudent-man rule on the managers of employee benefit plans[33];

(5) Accelerating legislative activity at the federal and state levels to establish, among other things, minimal standards of competence for investment managers.[34]

---

the federal securities laws. Thus, at the federal level at least, the doctrines comprehend more than mere negligence at their present stage of development. Cf. Ernst & Ernst v. Hochfelder, 425 U.S. 185 (1976). But there can be little question that they represent initial attempts to transpose the reasonable-care principle into a real standard controlling conduct. It is a violation of the suitability doctrine, either because of insufficient inquiry into a client's circumstances or because of the risky nature of a proposed commitment, if a broker (and, a fortiori, a manager) does not know that the proposed commitment involves excessive risk for the client. Similarly, the reasonable-basis doctrine charges brokers (and hence managers) with having made a sufficient investigation into the characteristics of a commitment to justify recommending it.

[32] See, e.g., Reg. § 53.4944-1(a)(2) (investment managers of a foundation subject to a tax for making imprudent investments); Rev. Rul. 69-421, Pt. 2(k)(1), 1969-2 C.B. 59 (pension plan may lose its tax-preferred status by engaging in imprudent investment practices).

[33] Employee Retirement Income Security Act of 1974 § 404(a)(1)(B), 29 U.S.C. § 1104(a)(1)(B) (hereinafter cited as ERISA). Exculpatory provisions overriding this (and other) statutory duties are expressly prohibited. ERISA § 410(a), 29 U.S.C. § 1110(a).

[34] In the early 1970s, after Congress had completed its work in reforming the Investment Company Act (Pub. L. 91-547, 84 Stat. 1413 (Dec. 14, 1970)), sentiment began growing to regulate investment management activities either by expanding the scope of the Investment Advisers Act or through state legislation and regulation. See, e.g., Hedberg, "Let's Regulate Investment Advice," 29 Fin. Anal. J. 24 (May-June 1973); Owens, "Investment Adviser Regulation: A Subject Too Long Neglected," id. at 12 (Jan.-Feb. 1973); Nelson, "Let's Make Investment Advisers Accountable," id. at 19 (Jan.-Feb. 1973). See also Wall Street Letter, May 26, 1975, p. 9 (speech by SEC Commissioner Sommer).

But with the attention of Congress on what it regarded as more pressing securities matters, consideration of federal action was delayed until adoption of the Securities Act Amendments of 1975 (Pub. L. 94-29, 89 Stat. 97 (June 4, 1975)), and most of the legislative activity occurred at the state level. For example, under the prodding of the New York Society of Securities Analysts, in early 1974, the New York Attorney General proposed legislation for certifying and regulating financial analysts. See Securities Week, Jan. 7, 1974, p. 4. The legislation ultimately was abandoned because of

In addition to tightening scrutiny of professional competence, the process of implementing the reasonable-care standard has also manifested itself by expanding the investment discretion of managers as developments in theory undercut the rationale for restrictive rules. The first to go was the notorious "legal list" approach to prudence.[35] Then, undermined by a report prepared for the Ford Foundation,[36] the established rule against invading principal, which limited a trustee's ability to invest in non-income-producing securities, began eroding to accommo-

---

serious and justifiable objections (see Wall Street Letter, Jan. 21, 1974, p. 3, and Feb. 11, 1974, p. 5), but it signaled a continuing effort in New York (see Karp, "NYSSA v. FAF," Barron's, April 26, 1976, p. 3) and the start of related movements in other jurisdictions. See, e.g., Testimony of Chairman of the Investment Counsel Association of America, in Hearings on S. 2849 Before the Subcomm. on Securities of the Senate Comm. on Banking, Housing and Urban Affairs, 94th Cong., 2d Sess. 275-276 (1976) (describing legislative and regulatory activity in Massachusetts, New York, New Jersey, and Florida). See generally Memorandum of the Division of Investment Management Regulation of SEC on State Regulation of Investment Advisers, Appendix to Letter of Transmittal by Chairman of SEC, id. at 19.

In late 1975, the SEC transmitted to Congress proposed legislation amending the Investment Advisers Act to prescribe, among other things, "standards of training, experience, competence, and such other qualifications . . . as the Commission finds necessary or appropriate in the public interest or for the protection of investors." Proposed amendment adding new Section 208(e), S. 2849, § 2, 94th Cong., 2d Sess. (1975). The bill also would "clarify" (Hearings on S. 2849, supra, at 9) the existence of private rights of action by amending Section 214. Id. § 6. It is unclear whether this would give advisory clients a federal right of action for violation of standards of competence under proposed Section 208(e) or is intended only to overrule cases holding no private right exists under Section 206, the statutory antifraud provision. See, e.g., Gammage v. Roberts, Scott & Co., [1974-1975 Transfer Binder] CCH Fed. Sec. L. Rep. ¶ 94,761 (S.D. Cal. 1974).

[35] An excellent summary of the progressive abandonment of legal lists can be found in Shattuck, "The Development of the Prudent Man Rule for Fiduciary Investment in the United States in the Twentieth Century," 12 Ohio St. L.J. 491, 499-504 (1951). See also Torrance, "50 Years of Trust Investment," 93 Trusts & Estates 250 (1954); Arenson, "1965 Legislation Affecting Law of Trusts and Estates," 12 N.Y.L.F. 1, 40-42 (1966).

[36] Advisory Committee on Endowment Management to the Ford Foundation, *Managing Educational Endowments* (Ford Foundation 1969). W. Cary & C. Bright, *The Law and the Lore of Endowment Funds* (Ford Foundation 1969). Compare J. Williamson, *Performance Measurement and Investment Objectives for Educational Endowment Funds* (The Common Fund 1972). The original Ford Foundation report has suffered, perhaps unfairly, from the timing of its issuance and the unwise implementation of its recommendations.

date the "total return" concept.[37] Most recently, even supposedly high-risk ventures, such as options-dealing and leveraging, have come to be recognized as safe for conservative accounts when carried out properly.[38]

[b] Regulation of practices involving divided loyalties

Far more than the reasonable-care principle, abuse of the loyalty principle prior to and after the Great Crash motivated Congress to adopt a federal scheme of securities regulation. A fundamental aim of the Glass-Steagall Act was to reduce the involvement of banks in underwriting the securities they were recommending to their customers.[39] One of the major reasons for the Securities Exchange Act was a perceived need to control manipulative trading practices by brokers and dealers in derogation of the interests of their customers.[40] The Trust Indenture Act was designed to restore balance to the relationship between indenture trustees and holders of publicly issued corporate debt by expressly disqualifying a trustee from serving in the presence of different conflicts of interest between it and the securities holders it was representing.[41] The Investment Company Act was needed, Congress found, because investment companies were being managed in the interests of their advisers, underwriters, and officers rather than in the interests of all securities holders.[42]

---

[37] The Uniform Management of Institutional Funds Act (7 *U.L.A.* (Supp. 1971-1976)) authorized trustees of charitable institutions to use principal to meet current expenditures so that such institutions could take advantage of higher-risk/higher-return growth stocks, an investment strategy which would otherwise have been difficult since the return on such securities is ordinarily in the form of capital appreciation.

[38] At least in contemporary investment theory, a broadly diversified trust portfolio can properly undertake commitments which, viewed only on their own merit, would be inappropriate for trust accounts according to traditional interpretations of the prudent-man rule. These include high-volatility securities, margin purchases, and options commitments. Legal restrictions have been adapting to recognition of this fact (see ¶ 7.05), but they have been doing so cautiously. For example, *In re* Bank of New York, 35 N.Y.2d 512, 364 N.Y.S.2d 164, 323 N.E.2d 700 (1974), might be given a restrictive reading with respect to the implementation of contemporary investment theory. The case is discussed more fully in ¶ 7.04.

[39] See Glass-Steagall Act §§ 16, 12 U.S.C. § 24 (Seventh), and 21, 12 U.S.C. § 378(a).

[40] See Securities Exchange Act §§ 2(3), 2(4), 15 U.S.C. §§ 78b(3), 78b(4).

[41] Trust Indenture Act § 310(b), 15 U.S.C. § 77jjj(b).

[42] Investment Company Act § 1(b)(2), 15 U.S.C. § 80a-1(b)(2).

But while the federal securities laws reaffirmed the loyalty principle and eliminated, or at least reduced the severity of, some of the worst abuses, the legislation stopped well short of establishing the supremacy of the duty of loyalty over ordinary business practices. It would be almost thirty years, for example, before banks would see anything wrong with allocating brokerage business according to the deposits of brokerage firms in their commercial departments, and even when the practice ended, it was because of an antitrust threat and not the loyalty question it raised.[43] Indeed, if there has been one constant throughout the period since the adoption of the federal securities laws, it is that the loyalty principle is continuously being tested by industry practices; and even though, ultimately, the duty of loyalty may prevail in some form, the gap between official recognition of a conflict-of-interest problem and its resolution is typically substantial.

In any event, the central issue involving the loyalty principle during this period has not been the validity of the principle—that seems beyond question at this stage of development of the law—but how practices raising duty-of-loyalty questions should be regulated. The primary technique has been to expand disclosure obligations to the point that, as a general rule, any material fact adverse to a client's interest in an investment management relationship must be disclosed. But there is also a growing dissatisfaction with disclosure as the means of resolving duty-of-loyalty questions. This dissatisfaction is expressing itself in the form of regulatory prohibitions of and restrictions on structural arrangements which place stress on an investment manager's duty of loyalty.

---

43 See 4 SEC, *Institutional Investor Study Report* 2283, H.R. Doc. No. 64, 92d Cong., 1st Sess. (1971). The allocation of brokerage business in this fashion can cause a sacrifice of best execution if a bank chooses an inferior executing broker-dealer in order to direct business to a broker-dealer depositor. Even though no purposeful sacrifice of best execution may be involved, a tie-in between deposits and brokerage presents a classic duty-of-loyalty question: Bank profits derive from commercial loans attributable to brokerage deposits, but trust department customers require the exercise of independent judgment as to the best executing broker-dealer for the transactions in which they participate. As with most duty-of-loyalty questions, the seriousness with which the problem is viewed depends in large part on how the fiduciary resolves the conflict of interest. In this case, there is no record of banks' disclosing brokerage allocation practices and their meaning to customers of the trust department or of banks' allocating directly any part of their profits from brokerage deposits in the form of lowered management fees, outright cash rebates, or in any other way, the relatively low profitability of trust departments during the period brokerage having been influenced by commercial deposits notwithstanding.

For example, federal pension legislation has two sets of prohibited-transaction provisions—one enforceable by the Secretary of Labor or a beneficiary, participant, or plan fiduciary and the other enforceable by the Secretary of the Treasury—which in essence render unlawful the provision of multiple services to or the transaction of different kinds of business with qualified plans.[44] The principal motivation for the sweeping prohibition in the statute, which exempts specific transactions and gives special exemptive power to the Secretaries of Labor and of the Treasury, was to deal with abuses by fiduciaries to employee benefit plans who were found to be using plan assets either for the benefit of employers or employee representatives, depending on the affiliation of those responsible for administering the plan.[45] But the effects of the prohibited-transaction provisions also extend well beyond plan trustees and affiliated administrative fiduciaries to unaffiliated investment managers. Assuming this was not inadvertent,[46] it indicates a rejection of the adequacy of the disclosure technique as a means by which plan fiduciaries can control the activities of plan investment managers when faced with duty-of-loyalty problems. The extent of this rejection is underlined by the limited exceptions afforded investment managers by the Secretaries of Labor and of the Treasury for certain principal and dual agency transactions, including block trading, underwriting, and market-making by broker-managers.[47]

Another manifestation of the growing skepticism of the adequacy of disclosure also concerns broker-managers. The Securities Acts Amendments of 1975[48] amended the Securities Exchange Act to make unlawful,

---

[44] ERISA § 406, 29 U.S.C. § 1106; ERISA § 2003, 26 U.S.C. § 4975. The prohibited-transaction provisions are discussed in more detail in ¶ 10.03.

[45] See, e.g., *Private Welfare and Pension Plan Study, Interim Report of the Subcomm. on Labor of the Senate Comm. on Labor and Public Welfare,* S. Rep. No. 634, 92d Cong., 2d Sess. (1972).

[46] While the effect of these prohibitions on unaffiliated investment managers did not receive a great deal of attention from either Congress or the securities industry (see ¶ 10.03[1]), there were at least some statements alerting Congress to the reach of the statute. See, e.g., Submission of Donaldson, Lufkin and Jenrette, Written Statements Submitted on H.R. 10474 [H.R. 2] to the House Comm. on Ways and Means, 93d Cong., 1st Sess. (1973). It is also notable, however, that shortly after ERISA was adopted, new proposed legislation was introduced for the purpose of substantially narrowing the effects of the prohibited-transaction provisions on independent investment managers. H.R. 7597, 94th Cong., 1st Sess. (1975).

[47] Prohibited Transaction Exemption 75-1, 40 Fed. Reg. 50,845 (Oct. 31, 1975), discussed more fully in ¶ 10.03[1].

[48] Pub. L. 94-29, 89 Stat. 97 (June 4, 1975).

subject to a three-year grandfather clause, combined management and brokerage on securities exchanges.[49] The SEC also began to show an increased tendency toward restricting practices raising duty-of-loyalty questions even in the face of full disclosure.[50] To be sure, Congress had previously separated investment banking from commercial banking in the Glass-Steagall Act and had eliminated transactions between and joint transactions with investment companies and investment company managers instead of relying on mere disclosure. But the recent restrictions seem different in kind. Arguably, there are no independent watchmen in the trust department of a commercial bank to protect customers from overreaching in investment banking activities, and the independent directors of an investment company, being selected by and serving at the whim of management, may not be sufficiently independent to be truly reliable guardians of shareholder interests. Disclosure in that event may not be an effective remedy against breaches of the duty of loyalty. But absolute prohibitions against approval by pension trustees, despite full disclosure, of the provision of multifaceted financial services by investment managers, or the absolute separation of brokerage and management, no matter how knowledgeable the client, is a rejection of disclosure by another order of magnitude.

And there is yet another notable phenomenon. The courts as well as the Congress and the SEC have been actively grappling with resolution of duty-of-loyalty questions. Whereas in an earlier day, the courts seemed overly willing to take a contract approach to such questions, they have more recently been assuming even an activist role in insisting on affirmative undertakings for managers whose activities subject them to divided loyalties. For the most part, the antifraud provisions of the federal securities laws have been the means of entry of the courts. Thus, for example, in *Chasins v. Smith, Barney & Co.*,[51] a broker-adviser's failure to disclose its status as market-maker, even though it revealed in confirmation slips that it had acted as principal, was held a violation of Rule 10b-5 of the Securities Exchange Act. And *Slade v. Shearson, Hammill & Co.*[52] virtually closed the door on a firm's conducting bro-

---

[49] Securities Acts Amendments of 1975 § 6(2), *amending* Securities Exchange Act § 11(a), 15 U.S.C. § 78k(a), discussed more fully in ¶ 10.02.

[50] See, e.g., John C. Tead Co., CCH Mutual Funds Guide ¶ 9896 (1973); Argus Sec. Management Corp., [1971-1972 Transfer Binder] CCH Fed. Sec. L. Rep. ¶ 78,366 (1971) (no-action letter request concerning fully disclosed referral fees denied).

[51] 438 F.2d 1167 (2d Cir. 1971).

[52] 356 F. Supp. 304 (S.D.N.Y.), *aff'd sub nom.* Odette v. Shearson, Hammill & Co., 486 F.2d 1395 (2d Cir. 1973).

kerage activity on an issue during its participation in the underwriting of a related issue.

But the courts have not restricted themselves to the statutory fraud provisions in enforcing the loyalty principle; they have also shown a renewed willingness to refine and apply traditional common-law rules without specific reliance on the antifraud provisions. In *Rosenfeld v. Black*,[53] for example, it was on the basis of the " 'well established principle of equity . . . that a . . . fiduciary . . . may not sell or transfer [his] office for personal gain' " that an investment adviser to an investment company was held to an accounting for the profits realized when it replaced itself with another adviser.[54]

[c] Extension of the public-duty principle

When Congress passed the Securities Exchange Act of 1934, it stated that "transactions in securities . . . are affected with a national public interest. . . ."[55] Since that time, Congress, the courts, and the SEC have moved progressively toward translating the principle that investors have a public duty to the securities markets into specific undertakings or prohibitions in furtherance of that principle.[56] While the full outline of the obligations encompassed by a public-duty rationale is not yet clear, the law has developed far enough so that effects on the marketplace must be regarded by investors.

To be sure, the obligations created under the public-duty principle affect all parties to securities transactions, not just persons providing investment management services. Nonetheless, the public-duty principle has special impact on persons providing investment management services because they, in effect, stand between investors and the securities markets. Though in theory the insider-trading proscriptions, for example, apply with equal force to individual investors and investment managers,[57] it is the manager, with his securities analysts actively seeking

---

[53] 445 F.2d 1337, 1342 (2d Cir. 1971).

[54] A number of other cases exhibit a similar attitude toward enforcing the loyalty principle. See, e.g., Morris v. Cantor, 390 F. Supp. 817 (S.D.N.Y. 1975).

[55] Securities Exchange Act § 2, 15 U.S.C. § 78b.

[56] See, e.g., SEC v. F.L. Salmon & Co., [1975-1976 Transfer Binder] CCH Fed. Sec. L. Rep. ¶ 95,335 (S.D.N.Y. 1975), in which the court explained that Rule 10b-5 of the Securities Exchange Act is intended to protect the public at large.

[57] Compare SEC v. Texas Gulf Sulphur Co., 401 F.2d 833 (2d Cir. 1968), *cert. denied sub. nom.* Kline v. SEC, 394 U.S. 976 (1969), with *In*

information on the basis of which client accounts can capitalize, who is far more exposed to inside-information transgressions than the individual investor who stumbles onto such information in connection with his job or a chance encounter with an acquaintance.[58]

To this point, application of the public-duty principle to securities transactions affects investment managers in three areas. The most well-developed, of course, concerns the use of nonpublic corporate information which has spawned the insider-trading cases. A more recent development concerns the use of market information—nonpublic facts not about an issuer but about the market for its securities.[59] Finally, in connection with the expanding influence of institutional investors over the securities markets, Congress provided in the Securities Acts Amendments of 1975 that institutional investment managers regularly report their aggregate portfolio holdings by individual security and, with respect to large trades, size, price, and other related information concerning each transaction.[60]

¶ 1.02. ANALYSIS OF THE REASONABLE-CARE PRINCIPLE

There is no real disagreement that investment managers are under a duty of reasonable care in carrying out their responsibilities. According to the *Restatement (Second) of Trusts*, a trustee is under a duty to make investments "as a prudent man would make of his own property having in view the preservation of the estate and the amount and regularity of the income to be derived." [61] Similarly, the *Restatement (Second) of Agency* describes a duty to invest as would "a prudent in-

---

re Investors Management Co., SEC Securities Exchange Act Release No. 9267 (July 29, 1971), [1970-1971 Transfer Binder] CCH Fed. Sec. L. Rep. ¶ 78,163.

[58] See, e.g., SEC v. Bausch & Lomb, 420 F. Supp. 1226 (S.D.N.Y. 1976), discussed more fully in note 131 *infra*; SEC v. Lum's, Inc., 365 F. Supp. 1046 (S.D.N.Y. 1973). See also Herman, "Equity Funding, Inside Information, and the Regulators," 21 U.C.L.A.L. Rev. 1 (1973).

[59] See Oppenheimer & Co., SEC Securities Exchange Act Release No. 12319 (April 2, 1976); Fleischer, Mundheim & Murphy, "An Initial Inquiry Into the Responsibility to Disclose Market Information," 121 U. Pa. L. Rev. 798 (1973).

[60] Securities Acts Amendments of 1975 § 10, Pub. L. 94-29, 89 Stat. 97 (June 4, 1975), *adding* Securities Exchange Act § 13(f), 15 U.S.C. § 78m(f).

[61] Section 227(a) (1959).

vestor for his own account, having in view both safety and income, in the light of the principal's means and purposes." [62]

The reference to prudence instead of reasonable care is of little significance in legal theory. It is indicative more of historical antecedents to modern doctrine than of the existence of any special purpose served by the term. The primary reason here for referring to reasonable care to describe the principle underlying the care and skill the law requires of investment managers is that prudence, as a term of art in investment management law, has acquired a particularized meaning with respect to the types of investments open to trustees, and it has acquired connotations of fiduciary duty more appropriately analyzed in connection with the duty of loyalty as well.

To avoid encumbering analysis of the duty of reasonable care, it is best to begin by restricting reliance on usages which have been forced by the law's evolutionary processes to shoulder different and often competing themes. Throughout the remainder of this work, the reader should treat prudence and reasonable care interchangeably unless prudence is being used in a technical sense in a case, statute, or regulation. In that way, distinctions between trusteeship and agency can be handled as factual questions affecting the application of the reasonable-care principle without affecting the unity of the principle itself.

[1] The Meaning of Reasonable Care

The more interesting question is what constitutes reasonable care in investment management. Though negligence law has been an object of study for many years, reasonable care in the best of circumstances is not a precise concept. Reasonable care asks whether an undertaking is carried on in a fashion which sufficiently tends to accomplish its aims. This does not mean that it must succeed or that failure proves lack of reasonable care. Reasonable care only requires that the teachings of experience be heeded so that unnecessary risks are avoided. For investment management, reasonable care normally translates into the use of methods and techniques which take into account principles, theories, customs, and conventions generally observed by the investment management community.

This does not imply that universal agreement about what should be done is necessary. Like everyone else, investment managers are entitled to disagree over the wisdom of different courses of action. Nor does it imply that new departures in method or technique are prohibited. On

---

[62] Section 425(b) (1958).

the contrary, one of the most serious contemporary criticisms of negligence law is that it underwrites progress at the expense of those suffering injury.[63] Reasonable care is simply a balance between experience and enterprise. It requires that whatever the course chosen, there be due regard for what is generally known.

[2] Applying the Reasonable-Care Standard

The problem with the reasonable-care standard is not in understanding the theory which supports it, but in applying it to real situations. It is all very well to say that investment managers are bound to exercise reasonable care in carrying out their professional responsibilities. It is quite another thing to identify the limits of reasonable care in a given case. There are two reasons why applying the reasonable-care standard to investment management practices can be hazardous:

(1) The theoretical basis of the reasonable-care standard reduces in the end to a value judgment as to what experience has taught about the risks involved in competing courses of action. By its nature, this kind of value judgment is not capable of quantification, and hence its limits cannot be precisely known in advance.

(2) The reasonable-care standard, as applied to investment management, is an objective rather than subjective test of how well an investment manager has chosen among competing courses of action. His personal beliefs about the reasonableness of his management activities are largely irrelevant. Rather, the standard to which he must adhere is an extended measure of the latitude to be afforded investment managers generally in carrying out their professional responsibilities. In effect, an investment manager is faced with the necessity of anticipating how an official body having enforcement power—a court, an administrative agency, an arbitration panel, or a professional society, for example—would evaluate his activities.

As an illustration of the complexity of the problem of applying the duty of reasonable care to particular management activities, consider the

---

[63] See, e.g., Franklin, "Replacing the Negligence Lottery: Compensation and Selective Reimbursement," 53 Va. L. Rev. 774 (1967). This article, like most contemporary attacks on negligence theory, concerns personal-injury cases. Nonetheless, even if pure economic loss is a less compelling catastrophe than personal injury, the policy argument underlying this criticism of negligence theory as a system of redress still stands.

obligation of a trustee to select investments suitable for a trust portfolio. In the nineteenth century, there developed two competing lines
of thought about how this issue should be resolved. The Massachusetts
approach, adopted by a distinct minority of jurisdictions, treated the
issue as a question of fact and used trustee practices as a base of reference.[64] The New York approach, initially far more popular, specified
as a matter of law the kinds of investments suitable for trust estates.[65]

That the Massachusetts approach ultimately was the more persuasive[66] is less important than recognizing the different assumptions underlying the disagreement. The Massachusetts courts conceded greater
competence to the trustee community to set standards of reasonable
care and assumed that trustees would receive adequate guidance on how
to meet their responsibilities by reference to generally accepted professional practices. The New York courts, on the other hand, rejected the
notion of the superior competence of the trustee community to set standards of reasonable care. The New York rule assumed that trustees
would not recognize all the considerations bearing on reasonable investment selection and that they were in need of instruction from outside
the trustee community on what to do.

[a] Reasonable care as a question of fact; professional standards

The tension between deferring to professional practices to set the
standard of care and setting the standard as a matter of law underlies
all the developments in connection with the evolution of the investment
manager's duty of reasonable care. Strong arguments can usually be
made in favor of both views, and neither is ever entirely correct. Consider, first, the concept of setting the standard of care according to generally accepted professional practices. As an abstract matter, there is
much to be said for relying on the investment management community
as the source of professional duty. Since a professional investment man-

---

[64] See *In re* Dickinson, 152 Mass. 184, 25 N.E. 99 (1890) (standard of
care established through evidence of practice of trustees). See also Kimball
v. Whitney, 233 Mass. 321, 123 N.E. 665 (1919).

[65] Beginning in 1889, the New York Legislature undertook to set forth
the kinds of securities permissible for trust investment. N.Y. Laws 1889,
Ch. 65. The prescribed categories were broadened from time to time, but it
was not until 1950 that securities other than of the fixed-income type were
approved. N.Y. Sess. Laws 1950, Ch. 464.

[66] See 3 Scott, note 12 *supra*, § 227; Shattuck, "The Development of the
Prudent Man Rule for Fiduciary Investment in the Twentieth Century," 12
Ohio St. L.J. 491 (1951); Torrance, "50 Years of Trust Investment," 93
Trusts & Estates 250 (1954).

ager represents to his clients that he knows the elements of his profession, the imposition of a duty to act accordingly does not seem unduly burdensome. Moreover, the great advantage of relying on the profession to set the standard of care is the ease with which the law can accommodate shifts in professional thinking. Particularly where there is significant but defensible disagreement over the proper course of action, an approach which accepts the exercise of discretion within professional limits seems preferable to one which relies on conformity to a narrow rule.

An excellent illustration of the advantage in treating reasonable care as a question of fact is the way in which Massachusetts trust law was able to respond as the importance of diversification to competent investment management emerged. By the late nineteenth century, diversification had come to be recognized in certain quarters as an important risk-reducing device appropriate for trust management.[67] There was serious judicial dispute in various jurisdictions, however, over the degree and method of diversification advisable,[68] and several courts simply abandoned the attempt to set standards for diversification.[69] Massachusetts resolved the problem by deferring to the practices of the professional community to set the standard.

---

[67] See 3 Scott, note 12 *supra*, § 228; Shattuck, "The Massachusetts Prudent Man Rule in Trust Investments," 25 B.U.L. Rev. 307, 323-325 (1945). Although there are some hints of recognition in Harvard College v. Amory, 26 Mass. (9 Pick.) 446 (1830), of the utility of diversification—the court's discussion at 461 of the attractiveness of insurance stocks, for example—it is difficult to identify serious concern with diversification as an issue, even though it could have been raised on the facts.

[68] The New York approach, of course, absolutely precluded diversification into equities. See notes 65, 66 *supra*.

[69] See, e.g., *In re* Adriance, 145 Misc. 345, 352, 260 N.Y.S. 173, 181 (1932), in which the court said:

"It is entirely true that many financial authorities advocate wide diversity of investment. It is equally true that others as strenuously affirm the contrary, and agree with the familiar admonition of the late Andrew Carnegie: 'Put all your eggs in one basket and watch the basket.' This divergence of sentiment . . . in favor of either school of thought [is] an *ultra* hazardous undertaking. For present purposes, . . . no such demonstration of improvidence on the part of the trustees in investing less than two-fifths of their fund in these securities has been made, as to justify the court in declaring as a matter of law that their action was improper."

See also *In re* Stupack, 154 Misc. 759, 278 N.Y.S. 403 (1935), *rev'd on other grounds* 274 N.Y. 198, 8 N.E.2d 485 (1937) (trust invested almost entirely in participation certificates).

In the case of *In re Dickinson*,[70] the Massachusetts Supreme Judicial Court, while recognizing the value of diversification, expressly declined to adopt a mandatory rule. Instead, it surcharged the trustee only for that portion of his investment program which, measured against evidence of trustee practices, was unreasonably concentrated. By this approach, the court allowed room for disagreement over and development of the diversification device. Thus, in Massachusetts, conventional trustee practice could evolve from investing about one-third of a portfolio in equities to investing about half some fifty years after *Dickinson* without any involvement of or interference by the legislature or the courts.[71] But while the Massachusetts approach allowed the trustee community to set diversification standards, it still circumscribed trustee discretion to the point that diversification considerations were made a mandatory element of trustee investment decision-making and could not be rejected except on professionally sound and defensible grounds.[72]

[b] Reasonable care as an issue of law

The law does not always permit a professional community to set its own standards for determining reasonable care. The justifications for treating reasonable care as a question of fact for investment managers are that the requisite expertise resides in the professional community and that due care requires too rapid adjustment of conduct for the law to accommodate through set rules. But if the requisite expertise is possessed by the lawmakers, and if a need for standardization of performance outweighs the importance of easy change, precise rules detailing reasonable care can be the result.

The argument that, in setting standards of care, courts, legislatures, and regulatory authorities should defer to the professional community on grounds of expertise is especially weak. With the rise of administrative agencies, supposedly expert in the matters they regulate, as a means of carrying out public policy, expertise has ceased to be a barrier to regulatory control. Thus, for example, the SEC might conclude as readily as the investment management community that extrasensory percep-

---

[70] 152 Mass. 184, 25 N.E. 99 (1890).

[71] Compare *id.* at 185 (case report incomplete in 25 N.E.) (trustees invest one-third of portfolios in "fluctuating securities"), with Shattuck, "The Massachusetts Prudent Man Rule in Trust Investments," 25 B.U.L. Rev. 307, 323 (1945) (Boston corporate fiduciaries balancing portfolios fifty-fifty between stocks and bonds).

[72] See, e.g., First Nat'l Bank v. Truesdale Hosp., 288 Mass. 35, 192 N.E. 150 (1934).

tion is not an acceptable means for an adviser to use in selecting investments for others.[73]

The strength behind the argument for treating reasonable care as a question of fact is the ease with which standards of care can change in line with professional thinking. Since regulatory agencies are more capable procedurally of adapting to shifts in professional thinking than are legislatures and courts, there is less risk of stifling professional advances than if rules are adopted by judicial decision or statute. Nonetheless, regulation is a drag on changes in professional practice, and the mere fact that it is less a drag than legislation hardly justifies it.

The affirmative reason for choosing rules of law to determine reasonable care is to achieve standardization, a goal which can be important both from the perspective of a potential victim and from that of an actor. Sometimes, variations in performance can be so excessive that specific rules of conduct are necessary to reduce the number of persons who would otherwise suffer seemingly fortuitous losses. Because specific rules efficiently convey information to actors about what is expected of them, and thereby increase the amount of conforming conduct, they reduce the incidence of injury and, by the same token, reduce the cost of avoiding injury to potential victims. Stop signs, for example, identify dangerous corners for drivers and tell them what they must do to reduce the chance of a traffic accident to reasonable dimension. Stop signs also inform pedestrians and other drivers of the conduct they can expect and allow them to continue on their way without trying to figure out (in the absence of a stop-sign rule) how an oncoming vehicle will negotiate the corner, how skillful the driver is and how fast his reflexes, whether he sees the other traffic, who has the right-of-way, and so forth. Moreover, specific rules are increasingly valuable as potential victims become less and less able to gather and evaluate the information necessary to determine what reasonable care for an actor would be. Thus, for example, detailed building codes specify minimum standards for construction in part because most purchasers and users of buildings are too uninformed to express their interest in safety either in contract negotiations or in market choice. With respect to investment manage-

---

[73] Cf. Advanced Analysis, Inc., SEC Investment Advisers Act Release No. 397 (Jan. 18, 1974), [1973-1974 Transfer Binder] CCH Fed. Sec. L. Rep. ¶ 79,369. The SEC deemed the disclosure fraudulent in this case because, among other things, the registrant represented ESP as an established method of investment advice. Whether accurate disclosure would have produced a different result cannot be determined.

ment, this attitude reflects itself through developments such as imposition of licensing and examination standards.[74]

Moreover, in the face of great uncertainty about the results of the enforcement process, actors will seek specific rules so that conformity with them will protect them from the vagaries of the fact-finding process. This is not a manifestation of the kind of anticompetitive motivation which frequently stands behind such standard-setting procedures as licensing. Rather, it reflects a willingness to sacrifice some discretion in order to achieve a uniform standard against which to be judged. Thus, for example, reputable contractors might disagree over what would be the proper wiring standards or plumbing standards or materials specifications, but agree to an administrative process whereby a firm decision is made on setting standards so that no retrospective evaluation will be made of whether the contractor's choices were proper. With respect to investment management, this kind of attitude might be shared by those trustees who, though agreeing in principle that full discretion over the mix of stocks and bonds is preferable, would support a rule bracketing permissible proportions in order to reduce the chances of being second-guessed on the basis of portfolio mix.

[c] When standard-setting is a matter of fact and when a matter of law

It is never entirely accurate to describe the reasonable-care issue as a question of fact or an issue of law. Even where reasonable care is generally treated as a question of fact, a reviewing authority will occasionally conclude that the actor's conduct so departed from ordinary care that it was negligent as a matter of law. Thus, for example, in an administrative proceeding, the SEC concluded, without reference to evidence of industry practices, that a mutual fund manager's representation of competence was fraudulent where he was found to have repeat-

---

[74] The SEC has proposed requiring examinations for statutory investment advisers. See note 34 *supra*. Professional associations already require qualifying examinations, the most rigorous being the three levels of examination on accounting and finance, economics, portfolio management, and professional ethics which must be passed to become certified as a Chartered Financial Analyst. See also Financial Programs, Inc., SEC Securities Exchange Act Release No. 11312 (March 24, 1977), [1974-1975 Transfer Binder] CCH Fed. Sec. L. Rep. ¶ 80,146, in which the SEC determined that representations that management was competent were fraudulent where a mutual fund "permitted inexperienced and incompetent persons to make significant investment decisions."

edly purchased excessive amounts of low-float unseasoned securities over the counter on the basis of a single salesman's recommendations.[75] By the same token, specific rules are qualified by the factual circumstances in which conduct takes place. Posted speed limits, for example, apply only if conditions permit. With respect to investment management, the same considerations affect rules of conduct. As Professor Scott points out, even in the legal-list states, trustees must choose among officially authorized investment opportunities with professional skill and care.[76]

Nonetheless, though setting standards of reasonable care necessarily mixes fact and law, it is clear that the distinction is important. To the extent standards of reasonable care for investment managers are treated as questions of fact, responsibility for determining those standards rests with the investment management community. To the extent they are treated as questions of law, it is the courts and regulatory authorities, with the advice of the investment management community to be sure, who determine professional conduct.

It is impossible to state in a fashion capable of perfect prediction the conditions under which one approach should prevail over the other. It is useful, however, to examine the interplay of the policies which support each in a particular context. Conveniently, the struggle over the definition of prudence in trust law provides an excellent vehicle for such an inquiry. In fact, it is especially interesting because, contrary to the usual flow of things in the administration of negligence theory, the standard of care progressed away from treatment as an issue of law toward treatment as a question of fact.

Shortly after the Civil War, the New York Court of Appeals held in *King v. Talbot*[77] that common stocks, unless authorized by a trustor, were unreasonable trust investments as a matter of law. In *King*, the settlor created a trust to provide for the maintenance of his children until majority, at which point the trust corpus was to be distributed to them. The defendants, business associates of the testator, invested in stocks and bonds found to be reputable, safe, and desirable.[78] The court held that the trustees were obliged to invest during the period of maintenance to obtain interest "without exposure to the uncertainties or fluctuations of adventures of any kind," [79] and that prudence precluded

---

[75] Thomas J. Herbert, SEC Securities Exchange Act Release No. 11496 (June 26, 1975).

[76] See 3 Scott, note 12 *supra*, § 227.12.

[77] 40 N.Y. 76 (1869).

[78] *Id.* at 79.

[79] *Id.* at 87.

exposing the fund "to the hazard of loss or gain." [80] Investments in stock, according to the court, deprived the estate of a return of principal and placed control of the fund beyond the trustees, liquidation in the market being "necessarily contingent and uncertain." [81] Moreover, to the argument that bonds suffer losses from depreciation and insolvency, the court replied that adequate security averts dependency on the success of the business.[82]

One can try to explain the result in *King* as a manifestation of a primitive understanding by the court of investment theory. Indeed, from a contemporary perspective, the arguments in *King* are almost disarming in their simplemindedness. Real estate interests and fixed-income securities fluctuate in value and are hardly "without exposure to . . . uncertainties." Any investment medium, even cash, exposes assets "to the hazard of loss or gain." Only if one values the fact that secured interests will almost always have some worth, even if only pennies on the dollar, or, that in the event of failure, bonds have a claim on assets prior to stock, can it be said that control of funds remains with the owner of bonds and not with the owner of stock. The return of principal is as beyond control when lent as it is when invested in stock, and, in many cases, liquidation of stock is easier to accomplish than liquidation of bonds.[83]

But in marked contrast to the naïveté shown in *King* is the analysis in *Harvard College v. Amory*,[84] decided almost forty years earlier. Placed in trust was a $50,000 fund, the income of which was to support the testator's widow and the remainder of which was bequeathed to Harvard College and the Massachusetts General Hospital. After negotiations between the trustee and the remaindermen over a guaranteed income for the life tenant broke down, the trustee invested the entire fund in shares of bank stock, insurance stock, and trading company stock. By these investments, the trustee was able to secure a better income for the beneficiary than the fixed income discussed during the negotiations. But when the trustee presented his account, the market value of the stock had fallen below fifty thousand dollars and the remaindermen objected. The opinion of the court, rejecting the claims of the remaindermen, is remarkable for its prescience.

---

[80] *Id*. at 88.

[81] *Id*.

[82] *Id*. at 89.

[83] See generally B. Graham, D. Dodd & S. Cottle, *Security Analysis* (4th ed. 1962).

[84] 26 Mass. (9 Pick.) 446 (1830).

Stock in prudently managed companies, the court said, "might be reasonably calculated upon as a safe and permanent capital." [85] Nor are public obligations necessarily less risky than other investments since the credit of governments can be impaired.[86] Moreover, dishonored governmental commitments can deny investors legal remedy and place them in the position of supplicants[87]—advice purchasers of today's moral-obligation bonds and certain municipal obligations might well have heeded.[88] To support its position of the error in prejudging an investment medium, the court pointed to the fluctuation in value of some government obligations as being comparable to that of some bank stocks[89] and the fluctuation of bank stocks as being comparable to that of some insurance and trading companies.[90] In a sober but accurate assessment of investment selection, the court said, "Do what you will, the capital is at hazard." [91]

Given the example of *Harvard College*, it is difficult to credit failure to appreciate the complexities of investment selection as the principal reason for the *King* rule that stocks were imprudent as a matter of law. Even if the *King* court was not capable of a more discriminating analysis, its lack of sophistication hardly explains the influence of its opinion in other jurisdictions. Certainly, the historical record never undercut the Massachusetts rule. True to *Harvard College*, the Massachusetts courts refused to prohibit investment opportunities as imprudent as a matter of law.[92] Instead, they required a showing that challenged investments exceeded the limits of discretion characteristic of trust manage-

---

[85] *Id*. at 459.

[86] *Id*. at 460.

[87] *Id*.

[88] See Bleiberg, "End of the Tunnel? For Port Authority Bondholders Not Much Light," Barron's, April 14, 1975, p. 7; Klapper, "Just How Binding Is a Moral Obligation? Bond Market Nervously Awaits Answer," Wall Street J., Feb. 28, 1975, p. 32, col. 1; see also "Review & Outlook, Moral Obligation," Wall Street J., Feb. 28, 1975, p. 10, col. 1; Lacey, "Shame of the Cities?" Barron's, Feb. 3, 1975, p. 3. Investors in municipal securities have been making some gains, however. See United States Trust Co. v. New Jersey, 52 L. Ed. 2d (1977); Flushing Nat'l Bank v. Municipal Assistance Corp., 40 N.Y.2d 731, 358 N.E.2d 848 (1976).

[89] 26 Mass. at 460.

[90] *Id*. at 461.

[91] *Id*.

[92] See, e.g., Clark v. Garfield, 90 Mass. (8 Allen) 427 (1864) (unsecured note); Hunt, Appellant, 141 Mass. 515, 6 N.E. 554 (1886) (certificate of deposit); Daland v. Williams, 101 Mass. 571 (1869) (dividend of stock instead of cash).

ment at the time a challenged investment was made.[93] There is no evidence that trust beneficiaries were faring worse under the Massachusetts approach than under the New York approach. On the contrary, the record shows repeated legislative modifications of judicial limitations on trustee discretion to select investments in jurisdictions following the New York approach.[94] Furthermore, even New York was not true to the spirit of *King*. With rare exception, the courts interpreted ambiguous language in deeds of trust to extend trustee discretion, particularly to investments in common stock.[95] Still more interesting is the test used to determine whether a trustee, given expanded investment authority by a trust instrument, had exercised due care: It was essentially the prudent-man rule of *Harvard College*.[96] In effect, *King* was restricted to those trust estates for which there were express limitations on a trustee's discretion or for which the trustee's authorization extended only to a general power to invest.

The more plausible explanation of the *King* rule is not that the courts did not appreciate the utility of common stock investments or understand the real differences between stocks and bonds, but that too many trustees lacked the expertise to select investments properly. From today's perspective, it is easy to forget that most trustees were not professional investment managers at the time *King* was decided and during the period its influence spread. Massachusetts may have been the home of the Boston trustee,[97] that hallmark of probity and good judgment, but most other jurisdictions had to wait for the development of corporate trusts and the higher standard of care the law would eventually impose on them,[98] since initially, at least, they too were viewed as

---

[93] See, e.g., Brown v. French, 125 Mass. 410 (1878) (stocks and bonds of incomplete railroad held improper investment); Trull v. Trull, 95 Mass. (13 Allen) 407 (1866) (investment in patent right and manufacturing company held improper investment).

[94] See note 65 *supra*.

[95] See, e.g., Lawton v. Lawton, 35 App. Div. 389, 54 N.Y.S. 760 (1898); Duncklee v. Butler, 30 Misc. 58, 62 N.Y.S. 921 (1899); *In re* Maloney, 120 Misc. 456, 198 N.Y.S. 788 (1923); *In re* Hall, 164 N.Y. 196, 58 N.E. 11 (1900).

[96] See, e.g., *In re* Vom Saal, 82 Misc. 531, 145 N.Y.S. 307 (1913), where a will which allowed the trustees "to *invest and reinvest* . . . although the said investments may not be of the character permitted for the investment of trust funds by the ordinary rules of law" was held not void as against public policy and the standard for the propriety of such investments was held to be a standard of prudence.

[97] See Friedman, "The Dynastic Trust," 73 Yale L.J. 547, 554 (1964).

[98] See, e.g., *Restatement (Second) of Trusts* § 227, Comment d (1959); Springfield Safe Deposit & Trust Co. v. First Unitarian Soc'y, 293 Mass.

possessing special competence. In fact, in the last part of the nineteenth century, even Massachusetts adopted a legal-list approach with respect to corporate trustees,[99] demonstrating how unproven a factor they were in investment management.

Unavoidably, the *King* approach to investment selection suffered from a double failing. Not only was its restrictive rule with respect to common stocks unsubstantiated by any knowledgeable professional source, but, even as modified by subsequent legislation, it was always out of date. Both these failings became increasingly obvious as the trustee community professionalized.[100] The effect of *King* was to cut trustees off from an entire range of investment opportunities, and trust portfolios restricted by the *King* rule suffered, occasionally even severely.[101] The most significant feature of the *King* rule, as a result, has been

---

480, 200 N.E. 541 (1936). A corporate trustee makes an implied representation of professional competence and is consequently held to a higher standard of care. See, e.g., *In re* Killey's Est., 457 Pa. 474, 326 A.2d 372 (1974), noted in 21 Vill. L. Rev. 151 (1975).

[99] Friedman, note 97 *supra*, at 565 n.62.

[100] It has also been argued that professional trustees may have supported the legal-list approach as a means of insulating themselves in advance from liability for inadequate management services (see Shattuck, "The Massachusetts Prudent Man Rule in Trust Investments," 25 B.U.L. Rev. 307, 311 (1945), and compare ¶ 1.02[2][b], *supra*), or that a greater availability of government obligations turned the courts away from common stocks as trust investments. See 3 Scott, note 12 *supra*, § 227.5. Another hypothesis for the contrasting approaches of Massachusetts and New York is that trusts differed in nature in the two jurisdictions, with Massachusetts trusts characteristically longer-term and hence more concerned with more flexible investment policy. Friedman, note 97 *supra*. Doubtless, the concern of trustees over possible liability and the differing attitudes of trustors played some part in shaping the law's response to the exercise of trustee discretion. But individually, these explanations seem much more like eddies than currents. The interest of professional trustees in protecting themselves can be better accomplished by insisting on trust provisions exculpating them for ordinary negligence rather than limiting their power to choose good investments. Such provisions were, in fact, common. Moreover, professional trustees generally recommended that they be authorized to exercise broad investment powers, an attitude more consistent with concern for competitive pressure than with personal protection. Finally, while it may be that the purposes of trustors differ, it is difficult to agree, in the absence of strong proof, that the nature of a trust also depended on the jurisdiction in which it was created, especially when comparing jurisdictions like New York and Massachusetts.

[101] During the depression of the 1930s, interest rates were very low; yet trustees, constrained by legal lists, were unable to diversify into equities. According to one authority, the yield on portfolios in legal-list states averaged about 2 percent, whereas, under the Massachusetts rule, it was com-

a long history of legislative retreat, until New York finally adopted the Massachusetts approach of referring to generally accepted trustee practices to set the standard of care for investment selection.[102]

The vindication of *Harvard College* and the decline of *King* illustrate the superiority of treating reasonable care as a question of fact in connection with the selection of investments by investment managers. The failure to adapt to changing investment theory has been demonstrated so costly in selecting investments that rules of law standardizing investment-selection practices cannot be maintained. But, in an important respect, the victory of *Harvard College* has not been complete, and this illustrates the circumstances in which reasonable care tends to be treated as an issue of law.

The selection of investments is really the second step of a two-step process. No investment can be prudent or imprudent in the abstract. It must be first related to someone's investment objectives. Thus, for example, a private placement may be an excellent opportunity for high return. Indeed, given the difficulty of finding sound private placements, the method of discovery and selection may reflect unusual acumen on the part of an investment manager. Nonetheless, a good private placement can still result in sharp losses. In view of the risk, committing a client's funds to such a venture might show a lack of due care if the client's investment objectives would exclude it, and no amount of professional support for the sagacity behind the decision to invest can change that conclusion.

This aspect of investment selection qualifies the prudent-man rule by requiring that the trustee keep "in view the preservation of the estate and the amount and regularity of the income to be derived. . . ." [103] Its analogue in contemporary securities law is the suitability doctrine, which generally treats the question whether an investment manager has exercised reasonable care in conforming the commitments he makes to his client's investment objectives as an issue of law,[104] the only factual questions being the nature of the documents controlling the investment management relationship, the degree of inquiry into the client's circum-

---

paratively easy to maintain 4 percent. Shattuck, "The Development of the Prudent Man Rule for Fiduciary Investment in the United States in the Twentieth Century," 12 Ohio St. L.J. 491, 501 (1951).

[102] N.Y. Laws 1970, Ch. 321, *amended* Estates, Powers and Trusts Law § 11-2.2 to provide for a general prudent-man rule with respect to investments by fiduciaries.

[103] *Restatement (Second) of Trusts* § 227(a) (1959). See also *Restatement (Second) of Agency* § 425 (1958).

[104] See Chapter 4.

stances by the manager, and the risk profile of the commitments chosen by the manager. In contrast to the expanding discretion being given to investment managers to select investments consistent with a client's objectives, the courts and the SEC are narrowing the discretion of investment managers to say what those objectives are.

This result also represents an understandable resolution of the policies supporting each of the two approaches to determining reasonable care. There is little need to accommodate suitability considerations to changing conditions. The attitude of a client toward risk and return is idiosyncratic to him and is not especially affected by shifting investment practices in the investment management community. Moreover, there is a need for standardization with respect to suitability because clients expect a manager to invest in relation to their investment objectives. Thus, for example, an individual trust presumptively is not designed with investment intent but to provide for support, education, or to make some other gift. In view of the established expectations of trustors and beneficiaries, while it might reflect contemporary practices of professional investment managers to include particular commitments in growth-oriented securities as elements of a diversified portfolio, it is highly doubtful that a court would accept a proffer of proof that trustees of such accounts are pursuing programs of substantial capital accumulation in managing such trusts or that the trustee was doing so with skill and care. More likely, it would reject such a program as unsuitable as a matter of law.

¶ 1.03. ANALYSIS OF THE LOYALTY PRINCIPLE

According to the *Restatement (Second) of Trusts*, the duty of loyalty charges a fiduciary to administer the trust "solely in the interest of the beneficiary." [105] According to the *Restatement (Second) of Agency*, the duty of loyalty charges an agent in connection with his agency to act "solely for the benefit of the principal." [106] The duty of loyalty has been codified in federal law,[107] and it has been defended so often[108]

---

[105] *Restatement (Second) of Trusts* § 170(1) (1959).

[106] *Restatement (Second) of Agency* § 387 (1958).

[107] See ERISA § 404(a)(1), 29 U.S.C. § 1104(a)(1):

"[A] fiduciary shall discharge his duties with respect to a plan solely in the interest of the participants and beneficiaries and—

"(A) for the exclusive purpose of:

"(i) providing benefits to participants and their beneficiaries. . . ."

[108] See, e.g., Weinrib, "The Fiduciary Obligation," 25 U. Toronto L.J. 1 (1975); Scott, "The Fiduciary Principle," 37 Calif. L. Rev. 539 (1949);

that its recognition as fundamental to every fiduciary relationship cannot seriously be questioned.

But though the principle of undivided loyalty may not be in doubt in the abstract, the achievement of the ideal of selfless devotion to the interests of another is a different thing entirely. Apart from the moral and ethical question, it is a practical impossibility to eliminate one's own self-interest as a possible influence when undertaking to act for the benefit of another. Virtually every such undertaking involves choices about how to carry it out, and, however sincerely done, the way those choices are resolved unavoidably affects the well-being of the fiduciary.

Except perhaps in politics, the phenomenon of conflicting interests is nowhere more an issue than in investment management. Any investment manager providing his clients multiple services is always faced with the question of how much use to make of those services. Any investment manager serving many managed accounts or offering other kinds of financial services to nonmanagement clients is always faced with how to avoid preferring one client over another. Any investment manager with authority to purchase services for his clients outside his own organization is always faced with how to evaluate the worth of those services to himself.

The conflicts can manifest themselves as deliberate perversions of duty, but the problem remains even in the presence of the utmost good faith. For example, when a bank deposits trust cash in its commercial department, the purpose may be to safeguard the cash while seeking appropriate investments. But the purpose, or at least the effect, may also be to support the commercial department's lending operations to the profit of the bank.[109] Even if the trust department's purpose is to safeguard the cash, can the client be sure the deposits were not held one or two or three extra days?[110] Equally important, can the manager? To

---

Committee on Trust Administration and Accounting, "The Trustee's Duty of Loyalty," 6 Real Prop., Prob. & Trust J. 528 (1971).

[109] Maintaining deposits for this purpose is a clear breach of trust. Blankenship v. Boyle, 329 F. Supp. 1089 (D.D.C. 1971), *supplemented in* 337 F. Supp. 296 (D.D.C. 1972); Comptroller of the Currency, *Comptroller's Manual for Representatives in Trusts* 90 (1963).

[110] Deposits of cash balances are no longer the problem they once were, in part because investors are more demanding about the performance of their accounts, in part because regulators have been paying more attention to the problem, and in part because banks have become far more earnest in the management of cash balances than once was the case. E. Herman, *Conflicts of Interest: Commercial Bank Trust Departments* 131-132 (Twentieth Century Fund 1975); D. Green & M. Schuelke, *The Trust Activities of*

take another example, a broker who refers clients to an investment manager may do so because he regards the manager highly. But he may also do so because he expects brokerage business in return.[111] If he in fact receives brokerage business, how much weight should one attribute to each factor? Further, consider the problem from the manager's point of view. All things being equal, he would probably choose to execute through the referring broker. But he may also do so despite loss of best execution in order to reward the referring broker.[112] Even if the manager intends to obtain best execution and trades through many brokers other than referring brokers, can the client be sure that the amount of business done through the referring broker really reflects the manager's best judgment about where to obtain best execution? Equally important, can the manager be sure of his own motives?

One of the most established rules in connection with the duty of loyalty is that a fiduciary cannot buy property from or sell it to his client without the client's knowing consent.[113] The obvious danger is that the price will not be fair. In the case of publicly traded securities, however, there is an objective market price which, even for trades large enough to introduce an element of uncertainty into price, can prevent a manager from taking advantage of his fiduciary position on that ground.[114] The problem is the commitment of the manager's investment judgment on the client's behalf. Unless the manager is totally agnostic about the security, he has an opinion of its worth relative to market price. Short of dumping overvalued securities on a client or purloining undervalued securities from a client, the manager must somehow measure investment potential for both himself and his client and take opposite action for each. It is difficult to see how a manager's own interests can be

---

the *Banking Industry* 46-48 (Stanford Research Institute 1975). In many large banks, cash management is treated as a specialty, and the personnel responsible for cash management, like those responsible for securities investments, are responsible for maximizing investment return.

111 See, e.g., Moses v. Burgin, 445 F.2d 369 (1st Cir.), *aff'd sub nom.* Johnson v. Moses, 404 U.S. 994 (1971).

112 See Casey, " 'Finders Fee' Compensation to Brokers and Others," 31 Bus. Law. 707 (1976); Friedman, "Problems Involving Investment Advisers and Broker-Dealers Serving Individual Accounts," in R. Mundheim, A. Fleischer & J. Schupper, *Fourth Annual Institute on Securities Regulation* 295, 297-308 (PLI 1973).

113 See 2 Scott, note 12 *supra*, § 170.1; W. Seavey, *Handbook of the Law of Agency* §§ 149-150 (1964).

114 Compare *In re* Flint's Will, 148 Misc. 474, 266 N.Y.S. 392, 405 (1933) ("an investment for which there is no market except the corporate fiduciary itself is improvident").

prevented from affecting his judgment, even if he goes to great lengths to ignore them.

There is a myriad of other conflicts of interest an investment manager may face in carrying out his responsibilities. What should a manager who has a commercial or investment banking relationship with an issuer do with respect to his managed accounts in the event of a takeover bid? How should such a manager vote its managed holdings when an issuer proposes to change its articles of incorporation or amend its by-laws to provide for a higher shareholder percentage approval for a merger in order to prevent takeover bids? How should a manager respond to directed brokerage orders from an institutional client when the manager believes sacrifice of best execution would be the result?

The question, given the pervasive nature of conflicts of interest in investment management, is how best to resolve these conflicts consistent with the loyalty principle. The rule is clear that in a conflict-of-interest situation, the burden is on the manager to resolve the conflict, and that, in the absence of resolution, any benefit accruing to the manager belongs to the client.[115]

Before examining several methods of resolving duty-of-loyalty problems, it is important to recognize that industry practices, so important to application of the reasonable-care principle, are of little value in determining whether a satisfactory resolution has been achieved. To a large extent, the market for investment management services disciplines against negligence since new clients are drawn primarily to investment managers with good performance records. But in conflict-of-interest situations, industry practices tend to deteriorate to the lowest common denominator because abuse of the loyalty principle occurs only where client ignorance permits a profit to be gained. Once the availability of extra profits becomes apparent, others will either join in voluntarily, as was the case when banks were directing brokerage according to the size of brokerage deposits in the bank; or, perversely, they may be forced by competition to follow suit, as was the case with mutual fund give-ups when the refusal of a fund to direct brokerage to firms selling fund shares would dry up selling activity. Thus, when industry practices are frequently raised as a defense to plaintiffs' claims based on violation of the duty of loyalty, that defense is almost uniformly rejected.[116]

---

[115] *Restatement (Second) of Trusts* §§ 203, 205, 206 (1959); *Restatement (Second) of Agency* §§ 388, 389, 391 (1958).

[116] See, e.g., Chasins v. Smith, Barney & Co., 438 F.2d 1167 (2d Cir. 1971) (assertion that all other brokerage firms followed same practice and that the SEC had never prosecuted that practice rejected); Steadman Sec.

Techniques for resolving conflict-of-interest problems, other than for those conflicts too modest to require any affirmative action, fall into four classes:

(1) Disclosure of information relevant to a manager's conduct;

(2) Isolation of investment management from the provision of other services offered by the manager;

(3) Obtaining a specific exemption from the appropriate regulatory agency or from a court; and

(4) Conforming to statutory or regulatory restrictions governing transactions potentially advantageous to the investor, but involving possible conflicts of interest.

These techniques are not mutually exclusive, and often it will be to the advantage of, if not actually a requirement for, a manager to undertake more than one. Furthermore, none is sufficient to remove the duty-of-loyalty issue from further consideration. If it should turn out that, despite technical compliance with the requirements of one or more of these techniques for resolving conflicts of interest, a manager has chosen a course of action preferring his own or someone else's interests over those of his client, it is still a breach of the duty of loyalty.[117] The crucial significance of a manager's having engaged in resolution of such conflicts of interest as occur in the course of administering a management relationship is that the manager is relieved of his burden of demonstrating that he acted in the best interests of his client and, in the absence of proof that he violated his duty of loyalty, he is not accountable for any additional profits he may have received. The burden shifts to the client to show that the manager obtained unfair advantage or unreasonable profit by his behavior.

The most effective method of resolving a conflict of interest is through disclosure. It is well established, both in the law of trusts[118]

Corp., [1974-1975 Transfer Binder] CCH Fed. Sec. L. Rep. ¶ 80,038 (1974) (assertion that conduct was not in violation of any statute or regulation rejected on ground that ad hoc adjudication particularly applicable where strong fiduciary relationship present).

[117] See, e.g., Steadman Sec. Corp., note 116 *supra,* in which, despite concluding that there had been no literal violation of Investment Company Act § 17(d) or 17(e)(1), an administrative law judge imposed sanctions on an investment manager to various mutual funds for using custodial accounts to obtain brokerage allocations for a brokerage affiliate and to facilitate loans to affiliates.

[118] *Restatement (Second) of Trusts* § 216 (1959).

and the law of agency,[119] that the informed consent of a beneficiary or principal makes lawful conduct that would otherwise be a breach of the duty of loyalty. The purpose of disclosure is to provide the person whose interests may be adversely affected by a conflict of interest with enough information to be aware of that possibility and to decide for himself whether to forego a transaction or set of transactions, or to supervise them closely, or to obtain the assistance of an independent watchman, or to take any other action, including none at all, which will satisfy him that his interests are being adequately protected.

Disclosure can take many different forms. A manager may provide advance disclosure of a proposed course of action or may seek ratification after one has been decided upon. He may disclose directly to the client or disclose instead to a supervising intermediary, such as the outside directors of an investment company or the fiduciaries of a pension fund. Whatever specific method is chosen, the capacity for disclosure to resolve a conflict of interest depends on whether the fiduciary has disclosed sufficient information for the beneficiary or principal or the chosen surrogate to make a considered response. If an investment manager knows or ought to know that his client does not appreciate the full significance of his proposed course of action and cannot fully evaluate what he has been told, disclosure does not serve its function of restoring fair balance to the relationship.

A second technique for resolving conflict-of-interest problems, one useful in an organization offering multifaceted financial services, is to isolate individual portfolio managers from other departments in the organization. Ignorance of the specifics of the activities of other departments in an organization makes support of those activities difficult. For example, if trust officers in a bank are unaware of which brokerage firms maintain deposits at the bank, or at least if they are ignorant of the size of the deposits, they will not be able to allocate brokerage business on that basis, even if they were inclined to do so. Furthermore, in theory, individual portfolio managers will use the financial services available through the firm's other departments only to the extent such services are offered at competitive prices. A portfolio manager, properly isolated, would execute through an affiliated broker, for example, only if the price and service package were, in his judgment, the best offered.

But there are two problems that undercut the value of the isolation technique. One, entirely subjective but real nonetheless, is a refusal by outsiders to credit isolation as being as strong as represented. Second, and more significant, isolation never can be complete because a saga-

---

[119] *Restatement (Second) of Agency* §§ 390, 392 (1958).

cious portfolio manager will always be aware of when his actions can benefit the firm even if he lacks the information to know specifically how much he can help.[120]

A third technique is to seek protection of an official agency. It is a well-established rule in the law of trusts that a court of competent jurisdiction can approve a transaction that otherwise might be a breach of the duty of loyalty.[121] To similar purpose are statutes authorizing regulatory agencies to approve transactions which would otherwise be prohibited under the statutes they administer. For example, the Investment Company Act gives the SEC general exemptive power with respect to all provisions of the Act[122] and specific exemptive power with respect to transactions between an investment company and an affiliate[123]; and federal pension legislation authorizes the Secretaries of Labor and of the Treasury to exempt otherwise prohibited transactions.[124]

Finally, conflicts of interest may be resolved through regulation. The advantages of a particular type of transaction may be substantial enough that it would be bad policy to prohibit it entirely or inhibit it excessively, even though the transaction may involve a substantial opportunity for abuse of the duty of loyalty. To accommodate these competing considerations for transactions which occur often enough to make a standard procedure useful, the legislature may include a provision in the organic statute or the appropriate supervisory authority may adopt a regulation which, while not preventing an investment manager from serving his own interests at the expense of the interests of a client, restricts the degree to which the manager may do so, thereby limiting the amount the client may lose in the event of a breach of duty of loyalty. For example, it is common in both state and federal legislation to permit a bank to deposit trust funds with itself, subject to express conditions concerning authorization, security, and rate of interest.[125] In a similar

---

120 See, e.g., Securities Week, May 3, 1976, p. 1, describing an SEC investigation of the relationship between a leading brokerage firm and an investment advisory subsidiary, allegedly for excess payment of brokerage fees to compensate for services in addition to pure execution.

121 See 2 Scott, note 12 *supra*, § 170.1.

122 Investment Company Act § 6(c), 15 U.S.C. § 80a-6(c).

123 *Id.* § 17(b), 80 U.S.C. § 80a-17(b).

124 ERISA §§ 408(a) (29 U.S.C. § 1108(a)), 2003(a) (I.R.C. § 4975 (c)(2)).

125 See, e.g., ERISA § 408(b)(4), 29 U.S.C. § 1108(4)(b) (deposits must be expressly authorized by a provision of the plan or by a fiduciary other than the bank); Uniform Trusts Act (9C *U.L.A.*) § 4 (1957) (bank must set aside security fund of legal securities of equal value or insure deposits, and interest must be paid at statutory rate or rate equivalent to similar nontrust funds).

vein, Investment Company Act Rule 10f-3 and ERISA Prohibited Transaction Exemption 75-1 permit investment companies and employee benefit plans to participate in underwritings by their managers, but to prevent them from suffering serious injury at the hands of managers inclined to use clients as repositories for underwritings of questionable value, the regulations limit extent of participation, size of underwriting fee, and eligibility of issuer.[126]

¶ 1.04. ANALYSIS OF THE PUBLIC-DUTY PRINCIPLE

Ordinarily, an investment manager in possession of information capable of enhancing the return of the portfolios he has under management would be required by his duty of reasonable care to apply that information to investment decisions. Furthermore, even if the manager knew that other parties to the transaction might not be aware of the information in his possession, his fiduciary duty to act in the best interest of his clients would require him to carry out such a transaction. Also firmly established as a fiduciary duty of investment managers is the maintenance of the confidences of the client,[127] so that information such as client holdings, trading activities, and the like would ordinarily be kept private. It is now clear under federal law, however, that an investment manager's public duty to the marketplace overrides his private duties of reasonable care and loyalty to his clients. He may not trade on inside information[128] or, to a lesser extent, on market information,[129] and, depending on the amount of assets under management, he must divulge the extent of his holdings, the prices at which they were acquired, and other related information.[130]

---

[126] See ¶ 10.03[3][c].

[127] *Restatement (Second) of Trusts* § 170, Comment s (1959); *Restatement (Second) of Agency* §§ 395-396 (1958).

[128] Inside information may usefully be defined as "information which emanates from the issuer or those connected with the issuer." Lipton & Katcher, "Liability of Buyers and Sellers in Market Transactions," in K. Bialkin, *The 10b Series of Rules* 129, 139 (PLI 1975). See also *ALI Model Federal Securities Code.*

[129] Market information may usefully be defined as information concerning the market for an issuer's securities not directly connected with facts about the issuer's operations, business prospects, or the like. See Lipton, "Market Information," in R. Mundheim, A. Fleischer & J. Schupper, *Fifth Annual Institute on Securities Regulation* 287 (PLI 1974). See ¶ 10.06 [2][a].

[130] Securities Exchange Act § 13(f), 15 U.S.C. § 78m(f). See also 12 C.F.R. §§ 9.101-9.104.

Because the public-duty principle is relatively recent in origin, it is difficult to prognosticate about the impact it will have on investment managers. With respect to the use of nonpublic information, the aspect of public duty about which most legal developments have occurred, it has been cogently argued that the law should not deny investors the legitimate rewards of the information they have acquired through their own efforts and insights.[131] This interpretation of the public-duty principle is consistent with its origins as an expression of public policy against manipulation or prices in the securities market.

But, whether it is because the concept of manipulation is becoming increasingly refined or because the public-duty principle is actually moving beyond its antimanipulation origins, the mere possession of material nonpublic information is being treated in some situations as sufficient grounds to invoke the public-duty principle. For example, the SEC has suggested as the logical conclusion of a line of cases ending with *Slade v. Shearson, Hammill & Co.*,[132] that an underwriter in possession of material inside information about an issuer is answerable to clients who either purchase or sell the issuer's securities during the period the underwriter is in possession of the information, even if a total separation is maintained between the underwriting and brokerage departments. The SEC took this position in an amicus brief filed in *Slade*,[133] and if it is

---

[131] Lipton & Katcher, note 128 *supra*, at 136-137; Fleischer, Mundheim & Murphy, "An Initial Inquiry into the Responsibility to Disclose Market Information," 121 U. Pa. L. Rev. 798 (1973). Determining the degree to which information is acquired by one's own efforts, however, may be problematic. The practice of meetings between company representatives and professional securities analysts has come under fire by the SEC. See SEC v. Bausch & Lomb, Inc., 420 F. Supp. 1226 (S.D.N.Y. 1976), in which the court rejected the SEC's request for an injunction against the company and an officer for disclosures to visiting analysts on grounds of nonmateriality, the absence of proof of the jurisdictional requirement of a purchase or sale, and the absence of *scienter* as an essential element of an antifraud action for injunctive relief. The SEC has noted its appeal.

[132] 356 F. Supp. 304 (S.D.N.Y.), *aff'd sub. nom.* Odette v. Shearson, Hammill & Co., 486 F.2d 1395 (2d Cir. 1973). See Shapiro v. Merrill Lynch, Pierce, Fenner & Smith, 353 F. Supp. 264 (S.D.N.Y.), *aff'd* 495 F.2d 228 (2d Cir. 1974); Investors Management Co., SEC Securities Exchange Act Release No. 9267 (July 29, 1971), [1970-1971 Transfer Binder] CCH Fed. Sec. L. Rep. ¶ 78,163. See also Financial Industrial Fund, Inc. v. McDonnel Douglas Corp., 315 F. Supp. 42 (D. Colo. 1971), *rev'd* 474 F.2d 514 (10th Cir.), *cert denied* 414 U.S. 874 (1973); Merrill Lynch, Pierce, Fenner & Smith, Inc., SEC Securities Exchange Act Release No. 8459 (Nov. 25, 1968).

[133] See Sec. Reg. & Trans. Rep., April 11, 1975, pp. 4-6.

an accurate statement of the law, it would seem also to preclude trading for the benefit of the underwriter's managed accounts. By the same token, the SEC's position in *Slade* would seem also to have grave implications for bank trust departments trading in securities issued by commercial customers of the bank, if the bank thereby came into possession of material nonpublic information. The SEC's concern plainly is directed much more toward appearances of or opportunities for price manipulation than it is toward proof of actual attempts to manipulate, and it goes well beyond the problems of financial analysts trying to get useful information about publicly traded companies.[134] Yet, to deny trust officers in a commercial bank and portfolio managers affiliated with an investment banker the opportunity to trade in such securities would lock in managed accounts under circumstances which, if a separation of functions actually exists, would not harm public investors.[135] Furthermore, such an interpretation of public duty places great strain on fiduciaries who, fearful of incurring liability for dealing on the basis of nonpublic information, forgo investment opportunities which would have been lawful.[136]

It may be that behind the developments in connection with the use of inside information and market information is an unstated assumption about the probable behavior of most financial institutions in their business activities, and especially with respect to their practices when investing as investment managers or for their own accounts. By their continually expanding application of the public-duty principle, the courts and the SEC seem to be reaching the conclusion that financial institutions in a position to affect or use market prices to their advantage (or the advantage of their customers) will usually do so.[137] In this view, financial institutions, in essence, are caught in the prisoner's dilemma. Each knows that if all behave, the securities markets will be a more

---

[134] See, e.g., Jennings & Smith, "Insider Trading and the Analyst," in R. Mundheim, A. Fleischer & J. Schupper, *Fifth Annual Institute on Securities Regulation* 261 (PLI 1974).

[135] See "Problems of Fiduciaries Under the Securities Laws," 9 Real Prop., Prob. & Trust J. 292, 295-312 (Fall 1974).

[136] See, e.g., Schuyler, "From *Sulphur* to *Surcharge?*—Corporate Trustee Exposure Under SEC Rule 10b-5," 67 Nw. U.L. Rev. 42 (1972). The author suggests incorporating an exculpatory provision on the management agreement. *Id.* at 57 n.68. See also "Problems of Fiduciaries Under the Securities Laws," note 135 *supra,* at 311. While such provisions might be valid, they also raise their own obvious duty-of-loyalty questions. See ¶ 5.02.

[137] See, e.g., Schotland, "Bank Trust Departments and Public Policy Today," 4 Sec. Reg. L.J. 389 (1977).

effective medium in which to conduct investment activities. But each also knows that the advantages of having economic strength over a portion of the market or of being in possession of information which, because of its nonpublic nature, has not been properly discounted, offer such significant opportunities for gain that others will take advantage of their position. As is the case with the duty of loyalty, the opportunity to profit or the competition for business can move the level of professional practice to the lowest common denominator. Indeed, this is the reason one frequently hears the term "fiduciary responsibility" used in connection with inside-information cases. Yet it is plainly a fiction to speak of a fiduciary duty either to a faceless investor who was prepared to buy or sell anyway or to a corporation which, in most circumstances, could not capitalize on its own inside information in the first place. The reference to fiduciary responsibility is simply an intuitive recognition that, as is often the case with duty-of-loyalty matters, business custom is seen as being in derogation of the principle to be applied and industry practices will not be permitted to set the standard by which to determine proper conduct.[138]

---

[138] See note 116 *supra*.

Chapter 2
THE GOVERNING STATUTORY AND COMMON-LAW SYSTEMS

¶ 2.01.   THE DIVERSE SYSTEMS REGULATING INVESTMENT MANAGEMENT ACTIVITIES

Chapter One discussed the fundamental principles around which study of investment management law can be organized. But one should not be misled by the generality of investment management law as a term of art. Investment management law is a collection of self-contained statutory and common-law systems, which, though related in principle, differ extensively in the investment management activities they affect and in the specific obligations they impose. No single statutory or common-law system is the entire locus of a manager's responsibilities, neither with respect to obtaining new business, nor to setting proper investment objectives, nor to choosing particular investments, nor to obtaining execution of his investment decisions.

In view of the diversity and cross-jurisdictional reach of these statutory and common-law schemes, it is important to understand how each connects with the investment management activities each regulates. Knowing the jurisdictional means by which regulation of investment management is possible simplifies identification of the controls that might be imposed in any case. The function of this chapter is to list the relevant statutory and common-law schemes and to explain the means by which each applies to matters of concern to investment managers.

¶ 2.02.   DEFINING THE COMMON-LAW RELATIONSHIP BETWEEN CLIENT AND MANAGER

Almost all investment management relationships are the product of an express contract or an instrument creating a trust. A contract to provide management services invokes agency law; a trust instrument, trust law. Even where an investment management arrangement is not documented, however, either agency or trust doctrine controls the acts of the manager. Together, agency and trust law cover every investment management service for which an investment manager expressly or impliedly has any degree of discretion to act in behalf of and bind a client or beneficiary.

[1] Trust Relationships

A trust is a relationship in which legal title to property resides in one party who is subject to equitable duties to deal with the property for the benefit of another.[1] Individuals, partnerships, associations, and corporations may all assume the office of trustee.[2] Compensation for assuming the duties of trustee is not required, though reasonable compensation is assumed unless provision to the contrary appears in the trust instrument or the trustee otherwise agrees to forgo compensation.[3] Once engaged in administering the trust, the trustee assumes the duties determined by the terms of the trust instrument, plus all general duties normally incident to trusteeship except those expressly excluded by the trust instrument.[4] Those duties normally incident to the trust include loyalty,[5] administration,[6] fair dealing among beneficiaries and between

---

[1] *Restatement (Second) of Trusts* §§ 2, 348 (1959).

[2] *Id.* §§ 89-99. The general principle is that natural persons can hold property in trust and administer it to the extent they could were the property owned beneficially by them. A corporation, association, or partnership can administer a trust only to the extent permitted by state law.

[3] *Id.* § 242. In some jurisdictions, trustee compensation is determined by statute. The English rule is that a trustee is not entitled to compensation unless the terms of the trust provide otherwise. See generally 3 A. Scott, *Law of Trusts* § 242 (3d ed. 1967) (hereinafter cited as Scott). Compensation of investment managers is discussed more fully in ¶ 5.03. It is worth noting, however, that restrictive compensation rules pressure investment managers to increase their revenues through additional services to their managed accounts. The provision of these extra services often creates conflicts of interest which are more subversive of an account's net return than higher management fees would be. How efficiently a trust officer in a bank manages the uninvested cash of its trust accounts may depend, for example, on whether the fees for trust management provide enough independent compensation to enable the trust department to retain the personnel necessary to use effectively uninvested cash by removing it from commercial department time and demand deposits and investing it in more productive short-term debt instruments. See, e.g., E. Herman, *Conflicts of Interest: Commercial Bank Trust Departments* (Twentieth Century Fund 1975). As another example, the power to hire an associated adviser under the Uniform Trustee's Powers Act (7 *U.L.A.*) § 3(c)(24) (1970) raises the question of when the adviser should be paid by the trustee and when by the trust. See Stillman v. Watkins, 325 N.E.2d 295 (Mass. App. 1975) (trustee not empowered to compensate retained investment adviser from estate). See also Heskell, "Some Problems With the Uniform Trustee's Powers Act," 32 L. & Contemp. Prob. 168, 177 (1967).

[4] *Restatement (Second) of Trusts* §§ 164-168 (1959).

[5] *Id.* § 170.

[6] *Id.* §§ 171-182.

beneficiaries and remaindermen,[7] and, with respect to the selection of investment, the duty to invest prudently with an eye to preservation of the estate and the production of regular income.[8]

Institutional trusts, such as the endowments of educational and charitable organizations, often receive special treatment. Unlike individual trusts, they rarely involve remaindermen who can realistically expect to receive trust assets.[9] Moreover, they are usually larger than individual trusts and hence more likely to seek professional assistance in managing their investments.

These characteristics of institutional trusts often raise problems concerning the delegation of investment responsibility and the application of capital gains and income to preservation of the trust corpus or to current expenses.[10] As a result, state law in most jurisdictions treats institutional trusts differently from individual trusts. Many states, for example, have adopted the Uniform Management of Institutional Funds Act. In general, the Uniform Act, which permits both delegation of investment management and the expenditure of capital appreciation,[11] is supportive of trustees seeking more discretion in applying endowment-fund assets to current expenditures and in seeking professional investment management services than traditional trust law may permit. Nonetheless, the Act still requires the exercise of ordinary skill and care,[12] and, in most cases, that standard probably demands either the skill and care of a professional or a high level of skill and care in the selection of a professional.[13]

---

[7] *Id.* §§ 183, 232.

[8] *Id.* §§ 227-231.

[9] See Saint Joseph's Hosp. v. Bennett, 281 N.Y. 115, 118, 22 N.E.2d 305, 306 (1939), defining an endowment as money permanently bestowed, "the income of which is to be used in the administration of a proposed work."

[10] See W. Cary & C. Bright, *The Law and the Lore of Endowment Funds* (Ford Foundation 1969); W. Cary & C. Bright, *The Developing Law of Endowment Funds: "The Law and the Lore" Revisited* (Ford Foundation 1974). See also Cary & Bright, "The Delegation of Investment Responsibility for Endowment Funds," 74 Colum. L. Rev. 207 (1974).

[11] Uniform Management of Institutional Funds Act (7 *U.L.A.*) §§ 2, 5 (Supp. 1971-1976). The Act was approved in 1972 largely in response to the arguments of Cary and Bright, cited note 10 *supra.*

[12] *Id.* § 6 ("ordinary business care and prudence").

[13] The Commissioner's comment to Section 6 of the Uniform Act states:

"Officers of a corporation owe a duty of care and loyalty to the corporation, and the more intimate the knowledge of the affairs of the corporation the higher the standard of care. . . . This is a proper standard for the managers of a nonprofit institution, whether or not it is incorporated."

[2] Agency Relationships

An agency relationship is created when one party, the principal, agrees that another shall act on his behalf, subject to the principal's control, and the other consents so to act.[14] Any person or entity legally empowered to contract is capable of being an agent.[15] An investment management arrangement which is not a trust thus subjects the manager to the constraints of the common law of agency. Compensation, though normally included in a management contract,[16] is not required to create an agency relationship.[17] Consequently, agency law would apply, for example, to voluntary investment management services provided an eleemosynary institution.[18]

Section 425 of the *Restatement (Second) of Agency* specifies three general duties investment managers owe investors in selecting investments:

(1) To invest promptly;

(2) To invest prudently; and

(3) To shift investments according to changes in the safety of existing investments or the needs of the investor.

In addition to these specific duties, agency law imposes on investment managers the other duties normally incident to an agency relationship.

In Stern v. Lucy Webb Hayes Nat'l Training School for Deaconesses & Missionaries, 381 F. Supp. 1003 (D.D.C. 1974), the court held that trustees of a charitable corporation owe a higher duty of care with respect to management of investments than to corporate investors in matters of judgment, the standard applicable to trustees being mere negligence. *Stern* raised questions both of mismanagement and self-dealing. For a useful analysis of the practical application of *Stern*, see Mace, "Standards of Care for Trustees," 54 Harv. Bus. Rev. 14 (1976).

[14] *Restatement (Second) of Agency* § 1 (1958).

[15] *Id.* § 21. A person acting as agent can bind the principal to a third party even though, due to an incapacity, the appointed agent cannot be held to fiduciary duties. *Id.*

[16] *Id.* § 441. Compensation is implied in an agency contract for the fair value of the services if a definite sum is not agreed upon. *Id.* § 443.

[17] Consideration is not a necessary element of an agency relationship. *Id.* §§ 16, 225. Nor is it necessary that there be an actual contract. *Id.* § 1, Comment b; § 26, Comment a.

[18] Most nonprofit institutions are operated as charitable trusts. Although the general trust rule is that despite a trustee's authority to appoint agents, trustees may not delegate investment management authority, it is now recognized that trustees of nonprofit institutions may delegate such authority to professional investment managers. See notes 10 and 11 *supra*.

An investment manager owes his client duties of service and obedience,[19] loyalty,[20] and any additional duties imposed by the investment contract.[21] Though a more recent source of investment management law than the law of trusts, agency law is ancient doctrine and, as a result, has a well-developed scheme of liabilities and remedies.[22] Absent contrary contractual arrangements that a court will enforce, they all apply to investment management relationships.

¶ **2.03. APPLICATION OF THE LAW BY TYPE OF TRANSACTION: THE ANTIFRAUD PROVISIONS OF THE SECURITIES ACT OF 1933 AND THE SECURITIES EXCHANGE ACT OF 1934**

The antifraud provisions of the Securities Act of 1933 and the Securities Exchange Act of 1934 apply broadly to a variety of activities in which investment managers engage. But the application of these provisions is triggered by the activity rather than anything deriving peculiarly from the fact of investment management. That is, the activities to be regulated taken together may represent an investment management relationship, but the antifraud provisions themselves apply to each of these activities severally, regardless of whether an investment manager is responsible. The fact of investment management, if relevant at all, only strengthens the resolve of a reviewing authority to insist on a high degree of fairness toward a client.[23]

The general antifraud provisions from which the federal courts and the Securities and Exchange Commission derive open-ended authority to regulate securities practices are Section 17(a)[24] of the Securities Act and Sections 10(b)[25] and 15(c)(1)[26] of the Securities Exchange Act.

---

[19] *Restatement (Second) of Agency* §§ 377-386 (1958).

[20] *Id.* §§ 387-398.

[21] *Id.* § 377.

[22] *Id.* §§ 399-409. Depending on the injury, a principal may sue in law or in equity. The principal's choice of remedies is, of course, broadest for breaches of duty of loyalty. *Id.* § 407. For a useful discussion of remedies available to limited partners of an investment partnership, see Note, "Procedures and Remedies in Limited Partners' Suits for Breach of the General Partner's Fiduciary Duty," 90 Harv. L. Rev. 763 (1977).

[23] See, e.g., Chasins v. Smith, Barney & Co., 438 F.2d 1167 (2d Cir. 1971) (broker-dealer, complying with rules in disclosing principal status, held liable to customer relying on its recommendations and advice for failing to disclose status as market-maker).

[24] 15 U.S.C. § 77q(a).

[25] 15 U.S.C. § 78j(b).

[26] 15 U.S.C. § 78o(c)(1).

Although they are similar in the nondistinct character of their reach, they are different in certain respects which can affect their respective application in a given case:

(1) Both Sections 17(a) and 10(b) apply to "any person." Section 15(c)(1) applies only to a broker or dealer.

(2) Section 10(b), and its supplementing regulation, Rule 10b-5, proscribe manipulative and fraudulent practices "in connection with the purchase or sale of any security." Section 17(a) applies to "the offer or sale of any securities." [27] This means that an actual transaction must take place to trigger Section 10(b),[28] whereas only an offer is necessary under Section 17(a). On the other hand, Section 17(a) would not apply to a purchase, whereas Section 10(b) expressly does so.

(3) Sections 17(a) and 10(b) apply to transactions in securities wherever carried out. Section 15(c)(1), since it appears in that part of the Act dealing with over-the-counter markets, applies only to transactions "other than on a national securities exchange."

(4) Section 17(a) is self-executing, but Sections 10(b) and 15(c)(1) must be implemented by rule. Rules 10b-5 and 15c1-2 substantially incorporate the language of Section 17(a).

Although the antifraud provisions are transaction-oriented, they can apply to a course of dealing. With respect to investment management relationships in particular, a management arrangement may be deemed a statutory investment contract, and hence a statutory security.[29] In that event, the proceedings leading up to the agreement that an investment management relationship be created and the circumstances under which it is carried out would be both "an offer of" and "in connection with" the purchase or sale of a security. With the jurisdictional means satisfied, the antifraud provisions would be available as a regulatory tool. Even if an investment management arrangement is not deemed a statutory investment contract, Section 10(b) and Rule 10b-5 may nonetheless apply to a manager's activities. Since one of the functions of investment management is expert assistance in selecting suitable securities, the very existence of a management arrangement would seem to

---

[27] Pub. L. 83-577 § 10, 68 Stat. 686 (1954), added the words "offer or."
[28] See Blue Chip Stamps v. Manor Drug Stores, 421 U.S. 723 (1975).
[29] See ¶ 3.03.

be in connection with the purchase or sale of securities. Thus, at least for purposes of SEC enforcement,[30] the Commission has applied Rule 10b-5 to the marketing of management services,[31] suitability determinations,[32] investment recommendations,[33] and execution practices.[34]

There are two respects in which the antifraud provisions may create special problems for investment managers. One concerns the enforcement of a client's rights against persons other than the manager. The law of trusts and the law of agency require trustees and agents to protect the legal rights of beneficiaries and principals, at least through information that legal steps may be available.[35] An investment manager, having expertise in the operation of the securities markets and the application of securities laws, may be under an obligation to use reasonable diligence to identify and preserve the legal rights of his managed accounts, particularly where the client is unsophisticated in these matters.

Second, the antifraud provisions may create obligations that override a manager's common-law fiduciary obligations to his clients. A manager may not defend his use of inside information by arguing a paramount duty to his clients.[36] The matter is similar in principle but less clear with respect to market information.[37] Also, a manager may

---

[30] The antifraud provisions may not apply equally extensively in regulatory proceedings and private litigation. In Ernst & Ernst v. Hochfelder, 425 U.S. 185 (1976), the Supreme Court held that "scienter" was a necessary element of a civil damages action under Section 10(b) of the Securities Exchange Act. *Id.* at 193 n.12. The Court reserved decision, however, on whether scienter must be proved in an action for injunctive relief. It may be that the administrative expertise of the SEC and its mission of investor protection will make available to it more liberal application of statutory fraud concepts, a greater showing of scienter being necessary in private litigation. This issue is discussed more fully in ¶ 6.01, note 5.

[31] See ¶ 3.02.

[32] See ¶ 4.01[2].

[33] See ¶ 7.07.

[34] See ¶¶ 10.04-10.06.

[35] *Restatement (Second) of Agency* § 381, Comment a (1958); *Restatement (Second) of Trusts* §§ 177-178 (1959). Cf. Auchincloss & Lawrence Inc., [1973-1974 Transfer Binder] CCH Fed. Sec. L. Rep. ¶¶ 79,762, 79,686 (1974) (exculpatory language must be removed from advisory contract which might be construed to relieve adviser from fiduciary duty).

[36] See *In re* Investors Management Co., SEC Securities Exchange Act Release No. 9267 (July 29, 1971), [1970-1971 Transfer Binder] CCH Fed. Sec. L. Rep. ¶ 78,163.

[37] See *In re* Oppenheimer & Co., SEC Securities Exchange Act Release No. 12319 (April 2, 1976), [1975-1976 Transfer Binder] CCH Fed. Sec. L. Rep. ¶ 80,551, discussed at 10.06[2][a], note 316. See also ¶ 1.04. But cf.

have conflicting fiduciary obligations where he manages a number of accounts or acts as agent for both parties to a transaction. In that event, he is under a duty of fair dealing to both clients and cannot argue fiduciary obligation to one as grounds for ignoring fiduciary obligation to the other.[38]

In addition to the antifraud provisions, the Securities Exchange Act contains two provisions which, though transaction-oriented, deal with the substance of investment management issues far more narrowly than do the antifraud provisions. The Securities Acts Amendments of 1975[39] amended Section 11(a) of the Act to separate brokerage and management for certain transactions on national securities exchanges and added new Section 28(e) to enable investment managers to pay excess commissions for supplementary services. Ostensibly added to federal law to ameliorate perceived conflicts of interest, Sections 11(a) and 28(e) have a complex genesis which is heavily connected to the transition from fixed to negotiated commission rates. Both provisions are analyzed in detail in subsequent chapters.[40]

¶ 2.04. APPLICATION OF THE LAW BY TYPE OF CLIENT

Several statutes, discussed below, regulate investment management activities only for specific types of clients that possess certain characteristics which are deemed worthy of extra concern as a matter of public policy. The principal effect of these statutes is to create rules of compliance and prohibitions or restrictions on conduct which apply only to statutory clients (though, of course, such rules, prohibitions, and limitations can become models for standards to be imposed under other statutory and common-law schemes). This is not to say that these stat-

---

Frigitemp Corp. v. Financial Dynamics Fund, Inc., [1974-1975 Transfer Binder] CCH Fed. Sec. L. Rep. ¶ 94,907 (S.D.N.Y. 1974).

[38] See ¶ 9.06[4].

[39] Pub. L. 94-29, 89 Stat. 97 (June 4, 1975).

[40] See Part IV.

Investment management activities are also subject to the antifraud provisions of state Blue Sky legislation (see, e.g., Conn. Gen. Stat. § 36-338) and other legislation which, as a refinement of common-law deceit and unfair competition, can apply to securities transactions (see, e.g., Mass. Gen. Laws Ann., Ch. 93, § 2). As a general rule, the federal antifraud provisions are more broad than state provisions, but state law has become increasingly responsive to securities matters, especially with respect to investment management activities. See, e.g., Cal. Reg., Tit. 10, Subch. 2, Art. 4, Subpts. 8-11, 1 CCH Blue Sky Rep. ¶¶ 8624-8627. See generally A. Bromberg, *Securities Law: Fraud, SEC Rule 106-5* § 2.7 (Supp. 1971).

utes are entirely technical in character. On the contrary, they can impose obligations which are as open-ended and indefinite as the antifraud provisions of the Securities Act and the Securities Exchange Act. The point is, however, that these statutes apply only to statutory clients and their managers. Therefore, even though the status of a client may be clear in most cases, errors on the issue resulting in regulatory action occur often enough to underline the hazard of providing investment management for an inadvertent statutory client.

[1] Publicly Owned Corporate Investors: The Investment Company Act of 1940

The Investment Company Act of 1940[41] is a comprehensive statute designed to deal with publicly owned corporate investors and face-amount certificate companies. Because they occupy the dominant position in the pooled-agency account market, however, open-end investment companies (mutual funds) and closed-end investment companies have been the principal objects of regulation under this statute. These companies buy and sell securities in accordance with investment programs previously constructed by their promoters. Normally, external advisers handle their selection of investments and their trading activities, though in some cases investment management is an internal operation conducted by officers and employees of the company. In any event, either because of deserved notoriety or because so many of their activities are a matter of public record, investment companies have been responsible for much legislative and regulatory activity not only in connection with administration of the Investment Company Act, but also with respect to the administration of other securities laws.

The Investment Company Act defines an investment adviser to an investment company in Section 2(a)(20).[42] The definition includes anyone regularly furnishing the company advice concerning investments in securities and other property; anyone empowered to determine the securities to be bought or sold by the company; and anyone under contract with a statutory investment adviser to perform substantially all duties of the adviser. The most serious danger facing one not deliberately evading regulation under the Act is that he will provide sufficient

---

41 15 U.S.C. §§ 80a-1 et seq. An excellent analysis of the Act in the context of contemporary reform appears in Rosenblat & Lybecker, "Some Thoughts on the Federal Securities Laws Regulatory External Investment Management Arrangements and the ALI Federal Securities Code Project," 124 U. Pa. L. Rev. 587 (1976).

42 15 U.S.C. § 80a-2(a)(20).

advisory assistance to a statutory investment adviser to be brought within Section 2(a)(20). Broker-dealers providing research assistance and investment recommendations to a statutory investment adviser are especially exposed.[43] Another difficult area concerns shifts in the composition of the investment adviser. Assignment terminates the advisory contract,[44] and in such case one assuming investment management

---

[43] For example, in Lutz v. Boas, 39 Del. Ch. 585, 171 A.2d 381 (1961), a broker-dealer to whom the advisers of an investment company delegated responsibility for selecting securities for the company's portfolio was held to be a statutory investment adviser.

[44] Investment Company Act § 15(a)(4), 15 U.S.C. § 80a-15(a)(4). See, e.g., Finomic Inv. Fund & Inv. Advisors, Inc., [1973 Transfer Binder] CCH Fed. Sec. L. Rep. ¶ 79,572 (1973) (issuance of 33 percent of stock on an assignment). Assignment does not depend on compensation by the assignee to the assignor, of course, but the presence of compensation certainly colors the question when an outgoing adviser presents shareholders with information describing arrangements for transfer of all or part of its business that it has negotiated with an incoming adviser and recommends approval of a new contract with the incoming adviser. Shareholder endorsement is virtually certain since control of the proxy machinery rests with the adviser. Whether the terms of the transfer suggest unacceptable influence on the part of the outgoing adviser may depend in turn on whether the arrangement between the outgoing adviser and the incoming adviser is contingent on such shareholder approval.

The item of value apparently being transferred is the discounted value of the advisory fee over the life of the fund. In litigation, mutual fund shareholders have asserted that this value belongs to them and that the fund's directors should use it as a means to buy less expensive advice. See, e.g., Rosenfeld v. Black, 445 F.2d 1337 (2d Cir. 1971), appeal dism'd sub nom. Lazard Freres & Co. v. Rosenfeld, 409 U.S. 802 (1972). But see Kukman v Baum, 346 F. Supp. 55 (N.D. Ill. 1972), which, aligning itself with SEC v. Insurance Secs., Inc., 254 F.2d 642 (9th Cir. 1958), held that the profits above book value realized on sale of the advisory office do not involve a breach of fiduciary duty under the Act. While Rosenfeld involved the sale of the adviser, Kukman involved only the sale of the controlling block of stock in the adviser. In this connection, consider Newman v. Stein, 464 F.2d 689 (2d Cir. 1972), in which the Rosenfeld court approved a modest settlement where a public offering was made of a large majority of the adviser's stock. The SEC has taken a similar position to that of Kukman in Fulton Reid & Staples Fund, Inc., [1969-1973 Transfer Binder] CCH Mutual Funds Guide ¶ 9168 (1970). It has also held that statutory mergers involving no change in control are not in violation of the Act. See Securities Management & Research, Inc., [1969-1973 Transfer Binder] CCH Mutual Funds Guide ¶ 9400 (1971); Lexington Research Fund, Inc., [1969-1973 Transfer Binder] CCH Mutual Funds Guide ¶ 9258 (1971). In any event, the issue, though highly celebrated (see Newman, supra at 695 n.14), has attenuated perceptibly since Section 28(1) of the Securities

duties for an investment company must be properly approved or qualify for one of the exclusions in Section 2(a)(20).[45]

As serious as mistaking one's status as a statutory investment adviser is the possibility of providing investment management services to a client erroneously not registered as a statutory investment company. Section 3(a)[46] of the Act, the statutory definition of investment com-

---

Acts Amendments of 1975 (Pub. L. 94-29 (June 4, 1975)) amended Section 15(f) of the Investment Company Act (15 U.S.C. § 80a-15(f)) to permit transfer of an interest in the advisory office if certain statutory conditions are met. Transfers of legal ownership without change in beneficial ownership are not treated as assignments. See, e.g., Tucker, Anthony Mgmt. Corp. (available Oct. 11, 1975), Sec. Reg. & L. Rep., Oct. 22, 1975, p. C-1.

[45] Excluded are persons distributing their publications to subscribers, persons providing statistical information without regularly furnishing advice or making recommendations concerning specific securities, persons compensated under the supervision of a court, and persons excluded by rule or regulation. Sections 2(a)(20)(i) through 2(9)(20)(v). None of these exclusions would ordinarily apply to an assignment, defined in Section 2(a)(4) (15 U.S.C. § 80a-2(a)(4)) to include "any direct or indirect transfer or hypothecation of a contract . . . or of a controlling block of the assignor's outstanding voting securities. . . ."

Ironically, the Act's strictness with respect to assignment and approval of the advisory contract makes it extremely difficult for a statutory company to rid itself of an unsatisfactory adviser and hire a new one. Section 15(a) (15 U.S.C. § 80a-15(a)) makes it unlawful to serve as a statutory investment adviser except "pursuant to a written contract, which . . . has been approved by the vote of a majority of the outstanding voting securities of such . . . company. . . ." Thus, except when the SEC obtains the appointment of a receiver (see Section 42(e), 15 U.S.C. § 80a-41(e)), an investment company must obtain an exemption under Section 6(c) (15 U.S.C. § 80a-6(c)) to permit an interim adviser to serve. See *In re* Ivy Fund, SEC Investment Company Act Release No. 8687 (Feb. 25, 1975), [1974-1975 Transfer Binder] CCH Fed. Sec. L. Rep. ¶ 80,120, and, on the same matter, SEC Investment Company Act Release No. 8646 (Jan. 21, 1975). See also Securities Week, Jan. 20, 1975.

[46] 15 U.S.C. § 80a-3(a) reads:

"When used in this subchapter, 'investment company' means any issuer which—

"(1) is or holds itself out as being engaged primarily, or proposes to engage primarily, in the business of investing, reinvesting, or trading in securities;

"(2) is engaged or proposes to engage in the business of issuing face-amount certificates of the installment type, or has been engaged in such business and has any such certificate outstanding; or

"(3) is engaged or proposes to engage in the business of investing, reinvesting, owning, holding, or trading in securities, and owns or pro-

pany, is broad enough to include every organization engaged in investing at least forty percent of its assets in the securities of other issuers. Section 3(b)[47] excludes certain holding companies, and Section 3(c)[48] contains special exclusions for various defined organizations. Nonetheless, such precision as Section 3 may have been able to attain has been dulled by regulatory efforts to restrict the exclusions as much as possible. The ectoplasmic theory, which concentrates on the structure of an investment vehicle instead of the structure of its sponsor, enabled the SEC to reach variable annuities and variable life insurance despite the specific exclusion provided insurance companies in Section 3(c)(3).[49] In an-

---

poses to acquire investment securities having a value exceeding 40 per centum of the value of such issuer's total assets (exclusive of Government securities and cash items) on an unconsolidated basis.

"As used in this section, 'investment securities' includes all securities except (A) Government securities, (B) securities issued by employees' securities companies, and (C) securities issued by majority-owned subsidiaries of the owner which are not investment companies."

[47] 15 U.S.C. § 80a-3(b) excludes companies holding securities in wholly owned subsidiaries not in the business of investing in securities, and companies the SEC finds to be not in the business of investing in securities either through majority-owned subsidiaries or controlled companies conducting similar types of business. "Control" means the power to exercise a controlling interest and is presumed for ownership of more than 25 percent of an issuer's voting securities. Investment Company Act § 2(a)(9), 15 U.S.C. § 80a-2(a)(9).

[48] 15 U.S.C. § 80a-3(c). Among the more significant organizations excluded under this provision are investment banking operations (§ 3(c)(2)), banks and insurance companies, including common trust funds (§ 3(c)(3)), real estate companies (§ 3(c)(5)(6)), oil and gas companies (§ 3(c)(9)), charitable organizations (§ 3(c)(10)), and qualified pension and profit-sharing plans (§ 3(c)(11)). These exclusions are construed narrowly, however. See, e.g., UMP, Unlimited, [1975-1976 Transfer Binder] CCH Fed. Sec. L. Rep. ¶ 80,492 (1976) (not-for-profit corporation administering strike-benefits trust fund not excluded); Continental Illinois Nat'l Bank & Trust Co., [1975-1976 Transfer Binder] CCH Fed. Sec. L. Rep. ¶ 80,411 (1976) (collective trust fund consisting of I.R.C. § 401 funds and § 408 funds not excluded). See also First Nat'l Bank of Akron, [1975-1976 Transfer Binder] CCH Fed. Sec. L. Rep. ¶ 80,441 (1976) (collective trust not excluded unless trustee bank maintains full investment responsibility).

[49] Benefits under variable life insurance (VLI) are not fixed, but are determined according to the asset value of a portfolio of securities. Although the insurance industry claimed that VLI was an insurance contract and hence should not be subject to regulation under the federal securities laws, the SEC insisted that VLI was a security and that the policyholders were investors in an investment company. Based on the SEC's successes in

other development, the SEC has taken the position that collectively managed individual accounts comprise a statutory investment company.[50] Because of its importance to all regulatory events bearing on

---

obtaining jurisdiction under the Securities and Investment Company Acts over the sale of variable annuities (see SEC v. Variable Annuity Life Ins. Co. of Am., 359 U.S. 65 (1959); Prudential Ins. Co. of Am. v. SEC, 326 F.2d 383 (3d Cir.), *cert. denied* 377 U.S. 953 (1964)), the industry capitulated and sought exemptive relief from various provisions in the federal securities laws, and especially from the Investment Company Act. After an extensive investigation, the Commission issued Investment Company Act Rule 3c-4 (17 C.F.R. § 270.3c-4 (1974)) and Investment Advisers Act Rule 202-1 (17 C.F.R. § 275.202-1 (1974)), which totally exempted VLI from regulation under the two statutes. See SEC Investment Company Act Release No. 7644 (Jan. 31, 1973), [1972-1973 Transfer Binder] CCH Fed. Sec. L. Rep. ¶ 79,207.

Although the life insurance industry was poised for issuance of its new insurance vehicle, the response of many interest groups whose competitive position would be adversely affected by total exemption was vigorous. Responding quickly, the SEC published proposed amendments to Rule 3c-4 and Rule 202-1, conditioning the exemptions available in those rules to a Commission determination that state insurance regulation provide VLI purchasers with protection comparable to that available under the Investment Act and the Investment Advisers Act. See SEC Investment Company Act Release No. 8000 (Sept. 20, 1973), [1973 Transfer Binder] CCH Fed. Sec. L. Rep. ¶ 79,518. Since most states do not provide comparable protections, and since most state insurance commissioners were not willing to have the SEC involved in the regulation of insurance sold within their jurisdictions, VLI still could not be actively marketed. See generally Blank, Keen, Payne & Miller, "Variable Life Insurance and the Federal Securities Laws," 60 Va. L. Rev. 71 (1974). The Commission then rescinded Rules 3c-4 and 202-1, the withdrawal proposal appearing in SEC Investment Company Act Release No. 8690 (Feb. 27, 1975), [1974-1975 Transfer Binder] CCH Fed. Sec. L. Rep. ¶ 80,117, and final action appearing in SEC Investment Company Act Release No. 8826 (June 18, 1975), [1975-1976 Transfer Binder] CCH Fed. Sec. L. Rep. ¶ 80,206. In proposing to rescind the rules, however, the SEC stated its intent to adopt a rule under Section 6(e) to exercise its exemptive authority to designate provisions in the Act from which VLI would be exempted and the conditions attaching to those exemptions. SEC Investment Company Act Release No. 8691 (Feb. 27, 1975), [1975-1976 Transfer Binder] CCH Fed. Sec. L. Rep. ¶ 80,118. Without waiting for the rule to be drafted, one insurer petitioned for exemptions from various provisions for its own case. SEC Investment Company Act Release No. 8888 (Aug. 13, 1975). The application was granted shortly thereafter. See Securities Week, Oct. 27, 1975, p. 3. See generally "Proceedings, Conference on Variable Annuities and Variable Life Insurance," 32 Bus. Law. 675 et seq. (1977).

[50] See, e.g., Far West Futures Fund, [1974-1975 Transfer Binder] CCH Fed. Sec. L. Rep. ¶ 79,968. Perhaps the best-known instance of the SEC's

investment enterprises that involve widespread passive participations but are not registered under the Act, this position is discussed more fully in Chapter 3.[51]

Statutory investment advisers to investment companies are subject to a number of legal restrictions, principally in regard to transactions between themselves and their companies and joint transactions with their companies.[52] In addition, investment advisers are under a general statutory fiduciary duty[53] and a specific fiduciary duty with respect to compensation for services.[54] Also extensively regulated are other details of the relationship between the adviser and the company, such as

---

taking action under this theory is the *First National City Bank* case, SEC Litigation Release No. 4534 (Feb. 6, 1970), discussed extensively in ¶ 3.04.

[51] See ¶ 3.03.

[52] Investment Company Act §§ 17(a)-17(e), 15 U.S.C. §§ 80a-17(a)-80a-17(e). See Comment, "Application of Section 17 of the Investment Company Act of 1940 to Portfolio Affiliates," 120 U. Pa. L. Rev. 983 (1972). See also Investment Company Act § 10(f) (15 U.S.C. § 80a-10 (f)), concerning an investment company's participation as a purchaser in affiliated underwritings.

[53] Investment Company Act § 36(a), 15 U.S.C. § 80a-35(a), *as amended*, Pub. L. 91-547 § 20, 84 Stat. 1428-1429 (Dec. 14, 1970), reads:

"The Commission is authorized to bring an action in the proper district court of the United States, or in the United States court of any territory or other place subject to the jurisdiction of the United States, alleging that a person serving or acting in one or more of the following capacities has engaged within five years of the commencement of the action or is about to engage in any act or practice constituting a breach of fiduciary duty involving personal misconduct in respect of any registered investment company for which such person so serves or acts—

"(1) as officer, director, member of any advisory board, investment adviser, or depositor; or

"(2) as principal underwriter, if such registered company is an open-end company, unit investment trust, or face-amount certificate company.

"If such allegations are established, the court may enjoin such persons from acting in any or all such capacities either permanently or temporarily and award such injunctive or other relief against such person as may be reasonable and appropriate in the circumstances, having due regard to the protection of investors and to the effectuation of the policies declared in section 1(b) [15 U.S.C. § 80a-1(b)] of this title."

[54] Investment Company Act § 36(b), 15 U.S.C. § 80a-35(b), *added by* Pub. L. 91-547 § 20, 84 Stat. 1429-1430 (Dec. 14, 1970). The legislative history and application of Section 36(b) are discussed more fully in ¶ 5.03[1].

dual employment,[55] terms of advisory contracts,[56] and other matters of administration.[57]

---

[55] Investment Company Act § 10 (15 U.S.C. § 80a-10) limits the extent to which statutory companies can choose as directors persons who are otherwise affiliated with the company (§ 10(a)), and restricts the discretion of a company not having a majority of independent directors on its board to use the services of brokers, of underwriters of the company, and of other investment bankers (§ 10(b)). Special rules also apply to persons connected with banks (§ 10(c)) and to certain open-end, no-load (i.e., no underwriting commission) companies (§ 10(d)).

[56] Investment Company Act § 15(a) (15 U.S.C. § 80a-15(b)) makes it unlawful for any person to serve as an investment adviser to a company except pursuant to a written contract which has been approved by vote of a majority of the outstanding voting securities of the company. This includes a contract by another investment adviser to offer investment advice to the fund's regular investment adviser. The written contract must precisely describe all compensation to be paid. "Compensation" is not defined in the Act. In Moses v. Burgin, 316 F. Supp. 31 (D. Mass. 1970), *rev'd on other grounds* 445 F.2d 369 (1st Cir. 1971), *cert. denied sub nom.* Johnson v. Moses, 404 U.S. 994 (1972), the district court held that brokerage awarded in exchange for research information is not compensation to be paid within the limits of this section. Compare ¶ 5.03[1] at notes 58-64. The advisory contract may not continue in effect for longer than two years, unless continuance is specifically approved at least annually ("annually" is defined in Rule 15a-2, 17 C.F.R. § 270.15a-2) by the board of directors or by a vote of the majority of the shareholders. It must provide for termination at any time without payment of penalty on sixty days' written notice to the investment adviser and for automatic termination in the event of assignment by the adviser.

Investment Company Act § 15(c) (15 U.S.C. § 80a-15(c)) requires that approval of the investment advisory contract or underwriting contract must be made by a vote of the majority of directors who are not parties to the contract or interested persons of any party to the contract. These disinterested directors have the duty to request and evaluate such information as may be reasonably necessary to evaluate the terms of the advisory contracts and the investment adviser has the duty to provide any such information. This duty on the part of the disinterested directors to inquire and the correlative duty of the adviser to inform, though implicit in the original version of the Act (see Moses v. Burgin, *supra,* 445 F.2d at 376-377; Brown v. Bullock, 194 F. Supp. 207 (S.D.N.Y. 1961)), was made express in Section 15(c) by statutory amendment in Section 8(c) of the Investment Company Act Amendments of 1970, Pub. L. 91-547, 84 Stat. 1420 (Dec. 14, 1970).

[57] See, e.g., Investment Company Act §§ 12, 16, 20, 15 U.S.C. §§ 80a-12, 80a-16, 80a-20. Section 12 covers a number of matters, including acquisitions and mergers, ownership of securities in insurance companies, and broker-dealers. Section 16 deals principally with the process for selection of directors, and Section 20 with proxy and voting trust matters and circular ownership.

[2] Employee Benefit Plans: The Employee Retirement Income Security Act of 1974

In a major legislative effort to protect retirement and other employment benefits normally paid for by employee contributions from, or in lieu of additional, salary, Congress passed the Employee Retirement Income Security Act of 1974 (ERISA).[58] Because of its recent enactment, the statute is as yet untested. Nonetheless, it plainly imposes requirements, duties, and liabilities either not a part of or not enforced under preexisting law.

ERISA is a complex statute. It is, in fact, an amalgam of two separate bills—a labor bill and a tax bill—and both portions have consequences for investment managers. The labor portion of the statute reaches investment management through a set of provisions pertaining to fiduciary responsibility.[59] With respect to investment managers, the tax provisions are less broad in scope, reaching primarily prohibited transactions (a defined term).[60]

---

[58] Pub. L. 93-406, 88 Stat. 829 (Sept. 2, 1974). Useful discussions concerning the background of ERISA and the administration of the fiduciary responsibility provisions of the Act appear in "Proceedings, ABA National Institute, Fiduciary Responsibilities Under the Pension Reform Act," 31 Bus. Law. 1 et seq. (1975). See also Chadwick & Foster, "Federal Regulation of Retirement Plans: The Quest for Parity," 4 Vand. L. Rev. 641 (1975).

[59] ERISA §§ 401-414, 29 U.S.C. §§ 1101-1114. For a useful analysis of the impact of these provisions on investment managers, see Gillis & Weld, "Securities Law and Regulation: Fiduciary Responsibility Under the 1974 Pension Act," 31 Fin. Anal. J. 10 (May-June 1975). The Department of Labor has issued a series of interpretive bulletins concerning the fiduciary responsibility provisions. These bulletins have been incorporated as regulations. 29 C.F.R. §§ 2509.75-1, 2509.75-2, 2509.75-7 (prohibited transactions); 29 C.F.R. § 2509.75-3 (investment in shares of investment companies); 29 C.F.R. § 2509.75-4 (indemnification of fiduciaries); 29 C.F.R. § 2509.75-5 (definition of fiduciary; lines of responsibility; funding; investment manager of qualifications; bonding); 29 C.F.R. § 2509.75-6 (advances on expenses to party in interest); 29 C.F.R. § 2509.75-8 (definition of fiduciary; fiduciary's right to rely on information provided by others; number of fiduciaries required; allocation and delegation of fiduciary responsibilities; performance-monitoring obligations).

[60] ERISA § 2003, *adding* § 4975 to the Internal Revenue Code. Although the emphasis of the tax provisions of ERISA is clearly on prohibited transactions, as was the case before ERISA, a plan can lose its tax-qualified status under Section 401(a) of the Code by engaging in imprudent investment practices. See Rev. Rul. 69-421, Pt. 2(k)(1), 1969-2 C.B. 59. Because removal of tax-exempt status is so devastating a weapon, and because its exercise impacts on blameless employees, it is not a remedy

In the labor portion, Section 3(21)[61] defines "fiduciary" broadly enough to include nearly everyone having a measurable influence in fashioning or carrying out an investment program for covered employee benefit plans. There is also a definition of investment manager in Section 3(38)[62] as a subclass of fiduciary. Its principal requirement is that a statutory investment manager be a registered investment adviser under the Investment Advisers Act of 1940, a bank, or a qualified insurance company. The reason for specially defining investment manager was not, however, to expand or diminish the responsibilities of investment managers as fiduciaries. Rather, the purpose was to permit plan fiduciaries and trustees to rely on investment management services without breaching common-law duties against delegation[63] and without incurring vicarious liability for statutory violations by the investment manager.[64] The Department of Labor and the Treasury Department have adopted implementing regulations which narrow somewhat the statutory definition of fiduciary,[65] but, that action notwithstanding, the SEC has adopted a rule refusing registration as an investment adviser solely for the purpose of triggering the provisions for insulating trustees from liability as co-fiduciaries.[66]

---

likely to see much use except in egregious cases. But see BNA Daily Tax Report No. 127, June 30, 1976, at G-3 (Teamsters Union pension fund reportedly in danger of losing tax-exempt status). The Internal Revenue Service has issued a series of interpretive bulletins concerning the tax provisions. These bulletins have not, however, focused much on prohibited transaction matters. See T.I.R. 1334, P-H Fed. Taxes ¶ 54,974 (1975).

[61] 29 U.S.C. § 1002(21).

[62] 29 U.S.C. § 1002(38).

[63] See *Restatement (Second) of Trusts* § 171 (1959). See notes 10-11 *supra*. Compare ERISA § 403(a)(2) (29 U.S.C. § 1103(a)), which places in the trustees "exclusive authority and discretion to manage and control the assets of the plan, except to the extent that . . . (2) authority to manage, acquire, or dispose of assets of the plan is delegated to one or more investment managers pursuant to section 402(c)(3)." That latter section vests authority in the named fiduciary to appoint investment managers.

[64] ERISA § 405(d)(1) (29 U.S.C. § 1105(d)(1)) relieves a trustee from liability for the acts or omissions of properly appointed statutory investment managers. The insulation from liability is far less than total, however. Section 405(d)(2) (29 U.S.C. § 1105(d)(2)) restricts the scope of Section 405(d)(1) so as not to affect a fiduciary's independent liability under Section 405. Thus, complicity with a statutory investment manager, for example, would deprive a fiduciary of the protection of Section 405(d)(1).

[65] 29 C.F.R. §§ 2510.3-21(c), 2510.3-21(d). These provisions are discussed extensively in ¶ 10.03[2].

[66] Rule 202-1, 17 C.F.R. § 275.202-1, SEC Investment Advisers Act Release No. 503 (March 12, 1976), [1975-1976 Transfer Binder] CCH

Not including the prohibited-transactions provisions, the fiduciary-responsibility provisions in the labor portion impose three principal obligations which affect investment managers:

(1) *Delegation requirement.* The controlling instrument, which must be in writing,[67] can delegate investment management responsibility only through a fiduciary named in the instrument.[68]

(2) *Fiduciary duties.* An investment manager must invest "solely in the interest" of plan participants and beneficiaries,[69] and he must do so in accordance with a statutory standard of prudence,[70] including prudence in diversification of investments.[71]

Fed. Sec. L. Rep. ¶ 80,403; SEC Investment Advisers Act Release No. 478 (Sept. 29, 1975), [1975-1976 Transfer Binder] CCH Fed. Sec. L. Rep. ¶ 80,304.

[67] ERISA § 402(a)(1), 29 U.S.C. § 1102(a)(1).

[68] ERISA § 402(1)(3), 29 U.S.C. § 1102(c)(3).

[69] ERISA § 404(a)(1), 29 U.S.C. § 1104(a)(1).

[70] ERISA § 404(C)(1)(B), 29 U.S.C. § 1104(a)(1)(B) ("with the care, skill, prudence and diligence under the circumstances then prevailing that a prudent man acting in a like capacity and familiar with such matters would use in the conduct of an enterprise of a like character and with like aims").

[71] ERISA § 404(a)(1)(C), 29 U.S.C. § 1104(a)(1)(C) ("by diversifying . . . so as to minimize the risk of large losses, unless under the circumstances it is clearly prudent not to do so"). In interposing the word "clearly," Congress intended to place the burden of proof on justification of nondiversification on the investment manager or such other parties as were responsible for diversification. Conference Report on H.R. 2, Employee Retirement Income Security Act of 1974, H.R. Rep. No. 1280, 93d Cong., 2d Sess. 304 (Aug. 12, 1974). Congress declined, however, to give more than general guidance with respect to diversification requirements, preferring to have the meaning of "diversification" turn on the facts of each case. For a discussion of the meaning of diversification measured by contemporary investment theory, see ¶ 7.08.

One obvious departure from meeting ordinary diversification (and perhaps prudence) standards is the employee stock option plan (ESOP). ERISA defines an ESOP in Sections 407(d)(6), 29 U.S.C. § 1107(d)(6), and 2003(a), I.R.C. § 4975(e)(7), as a qualified defined benefit plan "designed to invest primarily in employer securities." (Section 407 pertains, among other things, to holding employer securities.) Section 404(a)(2) of ERISA (29 U.S.C. § 1104(a)(2)) exempts an ESOP from statutory diversification requirements but not from statutory prudence requirements except as diversification is deemed an element of diversification. To the extent an ESOP is for the purpose of providing incentives to employees through participatory ownership, the meaning to be given statutory prudence as

(3) *Co-fiduciary duties.* An investment manager incurs liability for the acts of a co-fiduciary if he participates in, conceals, fails to take reasonable steps to remedy, or, by his own wrong, enables the commission of a breach of duty by the co-fiduciary.[72] The degree of responsibility to be imposed on investment managers for the acts of unrelated investment managers is unclear.[73]

The prohibited-transactions provisions bear special note. The remedies and liabilities applicable to prohibited transactions are far more extensive than those applicable to other breaches of duty under the statute. In addition to the general criminal, legal, and equitable remedies specified in Sections 501 through 502,[74] and the personal liability in damages in Section 409(a) against fiduciaries for their breaches of duty,[75] an investment manager participating in a prohibited transaction is answerable for civil fine under the labor provisions[76] and mandatory excise taxes under the tax provisions.[77]

The general principle is that, unless expressly exempted, any transaction (1) with an employee benefit plan by a fiduciary for his own

---

applied to investment in employer securities may receive guidance from Section 402(b)(1) (29 U.S.C. § 1102(b)(1)), which requires a plan to provide for "a funding policy and method consistent with the objectives of the plan." Another aspect of prudence might be the proper valuation of employer securities. See Section 407(e). See also 1975-50 I.R.B. 16, Rev. Rul. 69-65, 1969-1 C.B. 114. A useful discussion of the application of ERISA to an ESOP appears in Note, "Employee Stock Ownership Plans: A Step Toward Democratic Capitalism," 55 B.U.L. Rev. 195 (1975). See also Lund, Casey & Chamberlain, "A Financial Analysis of the ESOP," 32 Fin. Anal. J. 55 (Jan.-Feb. 1976); Burck, "There's More to ESOP Than Meets the Eye," 93 Fortune 128 (March 1976).

[72] ERISA § 405(a), 29 U.S.C. § 1105(a).

[73] 29 C.F.R. §§ 2510.3-21(c), 2510.3-21(d), and 26 C.F.R. §§ 54.4975-9(c), 54.4975-9(d), interpreting the statutory term "investment advice" as it appears in Sections 3(2) and 2003(a) of the Act, take the position that an investment manager who is a statutory fiduciary with respect to assets he manages shall not be deemed a fiduciary with respect to other assets, the management of which is not his responsibility. But while those regulations (discussed more fully in ¶ 10.03[2][a]) save an investment manager from fiduciary status with respect to such other assets, they do not on their face limit the scope of Section 405(a). Thus, for example, an investment manager, aware of imprudent investing by another investment manager, may have an obligation to take reasonable steps to remedy that situation.

[74] 29 U.S.C. §§ 1131, 1132.

[75] 29 U.S.C. § 1109(a).

[76] ERISA § 502(i), 29 U.S.C. § 1132(i).

[77] ERISA § 2003(a), I.R.C. §§ 4975(a), 4975(b).

account, or (2) between a party in interest (under the labor provisions) or a disqualified person (under the tax provisions) caused by a fiduciary is prohibited. Although there are linguistic differences, the definition of fiduciary with respect to investment management seems operatively the same in both parts of the statute[78]; and the definitions of party in interest (in the labor portion) and disqualified person (in the tax portion) also seem operatively equivalent.[79] In at least one respect, however, the two parts differ with potentially serious consequences. Liability under the labor provisions seems to depend on a form of scienter or awareness. The tax provisions have no comparable requirement.[80] On the other hand, the Department of Labor and the Internal Revenue Service have jointly issued a major prohibited-transaction exemption concerning various agency and principal transactions in securities by investment managers.[81] It is possible, therefore, that at least as regards the provision of investment advice and related investment management services, the two sections will be applied in concert.

In view of the uncertain consequences facing investment managers subject to ERISA, it is important that there be no mistake about the status of one's client. The labor and tax provisions affecting investment management activities apply to all employee benefit plans except those expressly excluded or exempted,[82] whether or not the covered plans

---

[78] The labor and tax regulations interpreting the term fiduciary with respect to investment management are identical. See note 65 *supra*.

[79] ERISA § 3(14) (29 U.S.C. § 1002(14)) defines party in interest to include "any fiduciary (including, but not limited to, any administrator, officer, trustee, or custodian), counsel, or employee of such employee benefit plan [or] a person providing services to such a plan."

ERISA § 2003(a), I.R.C. § 4975(e)(2), defines disqualified person as "a fiduciary [or] a person providing services to the plan."

[80] Compare ERISA § 406(a), 29 U.S.C. § 1106(a) ("knows or should know"), with ERISA § 2003(a), I.R.C. § 4975(a)(1) ("tax imposed . . . [on] any disqualified person who participates"). Another distinction to note is that a disqualified person is theoretically subject to a self-executing excise tax for engaging in a prohibited transaction, whereas the civil liability of a party in interest for doing so is discretionary with the Secretary of Labor and applies only to transactions not within the purview of Section 4975(e)(1) of the Code, that is, to transactions of nonqualified plans. ERISA § 502(i), 29 U.S.C. § 1132(i).

[81] Prohibited Transaction Exemption 75-1, 40 Fed. Reg. 50,845 (Oct. 31, 1975), concerns excess commission payments for brokerage services, general agency and principal transactions, underwriting, market-making, and credit extensions. It is discussed more fully in ¶ 7.04.

[82] See ERISA § 4, 29 U.S.C. § 1003. Application of the fiduciary responsibility provisions does not depend on the qualification of a plan. Un-

meet the funding, vesting, insurance, and other requirements of the Act. The definitions of employee welfare benefit plan in Section 3(1)[83] and employee pension benefit plan in Section 3(2)[84] include most plans offering employee fringe and retirement benefits established or maintained by an employer or employee organization, as those terms are defined in Sections 3(4)[85] and 3(5).[86]

[3] Charitable Endowment Funds

[a] Private foundations: The Internal Revenue Code

Before the Tax Reform Act of 1969[87] the only federal remedy for breaches of duty by investment managers serving private foundations was to disqualify such foundations from tax-preferred status. Now, according to Section 4944(a)(2)[88] of the Internal Revenue Code, as amended by the Tax Reform Act of 1969, and Regulation § 53.4944-1(a)(2)[89] (implementing the section), investment managers who are employees of a foundation are subject to tax sanctions for making investments without exercising ordinary business care and prudence. Investment managers who are officers, directors, or trustees of a foundation also are subject to the requirements of Section 4944(a)(2). In addition, they are defined in Section 4946(a)(1)(B)[90] of the Code as

---

funded deferred compensation plans for select employees and plans for retired partners, however, are specifically exempted from the fiduciary responsibility provisions. ERISA § 401(a), 29 U.S.C. § 1101(a).

[83] 29 U.S.C. § 1002(1).

[84] 29 U.S.C. § 1002(2).

[85] 29 U.S.C. § 1002(4).

[86] 29 U.S.C. § 1002(5).

[87] Pub. L. 91-172, 83 Stat. 487 (Dec. 30, 1969). See generally W. Smith & C. Chiechi, *Private Foundations Before and After the Tax Reform Act of 1969* (American Enterprise Institute for Public Research 1974).

[88] 26 U.S.C. § 4944(a)(2). There is also a tax imposed directly on the foundation. I.R.C. § 4944(a)(1), 26 C.F.R. § 4944(a)(1). The legislative history shows clearly that the tax on investments and on foundation managers be related to investment of foundation assets "in a way which jeopardizes their use for the organization's exempt purpose." Tax Reform Act of 1969, Report of the Senate Comm. on Finance on H.R. 13270, S. Rep. No. 552, 91st Cong., 1st Sess. 45 (Nov. 21, 1969). According to the Committee, investments are to be judged "in accordance with a 'prudent trustee' approach. . . ." *Id.* at 46. See also Summary of H.R. 13270, The Tax Reform Act of 1969, Staff Report of the Joint Comm. on Internal Revenue Taxation and the Comm. on Finance, 91st Cong., 1st Sess. 16-17 (Aug. 18, 1969).

[89] 26 C.F.R. § 53.4944-1(a)(2).

[90] 26 U.S.C. § 4946(a)(1)(B).

disqualified persons subject to tax in the event they engage in certain self-dealing transactions with the foundation. Aside from the possibility of incurring direct personal tax liability, an investment manager may also face civil sanctions as a result of his relationship with a private foundation. The Code imposes taxes for violations on foundations as well as on foundation managers. But whereas foundation managers can avoid personal liability if their involvement is not willful or due to lack of reasonable care, the foundation has no such defense. It may well be, therefore, that an investment manager whose investment policies are held to violate the requirements of the Code such that the foundation suffers tax sanctions will also incur common-law liability for making imprudent investments.

There are a number of organizations excepted from the Code's private-foundation classification, principally schools, churches, hospitals, and organizations receiving substantial support from governmental bodies.[91] Management of these organizations' investments plainly presents less of a hazard of regulatory action to investment managers since there is thus one less regulatory authority to worry about. But the very distinction in treatment afforded excepted organizations emphasizes the importance of properly identifying their status, especially since the statutory scheme, in Section 509(a),[92] provides that a foundation is classified as a private foundation unless exempted. Moreover, tax liabilities aside, on the question of investment policy, the standards of prudence developed for regulated foundations are equally well suited to setting standards of prudence for charitable endowment fund investing generally. The principal reason for tax regulation of private foundations is to end use of foundations as tax havens. By regulating investment purpose, therefore, Congress apparently was insisting that foundation endowments be managed consistent with the donative intent assumed to be the motive of contributors. Should the federal tax law experience any substantial development with respect to "prudent" investing for foundations, such development could well serve as a broader model than the actual regulatory scope of Regulation § 53.4944-1(a)(2).

[b] Charitable trusts: The Uniform Management of Institutional Funds Act

Although the enforcement problems for charitable institutions are

---

[91] 26 U.S.C. § 509(a)(1).
[92] 26 U.S.C. § 509(a).

different from those for private trusts,[93] the trust duties of prudence and loyalty are essentially the same.[94] In the investment environment after World War II, it became apparent that many of the restrictions on the administration of private trusts were harming charitable trusts. In particular, trustees of charitable trusts desired clear authority to delegate investment responsibility to professional investment managers and to participate in a wider range of investment opportunities, as well as more power to disregard the distinction between principal and income in order to meet current expenses. With the publication of two influential reports on these matters concerning college endowment funds as a catalyst,[95] the National Conference of Commissioners on Uniform State Laws undertook to fashion a statute which would be responsive to the investment needs of charitable institutions. In 1972, the Conference approved the Uniform Management of Institutional Funds Act,[96] which authorizes the prudent expenditure of capital appreciation "for the uses and purposes for which an endowment fund is established," [97]

---

[93] See Uniform Supervision of Trustees for Charitable Purposes Act (7 U.L.A.) § 821 (1970). Generally, the attorney general must enforce a trust, although persons with a special interest and settlors who have properly reserved enforcement authority may do so also. See 4 Scott, note 3 supra, § 391. But it seems that recent legal developments are opening enforcement powers to others. See Stern v. Lucy Webb Hayes Nat'l Training School for Deaconesses & Missionaries, 381 F. Supp. 1003 (D.D.C. 1974) (class action against charitable hospital by purchasers of health services); Daniel v. Brotherhood of Teamsters, 410 F. Supp. 541 (N.D. Ill. 1976) (involuntary noncontributory pension plans held securities). Cf. also James v. Gerber Prods. Co., 483 F.2d 944 (6th Cir. 1974) (beneficiary of testamentary trust has standing under Rule 10b-5 to sue purchaser of securities sold from trust).

[94] According to the Restatement (Second) of Trusts § 379 (1975), "the duties of the trustee of a charitable trust are similar to the duties of the trustee of a private trust." See note 13 supra.

[95] W. Cary & C. Bright, The Law and the Lore of Endowment Funds (Ford Foundation 1969); Advisory Committee on Endowment Management to the Ford Foundation, Managing Educational Endowments (Ford Foundation 1969). See also W. Cary & C. Bright, The Developing Law of Endowment Funds: "The Law and the Lore" Revisited (Ford Foundation 1974); J. Williamson, Performance Measurement and Investment Objectives for Educational Endowment Funds (The Common Fund 1972); Cary & Bright, "The 'Income' of Endowment Funds," 69 Colum. L. Rev. 396 (1969).

[96] (7 U.L.A.) § 269 (Supp. 1975).

[97] Id. § 2. On the wisdom of using principal for current expenses, see "The Harvard-Yale Game," 8 Institutional Investor 46 (Sept. 1972); "Let's Not Strangle the Golden Goose: An Open Letter to Harvard's President

the making of certain kinds of investments "without restriction to investments a fiduciary may make," [98] and the delegation of investment authority and payment of compensation to "independent investment advisors, investment counsel or managers, banks, or trust companies. . . ." [99]

[4] Holders of Debt Securities: The Trust Indenture Act of 1939

The purpose of the Trust Indenture Act of 1939[100] is to provide, through independent trustees, protection for holders of debt securities which, because of the size of the issue and the number of security holders, must be issued under indentures and administered through a central supervising authority. In normal circumstances, the work of an indenture trustee involves administrative duties far more than investment management. Nonetheless, issuers occasionally seek to alter the security underlying their obligations, and the process of deciding whether to approve or disapprove can require investment analysis of high quality from an indenture trustee. Furthermore, should it be necessary for an indenture trustee to avail itself of its creditor's remedies, issues involving more active investment management may arise. In all events, Section 315(c) of the Act[101] imposes on the trustee a statutory duty of prudence in carrying out all its responsibilities. Additionally, the theoretical independence of the indenture trustee frequently is not supported by the facts, since indenture trustees usually have commercial relations with the debtor and, indeed, may obtain office by virtue of those relations. With middling effectiveness, the Act also tries to deal with the conflicts of interest which occur when the indenture trustee is not truly independent.

¶ 2.05. APPLICATION OF THE LAW BY TYPE OF MANAGER

The primary sources of professional investment management services are the trust departments of banks, insurance companies, investment advisers and counselors, and brokerage firms. Although some cross-regulation occurs, separate regulatory systems control most of

---

from Paul Cabot," *id*. at 50. See also Shakin, "Down to Its Last $2 Billion: Ford Foundation Is Tightening the Purse-Strings," Barron's, June 2, 1975, p. 11.

[98] *Id*. § 4.
[99] *Id*. § 5.
[100] 15 U.S.C. §§ 77aaa-77bbbb.
[101] 15 U.S.C. § 77ooo(c).

these organizations. Moreover, they are subject not only to different sets of rules, but also to regulation by different administrative authorities.

[1] Bank Trust Departments: Regulation by the Federal Reserve Board and the Comptroller of the Currency

Because bank trust departments receive their authority to act from and are regulated by both state and federal authorities,[102] their investment management duties and obligations may differ depending on the jurisdiction exercising regulatory authority. Since federal law governing national banks is broader than state law in coverage and representative of relevant state law in design, federal law is the model throughout this book.

The Federal Reserve Act conferred authority on the Federal Reserve Board to grant trust powers to national banks.[103] Initial rudimentary controls over the trust activities of national banks appeared as early as 1933 in the Glass-Steagall Act.[104] In addition, the Federal Reserve Board has been given broad power, as yet unused, to promulgate rules under the Bank Holding Company Act of 1956.[105] At pres-

---

[102] See generally 2 Scott, note 3 *supra*, § 96.5. For a lengthy discussion of the regulation of bank trust departments in general, see Lybecker, "Regulation of Bank Trust Department Investment Activities: Seven Gaps, Eight Remedies," 90 Banking L.J. 912 (1973), and 91 Banking L.J. 6 (1974). National banks not having authority to act in a fiduciary capacity may accept individual retirement accounts and self-employed retirement trusts funded by time deposits. Banking Circular 61 (Jan. 27, 1975), CCH Fed. Banking L. Rep. ¶ 96,446.

[103] 12 U.S.C. § 92(a). The Federal Reserve Act has been amended so frequently that no useful catalogue of its codification is possible save a statement that, as amended, it is generally dispersed throughout Title 12 of the United States Code.

[104] Banking Act of 1933, Ch. 89, 48 Stat. 162 (Glass-Steagall Act), now distributed throughout Chs. 3 and 6 of 12 U.S.C. (1970). The Act, which is discussed in "Glass-Steagall Act—A History of its Legislative Origins and Regulatory Construction," 92 Banking L.J. 38 (1975), was designed primarily to "reduce the risk that inventory losses in speculative securities might jeopardize the stability of banks and the banking system" (*id.* at 41-42), and was directed mainly at banks dealing in securities for their own accounts. There is, however, some indication of concern with the activities of trust departments (see, e.g., 77 Cong. Rec. 3491-3493 (1933)) (remarks of Rep. McFadden), and many provisions of the statute could have application in that area. See, e.g., Investment Co. Institute v. Camp, 401 U.S. 617 (1971) (collective agency accounts prohibited).

[105] 12 U.S.C. §§ 1842, 1844; Lybecker, note 102 *supra*, 91 Banking L.J. at 43.

ent, the most significant regulations are those of the Comptroller of the Currency,[106] who was authorized in 1962 to grant fiduciary powers to national banks by special permit.[107] A number of traditional restrictions, such as a prohibition of commingling trust accounts and general funds,[108] were also enacted at that time.

During the intervening years, the Comptroller has promulgated Regulation 9[109] to deal with fiduciary powers of national banks and collective investment funds. The regulation requires that national banks "desiring to exercise fiduciary powers" apply to the Comptroller for a permit[110] and follow certain procedures[111] when employing such powers. Also, a 1974 addition to Regulation 9 calls for the reporting of fiduciary account holdings and securities transactions,[112] and Regulation 23 requires disclosure of various types of "business interest" held by directors and principal officers of national banks.[113] As a supplement to the regulations, the Comptroller publishes general guidelines in a manual of instructions[114] and issues opinions on specific matters.

Some of the most controversial recent developments are proposals that the Securities and Exchange Commission be provided with disclosure of data and with regulatory authority over trust departments.[115]

---

[106] 12 C.F.R. Pt. 9.

[107] 12 U.S.C. § 92a(a).

[108] 12 U.S.C. § 92a(c).

[109] 12 C.F.R. Pt. 9.

[110] 12 C.F.R. § 9.2.

[111] 12 C.F.R. §§ 9.7-9.18 (concerning administration, record-keeping, auditing, investment of funds, self-dealing, custodianship, and collective investment).

[112] 12 C.F.R. §§ 9.101-9.103. The SEC has power to control the form and type of disclosure, however. Securities Exchange Act § 13(f), 15 U.S.C. § 78m(f).

[113] 12 C.F.R. Pt. 23. The regulation requires disclosure of interests such as stock ownership or control of enterprises other than the bank and controlling or controlled companies. For a discussion of the provision, see Callaghan, "The Comptroller of the Currency's Disclosure Regulation and a Banker's Right to Privacy," 92 Banking L.J. 119 (1975).

[114] Comptroller of the Currency, *Comptroller's Manual for Representatives in Trusts* 21 (1963).

[115] The SEC's concern with the involvement of banks in investment management matters falling within the Commission's jurisdiction was probably catalyzed by the arrangement between First National City Bank and Merrill Lynch, Pierce, Fenner & Smith, wherein the two offered jointly advisory, execution, and custodian services to collectively managed small

It is reasonably clear that the disclosure required by the 1974 additions to Regulation 9 and by Regulation 23 was at least in part a response to these proposals.

---

accounts. See SEC Litigation Release No. 4534 (Feb. 6, 1970). The banks also helped draw attention to themselves by seeking (unsuccessfully) to have the Investment Company Act of 1940 amended during a major overhaul of that statute culminating in legislation in 1970. Pub. L. 91-547, 84 Stat. 413 (Dec. 14, 1970). The *Camp* case, note 104 *supra*, also spotlighted bank entry into nontrust advisory services. Rebuffed by Congress and the Supreme Court with respect to commingled agency accounts, the banks persisted in developing nontrustee investment services. See generally D. Green & M. Schuelke, *The Trust Activities of the Banking Industry* (Stanford Research Institute 1975). Perhaps the most publicized new program was automatic investment services (AIS). The SEC initially took a tolerant attitude toward AIS. See Security Pacific Nat'l Bank, [1973 Transfer Binder] CCH Fed. Sec. L. Rep. ¶ 79,412, and Investment Data Corp., *id.* at ¶ 79,411. In due course, the Comptroller of the Currency approved AIS. Letter of June 10, 1974, CCH Fed. Banking L. Rep. ¶ 96,272. The brokerage community and the investment company industry viewed AIS in its own right and in its role as harbinger of things to come as an improper competitive inroad into their respective domains. They unsuccessfully sued the Comptroller (NYSE v. Smith, 404 F. Supp. 1091 (D.D.C. 1975)), but at least managed to keep the issue of bank securities activities controversial. The SEC, reconsidering to some extent its earlier position on AIS, issued a wide-ranging study entitled "Inquiry Concerning Bank-Sponsored Investment Services" under the authority of the four major securities statutes it administers. SEC Securities Act Release No. 5491, [1973-1974 Transfer Binder] CCH Fed. Sec. L. Rep. ¶ 79,767. See also *id.* ¶ 79,775 (speech by Commissioner Evans) (April 30, 1974). Banking regulators also spoke of the difficulties presented by banks seeking legislative approval to broaden investment services while restricting regulation to banking authorities (see, e.g., Statement of FDIC Chairman, Securities Week, Sept. 16, 1974, pp. 3, 8-10), though, of course, they criticized SEC regulation of banks strongly (see, e.g., Statement of Deputy Comptroller, Securities Week, February 3, 1975). The issue remains unsettled, at least pending an SEC study of bank brokerage activities commissioned by Section 7 of the Securities Acts Amendments of 1975, Pub. L. 94-29, 89 Stat. 97 (June 4, 1975), *adding* Securities Exchange Act § 11A(e) (15 U.S.C. § 78K-16), and an inquiry by Congress into the need to amend the Glass-Steagall Act. See, e.g., Study of the Securities Activities of Commercial Banks, Hearings Before the Subcomm. on Securities of the Senate Comm. on Banking, Housing and Urban Affairs, 94th Cong., 2d Sess. (1976) (brokerage and related commercial bank services). See also Note, "The Legal Status of a National Bank's Automatic Stock Investment Service Under Sections 16 and 21 of the Glass-Steagall Act of 1933," 27 Vand. L. Rev. 1217 (1974).

[2] Investment Advisers: The Investment Advisers Act of 1940

The Investment Advisers Act of 1940,[116] originally designed as little more than a census-type licensing law,[117] has become a statute with substantive regulatory power over investment managers. Except for its registration requirements, its provisions extend, according to the statutory definition of investment adviser in Section 202(a)(11),[118] to

---

[116] 15 U.S.C. §§ 80b-1 et seq. In addition to the Investment Advisers Act, state Blue Sky laws also regulate investment advisers. See note 40 *supra*.

[117] In 1940, David Schenker, the Chief Counsel of the SEC Investment Trust Study, described the purposes of Title II of S. 3580, the SEC's proposal for regulating investment companies and investment advisers, in the following terms:

> "Now, I cannot impress too strongly upon the Senators the fact that our title 2 does not attempt to say who can be an investment counselor, . . . and does not even remotely presume to undertake to pass upon their qualifications. All we say is that in order to get some idea of who is in this business and what is his background, you cannot use the mails to perform your investment counsel business unless you are registered with us."

Hearings on S. 3580 Before a Subcomm. of the Senate Comm. on Banking and Currency, 76th Cong., 3d Sess. Pt. 1, at 50 (1940). It should be noted, however, that the title also contains antifraud and other prohibitory provisions directed at practices of advisers. E.g., Investment Advisers Act of 1940, § 206, 15 U.S.C. § 80b-6 (1970). These received some attention in debate: "The bill makes fraudulent practices by investment advisers unlawful and requires investment advisers . . . to register with the Commission which is empowered to deny registration to individuals convicted . . . for securities frauds." 86 Cong. Rec. 9809 (1940) (remarks of Rep. Cole). Despite the presence of these sections, until relatively recently, the statute has been administered largely as a registration measure, in contrast to the manner in which the similar provisions of the Securities Exchange Act of 1934 have been applied against broker-dealers.

[118] 115 U.S.C. § 80b-2(a)(11). See, e.g., Abrahamson v. Fleschner, [1976-1977 Transfer Binder] CCH Fed. Sec. L. Rep. ¶ 95,889 (2d Cir. 1977) (general partners of investment partnership). See generally Lovitch, "The Investment Advisers Act of 1940—Who Is an 'Investment Adviser,'" 24 Kan. L. Rev. 67 (1975).

A related question is whether a person is providing advice classifiable as investment advice. Whereas the SEC has traditionally taken a broad view as to what it considers investment advice, the Commission recently narrowed the scope of Section 202(a)(11), at least with respect to publishers of investment information. See Investment Advisers Act Release No. 563 (Jan. 10, 1977), 4 CCH Fed. Sec. L. Rep. ¶ 56,157. The tenor of the release strongly suggests that it was a response to the registration burden, however,

every person in the business of offering investment advice to others for a fee, unless a statutory or regulatory exclusion is available.

[a] Investment counsel

Section 208(c)[119] of the statute reserves the title "investment counsel" to investment advisers satisfying two conditions: (1) that their principal business be serving as statutory investment advisers; and (2) that their advisory services consist substantially of investment supervisory services for clients. The purpose of Section 208(c) was to protect the emerging industry of nontrustee investment management and to encourage development of professional standards.[120] But the content of the investment supervisory services required for entitlement to use of the name "investment counsel" is unclear. As defined in Section 202 (a)(13), "investment supervisory services" requires that investment advice be given continuously on the basis of individual needs.[121] But there has been little regulatory effort to interpret Section 202(a)(13) in context except in a 1973 report of an advisory committee to the SEC.[122] It is possible that use of the name "investment counsel" carries implied representations about professional competence, the failure to provide which may lead to sanctions enforceable under Section 206, the statutory fraud provision.[123]

---

and facts tending to connect a publication with some kind of manipulation, deception, or other like scheme would probably deprive the author of the exclusion afforded by the release. See, e.g., Municipal Advisory Council of Texas, [1975-1976 Transfer Binder] CCH Fed. Sec. L. Rep. ¶ 80,410 (1975).

[119] 15 U.S.C. § 80b-8(c). This provision was amended in 1960 (Pub. L. 86-750, 74 Stat. 887 (Sept. 13, 1970)) to eliminate the requirement that a person be engaged primarily in rendering investment supervisory services, Congress relying instead on the operative term "substantial part."

[120] See, e.g., Report on H.R. 10065, House Comm. on Interstate and Foreign Commerce, H.R. Rep. No. 2639, 76th Cong., 3d Sess. 27-28 (June 18, 1940).

[121] 15 U.S.C. § 80b-2(a)(13).

[122] SEC, *Report of the Advisory Committee on Investment Management Services for Individual Investors, Small Account Investment Management Services* 27-32 (Jan. 1973). The statutory definition in Section 202(a)(13) has been the subject of litigation, however. See Anderson Co. v. John P. Chase, Inc., [1974-1975 Transfer Binder] CCH Fed. Sec. L. Rep. ¶ 95,009 (S.D.N.Y. 1975), discussed at ¶¶ 4.01[2][b] and 4.03[2][b].

[123] 15 U.S.C. § 80b-6. See Anderson Co. v. John P. Chase, Inc., note 122 *supra.*

[b] Broker-Dealers

Most of the advisory activities of broker-dealers are regulated under the Securities Exchange Act, especially the antifraud provisions in Sections 10(b)[124] and 15(c)(1).[125] But were it not for a statutory exclusion in Section 202(a)(11)(C) of the Investment Advisers Act, broker-dealers would also almost unavoidably fall within the statutory definition of investment adviser. That subsection exempts from application of the Act "any broker or dealer whose performance of [investment advisory] services is solely incidental to the conduct of his business as a broker or dealer and who receives no special compensation therefor. . . ." [126] To be sure, a number of broker-dealers do not rely on the statutory exclusion to avoid registration because they or their advisory affiliates charge management fees for providing investment advice and hence are probably receiving "special compensation therefor." [127]

---

[124] 15 U.S.C. § 78j(b). See, e.g., Rolf v. Blyth Eastman Dillon & Co., 424 F. Supp. 1021 (S.D.N.Y. 1977).

[125] 15 U.S.C. § 78o(c)(1). See, e.g., Rolf v. Blyth Eastman Dillon & Co., note 124 *supra*.

[126] 15 U.S.C. § 80b-2(11)(C). It seems that broker-dealers were not intended to be excluded from the definition of investment adviser as the Investment Company and Investment Advisers Acts were originally contemplated by the drafters. The proposed legislation submitted by the SEC defined "investment adviser" for purposes of both titles as follows:

" 'Investment adviser' means any person who, for compensation, engages in the business of advising others, either directly or through publications or writings, as to the value of securities or as to the advisability of investing in, purchasing, or selling securities, or who, for compensation and as part of a regular business, issues or promulgates analyses or reports concerning securities; but does not include (A) a bank; (B) any lawyer, accountant, engineer, or teacher whose performance of such services is solely incidental to the practice of his profession; (C) the publisher of any bona fide newspaper or newsmagazine of general circulation; or (D) such other persons, not within the intent of this paragraph, as the Commission may designate by rules and regulations or order."

S. 3580, 76th Cong., 3d Sess. § 45(a)(16) (1940). Moreover, broker-dealers were expressly excluded from the application of Title I, the investment company portion (*id.* § 3(a)(2)), thus indicating that they were not intended to be excluded from Title II, the investment adviser portion. See also Hearings on S. 3580 Before a Subcomm. of the Senate Comm. on Banking and Currency, 76th Cong., 3d Sess. 181 (1940).

[127] The hearings on S. 3580 show that broker-dealers receiving advisory fees were intended to be included. Hearings on S. 3580 Before a Subcomm. of the Senate Comm. on Banking and Currency, 76th Cong., 3d Sess. Pt. 2, at 711 (1940). More important, the hearings on the draft of the bill

Moreover, to an extent, the registered investment adviser credential is a public relations asset which until now has outweighed the relatively light burdens imposed by registration under the Act.

But broker-dealers managing discretionary accounts may not realize the Act applies to them because they do not understand the limited scope of the statutory exclusion. It appears that those broker-dealers being compensated for managing discretionary accounts only by commissions generated through brokerage on clients' trades are particularly vulnerable. And broker-dealers who refer customers to affiliated or non-affiliated investment advisers in return for some form of payment from the adviser for the referral may also be vulnerable.

Section 202(a)(11)(C) sets up two conditions to be satisfied for broker-dealers to be excluded from the statutory definition of investment adviser:

(1) The provision of investment advice only as an incident of the broker-dealer function; and

(2) The absence of special compensation for the advice.

Furthermore, both conditions must be satisfied for the exclusion to operate because Section 202(a)(11)(C) lists them conjunctively.[128] Unfortunately, neither condition has had an authoritative interpretation. The legislative history of Section 202(a)(11)(C) is thin,[129] and there is no judicial construction on which to rely. Shortly after the Advisers Act was adopted, the SEC issued Investment Advisers Act Release No.

---

which became the Investment Company and Investment Advisers Acts of 1940 confirm that the Committee believed that the exclusion of broker-dealers in Section 202(a)(11)(C) (15 U.S.C. § 80b-2a(11)(C) (1970)) would not be available to broker-dealers receiving a fee for their investment advisory activities. See Hearings on H.R. 10065 Before a Subcomm. of the House Comm. on Interstate and Foreign Commerce, 76th Cong., 3d Sess. 87 (1940).

[128] The relevant portion of Section 202(a)(11)(C) reads:

" 'Investment adviser' means any person who, for compensation, engages in the business of advising others . . . as to the value of securities or as to the advisability of investing in, purchasing, or selling securities . . . but does not include . . . (C) any broker or dealer whose performance of such service is solely incidental to the conduct of his business as a broker or dealer and who receives no special compensation therefor. . . ."

[129] The meaning of the exclusionary language is unclear, since the meaning of "investment adviser" is discussed in the legislative history of the Act only in its broadest sense by repetition of the definition provided in the Act. It is clear that the definition was meant to encompass a wider

2,[130] taking the position that a commission surcharge based on advice to customers constitutes special compensation. But that release is of little help in evaluating arrangements in which the broker-dealer is ostensibly paid only standard brokerage fees for executing transactions,[131] such as would be the case where broker-dealers offer discretionary management services for commissions, or where investment advisers offer broker-dealers some kind of emolument, such as directing brokerage business to them, for referring clients.

The scope of the exclusion in Section 202(a)(11)(C) is even more problematic under a negotiated commission rate system. Arguably, any execution charge above best net price contains special compensation for advisory services. Presently, Rules 206(3)-1[132] and 206A-1(T)[133]

---

spectrum of "advisers" than members of the profession of investment counselors:

> "Investment advisers are persons who for compensation engage in the business of advising others . . . as to the value of securities or as to the advisability of investing in, purchasing or selling securities or who, for compensation and as part of a regular business, promulgate analyses or reports concerning securities."

H.R. Rep. No. 2639, 76th Cong., 3d Sess. 27 (1940). Similar language appears in S. Rep. No. 1775, 76th Cong., 3d Sess. 20 (1940). David Schenker, Chief Counsel of the SEC Investment Trust Study, stated that investment advisers are "that broad category ranging from people who are engaged in the profession of furnishing disinterested, impartial advice to a certain economic stratum of our population to the other extreme, individuals engaged in running tipster organizations, or sending through the mails stock market letters." Hearings on S. 3580 Before a Subcomm. of the House Comm. on Banking and Currency, 76th Cong., 3d Sess. Pt. 1, at 47 (1940). Apparently, the only direct interpretation of the exclusion at issue was made by Douglas T. Johnston, vice-president of the Investment Counsel Association of America, who said that the definition would still include "certain . . . brokerage houses which maintain investment advisory departments and make changes for services rendered. . . ." Id. Pt. 2, at 711. Thus, the only theme that appears widely in the legislative history is that the statute is meant to apply to those who render investment advice for compensation in the ordinary course of their business or as an independent aspect thereof.

130 Oct. 28, 1940, 4 CCH Fed. Sec. L. Rep. ¶ 56,156.

131 The release dealt only with the addition of an "overriding commission" or "service charge" over and above the regular commission which a broker-dealer would receive from executing the transaction. See id.

132 17 C.F.R. § 275.206(3)-1, SEC Investment Advisers Act Release No. 470 (Aug. 20, 1975), [1975-1976 Transfer Binder] CCH Fed. Sec. L. Rep. ¶ 80,268 (exemption for broker-dealers charging special fee for certain advisory support services).

133 17 C.F.R. § 275.206A-1(T), SEC Investment Advisers Act Release No. 471 (Aug. 20, 1975), [1975-1976 Transfer Binder] CCH Fed. Sec. L.

offer limited protection to broker-dealers providing investment management services. But the extent of their protection is not identical to that which was assumed under fixed rates.[134] Moreover, the existence of these rules strongly implies that the exclusions of Section 202(a)(11) (C) are not available to broker-dealers who do not qualify for application of the rules to their activities.

[c]   Other statutory investment advisers

Section 202(a)(11) was designed with two types of investment advisers principally in mind: investment counselors and purveyors of limited circulation market letters. But instead of restricting the statutory definition to those types of investment advisers, Congress structured Section 202(a)(11) for broad coverage subject to specific exclusions. In addition to broker-dealers, exclusions apply to banks and bank holding companies, professionals such as lawyers, accountants, and teachers, publishers of newspapers of general circulation, investment advisers dealing only in securities of the United States, and those investment advisers determined by the SEC not to require regulation under the Act. The exclusions must be read with some care. The exclusion applying to banks and bank holding companies may not apply to bank holding company subsidiaries[135]; and the exclusion applying to professionals can be lost through promotions, financial consulting, and referrals to investment managers.[136] Also still unsettled is whether non-

---

Rep. ¶ 80,269 (exemption for broker-dealers providing advisory services for which no special compensation is received).

[134] See ¶ 10.06[2][b].

[135] Section 202(a)(11)(A) (15 U.S.C. § 80b-2(a)(11)(A)) excludes a "bank, or any bank holding company as defined in the Bank Holding Company Act of 1956 which is not an investment company. . . ." "Bank" is further defined in Section 202(a)(2) (15 U.S.C. § 80b-2(a)(2)) to cover only United States banking institutions. See Brewer-Burner & Assoc., Inc., [1973-1974 Transfer Binder] CCH Fed. Sec. L. Rep. ¶ 79,719 (1974) (foreign trust company not a "bank"). The definition of bank holding company (12 U.S.C. § 1841(a)) is technical, depending either on actual or statutorily defined control.

[136] Section 202(a)(11)(B) (15 U.S.C. § 80b-2(a)(11)(B)) excludes "any lawyer, accountant, engineer, or teacher whose performance of such [investment advisory] services is solely incidental to the position of his profession. . . ." See Hines, [1972-1973 Transfer Binder] CCH Fed. Sec. L. Rep. ¶ 78,963 (1972) (class providing general instruction on developing an investment program not within exclusion).

bank trustees come within the purview of Section 202(a)(11).[137]

---

[137] Compare Loring, [1941-1944 Transfer Binder] CCH Fed. Sec. L. Rep. ¶ 75,299 (1942) (professional trustee under judicial appointment not intended to be covered by Section 202(a)(11)), with Philip Eiseman, [1976-1977 Transfer Binder] CCH Fed. Sec. L. Rep. ¶ 80,914 (1976) (trustee is statutory investment adviser) (distinguishing *Loring*), and Brewer-Burner & Assoc., Inc., [1973-1974 Transfer Binder] CCH Fed. Sec. L. Rep. ¶ 79,719 (1974) (foreign trust company is statutory investment adviser). *Eiseman* somewhat unsettles the status of lawyers. Lawyers often act as trustees or co-trustees of personal trusts, some firms administering a sufficient number of trust portfolios to require the retention of a professional investment adviser. Section 202(a)(11)(B) (15 U.S.C. § 806-2(a)(11)(B)) provides a statutory exclusion for a lawyer performing investment advisory services "solely incidental to the practice of his profession." The issue is whether portfolio management, particularly where common to many accounts, is incidental to a lawyer's profession. See, e.g., Winstead, McGuire, Sechrest & Trimble, [1974-1975 Transfer Binder] CCH Fed. Sec. L. Rep. ¶ 80,131 (1975).

But the expansive interpretation the SEC takes of Section 202(a)(11) notwithstanding, the Commission will not admit to adviser status persons seeking thereby to avoid other statutory responsibilities. Rule 202-1 (17 C.F.R. § 275.202-1, SEC Investment Advisers Act Release No. 503 (March 12, 1976), [1975-1976 Transfer Binder] CCH Fed. Sec. L. Rep. ¶ 80,403) denies pension-fund managers adviser status if they do not hold themselves out to the public generally as advisers.

Part II

ESTABLISHING THE CLIENT-MANAGER RELATIONSHIP

Chapter 3

DEVELOPING NEW BUSINESS

¶ 3.01.   CONSTRAINTS ON THE INVESTMENT MANAGER'S RELATIONSHIP WITH PROSPECTIVE CLIENTS

An investment manager, whether trust department in a commercial bank, insurance company, registered investment company, registered investment adviser, broker-dealer, or any other type of investment management organization, must promote its services in order to obtain clients. There are two stages to the promotional efforts leading to the establishment of investment management relationships. First, an investment manager makes contact with prospective clients. This may be done through advertising, calls by sales personnel, referrals by third parties, previous relations with investors in other business or social contexts, or a variety of other marketing techniques.[1] Second, once initial contact is made and a prospective client shows interest, the investment manager explains the nature of its operations, usually with emphasis on performance, philosophy, personnel, support services available to assist the client with related financial problems, and the like. To varying degrees, all these activities designed to encourage investors to enter an investment management relationship are subject to legal constraints.

Though technically an investment manager is not in a fiduciary relationship with a prospective client, since the manager has not assumed his office, something very much akin to fiduciary responsibility exists

---

[1] Particularly with institutional investors and knowledgeable individual investors, developing new business can be a gradual process. The essential task for investment managers seeking these types of clients is to build up a sense of respect for the manager's capability. For example, one technique apparently growing in popularity is for an investment manager to sponsor an educational program of some sort, such as a seminar, and, by virtue of the organization and contents of the program, to impress investors. Patocka, "The New Look in Marketing Pension Management," 9 Institutional Investor 61 (March 1975); Wall Street J., Aug. 8, 1975, p. 1, col. 5. A more conventional approach is to exploit existing financial ties. Insurance underwriting, commercial banking, investment banking, and actuarial services have often been routes to the creation of an investment management relationship. Patocka, *supra*, at 66.

during the promotional phase of an investment management relationship. Fraud, duress, undue influence, and mistake are grounds for rescinding or reforming trust agreements[2] and agency agreements.[3] Moreover, the traditions reflected in the tort doctrines of fraud, deceit, and misrepresentation provide a precedent for imposing civil damages for injury resulting from reasonable reliance on falsehoods and half-truths.[4] These common-law antecedents have given way to the federal securities laws, particularly the fraud provisions, as the primary source of regulation of the promotional activities of investment managers. Nonetheless, they have provided moral authority to contemporary regulation in this area, and even though many of the developments under the federal securities laws reflect substantial refinement of common-law principles, the notion that fiduciary principles control investment management conduct during the promotional phase is strongly entrenched.

Actually, the federal securities laws present two general problems with regard to the promotional activities of investment managers: (1) the application of the statutory fraud provisions; and (2) the application of the registration provisions of the Securities Act of 1933 and the Investment Company Act of 1940. The statutory fraud provisions control the form and substance of information investment managers make available to prospective clients. Some things are conditionally permitted, others absolutely prohibited, and still others absolutely required. The application of the registration provisions to the promotional activities of investment managers is the product of recent departures in the broadening of the statutory definition of a security. Although, as a practical matter, the application of the registration provisions could prevent the offering of some accounts, the sentiment to require registration reflects regulatory concern with the promotional activities of investment managers and their administration of their responsibilities. The discussion that follows examines the promotional activities of investment managers from the perspectives of both the statutory fraud and the registration provisions of the federal securities laws.

---

[2] *Restatement (Second) of Trusts* § 331 (1959); 38 A.L.R. 937 (Fidelity & Columbia Trust Co. v. Gwynn, 206 Ky. 823, 268 S.W. 537 (1925)), 977 (1925).

[3] *Restatement (Second) of Agency* § 15, Comment c (1958); *Restatement (First) of Contracts* §§ 476(1) (contract voidable for misrepresentation or fraud), 495 (voidable for duress), 497 (voidable for undue influence), 502 (voidable for mistake), 491 (reformation of contract for fraud or misrepresentation), 499, 504-506 (remedies—avoidance for duress and undue influence and reformation for mistake) (1932).

[4] *Restatement of Torts* §§ 871(e), 892(d) (1939).

¶ 3.02. APPLICATION OF THE ANTIFRAUD PROVISIONS OF THE FEDERAL SECURITIES LAWS TO PROMOTIONAL ACTIVITIES

[1] The Broad Reach of the Provisions

The promotional activities of all investment managers fall within the reach of one or more of the antifraud provisions of the federal securities laws. Section 10(b) of the Securities Exchange Act[5] and Section 17(a) of the Securities Act[6] apparently include all investment managers within their scope since they apply to "any person" engaged in a transaction which is fraudulent according to those provisions. Section 15(c) of the Exchange Act,[7] however, proscribes fraudulent activities only by over-the-counter brokers and dealers. And Section 206 of the Investment Advisers Act[8] applies only to persons who are statutory investment advisers as defined in Section 202(a)(11) of the Act.[9]

These jurisdictional discontinuities raise questions of the degree to which the statutory fraud provisions differ in their impact on the promotional activities of investment managers. That there is some variation, at least in technical detail, is evident. For example, Investment Advisers Act Rule 206(4)-1 mandates the location and content of a cautionary legend any time past investment recommendations are included in an advertisement.[10] None of the other antifraud provisions directly incorporates the same requirements, although requirements comparable to those of Rule 206(4)-1 may be incorporated by implication through application of rules under other provisions by analogy and by reference to stock exchange or association regulations.[11]

Moreover, the statutory fraud provisions have developed along separate paths in their treatment of the promotional activities of investment

---

[5] 15 U.S.C. § 78j(b).

[6] 15 U.S.C. § 77q(a).

[7] 15 U.S.C. § 78o.

[8] 15 U.S.C. § 80b-6.

[9] 15 U.S.C. § 80b-2(a)(11). See ¶ 2.05[2].

[10] 17 C.F.R. § 275.206(4)-1(a)(2).

[11] Van Gemert v. Boeing Co., 520 F.2d 1373 (2d Cir. 1975) (defendant's violation of NYSE publicity rule is "colorable claim" for civil liability). But see Jenny v. Shearson, Hammill & Co., [1974-1975 Transfer Binder] CCH Fed. Sec. L. Rep. ¶ 95,021 (S.D.N.Y. 1975) (violation of NYSE "know your customer" rule does not create implied civil liability under federal law). See also Colonial Realty Corp. v. Bache & Co., 358 F.2d 178 (2d Cir.), cert. denied 385 U.S. 817 (1966) (no blanket federal civil liability derivable from exchange rules; decision must be made case by case).

managers. Section 206 of the Advisers Act seems the most refined. In *Intersearch Technology, Inc.,*[12] the SEC cited the phrase *"client or prospective client"* in subparagraphs (1) and (2) of Section 206 as authority for the proposition that the Act has legislated a fiduciary relationship extending "to the whole process whereby a potential client becomes a client." [13] Section 10(b) of the Exchange Act, on the other hand, though it has been interpreted both on its own footing and in connection with Sections 15(c) and 17(a)[14] to apply to many promotional activities of banks,[15] broker-dealers,[16] lawyers,[17] and accoun-

---

[12] [1974-1975 Transfer Binder] CCH Fed. Sec. L. Rep. ¶ 80,139 (1975).

[13] *Id.* at p. 85,189.

[14] For a comparison of Sections 10(b), 15(c), and 17(a), see ¶ 2.03. See also R. Jennings & H. Marsh, *Securities Regulation* 821 (1972).

[15] SEC v. First Am. Bank & Trust Co., 481 F.2d 673 (8th Cir. 1973); Fenstermacher v. Philadelphia Nat'l Bank, 493 F.2d 333 (3d Cir. 1974); SEC v. National Bankers Life Ins. Co., 324 F. Supp. 189 (N.D. Tex.), *aff'd* 448 F.2d 652 (5th Cir. 1971); Blake, Stephens & Kittredge, Inc., [1973-1974 Transfer Binder] CCH Fed. Sec. L. Rep. ¶ 79,638 (1973); see also Investment Data Corp., [1973 Transfer Binder] CCH Fed. Sec. L. Rep. ¶ 79,411; Security Pacific Nat'l Bank, [1973 Transfer Binder] CCH Fed. Sec. L. Rep. ¶ 79,412.

In one case, investment advice by bank officers, allegedly misleading in violation of the federal securities laws, was held sufficient to be deemed "dishonest," as that term is applied to bankers' indemnity bonds. Baskin v. A.G. Becker & Co., [1966-1967 Transfer Binder] CCH Fed. Sec. L. Rep. ¶ 92,006 (N.D. Ill. 1967).

[16] Glickman v. Schweickart & Co., 242 F. Supp. 670 (S.D.N.Y. 1965) (misrepresentations by broker-dealer concerning the financing of a purchase of securities held actionable under Section 10(b)); *In re* Triangle Investors Corp., [1964-1966 Transfer Binder] CCH Fed. Sec. L. Rep. ¶ 77,356 (1966) (broker-dealer's "boiler room" sales tactics held violation of Sections 10(b), 15(c), and 17(a)); *In re* Delafield & Delafield, [1967-1969 Transfer Binder] CCH Fed. Sec. L. Rep. ¶ 77,648 (1968) (broker-dealer's inducing the price of a security to fall in order to cause holders of that security to sell to the broker-dealer's customers, held violation of Sections 10(b) and 17(a)).

[17] United States v. Peltz, 433 F.2d 48 (2d Cir.), *cert. denied* 401 U.S. 955 (1971) (attorney's representation to a board of directors that his sale of stock was "long" when it was in fact "short" held a violation of Section 10(b)); SEC v. American Associated Sys., Inc., 482 F.2d 1040 (6th Cir. 1973), *cert. denied* 414 U.S. 1130 (1974) (corporate counsel's failure to disclose certain cash-flow problems and his participation in the issuance of a misleading registration statement held violation of Section 10(b)); see also Speech of SEC Commissioner Sommer, "The Emerging Repsonsibilities of the Securities Lawyer," [1973-1974 Transfer Binder] CCH Fed. Sec. L. Rep. ¶ 79,631 (1974), for a discussion of potential liabilities of attorneys under the federal securities laws.

tants,[18] has not so precisely identified a standard of care to which investment managers must adhere in their dealings with prospective clients. Rather, as implemented by Rule 10b-5,[19] Section 10(b) has produced a set of authorities concerning promotional activities co-ordinated only by vague references to a duty to meet "high standards" [20] or to the reasonable-basis[21] and suitability[22] doctrines, or to the shingle theory.[23] Similarly, Sections 17(a) and 15(c), when relied on in their own right, have been no more exacting or precise than Section 10(b).[24]

Nonetheless, the fiduciary-responsibility standard of Section 206 of the Advisers Act probably represents the standard of care implied by the other statutory fraud provisions for investment managers promoting their services. Caution, at least, suggests assuming that to be the case. The most significant categories of persons excluded from the statutory definition of investment adviser are banks and bank holding companies, broker-dealers, and lawyers and accountants. But of these, only banks and bank holding companies may perform investment management services indiscriminately without losing their statutory exclusion.[25] Since

---

[18] E.g., Fischer v. Kletz, 266 F. Supp. 180 (S.D.N.Y. 1967) (accountant's failure to disclose the falsity of certain financial statements in an annual report could constitute a violation of Section 10(b)).

[19] 17 C.F.R. § 240.10b-5, SEC Securities Exchange Act Release No. 3230 (May 21, 1942).

[20] Hanly v. SEC, 415 F.2d 589 (2d Cir. 1969).

[21] Kahn v. SEC, 297 F.2d 112 (2d Cir. 1961).

[22] See R. Jennings & H. Marsh, *Securities Regulation* 810 (1972).

[23] Kahn v. SEC, 297 F.2d 112 (2d Cir. 1961).

[24] United States v. Benjamin, 328 F.2d 854 (2d Cir.), *cert. denied sub nom.* Howard v. United States, 377 U.S. 953 (1964) (accountant, lawyer, and corporation all held to have violated Section 17(a) in making false statements about the assets of a corporation in attempting to sell its stock); United States v. White, 124 F.2d 181 (2d Cir. 1941) (accountant liable under Section 17(a) for false financial statements in prospectus); Newkirk v. Hayden, Stone & Co., [1964-1966 Transfer Binder] CCH Fed. Sec. L. Rep. ¶ 91,621 (S.D. Cal. 1965) (broker-dealer's "churning" activities held a violation of Sections 17(a) and 15(c)); Hughes v. SEC, 174 F.2d 969 (D.C. Cir. 1949) (investment adviser's failure to disclose to clients the nature of certain "adverse interests" held a violation of Sections 17(a) and 15(c)); Armstrong, Jones & Co. v. SEC, 421 F.2d 359 (6th Cir.), *cert. denied* 398 U.S. 958 (1970) (broker-dealer's failure to disclose to customer the fact of common control of the broker-dealer and issuer held a violation of Section 15(c)).

[25] Investment Advisers Act § 202(a)(11), 15 U.S.C. § 80b-2(a)(11); note the requirement that in order for a lawyer, accountant, or broker-dealer to enjoy the exemption, the "performance of such [investment management]

banks offering investment management services are subject to the other antifraud provisions of the federal securities laws,[26] banks could avoid the fiduciary-duty standard set by the Investment Advisers Act only if Sections 10(b) and 17(a) imposed a lesser standard on promotional activities than Section 206.[27] If that were so, banks alone among investment managers would be subject to a lesser federal standard than fiduciary responsibility in promoting their investment management services.[28]

Aside from the anomaly of subjecting banks to a lesser duty than that of other investment managers, other things suggest that the fiduciary-responsibility standards apply uniformly to the promotional activities of all investment managers. The operative language of Section 206, Section 17(a), and Rule 10b-5 is similar; each is an open-ended provision designed to encompass questionable practices as they develop. More significantly, no promotion forbidden under one has been permitted

---

services [must be] solely incidental" to "the practice of his profession" or "the conduct of his business." In addition, a broker-dealer must receive no special compensation for such services. As an example of lawyers losing their Section 202(a)(11) exemption for activities not "solely incidental" to the practice of law, see Winstead, McGuire, Sechrest & Trimble, [1974-1975 Transfer Binder] CCH Fed. Sec. L. Rep. ¶ 80,131 (1975); see also Bines, "Regulating Discretionary Management: Broker-Dealers as Catalysts for Reform," 16 B.C. Ind. & Comm. L. Rev. 347, 362-374 (1975); Lybecker, "Advisers Act Developments," 8 Rev. of Sec. Reg. 927, 929 (1975).

26 See note 15 *supra*. See also Commissioner Evans' Speech Before the Ninth Annual Banking Law Institute, [1973-1974 Transfer Binder] CCH Fed. Sec. L. Rep. ¶ 79,775, at 84,102-84,103 (1974).

27 Securities Exchange Act § 15(c) does not apply to banks at all, because Sections 3(a)(4) and 3(a)(5) of the Act expressly exempt banks from the definition of "broker" and "dealer." A bank is considered a "customer," however. SEC Securities Exchange Act Release No. 1462 (Nov. 15, 1937), 2 CCH Fed. Sec. L. Rep. ¶ 25,093.

28 In his speech before the Banking Law Institute (see note 26 *supra*), Commissioner Evans indicated that the investment management activities of banks have been of great concern to the SEC and that the Commission has opposed holding banks to a lower fiduciary standard than other investment managers; see also SEC Chairman Garrett, "The SEC and Its Concern With Bank Trust Activities," 113 Trusts & Estates 280 (1974). Since passage of the Securities Acts Amendments of 1975, Pub. L. 94-29, 89 Stat. 97 (June 4, 1975), which commissioned an SEC study of bank securities activities, investigations by the SEC and Congress have accelerated. See also SEC Securities Act Release No. 5491 (April 30, 1974), [1973-1974 Transfer Binder] CCH Fed. Sec. L. Rep. ¶ 79,767 (bank-sponsored investment activities), discussed more fully in ¶ 2.05[1], note 115.

by either of the others.[29] On the contrary, Section 206 and Rule 10b-5 are increasingly relied on in common when abuses in promotions are thought to occur.[30] Moreover, banking regulators have warned banks to respect their fiduciary position in promoting their services, specifically noting that the federal antifraud rules apply to any excesses they may perpetrate.[31]

[2] The Disclosure Rules: Advertising as the Focus of Regulatory Activity

More important than whether fiduciary responsibility is the standard is the question of what it means to be in a fiduciary relationship during the promotional phase of one's operations. A fiduciary-responsibility standard creates an unavoidable conflict of interest between an investment manager and a prospective client. Although an investment manager's business interest leans toward securing an account, fiduciary principles would enjoin the investment manager to act solely in the best interest of the prospective client. In the extreme, this would mean that the investment manager must determine whether his services are ap-

---

[29] For example, compare Hamilton Waters & Co., [1964-1966 Transfer Binder] CCH Fed. Sec. L. Rep. ¶ 77,298 (1965) (§§ 10(b) and 17(a)), with Shearson, Hammill & Co., *id.* ¶ 77,306 (1965) (§ 206); and compare Amalgamated Inv. Inc., [1967-1969 Transfer Binder] CCH Fed. Sec. L. Rep. ¶ 77,536 (1968) (§§ 10(b) and 17(a)), with Patrick Clements, d/b/a Patrick Clements & Associates; Capital Gains Instruments, Inc., [1964-1966 Transfer Binder] CCH Fed. Sec. L. Rep. ¶ 77,146 (1964) (§ 206).

[30] See, e.g., Shortline Reports Inc., [1970-1971 Transfer Binder] CCH Fed. Sec. L. Rep. ¶ 77,962 (1971); George L. Bedford, [1972-1973 Transfer Binder] CCH Fed. Sec. L. Rep. ¶ 78,911 (1972); Thomas J. Herbert, d/b/a Pembroke Management Co., SEC Securities Exchange Act Release No. 11496 (June 26, 1975). See also Capbell, Henderson & Co., SEC Investment Advisers Act Release No. 482 (Oct. 24, 1975).

[31] In a letter from the Administrator of National Banks to the presidents of all national banks ([1966-1967 Transfer Binder] CCH Fed. Sec. L. Rep. ¶ 77,421 (Dec. 16, 1966)), banks were warned to follow certain "minimum principles" in "their advertisements directed toward attracting funds," in that advertisements contrary to such principles might violate the antifraud provisions of the securities acts. See also "Fiduciary Powers," CCH Fed. Bank. L. Rep. ¶ 96,355 (Aug. 8, 1973), in which the Deputy Comptroller of the Currency for Trusts stated that advertising by banks for their fiduciary services is limited to publicity that annual reports are available with regard to common trust funds. He also pointed out that the antifraud sections of the securities laws are applicable to bank pooled-pension and profit-sharing trusts, and that banks "should at least conform to the standards applicable to non-bank competitors in this area."

propriate to the prospective client's needs and whether services of comparable quality are available at competitive prices. But, except in unusual cases where investment needs, management services, and management costs are plainly out of balance, it is unreasonable to expect an investment manager to reject prospective clients, much less to send them to another firm.

Instead, disclosure is the device relied on to minimize the effects of the inherent conflict of interest involved in marketing the management office. In essence, the law recognizes that a prospective client will have to decide for himself which investment manager is best for him. But, in deference to the fiduciary character of the relationship, the law insists that an investment manager furnish a prospective client with enough information to make an intelligent decision about whether to retain the manager's services. Disclosure in this context thus denies investment managers the puffing privileges and tactical silences permitted other types of businessmen. More than avoiding outright misrepresentation, investment managers must present information with a completeness and accuracy adequate to permit a prospective client to make a reasonable evaluation of the services he will obtain. An investment manager also must not omit disclosure of material facts, that is, "facts to which a reasonable man would attach importance under the circumstances," [32] regardless of the effect disclosure would have on the success of a sales promotion. Material omissions are as violative of the antifraud provisions as deliberate misrepresentations.[33]

Because of the open-ended quality of the standards set by the antifraud provisions, it is impossible to describe precisely the line separating legitimate promotional activity from the illegitimate. The very purpose of such provisions is to maintain the capability of dealing with practices as they develop by insisting that they hew to established principles. Nonetheless, some observations on what constitutes misleading statements or material omissions are possible. Disclosure during the promotional phase of an investment management relationship should

---

[32] Intersearch Technology, Inc., [1974-1975 Transfer Binder] CCH Fed. Sec. L. Rep. ¶ 80,139, at 85,188 (1975); see also Datapax Computer Sys. Corp., [1972-1973 Transfer Binder] CCH Fed. Sec. L. Rep. ¶ 78,958 (1972). In a case involving the materiality of an omission from a proxy statement, the Supreme Court stated that "an omitted fact is material if there is a substantial likelihood that a reasonable shareholder would consider it important in deciding how to vote." TSC Indus., Inc. v. Northway, Inc., [1976-1977 Transfer Binder] CCH Fed. Sec. L. Rep. ¶ 95,615, at 90,069 (1976).

[33] Hughes v. SEC, 174 F.2d 969 (D.C. Cir. 1949).

bring balance to an investment manager's natural tendency to emphasize the strengths of his organization over its weaknesses. Against talk
of opportunities for gain should appear information permitting a realistic assessment of potential for loss. Against the ostensible advantages
of the techniques and procedures employed by an investment manager
should appear a frank appraisal of their limitations. Moreover, the degree of disclosure necessary to achieve a harmonious balance in a sales
presentation depends on the prospective client. If an investment manager knows, or ought to know, that because of a lack of sophistication
or otherwise, a prospective client may be unaware of the need for
additional facts or of the implications of the facts he has been given, the
burden rests with the manager to provide the additional information
needed to make disclosure serve its balancing function.

But more than this can be said about the implications of the disclosure rules for marketing the management office. Even though the
open-ended nature of the antifraud provisions makes it impossible to
be certain in advance about the legitimacy of all promotional activities
of investment managers, the restrictions which the rules have previously
imposed offer a reasonably definite means for assessing many promotional practices. In addition, existing authorities furnish excellent illustrations of how disclosure requirements mature in response to marketing developments. Consequently, these authorities spotlight many
of the considerations that might impact on other marketing practices
not yet tested in a regulatory environment.

As a prefatory matter, it is important to note that most of the regulatory efforts directed at promotional activities have focused on advertising.[34] Investment managers rely on many other marketing tech-

---

[34] The form, as well as substance, of advertising is closely scrutinized,
the principal regulatory controls being found in the Securities Act and the
Investment Advisers Act. Most restrictive is Rule 134 under the Securities
Act, though it has been liberalized somewhat recently. With respect to
investment companies, the use of past performance figures is still forbidden;
sales literature may now, however, contain the names of principal managing
officers and direct the reader's attention to the prospectus for information on
fees and expenses. "Tombstones" may include the period of existence of
the fund and the length of service of the investment adviser, the aggregate
investment corporate net assets under the adviser's management, and the
adviser's logo or corporate symbol (SEC Securities Act Release No. 5536,
(Nov. 4, 1974), [1974-1975 Transfer Binder] CCH Fed. Sec. L. Rep.
¶ 80,000). Additionally, pictorial illustrations are permitted, and the scope
of the liberalized rule has been expanded to include access by companies not
making a continuous offering of their shares, such as certain bond funds,
variable annuities, unit investment trusts, and other investment companies

niques, however, some using advertising hardly at all.[35] Nonetheless, the lessons of the advertising cases are broadly applicable to other kinds of promotional activities.

From the perspective of disclosure, the distinguishing feature of advertising is its impersonality. An advertisement cannot answer the questions it raises in a prospective client's mind,[36] and it can mask the information it does provide by such devices as type size or prominence of display, or, in the case of radio and TV, inflection and emphasis.[37] Yet, the basis for most of the regulatory concern in the advertising

---

issuing redeemable securities (SEC Securities Act Release Nos. 5566 (Feb. 6, 1975), [1974-1975 Transfer Binder] CCH Fed. Sec. L. Rep. ¶ 80,102, 5591 (June 16, 1975), [1974-1975 Transfer Binder] CCH Fed. Sec. L. Rep. ¶ 80,211). In SEC Securities Act Release No. 5582 (April 28, 1975), [1974-1975 Transfer Binder] CCH Fed. Sec. L. Rep. ¶ 80,166, and in SEC Securities Act Release No. 5591, *supra* ¶ 80,211, the SEC adopted an amendment to its Statement of Policy to permit investment companies issuing variable annuity contracts to employ standardized illustrations based upon hypothetical rates of return of 0 percent, 4 percent, and 8 percent. Tailored illustrations, however, are not allowed. (Legends are sufficient if the type is different from but at least as large as a major portion of the ad.)

Investment Advisers Act Rule 206(4)-1 complements Rule 134 by dealing with advertising not connected with an offering by prospectus, though its scope is limited to statutory investment advisers. Furthermore, this rule combines specific limitations with a general antifraud provision. See notes 38-40 *infra*. See also Securities Evaluation, Inc., [1971-1972 Transfer Binder] CCH Fed. Sec. L. Rep. ¶ 78,786 (1972) (failure of firm to disclose the limitations of an analysis device mentioned in a sales brochure constituted a violation of Rule 206(4)-1); Axe Sec. Corp., [1964-1966 Transfer Binder] CCH Fed. Sec. L. Rep. ¶ 77,148 (1964) (article in book describing shares of an investment company and recommending purchase without disclosing that the article was prepared and paid for by the company violated Sections 17(a) and 206).

[35] One liquid-assets mutual fund, for example, relies heavily on programmed advertising, and it closely analyzes the extent and quality of the responses produced by different types of advertising campaigns (Securities Week, March 31, 1975, p. 8). On the other hand, some managers of institutional clients claim they neither advertise nor make unsolicited calls. Patocka, "The New Look in Marketing Pension Management," 9 Institutional Investor 61 (March 1975).

[36] See First Trust of Insured Municipal Bonds, [1973-1976 Transfer Binder] CCH Mutual Funds Guide ¶ 10,129 (1974) (unit investment trust may not include Standard & Poor's rating of units in tombstone advertisement because rating based on underlying bonds). But see Municipal Income Fund, Sec. Reg. L. Rep. No. 316, Aug. 20, 1975, at C-1.

[37] For this reason, the regulation of investment company advertising through Rule 134 shows special concern for type size, pictorial descriptions,

cases has been the character of the statements rather than the medium through which they are made. The medium is relevant for regulatory purposes only to the degree it bears on the completeness and accuracy of what is said measured against a prospective client's personal needs.

A sales presentation which might be unacceptable as an advertisement, for example, might not violate antifraud rules if a prospective client fills in gaps in information with appropriate questions, or if a prospective client is sufficiently sophisticated not to need the missing information. But the mere fact that statements are made in a sales presentation does not automatically merit different treatment for them from that which they would receive if they appeared in an advertisement. If statements are misleading because the prospective client fails to ask the right questions, or because he lacks the experience to dispense with the missing information, the consequences are the same for him regardless of the promotional technique which motivates his decisions to establish an investment management account.

Besides, even if there is a relevant consideration affecting the impact of the advertising cases on other promotional activities, the antifraud rules include a great number of marketing techniques under the heading "advertisement." Investment Advisers Act Rule 206(4)-1(b) defines advertisement to include any "written communication addressed to more than one person." [38] Plainly, this provision goes far beyond what is thought of as the traditional domain of advertising. Significant also is the open-ended character of Rule 206(4)-1. In addition to specific requirements with respect to testimonials, past recommendations, the use of charts and formulas, and the provision of free services, it includes a general antifraud subsection, Section 206(4)-1(a)(5), which, in the standard prose, proscribes any advertisement "which contains any untrue statement of a material fact, or which is otherwise false or misleading." [39] Thus, the Commission is not constrained to deal only with the specific practices enumerated in the rule. Moreover, because of the similarity of Section 206(4)-1(a)(5) to Rule 10b-5(2)

---

and the like. See note 34 *supra.* Such regulation is necessary in order to prevent mere advertising from becoming what would in effect be an offer to sell (made in violation of Securities Act § 5(a), 15 U.S.C. 77e(c), or a prospectus not in compliance with Securities Exchange Act § 10, 15 U.S.C. 78), as well as to prevent statements or representations which might be fraudulent or misleading.

[38] 17 C.F.R. § 275.206(4)-1(b).

[39] Investment Advisers Act Rule 206(4)-1(a)(5), 17 C.F.R. § 275.206(4)-1(a)(5).

under the Exchange Act, and because of the frequency with which Section 206(4)-1(a)(5) is cited jointly with the other subsections of Rule 206(4)-1,[40] it is reasonable to expect the Commission to impose comparable demands under both rules and thereby regulate the conduct of persons not subject to the Investment Advisers Act.[41]

Another important consideration in the evaluation of these authorities is what kinds of remedies are applicable to violations of the disclosure rules in the marketing of investment management services. Most of the authorities consist of administrative proceedings and staff action on requests for no-action letters. Private litigation based on misrepresentations during the marketing phase has been notably unsuccessful, if only because of problems of proof.[42] Moreover, the law is not yet settled on how far private rights of action are to be implied into the principal antifraud provisions other than Rule 10b-5.[43] Also unsettled

---

[40] E.g., George L. Bedford, [1972-1973 Transfer Binder] CCH Fed. Sec. L. Rep. ¶ 78,911 (1972); Anametrics, Inc., [1970-1971 Transfer Binder] CCH Fed. Sec. L. Rep. ¶ 78,057 (1971).

[41] In fact, in Bolger v. Laventhol, Krekstein, Horwath & Horwath, 381 F. Supp. 260 (S.D.N.Y. 1974) (noted in 43 Fordham L. Rev. 493 (1974)), the court denied a motion to dismiss by defendant accountants of an action under Section 206, even though the accountants did not meet the statutory definition of "investment adviser." The court seemed to use an analysis akin to that used under Section 10(b), pointing out that the defendant's actions were "inexorably intertwined with the fraud being perpetrated by the investment advisers," and that they were, in short, "aiders and abettors." The decision was qualified somewhat by the court's noting that even if Section 206 did not apply, a claim under common law had been sufficiently stated. Nevertheless, the implications of the court's liberal construction of Section 206 seemed to indicate that the scope of the Act may broaden considerably in the hands of the judiciary.

[42] E.g., Kutner v. Gofen & Glossberg, [1970-1971 Transfer Binder] CCH Fed. Sec. L. Rep. ¶ 93,109 (7th Cir. 1971); Skydell v. Mates, 59 F.R.D. 297 (S.D.N.Y. 1972), reported in [1972-1973 Transfer Binder] CCH Fed. Sec. L. Rep. ¶ 93,538.

[43] The cases concerning Section 15(c) seem to indicate that a private right of action rather firmly exists under the section. Franklin Nat'l Bank v. L.B. Meadows & Co., 318 F. Supp. 1339 (S.D.N.Y. 1970); Osborne v. Mallory, 86 F. Supp. 869 (S.D.N.Y. 1949); Newkirk v. Hayden Stone & Co., [1964-1966 Transfer Binder] CCH Fed. Sec. L. Rep. ¶ 91,621 (S.D. Cal. 1965); cf. Rekant v. Desser, 425 F.2d 872 (5th Cir. 1970). With regard to Sections 17(a) and 206, however, the cases are still unsettled. See Fund of Funds, Ltd. v. Vesco, CCH Fed. Sec. L. Rep. ¶ 95,644 (S.D.N.Y. 1976) (private action under § 206 allowed); Angelakis v. Churchill Management Corp., [1975-1976 Transfer Binder], CCH Fed. Sec. L. Rep. ¶ 95,285 (N.D. Cal. 1975) (private action under § 206 allowed); Jones v. Equitable Life Assurance Soc'y of the U.S., [1974-1975 Transfer

is the degree of awareness or scienter required to give rise to a private

---

Binder] CCH Fed. Sec. L. Rep. ¶ 94,986 (S.D.N.Y.) (private action under § 206 allowed); Bolger v. Laventhol, Krekstein, Horwath & Horwath, 381 F. Supp. 260 (S.D.N.Y. 1974) (private action under § 206 allowed). But see Greenspan v. Del Toro, [1975-1976 Transfer Binder] CCH Fed. Sec. L. Rep. ¶ 95,488 (S.D. Fla. 1974) (no private action under § 206 allowed); Gammage v. Roberts, Scott & Co., [1974-1975 Transfer Binder] CCH Fed. Sec. L. Rep. ¶ 94,761 (S.D. Cal. 1974) (no private action under § 206 allowed). With respect to Section 17(a), compare Cass v. Prior, [1975-1976 Transfer Binder] CCH Fed. Sec. L. Rep. ¶ 95,433 (D. Minn. 1976), Vogel-Lorber, Inc. v. Options on Shares, Inc., [1974-1975 Transfer Binder] CCH Fed. Sec. L. Rep. ¶ 94,911 (S.D.N.Y. 1974), and Barnes v. Peat, Marwick, Mitchell & Co., 69 Misc. 2d 1068, 332 N.Y.S.2d 645 (1972), *mdf'd* 42 App. Div. 2d 15, 344 N.Y.S.2d 281 (1973), reprinted in [1972-1973 Transfer Binder] CCH Fed. Sec. L. Rep. ¶ 93,511 (private action allowed), with Russell v. Travel Concepts Corp., [1975-1976 Transfer Binder] CCH Fed. Sec. L. Rep. ¶ 95,230 (S.D.N.Y. 1975), and Dyer v. Eastern Trust & Banking Co., 336 F. Supp. 890 (D. Me. 1971) (no private action allowed). Cf. Thompson v. Merrill Lynch, Pierce, Fenner & Smith, Inc., [1975-1976 Transfer Binder] CCH Fed. Sec. L. Rep. ¶ 95,383 (W.D. Okla. 1975) (negligent misrepresentations not actionable under Section 17(a)). See also ¶ 4.01[2][b], note 54. For a further discussion of this problem, see Note, "Securities Investment Advisers Act of 1940 and Private Right of Action for Damages Allowed Against an Investment Advisor and his Accountant," 43 Fordham L. Rev. 493 (1974).

The questions of whether private rights of action exist under Sections 206 and 17(a) are aspects of the general problem of when private enforcement is an appropriate supplement to official enforcement of the securities laws. See, e.g., Walsh v. Butcher & Sherrerd, [1975-1976 Transfer Binder] CCH Fed. Sec. L. Rep. ¶ 95,325 (E.D. Pa. 1975) (no private enforcement of SEC order pursuant to Section 21(f) of Exchange Act); Morris v. Cantor, 390 F. Supp. 817 (S.D.N.Y. 1975) (private right of action under Section 315(d) of Trust Indenture Act); Index Fund, Inc. v. Insurance Co. of North America, [1974-1975 Transfer Binder] CCH Fed. Sec. L. Rep. ¶ 94,952 (S.D.N.Y. 1975) (claim of investment company on fidelity bond not cognizable under Section 17(g) of Investment Company Act); Little v. First Cal. Co., CCH Fed. Bank. L. Rep. ¶ 96,305 (D. Ariz. 1974) (private right of action recognized under Comptroller's regulations regarding offering circulars, 12 C.F.R. § 16.4). See generally Pitt, "An SEC Insider's View of the Utility of Private Litigation Under the Federal Securities Laws," 5 Sec. Reg. L.J. 3 (1977). In Abrahamson v. Fleschner, [1976-1977 Transfer Binder] CCH Fed. Sec. L. Rep. ¶ 95,889 (2d Cir. 1977), the court considered the status of private actions under Section 206 of the Investment Advisers Act. In that connection, it surveyed the securities cases in which private rights of action had been implied, and it applied the four-factor test developed by the Supreme Court in Cort v. Ash, 422 U.S. 66, 78 (1975), respecting implied rights of action. Based on its analysis, the court concluded in a 2-to-1 decision that a private right of action exists under Section

claim.[44] This much is certain, however: If misrepresentations or omissions are material and the element of reliance is present, the cause-in-fact connection between wrongful management action and investor injury will be established, and defendants will be forced to search for policy justifications emphasizing administrative convenience or legislative intent to avoid personal answerability.

[a] Testimonials

Testimonials may be either solicited or unsolicited. If unsolicited, they impose no obligations on an investment manager unless he effectively adopts them. Thus, for example, an investment manager should disavow inaccuracies coming to his attention, particularly if circumstances make it reasonable for a prospective client to believe that the testimonials were sponsored by the manager.[45] Furthermore, it is doubt-

---

206. The opinions of the majority and the dissent are useful for the contrasting views they take on the application of the broad principles announced in *Cort* to securities matters.

[44] In Carras v. Burns, 516 F.2d 251 (4th Cir. 1975), the court held that where the executors of an estate relied on the assurances of a broker rather than seeking out an attorney, it was not necessary for the plaintiff to prove intent by the broker to defraud in order to recover. Instead, the standard was whether the broker knew that margin trading was dangerous without disclosing it to the client. But in White v. Abrams, 495 F.2d 724 (9th Cir. 1974), the court held that material misrepresentation was not sufficient to allow recovery, if the broker did not know that the statements were false. Both courts emphasized the degree of trust which the broker had instilled in the client. In *Carras*, the court noted that the broker was placed in a position of extreme trust and confidence to the extent of complete reliance upon him, and that the relationship was greater than the ordinary broker-client relationship. The *White* case found this high degree of trust to be lacking, and therefore imposed a lower duty of care upon the broker. These cases are to be contrasted with the Supreme Court's holding in Ernst & Ernst v. Hochfelder, 425 U.S. 185 (1976), in which the Court held that, at least where no fiduciary relationship is involved, scienter must be alleged and proved in a civil action for damages under Rule 10b-5. *Hochfelder* is discussed in depth in ¶ 6.01, note 5.

[45] See General Statistics, Inc., [1975-1976 Transfer Binder] CCH Fed. Sec. L. Rep. ¶ 80,234 (1975). The staff concluded that a proposed simulated investment services program through which participating advisers' "performance" on a hypothetical portfolio would be transmitted to clients of the adviser could violate the securities laws, and pointed out that the awarding of "experience points" could be considered providing testimonials in violation of Rule 206(4)-1(a)(1).

ful that a testimonial will be regarded as unsolicited if the maker can expect to receive some consideration from an investment manager as a consequence. Problems involved in shepherding indirect benefits to persons not employed by an investment manager as a means of developing new business are discussed in more detail below.[46]

The SEC regards testimonials with suspicion. Investment Advisers Act Rule 206(4)-1(a)(1)[47] prohibits statutory investment advisers from using testimonials of any type in advertisements. The Commission's position with regard to broker-dealers who are not statutory investment advisers is less severe; it defers to stock exchange rules which, though not totally prohibitory of testimonials, greatly restrict their use. The National Association of Securities Dealers (NASD) requires broker-dealers to disclose that the experience of the maker of the testimonial may not reflect the experience a prospective client can anticipate.[48] Additionally, NASD rules[49] require testimonials to disclose whether the maker is receiving compensation[50] for his actions. The New York Stock Exchange and American Stock Exchange rules set four conditions on the use of testimonials.[51] A testimonial must contain a statement:

(1) That it may not be representative of the experience of other clients;

(2) That it cannot be indicative of future performance or success;

(3) If applicable, that it is a paid testimonial; and

(4) To the extent technical aspects of investing are involved, that the maker has adequate knowledge and experience to form a valid opinion.

The reason solicited testimonials are so tightly controlled is that they create serious risks of being misleading. Even if every statement made by one offering a testimonial is true, no useful evaluation of the testi-

---

[46] See ¶ 3.02[2][b], *infra.*

[47] 17 C.F.R. § 275.206(4)-1(a)(1).

[48] NASD Rules of Fair Practice, Art. III, § 1, Board of Governors, "Advertising Interpretation," CCH NASD Manual ¶ 2151.

[49] *Id.*

[50] See ¶ 5.03, notes 59-64, on the meaning of compensation. See also Casey, " 'Finders Fee' Compensation to Brokers and Others," 31 Bus. Law. 707 (1976).

[51] NYSE Rule 473, CCH NYSE Guide ¶ 2474A.10; AMEX Rule 484, CCH AMEX Guide ¶ 9495.

monial is possible unless at least three facts are known: (1) the investment objectives of the maker; (2) the degree of risk undertaken to achieve the results that were so obviously satisfactory to the maker, especially if the testimonial refers to an investment period of less than a full market cycle[52]; and (3) how closely the experience of the maker reflects the experience of a significant number of the investment manager's other clients. Moreover, in addition to the potential of testimonials to mislead prospective clients by substituting the opinions of the maker for the client's independent evaluation of the record, testimonials typically contain little positive information, such as qualifications of personnel or methods of operation.

With testimonials having such little substantive value in meeting the function of disclosure in marketing investment management services, the fear is that they will appeal only to unsophisticated and credulous investors who are most in need of extensive disclosure. For these reasons, investment managers using testimonials should include more than the opinion of the maker. They should be used only in conjunction with a comprehensive marketing program. And they should also contain facts sufficient for a prospective client to reach an independent judgment about whether the maker of the testimonial got what he claimed, or at least an offer to make such facts available.

[b] Referrals

Referrals can be an attractive method of acquiring new investment management business,[53] and they present no legal problems if they are neither solicited nor rewarded. Furthermore, many investors prefer persons in whom they have confidence to refer them to competent investment managers. But referrals can test severely an investment manager's fiduciary duty of loyalty if, to reciprocate, the manager directs business

---

[52] Indeed, there is some feeling that a full market cycle is an inadequate period for measuring performance and that it should be a full business cycle if that is greater. The selection of a period for performance measurement is considered more fully in ¶ 5.03[2][c][vii].

[53] See SEC, *Institutional Investor Study*, H.R. Doc. No. 64, 92d Cong., 1st Sess. 2, 196 (1971). In Patocka, "The New Look in Marketing Pension Management," 9 Institutional Investor 61 (March 1975), the author reports that referrals are an increasingly important means of acquiring institutional as well as individual clients, especially "in the wake of the long bear market" when the effectiveness of "cold calls" (that is, the practice of unsolicited calling on potential clients in order to make sales presentations) has dropped significantly.

to the one responsible for the referral. The risk is that prospective clients will lose two ways: The one making the referral might recommend an investment manager based on the advantages he can expect for sending the account rather than on his best judgment of which investment manager is most suitable for the client; and an investment manager might select sources of support services for management of the account based not on the manager's best judgment of who can best provide them, but on who has been most valuable in expanding the manager's business.

Reciprocal arrangements conditioned on referral business vary extensively. A primary source of referrals to investment managers has been broker-dealers, but financial consultants, lawyers, accountants, insurance agents, and many other persons connected in some fashion with the securities industry have also been involved. Moreover, the type of consideration referrals have generated also varies considerably. Some investment managers engage in fee-splitting arrangements or pay referral fees, but there have also been many forms of less concrete consideration. Directed brokerage and custodianship are common, but other arrangements, such as participation in underwritings and private placements, are known also. The point, however, is that, limited only by the ingenuity of the reciprocating parties, referral business has tended to compromise the duty-of-loyalty requirement that investment management relationships be established and carried on solely in the best interests of the clients.

For reasons indicated above,[54] during the preemployment phase, an investment manager breaches no duty stemming from the common law of trusts or agency by accepting referral business. Of course, the party making the referral is an agent of the prospective client for purposes of selecting an investment manager[55] and is subject to the attendant consequences arising out of that relationship. As a result, he may be subject to common-law duties of supervision and care, especially if he receives a form of consideration for making the referral as part of a continuing

---

[54] See text at notes 2-4 *supra*.

[55] The referring party is not a mere middleman if he exercises the slightest amount of discretion in the choice of an investment manager. A middleman's sole function is to bring interested parties together, and it is understood by all that the middleman's employer has no right to rely on the middleman's judgment in selecting an appropriate party with whom the employer can deal. See *Restatement (Second) of Agency* § 258, Comment b (1958); *Am. Jur. 2d* "Brokers" § 173 (1964).

arrangement.[56] Moreover, the making of referrals regularly can result in classification of one engaging in that course of conduct as a statutory investment adviser[57] and would consequently require compliance with the technical and antifraud provisions of the Investment Advisers Act.

The danger for investment managers directly or indirectly rewarding those who refer business to them arises once referral clients enter a management relationship with them. Trustees and agents must use the assets in the accounts they control in the best interest of the beneficiaries and principals.[58] By paying fees or directing business to those making referrals, investment managers may be using those assets to aid their own promotional activities. Furthermore, depending on the formality and regularity of the relationship between an investment manager and those making referrals, the manager might be determined to be in a joint venture with those making the referrals, and hence responsible for their actions, including representations made in encouraging the client to seek the manager's services.[59]

In addition to the application of the common-law rules, it is probable that, absent disclosure, referrals as a means of promoting investment management services now violate the antifraud provisions of the federal securities laws.[60] Moreover, even with disclosure, the status of

---

[56] To the extent a securities professional, expecting some form of consideration, aids in the selection of an investment manager, he is, in effect, an agent soliciting a sub-agent, and is merely under a duty of care in the appointment and supervision of the manager unless otherwise agreed. *Restatement (Second) of Agency* § 405(2) (1958). In furtherance of this principle, the antifraud provisions of the Exchange Act have been adapted to impose supervisory and due-diligence duties on a broker-dealer who referred a customer to an investment adviser. Rolf v. Blyth Eastman Dillon & Co., 424 F. Supp. 1021 (S.D.N.Y. 1977).

[57] Dillon, Read & Co., [1973-1976 Transfer Binder] CCH Mutual Funds Guide ¶ 9903, at 12,573 (1973) (broker-dealer splitting advisory fees with operator of information-retrieval system is investment adviser to clients of operator). See also FPC Secs. Corp., [1974-1975 Transfer Binder] CCH Fed. Sec. L. Rep. ¶ 80,072 (1974); Reinholdt & Gardner, [1969-1973 Transfer Binder] CCH Mutual Funds Guide ¶ 9213 (1971). See Bines, "Regulating Discretionary Management: Broker-Dealers as Catalysts for Reform," 16 B.C. Ind. & Comm. L. Rev. 347, 377-378 (1975).

[58] See discussion of the duty of loyalty in ¶ 1.03.

[59] Cf. Lutz v. Boas, 39 Del. Ch. 585, 171 A.2d 381, supplemented in 40 Del. Ch. 130, 176 A.2d 853 (1961).

[60] SEC v. MONEX Int'l, Ltd., d/b/a Pacific Coast Coin Exch., SEC Litigation Release No. 6645 (Dec. 18, 1974). See also Moses v. Burgin, 445 F.2d 369 (1st Cir.), cert. denied sub nom. Johnson v. Moses, 404 U.S. 994 (1971); SEC, *Report of the Advisory Committee on Investment Manage-*

referral business is unclear. The NASD Rules of Fair Practice[61] and Securities Exchange Act Rule 15b10-10[62] forbid broker-dealers to sell mutual fund shares in anticipation of brokerage or other reciprocal dealings, and the SEC staff at one stage was taking a position against fee-sharing arrangements between investment advisers and broker-dealers.[63]

Given the antipathy of the SEC to referrals as a means of marketing the management office, and in view of the importance of referrals to some investment managers, it is worthwhile tracing the regulatory history, the better to appreciate why referral business is subject to such suspicion. In the 1960s, as a result of the fixed-rate regime, large transactions generated high commissions which did not reflect the true costs of execution.[64] Stock exchange rules prohibited members from rebating excessive commissions, but also permitted members to share commissions regardless of whether each had participated in carrying out a trade. Large investors whose trading activities generated these excess commissions frequently found that they could pay for services provided by different houses by requiring executing brokers to share commissions with the houses providing those services.[65] In short order, the broker-dealer community also developed techniques for sharing excess commissions among members and nonmembers of an exchange so that these large investors could obtain valuable services from any broker-dealer

---

ment Services for Individual Investors, Small Account Investment Management Services, CCH Fed. Sec. L. Rep. No. 465, Pt. III, at 39-42 (1973).

[61] Art. III, § 26(k)(5), Board of Governors' Explanation, CCH NASD Manual ¶ 2176.

[62] 17 C.F.R. § 240.15b10-10.

[63] See, e.g., John C. Tead Co., [1973-1976 Transfer Binder] CCH Mutual Funds Guide ¶ 9896 (1973); Argus Sec. Management Corp., [1971-1972 Transfer Binder] CCH Fed. Sec. L. Rep. ¶ 78,366 (1971); Reinholdt & Gardner, [1969-1973 Transfer Binder] CCH Mutual Funds Guide ¶ 9213 (1971). But see text at notes 77-78 infra.

[64] It may be that, absent the rebative practices described below, commission rates would not have become completely cost-related; at least the progress toward fully negotiated commissions may have been much slower. It is not so long ago that the stock exchanges were perceived in part as a public utility, and, indeed, it was probably that perception which kept the brokerage community from recognizing the inevitability of the shift to negotiated commissions. These matters are discussed in detail in ¶ 8.02.

[65] Independent Broker-Dealers Trade Ass'n v. SEC, 442 F.2d 132 (D.C. Cir. 1971). A detailed discussion of the execution practices of investment managers during the transition from fixed brokerage commission rates to negotiated rates appears in ¶ 8.02[3].

and still retain the ability to execute with the broker-dealer best suited to handle a given trade.[66]

The name commonly applied to the technique of investors' directing executing brokers to share part of their commissions with nonparticipating brokers was "customer-directed give-ups." (Not all give-ups occurred at the direction of the brokerage clients.) On its face, the practice of directing give-ups was benign because fixed rates required the commissions to be paid anyway. And the rules established in the brokerage community and supported through federal regulation made it impossible to get back the excess charges for trading activities except through the acquisition of services in addition to pure execution. But in actuality, the practice of directing give-ups was less benign than first appeared, for it began to place strains on the fiduciary duty of loyalty investment managers owed their clients. For example, in its *Report on the Public Policy Implications of Investment Company Growth*, the SEC pointed out that the purchase of research assistance with brokerage commissions should have led to reduced advisory fees, but that only a few investment advisers had elected to apply the value they got from supplementary research in this way.[67]

The practice that really destroyed give-ups, however, was the mutual fund industry's use of give-ups to promote referral business. As early as 1964, the SEC noted critically that mutual fund investment advisers were directing commissions to houses that sold shares in the fund.[68] Unlike supplementary research, there was no doubt of the financial benefit the advisers derived from this tactic, since the method of compensating mutual fund investment advisers was to charge a percentage of the assets under management. An increase in fund size meant an increase in management fees. On the other hand, those same commission dollars could have been used to purchase research or other support services which might have been more valuable to the fund shareholders by aiding investment performance or at least reducing administrative costs.

Although the choice between rewarding referring brokers or pur-

---

[66] See Jennings, "The New York Stock Exchange and the Commission Rate Struggle," 53 Cal. L. Rev. 1119, 1121-1124 (1965); R. Jennings & H. Marsh, *Securities Regulation* 762-766 (1972); SEC, *Report on the Public Policy Implications of Investment Company Growth,* H.R. Rep. No. 2337, 89th Congress, 2d Sess. 171-172 (1966).

[67] *Id.* at 108-110, 172-174.

[68] SEC, *Report of Special Study of Securities Markets,* H.R. Doc. No. 95, 88th Cong., 1st Sess. Pt. 4, at 220 et seq. (1963).

chasing other services was enough to test the investment advisers' duty of loyalty to the funds they managed, other developments made the strain intolerable. There was a greater danger to fund shareholders in the practice of directing excess commissions to brokers selling fund shares than simply the loss of possibly valuable services. Some mutual fund investment managers increased portfolio turnover in order to generate greater sales efforts by referring brokers.[69] And, more telling with respect to these referral arrangements, it soon became possible for the underwriter affiliates of mutual fund investment advisers to join regional exchanges and to recapture part of the fund assets expended on commissions.

The consequences of the conflicting interests involved in deciding whether to use excess commission dollars to reward referral business or to recapture those dollars for the benefit of the mutual fund ultimately resulted in substantial liability for the defendants in the case of *Moses v. Burgin*.[70] The defendants argued that increasing the size of the fund was in the interest of the shareholders as well as management because the constant inflow of money would render it unnecessary for management to liquidate part of its portfolio in the event of heavy redemptions. They also argued that seeking exchange membership was a serious undertaking and that in the exercise of sound business judgment, they could decide to forego such a program, even though it would deprive them of the opportunity to recapture commissions—a position which has since received judicial support.[71] Though the court did not reject the defendants' claim that their actions may have been in the best interests of the fund shareholders, it held that because of the conflicting interests involved, it was beyond the power of the investment advisers to decide on their own which course to take. They were under a duty of disclosure to the outside directors whose responsibility it was to resolve the conflict for the benefit of the fund.

The question is whether the position taken in *Moses* that the potential breach of the duty of loyalty involved in referral business can be

---

[69] See Continental Inv. Corp., [1972-1973 Transfer Binder] CCH Fed. Sec. L. Rep. ¶ 79,024 (1972). See also Romanski, "The Role of Advertising in the Mutual Funds Industry," 13 B.C. Ind. & Comm. L. Rev. 959, especially 968-974 (1972).

[70] 445 F.2d 369 (1st Cir.), *cert. denied sub nom.* Johnson v. Moses, 404 U.S. 994 (1971).

[71] See Tannenbaum v. Zeller, 399 F. Supp. 945 (S.D.N.Y. 1975), *rev'd on other grounds* [1976-1977 Transfer Binder] CCH Fed. Sec. L. Rep. ¶ 95,900 (2d Cir. 1977). But see Fogel v. Chestnutt, 533 F.2d 731 (2d Cir. 1975). *Moses, Tannenbaum,* and *Fogel* are discussed in detail at ¶ 9.07[2].

resolved through full disclosure is a proper expression of the law. As indicated above, shortly after *Moses* was decided, the SEC exercised its rule-making authority to prohibit all use of commissions to reward brokers selling mutual fund shares.[72] Furthermore, the attitude of the SEC toward referral business in the mutual fund industry has carried over into its consideration of referral business for other investment management relationships. The staff has denied no-action-letter requests involving referral arrangements between broker-dealers and investment advisers, even in the face of full disclosure to the investor.[73] The staff's position apparently was that regularized fee-sharing through receipt of a portion of the management fee or through reciprocal brokerage creates conflicts of interests so fundamental as to render the relationship inherently fraudulent or deceptive.

The staff's position was severely criticized.[74] In particular, the SEC Advisory Committee on Investment Management Services for Individual Investors[75] sharply disagreed with the staff's conclusion that fee-sharing arrangements, when fully disclosed, could be fraudulent or deceptive. But even the Advisory Committee took the position that continuous fee-sharing puts excessive strain on the fiduciary relationships between the broker-dealer and the investor, and the investment adviser and the investor. Consequently, it recommended that only a one-time finder's fee, reasonable in amount and fully disclosed, be permitted referring broker-dealers.[76]

But the SEC staff has apparently changed its attitude respecting referral arrangements. It has taken a position, seemingly inconsistent with the total prohibition of referral arrangements, that associations between investment advisers and broker-dealers are permissible if three conditions are satisfied:

(1) The broker-dealer may not receive a portion of the advisory fee, but only the ordinary brokerage associated with executing trades recommended by the adviser (and, presumably, only the ordinary brokerage from unrelated advisory accounts);

(2) The customer must have the option to choose a different broker-dealer; and

---

[72] See text at notes 61-62 *supra*.

[73] See note 63 *supra*.

[74] Friedman, "Problems Involving Investment Advisers and Broker-Dealers Serving Individual Accounts," in R. Mundheim, A. Fleischer & J. Schupper, *Fourth Annual Institute on Securities Regulation* 295, 297-308 (PLI 1973).

[75] Note 60 *supra*, at 42.

[76] *Id.*

(3) There must be full disclosure of the relationship.[77]

Another development indicating a mellowing of the staff's strict position occurred in a no-action request by a broker-dealer firm offering to assist investors in the selection of investment advisers.[78] Though the staff denied the request, it did so because of the specifics of the resultant brokerage arrangement rather than on the grounds that a fully disclosed referral was inherently fraudulent.

A large part of the explanation of why the SEC seems uncompromising with respect to referral business is a concern that referral arrangements have adverse consequences, mostly for unsophisticated investors.[79] The principal appeal of mutual funds is to small investors. In the 1960s' mutual fund shareholders were not likely to know that their funds' brokers were receiving handsome rewards in addition to the underwriting commission for having sold them their shares. Nor were they likely to know that the commissions spent by their mutual funds were for anything but execution services, much less that the advisers to their funds could have recaptured part of those commissions or used them to obtain other services.[80] Moreover, virtually all of the regulatory attention the SEC has given referrals has focused on investment management services for individual investors, and almost without exception the referral arrangements under scrutiny were between investment managers and referring broker-dealers.[81] Again, the potential for harm resulting

---

[77] See Hartzmark & Co., [1973-1976 Transfer Binder] CCH Mutual Funds Guide ¶ 9900, at 12,563 (1973); Thomas L. Gordon, [1973-1976 Transfer Binder] CCH Mutual Funds Guide ¶ 9831, at 12,434 (1973); Bacon, Whipple & Co., [1969-1973 Transfer Binder] CCH Mutual Funds Guide ¶ 9673, at 12,308 (1972). Cf. John G. Kinnard & Co., CCH Mutual Funds Guide ¶ 9941, at 12,631 (1973). Investor's Diversified Servs., Inc., Sec. Reg. L. Rep., No. 319, Sept. 17, 1975, at C-1. As one commentator has pointed out, when compensation for referral business is not disclosed, it is hard to believe that a prospective client is getting the objectivity he is seeking. See Casey, " 'Finders Fee' Compensation to Brokers and Others," 31 Bus. Law. 707 (1976).

[78] FPC Secs. Corp., [1974-1975 Transfer Binder] CCH Fed. Sec. L. Rep. ¶ 80,072 (1974).

[79] If, by the term unsophisticated investors, one excludes institutions from consideration, it is definitely not true that referral arrangements affect only unsophisticated investors. Indeed, since the introduction of negotiated rates, several brokerage houses have threatened to withhold referrals from investment managers who fail to execute with them. See, e.g., Wall Street Letter, Aug. 18, 1975, p. 1. See also note 53 supra.

[80] See, e.g., In re Mates Fin. Servs., [1969-1970 Transfer Binder] CCH Fed. Sec. L. Rep. ¶¶ 77,721, 77,790 (1970).

[81] See notes 63, 77 supra.

from the inexperience of individuals seems manifest, at least to the Commission.

It is thus possible that a regulatory distinction will be made between investment management services designed primarily for individual investors and those intended to serve institutional investors, a supposedly more sophisticated clientele.[82] Or it may be the case, as the staff's most recent statements seem to indicate, that referrals will be acceptable for most investors.[83] But whatever the degree of prohibition, the *Moses* case makes clear that, for those investors who lawfully may be made the object of marketing by referrals, full disclosure is essential.

There are two levels to disclosure in this context:

(1) Insofar as investors who have a broad understanding of the securities market and investment management practices are concerned, it should suffice to disclose the relationship between the referring party and the investment manager, including a precise description of the type of consideration being provided for the referral.

(2) A less knowledgeable investor, however, probably requires a more detailed explanation of what is involved, for that type of investor may not understand the implications of the referral relationship even though it is fully disclosed.

Although the law remains unsettled over what full disclosure includes when dealing with unsophisticated investors, the best policy in such case might be for the investment manager to explain the risks that the potential conflict of interest can produce. If the referral relationship is with a broker granted custody and execution authority for an account, for example, the investment manager should tell the prospective client that

---

[82] On the other hand, Securities Exchange Act § 11(a) (15 U.S.C. § 78k(a)), as amended by the Securities Acts Amendments of 1975 (Pub. L. No. 94-29, 89 Stat. 97, § 6(2) (June 4, 1975)), distinguishes between individual and institutional investors by separating management and brokerage services only in the case of institutions. Why Congress deemed individuals less worthy of protection from the conflict of interest ostensibly inherent in combined management and brokerage is not entirely clear. For a fuller discussion of this point, see ¶ 10.02[1][c][iii].

[83] See notes 77-78 *supra*. Note also that Securities Exchange Act § 28(e) (15 U.S.C. § 78bb(e)), the "paying up" provision of the Securities Acts Amendments of 1975 (note 82 *supra*, § 21(2)), refers to all investors, no distinction being made between individual investors and institutions, despite the greater potential for harm to individuals. A detailed discussion of Section 28(e) appears in ¶ 9.03[2].

there is at least a theoretical risk of overtrading or sacrifice of best price execution to reciprocate for the referral, and that the judgment of the referring broker-dealer may have been colored by the degree to which he expected to profit from a resulting investment management arrangement. The manager might even find it a selling advantage to explain how he prevents these theoretical risks from maturing into actual harm. In any event, disclosure at this level of precision should insulate an investment manager against subsequent claims based on allegations of misleading statements arising out of the referral but in fact attributable to client dissatisfaction with some other facet of the management of the account.

[c] Past investment recommendations as a measure of performance

Another marketing device which is a snare principally for unsophisticated investors is the use of past recommendations to persuade prospective clients that an investment manager possesses superior ability to select securities. Apparently, a number of persons offering investment management services have been able to impress prospective clients by displaying incomplete or unrepresentative lists of recommendations the manager has made in the past,[84] though it would seem that an investor who would rely on such information without inquiring whether it was complete is beyond regulatory redemption. In any event, Investment Advisers Act Rule 206(4)-1(a)(2)[85] permits statutory Investment Advisers to rely on past recommendations for marketing purposes if all of the following conditions are met:

(1) All recommendations must be listed, or there must be an offer to furnish such a list;

(2) The list must cover a period of not less than one year;

(3) The list must show the date each recommendation was made;

(4) The list must describe the nature of each recommendation, that is, whether the investment adviser counseled buying, selling, or holding;

(5) The list must present the market price at the time of the recommendation;

---

[84] E.g., George L. Bedford, [1972-1973 Transfer Binder] CCH Fed. Sec. L. Rep. ¶ 78,911 (1972); Killgore Management, Inc., [1972-1973 Transfer Binder] CCH Fed. Sec. L. Rep. ¶ 78,977 (1972); Paul K. Peers, Inc., [1964-1966 Transfer Binder] CCH Fed. Sec. L. Rep. ¶ 77,222 (1965).

[85] 17 C.F.R. § 275.206(4)-1(a)(2).

(6) The list must present the price at which the recommendation was to be acted upon;

(7) The list must present the market price of each security recommended as of the most recent date practicable; and

(8) The list must contain a cautionary legend warning that future recommendations might not be profitable and might not equal the performance of the securities previously recommended.

It is safe to say that, insofar as investment managers not subject to the Investment Advisers Act are concerned, the nontechnical features of this rule would be implied under other antifraud provisions to test the use of past recommendations as a marketing device.[86]

Although Rule 206(4)-1(a)(2), stock exchange rules, and other authorities require past recommendations to cover at least a one-year period,[87] there is also the question of how ancient recommendations may be. The SEC staff has taken the puzzling position that any use of past recommendations over two years old would be misleading and fraudulent.[88] The staff took that position without citing any authority for support and in opposition to the conclusion of the *Institutional Investor Study* that the appropriate period for measuring performance is from one to three years.[89] Other commentators also agree that periods well in excess of one year are useful in measuring an investment manager's performance.[90] In view of the authority against the staff, it is highly likely that lists of past recommendations extending back for several years, if complete and in other respects not misleading, would not be disqualified on the grounds of vintage.

Incompleteness is not the only problem associated with the use of past recommendations. No useful assessment of an investment man-

---

[86] See Spear & Staff, [1964-1966 Transfer Binder] CCH Fed. Sec. L. Rep. ¶ 77,216 (1965).

[87] NYSE Rule 473, 2 CCH NYSE Guide ¶ 2474A; AMEX Rule 484, 2 CCH AMEX Guide ¶ 9495; Interpretation of the Board of Governors, NASD Rules of Fair Practice, Art. III, § 1, CCH NASD Manual ¶ 2151. See also Cubitt-Nichols Associates, [1971-1972 Transfer Binder] CCH Fed. Sec. L. Rep. ¶ 78,659 (1971).

[88] Hardy & Co., [1972-1973 Transfer Binder] CCH Fed. Sec. L. Rep. ¶ 78,947 (1972).

[89] See SEC, *Institutional Investor Study*, Ch. 2, H.R. Doc. No. 64, 92d Cong., 1st Sess. 265 (1971).

[90] See J. Lorie & M. Hamilton, *The Stock Market: Theories and Evidence* 247 (1973); R. Sprecher, *An Introduction to Investment Management* 370 (1975).

ager's ability to select securities is possible without taking into account the influence of general market movements. For this reason, NYSE and AMEX rules require disclosure of rising markets during the period covered by a list of recommendations.[91] (There is no comparable requirement for disclosure of a falling market. This doubtless reflects a realistic view that anyone able to pick more winners than losers during a falling market is not likely to hide that fact, and that others who were less fortunate will surely refer to market conditions to explain their results.) Thus, full disclosure almost surely includes a statement concerning upward market movement, if such were the case.

Suitability is another important consideration which the use of past recommendations tends to mask. Without knowing the riskiness of the securities appearing on a list, a prospective client would not be able to tell how a portfolio designed to meet his investment objectives would have fared. Furthermore, there is the complementary danger that, in an oral sales presentation, a model portfolio meeting the investor's objectives could be fashioned from successful security selections taken from a list of past recommendations while less profitable securities, equally likely to have been chosen, would be ignored. Though detection and proof might be difficult, there is little question that extrapolating from a list of past recommendations to demonstrate typical results a prospective client could have experienced would violate the antifraud rules.[92]

But the greatest shortcoming of past recommendations as a means for evaluating the sagacity of an investment manager is the hypothetical nature of the performance indicated by the list. In order for past recommendations to provide a realistic indication of an investment manager's abilities, it would be necessary for the client to have invested precisely in accordance with the recommendations as they were made. Suitability problems aside, one immediate difficulty arising out of such a supposition is that one must choose how to weight the expenditures made in acquiring each security recommended. Plainly, the investment results will differ depending on whether a client invests equal dollar amounts in each recommended security, or whether he invests in equal numbers of shares, or whether he uses some other weighting system.[93] The choice of system is particularly critical if the performance of past

---

[91] NYSE Rule 473, 2 CCH NYSE Guide ¶ 2474A; AMEX Rule 484, 2 CCH AMEX Guide ¶ 9495.

[92] E.g., Killgore Management, Inc., [1972-1973 Transfer Binder] CCH Fed. Sec. L. Rep. ¶ 78,977 (1972); Hardy & Co., *id.* ¶ 78,947.

[93] See J. Lorie & M. Hamilton, *The Stock Market: Theories and Evidence* 51-69 (1973).

recommendations is to be compared with the performance of a broad market index since each index has its own weighting system. If the list and the index are not weighted in the same way, it is likely that the full effects of market movements will not be adequately taken into account in any comparison.[94]

An even more serious consideration is the improbability that any account could adopt an investment program following precisely an investment manager's recommendations as they occur. For one thing, the staffs of many investment managers are structured to develop lists of approved securities from which portfolio managers make individual decisions about what to do for the accounts they control. It is not even intended that every recommendation lead to investment action. More fundamental, however, it is doubtful that many accounts will have available the occasional inflows of cash necessary to consummate each recommendation even if that were the manager's policy. In actuality, the decision a portfolio manager must make when a new recommendation appears is whether it is good enough to merit changing an existing portfolio. A recommendation to buy, for example, must promise greater gains at no greater risk than the securities the new purchase would replace, and the difference must be great enough to warrant the requisite expenditure on commissions. There is simply no way to transpose a list of past recommendations into an accurate representation of what an invesment manager would have done with an existing portfolio during the period covered by the list.[95]

For these reasons, stock exchange rules require that if a record is averaged or summarized, it be disclosed that the reported results would have been obtained only if each issue had been purchased when recommended and sold at the end of the period covered or when sale was recommended.[96] In addition, the rules require that the cost of commissions be mentioned. Caution suggests that investment managers relying on past recommendations as a marketing device disclose at least that much if their sales presentations contain any suggestion that the list might have been representative of client experience.[97]

---

[94] *Id.* Note that different stock market indices provide different rates of return.

[95] E.g., George L. Bedford, [1972-1973 Transfer Binder] CCH Fed. Sec. L. Rep. ¶ 78,911 (1972).

[96] See note 91 *supra.*

[97] In Anametrics, Inc., [1970-1971 Transfer Binder] CCH Fed. Sec. L. Rep. ¶ 78,057 (1971), the staff took the position that although the use of individual percentage gain or loss for each recommendation listed would

[d]   Other measures of performance

Because performance figures are so important to investors, success-ful marketing virtually requires either that performance figures be strong or that attention be diverted from them. As a result, the potential for misleading information to be provided in connection with statements of performance is enormous. For example, some investment managers quote figures based on the experience of a relatively few accounts.[98] Others present an average performance figure without identifying the types of accounts comprising the average or the frequency and range of deviations from the average.[99] Another ploy investment managers rely on is the creation of standards of comparison to improve the appearance of the results they have achieved. They invent their own market indexes[100] and model portfolios,[101] or they make incomplete comparisons to the performance of others.[102]

Although the SEC has taken a fairly firm position against misleading statements of performance, it has been relatively uncommunicative about its rationale for rejecting particular practices. For example, the Commission has amended Rule 134 of the Securities Act to permit more open advertising by investment companies, but, without much expla-nation, it remains adamant in prohibiting publication of performance

---

not be misleading, the use of a simple cumulative arithmetic average would violate Rule 206(4)-1(a)(5) in that it would "obscure the impact of un-successful recommendations."

[98] See, e.g., Avatar Investors Associates Corp., [1973-1976 Transfer Binder] CCH Mutual Funds Guide ¶ 10,285 (1975).

[99] See, e.g., Anametrics, Inc., [1970-1971 Transfer Binder] CCH Fed. Sec. L. Rep. ¶ 78,057 (1971).

[100] See, e.g., George L. Bedford, [1972-1973 Transfer Binder] CCH Fed. Sec. L. Rep. ¶ 78,911 (1972).

[101] See, e.g., Killgore Management Inc., [1972-1973 Transfer Binder] CCH Fed. Sec. L. Rep. ¶ 78,977 (1972); Jerry W. Smith, [1972-1973 Transfer Binder] CCH Fed. Sec. L. Rep. ¶ 78,856 (1972); S.H. Dike & Co., [1975-1976 Transfer Binder] CCH Fed. Sec. L. Rep. ¶ 80,246 (1975); General Statistics, Inc., [1975-1976 Transfer Binder] CCH Fed. Sec. L. Rep. ¶ 80,234 (1975).

[102] *In re* Dow Theory Forecasts, Inc., SEC Investment Advisers Act Re-lease No. 223 (July 28, 1968), [1967-1969 Transfer Binder] CCH Fed. Sec. L. Rep. ¶ 77,580. But when an independent agency proposed to publish a comparison of investment managers based on information received from them, it obtained a no-action letter virtually without comment. Evaluation Associates, Inc., [1976-1977 Transfer Binder] CCH Fed. Sec. L. Rep. ¶ 80,874 (1976).

figures.[103] It has behaved similarly in the case of statutory investment advisers. In considering the validity of statements of average performance as a marketing device, the SEC staff has rejected one request for a no-action letter on the ground that averaging past recommendations can obscure the impact of unsuccessful recommendations, although the staff did not say how.[104] Similarly, the staff has warned an investment manager that advertising average performance figures requires a high degree of disclosure, again without saying what had to be disclosed.[105]

Nonetheless, there is good reason to believe that, in the future, the Commission will be taking a more considered approach to the use of performance figures in the marketing of investment management services. Section 25 of the Investment Company Act Amendments of 1970[106] amended Section 205 of the Investment Advisers Act[107] to deal with performance fees, and in issuing implementing regulations, the SEC has been forced to analyze closely the components of performance measurement.[108] Moreover, the *Institutional Investor Study* gave extensive consideration to the measurement of performance.[109] As a consequence of these developments, it is reasonable to expect the SEC, with its recently acquired expertise on performance, to insist that use of per-

---

[103] See note 34 *supra*. See especially SEC Securities Act Release No. 5536 (Nov. 4, 1974), [1974-1975 Transfer Binder] CCH Fed. Sec. L. Rep. ¶ 80,000. Note that the Commission, while declaring its intention to continue to study the issue of utilization of past performance data, feels that development of clearer and more readily understandable illustrations of performance are needed, and that to date such information "might constitute a selling argument." *Id.* at p. 84,583.

[104] Anametrics, Inc., [1970-1971 Transfer Binder] CCH Fed. Sec. L. Rep. ¶ 78,057 (1971).

[105] Executive Analysts, Inc., [1972-1973 Transfer Binder] CCH Fed. Sec. L. Rep. ¶ 78,946 (1972).

[106] Pub. L. 91-547, 84 Stat. 1432 (Dec. 14, 1970).

[107] 15 U.S.C. § 80b-5.

[108] See SEC Investment Advisers Act Release No. 316 (April 6, 1972), [1971-1972 Transfer Binder] CCH Fed. Sec. L. Rep. ¶ 78,693 (proposed rule); SEC Investment Advisers Act Release No. 315 (April 6, 1972), [1971-1972 Transfer Binder] CCH Fed. Sec. L. Rep. ¶ 78,694 (factors to be considered in connection with incentive fees); and SEC Investment Advisers Act Release No. 327 (Aug. 8, 1972), [1972-1973 Transfer Binder] CCH Fed. Sec. L. Rep. ¶ 78,934 (adoption of Rule 205-1).

[109] SEC, *Institutional Investor Study*, H.R. Doc. No. 64, 92d Cong., 1st Sess. 400-410 (1971).

formance figures in marketing activities comport with emerging doctrine on performance measurement.[110]

Although the components of performance measurement are considered in depth in Chapter 5,[111] for purposes of discussing marketing problems, the principal points can be summarized:

(1) Since performance is relative, the results an investment manager achieves must be compared with those of someone else or with the market or with some other standard. Calculations of total return ignore the effect of market movements and, though relevant data, are therefore a misleading measurement of performance.

(2) Performance distinctions which fail to take into account a difference in level of risk between that undertaken by an investment manager and that of the standard to which he is compared will render any measurement of performance inadequate. Risk adjustment is essential to accuracy.

(3) Distributions and other returns must be included in calculating the results achieved both by the investment manager and by the standard of comparison. Performance is measured by the difference in the total return of both.

---

[110] For example, consider the SEC's discussion of the use of performance figures in investment company sales literature, SEC Securities Act Release No. 5537 (Nov. 4, 1974), [1974-1975 Transfer Binder] CCH Fed. Sec. L. Rep. ¶ 80,001 (proposed revision of policy with respect to charts in sales literature).

The regulatory sufficiency of criteria advanced as a basis for performance measurement is subtly different when an external independent agency is doing the measuring from when an investment manager prepares his own performance figures for promotional purposes. It is less important that the performance criteria selected by the independent agency measure performance accurately and completely since, assuming honest reporting, all managers are evaluated on the same grounds. Whatever the inherent limitations of the data requested of each manager, any deficiencies would at least apply equally to all managers covered. An investment manager's own promotional materials on performance, however, lack collective comparability and therefore must be more accurate and complete to be useful to a prospective client. See, e.g., Evaluation Associates, Inc., [1976-1977 Transfer Binder] CCH Fed. Sec. L. Rep. ¶ 80,874 (1976), in which the staff approved the no-action request of a registered adviser proposing to publish profiles of a number of investment managers to permit a generally sophisticated audience to compare managers.

[111] See ¶ 5.03[2].

(4) Similarly, to eliminate miscalculations of investment returns to a managed portfolio, it is essential to exclude the effects of cash flow. Consequently, there must be an adjustment of the results achieved by the investment manager for receipts and disbursements during the evaluation period.

(5) Finally, the time interval chosen for the evaluation of performance must be appropriate. Too short a period can emphasize random factors, and too long a period can mask recent experience.

Given the complexity involved in measuring performance, it is difficult to say what full disclosure means in the marketing context. At one extreme is the possibility, at least in the case of unsophisticated investors, that full disclosure will require the factors described above to be included in the calculation of performance figures intended for use in sales presentations. Perhaps full disclosure will be less demanding and require merely that, for marketing purposes, there be a statement identifying the factors not included in the calculations or not calculated precisely. Or the Commission may maintain its existing posture of restricting the use of performance figures only where they would be blatantly misleading or beyond the competence of most of the intended audience to evaluate. Developments in applying the theory of performance measurement in a regulatory environment are too new to predict their regulatory impact with confidence.

[e] Special services

A matter frequently of concern to investors is the degree of personal attention they can expect in the management of their accounts. The Investment Advisers Act endorses the importance of personalized service by prohibiting registered investment advisers from using the name "investment counsel" [112] unless their business consists substantially of giving "continuous advice as to the investment of funds on the basis of the individual needs of each client." [113] Moreover, many types of investment managers, whether statutory investment advisers or otherwise, often compete on the basis of the personalized service they provide. For many years, banks, for example, have emphasized the attention they

---

[112] Investment Advisers Act § 208(c), 15 U.S.C. § 80b-8(c).
[113] Investment Advisers Act § 202(a)(13), 15 U.S.C. § 80b-2(a)(13).

give to beneficiaries of testamentary and inter vivos trusts.[114] More recently, professional pension-fund managers have begun making frequent contact with pension trustees to provide them a full description of investment activity, an important element in the marketing of their services.[115]

The term used by the investment management community to describe a close and continuous relationship between an investment manager and client is "hand-holding." In some quarters, it has a pejorative connotation because many portfolio managers view contacts with clients as burdensome and inefficient. Hand-holding is said to take up a great deal of time which could be better spent analyzing investment opportunities.[116] Nonetheless, to the extent it is part of an investment manager's marketing program, hand-holding is material information which must accurately portray the way an account is actually handled.[117]

[f]   Portfolio appraisal and management by formula

Another technique used by some investment managers to attract business, especially from individual investors, is to promote some form of technical analysis as an investment tool. In some cases, investment managers offer to evaluate the quality of an existing portfolio. Other investment managers promote their services by promising to run an investment program on the basis of a formula plan. Typically, computer analysis is at the core of these services, and the print-outs of recommendations for action or the charts, graphs, and the like generated by the computer can be very impressive.

---

[114] For other material on marketing investment management by bank trust departments, see M. Mayer, *The Bankers* 500 et seq. (1974); D. Leinsdorf & D. Etra, *CITIBANK, A Ralph Nader Report* 163 et seq. (1973); C. Whittlesey, A. Freedman & E. Herman, *Money and Banking* 68-69 (1968); SEC Chairman Cook's Speech to the Investment Company Institute, [1973 Transfer Binder] CCH Fed. Sec. L. Rep. ¶ 79,366 (1973). See also D. Green & M. Schuelke, *The Trust Activities of the Banking Industry* (Stanford Research Institute 1975).

[115] See Patocka, "The New Look in Marketing Pension Management," 9 Institutional Investor 61 (March 1975).

[116] See SEC, *Report of the Advisory Committee on Investment Management Services for Individual Investors, Small Account Management Services,* CCH Fed. Sec. L. Rep. No. 465, Pt. III, at 30 (1973).

[117] Finanswer America/Investments, Inc., [1970-1971 Transfer Binder] CCH Fed. Sec. L. Rep. ¶ 78,111 (1971) (misrepresentation concerning individualized services).

The problem with these formula evaluations and investment techniques is that, despite the technical trappings, there is as yet no precise quantitative means of determining the intrinsic worth of a security or a portfolio.[118] Some judgment is always involved. Consequently, the SEC has taken a firm and consistent position with respect to the use of portfolio analysis by formula as a marketing technique. Investment Advisers Act Rule 206(4)-1(a)(3)[119] requires that advertisements promoting graphs, charts, formulas, or other similar devices must disclose prominently the limitations inherent in their use. In administrative cases and responses to requests for no-action letters, the Commission has consistently maintained that Rule 206(4)-1(a)(3) and general anti-fraud principles do not allow investment managers the pretense of absolute objectivity in the use of formula programs.[120]

But in this area also, the Commission has not been specific about the type of information which must be disclosed. It has not ventured much further than to state that the elements of formula programs involving judgment must be identified as such. Yet the applications of technical analysis have been growing apace. Not only are formula programs used to evaluate portfolios and identify investment opportunities, they are also being constructed now to evaluate investment managers for their ability to structure portfolios and trade effectively.[121] Since, at the same time, the predictive value of technical analysis at all levels has come under severe attack from modern investment theory,[122] it probably will become increasingly important for purveyors of technical analysis to disclose more than the point at which investment judgment must enter.

---

[118] See ¶ 7.07[2][d].

[119] 17 C.F.R. § 275.206(4)-1(a)(3).

[120] Sackville-Pickard, [1967-1969 Transfer Binder] CCH Fed. Sec. L. Rep. ¶ 77,620 (1968); Security Evaluation, Inc., [1971-1972 Transfer Binder] CCH Fed. Sec. L. Rep. ¶ 78,786 (1972); Alphadex Corp., [1971-1972 Transfer Binder] CCH Fed. Sec. L. Rep. ¶ 78,624 (1972); Investment Quality Measurement Corp., Sec. Reg. L. Rep., No. 309, July 2, 1975, at C-2; The Mottin Forecast, Sec. Reg. L. Rep., No. 331, Dec. 10, 1975, at C-2.

[121] Levy, "How to Measure Research Performance," 1 J. Portfolio Management 44 (1974); R. Sprecher, *An Introduction to Investment Management*, Ch. 17 (1975); J. Cohen, E. Zinbarg & A. Zerkel, *Investment Analysis and Portfolio Management* 812-825 (1973).

[122] See ¶ 7.07[2][d]. See generally J. Lorie & M. Hamilton, *The Stock Market: Theories and Evidence* (1973). As an indicator that the academic attitude doubting technical analysis is becoming better accepted in professional circles, see "Ehrbar, Techncial Analysis Refuses to Die," 92 Fortune 99 (Aug. 1975).

Underlying every form of technical analysis is a set of assumptions which ostensibly rationalizes the conclusions it produces. These assumptions probably should be disclosed to the extent consistent with the protection of proprietary information. Furthermore, assuming that technical analysis can be a useful tool for investment management, it still deals only in probability and not certainty. The conclusions it reaches will vary both in frequency and in degree of error. Disclosure in marketing probably requires that there be some acknowledgment of this fact, and perhaps also some attempt to bracket the error characteristic of the formula involved.

[g] Mandatory disclosures

Members of the investment management community have also sought new clients through other marketing techniques thought to provide a competitive edge. Some of these have been subject to regulatory consideration, and their treatment demonstrates the same approach to the promotional activities of investment managers that the preceding discussion has exposited. In all events, the disclosure rules require representations to be both accurate and complete. Statements concerning the qualifications of staff members or the reputation and history of a firm, for example, must not only be truthful, but must also reveal adverse information to the extent it is material.[123] In the case of representations concerning management fees, it would violate the antifraud rules not to disclose related sources of income deriving from control of a prospective client's account.[124]

But there are also mandatory disclosures an investment manager must make regardless of the harm such disclosures may do to his marketing efforts. These kinds of disclosures are of two types. The first covers information thought so important to a prospective client that no investment management agreement should be entered without it. In most of these cases, the mandatory disclosure requirements result from

---

123 Financial Programs, Inc., [1974-1975 Transfer Binder] CCH Fed. Sec. L. Rep. ¶ 80,146 (1975); Paul K. Peers, Inc., [1964-1966 Transfer Binder] CCH Fed. Sec. L. Rep. ¶ 77,222 (1965); "Benchmark," Sec. Reg. L. Rep., No. 340, Feb. 18, 1976, at C-2. (An extensive description of the bench-mark system of evaluation involved in this no-action request appears in Anderson, "How One System Helps Measure Stock Portfolio Quality," P-H Control of Banking ¶ 124 (1975).)

124 Mates Fin. Servs., [1969-1970 Transfer Binder] CCH Fed. Sec. L. Rep. ¶¶ 77,721, 77,790 (1969); TISE, Inc., [1974-1975 Transfer Binder] CCH Fed. Sec. L. Rep. ¶ 80,070 (1974).

some practice or procedure which severely tests an investment manager's duty of loyalty. For example, the Securities Acts Amendments of 1975[125] permit the use of brokerage commissions to obtain additional services [126] but, in order to reduce the conflicts of interest, make such practices subject to, among other things, disclosure rules established by the appropriate regulatory agency.[127] As another example, in a no-action letter,[128] the SEC staff warned an investment manager of its special disclosure duties to prospective clients where the manager was to be compensated by receiving limited or general partnership interests in investments it recommended to its clients. The staff regarded the conflict of interests inherent in this kind of compensation scheme so fundamental as to make full disclosure of the proposed arrangement mandatory.

One continuing source of controversy is the degree to which investment managers must disclose risk of loss as well as opportunity for gain. The Commission has long insisted that talk of rewards be balanced by warning about risk and has acted against marketing appeals that flagrantly promise profits or that guarantee against losses.[129] Aside from their attraction for the gullible, these techniques tend to divert attention from more important matters, such as actual performance records, and they may impose competitive pressures on otherwise responsible managers similarly to lower marketing standards. But, even assuming that a balanced presentation is intended, it is doubtful whether general warnings about the risk of loss will still suffice, if indeed they ever could. Modern investment theory has made some quantification of risk possible,[130] and it seems that the Commission is inching toward

---

[125] Pub. L. 94-29, 89 Stat. 97 (June 4, 1975).

[126] Securities Exchange Act § 28(e), 15 U.S.C. § 78bb(e).

[127] Appropriate regulatory agency is defined in Section 3(a)(34) of the Act, 15 U.S.C. § 78c(a)(34). The SEC has issued proposed disclosure rules applicable to persons under its jurisdiction. SEC Securities Act Release No. 5772 (Nov. 30, 1976), [1976-1977 Transfer Binder] CCH Fed. Sec. L. Rep. ¶ 80,815.

[128] TISE, Inc., [1974-1975 Transfer Binder] CCH Fed. Sec. L. Rep. ¶ 80,070 (1974).

[129] Dow Theory Forecasts, [1967-1969 Transfer Binder] CCH Fed. Sec. L. Rep. ¶ 77,580 (1968); SEC v. Seipel, [1952-1956 Transfer Binder] CCH Fed. Sec. L. Rep. ¶ 90,735 (D.D.C. 1955); Spear & Staff, Inc., [1964-1966 Transfer Binder] CCH Fed. Sec. L. Rep. ¶ 77,216 (1965). See also Benchmark Securities, Inc., [1975-1976 Transfer Binder] CCH Fed. Sec. L. Rep. ¶ 80,424.

[130] See ¶ 6.03.

a requirement that there be some disclosure of this type. Investment Advisers Act § 205 regulates incentive fees by requiring basic fees to be adjusted both up and down in proportion to performance, and, in an implementing release, the SEC has made it clear that adjustment for portfolio risk is necessary.[131]

Nonetheless, as a practical matter, it is difficult to quantify risk in marketing investment services unless reference is being made to the experience of a single investor or a collective investment vehicle. Risk analysis is a feature of profiling an investor rather than a method of attracting an investor's interest. Thus, the effect of expanding the disclosure requirements to obtain increased quantification of risk probably means that a higher standard of care is developing for profiling an investor than previously may have been the case.[132]

The other type of mandatory disclosure insisted on by the SEC is, despite appearances, not really disclosure in the marketing context at all. It is rather a method by which the Commission justifies enforcement action in cases involving shoddy management practices which do not seem to violate any substantive rule otherwise within the Commission's jurisdiction. For example, the Commission takes the position that the failure to disclose an insolvent condition is fraudulent.[133] Of course, disclosures of this kind would put an investment manager out of business—which is precisely the point motivating the SEC.

¶ 3.03. APPLICATION OF THE REGISTRATION PROVISIONS OF THE SECURITIES ACT OF 1933 TO PROMOTIONAL ACTIVITIES

The Supreme Court has characterized the Securities Act of 1933 as a remedial statute to be broadly construed.[134] Thus commissioned, the federal courts and the SEC have been expanding the definition of secu-

---

131 15 U.S.C. § 80b-5. See SEC Investment Advisers Act Release No. 315 (April 6, 1972), [1971-1972 Transfer Binder] CCH Fed. Sec. L. Rep. ¶ 78,694. See also "The Municipal Income Fund," Sec. Reg. L. Rep., No. 316, Aug. 20, 1975, at C-1 (unit investment trust investing in municipals may include Standard & Poor's rating in advertising literature).

132 See ¶ 4.02.

133 SEC v. First Am. Bank & Trust Co., 481 F.2d 673 (8th Cir. 1973); Intersearch Technology, Inc., [1974-1975 Transfer Binder] CCH Fed. Sec. L. Rep. ¶ 80,139 (1975); In re Jerry Richman, SEC Securities Exchange Act Release No. 11314 (March 27, 1975); SEC v. Phillips Publishing, Inc., SEC Litigation Release No. 7044 (Aug. 18, 1975).

134 Tcherepnin v. Knight, 389 U.S. 332, 336 (1967).

rity to include arrangements between investment managers and their clients. Although the issue is not yet settled, Supreme Court precedent has established that at least some investment management arrangements are statutory securities,[135] and the issue now is how encompassing a statutory classification will result. To the extent status as securities attaches to managed investment accounts, investment managers become statutory underwriters and must register each account or rely on some exception or exclusion from, or safe harbor in, the Securities Act.

[1] Managed Investment Accounts as Statutory Securities: The Howey Test

The route to classification of managed accounts as securities is complex, but by now it has been traveled enough to be familiar. The starting point is *SEC v. W.J. Howey Co.*[136] In that case, the Supreme Court set out a three-pronged test for defining the term "investment contract" as that term is used in Section 2(1) of the Securities Act, the section which defines "security" for statutory purposes.[137] An arrangement becomes a statutory security if it involves (1) a contract for investing money; (2) profits expected solely from the efforts of a promoter or a third party; and (3) a common enterprise.[138] It is possible to construe each of these elements to encompass almost the full range of ordinary investment management relationships.

[a] A contract for investing money: The status of trust relationships

No particular form of arrangement between an investment manager and a client is necessary to create a statutory security. On the contrary, the term of art, "investment contract," has demonstrated an amazing capacity to absorb the brain-children of promoters. Limited partnerships,[139] interests in short-term debt instruments,[140] participations in oil

---

135 SEC v. Variable Annuity Life Ins. Co. of Am., 359 U.S. 65 (1959); SEC v. United Benefit Life Ins. Co., 387 U.S. 202 (1967); see also Prudential Ins. Co. of N. Am. v. SEC, 326 F.2d 383 (3d Cir.), *cert. denied* 377 U.S. 953 (1964).

136 328 U.S. 293, *rehearing denied* 329 U.S. 819 (1946).

137 15 U.S.C. § 77b(1).

138 328 U.S. at 298-299.

139 McGregor Land Co. v. Meguiar, [1975-1976 Transfer Binder] CCH Fed. Sec. L. Rep. ¶ 95,273 (9th Cir. 1975); Hirsch v. duPont, 396 F. Supp. 1214 (S.D.N.Y. 1975); NYSE, Inc. v. Sloan, 394 F. Supp. 1303 (S.D.N.Y. 1975).

140 American Express Income Shares, Inc., [1974-1975 Transfer Binder]

and gas schemes,[141] pyramid and franchising promotions,[142] condominium sales,[143] and a variety of other investment relationships[144] have all been held to satisfy the *Howey* requirement of a contract for investing money. It is not even necessary that there be a formal contract. In *Scheer v. Merrill Lynch, Pierce, Fenner & Smith, Inc.,*[145] the court held that no proof of entry into a formal contract was required to classify a discretionary commodities account as a security.

Because virtually all agency investment management arrangements are contractual in nature, the issue the contract requirement poses for investment managers is the degree to which trust relationships may be deemed statutory securities. The SEC has not yet openly evidenced an intent to treat trust and agency arrangements alike under the Securities Act. But neither the Commission nor the courts have been willing

---

CCH Fed. Sec. L. Rep. ¶ 80,074 (1974); Arthur E. Fox, [1974-1975 Transfer Binder] CCH Fed. Sec. L. Rep. ¶ 80,082 (1974).

[141] SEC v. C.M. Joiner Leasing Corp., 320 U.S. 344 (1943).

[142] SEC v. Bull Inv. Group, Inc., [1974-1975 Transfer Binder] CCH Fed. Sec. L. Rep. ¶ 95,010 (D. Mass. 1975) (franchise arrangement); SEC v. Glenn W. Turner Enterprises, Inc., 474 F.2d 476 (9th Cir. 1973) (pyramid scheme); SEC v. Steed Indus., Inc., [1974-1975 Transfer Binder] CCH Fed. Sec. L. Rep. ¶ 94,917 (N.D. Ill. 1974) (pyramid scheme); see also SEC Securities Act Release No. 5211 (Nov. 30, 1971), [1971-1972 Transfer Binder] CCH Fed. Sec. L. Rep. ¶ 78,446 (applicability of the securities laws to multilevel distributorship and pyramid sales plans). But see A.B.A. Auto Lease Corp. v. Adams Indus., Inc., 387 F. Supp. 531 (E.D. Pa. 1975) (franchise arrangement).

[143] SEC Securities Act Release No. 5347 (Jan. 4, 1973), [1972-1973 Transfer Binder] CCH Fed. Sec. L. Rep. ¶ 79,163 (condominium offerings as securities).

[144] The classification of certain types of insurance contracts as securities is another example. See cases cited in note 135 *supra*. See also Safeway Portland Employees' Federal Credit Union v. FDIC, 506 F.2d 1213 (9th Cir. 1974), and Safeway Portland Employees' Federal Credit Union v. C.H. Wagner & Co., 501 F.2d 1120 (9th Cir. 1974) (broker loan transactions as investment contracts); Bank of North Carolina, N.A., [1974-1975 Transfer Binder] CCH Fed. Sec. L. Rep. ¶ 80,053 (1974) (plan whereby bank's checking-account customers could purchase shares of bank's parent through their accounts held a security). With respect to employee benefit plans, see Overman, "Registration and Exemption From Registration of Employee Compensation Plans Under the Federal Securities Law," 28 Vand. L. Rev. 455 (1975).

[145] [1974-1975 Transfer Binder] CCH Fed. Sec. L. Rep. ¶ 95,086 (S.D.N.Y. 1975).

to permit the characterization of an investment vehicle as a trust to deter them from applying the Act. Thus, early in its administration, the SEC successfully sued for injunctive relief against an unregistered scheme to issue trust certificates, the proceeds of which were to be commingled and applied to acquire stock in a bank.[146]

As the Supreme Court has emphasized, substance and economic realities rather than form determine classification as a security.[147] This view is entirely consistent with the policy, well established in federal tax law, that formal compliance with state trust-law requirements cannot control application of federal law.[148] Moreover, the federal securities laws themselves help to establish the intent of Congress to include at least some trust arrangements within the definition of security. Section 3(a)(2) of the Securities Act exempts common trust funds maintained by a bank in its capacity as a trustee, executor, administrator, or guardian, and collective trust funds maintained by a bank for qualifying stock bonus, pension, profit-sharing, or annuity plans.[149] Such an exemption, of course, would not be necessary if Congress intended status as a trust to be sufficient to avoid application of the Securities Act. Additionally, the combined definitions of "company," "issuer," and "person," in Sections 2(a)(8), 2(a)(22), and 2(a)(28) of the Investment Company Act[150] establish that participations in collective trusts are securities under that statute; and the definition of security under Section 2(a)(36)

---

[146] SEC v. Timetrust, Inc., 28 F. Supp. 34 (N.D. Cal. 1939), *appeal dism'd on stipulation sub nom.* Timetrust, Inc. v. SEC, 118 F.2d 718 (9th Cir. 1941). See also Independent Bankers' Ass'n of Ga., Inc., [1972-1973 Transfer Binder] CCH Fed. Sec. L. Rep. ¶ 79,198 (1973) (two-level collective employee retirement trusts deemed to create a security even though employees received only cash proceeds of the trusts and contributions came exclusively from participating companies). With these cases, compare Woodmoor Corp., [1970-1971 Transfer Binder] CCH Fed. Sec. L. Rep. ¶ 78,140 (1971) (limited transferability of shares in trust tied to separate ownership deed on real estate placed trustee essentially in position of a custodian; hence, trust participations deemed *not* to be securities).

[147] United Housing Foundation, Inc. v. Forman, 421 U.S. 837, 847-851 (1975); Tcherepnin v. Knight, 389 U.S. 332, 336 (1967).

[148] See I.R.C. §§ 671-678 (treatment of grantor-trusts).

[149] 15 U.S.C. § 77c(a)(2). But see Daniel v. International Brotherhood of Teamsters, [1975-1976 Transfer Binder] CCH Fed. Sec. L. Rep. ¶ 95,453 (N.D. Ill. 1976) (participation in involuntary noncontributory pension plan a security); Sterling Nat'l Bank & Trust Co., [1975-1976 Transfer Binder] CCH Fed. Sec. L. Rep. ¶ 80,433.

[150] 15 U.S.C. §§ 80a-2(a)(8), 80a-2(a)(22), 80a-2(a)(28).

of the Investment Company Act and under Section 2(1) of the Securities Act are the same.[151]

This is not to say that structuring an account as a trust not specifically exempted from the Securities Act has no bearing on its status as a security. On the contrary, federal law implicitly recognizes that there is a structural distinction between trust and agency accounts which permits different treatment for each under the Securities Act. The best example of this phenomenon is the contrasting classifications afforded participations in collective investment vehicles. Congress has established the power of national banks to manage collective trust funds of various types,[152] and, as stated above, has exempted participations in such vehicles from classification as statutory securities under the Securities Act.[153] In *Investment Company Institute v. Camp*,[154] however, the Supreme Court interpreted Sections 16 and 21 of the Glass-Steagall Act[155] to prohibit banks from managing commingled agency accounts regardless of compliance with the federal securities laws. Since, as a practical matter, investment management activities in behalf of commingled trust funds are similar to those performed for commingled agency accounts, both of which in turn are much the equivalent of managing open-end investment companies, popularly called mutual funds,[156] the Court's construction of the Glass-Steagall Act represents a recognition, at least at the federal level, of an important difference in the status of participations of trust and agency vehicles under the Securities Act.

The precise holding in *Camp* was that participations in commingled agency accounts are securities which, when marketed by a commercial bank, make the bank an underwriter in violation of the separation of commercial banking and investment banking activities imposed by the Glass-Steagall Act. Of greater moment for purposes of determining whether structuring an investment management arrangement as a trust can evade application of the Securities Act, however, is the Court's

---

[151] As one might expect, Investment Company Act § 3(c)(3) (15 U.S.C. § 80a-3(c)(3)) provides an exemption, analogous to that of Securities Act § 3(a)(2) (15 U.S.C. § 77c(a)(2)), from application of the Investment Company Act to collective trusts.

[152] 12 U.S.C. § 248.

[153] See note 149 *supra*.

[154] 401 U.S. 617 (1971).

[155] Banking Act of 1933, Ch. 89, 48 Stat. 162 (June 16, 1933) (distributed throughout 12 U.S.C., Chs. 2, 3, 6).

[156] Investment Company Act § 4(3), 15 U.S.C. § 80a-4(3).

rationale for distinguishing participations in commingled agency accounts from other investment accounts commonly managed by the trust departments of commercial banks. Expressing concern over promotional pressures capable of undermining traditional bank conservatism, the Court contrasted client expectations in the establishment of trust accounts with the attitude which might characterize participants in a commingled agency vehicle. Because the demands of the latter group would be for investment return alone, the Court concluded that "there is a plain difference between the sale of fiduciary services and the sale of investments." [157]

But while the *Camp* court's investment-intent rationale may have appeal as an explanation of why participations in commingled agency accounts are securities, it does not offer a satisfactory rule for determining when participations in trust vehicles are not. Interests in some trusts plainly are securities.[158] The question is whether there are any structural attributes includable in a trust arrangement which facially establish that security status does not exist. In this respect, the Court's emphasis on the "true fiduciary purpose" [159] of a trustee relationship may have some bearing. The sense is strong that, in the Court's judgment, the notion of the fiduciary service underlying a trust relationship which is not a security includes much more than mere investment management services.

If this is so, testamentary and irrevocable inter vivos trusts would seem presumptively to escape security status. While the Court's view of classical trusteeship might not describe the kinds of services desired by institutional and individual revocable trust and agency accounts, it is safe to say that most testamentary and irrevocable inter vivos trusts reflect an intent on the part of settlors to provide services and care to their beneficiaries beyond a mere desire to obtain an investment return.[160] The importance of protecting the corpus of testamentary and

---

[157] 401 U.S. 617, 638 (1971).

[158] See note 146 *supra*.

[159] 401 U.S. 617, 638 (1971). Possibly instructive on the meaning of true fiduciary purpose is a comparison of the definition of "investment supervisory services" in Investment Advisers Act § 202(a)(13) (15 U.S.C. § 80b-2(a)(13)), and the use of "managed account" in SEC Securities Exchange Act Release No. 12055 (Jan. 27, 1976), [1975-1976 Transfer Binder] CCH Fed. Sec. L. Rep. ¶ 80,367.

[160] It is somewhat ironic that the portfolio managers for these types of trusts handle proportionately many more accounts than do pension fund and investment advisory account managers, while they are usually less ex-

irrevocable inter vivos trusts cannot be gainsaid, of course. But it is also true that protection of the corpus is typically secondary to, or at least no more important than, meeting other objectives, including fairly apportioning benefits among beneficiaries and balancing the interests of immediate beneficiaries against those of remaindermen. Should investment intent be the test for classification of a trust account as a security, a good objective indicator of that intent would be helpful if case-by-case determinations are to be avoided, and revocability might fill that function well.

But there is an important caveat to this analysis. *Camp* involved the definition of security under the Glass-Steagall Act, not the Securities Act. Although the Court did say, in reversing the Court of Appeals,[161] that the definition of security under the Glass-Steagall Act was not to be construed narrowly, it stopped short of equating it to Section 2(1) of the Securities Act.[162] It is thus possible that trust participations which are not securities under the Glass-Steagall Act may be securities under the Securities Act. On the other hand, the Court's emphasis in *Camp* on investment intent as the essential feature of a Glass-Steagall Act security suggests that participations in testamentary trusts and irrevocable inter vivos trusts would not be securities under either statute. It is highly doubtful that settlors and beneficiaries of testamentary and irrevocable inter vivos trusts require the separate protection of the Securities Act, especially since disclosure under that Act would be inadequate in any event. Moreover, since the *Howey* interpretation of investment contract is based on a requirement of investment intent to create a security,[163] *Howey* also would seem to exclude trusts of the classical variety.

[b] Profits expected solely from the efforts of a promoter or a third party: The degree of managerial control over the investment

The second element of the *Howey* test, that profits be expected solely from the efforts of a promoter or third party, ties security status

---

perienced and competent than the latter. See E. Herman, *Conflicts of Interest: Commercial Bank Trust Departments* 59 (Twentieth Century Fund 1975).

161 420 F.2d 83 (D.C. Cir. 1969).

162 401 U.S. 617, 635 (1971).

163 See note 138 *supra.* Another useful indicator of a settlor's interest is the nature of the marketing program which attracted him to the trustee in the first place. The effects of marketing programs are discussed more fully at ¶ 3.03[2][b] *infra.*

to the control an investor retains over his investment. Thus, because of the degree of managerial control involved, a general partnership interest is not a security while a limited partnership interest is.[164] But this element of the *Howey* test has undergone substantial refinement, so that "solely" is now to be read "largely." The classification of franchising arrangements, for example, does not depend on total passivity by franchisees, but rather on the degree of involvement of the promoter or a third party in the subsequent management of franchise interests. In one case, the obligation of franchisees to locate prospective lessees and forward lease contracts to the franchisor for processing was held to preclude classifying the arrangement as a security.[165] In contrast, a franchise program in which the franchisor took promotional responsibility for selling to potential customers of franchisees was held to involve the issue of securities.[166]

Where more direct investment management services are involved, the same kind of analysis applies. For example, the classification of

---

[164] Hirsch v. duPont, 396 F. Supp. 1214 (S.D.N.Y. 1975) (general partnership interest not a security since partners all vested with complete managerial control); Herman v. Doug Frank Dev. Corp., 385 F. Supp. 767 (S.D.N.Y. 1974) (limited partnership interest deemed a security). Similarly, real property interests in vacation developments marketed on their investment appeal are securities, whereas mere purchases of land in a development are not. The SEC set out guidelines on this subject in SEC Securities Act Release No. 5347 (Jan. 4, 1973), [1972-1973 Transfer Binder] CCH Fed. Sec. L. Rep. ¶ 79,163, at 82,539, stating that "condominiums, coupled with a rental arrangement, will be deemed to be securities if they are offered and sold through advertising, sales literature, promotional schemes or oral representations which emphasize the economic benefits to the purchaser to be derived from the managerial efforts of the promoter, or a third party designated or arranged for by the promoter, in renting the units." Thus, in Davis v. Rio Rancho Estates, Inc., 401 F. Supp. 1045 (S.D.N.Y. 1975), the court held that where the promotion of a real estate development placed more emphasis on development of a residential community than on investment potential, and where the vendor did not promise to run the development and distribute profits to the vendee, no sale of a security was involved. Expectation of profit in resale alone was not enough. See also First Inv. Annuity Co. of Am., [1971-1972 Transfer Binder] CCH Fed. Sec. L. Rep. ¶ 78,371 (1971), citing the SEC's position that a security may not exist in an investment program where the investor retains extensive powers to direct the investment and reinvestment of his funds in the program.

[165] A.B.A. Auto Lease Corp. v. Adam Indus., Inc., 387 F. Supp. 531 (E.D. Pa. 1975).

[166] SEC v. Bull Inv. Group, Inc., [1974-1975 Transfer Binder] CCH Fed. Sec. L. Rep. ¶ 95,010 (D. Mass. 1975).

interests in precious metals or rare coins depends on the extent to which someone other than the purchaser will be responsible for carrying out the latter's investment aims. Thus, sellers of precious metals to commercial buyers, hedging against future market developments, would not be selling securities[167]; nor would coin dealers selling their inventory to bona fide numismatists.[168] But precisely the same items are deemed securities if the purchasers, relying on those commodities to preserve or enhance the value of their personal estates, give substantial weight to the opinions and recommendations of promoters concerning how to minimize risk while maximizing chances of appreciation.[169]

For investment managers, the most important implication of the requirement that profits be obtained through the efforts of others is that discretionary authority is not necessary for a managed account to acquire security status. In *SEC v. Brigadoon Scotch Distributors, Ltd.*,[170] in which the sale of rare-coin portfolios was held to be an offer of securities, the court took the position that the advisory assistance the defendants provided investors combined with the other administrative services they offered was enough managerial control to satisfy *Howey*. A general extrapolation of this holding would mean that, even if clients retain authority to approve or disapprove the recommendations of investment managers, their accounts may nonetheless be securities.

Although it is possible that the Supreme Court may decide to reaffirm its holding in *Howey* that profits be obtained solely through the efforts of others, it is likely that the position taken in *Brigadoon Scotch Distributors* that the investor's delegation of discretionary authority is not necessary will prevail. As a practical matter, the crucial element for managed accounts is investment advice, not discretionary authority, since investment managers are not normally hired with the expectation that their advice will be rejected. Moreover, the philosophical question raised by this entire line of development under the Securities Act is when the office of investment manager becomes itself an investment such that promoting it requires that management contracts be treated as securities.[171] Although there is much to be said on both sides about

---

[167] Mocatta Metals Corp., [1974-1975 Transfer Binder] CCH Fed. Sec. L. Rep. ¶ 79,940 (1974).

[168] Steve Ivy Rare Coin Co., [1975-1976 Transfer Binder] CCH Fed. Sec. L. Rep. ¶ 80,233 (1975).

[169] SEC v. Brigadoon Scotch Distribs., Ltd., 388 F. Supp. 1288 (S.D.N.Y. 1975).

[170] *Id.*

[171] The Advisory Committee on Investment Management Services for Individual Investors argued this very point in its report to the SEC. See

characterizing an offer of investment management services as an issue of securities, the only sound argument for drawing the line between investment management arrangements which are securities and those which are not at the existence of discretionary authority is that there is a need for an objective basis for determining when the managerial control element of *Howey* has been satisfied. Based on the experience of the franchising cases, however, no such need is likely to be recognized.[172]

Also relevant to this question are recent legislative developments which indicate strongly that, even if discretionary authority were regarded as essential, the meaning of the term will be expanded to include arrangements in which investors retain some control over the carrying out of their managers' investment decisions. The Securities Acts Amendments of 1975 amended the Securities Exchange Act to define "investment discretion" in a way which undermines the notion that absolute authority to carry out an investment program is a prerequisite to security status. Section 3(a)(35)[173] reads:

> "A person exercises 'investment discretion' with respect to an account if, directly or indirectly, such person (A) is authorized to determine what securities or other property shall be purchased or sold by or for the account, (B) makes decisions as to what securities or other property shall be purchased or sold by or for the account even though some other

---

SEC, *Report of the Advisory Committee on Investment Management Services for Individual Investors, Small Account Investment Management Services,* CCH Fed. Sec. L. Rep. No. 465, Pt. III, at 23-24 (1973). The Committee also argued, however, that status as a security should depend on the existence of discretionary authority. *Id.* at 24-25.

[172] Thus far, the courts have proceeded on a case-by-case basis in determining whether or not a franchise is a security. See L.H.M., Inc. v. Lewis, 371 F. Supp. 395 (D.N.J. 1974) (theater franchise held not a security due to participants' "significant contributions" to the management and operation of the theater); Bitter v. Hoby's Int'l, Inc., 498 F.2d 183 (9th Cir. 1974) (restaurant franchise not a security since franchisees responsible for day-to-day management and operation of restaurant, despite strict franchise guidelines), *accord* Nash & Associates, Inc. v. Lum's of Ohio, Inc., 484 F.2d 392 (6th Cir. 1973); Mizner v. Cardet Int'l Inc., 358 F. Supp. 1262 (N.D. Ill. 1973) (distributorship franchise held a security where franchisee's role purely mechanical and ministerial, devoid of any power to make "meaningful or independent *business* decisions"); SEC v. Bull Inv. Group, Inc., [1974-1975 Transfer Binder] CCH Fed. Sec. L. Rep. ¶ 95,010 (D. Mass. 1975) (arrangement whereby local "dealers" (franchisees) would solicit new customers in return for a commission held a security since ultimate success or failure of the recruitment depended upon franchisor's sales-presentation efforts).

[173] 15 U.S.C. § 78c(a)(35).

person may have responsibility for such investment decisions, or (C) otherwise exercises such influence with respect to the purchase and sale of securities or other property by or for the account as the Commission, by rule, determines, in the public interest or for the protection of investors, should be subject to the operation of the provisions of this title and the rules and regulations thereunder."

Though the purpose of adding Section 3(a)(35) to the Exchange Act was to implement the provisions regarding brokerage fees paid by fiduciaries and separation of brokerage and money management,[174] it is significant that the entity with which Congress was concerned was a managed account rather than a subclass of that entity, a fully discretionary account. Less direct but also important as an indicator of the sentiment of Congress against distinguishing discretionary accounts from other closely managed accounts is the provision in the Employee Retirement Income Act of 1974 defining fiduciary. Section 3(21)[175] defines fiduciary to an employee benefit plan to include both persons exercising discretionary authority and persons rendering investment advice for compensation. Though again the purpose of this provision was not to settle the status of managed accounts for Securities Act purposes, it does indicate the determination of Congress to reject attempts to avoid regulation of investment management by reposing nominal control over an investment account with the client.[176]

---

[174] See ¶¶ 9.03[2], 10.02. See also Bines, "Regulating Discretionary Management: Broker-Dealers as Catalysts for Reform," 16 B.C. Ind. & Com. L. Rev. 379-385 (1975).

[175] 29 U.S.C. § 1002(21).

[176] The Department of Labor, in 29 C.F.R. § 2510.3-21, and the Internal Revenue Service, in 26 C.F.R. § 54.4975-9, have defined investment advice to give meaning to the statutory term "fiduciary." In brief, an investment manager is a statutory fiduciary if he has actual discretionary authority or, expecting his advice will strongly influence plan investment decisions, he provides advisory assistance on a regular basis pursuant to an established understanding. See ¶ 10.03[2]. Whatever the degree of managerial influence necessary to elevate a relationship to status as a security, it is clear that without some influence over an investment program, no security is created. Compare First Life Assurance Co., [1975-1976 Transfer Binder] CCH Fed. Sec. L. Rep. ¶ 80,385 (1976) (investment annuity program deemed a security because, although company refrained from making investment recommendations, annuitant could invest in securities issued by company, affiliate or custodian), with Massachusetts Co., [1975-1976 Transfer Binder] CCH Fed. Sec. L. Rep. ¶ 80,338 (1975) (custodial accounts for transfer of money from fund shares to short-term debt instruments not a security). See also Stuyvesant Life Ins. Co., [1975-1976 Transfer Binder] CCH Fed. Sec. L. Rep. ¶ 80,294 (1975) (investment annuities deemed securities where issuer participates in decisions on investments).

[c] A common enterprise: Reliance on the manager's acumen

A strict application of the third element of the *Howey* test, that a common enterprise is necessary to creation of a statutory security, would seem to exclude managed accounts from classification as investment contracts unless a number of them are being managed in common fashion. Until very recently, that seems to have been the position the Commission and the courts were taking as authoritative.[177] In fact, as recently as 1972, in *Milnarik v. M-S Commodities, Inc.*,[178] the Seventh Circuit rejected the argument that a discretionary account for trading in commodity futures is a security on the grounds that investors in these accounts "were not joint participants in the same investment enterprise." [179]

Nonetheless, there were indications both before and after *Howey* was decided that a managed account, at least one characterized by discretionary authority, might be an investment contract.[180] The SEC

---

[177] Despite the well-known existence of discretionary management services, the SEC has apparently never taken action, either through enforcement or through its rule-making authority, to have discretionary accounts registered absent a common investment management scheme. For example, in 1970, the Commission attacked a managed account arrangement as a security on the ground, among others, that investment decisions were being applied to all accounts on a uniform basis, but not simply on grounds that the accounts were being managed on a discretionary basis. See SEC Litigation Release No. 4534 (Feb. 6, 1970), discussed in text at note 239 *infra*.

[178] 457 F.2d 274 (7th Cir.), *cert. denied* 409 U.S. 887 (1972).

[179] 457 F.2d at 277.

[180] E.g., SEC v. Wickham, 12 F. Supp. 245, 248-249 (D. Minn. 1935), where the court stated:

"Whether one invests money in the proverbial gold mine . . . or invests in a speculative venture by reason of the claimed skill and experience of a grain and stock market manipulation to make profits, the transactions cannot be rationally distinguished in determining the dealings which Congress intended to regulate in using the term 'investment contract.' Both are investments. . . . Both entail the issuance of a security. In one the investor expects profits by reason of the gold to be mined; in the other, by reason of the skill and experience of the defendant in the market. In both, the opportunities for fraud are notorious."

Following *Howey*, a number of cases came to the same conclusion. E.g., Marshall v. Lamson Bros. & Co., 368 F. Supp. 486, 490 (S.D. Iowa 1974); Johnson v. Espey, [1971-1972 Transfer Binder] CCH Fed. Sec. L. Rep. ¶ 93,376 (S.D.N.Y. 1972); Berman v. Orimex Trading, Inc., 291 F. Supp. 701, 702 (S.D.N.Y. 1968); Maheu v. Reynolds & Co., 282 F. Supp. 423, 429 (S.D.N.Y. 1967). Cf. Commercial Iron & Metal Co. v. Bache & Co., 478 F.2d 39 (10th Cir. 1973); Booth v. Peavey Co. Commodity Servs., 430 F.2d 132 (8th Cir. 1970).

and, to an increasing degree, the federal courts, now seem to believe that strict commonality in provision of investment management services is not required to create an investment contract. The Commission's first forays against managed accounts emphasized the commonality of investment programs offered customers of discretionary management services.[181] Subsequently, the Commission began taking the position that the reliance each investor places in the manager's acumen is a common element of discretionary accounts sufficient to satisfy *Howey*, a position quickly endorsed by the Fifth Circuit. In *SEC v. Continental Commodities Corp.*,[182] that court held that a discretionary commodity futures account is a security on the grounds that collective investment success is dependent on the skill of the manager. Thereafter, since common reliance on a manager's investment decisions does not depend on the existence of discretionary authority, it was a short step to abandoning managerial discretion as a necessary factor in establishing the element of common enterprise. Consequently, in *SEC v. Brigadoon Scotch Distributors, Ltd.*, the Commission contended[183] and the court agreed[184] that, despite the absence of discretionary authority, investment guidance and counseling offered by a rare-coin investing service gave rise to a common enterprise.[185]

---

181 See SEC Litigation Release No. 4534 (Feb. 6, 1970), discussed in the text at note 239 *infra*.

182 497 F.2d 516 (5th Cir. 1974). Accord, Wasnowic v. Chicago Bd. of Trade, 491 F.2d 752 (3d Cir. 1973), *cert. denied* 416 U.S. 994 (1974). The Commodity Futures Trading Commission Act of 1974 (Pub. L. 93-463 (Oct. 23, 1974)) substantially reduced SEC jurisdiction over commodities transactions, the statute providing that the Commodity Futures Trading Commission has "exclusive jurisdiction . . . over transactions involving contracts of sale of a commodity for future delivery." 7 U.S.C. § 2. Compare SEC v. American Commodity Exch., Inc., 546 F.2d 1361 (10th Cir. 1976), and SEC v. Norton, [1976-1977 Transfer Binder] CCH Fed. Sec. L. Rep. ¶ 95,709 (N.D. Ill. 1976), with SEC v. Univest, Inc., [1975-1976 Transfer Binder] CCH Fed. Sec. L. Rep. ¶ 95,369 (N.D. Ill. 1975). See also SEC—CFTC Jurisdictional Correspondence, [1975-1976 Transfer Binder] CCH Fed. Sec. L. Rep. ¶ 80,336 (1975).

183 SEC Litigation Release No. 6640 (Dec. 12, 1974).

184 388 F. Supp. 1288 (S.D.N.Y. 1975).

185 The court did give some weight to the fact that in many instances, the defendants' clients entrusted the actual selection of coins purchased for the client to be made by the defendants' agents in a manner which amounted to discretionary action by the agent. Yet the court held all the investment arrangements to be securities, even when the option to allow the agent to select was not exercised, indicating that the crucial factor was that this option be *offered. Id.* at 1292-1293.

It may happen, of course, that the Supreme Court or Congress will reject this extension of *Howey* and insist on greater commonality than shared management. For one thing, the discretionary accounts described in *Continental Commodities* can be distinguished from normal discretionary accounts, and consequently the *Continental Commodities* line of cases[186] can be limited on the facts. In most discretionary accounts, the investor owns the assets purchased for his account and the risk of loss is directly attributable to the wisdom of the investment decision. *Continental Commodities*, however, involved a firm placing its clients into naked options written by the firm.[187] Thus, the investor's return depended on two factors: (1) the wisdom of the investment decision; and (2) the ability of the firm to pay the claims of its clients for successful options purchases. Once one recognizes the importance of the second element to the result, one can see that *Continental Commodities* is not quite the departure from *Howey* it appears because all the investors in *Continental Commodities* had in common an unstated but very real investment in the financial health of the firm.[188]

A complaint filed by the SEC against the Pacific Coast Coin Exchange (PCCE) gives added substance to the argument that commonality derives from the mutual interest of investors in the financial health of the manager.[189] In that case, the Commission alleged that the

---

[186] Scheer v. Merrill Lynch, Pierce, Fenner & Smith, Inc., [1974-1975 Transfer Binder] CCH Fed. Sec. L. Rep. ¶ 95,086 (S.D.N.Y. 1975) (commodity futures account held a security where defendant asserted experience and expertise, and emphasized prospects of a good rate of return to customer who, in fact, always relied upon and followed defendant's advice); Rochkind v. Reynolds Secs., Inc., 388 F. Supp. 254 (D. Md. 1975) (commodity-futures account held a security, even absent a "pooling" of funds of several investors, where customer relied solely on broker's expertise in allowing broker to make investment decisions for him).

[187] 497 F.2d at 518.

[188] In essence, the agreements between client and manager were the equivalent of evidences of indebtedness. See SEC v. Western Pacific Gold & Silver Exch. Corp., [1974-1975 Transfer Binder] CCH Fed. Sec. L. Rep. ¶ 95,064 (D. Nev. 1975) (sales agreements for client investments in gold coins and silver bars as commodities constituted "evidences of indebtedness" where clients did not acquire title to the gold or silver, but did acquire claims for money against the defendant, and where clients' moneys were subjected to the "risks of the enterprise"). See text at note 190 *infra*.

[189] SEC v. MONEX Int'l Ltd., SEC Litigation Release No. 6645 (Dec. 18, 1974) (SEC alleged that a security existed where customers' funds were commingled in defendant's coin-investment enterprise, managed by defendant, subjected to the risks of that enterprise, and where investors relied on defendant's efforts for the safe return of their investments); SEC Litiga-

defendants sold their clients silver coins and other commodities on margin without purchasing or holding the coins or commodities until the margin accounts were paid in full. Instead, according to the Commission's complaint, PCCE commingled investor funds and subjected them to the risk of the PCCE venture. In effect, investors became creditors of the firm, an arrangement which may well have been classifiable as the issuance of a security in any event, on the grounds that the underlying investment arrangements were evidences of indebtedness.[190]

Nonetheless, this explanation of *Continental Commodities* does not give due regard to the rationale adopted by the court in that case. Even though the court seemed to understand the dual characteristics of the type of account at issue as being an investment in both commodities options and the financial health of the firm, it did not emphasize common investment in the firm as a basis for concluding that the accounts were securities. The court stated that investment success was "essentially dependent upon promoter expertise," that guidance was "uniformly extended to all . . . investors," and that the results of the enterprise as a whole and customer investments individually were "contingent upon the sagacious investment counseling of *Continental Commodities*." [191] Thus, the court was focusing more on the commonality of the services the promoter contracted to provide than on the investors' collective interest in the success of the enterprise.

This latter interpretation of *Continental Commodities* finds support in the *Brigadoon Scotch Distributors* case.[192] The facts there show that the defendants actually sold investors the goods they thought they were buying. Rather then trading on their clients' money, like PCCE, the defendants only engaged in questionable marketing practices. But the court was satisfied that the common package of services offered to clients by defendants met the *Howey* commonality requirement. Acknowledging that commonality normally implies participations in a common fund, the *Brigadoon* court held that "the requisite commonality

---

tion Release No. 7057 (Aug. 25, 1975) (declaration that a permanent injunction had been granted against the defendants (mentioned in SEC Litigation Release No. 6645, *supra*) from violating federal securities laws).

190 See SEC v. Western Pacific Gold & Silver Exch. Corp., note 188 *supra*. The court in Jenson v. Continental Financial Corp., 404 F. Supp. 792 (D. Minn. 1975), also concluded that contracts to purchase gold and silver coins were investment contracts. The opinion places substantially more weight than do *Continental Commodities* and *PCCE* on the degree to which the investors were co-venturers with the firm.

191 497 F.2d at 522-523.

192 388 F. Supp. 1288 (S.D.N.Y. 1975), note 184 *supra*.

of enterprise may also be achieved when 'the fortunes of all investors are inextricably tied to the efficacy [of the promoters' efforts].' " [193]

This is not to say that *Brigadoon Scotch Distributors* was wrongly decided. The point is only that, if that decision is correct, the *Howey* commonality requirement has become so refined in concept as not to exclude any investment scheme offered to more than one person. In this respect, *Brigadoon Scotch Distributors* has captured an idea attaining increasing support among commentators—that an arrangement or promotion should be regarded as a statutory investment contract whenever the assets at risk in an investment arrangement belong substantially to one party and the realization of a return depends primarily on the efforts of the promoter or manager.[194]

How acceptable the risk theory will become is difficult to say. The Supreme Court has acknowledged it without accepting or rejecting it.[195]

---

[193] *Id.* at 1291, citing SEC v. Koscot Interplanetary, Inc., 497 F.2d 473 (5th Cir. 1974).

[194] See Hannan & Thomas, "The Importance of Economic Reality and Risk in Defining Federal Securities," 25 Hastings L.J. 219 (1974), where, after a discussion of the history of the definition of a security, the authors state that "the problem with the *Howey* formula is not that it is wrong, but that it is often applied restrictively without recognizing that it is merely a statement of a result based upon the facts in the *Howey* case." *Id.* at 236. Emphasizing the importance of the location of the risk of loss and the control of the return on investment, Hannan and Thomas design a framework of seven questions to be answered in formulating a definition of a statutory security, and then discuss the application of their analysis to various categories of enterprises and promotions about which there is disagreement whether participations in them are statutory securities. See also Long, "An Attempt to Return 'Investment Contracts' to the Mainstream of Securities Regulation," 24 Okla. L. Rev. 135 (1971), in which it is suggested that a security should be defined as "the investment of money or money's worth in the risk capital of a venture with the expectation of some benefit to the investor when the investor has no direct control over the investment or policy decisions of the venture." *Id.* at 174 (emphasis deleted). This article, in part, attempts to expand upon treatment of the subject in Coffey, "The Economic Realities of a 'Security': Is There a More Meaningful Formula?" 18 W. Res. L. Rev. 367 (1967).

[195] United Housing Foundation, Inc., v. Forman, 421 U.S. 837, 857 n.24 (1975). The issue of whether and under what circumstances to classify a managed account as a statutory security is apparently disputed within the SEC. If managed accounts are securities, they must be registered or exempted from registration in accordance with the Securities Act. Although the Division of Enforcement has pursued the Securities Act theory (see notes 186-192 *supra*), the Division of Corporate Finance has issued no

On the other hand, if the commonality requirement can be satisfied by viewing each investor as having a common interest in the ability of investment manager, the concept of commonality would become analytically extinct. By relying on a common interest in managerial ability, the determination of security status depends on the degree of managerial assistance provided. That is, to establish the existence of a common enterprise, security status would be a function of when management assistance reached a substantial enough level that managerial sagacity reflected something highly important to investors. But the degree of managerial assistance is precisely the question raised by the second element of the *Howey* test: Do profits come from the efforts of others? This merging of the managerial control and common-enterprise elements of *Howey* explains why the court in the *Brigadoon Scotch Distributors* case pointed to a variety of promised services, including the initial purchase of rare-coin portfolios and various administrative support services thereafter, to establish the existence of commonality.[196] Such an argument was compelled by the fact that the generalized offer of professional services by the defendant was the only thing shared by all the clients.

Actually, the commonality issue is far less polar than these two explanations of the *Continental Commodities* line of cases would suggest. Although the discussion above assumes, as the facts in *Brigadoon Scotch Distributors* indicate, that investment accounts under one house's management have little in common except for the person or the manager and the advisory and administrative services they receive, a more realistic assumption would recognize that each account will overlap many others in portfolio composition and mix. The reasons for such overlapping follow from the management approach taken by most investment advisers. Managers do not seek out investment opportunities account by account as an individual might do with his own portfolio.

---

proposed exemptive rules or registration guidelines to deal with managed accounts. On the other hand, the Division of Enforcement has proposed a disclosure rule for statutory investment advisers concerning promotional brochures. Proposed Rule 206(4)-4, SEC Investment Advisers Act Release No. 442 (March 5, 1975), [1974-1975 Transfer Binder] CCH Fed. Sec. L. Rep. ¶ 80,128. While such a rule would not displace any obligation created under the Securities Act, it would certainly disarm proponents of the view that a managed account is a security since the Commission did not suggest that compliance with the Securities Act was also required and since a registration statement under the Securities Act is itself a disclosure document.

196 388 F. Supp. 1288, 1291-1292 (S.D.N.Y. 1975).

For purposes of efficiency, managers evaluate investment opportunities first, and, where action is indicated, identify all accounts suitable for the proposed action.[197] Although not every suitable account would be affected, it is plain that the correspondence in activity among accounts with similar objectives would be high.[198] Moreover, the correspondence tends to increase over time because investment managers necessarily follow only a limited selection of investment opportunities rather than the entire investment universe. If it were otherwise, it would be virtually impossible, even with computerization, to provide clients with professional management services. No investment manager can follow all the listed common stocks with sufficient depth to reach an informed investment decision, much less follow all publicly traded common stocks, debt instruments, private placements, tax shelters, and other kinds of investment opportunities. In any event, the practical realities of investment management which lead to overlapping portfolios only make the Securities Act problem worse. Certainly, if common management is to be grounds for regarding investment accounts as statutory securities, commonality of portfolio will only reinforce that position.

[2] Deflecting Extension of the Securities Act to All Managed Accounts

If *SEC v. Brigadoon Scotch Distributors, Ltd.*,[199] is an accurate prognosis of how the *Howey* definition of investment contract can be extended to managed accounts, the consequences for investment managers will be enormous. Thousands of investors of all types are receiving a variety of investment management services under arrangements which have not been registered as "securities" and are therefore potentially in violation of the statute. Aside from the mischief possible through selective exercise by the SEC of its enforcement power, the absence of registration could place investment managers in serious jeopardy of civil liability, since Section 12[200] of the Securities Act gives a purchaser of unregistered securities the right to recover the value of his account. In essence, if managed accounts are securities, every client

---

[197] Suitability is discussed extensively in Chapter 4.

[198] When possible, many investment managers tend toward keeping accounts alike due to the "pressure of comparisons and complaints" by account customers. This is especially true in the area of pension funds, where the customers are more sophisticated. E. Herman, *Conflicts of Interest: Commercial Bank Trust Departments* 61 (Twentieth Century Fund 1975).

[199] 388 F. Supp. 1288 (S.D.N.Y. 1975).

[200] 15 U.S.C. § 77l.

of an investment manager has a "put" [201] against his manager in the amount of his initial investment, regardless of how skillfully his investment program has been run.

The most apparent statutory routes for avoiding registration would seem to be: (1) Section 3(a)(11),[202] the intrastate exemption; (2) Section 3(b),[203] the small-offering exemption; and (3) Section 4(2),[204] the private-offering exemption. But few investment managers would find the intrastate exemption attractive because of the limit on obtaining new clients this would entail. The small-offering exemption also is of limited efficacy, since compliance with a statutory ceiling of $500,000 virtually eliminates all institutional accounts. Even if an investment manager were willing to restrict management activities to accounts of $500,000 or less, registration might still be required. The Commission could conclude that each separate account belongs to a set of securities so related in character that the accounts should be integrated—that is, combined in value—to determine the size of the offering.[205] Finally, the private-offering exemption seems an equally doubtful method of avoiding registration. For one thing, investment managers relying on advertising to attract clients would be engaging in a public offering.[206] Furthermore, even if the advertising problem could be solved, the integration doctrine might again come into play and put a ceiling on the

---

[201] Literally, a "put" is a contract which grants the holder the option to sell to the maker, at any time within a given period and at a fixed price, a certain number of shares of stock. G. Munn, *Encyclopedia of Banking and Finance* 767 (7th ed. 1973).

[202] 15 U.S.C. § 77c(a)(11).

[203] 15 U.S.C. § 77c(b).

[204] 15 U.S.C. § 77d(2).

[205] Under the most common application of the doctrine of integration, a number of ostensibly private offerings, which are ordinarily exempt from registration under Section 4(2) of Securities Act of 1933 (15 U.S.C. § 77d(2)), may be considered components of a single public offering in violation of the registration requirements. The integration doctrine has been applied to other exemptions, although it has been restricted to exemptions based on the type of offering or sale involved rather than upon the type of securities issued. For a discussion of the doctrine, see Shapiro & Sachs, "Integration Under the Securities Act: 'Once An Exemption, Not Always. . . .,'" 31 Md. L. Rev. 3 (1971).

[206] See SEC Rule 146, Transactions by an Issuer Deemed Not to Involve Any Public Offering, adopted in SEC Securities Act Release No. 5487 (April 23, 1974), 1 CCH Fed. Sec. L. Rep. ¶ 2710. Reasons for the new changes appear in SEC Securities Act Release No. 5336 (Nov. 28, 1972), [1972-1973 Transfer Binder] CCH Fed. Sec. L. Rep. ¶ 79,108.

number of offerees eligible for management services without registration.[207]

The expansion of the definition of investment contract to include managed accounts can be understood from several perspectives. From the point of view of dissatisfied investors, the Securities Act provides a neat remedy for recovering the lost value of an account without any need to show fraud by the manager. All that is required is a showing of nonregistration.[208] In contrast, the other federal securities laws, in particular the Investment Advisers Act of 1940, have a highly underdeveloped regulatory posture regarding investment management services. The degree of expertise required, the correlation between the statutory fraud provisions and notions of fiduciary duty, the existence of private rights of action, and other issues remain unresolved. Recoveries are thus less certain than under the Securities Act, and litigation is likely to be more complex. Moreover, even if the remedies provided by other federal securities laws were more certain, there may be no subject-matter jurisdiction under them unless the underlying agreement were determined to be a security in the first place. This would be the case, for example, where an investment management arrangement deals in commodities, precious metals, rare coins and stamps, or objects of art, which are not statutory securities of themselves.

From the point of view of the SEC, the Securities Act can be a useful vehicle to reduce marketing excesses which take advantage of investor gullibility and to restrict penetration of the marketplace by purveyors of investment management services of doubtful merit. By enjoining the marketing of an investment program on grounds of nonregistration, the Commission can weed out programs it believes may be fraudulent without the necessity of proving statutory fraud. In this respect, of course, the Commission is less interested in applying the disclosure philosophy of the Securities Act to make information available to investors before they engage investment managers than it is in preventing or stopping the marketing of services of which it disapproves. Otherwise, the Commission would long since have issued a special registration form applicable to the offer and sale of investment management services and, unlike Form S-1, responsive to the type of information required by persons interested in such services.

A third explanation for the intrusion of the Securities Act into arrangements between investment managers and their clients lies in the

---

[207] See note 205 *supra*.
[208] Securities Act § 12, 15 U.S.C. § 77*l*.

balkanization of federal regulation of investment management. For some time, underwriters, broker-dealers, insurance companies, investment counselors, and banks, the principals in the securities industry, have had their investment management activities regulated by separate administrative authorities. Even where regulated by a single authority, their activities have fallen under the jurisdiction of separate organic statutes. At some point, compartmentalized regulation of comparable activities creates discontinuities that generate regulatory strain. The natural response is to find a common basis for regulation. To a degree, the extension of the definition of investment contract can be seen as a movement toward consolidation.

But however accurate these observations are, they hardly justify reliance on the Securities Act to regulate investment management. Strong argument can be made that investors already have ample remedies to deal with fraud in the marketing of investment management services, and fraud and mismanagement thereafter, without adding a guarantee against investment failure under Section 12 of the Securities Act. Moreover, to the degree the Commission succeeds in applying the Act selectively to offers of investment management services of which it disapproves, it also threatens investment management arrangements which are carried on honestly and properly.

Consider, for example, the effect on commercial banks of extending the *Howey* definition of investment contract to managed accounts. According to the Supreme Court in *Investment Co. Institute v. Camp*,[209] the Glass-Steagall Act prohibits banks from marketing participations in investment accounts which are securities. Thus, if managed accounts are securities, either most of the investment management arrangements offered by banks are unregistered securities which violate the underwriting prohibitions of the Glass-Steagall Act, or the definition of security under that statute is different from that in the Securities Act. But it is doubtful that different definitions of a security will be given to each. The Court, though it did not equate the term security in both statutes, emphasized the broad interpretation to be given the term in the Glass-Steagall Act, particularly in the case of participations in an investment fund.[210] It would seem, therefore, that in desiring to attach different meanings to "security," as used in each statute, one would have to come up with a better reason than that the underwriting prohibitions in the Glass-Steagall Act could not otherwise be avoided.

---

[209] 401 U.S. 617 (1971).
[210] *Id.* at 638.

If argument is to be made that banks should be excluded from marketing investment management services, a long-established activity of bank trust departments, surely a more precise legislative judgment to that effect is required than can be sustained in the growth in scope of the *Howey* interpretation of investment contract. Yet the seemingly logical extensions of *Howey* to the management relationships described in *Continental Commodities Corp.*[211] and *Brigadoon Scotch Distributors*[212] require some rational distinction to be made between them and more ordinary investment management arrangements for the latter to also avoid classification as securities.

[a] Defining security status on the basis of risk

One suggestion for distinguishing different types of investment management relationships appears in the report of the Advisory Committee on Investment Management Services for Individual Investors.[213] The Committee concluded that investment management highly tailored to the individual needs of an investor should not be regarded as a security, or at least should be regarded as a private offering.[214] This private-offering outcome would be of no use to the banks, of course, because, although it suggests a means for avoiding registration, it concedes that managed accounts are securities. Moreover, the problem created by the underwriting prohibitions of the Glass-Steagall Act would still exist. The concept of individualization as a basis for avoiding security status has appeal, however, since it connotes a close personal relationship in which an investor would have a regular flow of information permitting a continual evaluation of the services being provided. On the other hand, individualization is an ill-defined concept[215] which may be too

---

[211] See text at note 182 *supra.*

[212] See text at note 192 *supra.*

[213] SEC, *Report of the Advisory Committee on Investment Management Services for Individual Investors, Small Account Investment Management Services,* CCH Fed. Sec. L. Rep. No. 465, Pt. III (1973).

[214] *Id.* at 24-25. The Committee's position will be difficult to sustain in light of Rule 146. Even if the clients (i.e., offerees) enjoy the level of knowledge, expertise, or financial resources required by the rule, the restraints on advertising, and other forms of general solicitation, as well as restraints on the number of clients, make it impractical for an adviser to conduct any substantial investment advisory business and avoid the ambit of Rule 146.

[215] See SEC, *Report of the Advisory Committee on Investment Management Services for Individual Investors, Small Account Investment Management Services,* CCH Fed. Sec. L. Rep. No. 465, Pt. III, at 24-38 (1973).

difficult to apply to be useful. Moreover, as a feature of an investment management relationship which can only be assessed subsequent to the initiation of that relationship, individualization fails to fulfill the pri-

---

The Committee took the position that in a case of true individualization, the need for disclosure is less immediate than where securities of industrial and investment companies are acquired, because close communication between client and adviser provides a perpetual feedback mechanism for indication of the client's approval or disapproval of investment decisions. The Committee also pointed out that the protective devices found in the Investment Advisers Act and, to some extent, in the Securities Exchange Act of 1934 would still check unsavory practices. Further, the Committee suggested a new Advisers Act rule for these accounts, requiring the persons offering these services to give clients an information statement as would be specified in such a rule. In the view of the Committee, an information statement would be less costly, would afford greater flexibility as to content, and would be subject to a less formal review process than would a Securities Act registration statement, thus encouraging the growth of mini-accounts. (In this connection, the Commission has proposed Rule 206(4)-4 (SEC Investment Advisers Act Release No. 442 (March 5, 1975), [1974-1975 Transfer Binder] CCH Fed. Sec. L. Rep. ¶ 80,128) detailing disclosure requirements for investment advisers to prospective clients.)

With regard to nondiscretionary accounts, the Committee pointed out that even though the client retains the authority to reject or act upon any recommendation, a number of advisers make merely blanket recommendations to many of these accounts. While maintaining its position that such accounts should not be subject to formal registration, in the face of this observed disregard of individual client needs, the Committee suggested that the SEC require firms servicing nondiscretionary accounts to describe the basis for all recommendations made to the client in order to enable the client to exercise independent judgment. (Proposed Rule 206(4)-4 responds at least in part to this concern.)

The Committee also considered the applicability of the Investment Company Act to individualized accounts. This problem is considered in detail in ¶ 3.04. Briefly, recognizing that the policies underlying the Securities Act and the Investment Company Act are not identical, the Committee recommended that accounts not receiving individualized services be registered as investment companies, while those receiving individualized services not be registered.

It is worth noting that Investment Advisers Act § 202(a)(13) (15 U.S.C. § 80b-2(a)(13)), lends some support for the Committee's approach to avoiding registration under the Securities Act and the Investment Company Act. It defines "investment supervisory services" as "continuous advice" based on the "individual needs of each client." Under Section 208(c) (15 U.S.C. § 80b-8(c)), only those persons a substantial portion of whose activities consist of providing "investment supervisory services" may use the title "investment counsel." This trade advantage granted by the Act indicates that Congress made at least one important distinction based on the presence of individualized services.

mary mission of the Securities Act. The purpose of the Act is to provide information in advance of investment—that is, during the marketing phase—to permit a prospective investor to reach a considered
judgment about the nature of the offering. It would be a strange outcome to condition security status on what happens to an investor
after he parts with his money. In any event, the question of individualized services has not yet been resolved, and present indications are
that the Committee's recommendation will be rejected.[216]

The *Camp* opinion offers another basis for excluding ordinary investment management arrangements from classification as securities.
By pointing to individually managed agency accounts as an example
of a traditional bank service which is not a security under the Glass-
Steagall Act,[217] the Court may have been implying approval of a pool-
ing/nonpooling distinction,[218] at least insofar as investment management services on an agency basis are concerned. Unfortunately, however
reassuring the Court's attempt to distinguish commingled agency accounts from more traditional bank-sponsored investment management
services may have been, *Camp* is of little help in establishing pooling
as the basis for distinguishing investment management arrangements
which are securities from those which are not. In classifying commingled agency accounts as securities, the Court characterized them
as vehicles operated in pursuit of investment objectives likely to pro-

---

[216] See SEC Securities Act Release No. 5491 (April 30, 1974), [1973-
1974 Transfer Binder] CCH Fed. Sec. L. Rep. ¶ 79,767. This release requested public comment on the role of the Commission in dealing with
bank-sponsored investment services. According to the release, discretionary
accounts managed for individual investors may be regarded as securities. No
mention appears of any effect individualized services might have on the
status of a discretionary account as a security. This is not to say that individualization has no role to play, however. The SEC staff regularly refers
to the absence of individualization as evidence that an investment manager
is issuing securities and managing an investment company. See, e.g., S.H.
Dike & Co., [1975-1976 Transfer Binder] CCH Fed. Sec. L. Rep. ¶ 80,246
(1975). Whether individualization of itself can be a basis for avoiding Securities Act application is another question. Under neither the risk theory
nor the marketing theory is individualization recognized as sufficient to
avoid security status. See the text at note 194 *supra*, and notes 225-228
infra.

[217] 401 U.S. at 638.

[218] A pooled investment vehicle is one in which all contributions of
investors are treated as part of the same unit and the interests of investors
are represented by participation in that unit. Common examples of pooled
vehicles are commingled trust funds and investment companies.

duce promotional and performance pressures deleterious to other banking activities. The Court argued that unsuccessful management could
lead, among other things, to imprudent investment, to the distortion
of credit decisions in favor of companies in which a bank's commingled
agency accounts had invested, to the exploitation of confidential relationships between banks and commercial and industrial clients, and to
the opening of credit facilities to commingled agency accounts in ways
inconsistent with the best interest of depositors.[219] Contending that
comparable hazards are not present when a bank acts as managing
agent for single accounts or when it commingles assets received as
trustee, the Court concluded, "there is a plain difference between the
sale of fiduciary services and the sale of investments." [220]

That rationale is unreliable. Any argument that the promotional
and performance pressures that can characterize commingled agency
accounts are more intense than the same pressures generated by the
marketing and operating of other bank-sponsored investment management services simply ignores the facts. Banks aggressively promote
their investment management services to pension and profit-sharing
accounts and other institutional investors, and they actively market
their extensive investment management services to individuals.[221] Moreover, just like other types of investment managers, banks compete for
the acquisition and retention of business on the basis of their performance records.[222] A pooling/nonpooling distinction based on the

---

[219] 401 U.S. 636-638.

[220] 401 U.S. at 638.

[221] See E. Herman, *Conflicts of Interest: Commercial Bank Trust Departments* 22-23 (Twentieth Century Fund 1975); D. Green & M. Schuelke,
The Trust Activities of the Banking Industry (Stanford Research Institute
1975).

[222] SEC, *Institutional Investor Study*, H.R. Doc. No. 64, 92d Cong., 1st
Sess. 454 (1971); Levi, "The Trust New Business Division: An Opportunity for Profit," 114 Trusts & Estates 540 (1975); Richards, "Reflections
on Incentive Compensation in Trust Marketing," *id.* at 534. Recognition of
the similarity of promotional and performance pressures produced by commingled agency accounts and other bank-sponsored investment management
services appeared in Judge Bazelon's opinion in *Camp* at the Court of
Appeals level. See NASD v. SEC, 420 F.2d 83, 89-90 (D.C. Cir. 1969).
Commentators also have spotlighted the tenuousness of the Supreme Court's
attempted distinction between commingled agency accounts and other bank-
sponsored and bank-managed investment services. See, e.g., Church &
Seidel, "The Entrance of Banks Into the Field of Mutual Funds," 13 B.C.
Com. & Ind. L. Rev. 1175 (1972); Comment, "National Banks and Mutual
Funds: Where Can They Go After *Investment Company Institute v.
Camp?*" 60 Ky. L.J. 757 (1972).

Court's analysis in *Camp* does not make sense for the additional reason that banks are permitted to manage many pooled vehicles which are the same in their potential consequences for depositors as commingled agency accounts would be. It strains credulity to believe, for example, that banks and bank holding companies operating closed-end investment companies or advising open-end investment companies, activities not prohibited by the Court's interpretation of the Glass-Steagall Act,[223] experience less intense promotional and performance pressures than they would if they were also marketing participations in commingled agency accounts.

One gets the impression that the *Camp* case was less a response to the imperatives of the Glass-Steagall Act than a sensing on the part of the Court that bank entry into the provision of investment management services had come so far as to require the kind of general review possible only for Congress. Since, under a literal reading of the statute, the sale of participations in commingled agency accounts could easily be regarded as contrary to the statutory prohibitions against underwriting, and since the Court knew that Congress was examining the commingled agency account issue in connection with its hearings on amending the Investment Company Act,[224] the Court's decision to hold the line against further bank encroachments is entirely understandable,

---

[223] 12 C.F.R. § 9.18 (collective investments by national banks); Fed. Res. Bd. Reg. Y §§ 225.125, 225.4(a)(5)(ii), 12 C.F.R. §§ 225.125, 225.4(a)(5)(ii) (investment adviser activities of bank holding companies); Investment Co. Institute v. Board of Governors of the Federal Reserve Sys., 398 F. Supp. 725 (D.D.C. 1975).

[224] See, e.g., Hearings on Mutual Fund Legislation of 1967 Before the Senate Comm. on Banking and Currency, 90th Cong., 1st Sess., Pt. 3, 1249 (1967); Hearings on Mutual Fund Amendments Before the House Subcomm. on Commerce and Finance of the Comm. on Interstate and Foreign Commerce, 91st Cong., 1st Sess. 139, 179, 456-458 (1969). In the Report of the Senate Committee on Banking and Currency (91st Cong., 1st Sess. 10-12, 23 (1969)), it can be seen that Senate Bill 5224 proposed expressly to authorize banks or savings and loan associations to operate a collective fund for managing agency accounts. The House Committee on Interstate and Foreign Commerce, in its Report (91st Cong., 2d Sess. 9 (1970)), refused to take a position whether commingled agency accounts were considered permissible under the Glass-Steagall Act. Recognizing that the *Camp* case was pending before the Supreme Court, however, the Committee did take the position that if such accounts were permitted, they ought to be regulated as investment companies. Both the House approach and the Senate approach were eliminated in conference (Conference Report, Investment Company Act Amendments of 1970, No. 163, 91st Cong., 2d Sess. 28-29 (1970)).

if somewhat disingenuous. Nonetheless, the question remains whether, in view of the developments reflected in *Continental Commodities* and *Brigadoon Scotch Distributors*, the Court's dicta in *Camp* about individually managed agency account can be sustained. To put the question precisely, if neither substantial commonality in treatment of investors nor vesting total control over achieving investment objectives in an investment manager are necessary to security status, is there a rationalizing principle through which most managed accounts can escape classification as securities?

[b] Defining security status on the basis of marketing method

Competing with the risk theory for defining security status is the marketing theory, which offers a principle for determining the status as a security of a managerial investment account. While the marketing theory is in its earliest stages of articulation,[225] its essence seems to be this: The security status of investment arrangements depends not only on investor reliance on manager acumen and service, but also on how the management service is marketed. Although the risk theory may describe arrangements which, because of the separation of risk of loss from responsibility for investment success, may be classifiable as securities, of itself, it is inadequate to make a final determination of security status. There must also be inquiry into the nature of the offering—how clients are sought, what promises are made, what information is disclosed and withheld, and so forth.

There are several sources of support for the marketing theory. The Securities Act itself was a response to the perceived need among investors for accurate material information before committing resources to investment ventures.[226] Consequently, the regulatory impact of the

---

[225] See SEC v. Steed Indus., [1974-1975 Transfer Binder] CCH Fed. Sec. L. Rep. ¶ 94,917 (N.D. Ill. 1974) (pyramid scheme); SEC v. Glenn W. Turner Enterprises, Inc., 474 F.2d 476 (9th Cir. 1973) (pyramid scheme); SEC Securities Exchange Act Release No. 9387 (Nov. 30, 1971), [1971-1972 Transfer Binder] CCH Fed. Sec. L. Rep. ¶ 78,446 (applicability of securities laws to multi-level distributorships). But see SEC v. Bull Inv. Group, Inc., [1974-1975 Transfer Binder] CCH Fed. Sec. L. Rep. ¶ 95,010 (D. Mass. 1975) ("hard sell" and "high pressure" marketing methods not objectionable so long as there were no implied or explicit misrepresentations).

[226] See the "Preamble" of the Securities Act of 1933, 1 CCH Fed. Sec. L. Rep. ¶ 514 ("to provide full and fair disclosure of the character of securities sold in interstate and foreign commerce . . . and to prevent frauds in the sale thereof").

statute falls primarily on the preinvestment or marketing phase of an offering. The *Camp* opinion also supports the marketing theory. Whatever might be said about the factual validity of the Supreme Court's distinction in *Camp* between commingled agency accounts and other bank-sponsored investment management arrangements, the Court did attempt to tie security status to concern over the methods of promotion banks might adopt.[227] This again identifies the method of marketing as the critical element in determining security status. Finally, even *Brigadoon Scotch Distributors* can be limited in application to cases involving questionable marketing. There, the court relied heavily on statements in defendants' sales brochure describing the services they would provide to establish the existence of a continuing management relationship between defendants and their clients. In addition, the court rejected defendants' argument that these additional services in fact had no effect on the value or sales price of client rare-coin portfolios because the contrary was claimed in defendants' "investment-oriented advertising." [228]

Because the marketing theory of security status for managed accounts is not well-developed,[229] it is difficult to identify its precise outline. Nonetheless, some observations are possible:

(1) Material omissions concerning risk of loss based on failure of the management firm can render an account a security. Thus, investment management arrangements were classified as securities in *Continental Commodities*[230] in behalf of the options buyers, and in *Pacific Coast Coin Exchange*[231] in behalf of the buyers of commodities on margin, who became general creditors of the firm without having that fact disclosed to them.

(2) Overemphasis on the opportunity for gain offered by a particular investment medium or, conversely, unjustified emphasis on its safety, at least if there is insufficient reference to an explanation of risk of loss, can be an important factor in establishing security status. For example, the SEC staff withdrew

---

[227] 401 U.S. at 629-638.

[228] SEC v. Brigadoon Scotch Distribs., Ltd., 338 F. Supp. 1288, 1292 (S.D.N.Y. 1975).

[229] See note 225 *supra*.

[230] 497 F.2d 516 (5th Cir. 1974), note 182 *supra*.

[231] SEC Litigation Release No. 6645 (Dec. 18, 1974); SEC Litigation Release No. 7057 (Aug. 25, 1975).

from a no-action position in *Dreyfus Gold Deposits, Inc.*[232] on the grounds that Dreyfus implied in a letter that the SEC had cleared its plan "based on its security, convenience and inexpensiveness."

(3) Finally, a generalized advertising campaign which goes beyond mere solicitation of interest by investors seeking personal investment counselling may give rise to an offering of securities. If, as was the case in *Brigadoon Scotch Distributors*, a marketing program ballyhoos a management operation to a wide audience and suggests that, at most, only modest efforts on the part of the investor are necessary to investment success, each resulting arrangement may well be a security.

The marketing theory can thus be seen as more of a supplement to *Howey* than a refinement of it. *Howey* focuses on participations in a definite investment scheme and it emphasizes both passivity on the part of investors and the creation of substantially similar, if not identical, types of interests in the scheme. Under a *Howey* analysis, red flags for security status for managed accounts would be heavy portfolio overlap[233] or joint management of an excessive number of accounts.[234] The marketing theory, on the other hand, focuses on how investment management services are sold rather than on any particular scheme in which the manager promises to invest for one client. It imposes security status on promotions which, in effect, make the ultimate object of investment secondary to the manager as the motivating force for investors to part with their money. Through the marketing theory, the Securities Act applies to protect persons who might be attracted to investments in esoteric untested media such as commodities,[235] gold bullion,[236] or rare coins,[237] or who might be attracted to investments in

---

[232] [1974-1975 Transfer Binder] CCH Fed. Sec. L. Rep. ¶ 80,069 (1975).

[233] See SEC Litigation Release No. 4534 (Feb. 6, 1970); Finanswer America/Investments, Inc., [1970-1971 Transfer Binder] CCH Fed. Sec. L. Rep. ¶ 78,111 (1971).

[234] SEC, *Report of the Advisory Committee on Investment Management Services for Individual Investors, Small Account Investment Management Services,* CCH Fed. Sec. L. Rep. No. 465, Pt. III, at 19 (1973).

[235] SEC v. Continental Commodities Corp., 497 F.2d 516 (5th Cir. 1974); Scheer v. Merrill Lynch, Pierce, Fenner & Smith, Inc., [1974-1975 Transfer Binder] CCH Fed. Sec. L. Rep. ¶ 95,086 (S.D.N.Y. 1975).

[236] Dreyfus Gold Deposits, Inc., [1974-1975 Transfer Binder] CCH Fed. Sec. L. Rep. ¶ 80,069 (1975).

[237] SEC v. Brigadoon Scotch Distribs., Ltd., 388 F. Supp. 1288 (S.D.N.Y. 1975).

more traditional media, such as securities or real estate, without adequate attention to the suitability of the investment programs they may encounter for their individual interests.[238]

¶ 3.04. APPLICATION OF THE REGISTRATION PROVISIONS OF THE INVESTMENT COMPANY ACT OF 1940 TO MANAGED ACCOUNTS

Individual accounts in an investment management enterprise may have implications beyond the Securities Act. Taken collectively, managed accounts may also be deemed participations in an investment company. Several years ago, First National City Bank and Merrill Lynch, Pierce, Fenner & Smith, Inc., jointly offered a discretionary management program designed to place investors into one of two portfolios depending on whether the objective was income or growth. In a 1970 lawsuit, the SEC took the position that the similarity of portfolios rendered each separate account a security, and that Citibank was operating an unregistered investment company.[239] The Commission settled the *Citibank* case, but since that time the staff has been taking the position that the Investment Company Act would apply where substantially similar advice is rendered to each of a group of accounts.[240] Furthermore, in a related development, the staff has been asserting that, taken individually, participations in a security are securities, and that, taken collectively, they constitute an investment company.[241] Consequently, because under the

---

[238] See, e.g., S.H. Dike & Co., [1975-1976 Transfer Binder] CCH Fed. Sec. L. Rep. ¶ 80,246 (1975).

[239] SEC Litigation Release No. 4534 (Feb. 6, 1970).

[240] The SEC stated in Finanswer America/Investments, Inc., [1970-1971 Transfer Binder] CCH Fed. Sec. L. Rep. ¶ 78,111, at 80,406 (1971):

"Registration of such an arrangement under the Investment Company Act would be necessary where substantially the same, or substantially overlapping, advice is rendered to each account or to a discernible group or groups of accounts, and where such accounts engage in the same securities transactions. Also, the interests offered in such an arrangement (the accounts) may be securities required to be registered. . . ."

See also Benchmark Securities, Inc., [1975-1976 Transfer Binder] CCH Fed. Sec. L. Rep. ¶ 80,424 (1976).

[241] See Arthur E. Fox, [1974-1975 Transfer Binder] CCH Fed. Sec. L. Rep. ¶ 80,082 (1974) (SEC opinion that participations in a large-denomination certificate of deposit are securities and offeror of the participations is an investment company); Josephthal & Co., [1974-1975 Transfer Binder]

line of cases beginning with *SEC v. Continental Commodities Corp.*,[242] a managed account may be a security, and because participations in a security may give rise to an investment company, the staff has suggested that participations in nonsecurities such as commodities futures may be treated as both securities and interests in a statutory investment company, should the investment program be run by an external investment manager.[243]

The argument that a set of managed accounts is an investment company is somewhat technical, but it follows logically from the statute. An investment company is defined in Section 3(a) as "any issuer which— (1) is or holds itself out as being engaged primarily . . . in the business of investing . . . in securities." [244] An issuer is any "person who issues . . . any security." [245] Included in the definition of person is "a company," [246] and a company includes "any organized group of persons whether incorporated or not." [247] Given this structure, a set of managed accounts might be regarded as an organized group and therefore a statutory company. Since the definition of security in both the Securities

---

CCH Fed. Sec. L. Rep. ¶ 80,116 (1974) (participations in certificates of deposit and other commercial instruments are securities and offeror may be an investment company).

[242] 497 F.2d 516 (5th Cir. 1974).

[243] Far West Futures Fund, [1974-1975 Transfer Binder] CCH Fed. Sec. L. Rep. ¶ 79,968 (1974). While commodities futures contracts are not securities, an investment in *option* contracts relating to commodities and commodities futures is deemed by the SEC to be an investment in securities. Further, when a company selling participations in its investments in commodities relies upon the discretion of an external adviser, the company may be investing in securities in the form of investment contracts relative to such commodities, particularly when the company's assets are externally managed together with assets of other entities.

[244] 15 U.S.C. § 80a-3(a)(1).

[245] 15 U.S.C. § 80a-2(a)(22), which provides in full that an issuer is "every person who issues or proposes to issue any security, or has outstanding any security which it has issued."

[246] 15 U.S.C. § 80a-2(a)(28), which defines "person" to include "a natural person or a company."

[247] 15 U.S.C. § 80a-2(a)(8), which provides:

" 'Company' means a corporation, a partnership, an association, a joint-stock company, a trust, a fund, or any organized group of persons whether incorporated or not; or any receiver, trustee in bankruptcy or similar official or any liquidating agent for any of the foregoing, in his capacity as such."

Act[248] and the Investment Company Act[249] is the same, such a group (company) would be issuing investment contracts (statutory securities) to each account owner. Thus, the group would fit the "any issuer" language of Section 3(a). Finally, because the purpose of creating such an account is to invest in the securities markets, the group of accounts would be an issuer engaged in investing in securities.[250]

Nor is it necessary that the portfolio of each managed account consist exclusively of securities. Section 3(a)(1) only requires only that an issuer be engaged "primarily" in securities investment. In addition, Section 3(a)(3) provides a numerical test; it includes any issuer which "is engaged or proposes to engage in the business of investing, reinvesting, owning, holding, or trading in securities and owns or proposes to acquire investment securities having a value exceeding 40 per centum of the value of such issuer's total assets. . . ." [251] In fact, there is a good argument that Section 3(a)(3) would provide the jurisdictional basis for regulating managed accounts under the Investment Company Act. Since, in many cases, there would be no intent to form a statutory investment company, a set of managed accounts, if subject to the Act, would be an "inadvertent" investment company.[252] It has been argued that Section 3(a)(3) was intended to be the jurisdictional basis for reaching inadvertent investment companies.[253]

The technical argument that a set of managed accounts is an investment company is not without policy support since most of the dangers recited in Section 1(b) of the Investment Company Act[254] are present to a large degree when many individual accounts are under the control of a single investment manager. Like investment advisers to investment companies, investment managers, able to exert control over their clients' investment decisions, can serve their own purposes by placing over-

---

[248] 15 U.S.C. § 77b(1).

[249] 15 U.S.C. § 80a-2(36).

[250] See 15 U.S.C. § 80a-3(a)(1). This construct under which a set of managed accounts may be deemed a statutory investment company (even though the investors and the manager may not realize its status as such) is sometimes called the ectoplasmic theory.

[251] 15 U.S.C. § 80a-3(a)(3).

[252] See note 250 supra.

[253] Kerr, "The Inadvertent Investment Company: Section 3(a)(3) of the Investment Company Act," 12 Stan. L. Rev. 29 (1959). But see SEC v. Fifth Ave. Coach Lines, Inc., 289 F. Supp. 3 (S.D.N.Y. 1968). See also Cohen & Hacker, "Applicability of the Investment Company Act of 1940 to Real Estate Syndications," 36 Ohio St. L. J. 482 (1975).

[254] 15 U.S.C. § 80a-1(b).

valued securities in their clients' portfolios[255]; they can engage in over-trading or other questionable trading practices to generate commissions for their own purposes[256]; and they can subject their clients' accounts to unsafe leveraging in hopes of improving investment performance.[257] Moreover, unlike investors in investment companies, owners of managed accounts are without the protection provided registered investment companies by outside directors or the specific statutory restrictions on transactions with affiliates and interested persons.[258] Most such constraints against self-dealing as exist are aspects of the general antifraud provisions rather than detailed rules of conduct.

If it becomes settled law that certain managed accounts are securities,[259] there are few arguments that those accounts should not be treated collectively as an investment company. The strongest argument that the Investment Company Act does not apply to a group of investment accounts classifiable as securities is that the Act was intended to apply only to pooled management and that most investment management arrangements do not involve pooling. The first suggestion that this distinction be made came from the SEC's Advisory Committee on Investment Management Services for Individual Investors. The Committee took the position that individual ownership of securities in an investment account is so unlike the status of shareholders of traditional investment companies as to justify treating them differently.[260]

That argument, although it has its appeal, is unlikely to prevail. The distinction between pooled and nonpooled accounts finds no support in the statute unless the meaning of "organized group" in the definition of company in Section 2(a)(8) of the Act is to turn on whether the securities belonging to investment accounts are kept segregated from each other. Such an interpretation, however, is sharply inconsistent with the commonality argument the SEC has put forward for classifying man-

---

255 This practice, sometimes called dumping, is discussed more fully in ¶ 10.06[2].

256 This practice, sometimes called churning, is discussed more fully in ¶ 10.06[1].

257 This practice is discussed more fully in ¶ 5.03[2].

258 See Investment Company Act §§ 10, 15, 17(a)-17(e), 15 U.S.C. §§ 80a-10, 80a-15, 80a-17(a)-17(e), respectively. But cf. Investment Advisers Act § 206(3) (15 U.S.C. § 80b-6(3)) (disclosure and written approval necessary if adviser purchases or sells as principal).

259 See ¶ 3.03[1], supra.

260 See SEC, Report of the Advisory Committee on Investment Management Services for Individual Investors, Small Account Investment Management Services, CCH Fed. Sec. L. Rep. No. 465, Pt. III, at 22-24 (1973).

aged accounts as investment contracts and hence statutory securities. The Commission would be hard-pressed to explain how a group of managed accounts can be sufficiently related to be statutory securities but at the same time be sufficiently unrelated not to be members of an organized group.

Furthermore, the pooling/nonpooling distinction makes little policy sense, since the opportunities for investment managers to perpetrate the abuses which led to the passage of the Investment Company Act are not less likely simply because accounts are not pooled. An investment manager willing to dump an overvalued underwriting into his client's account will find it little more difficult to do so when portfolios are maintained separately than when they are maintained in common. Similarly, an investment manager anxious to stimulate referrals by broker-dealers might trade his clients' portfolios more rapidly than otherwise regardless of whether the custody of each account is maintained separately or in common.

The conclusion seems to be that investment-company status for a set of managed accounts is virtually tied to security status for an individual account.[261] Particularly under a *Howey* analysis, the same commonality that establishes an investment management operation as a statutory security also establishes it as a statutory investment company. To be sure, the SEC possesses discretionary authority to waive compliance with all or part of the Investment Company Act, and it could exempt managed accounts that comply with some form of safe-harbor rule.[262] But realistically, the discretionary exemption power is used sparingly and restrictively, as the experience of variable life insurance indicates.[263] As a consequence, some limitation on the extension of

---

[261] See ¶ 3.03[1][c]. Conversely, if the individual interests are not statutory securities, no investment company is created. See Foundation Community Health Plan, [1974-1975 Transfer Binder] CCH Fed. Sec. L. Rep. ¶ 80,150 (1975).

[262] 15 U.S.C. § 80a-6(c).

[263] The SEC had for some time maintained that variable life insurance (VLI), under which benefits are determined according to the asset value of a portfolio of securities, was itself a security and, therefore, that a set of VLI contracts constituted an investment company (under the ectoplasmic theory; see note 250 *supra*). After much controversy, the Commission issued Investment Company Act Rule 3c-4 (17 C.F.R. § 270.3c-4 (1974)) and Investment Advisers Act Rule 202-1 (17 C.F.R. § 275.202-1 (1974)), which exempted VLI from both of these statutes. Yet the ensuing opposition by interest groups opposed to these blanket exemptions (particularly the investment company industry) led to the qualification that state protective

security status to managed accounts is essential for these correlative problems posed by the Investment Company Act to be avoided,[264] and the marketing theory of status of a managed account as a security [265] may necessarily be forced into double duty.

---

regulation comparable to that under the two federal statutes must exist before a federal exemption would attach. See SEC Investment Company Act Release No. 8000 (Sept. 20, 1973), [1973 Transfer Binder] CCH Fed. Sec. L. Rep. ¶ 79,518. Since most states do not have such comparable regulation, and since most state insurance commissioners were not willing to have the SEC involved in the regulation of insurance sold within their jurisdictions, VLI could not be actually marketed. See generally Blank, Keen, Payne & Miller, "Variable Life Insurance and the Federal Securities Laws," 60 Va. L. Rev. 71 (1974). The Commission then rescinded Rules 3c-4 and 202-1 and proposed instead to adopt a narrower exemptive rule under Section 6(e) (15 U.S.C. § 80a-6(e)). These developments are discussed more fully in ¶ 2.04[1].

[264] Because the definitions of security are the same in the Securities Act and the Investment Company Act (see text at notes 248-249 *supra*), it would be practically impossible to limit the reach of the Investment Company Act by refusing to treat managed accounts deemed securities under the Securities Act any differently under the Investment Company Act.

[265] See ¶ 3.03[2][b], *supra*.

Chapter 4

SETTING INVESTMENT OBJECTIVES

¶ 4.01.　DETERMINING THE CLIENT'S TOLERANCE FOR RISK

The investment objectives of an account determine the return an investor seeks and the risk he is willing to undertake. It is basic, therefore, that an investment manager know his client's investment objectives in order to provide useful management services. If investment objectives inappropriate for the client control an investment program, the results can be disastrous even though the program itself is carried out skillfully.

In principle, the responsibility for setting investment objectives is a matter of contract. A client can retain as much control as he wants over how the competing considerations of risk and return will be accommodated, and the manager can design an investment program accordingly. But, since contracts do not always expressly allocate between client and manager the responsibility for determining whether an investment satisfies a client's objectives, legal doctrine must carry out that task. In addition, the law places some limits on an investment manager's power to let his clients be foolhardy. Thus, given the degree of control the client contractually retains, the question is how great a burden the law should impose on the manager to assure that the investment objectives agreed upon are, in fact, appropriate for the client.

To illustrate the nature of the problem, assume that two parents, wishing to set aside a sum of money to provide for their child's education, approach an investment manager for professional assistance. Plainly, to do his job properly, the manager needs to know more than simply how much money he is being given to manage. He must also know the return the parents expect the account to show. This can be calculated by determining when the funds set aside will be required, what the costs of the child's education will be, and how much of those costs the fund is intended to offset.[1] The parents could rely entirely on the manager to make the calculations, of course, and if that were the case, the manager would have to carry out that task with ordinary skill and care. If, for example, the manager made no serious inquiry into the rate of growth of educational costs, had no expertise in the area himself, and, as a result, made an error in calculating the probable expenses, it is doubtful that he could devise an appropriate investment program, and he might well be answerable for any consequent losses.

But suppose that the manager's participation in the process of setting investment objectives is not so detailed and that the parents already have calculated for themselves the level of return they desire to achieve. Does the fact that clients can set their own investment objectives without much help from an investment manager mean that in the absence of a request for assistance, a manager can assume they have done so? Suppose, for example, the parents ask the manager to invest aggressively and seek a high rate of return for the fund they place under his

---

[1] These things cannot be known with certainty, of course, but reasonable estimates are possible. One would expect demands on the funds to begin shortly after completion of the child's secondary education. That fact would determine the time at which the portfolio should be ready to begin pay-outs. The amount required would depend on the projected cost of tuition, books and supplies, room and board, and so forth. To estimate these costs, it would be necessary to make certain assumptions about the rate of increase of college expenses and, using that rate, to extrapolate from existing figures. The rate of return required from the portfolio would be determined by subtracting the initial contribution from the portion of the total education expenses the fund is to pay, adjusted for the length of time until the funds would be needed. The calculus becomes even more complex if it is expected that the parents will contribute additional sums from time to time.

control. If the investment program, though carried out competently, should suffer sharp losses and the manager were then to discover that the fund was intended for their child's education, and that they had no other assets to make up for the losses, could the manager defend his action on the grounds that he was merely carrying out his client's instructions?[2]

The issue these questions raise is how responsible an investment manager should be for the risk his clients undertake.[3] Competent in-

---

[2] Cf. *In re* Shearson, Hammill & Co., [1964-1966 Transfer Binder] CCH Fed. Sec. L. Rep. ¶ 77,306 (1965), in which a brokerage firm was held answerable for inducing some of its clients to make investments not indicated by their investment objectives. In one instance, an account executive persuaded a client to invest in a risky issue without any inquiry into the client's purpose in making the investment. As it turned out, the client was investing part of a custodial fund maintained to provide for his child's education.

[3] The argument is sometimes made that risk cannot be considered in isolation, and that the appropriateness of a commitment or an investment also depends on its return. See, e.g., Note, "The Regulation of Risky Investments," 83 Harv. L. Rev. 603 (1970). But this argument suffers from two failings if it is intended to make more than the obvious point that investors will risk more for greater reward and rather to make a point of policy that investment managers *can* undertake greater risk because of possible gains. First, it treats the relationship between return and risk as if they were at least partially independent variables. Much evidence indicates that, to the contrary, over a large range of risk, a linear relationship approximates the actual relationship between risk and return in the securities markets. This phenomenon is discussed extensively in ¶ 7.03[2]. See generally J. Lorie & M. Hamilton, *The Stock Market: Theories and Evidence* (1973). Even if one assumes, however, that at a given level of risk, commitments can promise different levels of return, such that a higher return might warrant undertaking an otherwise unacceptable risk, the tolerance of an investor for risk and not the risk of the commitment itself is the dominant consideration in setting investment objectives.

To be sure, the higher the returns, the more acceptable the risk associated with a particular commitment. But the issue an investor is concerned with is whether, given the expected return of a commitment and the probability that return will be achieved, the risk falls within his personal and idiosyncratic tolerance for risk. Indeed, for most investors, there is a range of risk which is unacceptable no matter how high the return. A trustee of an ordinary testamentary trust could not, for example, risk the entire corpus of the trust for a commitment which, if successful, would increase the trust corpus many times over. Cf. Cohen, "The Suitability Rule and Economic Theory," 80 Yale L.J. 1604, 1624-1625 (1971).

The critical inquiry in accommodating high return and high risk to an investor's circumstances is the investor's attitude toward increases in his

vestment managers can design investment programs to achieve a wide range of returns, but, as a general rule, the higher the return sought, the greater the chances it will not be realized. The law has not yet imposed an absolute obligation on everyone offering investment management services to guarantee that the risk involved in an investment program be precisely the risk appropriate for the client. If the parents chose, for example, to purchase shares in a no-load mutual fund for their child's education, the burden would be on them to determine the appropriateness of the risk engendered by the fund's investment program.[4] On the other hand, the law does seek to assure at least that investors appreciate the risk they undertake. Thus, through the registration process required by Section 8(b) of the Investment Company Act of 1940[5] and the disclosure requirements of the Securities Act of 1933,[6] the parents would have the opportunity to ascertain in advance to a substantial degree the risk involved in the fund's investment program. Furthermore, they would know that disclosure would be continuous, since any fundamental variation from those policies without shareholder approval would violate the Investment Company Act and the antifraud provisions of other federal securities laws.[7]

But often, disclosure of the level of risk involved in an investment program will not satisfy an investment manager's duty to his client.

---

wealth. Most investors gain less and less satisfaction from each incremental gain in wealth, and most investors suffer greater pain from an incremental loss than they get satisfaction from an incremental gain. If the pain that would be produced by losses possible from making a particular commitment exceeds the satisfaction that would be derived from achieving its possible gains, the commitment should not be made, no matter what the nominal values of the losses and gains. This point is expressed in the economic principle called the diminishing marginal utility of wealth. Its nature and its implications are discussed more fully in ¶ 4.02 *infra*.

[4] If they purchased shares in a mutual fund with a sales load, the selling broker or salesman would have some obligation to see that the objectives of the fund comported with their own objectives. See text at notes 18-27 *infra*. Bines, "Regulating Discretionary Management: Broker-Dealers as Catalysts for Reform," 16 B.C. Ind. & Com. L. Rev. 347, 376 n.124 (1975).

[5] 15 U.S.C. § 80a-8(b). See text at notes 147-150 *infra*.

[6] 15 U.S.C. §§ 77a-77aa. The Securities Act registration forms for closed-end companies, Form S-4, and, for mutual funds, Form S-5, which dictate the contents of the prospectus, draw heavily from the disclosure requirements imposed by Section 8(b) (15 U.S.C. 80a-6) of the Investment Company Act.

[7] 15 U.S.C. §§ 80a-13(a), 80a-48; 15 U.S.C. § 77q(e); 15 U.S.C. § 78j(b); 15 U.S.C. § 80b-6. See Monheit v. Carter, 376 F. Supp. 334 (S.D.N.Y. 1974).

The law also imposes limits on a manager's power to disregard the capacity of those purchasing investment management services to bear risk. One method by which the law forces managers to take into account a client's capacity to bear risk is to impose a duty of inquiry into the client's circumstances, particularly in the event he requests to be put or the manager proposes to put him into a risky commitment or a risky investment program.[8] Moreover, the manager's obligations may not be satisfied merely by making the inquiry. A manager must use the knowledge he acquires at least to advise a client that a proposed commitment or investment program may involve an inappropriate level of risk.[9] Indeed, when the risk is plainly excessive, the manager may be forced to refuse to make a commitment or to forego an investment program on the client's behalf, however willing the client.[10]

Another method for pressuring investment managers to take the client's capacity to bear risk into account is to establish presumptive limits on risk based on the type of investment program undertaken. If the parents had created an ordinary trust to pay the costs of their child's education, their choice of the trust form would have set preservation of capital as a general risk limitation on any investment program designed by the manager, unless the trust documents expressly authorized something different.[11] Furthermore, even within the limits set by presumptive standards, the type of investment management arrangement created may place the entire responsibility for determining the appropriate level of risk on the manager. Subject to the instructions in

---

[8] See, e.g., Securities Act Rule 146(d) (17 C.F.R. § 230.146(d), 1 CCH Fed. Sec. L. Rep. ¶ 2709), which requires issuers of private placements and agents acting on behalf of such issuers to determine that offerees are either capable of evaluating the risk or capable of bearing the risk. See also Rolf v. Blyth Eastman Dillon & Co., [1976-1977 Transfer Binder] CCH Fed. Sec. L. Rep. ¶ 95,843 (S.D.N.Y. 1977) (broker-dealer did not know type of investor or intent of investor in recommending adviser).

[9] See, e.g., Anderson Co. v. John P. Chase, Inc., [1974-1975 Transfer Binder] CCH Fed. Sec. L. Rep. ¶ 95,009 (S.D.N.Y. 1975), cert. denied 424 U.S. 969 (1976) (client advised not to purchase on margin or make short sales).

[10] See Powers v. Francis I. DuPont & Co., 344 F. Supp. 429 (E.D. Pa. 1972) (broker-dealer not liable for churning an account where client initiated and authorized all transactions, but court indicated result would have been different if broker knew client could not make informed investment choice; court further suggested that broker-dealer, in allowing such high assumption of risk to continue, was unprofessional, and called for "governmental scrutiny and control" to prevent such financial waste in the future).

[11] Restatement (Second) of Trusts § 227, Comment e (1959).

the trust documents, a trustee, for example, must exercise independent judgment as to how the needs of the beneficiaries affect the risk the trust should undertake.[12]

[1] Presumptive Standards of Risk

Since an investment manager's responsibility for maintaining an account at the proper level of risk can vary from virtually nothing to an obligation actually to set the level of risk, the crucial question is how to determine the extent of a manager's responsibility in a given case. Presumptive standards of risk are a partial answer. It helps to know, for example, that presumptively, no commitment or investment program is appropriate for an ordinary trust if it unreasonably risks preservation of the trust's capital base,[13] or that a participation in a tax shelter will be deemed inappropriate for an investor unless he meets certain minimum standards of financial responsibility and need for shelter,[14] or that writing an option on securities not owned by an investor is unsuitable unless the investor has sufficient experience to appreciate the risk and the financial means to absorb a large loss.[15]

---

[12] *Restatement (Second) of Trusts* § 227(a) (1959); 3 A. Scott, *Law of Trusts* § 227.3 (3d ed. 1967) (hereinafter cited as Scott).

[13] *Id.*

[14] See proposed NASD Art. III, § 33, App. B, § 5, reported in SEC Securities Exchange Act Release No. 10260 (July 2, 1973), [1973 Transfer Binder] CCH Fed. Sec. L. Rep. ¶ 79,417. See also Faust, "Suitability," Rev. of Sec. Reg. 899, 901 (July 17, 1974).

[15] In proposed Securities Exchange Act Rule 9b-2 (17 C.F.R. § 240.9b-2), the SEC has established extensive disclosure and suitability requirements for broker-dealers. The Exchanges have given additional content to the proposed Rule. See, e.g., Chicago Board of Options Exchange Rule 9.9, CCH CBOE Guide ¶ 2309, which states:

> "A recommendation to a customer of the writing of a call option contract when the customer does not have a corresponding long position in the underlying security shall be deemed unsuitable for such customer unless, upon the information furnished by the customer, the person making the recommendation has a reasonable basis for believing at the time of making the recommendation that the customer has such knowledge and experience in financial matters that he may reasonably be expected to be capable of evaluating the risks of such transaction, and such financial capability as to be able to carry such uncovered position in the option contract."

More detailed codification of CBOE suitability requirements has been suggested, but the sharply varying purposes of investors has delayed action.

On the other hand, presumptive standards of risk are really only an initial guide to setting the proper level of risk for an account. For one thing, the strength of the presumption is debatable in most cases. Even in the case of an investment arrangement as well settled as an ordinary testamentary trust, the meaning of "preservation of capital" is subject to widely different interpretations. To see why this is so, contrast the investment program that would be carried out for a trust created for the maintenance of a testator's spouse with that of a trust created to accumulate the proceeds of investment until distribution at a certain age to the testator's child. Obviously, the maintenance trust cannot undertake the level of risk of the accumulation trust. More important than the variation in risk that is possible within a set of presumptive standards, however, is the fact that most investment management arrangements are not subject to presumptive standards except in the broadest sense. Contract, for more than presumptive standards, determines the range of risk at which an account must be maintained. Even with ordinary trusts, a trustor can easily enlarge or restrict an investment manager's discretion to assume risk by fixing the terms of trust management in the trust documents.[16]

[2] The Suitability Doctrine

The legal supplement to presumptive standards, and, indeed, the primary source of a manager's duty to take due account of a client's circumstances in setting investment objectives and maintaining an investment program, is the suitability doctrine.[17] The policy underlying the doctrine is that an investor should neither be influenced nor permitted to make commitments outside his tolerance for risk when he relies on an investment manager to identify levels of risk and return

---

[16] *Restatement (Second) of Trusts* § 227(c)(1959). Presumptive standards can also have an unfortunately counter-productive effect. The fact that a client satisfies a presumptive standard may be taken as tantamount to a determination that the risk involved in an investment program is appropriate for the client. Yet such a conclusion does not automatically follow. For example, because of fluctuations in asset value, an equity-based common trust fund, though ostensibly meeting the presumptive trust standard of preservation of principal, may be too risky a venture for the income beneficiary of a maintenance trust.

[17] Thus, for example, although banks have been authorized to purchase and sell options for trust accounts, because options are regarded as risky investments, if they do so, they must make an independent suitability determination. See Trust Banking Circular No. 2 (July 2, 1974), CCH Fed. Bank. L. Rep. ¶ 96,295. See note 116 *infra*.

which are suitable for him. In this respect, the suitability doctrine performs a function similar to that of presumptive standards. It forces an investment manager to make some effort at accommodating a client's investment program to the risk he can bear. But, unlike presumptive standards, the suitability doctrine does not set objective risk criteria to which a manager can refer for the purpose of determining his legal obligations. Rather, the doctrine requires a manager to make independent inquiry into and an evaluation of a client's circumstances to identify the range of risk appropriate for that particular client.

The suitability doctrine is almost entirely a development of federal and state securities regulation.[18] It can be traced to the need to deal with boiler-room operations by broker-dealers in which high-pressure sales techniques were used to solicit investors often not previously known to the soliciting broker-dealer.[19] The boiler-room cases typically involved outright misrepresentation or material nondisclosure.[20] But, together with the application of established securities antifraud doctrine, there began to develop the notion that a security being sold must reasonably fit the requirements of the person being solicited.[21] Once

---

[18] See L. Loss, *Securities Regulation* 3708-3727 (2d ed., Supp. 1969); Mundheim, "Professional Responsibilities of Broker-Dealers: The Suitability Doctrine," 1965 Duke L.J. 445 (1965); Comment, "Investor Suitability Standards in Real Estate Syndication: California's Procrustean Bed Approach," 63 Cal. L. Rev. 471 (1975).

[19] See L. Loss, *Securities Regulation* 3708-3709 (2d ed., Supp. 1969).

[20] See, e.g., Gerald M. Greenberg, 40 S.E.C. 133 (1960); Best Secs., Inc., 39 S.E.C. 931 (1960); Hamilton Waters & Co., [1964-1966 Transfer Binder] CCH Fed. Sec. L. Rep. ¶ 77,298 (1965); Triangle Investors Corp., [1964-1966 Transfer Binder] CCH Fed. Sec. L. Rep. ¶ 77,356 (1966). See also SEC, *Report of the Special Study of Securities Markets*, H.R. Doc. No. 95, 88th Cong., 1st Sess., Pt. I, at 238-240 and 298-299, and Pt. V, at 55.

[21] See Mundheim, "Professional Responsibilities of Broker-Dealers: The Suitability Doctrine," 1975 Duke L.J. 445, 449-450, 464-465 (1965).

In considering the impact of negotiated rates on the quality of research furnished to an investor, the Chairman of the SEC said:

> "[T]he suitability rules are cast in terms of the needs of the customer based on the information he furnishes to the broker. Unarticulated but implicit in such rules is also the broker's obligation to obtain current basic information regarding the security and then to make an evaluation as to the suitability of a recommendation for a particular customer in view of both the information concerning the security and the customer's needs."

SEC, *Policy Statement on Future Structure of the Securities Markets* (Feb. 2, 1972), [Special Reports Binder] CCH Fed. Sec. L. Rep. ¶ 74,811, at 65,620.

launched, the suitability doctrine grew rapidly. With Securities and Exchange Commission encouragement, the stock exchanges and the National Association of Securities Dealers (NASD) adopted know-your-customer rules,[22] and the SEC adopted a parallel regulation for nonmember broker-dealers.[23] Additionally, the SEC has forced suitability considerations on broker-dealer self-regulatory organizations for dealings in particular securities such as "hot issues" [24] and tax shelters.[25]

---

[22] The relevant rules are NYSE Rule 405, 2 CCH NYSE Guide ¶ 2405; AMEX Rule 411, 2 CCH AMEX Guide ¶ 9431; NASD Rules of Fair Practice, Art. III, § 2, CCH NASD Manual ¶ 2152; CBOE Rule 9.9, CCH CBOE Guide ¶ 2309.

[23] Securities Exchange Act Rule 15b 10-3 (17 C.F.R. § 240.15b 10-3) provides:

> "Every nonmember broker or dealer and every associated person who recommends to a customer the purchase, sale or exchange of any security shall have reasonable grounds to believe that the recommendation is not unsuitable for such customer on the basis of information furnished by such customer after reasonable inquiry concerning the customer's investment objectives, financial situation and needs, and any other information known by such broker or dealer or associated person."

There is a construction of the NASD rule (see note 22 *supra*) which suggests that a broker-dealer may have no duty to inquire into a client's financial circumstances, but may remain passive and use only the information the client furnishes on his own initiative. The rule reads that a recommendation must be suitable "on the basis of the facts, if any, disclosed" by the client about his finances and needs. But Rule 15b10-3 is not open to such an interpretation, and it would probably control the construction of the NASD rule. See Faust, "Suitability," Rev. of Sec. Reg. 899 (July 17, 1974).

[24] SEC pressure came in the form of enforcement actions (see, e.g., Gerald M. Greenberg, 40 S.E.C. 133 (1960)) and Proposed Rule 15c2-6 (SEC Securities Exchange Act Release No. 6885 (Aug. 16, 1962), [1961-1964 Transfer Binder] CCH Fed. Sec. L. Rep. ¶ 76,862). See also Comment, "A Symptomatic Approach to Securities Fraud: The SEC's Proposed Rule 15c2-6 and the Boiler Room," 72 Yale L.J. 1411 (1963). As a consequence, the NASD Rules of Fair Practice, Art. III, § 2, lists as a clear violation the recommendation of speculative low-priced securities without making a suitability inquiry, on the grounds that such a practice is bound to ensnare some persons for whom the recommendation will not be suitable. For the precise language, see note 88 *infra*. See also SEC Securities Act Release No. 5275 (July 26, 1972), CCH Fed. Sec. L. Rep. No. 434 (discussing the reasonable-basis doctrine with respect to "hot issues," requiring, among other things, familiarity on the part of a recommending broker with the registration statement).

[25] Proposed NASD Art. III, § 33, App. B, § 5. A summary of the proposed rule appears in SEC Securities Exchange Act Release No. 10260

For its own part, the Commission has included a suitability standard in Securities Act Rule 146, concerning persons eligible for private placements,[26] and in Securities Exchange Act Rule 15c2-5, concerning arrangements involving the extension of credit.[27]

[a] Application of the doctrine to investment managers

The broker-dealer origin of the suitability doctrine raises the question of whether it should apply equally forcefully to investment managers. It would be facile analysis to extend the doctrine to investment managers just because both broker-dealers and investment managers are connected with the securities industry or because the clients each deals with are interested in investing in securities, for there is an important difference between broker-dealers and investment managers where questions of suitability arise. Although it may be to their advantage to make sound recommendations and thereby develop customer loyalty, broker-dealers have an interest adverse to that of their clients when they solicit sales from or make recommendations to their clients. Virtually all their income depends on commissions and spreads earned only when sales are actually made. Assuming there is a fiduciary relationship between a broker-dealer and its client,[28] the suitability doctrine is an ap-

---

(July 2, 1973), [1973 Transfer Binder] CCH Fed. Sec. L. Rep. ¶ 79,417. An excellent discussion of the background to the proposal and the SEC's reaction to it appears in Comment, "Investor Suitability Standards in Real Estate Syndication: California's Procrustean Bed Approach," 63 Cal. L. Rev. 471, 486-488 (1975).

[26] 17 C.F.R. § 230.146(d), 1 CCH Fed. Sec. L. Rep. ¶ 2790. The language of the rule was originally proposed to impose two conditions conjunctively: (1) The offeree must be capable of evaluating the risk; and (2) the offeree must be in a position to bear the risk. As adopted, the rule lists the conditions disjunctively. See text at notes 106-111 *infra*.

[27] 17 C.F.R. § 240.15c2-5(a)(2) requires that, before any broker-dealer arranges an extension of credit to a client, he must obtain from that client "information concerning his financial situation and needs"; reasonably determine that the transaction, including the credit arrangement, is suitable for the client; and retain a written statement, available to the client upon request, setting forth the basis upon which the broker-dealer made his determination.

[28] The existence of a fiduciary relationship between a broker and customer is well recognized, but its extent and continuity are unsettled. The law of agency makes a broker a fiduciary in executing all trades, but some courts limit the fiduciary relationship to each separate transaction even though a customer may rely on the broker for regular and accurate information and advice. See, e.g., Walston & Co. v. Miller, 100 Ariz. 48, 410 P.2d 658 (1966). Federal authorities, on the other hand, take the view that,

plication of the duty of loyalty and is necessary as a counterweight to the broker-dealer's inclination to serve its immediate interests by stimulating sales.[29]

The suitability doctrine does not perform a like function for investment managers, at least in principle. Investment managers should have every incentive to see that the commitments they select and investment programs they design are suitable for their clients. They sell performance, not securities, and they earn the same fee, usually a percentage of the assets under management, whatever securities they put into the portfolios they control. Of course, not all investment management arrangements are free of pressures that would induce a manager to introduce undue risk into an account. For example, a manager may try to remedy a poor performance record by hazarding the portfolio.[30] Or a manager may be a broker-dealer, or affiliated with one, so that all or part of his compensation depends on commission business.[31] He may depend on referral business from broker-dealers[32] or be able to reduce

---

where reliance is present, a broker-dealer has a continuing fiduciary relationship with a customer. See, e.g., Cant v. A.G. Becker & Co., 374 F. Supp. 36, supplemented in 379 F. Supp. 972, supplemented in 384 F. Supp. 814 (N.D. Ill. 1974); Chasins v. Smith, Barney & Co., 438 F.2d 1167 (2d Cir. 1971); In re Gorski, [1967-1969 Transfer Binder] CCH Fed. Sec. L. Rep. ¶ 77,514 (1967). With regard to the continuing obligations of an investment adviser, see John C. Tead Co., [1973 Transfer Binder] CCH Fed. Sec. L. Rep. ¶ 79,557 (1973).

[29] See, e.g., In re Merrill Lynch, Pierce, Fenner & Smith Inc., [1975-1976 Transfer Binder] CCH Fed. Sec. L. Rep. ¶ 80,216 (1975) (sales quota system and mandatory weekend sales-solicitation sessions caused salesmen to encourage customers "to liquidate securities, some of which were of equally high quality [to those recommended] and which at the time of sale were the subject of buy or hold recommendations by Merrill Lynch's research department").

[30] See, e.g., John G. Kinnard & Co., [1973-1974 Transfer Binder] CCH Fed. Sec. L. Rep. ¶ 79,662 (1973). A statement by the Bank of America recognizes that marketing promises made to acquire small-investor accounts can produce the kinds of performance pressures which lead to introducing higher risk into those accounts than proper. See Securities Week, Aug. 11, 1975, p. 4.

[31] See, e.g., Hecht v. Harris, Upham & Co., 283 F. Supp. 417 (N.D. Cal. 1968), mdf'd and aff'd 430 F.2d 1202 (9th Cir. 1970); Mates Fin. Servs., [1969-1970 Transfer Binder] CCH Fed. Sec. L. Rep. ¶ 77,790 (1970) (investment adviser violated Securities Exchange Act § 10(b) in allocating brokerage of private clients to brokers in exchange for rebates which gave the adviser a "personal interest in the volume of transactions").

[32] See ¶ 3.02[2][b]. See generally Casey, " 'Finders Fee' Compensation to Brokers and Others," 31 Bus. Law. 707 (1976).

his operating and research expenses by dealing with a broker-dealer.[33] Where these kinds of conflicts of interest are present, the suitability doctrine serves a purpose with respect to investment managers similar to that applicable to broker-dealers. That is, the suitability doctrine acts as a response to duty-of-loyalty considerations exposed by virtue of the manager's conflicting interests with his client. But where these kinds of conflicts are not present, it is doubtful that a suitability obligation can be extended to investment managers by simple analogy to rules applying to broker-dealers.[34]

This is not to say that, where potential conflicts of interest do not exist, investment managers have no duty to design suitable investment programs. On the contrary, a strong argument can be made that, in the event suitability responsibility is not express, investment managers owe their clients a duty to make suitable commitments and to design suitable investment programs on the independent policy grounds that their express or implied holding out of professional expertise requires them to determine the range of risk their clients are in a position to bear, that their clients are ordinarily not as capable of doing so, and consequently that client reliance on the exercise of that expertise should be an assumed part of a management relationship. Moreover, the transposition of that policy into legal duty has solid common-law antecedents. The *Restatement (Second) of Agency* states that an agent should invest "in the light of the principal's means and purposes," [35] and the *Restatement (Second) of Trusts* cautions that a trustee's discretion is limited by "the purposes of the trust." [36]

---

[33] See ¶ 9.06 for a discussion concerning "paying up" and suitability in the context of the recent amendment to the Securities Exchange Act § 28(e) (15 U.S.C. § 78bb(e)), and the legislative history of that amendment to the Securities Exchange Act in the Securities Acts Amendments of 1975, Pub. L. 94-29, 89 Stat. 97 (June 4, 1975).

[34] Thus, in Anderson Co. v. John P. Chase, Inc., [1974-1975 Transfer Binder] CCH Fed. Sec. L. Rep. ¶ 95,009 (S.D.N.Y. 1975), *cert. denied* 424 U.S. 969 (1976), the court held that where plaintiff took an active part in making investment decisions, defendant investment adviser owed plaintiff little more than an obligation to inform plaintiff of the risks involved in the proposed investment program and to keep reasonably abreast of the client's financial circumstances. Plaintiff argued that the Investment Advisers Act imposes a general duty to provide investment supervisory services and cited a number of authorities in support of that proposition. *Id.* at p. 97,509. The court distinguished plaintiff's authorities on the ground they all involved self-dealing.

[35] Sections 70, 425(b) (1958).

[36] Section 187, Comment d (1959).

As was the case with broker-dealers, the development of the duty of suitability for investment managers is likely to occur at the federal level.[37] For one thing, parallels to the broker-dealer authorities are too easy to draw, despite the conceptual difference in the position of broker-dealers and investment managers in their relationship with clients. More important, however, there are many excellent authorities on which a federal duty of suitability can be based. Some federal statutes and regulations already impose suitability responsibilities on particular types of investment managers. Part 4 of the Employee Retirement Income Security Act of 1974 (ERISA) requires that pension-plan fiduciaries having investment management responsibilities carry out their contractual obligations constrained by the objectives of the plan[38]; and the Investment Advisers Act of 1940 makes essential to the use of the title "investment counsel" the provision of investment supervisory services,[39] defined in Section 202(a)(13) of the Act as "the giving of continuous advice as to the investment of funds on the basis of the individual needs of each client." [40]

In addition, through reliance on the federal antifraud provisions, the SEC has been extending a suitability duty to investment managers other than statutory investment counsel. In enforcement actions, the Commission has taken the position that the failure to carry out representations about designing an investment program to fit client needs is fraudulent.[41] And, in no-action letters, it has taken the position that

---

[37] State law, however, especially through state securities regulation, is beginning to take on increasing importance in responding to the suitability issue. See Comment, "Investor Suitability Standards in Real Estate Syndication: California's Procrustean Bed Approach," 63 Cal. L. Rev. 471 (1975).

[38] See text at notes 155-169 *infra*.

[39] Investment Advisers Act § 208(c) (15 U.S.C. § 80b-8(c)) provides that:

"[I]t shall be unlawful for any person registered under section 203 of this title to represent that he is an investment counsel or to use the name 'investment counsel' as descriptive of his business unless (1) his or its principal business consists of acting a investment adviser, and (2) a substantial part of his or its business consists of rendering investment supervisory services."

[40] 15 U.S.C. § 80b-2(a)(13).

[41] Finanswer Am./Investments, Inc., [1970-1971 Transfer Binder] CCH Fed. Sec. L. Rep. ¶ 78,111 (1971); SEC v. A.J. Groesbeck Fin. Advisers, Inc., Civil No. 73-2678 (C.D. Cal. 1973), [1973 Transfer Binder] CCH Fed. Sec. L. Rep. ¶ 94,237 (summary of complaint).

discretionary management imposes a duty of suitability.[42] Also, Investment Advisers Act Proposed Rule 206(4)-4, which prescribes the disclosure of certain information to prospective clients by investment advisers,[43] requires all investment advisers actually providing investment supervisory services, whether claiming the title of investment counsel or not, to disclose "the factors relating to the individual circumstances of any client" on which the adviser .relies in managing the account.[44] It seems likely that the law will insist that investment advisers actually perform the services they say they offer.

At least partial support for the SEC's position can be found in *Anderson Co. v. John P. Chase, Inc.*[45] Plaintiffs claimed that an investment adviser who is a statutory investment counsel is obliged to provide investment supervisory services to every client and that defendant, in failing to do so, violated Section 206 of the Investment Advisers Act, the antifraud provision. The court held that the requirements of Section 202(a)(13) are not implied into every contract for advisory services, but apply only to statutory investment counsel.[46] But the court also said, though in dictum to be sure, that representations that investment supervisory services will be provided are enforceable under Section 206.[47]

[b] Substance questions and enforcement problems

Because the extension under federal law of the suitability doctrine to investment managers is so recent a development, there remain serious questions about the substantive content of the doctrine. In the absence of conflicts of interest, the analogy between the suitability duty of investment managers and the suitability duty of broker-dealers breaks down.[48] Most likely, the suitability responsibilities of investment managers where self-dealing is not in issue will derive from the negligence principles established in agency law and trust law.[49] In accordance with traditional negligence doctrine, private codes of conduct by professional

---

[42] See, e.g., John G. Kinnard & Co., [1973-1974 Transfer Binder] CCH Fed. Sec. L. Rep. ¶ 79,662 (1973).

[43] See SEC Investment Advisers Act Release No. 442 (March 5, 1975), [1974-1975 Transfer Binder] CCH Fed. Sec. L. Rep. ¶ 80,128.

[44] Proposed Rule 206(4)-4(c)(4), 17 C.F.R. § 275.206(4)-4(c)(4).

[45] [1974-1975 Transfer Binder] CCH Fed. Sec. L. Rep. ¶ 95,009 (S.D.N.Y. 1975), *cert. denied* 424 U.S. 969 (1976).

[46] [1974-1975 Transfer Binder] CCH Fed. Sec. L. Rep. at 97,508.

[47] *Id.* at 97,509.

[48] See text at notes 28-34 *supra.*

[49] *Restatement (Second) of Agency* § 379 (1958); *Restatement (Second) of Trusts* § 174 (1959). See also Piper, Jaffray & Hopwood, Inc. v. Ladin,

associations of investment managers,[50] for example, might be elevated to law to establish the standard for negligence.[51]

Another complicating factor in applying the suitability doctrine to investment managers is enforcement. In part, this is because federal law is still in the process of determining the degree to which it will incorporate a negligence standard.[52] In part also, it is because enforcement of the suitability rules under the federal antifraud provisions has been proceeding differently depending on the party seeking the remedy and the type of remedy sought. Although disciplinary sanctions are apparently available for violation of suitability standards,[53] still unresolved

---

399 F. Supp. 292 (S.D. Iowa 1975) (recommendation by broker-dealer of low-grade corporate bonds to trustee held actionable negligence).

[50] The Investment Counsel Association of America, Inc., states in its Standards of Practice: "Investment counsel is oriented to the respective needs of each client as well as to the relative merits of various investments. Thus, investment counsel provides advice which is continuous rather than incidental or occasional and which is predicated upon a full understanding of the objectives, investments, tax status and general circumstances of each client rather than advice which is distributed on a wholesale or mass basis." (Reprinted in *Counseling the Investment Adviser* 470 (PLI Corporate Law & Practice Course Handbook No. 177, 1975).) Cf. SEC v. Capital Gains Research Bureau, Inc., 375 U.S. 180, 188 (1963) (reliance on investment counsel code of ethics).

[51] See Piper, Jaffray & Hopwood, Inc. v. Ladin, 399 F. Supp. 292 (S.D. Iowa 1975).

[52] ERISA (Pub. L. 93-406, 88 Stat. 829 (Sept. 2, 1974)) incorporates the prudent-man rule into federal law. ERISA § 404(a)(1)(B), 29 U.S.C. § 1104(a)(1)(B). The Supreme Court, on the other hand, has held that Section 10(b) will not support an action for damages based on a pure negligence theory (Ernst & Ernst v. Hochfelder, 425 U.S. 185 (1976)), though it reserved decision on the applicability of a negligence standard in enforcement actions. See note 54 *infra*.

To the extent suitability obligations of investment managers are held to arise out of their fiduciary responsibilities rather than merely their professional responsibilities, however, the viability of a negligence standard remains unsettled. Relevant also in this regard are the cases of White v. Abrams, 495 F.2d 724 (9th Cir. 1974), and Sanders v. John Nuveen & Co., 524 F.2d 1064 (7th Cir. 1975) (per Stevens, J.), reviewed for further consideration in light of *Hochfelder*. Both courts held that the standard is flexible, determined by the closeness of the relationship between the parties and the degree of the plaintiff's dependency on the defendant.

[53] See SEC v. A.J. Groesbeck Fin. Advisors, Inc., Civil No. 73-2678 (C.D. Cal. 1973), [1973 Transfer Binder] CCH Fed. Sec. L. Rep. ¶ 94,237 (summary of complaint); *In re* Tallman, SEC Securities Exchange Act Release No. 8830 (March 2, 1970), [1969-1970 Transfer Binder] CCH Fed. Sec. L. Rep. ¶ 77,800.

is the availability under federal law of civil damages to an aggrieved client.[54]

But most of the enforcement problems stem from the vagueness of the suitability concept. Despite the free usage of the term "suitability," its application to concrete situations has been limited, and one frequent-

---

[54] The reasons for this dichotomy between disciplinary sanctions and civil liability are several. First, as a matter of federal law, the suitability doctrine in its refined stages is supplementary to the traditional full disclosure and antifraud philosophy of the federal securities laws. In fullest effect, the doctrine requires provision not only of accurate and complete information to clients, but also of an evaluation of that information from the perspective of each customer's personal financial situation and attitude toward risk. This is a far cry from the notion of manipulation or deception which, as Professor Loss points out (7 Sec. Reg. & Trans. Rep., No. 24, at 2 (Feb. 7, 1975)), represents the original conception of statutory fraud. See also Ernst & Ernst v. Hochfelder, 425 U.S. 185 (1976).

Moreover, implying such an affirmative duty through reliance on open-end antifraud provisions instead of insisting on conduct involving at least some degree of scienter also makes it more difficult to control fairly the obligations it places on those to whom the doctrine applies. In its present stage of development, the suitability doctrine leaves unresolved many questions which could lead to harsh results if there were an absolute rule that violation of suitability standards would lead to civil liability. Still open, for example, are questions of how one's duty might be affected by whether the client is an individual or an institution, sophisticated or unsophisticated, purchasing on his own or through an investment adviser, and so forth. See Lipton, "The Customer Suitability Doctrine," in *Fourth Annual Institute on Securities Regulation* 278-287 (PLI 1973). It is one thing to discipline a broker-dealer for repeatedly making overtures to unsophisticated investors to purchase risk-laden securities (see *In re* Shearson, Hammill & Co., [1964-1966 Transfer Binder] CCH Fed. Sec. L. Rep. ¶ 77,306 (1965)); it is quite another to open up the adjudicative process to every dissatisfied client who concludes that his investment manager's blandishments seduced him into adopting an unnecessarily risky investment program (see Architectural League of N.Y. v. Bartos, [1975-1976 Transfer Binder] CCH Fed. Sec. L. Rep. ¶ 95,329 (S.D.N.Y. 1975)).

At the present time, virtually all legal developments concerning civil liability arising out of suitability violations have dealt with broker-dealers. See Lipton, "The Customer Suitability Doctrine," *supra*; Comment, "Investor Suitability Standards in Real Estate Syndication: California's Procrustean Bed Approach," 63 Calif. L. Rev. 471, 533-544 (1975). The most informative authorities on the question of whether the negligent design of an unsuitable investment program might lead to civil liability under the antifraud provisions of the federal securities laws are the cases in which attempts were made to predicate liability on the violation of the "know your customer" rules of the self-regulatory organizations. On whether those rules imply a damages action into the federal antifraud provisions, however, there

ly gets the impression that the term is being used to cover more than the allocation of responsibility for identifying and setting proper risk and return constraints. Once the substantive issue is resolved, most of the enforcement problems should fall into line. Consequently, the discussion which follows attempts to develop some objective guideposts as to

---

is currently a conflict among the circuits. It is the view of the Second Circuit that there is a right of action only on rules designed to prevent fraud (see Colonial Realty Corp. v. Bache & Co., 358 F.2d 178 (2d Cir.), *cert. denied* 385 U.S. 817 (1966)), a view which has been interpreted to exclude actions implied from the rules in question both by district courts within the Second Circuit (e.g., Jenny v. Shearson, Hammill & Co., [1974-1975 Transfer Binder] CCH Fed. Sec. L. Rep. ¶ 95,021 (S.D.N.Y. 1975); but see Starkman v. Seroussi, 377 F. Supp. 518 (S.D.N.Y. 1974), and Rolf v. Blyth Eastman Dillon, [1976-1977 Transfer Binder] CCH Fed. Sec. L. Rep. ¶ 95,843 (S.D.N.Y. 1977)), and some district courts outside (e.g., Piper, Jaffray & Hopwood, Inc. v. Ladin, 399 F. Supp. 292 (S.D. Iowa 1975); Utah v. duPont Walston, Inc., [1974-1975 Transfer Binder] CCH Fed. Sec. L. Rep. ¶ 94,812 (D. Utah 1974)). See also Rothstein v. Seidman & Seidman, [1975-1976 Transfer Binder] CCH Fed. Sec. L. Rep. ¶ 95,462 (S.D.N.Y. 1976) (no private right of action implied in exchange special instruction). The Seventh Circuit takes the opposite view, having stated in Buttrey v. Merrill Lynch, Pierce, Fenner & Smith, Inc., 410 F.2d 135 (7th Cir.), *cert. denied* 396 U.S. 838 (1969), that where such violations constitute a breach of fair practice, they are actionable under the federal securities laws. See also Van Gemert v. Boeing Co., 520 F.2d 1373 (8th Cir. 1975) (NYSE listing agreement violation); Evans v. Kerbs & Co. [1975-1976 Transfer Binder] CCH Fed. Sec. L. Rep. ¶ 95,459 (S.D.N.Y. 1976) (minimum equity in margin account). See generally Note, "Implication of Civil Liability Under the New York Stock Exchange Rules and Listing Agreement," 22 Vill. L. Rev. 130 (1976).

Some of the cases which have rejected use of the know-your-customer rules to establish a federal duty of suitability under the antifraud provisions have done so in part on the grounds that these rules are not intended by the SEC to supplement its supervisory responsibilities under the federal securities laws. For example, in Piper, Jaffray & Hopwood, Inc. v. Ladin, *supra,* in which a trustee sued a broker-dealer for breach of duty of suitability, the court dismissed the portion of the complaint based on federal law (but sustained the complaint on the same facts on a common-law negligence theory), saying that the trustee had failed to demonstrate "that the Suitability Rule or the Know Your Customer Rule were intended to substitute for direct SEC regulation. There is no indication that the SEC contemplated that the stock exchange rules in question were part of a federal scheme to prevent fraudulent practices." 399 F. Supp. at 297. This reasoning could not be more mistaken. The suitability rules are a direct result of SEC pressure and they substitute for direct regulation under such provisions as the SECO suitability rule, Rule 15b10-3 (17 C.F.R. § 240.15b10-3), only because of the congressional scheme of permitting self-regulation by broker-

the allocation of suitability responsibility based on existing legal authorities and business practice. First, however, it is necessary to add some precision to the meaning of suitability. To aid the analysis, therefore, we begin with a simplified discussion of some economic theory, in order to arrive at a sharper definition of suitability than is found in most legal authorities.[55]

---

dealers to the extent consistent with federal regulation. (Some of the SEC actions designed to instigate the creation and adoption of stock exchange suitability rules are detailed in notes 18-27 *supra*.) Nonetheless, it remains the dominant view that violation of stock exchange suitability rules alone does not amount to fraud cognizable under Rule 10b-5 (17 CFR § 240.10b-5).

Although Investment Advisers Act § 206 (15 U.S.C. § 80b-6), an antifraud provision which would apply to the activities of many investment managers, separately imposes a duly of suitability (see *In re* Shearson, Hammill & Co., [1964-1966 Transfer Binder] CCH Fed. Sec. L. Rep. ¶ 77,306 (1965)), there is also a split of authority over whether it makes available private rights of action. See, e.g., Fund of Funds, Ltd. v. Vesco, [1976-1977 Transfer Binder] CCH Fed. Sec. L. Rep. ¶ 95,644 (S.D.N.Y. 1976 (implied right of action); Bolger v. Laventhol, Krekstein, Horwath & Horwath, 381 F. Supp. 260 (S.D.N.Y. 1974) (implied right of action); Courtland v. Walston & Co., Inc., 340 F. Supp. 1076 (S.D.N.Y. 1972) (implied right of action); Angelakis v. Churchill Management Corp., [1975-1976 Transfer Binder] CCH Fed. Sec. L. Rep. ¶ 95,285 (N.D. Cal. 1975) (implied right of action); Gammage v. Roberts, Scott & Co., Inc., [1974-1975 Transfer Binder] CCH Fed. Sec. L. Rep. ¶ 94,761 (S.D. Cal. 1974) (no private right of action); Jones Memorial Trust v. Tsai Inv. Servs., Inc., 367 F. Supp. 491 (S.D.N.Y. 1973) (dictum) (no private right of action); Greenspan v. Del Toro, [1975-1976 Transfer Binder] CCH Fed. Sec. L. Rep. ¶ 95,488 (S.D. Fla. 1974) (no private right of action). See also Abrahamson v. Fleschner, [1976-1977 Transfer Binder] CCH Fed. Sec. L. Rep. ¶ 95,889 (2d Cir. 1977); ¶ 3.02 note 43. See generally Note, "Securities—Investment Advisers Act of 1940—Private Right of Action for Damages Allowed Against an Investment Adviser and His Accountant," 43 Ford. L. Rev. 493 (1974).

Congress has had before it proposed legislation which would, among other things, establish the availability of Section 206 for civil damage actions. See Investment Advisers Act Amendments of 1976, S. 2849, 94th Cong., 2d Sess., § 7 (1976). But plainly, until legislation is adopted, if Section 206 will not support any kind of action for civil damages, investors cannot rely on it to remedy breaches of the duty of suitability by their investment managers.

[55] For a different approach to analysis of the suitability question by use of economic theory, see Cohen, "The Suitability Rule and Economic Theory," 80 Yale L.J. 1604 (1971). Professor Cohen's analysis, which focuses on broker-dealers, treats the suitability issue as being controlled by an investor's existing portfolio. The suitability of a recommendation de-

¶ 4.02. AN EXAMINATION OF SUITABILITY ACCORDING TO ECONOMIC THEORY

The purpose of this discussion of economic theory is not to suggest that prior to constructing an investment program, investment managers must quantify risk and return with the exactitude hypothesized herein, but to introduce an objective measurement into the highly subjective explanations of suitability which have heretofore sufficed in legal doctrine.[56] With this qualification in mind, let us define suitability in negative terms, as follows: A change in an investment program is unsuitable if, taking into account both possible gains and possible losses, it unreasonably exceeds an investor's tolerance for risk.[57] This means that measuring the risk of loss of an investment opportunity is not sufficient to determine suitability. To ignore possible gain is to ignore the very reason an investor is willing to hazard the possibility of loss. Nonetheless, opportunities for greater gain can offset chances of greater loss and still be unsuitable unless the investor can tolerate the uncertainty about which will occur. Additionally, no investment opportunity is always either suitable or unsuitable for an investor. A given opportunity can be suitable for an investor at one level of wealth and unsuitable at another. To measure the suitability of a commitment or investment program, therefore, it is necessary to take into account both

---

pends on whether it improves diversification, improves return without affecting risk, or raises risk only to a point within a customer's risk threshold. *Id.* at 1626-1627. The analysis in this chapter treats an existing portfolio as at best evidentiary of an investor's attitude toward risk but not as the standard against which suitability as applied to subsequent investment decisions is to be determined since an existing portfolio may already be bearing an unsuitable level of risk and since suitability shifts over time depending on what is experienced by an investor.

[56] For purpose of analysis, the textual discussion treats the universe of investments as if their risk and return characteristics were perfectly determinable, a circumstance which is obviously not true. But the problem of identifying the risk and return characteristics of investment opportunities, see generally ¶ 6.03, is distinct from determining an investor's capacity for assuming risk. It is this latter question which is being explored in this section.

[57] Risk, as used in this discussion, has the same meaning given it in the exposition of portfolio theory in ¶ 6.03[2]. That is, the measure of the risk of a commitment or an investment program is the tendency of actual outcomes to vary from expected return. For purposes of examining the concept of suitability, however, the meaning of risk does not require the extensive development it receives in ¶ 6.03[2], and consequently, it is here used synonymously with uncertainty about what a commitment or investment program will actually return.

the wealth of the investor at the time he contemplates a change in his investment program and his attitude toward increases and decreases in his wealth from that position.[58]

[1] The Effect of Shifts in Wealth

In theory, most persons prefer more wealth to less. As wealth increases, however, the satisfaction gained from each increment of wealth diminishes. This principle, called the "declining marginal utility of wealth," means simply that if one is worth $100, the joy of getting to $101 is less intense than the pain of falling to $99.[59] Not everyone has the same attitude toward increasing his wealth, of course; getting from $100 to $101 could mean more to one person than to another. But almost everyone's attitude towards increasing his wealth is of the same character. Each dollar up offers progressively less pleasure, while each dollar down gives progressively more pain.

The implications of the declining-marginal-utility-of-wealth principle can best be illustrated graphically. Figure 4-1 maps the satisfaction a hypothetical investor gets from increases in his wealth, technically called utility, against wealth. This relationship between utility and wealth is called the utility function. As hypothesized above, Figure 4-1 shows utility always rising as wealth increases, but at a diminishing rate relative to wealth.[60] This indicates that the investor always would prefer greater wealth, no matter how wealthy he is initially, but that the wealthier he is, the less intense is the satisfaction he receives from each increment of it.

[2] The Dependency of Suitability on Shifts in Utility

Suppose that an investor's initial wealth is W_0 and that he can engage in an investment program which has an equal probability of either

---

[58] A more rigorous exposition of the points made in the textual discussion is obtainable from several sources. See, e.g., W. Sharpe, *Portfolio Theory and Capital Markets* 187-201 (1970); J. Lorie & M. Hamilton, *The Stock Market: Theories and Evidence* 191-197 (1973); Kassouf, "Towards a Legal Framework for Efficiency and Equity in the Securities Markets," 25 Hastings L.J. 417, 419-422 (1974); Friedman & Savage, "The Utility Analysis of Choices Involving Risk," 56 J. Pol. Econ. 279 (1948).

[59] Strictly speaking, the concept of wealth includes more than total assets in dollars. For simplicity, however, this discussion measures wealth monetarily. See W. Sharpe, *Portfolio Theory and Capital Markets* 9-10 (1970).

[60] If utility increased at the same rate as wealth, the line would be straight.

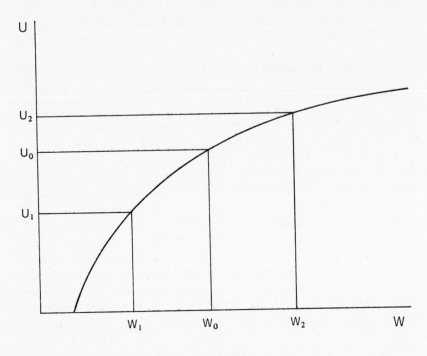

Fig. 4-1

decreasing his wealth to W_1 or increasing it to W_2. Since each outcome is equally probable, the investor would evaluate the investment potential of the program by averaging the two outcomes.[61] As Figure 4-2 shows, this program offers greater opportunity for gain than for loss. On the average, it will increase the investor's wealth. ($W_2 - W_0 > W_0 - W_1$.)

But an investment program is not necessarily suitable for an investor just because on the average it offers positive results. The crucial question for the investor is how he feels about being given the opportunity to pursue that program. If the actual result is W_1, his utility will drop to U_1; if it is W_2, it will rise to U_2. Since each outcome is equally probable, the investor would evaluate the opportunity to engage in the program by averaging the two outcomes measured by change in utility. Thus, if $(U_1 + U_2)/2 > U_0$, he would consider engaging in the pro-

---

[61] For a fuller explanation of why the average of the possible outcomes, called the expected value, represents the investment potential of the program measured prospectively, see ¶ 6.03[1].

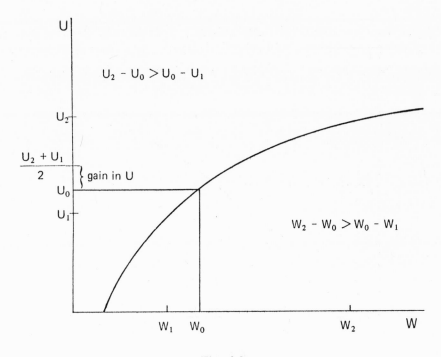

$$U_2 - U_0 > U_0 - U_1$$

gain in U

$$W_2 - W_0 > W_0 - W_1$$

Fig. 4-2

gram an improvement in his position; that is, the program would be suitable for him. Conversely, if $(U_1 + U_2)/2 < U_0$, he would forego the opportunity to engage in the program; the program would be unsuitable for him.

Extending this analysis to the general case, if risk is considered to be the uncertainty over what will actually be realized from an investment program, the suitability of an investment program for any investor can easily be determined by measuring the change in utility that would occur by undertaking the program. Simply calculate all possible outcomes of an investment program, determine the corresponding utility associated with each, average those values and compare that average with the initial utility level.[62] If utility would increase, the program is suitable; otherwise, it is not. Thus, Figure 4-2 illustrates a suitable investment program and Figure 4-3, an unsuitable investment program. As Figures 4-2 and 4-3 indicate, the opportunity for great gains is not

---

[62] To determine the average value, simply obtain the sum of possible outcome weighted by the probability it will occur. See ¶ 6.03[1].

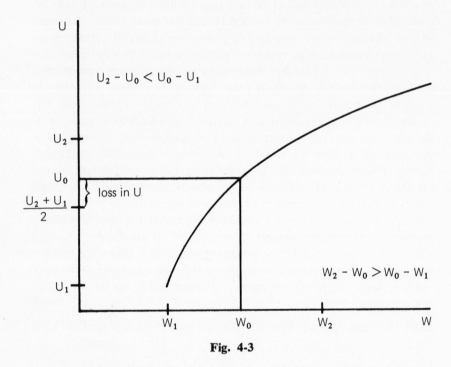

Fig. 4-3

enough to justify a program, nor does the chance of substantial loss preclude it. The answer depends on how much the investor values the program's possible gains and how much he values avoiding its possible losses.

[3] The Dependency of Suitability on Attitude Toward Risk

Now consider two investors with the utility functions depicted in Figure 4-4. For any given level of wealth, B values another dollar more than A does. For that reason, there are many investment programs which would be suitable for B but not for A. Suppose, for example, that the initial wealth of both A and B is W_0, and that a particular investment program will either reduce their wealth to W_1 or raise it to W_2 with equal probability. A will not undertake the program because $(U_{A1} + U_{A2})/2 < U_{A0}$. In other words, A would view himself as less well off if he exchanges the certainty of his current wealth, W_0, for the uncertainty of winding up at either W_1 or W_2. B's attitude, however, is exactly the opposite. Because $(U_{B1} + U_{B2})/2 > U_{B0}$, B would view himself as better off by taking the opportunity to increase his wealth to

W_2 even though he might lose money and fall to W_1. This analysis emphasizes an important point. Investment programs can differ in suitability for investors whose financial circumstances are identical in all respects. The determining factor is attitude toward change in wealth. The more an investor values additional wealth, the more uncertainty, or risk, he will bear in seeking to increase it. The more he values avoiding losses, the less risk he will bear in seeking to increase wealth.

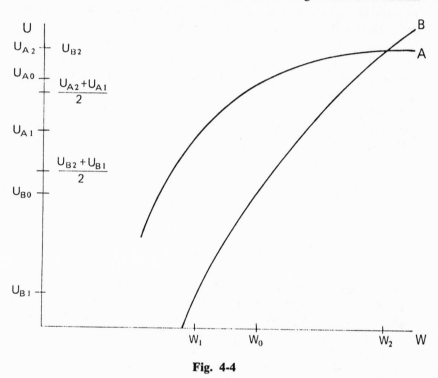

Fig. 4-4

[4] Problems in Seeking to Maximize Suitability

Now suppose an investor wants to know more than whether a particular investment program is suitable or unsuitable from his point of view. He wants to know which investment program of all those suitable is the best for him. One way to make this determination is to plot the possible outcomes of every available program on a graph of the investor's utility function and to select the one which raises his utility the most. But this method of selecting the best program has serious drawbacks. Because of the number of securities available for investment and all the combinations in which they could be bought, too many invest-

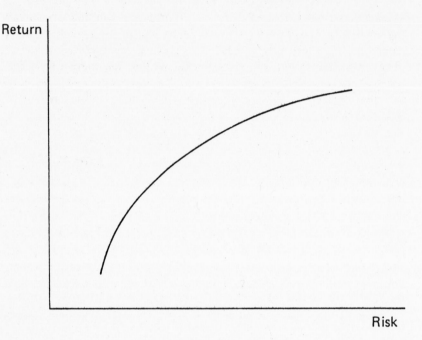

Fig. 4-5

ment programs would have to be evaluated in this fashion. Moreover, the process would have to be repeated for every different investor since each investor's attitude toward opportunities to increase wealth—that is, his utility function—plots out at different values.

Consider instead the graph in Figure 4-5. The solid line plots the relationship between risk and return for all portfolios having these significant characteristics: At any level of risk, no portfolio can be constructed offering a higher rate of return; and for any rate of return, no portfolio can be constructed at a lower level of risk.[63] In other words,

---

[63] Note that the line representing these portfolios is concave from below. One can see that this suggests two things: (1) The rate of return on the best portfolios increases as the risk of the portfolio increases, hardly a revolutionary concept (see J. Lorie & R. Brealey, *Modern Developments in Investment Management* 393-394 (1972)); and (2) the investment in return available decreases for each increment in risk, a more sophisticated observation, but one most investors sense intuitively. For a fuller discussion on why the curve representing the portfolios offering the greatest return possible at each level of risk has the shape depicted in Figure 4-5, see W. Sharpe, *Portfolio*

this line represents the set of all "best" portfolios.[64] By transposing the information contained in the graph of the investor's utility function in Figure 4-1 to the graph of all best portfolios in Figure 4-5, one can determine which portfolio in the set is also best for the investor.

To illustrate, suppose the investor begins with wealth W_0. His satisfaction from having that wealth is, by definition, U_0. Now suppose he is presented with an investment opportunity which, if he takes advantage of it, will raise his satisfaction to U_1 ($U_1 > U_0$). Plainly, he will want to invest because to do so improves his position. The investment opportunity meets our definition of suitability.[65] Suppose further that the investor is presented with another investment opportunity which will raise his satisfaction to U_2 ($U_2 > U_0$). U_2, therefore, is also a suitable investment. Also, as we know from the earlier discussion, the investor will choose between the investments yielding U_2 and U_1 on the basis of which provides the greater increase in satisfaction. If $U_2 > U_1$, he will prefer the second opportunity; conversely, if $U_1 > U_2$, he will prefer the first. But if $U_2 = U_1$, he will be indifferent about them. Furthermore, he will be similarly indifferent about any opportunity which raises his satisfaction only to the point where it is the same as U_2 or U_1. Figure 4-6 shows three investment opportunities, each of which is capable of realizing different gains and losses, but each of which produces the same level of utility. This process can be repeated for every level of utility. From an initial wealth position, therefore, it is possible to calculate all values for risk and return which will produce an identical change in utility.

Let us transpose the information provided by Figure 4-6 to a graph relating return and risk in order to determine which of the set of best portfolios is the most suitable for the investor. Figure 4-7 plots three curves, each representing a set of values for risk and return over which the investor would be indifferent[66] because he would experience no change in utility by a move along any one of the curves. Note that to maintain his attitude of indifference, the investor requires progressively

---

Theory and Capital Markets 52-53 (1970). By taking into account the opportunity to borrow, it is possible to approximate the best-portfolio frontier by a straight line. See ¶ 7.03.

[64] A portfolio can consist of one security, two securities, or many securities. It is simply synonymous with an investor's holdings at any given time.

[65] See also Cohen, "The Suitability Rule and Economic Theory," 80 Yale L.J. 1604, 1626-1627 (1971).

[66] Indifference curves are infinite in number, of course, since for every person, the number of utility levels possible is infinite.

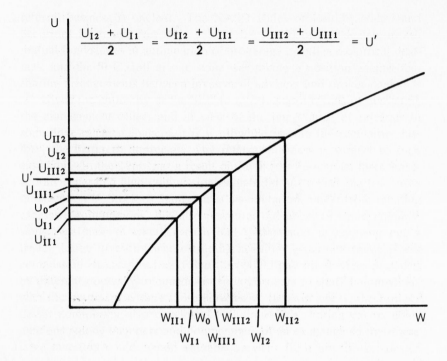

$$\frac{U_{I2} + U_{I1}}{2} = \frac{U_{II2} + U_{III}}{2} = \frac{U_{III2} + U_{IIII}}{2} = U'$$

Fig. 4-6

greater increments of return for each additional increment of risk he is asked to bear. This conclusion follows logically from the information contained in Figure 4-6. As uncertainty—that is, the distance between the final wealth positions possible as a result of investing in a particular program—increases, it takes greater and greater amounts of reward to maintain utility at a constant level.

The ideal combination of risk and return for the investor can be identified from Figure 4-8, which imposes the plot of the investor's indifference curves on the graph depicting the risk-return relationship for the set of best portfolios. All indifference curves which, like curve *c*, lie above and to the left of curve *b* represent investment programs which the investor would prefer but which cannot be carried out. At any level of risk along curve *c*, which is above and to the left of curve *b*, no portfolio exists which is capable of providing the level of return indicated by curve *c*. The return from all best portfolios at every level of risk is always below that capable of providing the level of utility indicated by curve *c*. On the other hand, though many portfolios having realizable risk and return characteristics lie along curve *a*, none of those

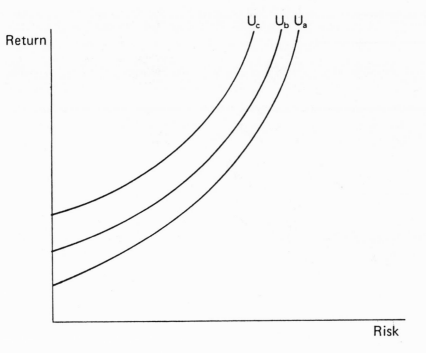

Fig. 4-7

portfolios is the most suitable for the investor. He will always prefer any portfolio lying along curve *b*, which is above and to the left of curve *a*, to any portfolio lying along curve *a*. For the same risk, every portfolio lying on curve *b* provides a higher return than a portfolio lying along curve *a*, and for any level of return, every portfolio lying along curve *b* has less risk than a portfolio lying along curve *a*. But curve *b* has realizable risk and return characteristics at only one point, and that is at the point of tangency between curve *b* and the line representing the set of best portfolios. Any other level of return at which the investor would be equally satisfied—that is, lying along curve *b*—is achievable only at a level of risk that the set of best portfolios cannot accommodate.

[5] How Suitability Continually Changes

But the task of determining the values of risk and return for the most suitable investment program is not complete, and indeed never can be complete, for as investment results are realized (and as the investor's fortunes change otherwise), the shift in wealth an investor experi-

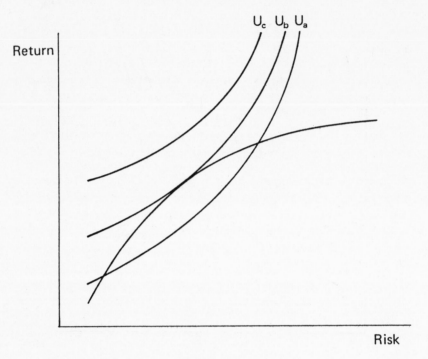

Fig. 4-8

ences affects his attitude toward investment opportunities. Technically, as wealth shifts, the change in utility offered by an investment opportunity changes even though the risk and return characteristics of the opportunity itself remain the same. This means that the sets of values for risk and return which determine the track of each of the investor's indifference curves will change also; consequently, there will be movement along the frontier of best portfolios of the point of tangency, the indicator of the most suitable level of risk and return.

The point that investors change their attitude toward investment opportunities as they realize investment results can be illustrated simply by the graph in Figure 4-9. Suppose an investor having the utility function pictured in Figure 4-9 has an initial wealth of W_0 and a consequent utility of U_0. Suppose further that over a designated period, investment opportunity A will either show a given rate of return or produce a given rate of loss with equal probability. By taking advantage of investment opportunity A, the investor's wealth will either rise to W_{A2} or fall to W_{A1}. Over an identical period, investment opportunity B will show a different rate of return or produce a different rate

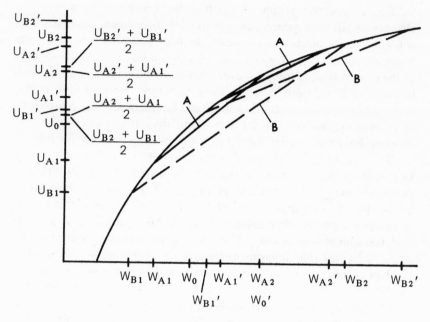

Fig. 4-9

of loss with equal probability. By taking advantage of investment opportunity B, the investor's wealth will either rise to W_{B2} or fall to W_{B1}. Note, however, that, considered prospectively, the opportunity to invest in each offers the same increase in utility from U_0 ($(U_{A2} + U_{A1})/2 = (U_{B2} + U_{B1})/2$.[67] From the investor's point of view, therefore, both A and B are equally attractive.

Suppose that the investor chose investment opportunity A, and that at the close of the investment period, he was fortunate enough to realize the gain A is capable of producing. The investor's new wealth position, therefore, is W_{A2}. Let us label that point also as W_0' to indicate it as his initial wealth position at the beginning of the second investment period. If he has the chance to choose again, the investor will no longer remain

---

[67] Note that neither A nor B is the most suitable opportunity for the investor at W_0. Since, by hypothesis, both A and B produce the same increase in utility, but differ in risk and return characteristics, they lie on an indifference curve which intersects the frontier of best portfolios at two points. That curve, of course, lies below and to the right of the curve tangent to the frontier of best portfolios, and hence contains portfolios which fail to raise utility as much as possible. See Figure 4-8. The analysis is simpler to illustrate, however, by use of the assumptions in the text.

indifferent between investment opportunities A and B, assuming neither changes its risk and return characteristics.[68] Investment opportunity A will either raise the investor's wealth to W_{A2}' or lower it to W_{A1}'. Investment opportunity B will either raise the investor's wealth to W_{B2}' or lower it to W_{B1}'. Note, however, that this time and for this investor, investing in B will raise his utility more than investing in A will. $((U_{A2}' + U_{A1}')/2 < (U_{B2}' + U_{B1}')/2.)$ From his point of view, therefore, investment opportunity B is more desirable than investment opportunity A, even though both offer the same prospects they have always offered.

This conclusion, although derived by graph, is realistic. A change in attitude toward investment opportunities that a shift in wealth produces is exactly what one would expect. The analysis drawn from Figure 4-9 suggests that chance of loss has relatively less influence on an investor's attitude than chance of gain as his wealth increases. Note that investment opportunity B offers a much greater opportunity for gain and for loss than investment opportunity A. Figure 4-9 shows that, if a loss occurs, investment opportunity B will yield a loss of about half again as much as investment opportunity A. If there is a gain, however, investment opportunity B will return over twice as much as investment opportunity A. At one point (W_0), B's capability of producing higher gains than A is offset in the investor's mind by the possibility that B will produce greater losses than A. Because the consequences of loss on standard of living diminish as wealth increases, the advantage of enhancing possible gains outstrips in impact the corresponding advantage of minimizing possible losses.

[6] The Limits on Lessons to Be Derived From Economic Theory

Economic theory offers some powerful insights into the meaning of suitability and, at the very least, focuses attention on the variables which determine whether an investment program is suitable. For example, an obvious implication of the preceding discussion is that an investment program which suffers setbacks should be reformed to a more conservative posture. Yet it is often the case that an investment manager will

---

[68] That is, for both investment opportunities, the probability of gain or loss is equal, and the amount of gain or loss remains the same:

Opportunity A:
$$W_{A2}' - W_0' = W_{A2} - W_0 \quad \text{(gain)}$$
$$W_0' - W_{A1}' = W_0 - W_{A1} \quad \text{(loss)}$$

Opportunity B:
$$W_{B2}' - W_0' = W_{B2} - W_0 \quad \text{(gain)}$$
$$W_0' - W_{B1}' = W_0 - W_{B1} \quad \text{(loss)}$$

react exactly the opposite and undertake greater risk in order to recoup losses as quickly as possible. But the lessons of economic theory are, at this stage, aids to analysis only. For as helpful as the principle of declining marginal utility of wealth may be in conceptualizing suitability, the precision to which it pretends is not yet fully translatable into practical usage.

The major difficulty is in determining any individual's utility function. Although some work has been done in developing techniques to map an individual's utility function,[69] the results remain far from conclusive. Still, the principle does have important implications for everyday practice. In theory, there exists for each investor a level of risk and return which best quantifies his investment objectives, however subjectively they may be expressed. In effect, the values of risk and return determined by the point of tangency of the key indifference curve and the line representing the set of best portfolios defines suitability for the investor. The legal question then becomes how much responsibility an investment manager should have to assure that the client's actual investment program approximates the values for risk and return that would be represented by the point of tangency. For example, to the extent the law permits a manager to handle an account for a client who states his investment objectives in such general terms as income, balance, growth, and aggressive growth, the manager's responsibility for determining suitability is small. He needs to know little more than the range of values along the frontier of best portfolios to which those terms ordinarily apply. He has virtually no obligation to take into account the crucial suitability variables—the client's wealth and attitude toward changes in wealth—except perhaps as those quantities are implied by the stated objectives.

Or, the law could place a far more demanding burden on a manager. It could insist that the manager design an investment program aimed at the values of risk and return indicated by the point of tangency in Figure 4-8. That would require that, before setting up an investment program, a manager determine a client's full financial condition and how the client would regard changes in that condition. Additionally, it would require the manager to adjust the investment program from time to time as realized results produce a shift in the client's wealth. The circumstances causing the legal standard to vary between these two extremes is the subject considered in ¶ 4.03.

---

[69] See Kassouf, "Towards a Legal Framework for Efficiency and Equity in the Securities Markets," 25 Hastings L.J. 417, 421 (1974).

¶ 4.03. AN EXAMINATION OF SUITABILITY ACCORDING TO LEGAL THEORY

On first impression, at least if conflicts of interest between manager and client are not present, it is difficult to see how imposing a duty of suitability on investment managers leads to much that is constructive. If an investment opportunity is accurately defined as suitable as long as it enhances an investor's satisfaction with his position, it seems that only an irrational person would undertake an investment program or make a commitment which makes him feel worse off.[70] Assuming that a client will not agree to investment programs which make him feel worse off, only by measuring suitability by an objective standard—that is, by what is good for the investor rather than what he thinks is good for him—can a conclusion of unsuitability with respect to an investment program the investor desires be sustained.[71] Furthermore, to hold an investment manager answerable on the basis of an objective suitability standard runs a substantial risk of unfairness. Suitability should be determined prospectively, according to the appropriateness of an investment program or a commitment before execution. But as a practical matter, compliance with a duty of suitability is determined after the returns are in. Client dissatisfaction with actual results might well influence a court or regulatory agency to find unsuitability and rationalize that conclusion under a standard appropriate for measuring the risk and

---

[70] Some persons may prefer risk, especially if the opportunities for gain are very high, even though the probability of loss causes the commitment to lose money on the average. See Friedman & Savage, "The Utility Analysis of Choices Involving Risk," 56 J. Pol. Econ. 279 (1948). Most investors, however, prefer to avoid risk, and it may be assumed that where a client repeatedly takes on risky commitments in an investment program of doubtful value, the client is acting sufficiently irrationally to preclude continuing an investment management relationship. Cf. Powers v. Francis I. DuPont & Co., 344 F. Supp. 429 (E.D. Pa. 1972), [1972-1973 Transfer Binder] CCH Fed. Sec. L. Rep. ¶ 93,584.

[71] Securities Act Rule 146(d), as proposed in its most recent revision, initially took the position that issuers and agents in private placements should have a suitability duty requiring both that the prospective investor be able to evaluate the issue and that the issue in fact be suitable. Rule 146(d) thus was positing both a subjective and an objective standard of suitability. As the rule was ultimately adopted, however, it required a determination either that the investor be capable of evaluating the risk involved on his own or that it be suitable. See Note, "Investor Suitability Standards in Real Estate Syndication: California's Procrustean Bed Approach," 63 Cal. L. Rev. 471, 495 (1975).

return preferences of an average investor instead of the complaining party.[72]

But this analysis holds only for investors who fully understand the risk and return characteristics of investment opportunities in which they may be placed. Yet a lack of such understanding can occur in two ways. First, an investor may be unable to evaluate investment opportunities presented to him. Suppose that an investment manager offers to place an investor's funds in one of several portfolios consisting of stocks and bonds. Unless the investor is capable of determining the risk and return characteristics of those portfolios and relating those values to his own tolerance for risk, he would be unable to decide whether any of those portfolios were suitable for him, much less which one was most suitable. Second, even if an investor is able to determine the risk and return characteristics of a portfolio, he may be unable to appreciate them sufficiently well to relate those values to his own tolerance for risk. To be told or to determine, for example, that a particular portfolio is one and one-half times as risky as another portfolio does little good unless the investor understands what is meant by portfolio risk in the first place. For purposes of analysis, the risk of an investment can be defined as the tendency of its actual return to vary from its predicted average return.[73] Many investors will find this concept too abstract to relate descriptions of portfolio risk to their own attitudes. If they cannot fully appreciate the terms in which investment risk is measured, they cannot determine the appropriateness to their own objectives of an investment opportunity of a stated level of risk and return.

The mere fact that clients may be unable to evaluate risk on their own does not justify imposing suitability responsibility on an investment manager. For one thing, it is often no mean task for a manager to arrive at the risk and return level appropriate for the client. The manager must calculate the client's wealth and tolerance for risk. Although calculating wealth is usually straightforward, it can require considerable effort, depending on the complexity of the client's financial posture. Even more difficult is calculating tolerance for risk. Although deductions made from a client's investment history and statements about plans and goals are helpful, these sources of information are hardly precise.

---

[72] See SEC v. American Agronomics Corp., Civil No. C72-331 (N.D. Ohio 1972) (unsuitable purchasers of grove securities entitled to rescission under judicial injunction).
[73] See ¶ 6.03[2].

In fact, they can be highly unreliable if the client is overstating his willingness to suffer losses or does not fully appreciate the relationship between risk and return in the marketplace.

Furthermore, the unreliability of statements about plans and goals can be exacerbated if the manager is hired by someone other than the client or there are competing interests to be served in the management of an account. The client of a trustee, for example, is the trust. It is not unusual for a trustee responsible for investment management to be hired by the settlor or by a co-trustee not only to select investments, but also to set investment objectives which balance the contending claims of income beneficiaries and remaindermen. In complex trust arrangements, the problem of competing interests can be particularly severe. In the case of a company-managed pension fund, for example, the client is ostensibly the fund. But often, the ones retaining the manager's services are officers of the company. They may have unrealistic attitudes about the prospects of investment.[74] Moreover, even if the officers have a realistic view of what is possible in the marketplace, they may be inclined to undertake excessive risk in order to keep company contributions to the fund low.[75] This not only hazards the pension rights of the employees, it also risks the capital of the stockholders in the event the company's investment program does not realize the return necessary to satisfy pension claims.[76] In either case, through their statements about investment objectives, the company officers may encourage the manager to take more risk than the client should bear.

There is another reason for not shifting the responsibility for suitability onto investment managers simply because a client may not be able to evaluate risk on his own. If every arrangement for providing investment management services imposed a corresponding duty that those services place clients only in suitable investments, it would be im-

---

[74] See Jansson, "Is Preservation of Capital Making a Comeback?" Institutional Investor 55, 56-57 (April 1974) (chief financial officer of a major foundation states that "investors almost always overstate their tolerance for volatility").

[75] See Bauer, "Are Unfunded Pension Liabilities Getting Out of Hand?" Institutional Investor 85 (April 1974).

[76] ERISA (29 U.S.C. §§ 1001 et seq.) establishes a nonprofit public corporation to guarantee partial payment of pension benefits to employees whose pension funds are inadequate to satisfy claims against them. ERISA, Title IV, Subtitles A and D. The assets of the employer setting up the pension fund are subject to "a lien in favor of the [pension benefit guaranty] corporation upon all property and rights to property, whether real or personal. . . ." ERISA § 4068(a), 29 U.S.C. § 1368(a).

possible to offer portfolio advisory services or portfolio management services alone. This would mean, among other things, that investment companies could not operate since the only service they provide is portfolio management. Nor could mass-published or limited-client investment advisory services operate, since their only service is to make recommendations about securities. Indeed, if a suitability determination were a mandatory legal requirement for every person offering investment management services, about all that organizations not equipped to make suitability determinations could offer would be information about securities published in a form which would require clients to determine the relative merits of the covered securities themselves.

The reason that the responsibility for suitability does not rest exclusively with the investment manager is that both parties can control the allocation of responsibility for suitability through contract. An investor desiring assistance in ascertaining the level of risk and return appropriate for him is entitled to rely entirely on an investment manager to make that determination and to design an investment program to accommodate it. But freedom of contract also permits investors to establish their own investment goals even if, in view of the means of the investor and the level of risk involved, others might regard those goals as unwise. Furthermore, investment managers can offer assistance in making suitability determinations if they believe that will help business or for any other reason. But freedom of contract also permits investment managers to establish limits on the services they provide even if that throws the burden on investors to determine for themselves the appropriateness of the offered services. Thus, in an action against a registered investment adviser on the grounds that a general suitability responsibility for statutory advisers is implied in the Investment Advisers Act of 1940,[77] the court said that "there would appear to be no reason for mandating such a standard across the board as long as the particular agreement is not inherently fraudulent and the parties clearly understand the nature of the services to be provided." [78]

---

[77] Anderson Co. v. John P. Chase, Inc., [1974-1975 Transfer Binder] CCH Fed. Sec. L. Rep. ¶ 95,009 (S.D.N.Y. 1975), *cert. denied* 424 U.S. 969 (1976).

[78] *Id.,* CCH Fed. Sec. L. Rep. at p. 97,509. Expanding on that theme, the court went on to say that "the parties were free to contract for the particular nature of the investment supervisory service to be provided, and . . . they indeed mutually agreed upon a far less extensive investment service than that represented by the full panoply of 'investment supervisory services' [referring to Investment Advisors Act § 202(a)(13), 15 U.S.C. § 80b-2; see note 130 *infra*] which plaintiffs presently discuss."

But although the parties can allocate responsibility for suitability themselves, many clients and investment managers enter into arrangements in which control of the allocation of that responsibility is not express. Moreover, it is widely assumed that clients lack the sophistication to make judgments about suitability as judiciously as can investment managers.[79] As a consequence, when investment management arrangements are silent about the allocation of responsibility for suitability, courts and regulatory authorities rely heavily on the circumstances surrounding the establishment and management of an account for the purpose of determining whether the client realized the degree of responsibility for suitability he was assuming. If an investment program or commitment does not actually prove to be suitable, and the facts fail to show that the client was aware he was assuming all or part of the responsibility for ascertaining suitability, the legal consequences of unsuitability will fall on the manager.[80]

The simplest way for an investment manager to satisfy himself that a client is making suitable investments is to make inquiries of the client as if the responsibility for making the suitability determination actually belonged to the manager. If the client's stated objectives seem outside the average levels of risk and return ordinarily undertaken by investors of comparable means, the manager could then advise the client of that fact and recommend an appropriate shift in investment approach. This is standard practice in the industry, and in *Anderson Co. v. John P. Chase, Inc.*, such practice was sufficient to insulate a manager from answerability for a client's insistence on margin trading and short selling to enhance investment profits.[81]

But it is not always possible to make full inquiry of the financial circumstances of a client. The client may keep crucial details confidential, or the type of arrangement—mass-marketed advisory letters, for example—may preclude gathering such information. Nevertheless, even

---

79 See, e.g., Cohen, "The Suitability Rule and Economic Theory," 80 Yale L.J. 1604, 1622 (1971).

80 In private placements, for example, if a prospective investor cannot evaluate the risk of the investment, the offeror and his agents must establish "that the offeree is able to bear the economic risk of the investment." Securities Act Rule 146(d)(2)(ii), 17 C.F.R. § 230.146(d)(2)(ii). See also Rolf v. Blyth Eastman Dillon & Co., [1976-1977 Transfer Binder] CCH Fed. Sec. L. Rep. ¶ 95,843 (S.D.N.Y. 1977)) (failure to inquire into investor's circumstances or intent).

81 Anderson Co. v. John P. Chase, Inc., [1974-1975 Transfer Binder] CCH Fed. Sec. L. Rep. ¶ 95,009 (S.D.N.Y. 1975), *cert. denied* 424 U.S. 969 (1976).

incomplete inquiry can suffice to make the determination that a proposed program or recommended commitment is suitable. There are many investment opportunities which are suitable in the sense that, taking both possible gain and loss into account, they lie within the investor's tolerance for risk. Where the relationship between the manager and client is sufficiently loose that no more is required of the investment manager than to choose investments lying within the client's tolerance for risk, rather than to identify the most suitable investment, it is plain that basic information about the client, of the type required by the stock exchange know-your-customer rules,[82] will ordinarily satisfy that standard. On the other hand, the more the client relies on the manager to find most suitable level of risk and return, the greater the amount of information the manager will need.

In view of the number of considerations which can influence the allocation of responsibility for suitability, it may be helpful to identify the factors which seem to control the authorities and to explain why those factors exert the control they do. As will be apparent from the discussion, each of the factors listed has one characteristic in common with the others: They all help establish as the critical consideration awareness on the part of either the investment manager or the client that the investment program or commitment at issue may be unsuitable for the client's account. This, of course, is just what one would expect. If the manager is or ought to be aware that the client does not recognize his own limited ability to evaluate the risk and return properties of a proposed investment program or commitment, the client's power to contract offers the client little protection against selection of unsuitable investments by the manager. On the other hand, if the client is or ought to be aware that the risk and return properties of investment opportunities offered to him may be unsuitable, the client can then contract to have a suitability determination made if he is so inclined.

---

[82] See NYSE Rule 405 (2 CCH NYSE Guide ¶ 2405), which requires that the broker generally obtain the "essential facts relative to every customer," particularly with regard to whether the orders are coming from an authorized source, and, if the customer is a corporation, whether the nature of the dealings is allowed by the corporation, by-laws, charter, or authorizations. AMEX Rule 411 (2 CCH AMEX Guide ¶ 9431) similarly requires the broker to acquire the "essential facts relative to the customer and to the nature of the account." Finally, the NASD Rules of Fair Practice, Art. III, § 2 (CCH NASD Manual ¶ 2152), mandate that a broker make recommendations "upon the basis of the facts, if any, disclosed by the customer as to his other security holdings and as to his financial situation and needs."

[1] Factors Tending to Shift Responsibility for Suitability to the Manager

[a] The level of risk in a proposed investment program or recommended commitment

A rational investor who would make unsuitable investments is, by definition, incapable of evaluating the suitability of a proposed investment program or recommended commitment. To the extent he seeks investment management services, therefore, he is relying on the judgment of others about suitability. If one providing these services is aware of his client's reliance, but causes the client to make unsuitable investments nonetheless, he violates his duty of suitability. Thus, in *Shearson, Hammill & Co.*, the SEC imposed sanctions on a brokerage firm and a number of its employees for "glaring examples of recommendations . . . to customers contrary to their needs." [83] The evidence showed that most of the respondents were serving their own interests in inducing the transactions at issue.[84] It also showed that some of the business stimulated developed from an overexuberant devotion to a very risky stock.[85] Regardless of the motivation, however, the Commission concluded that suitability violations under Section 10(b) of the Securities Exchange Act and Section 206 of the Investment Advisers Act had occurred.

But if deliberately causing clients to undertake investment programs or make commitments known to exceed the client's tolerance for risk plainly violates the duty of suitability, it is not a difficult step to the position that causing a client to undertake an investment program or a commitment which the manager ought to know exceeds the client's

---

[83] SEC Securities Exchange Act Release No. 7743 (Nov. 12, 1965), [1964-1966 Transfer Binder] CCH Fed. Sec. L. Rep. ¶ 77,306, at 82,525.

[84] The Commission found, among other things, indefensibly high turnover—over seventy times in approximately nine months in one case—in the accounts of small investors, the switching of mutual funds with no apparent aim except to earn underwriting commissions, and the splitting of mutual fund purchases among several funds in order to raise the total underwriting commission. One salesman who had caused a customer to switch mutual funds admitted that he had placed the customer in the first fund while working at another brokerage house in order to win a vacation trip. *Id.* at 82,534.

[85] The record showed that several of the respondents invested in the stock on no better information than they provided their customers. To this the Commission replied that "a salesman's willingness to speculate with his own funds without reliable information gives him no license to make false and misleading representations to induce his customer to speculate." *Id.* at 82,525.

tolerance for risk is equally a violation of that duty. Again, there is the requisite reliance on the part of the client. The only difference is that the manager's exposure of his client to risk beyond the client's tolerance results not from a deliberate decision to do so, but as a side effect of other objectives which induce the manager simply to ignore the suitability issue. For example, the SEC proceeded against a leading brokerage house for establishing a quota sales system for its account executives.[86] The account executives, to make their quotas, were intentionally encouraging clients to make unsuitable commitments, sometimes by selling securities which were subject to buy or hold recommendations by respondent's own research department, a fact of which respondent was not shown to be aware. Nonetheless, respondent should have realized the tendency for the quota system to lead to unsuitable recommendations, and, in its offer of settlement, it agreed to review and revise its selling practices.

This principle, establishing as a violation of the duty of suitability knowingly or negligently causing a client to make unsuitable investments, has particularly strong application where a proposed investment program or recommended commitment involves an above-average degree of risk. If, in such case, an investment manager makes no suitability inquiry, he should realize that there is a high probability that at least some of his clients will not be suited to participate. The conclusion that high-risk portfolio management must be informed by a suitability inquiry found its earliest expression in cases involving recommendations of speculative securities by broker-dealers who made virtually no suitability inquiry,[87] a position reinforced by the National Association of Securities Dealers (NASD) Rules of Fair Practice.[88] In enforcement proceedings[89] and

---

[86] *In re* Merrill Lynch, Pierce, Fenner & Smith, Inc., SEC Securities Exchange Act Release No. 11515 (June 30, 1975), [1975-1976 Transfer Binder] CCH Fed. Sec. L. Rep. ¶ 80,216.

[87] See, e.g., *In re* Tallman, SEC Securities Exchange Act Release No. 8830 (March 2, 1970), [1969-1970 Transfer Binder] CCH Fed. Sec. L. Rep. ¶ 77,800.

[88] Art. III, § 2 (CCH NASD Manual ¶ 2152) describes as unsuitable:

"Recommending speculative low-priced securities to customers without knowledge of or attempt to obtain information concerning the customers' other securities holdings, their financial situation and other necessary data. The principle here is that this practice, by its very nature, involves a high probability that the recommendation will not be suitable for at least some of the persons solicited. . . ."

[89] SEC v. Goldstein-Samuelson, Inc., [1972-1973 Transfer Binder] CCH Fed. Sec. L. Rep. ¶ 93,800 (C.D. Cal. 1973) (summary of complaint).

in no-action letters,[90] the SEC quickly extended application of the rule to high-risk options investment programs and to discretionary management of accounts engaging in margin purchasing and short selling.[91]

[*i*] *Source of Risk:* There are three contexts in which investment managers should be alert to the possibility that, because of the attendant high risk, their actions may involve unsuitability and therefore require suitability inquiries to reasonably insure that their proposals are suitable for each client. The first and most obvious of these is the inclusion in a client's portfolio of one or more risky securities. Although the suitability doctrine developed out of high-pressure broker-dealer promotions of risky securities, it has matured well beyond the boiler room cases and now is concerned with all types of risky securities. Through direct SEC action and through pressure on the self-regulatory organizations, the past few years have seen the establishment of suitability rules dealing with new issues,[92] tax-shelters,[93] hot issues,[94] private place-

---

The SEC alleged that an investment corporation, offering customers "options" in commodities futures which were in fact unrelated to the commodities futures market, was subjecting its customers to the general risks of the success of the corporation (which was not obligated to deal in futures and might instead invest clients' funds as it saw fit). The complaint asked for a temporary and permanent injunction.

[90] See Goldman, Sachs & Co., [1970-1971 Transfer Binder] CCH Fed. Sec. L. Rep. ¶ 78,159 (1971).

[91] See John G. Kinnard & Co., [1973-1974 Transfer Binder] CCH Fed. Sec. L. Rep. ¶ 79,662 (1973).

[92] SEC Securities Act Release No. 5275 (July 26, 1972), 1 CCH Fed. Sec. L. Rep. ¶ 4506B.

[93] See Section 5 of proposed Section 33, Art. III, NASD Rules of Fair Practice, summarized in SEC Securities Exchange Act Release No. 10260 (July 2, 1973), [1973 Transfer Binder] CCH Fed. Sec. L. Rep. ¶ 79,417. The original proposal was issued on May 9, 1972. The SEC objected to the NASD proposed rule on the grounds that its substantive regulation requirements affected nonmembers, especially issuers desiring access to the capital markets. The Commission endorsed the general approach of the rule, however, and suggested that it could act as an effective set of guidelines to satisfy suitability requirements in tax-shelter programs. In effect, the Commission proposed to give the rule the force of law without rendering it a mandatory standard: To contravene it, a broker-dealer would need to be able to justify doing so in advance. Apparently, the SEC is also desirous of bringing the regulation of real estate tax shelters and oil and gas tax shelters under its own roof. See Note, "Investment Suitability Standards in Real Estate Syndication: California's Procrustean Bed Approach," 63 Cal. L. Rev. 471, 487 n.94 (1975).

[94] See note 92 *supra*.

ments,[95] and, most recently, investments in options.[96]

Another context in which responsibility for suitability tends to be shifted to investment managers is risky trading. Portfolio management policies involving heavy turnover are doubtful means of enhancing profits[97] and are viewed with a great deal of suspicion.[98] Especially where the profits of the person providing management services depend at least in part on the amount of trading a client does, there is a strong obligation to show that trading policies accord with the objectives and financial circumstances of a client.[99] But suitability responsibility also lies with the manager for accounts dealing with sophisticated trading techniques such as purchasing on margin and short selling. For example, in *John G. Kinnard & Co.*,[100] a request for a no-action letter by a registered investment adviser planning to offer margin-purchasing and short-selling services to clients with a minimum account size of $15,000, the staff took the position that "many potential clients willing and able to invest this amount may nevertheless be unsuitable prospects for the service. This suggests the need for the formulation of adequate suitability standards and very thorough screening procedures in determining the acceptability of potential clients."

---

[95] Securities Act Rule 146(d), 17 C.F.R. § 230.146(d).

[96] See Goldman, Sachs & Co., [1970-1971 Transfer Binder] CCH Fed. Sec. L. Rep. ¶ 78,159 (1971). See also the directive of the Comptroller of the Currency (July 2, 1974), approving options dealing by banks in behalf of trust accounts for which options dealing is suitable. CCH Bank. L. Rep. ¶ 96,295.

[97] See Sharpe, "Likely Gains for Market Timing," 31 Fin. Anal. J. 60 (March-April 1975).

[98] See *In re* Shearson, Hammill & Co., [1964-1966 Transfer Binder] CCH Fed. Sec. L. Rep. ¶ 77,306 (1965). See also SEC, *Report of the Advisory Comm. on Investment Management Services for Individual Investors, Small Account Investment Management Services,* reprinted in CCH Fed. Sec. L. Rep., No. 465, Pt. III, at 43; SEC, *Institutional Investor Study,* Vol. I at pp. xii-xiii, and Vol. II, ch. 4, H.R. Doc. No. 64, 92d Cong., 1st Sess. (1971); SEC, *Report of Special Study of the Securities Market,* H.R. Doc. No. 95, 88th Cong., 1st Sess. Pt. 5, 49-56 (1963).

[99] See NYSE Rule 408(c) (2 CCH NYSE Guide ¶ 2408), which states:

"No member . . . exercising discretionary power in any customer's account shall . . . effect purchases or sales of securities which are excessive in size or frequency in view of the financial resources of such customer."

See also AMEX Rule 3(a) (2 CCH AMEX Guide ¶ 9223).

[100] [1973-1974 Transfer Binder] CCH Fed. Sec. L. Rep. ¶ 79,662 (1973).

Finally, an investment manager may increase his responsibility for suitability as his proposals increase the strain on a client's financial ability to carry them out. There is a specific prohibition imposed by the NASD Rules of Fair Practice against inducing a client to invest beyond his immediate resources.[101] To do so forces the client, in effect, to leverage his account and thereby subjects the client to the possibility of catastrophic losses as the result of short-term market fluctuations. In one case, for example, a broker-dealer recommended that a nonprofit institution purchase Government National Mortgage Association when-issued commitments and other short-, intermediate-, and long-term government securities in excess of the client's financial capacity.[102] Since the overcommitment forced the client to sell prior to settlement date, the success of the investment program depended entirely on interest-rate movement. The broker-dealer eventually settled the unsuitability claims of the client and agreed in administrative proceedings to undertake steps which would reduce the possibility of a recurrence.

[ii] *Relationship Between Risk and Suitability Duty:* It is not astonishing that the authorities tend to impose a greater burden on investment managers to make a suitability inquiry as the risk of the vehicle they offer to their clients increases. This only reflects application of standard negligence doctrine which adds to the burden of adequate precautions for any activity as the probability and gravity of harm increase.[103] But less clear than the fact that a suitability duty exists in connection with a manager's excursions into risky ventures is the nature of the duty. Although stock exchange rules suggest that suitability determinations ordinarily may be made on the basis of information furnished by the client,[104] where the venture is especially

---

101 NASD Rules of Fair Practice, Art. III, § 2 (CCH NASD Manual ¶ 2152), lists as a violation of suitability requirements:

"5. Recommending the purchase of securities or the continuing purchase of securities in amounts which are inconsistent with the reasonable expectation that the customer has the financial ability to meet such a commitment."

102 *In re* Merrill Lynch, Pierce, Fenner & Smith, Inc., SEC Securities Exchange Act Release No. 11515 (June 30, 1975), [1975-1976 Transfer Binder] CCH Fed. Sec. L. Rep. ¶ 80,216.

103 See, e.g., United States v. Carroll Towing Co., 159 F.2d 169 (2d Cir. 1947) (per Learned Hand, J.).

104 See, e.g., NASD Rules of Fair Practice, Art. III, § 2 (CCH NASD Manual ¶ 2152), which states:

risky, the SEC apparently feels that broad-based public sales are suspect. For example, the Commission staff refused to take a no-action position on suitability in the case of a proposal to market down-and-out options only to highly sophisticated individual and institutional investors of substantial wealth.[105] The staff said that full disclosure of the risk, with the adequacy of disclosure measured on a case-by-case basis, would also be required.

Another indicator of the unsettled state of the Commission's attitude toward suitability determinations with respect to risky securities can be drawn from the background to adoption of Rule 146, the private-placement rule.[106] As the most recent version was originally proposed by the SEC, Rule 146(d) imposed two suitability conditions conjunctively; both had to be satisfied for an investor to be eligible to participate in a private placement. First, the offeror had to determine "that the purchaser or his adviser be sophisticated" [107]—that is, that the investor be capable of evaluating the risk of the private placement. And second, the offeror had to make the independent determination that the investor be "able to bear the economic risks of the investment." [108] In the face of criticism of the proposed rule, the Commission gave ground and adopted the two conditions disjunctively. Under existing law, only one or the other must be satisfied.[109] Nonetheless, the Commission's

---

"In recommending to a customer the purchase, sale or exchange of any security, a member shall have reasonable grounds for believing that the recommendation is suitable for such customer upon the basis of the facts, if any, disclosed by such customer as to his other security holdings and as to his financial situation and needs."

[105] Goldman, Sachs & Co., [1970-1971 Transfer Binder] CCH Fed. Sec. L. Rep. ¶ 78,159. See also SEC Proposed Rule 9b-2, SEC Securities Exchange Act Release No. 105540 (Dec. 13, 1973), 2 CCH Fed. Sec. L. Rep. ¶ 22,623.

[106] 17 C.F.R. § 230.146.

[107] See Securities Act Release No. 5336 (Nov. 28, 1972), [1972-1973 Transfer Binder] CCH Fed. Sec. L. Rep. ¶ 79,108.

[108] Id.

[109] The term "sophisticated investor" was also replaced by a phrasing intended to be equivalent in effect, but more descriptive of the regulatory intent. Rule 146(d), 17 C.F.R. 230.146(d), provides:

"The issuer and any person acting on its behalf who offer, offer to sell, offer for sale or sell the securities shall have reasonable grounds to believe and shall believe:

. . . .

"(2) Immediately prior to making any sale, after making reasonable inquiry, either:

initial position on suitability determinations in private placements, particularly when read against some of its other statements on suitability,[110] raises the question of how intensely a manager must review a client's financial position and even suggests that a manager may act only on the basis of his own independent suitability evaluation regardless of the client's stated preference.[111]

[iii] *Presumptive Risk and Sophisticated Investment Techniques:* There is another problem in determining the scope of an investment manager's responsibility for determining suitability. The courts and the regulatory authorities take a rather simpleminded approach to determining when a vehicle is to be treated as involving high risk. Typically, the high-risk label attaches to particular securities, investment programs, trading techniques, and so forth without regard to whether they are truly unusually risky in the individual case. As the discussion above has shown,[112] this attitude has resulted in classifying the purchase and sale of options, new issues and hot issues, margin purchasing, and short selling as speculative without regard to whether, individually or in combination, they might actually help produce a relatively safe and sound investment approach.[113] Actually, as contemporary portfolio theory demonstrates, many securities, investment vehicles, and invest-

---

"(i) That the offeree has such knowledge and experience in financial and business matters that he is capable of evaluating the merits and risks of the prospective investment, or

"(i) That the offeree and his offeree representative(s) together have such knowledge and experience in financial and business matters that they are capable of evaluating the merits and risks of the prospective investment and that the offeree is able to bear the economic risk of the investment."

[110] See, e.g., SEC, *Policy Statement on Future Structure of the Securities Markets* (Feb. 2, 1972), CCH Fed. Sec. L. Rep. [Report Binder] ¶ 74,811 at 65,620.

[111] Should the suitability doctrine reach this point, it would be a regrettable extension of the law, for it fails to take into account the fact that the attitude toward risk of clients standing in an identical financial posture can differ markedly. See ¶ 4.02 *supra*. The practical result of extending the law to this point is to treat all investors having a comparable financial posture alike. This either denies investors who are more amenable to risk than others the opportunity to engage in investments which suit them, or it gives them an opportunity to charge their managers with suitability violations if their investment programs turn out to be unsuccessful even though they were in fact suitable.

[112] See text at notes 92-102 *supra*.

[113] See ¶ 6.02[1].

ment techniques which, when considered in isolation, appear to be very risky, can reduce the risk in a portfolio when they are properly co-ordinated. The discussion in Part III deals extensively with why this is so.[114] But since it is so, a strong argument can be made that an investment manager's responsibility for making a suitability inquiry should depend on the factual question of whether the manager's actions actually cause a client to increase the risk of his portfolio measurably.[115]

On the other hand, although many of these tools of investment management have the power to reduce risk if handled properly, their unskilled use can raise the risk of a portfolio dramatically. Moreover, skill in their use is not easy to acquire. Perhaps, since many persons offering investment management services lack the requisite skill to handle these investment techniques properly, it is justifiable policy to place them automatically in a suspect classification and increase a manager's suitability duty if he relies on them. Certainly, in view of the potential for harm in the event of misuse, it is easy to understand why the courts and the regulatory authorities uniformly treat these techniques as of high risk regardless of how they are utilized on behalf of a particular account and regardless of the qualifications of an investment manager. For example, the Comptroller of the Currency has authorized national banks to engage in options dealing for trust accounts so long as that authority is conferred by the trust. But the Comptroller's directive also imposes a correlative duty of suitability which makes no distinction between the purchase and sale of options to enhance returns by raising risk and the purchase and sale of options to stabilize returns to reduce risk.[116]

---

[114] See ¶¶ 7.02[1], 7.03[3][a], 7.05.

[115] See Cohen, "The Suitability Rule and Economic Theory," 80 Yale L.J. 1604, 1625-1633 (1971).

[116] See Trust Banking Circular No. 2 (July 2, 1974) (CCH Fed. Bank. L. Rep. ¶ 96,295), in which the Administrator of National Banks states in part, ". . . we shall not object to the writing of call options on securities held in trust department accounts where specific authority for such trans-actions is contained in the governing instrument of the particular account, and where the particular transaction is appropriate for the account." *Id.* at 81,411. Although skillful options dealing can help attenuate fluctuations in the return of an account and therefore can be an effective risk-control device, to accomplish this, options purchases and sales must be carried out in co-ordination with other portfolio management techniques. The mere purchase or sale of options without regard to the effect on the remainder of a port-folio only enhances the consequences of movement in the optioned securities and thus increases risk. The Comptroller could have taken the position in

But while the inclination of courts and regulatory authorities to treat sophisticated investment techniques as inherently risky may be understandable, such a regulatory approach creates a problem for investment managers. Suppose a manager, possessing the requisite skills, can design an options program which will effectively reduce the risk in a client's portfolio without substantially affecting the client's average returns. He may, for example, desire to write calls[117] against a small portion of an existing position in a security he is holding for long-term investment. Executed properly, this kind of program can reduce the volatility[118] of the portfolio and thus control risk.[119] But despite the power of a properly run options program to control risk, a regulatory approach which treats all sophisticated investment techniques as inherently risky would seem to require a suitability inquiry to determine that all options dealing is suitable for the client. Suppose, then, that the manager makes a suitability inquiry and concludes that his proposed options program is suitable for the client.[120] Suppose further that a program of straight options buying to achieve high returns by leveraging the capital appreciation of the underlying securities would be too risky for that client because if the anticipated market rise failed to occur, the entire investment in the options would be lost.[121] If the

---

the directive that suitability determinations were required only for the latter type of options dealing. Instead, the directive imposes a duty to make a suitability inquiry on all banks engaging in options dealing regardless of the purpose of the program. A fuller discussion of the use of options as a risk-control device appears in ¶ 7.05.

[117] Calls are options to buy securities at a specified price and within a specified time period.

[118] The volatility of a security or a portfolio is the amount it rises and falls in price relative to changes in market price levels. See ¶ 7.03[1]. Volatility is also used more loosely simply to mean the general tendency of a security or a portfolio to vary in price.

[119] See, e.g., Brody, "Options and the Mathematics of Defense," J. Portfolio Management 35 (Winter 1975). See also B. Malkiel & R. Quandt, *Strategies and Rational Decisions in the Securities Options Market* (1969).

[120] It is difficult to imagine how the proposed program would not be suitable for the client since, by hypothesis, the inclusion of options in the client's portfolio reduces risk without significantly affecting return.

[121] The leveraging effect of purchasing options works both ways. If the price of the underlying security moves in the direction of the option purchased, the returns are far greater than would be the case if only the underlying security were owned, because a given amount of money invested in options permits the control of many more shares of stock than would be the case if the money were put entirely into the stock. The problem is that if the price of the stock does not move in the direction of the option, no

suitability doctrine were interpreted to impose uniform, or at least minimum, suitability criteria for all clients without regard to the purpose of a given options program, it would preclude options programs for all investors for whom straight options buying as a means of seeking high profits at admittedly high risk is not suitable. In that event, a manager would not be able to avail his clients of options programs designed to reduce risk.

[iv] *Questions of Professional Competence Masquerading as Questions of Suitability:* Since such a result would be foolish, one can expect that the suitability doctrine will not develop in this way, and indeed, the record shows that, in the case of options, many investment managers have begun running programs for clients who could not possibly qualify as suitable for high-risk options programs.[122] But at the same time, a nagging worry remains that, in the event of a lawsuit by a disgruntled client, the imposition of a special suitability obligation on a program designed to control risk—simply because the program is based on an investment technique which, applied differently or misused, can raise risk—will complicate the defense for the manager. Suppose, for example, a client sues for damages, alleging that options dealing was unsuitable for his account. If some kind of special suitability obligation associated with options programs is permitted to color the litigation, it may happen that a program designed to control risk will actually be treated as if it were of high risk, and on that basis be found unsuitable for the client. Such a result would, in effect, turn questions of competence into questions of suitability in a way that would blur distinctions between the purposes underlying the use of different investment techniques.

Furthermore, the problem of translating questions of competence into questions of suitability is more severe the less widely recognized a particular program is. Options programs, despite the presence of special suitability requirements, at least have the implied assent of important regulatory authorities. In addition to the Comptroller of the Currency, state insurance commissions have begun expressly authorizing options dealing on the part of insurance companies.[123] But

---

profit is possible. Furthermore, after a stated period, the option expires. If the investor had purchased the stock instead, he would still own his equity share in the company, albeit at an unchanged or reduced market value. Nonetheless, his losses would plainly be much less unless the stock also dropped to zero value during the option period.

[122] See ¶ 7.05 at notes 72-86.

[123] See, e.g., 11 New York Code of Regulations, Pt. 174 (1975).

in *Trustees of Hanover College v. Donaldson, Lufkin & Jenrette*,[124] the plaintiffs alleged the unsuitability of individual securities in a program that apparently was intended to control risk through a total-return approach by blending low-volatility and high-volatility securities.[125] The case was eventually settled, so it is impossible to determine what the resolution of the suitability issue would have been. Nonetheless, the fact that the plaintiffs made an unsuitability claim amply demonstrates how easy it is to shift attention from the competence with which a program is conceived and executed to the suitability of investment objectives that may never have been contemplated in the first place.[126]

[b] The nature of the management relationship; discretionary authority

Also important to determining the responsibility of an investment manager for suitability is the nature of the management relationship. If the formal arrangements indicate that the client is placing heavy reliance on the manager's judgment, the manager has more responsibility than if he were serving merely a supportive role in setting investment

---

[124] Civil No. 71-C686 (S.D. Ind. 1971). For a reportorial description of the litigation, see Belliveau, "Discretion or Indiscretion?" 6 Institutional Investor 65 (Aug. 1972).

[125] A fuller discussion of the *Hanover College* case and the use of high-volatility securities to control risk appears in ¶¶ 7.04, 7.05.

[126] A suitability claim may also reflect an attempt to shift inquiry away from the question of whether investment authority has been properly delegated. Trustees have a duty not to delegate "the doing of acts which the trustee can reasonably be required personally to perform." *Restatement (Second) of Trusts* § 171 (1959). See also *id.* § 379, Comment a. On the other hand, a trustee is not answerable for the acts of agents if the tasks they perform are proper in carrying out the trust. See *id.* § 225(1). In recent years, it has become acceptable practice for trustees to delegate investment management responsibility to professional investment managers. See, e.g., Uniform Management of Institutional Funds Act (7 *U.L.A.*) § 5 (1971-1976 Supp.) (1972). Indeed, delegation to professionals is actively encouraged. See ERISA §§ 402(c)(3), 405(d), 29 U.S.C. §§ 1102(c)(3), 1105(d). But it is not clear that trustees also can delegate suitability responsibility to investment managers. Thus, in *Hanover College*, the trustees may have been facing personal liability if they permitted the defendant-manager to set suitability constraints and then invest accordingly. By suing on grounds that particular securities were unsuitable, the trustees effectively shifted attention away from their own suitability responsibility for setting the objectives for the entire account and the degree to which they lawfully can delegate that responsibility.

objectives and making investment decisions. A trust, for example, suggests a more exacting duty of suitability[127] than an agreement to provide "a flow of investment information." [128] Implied in proposed Investment Advisers Act Rule 206(4)-4[129] is a like distinction between an agency agreement for "investment supervisory services" [130] and an agreement for advisory support services. The rule requires advance disclosure of "the factors relating to the individual circumstances of any client which the investment manager considers" [131] for advisers providing investment supervisory services, but not for other statutory advisers.

Especially significant in tipping suitability responsibility toward the manager is the existence of discretionary authority because such authority is an obvious indication that the client places great reliance on the judgment of the manager. This is not to say that the absence of discretionary authority insulates a manager from responsibility for suitability. The course of dealing between a client and manager may show that although the client retained nominal authority, he followed his manager's advice with enough consistency to make the relationship virtually a discretionary account.[132] Furthermore, recent legislation has largely discarded the approach of making investor protection contingent on whether actual discretionary authority is vested in the manager and has adopted the idea of control or influence on the part of the manager in the investment process as the critical determinant. The Employee Retirement Income Security Act of 1974 (ERISA) defines "fiduciary" [133]

---

[127] See, e.g., Piper, Jaffray & Hopwood, Inc. v. Ladin, 399 F. Supp. 292 (D. Iowa 1975).

[128] Anderson Co. v. John P. Chase, Inc., [1974-1975 Transfer Binder] CCH Fed. Sec. L. Rep. ¶ 95,009 (S.D.N.Y. 1975), cert. denied 424 U.S. 969 (1976), at 97,509.

[129] SEC Investment Advisers Act Release No. 442 (March 5, 1975), [1974-1975 Transfer Binder] CCH Fed. Sec. L. Rep. ¶ 80,128.

[130] Investment supervisory services are defined in Investment Advisers Act § 202(a)(13) (15 U.S.C. § 80b-2(a)(13)) as "[T]he giving of continuous advice as to the investment of funds on the basis of the individual needs of each client."

[131] Proposed Rule 206(4)-4(c)(4), [1974-1975 Transfer Binder] CCH Fed. Sec. L. Rep. ¶ 80,128.

[132] See SEC, *Report of the Advisory Comm. on Investment Management Services for Individual Investors, Small Account Investment Management Services,* CCH Fed. Sec. L. Rep. No. 465, Pt. III, at 19 (1973).

[133] ERISA § 3(21)(A) (29 U.S.C. § 1002(21)(A)) treats equally as fiduciaries those who exercise discretionary authority and those rendering investment advice for a fee. It provides that ". . . a person is a fiduciary with respect to a plan to the extent (i) he exercises any discretionary author-

and the Securities Acts Amendments of 1975 define "investment discretion" [134] to equate the existence of influence and control over the purchase and sale of securities with contractual discretionary authority. To the extent that the form of the relationship puts the manager on notice of the existence of a greater responsibility for suitability, the existence of discretionary authority or its statutory equivalent is an especially significant feature.

But there is danger of too great a reliance on formal arrangements giving a manager control over the selection of investments and maintenance of a portfolio to determine the extent of a manager's suitability obligations. An investment manager for a directory trust, for example, might find himself obliged to evaluate the suitability of a proposed investment program even though his authority extends only to selecting securities for and maintaining a portfolio within determined risk and return constraints. The problem of relying on form to expand suitability responsibilities is especially acute in the case of institutional clients, where hybrid arrangements often characterize management relationships. The law now permits the trustees of pension funds and endowment funds to extend a great deal of management responsibility to professional investment managers.[135] Plainly, authorizing the manager to set risk and

ity or discretionary control respecting management or disposition of its assets, (ii) he renders investment advice for a fee or other compensation, direct or indirect, with respect to any moneys or other property of such plan, or has any authority or responsibility to do so . . . ." Investment advice has been defined more fully by regulation. See 29 C.F.R. § 2510.3-21 and 26 C.F.R. § 54.4975-9, discussed more fully in ¶ 10.03[2].

[134] Securities Act Amendments of 1975 § 3(6) amended Securities Exchange Act of 1934 § 3 (15 U.S.C. § 78c) to include new Section 3(a)(35), defining investment discretion as follows:

"A person exercises 'investment discretion' with respect to an account if, directly or indirectly, such person (A) is authorized to determine what securities or other property shall be purchased or sold by or for the account, (B) makes decisions as to what securities or other properties shall be purchased or sold by or for the account even though some other person may have responsibility for such investment decisions, or (C) otherwise exercises such influence with respect to the purchase and sale of securities or other property by or for the account as the Commission, by rule, determines, in the public interest or for the protection of investors, should be subject to the operation of the provisions of this title and the rules and regulations thereunder."

[135] See ERISA § 402(c)(3), 29 U.S.C. § 1102(c)(3); Uniform Management of Institutional Funds Act § 5 (1972); Cary & Bright, "The Delegation of Investment Responsibility for Endowment Funds," 74 Colum. L. Rev. 207 (1974).

return objectives for an account is a different case from entrusting the manager with discretionary authority only to construct and maintain a portfolio within preset objectives. Yet there is a possibility that the underlying formal structure will mask this critical distinction, and that a manager will be invested with suitability responsibility when his authority does not include the power to determine suitability limits.

[i] *Working Within Preset Risk-Return Constraints: The Investment Company Model:* A good way to illustrate the importance to the allocation of suitability responsibility of the distinction between general discretionary authority and discretionary authority limited to structuring and maintaining a portfolio within predetermined risk and return constraints is to consider the suitability obligations of open-end and closed-end management investment companies. The shareholders of these companies entrust their officers and investment advisers with extensive discretionary authority to purchase and sell securities. Indeed, as a practical matter, the discretionary authority afforded management is virtually without restriction. The only practical recourse for a shareholder in an investment company who disagrees with the portfolio selections of management is to sell his shares and terminate the management relationship.[136] Despite this broad discretionary authority, however, the suitability responsibilities of management are modest. Shares in no-load investment companies are ordinarily sold through the mail, and there is no suggestion that management be required to make a suitability inquiry of every investor requesting to purchase

---

[136] A successful derivative action or management ouster is highly unlikely, although there have been one or two reports in recent years of management shifts under pressure. For example, see "Fund Group Becomes First to Fire Its Manager," Wall Street Letter, Dec. 17, 1973, p. 5. A suit for breach of statutory fiduciary duty under Investment Company Act § 36(a) (15 U.S.C. § 80a-35(a)) is also a possibility. That section, however, is limited to a "breach of fiduciary duty involving personal misconduct," and by its terms is available only for enforcement by the SEC (but see Rosenfeld v. Black, 445 F.2d 1337 (2d Cir. 1971), *appeal dism'd sub nom.* Lazard Freres & Co. v. Rosenfeld, 409 U.S. 802 (1972)). When mismanagement is egregious, the SEC has statutory authority to seek the appointment of a receiver. Investment Company Act § 42(r), 15 U.S.C. § 80a-41(e). In a case allegedly involving the payment of fictitious finders' fees, "mismanagement, negligence, fraud and outright conversion," primarily by insiders scalping on investment company purchases, the SEC successfully petitioned for appointment of a receiver. SEC v. Seaboard Corp., SEC Litigation Release No. 6269 (C.D. Cal. 1974), [1973-1974 Transfer Binder] CCH Fed. Sec. L. Rep. ¶ 94,415 (summary of complaint).

shares.[137] Even in the case of companies whose shares are offered subject to a sales load or underwriting commission, management's suitability responsibilities are not significant, except, perhaps, to the extent management is or should be aware of sales representatives selling shares to unsuitable customers. From management's point of view, the major regulatory concern with selling practices has been that sales loads not be excessive.[138] Suitability obligations to purchasers of investment com-

---

[137] Suitability responsibility in the sale of no-load investment company shares may fall on brokers who charge a fee for services rendered in connection with the purchase or sale of such shares, unless it was clear from the transaction that the broker's duties were purely ministerial and did not involve any advice or assistance in selecting among available no-load companies. Although the SEC permits brokers to charge reasonable fees for their services, Commission approval is strictly conditioned in circumstances in which temptations to ignore suitability obligation are severe. No charge is permitted if an affiliation exists between the broker and the company, its investment adviser, or principal underwriter. The fund may not encourage the broker to make the charge or give the broker any special treatment. The fund's prospectus must disclose that such a charge may be made. The prospectus must state that if shares are purchased directly from the fund, there is no service charge. See Fahnestock & Co., [1974-1975 Transfer Binder] CCH Fed. Sec. L. Rep. ¶ 80,079 (1974). Compare note 139 infra. The staff also takes the position that fees for no-load purchases are excessive if they are unreasonable in relation to the cost of providing "ministerial" services. Parker/Hunter, Inc., [1975-1976 Transfer Binder] CCH Fed. Sec. L. Rep. ¶ 80,226 (1975). Limiting broker-dealers to ministerial services seems to exclude suitability responsibility.

[138] Investment Company Act § 22(d) (15 U.S.C. § 80a-22(d)) has, in conjunction with court interpretation, established a system of retail price maintenance with respect to the sale of mutual funds whose share values are determined by asset value plus a sales fee ("load funds"). The policy underlying such a system, however, has had little to do with imposing a duty on the underwriter to make a suitability inquiry concerning prospective purchasers of fund shares. Part of the history of this subsection involved the presence of a two-price backward pricing system for fund shares in which each day's selling price was determined by the asset valuation of the previous day. This setup created dilution of holders' shares in a rising market, and spurred quick buy-sell transactions, leading to numerous industry abuses. During congressional hearings surrounding Section 22 in the original 1940 Act, which at first omitted Section 22(d), various congressmen cited these abuses. Since the securities industry was opposed to granting the SEC broad price-regulation powers, Section 22(d) was added to supplement the other provisions of Section 22 by imposing a full load on all purchasers to prevent insiders from purchasing shares at asset value and quickly selling at a price which, due to backward pricing, they were assured would rise. In the hearings on the proposed 1970 amendments to

pany shares fall, for the most part, on the shoulders of the salesmen or brokers who deal directly with the shareholders and are derived from the same broker-dealer suitability rules which apply to ordinary securities transactions.[139]

[ii] *Authority to Set Risk-Return Constraints: The Pension Fund Model I:* If the analogy to the investment company model were perfect, all other investment management arrangements limiting the authority of the manager to portfolio selection and maintenance should similarly relieve him of most suitability responsibility. But some investment management arrangements are structurally different from the investment company model in a way which suggests that, for purposes of setting standards of suitability, the investment company model is inadequate, and that the separation of authority to set the risk and return constraints for an account from the authority to design and carry out an investment program within those constraints does not relieve an investment manager of suitability responsibility. In many cases, intermediaries who are not beneficiaries and may have other interests to serve have the power to set risk and return constraints for the manager. Because of this separation of the power to set suitability limits from the beneficiary of the account, investment objectives which investment managers are ordered to follow may not be appropriate.

Investment managers are aware of this problem, but they also know that if they insist on more suitable investment objectives, they may

---

the 1940 Act, the SEC opposed abolition of Section 22(d), favoring instead SEC-supervised self-regulation of sales loads by the industry. Yet the 1970 Amendments to the Act did not change the essential nature of Section 22(d), even though they did authorize security trade associations to regulate excessive loads. For a fuller discussion of the legislative and administrative history of Section 22(d), see Heffernan & Jorden, "Section 22(d) of the Investment Company Act of 1940," 1973 Duke L.J. 975-1008. See also United States v. NASD, 422 U.S. 694 (1975), in which the Supreme Court held that Section 22(d) embodied Congress's intent to eliminate price competition in the primary distribution of mutual fund shares, that Section 22(f) enabled the SEC to eliminate certain price competition on the secondary market, and that defendant broker-underwriter's refusal to participate in the resale of fund shares below the initial prospectus offering price was not a violation of antitrust law. See also Haddad v. Crosby Corp., [1975-1976 Transfer Binder] CCH Fed. Sec. L. Rep. ¶ 95,493 (D.C. Cir. 1976).

[139] The stock exchange suitability rules apply to the sale of mutual fund shares as well as shares in other publicly owned corporations. See, e.g., NYSE Rule 405, 2 CCH NYSE Guide ¶ 2405; NASD Rules of Fair Practice, Art. III, § 2, CCH NASD Manual ¶ 2152; Securities Exchange Act Rule 15b10-3, 2 CCH Fed. Sec. L. Rep. ¶ 25,074.

lose the account.[140] From the manager's point of view, the problem is a classic duty-of-loyalty issue: The manager's earnings may be directly affected by insisting on doing the right thing for the beneficiaries. Moreover, should the facts show that the objectives set by the intermediaries are unsuitable, the manager cannot resolve his dilemma by preferring ignorance and making no suitability inquiry. Deliberate ignorance in that context is akin to knowing complicity. The question is whether investment managers, retained by intermediaries, are responsible only to that source and can serve their own interests by doing merely as they are told, or whether, by undertaking management responsibilities for an account, they also become subject to a separate duty to act for the benefit of the account.

To see the problem in a particular context, consider the example of pension funds. Subject to the directory power of a named fiduciary and delegation to an investment manager, full authority for management of pension funds is vested in a trustee or group of trustees for the benefit of specified employees.[141] One or more of this set of statutory fiduciaries may be, but need not be, employees entitled to participate in the pension fund.[142] In setting the investment objectives for the fund, the trustees and investment managers must take into account the future claims of the work force on the pension fund; the contributions made to the fund by either the employer or the employees, or both; and the previous investment experience of the fund. Each of these factors is subject to considerable variation and, as a consequence, affords a great deal of discretion in setting investment objectives. On the basis of actuarial

---

140 The pressure exerted on a manager can be more subtle than an outright threat of termination of the management contract, since such a step might call attention to the intermediary's own breach of duty. Instead, the manager may find the client's cash flow being diverted to other managers whose investment programs produce higher returns during rising markets because they assume unsuitable risk.

141 See ERISA § 403(a), 29 U.S.C. § 1103(a). The diffusion of management control can be spread through several intermediate levels. The instrument creating an employee benefit plan must identify a named fiduciary who has the power to appoint trustees to administer the fund, including the "exclusive authority and discretion to manage and control" plan assets except to the extent the plan subordinates the trustees to the direction of the named fiduciary. Even then, however, the trustees remain "subject to proper directions" of the named fiduciary. ERISA § 403(a)(1), 29 U.S.C. § 1103(a)(1). The authority of the trustees is also limited through delegation of investment management to one or more investment managers. ERISA § 403(a)(2), 29 U.S.C. § 1103(a)(2).

142 ERISA § 408(c), 29 U.S.C. § 1108(c).

assumptions, estimates of future claims and contributions must be made. These estimates can depend on the age of the work force and different kinds of assets which comprise the fund and on the valuation techniques chosen. Furthermore, the process of relating the inflow of contributions to investment objectives is made more complex because of the discretion a plan's fiduciaries have over the amortization of unfunded liabilities. The funding rules of ERISA are sufficiently flexible to leave room to adapt funding requirements to circumstances the fiduciaries deem important, particularly to take into account the impact of investment gains or losses.[143]

Neither the complexity of the calculations nor the flexibility afforded pension fund fiduciaries justifies placing suitability responsibility with the investment manager, of course. But such matters do highlight the extent to which pension fund beneficiaries are dependent on proper determination of the investment objectives for the fund, a fact of which the investment manager is aware. On general fiduciary principles, the fact of such reliance would go a long way toward imposing a legal duty on the trustees and the investment manager, if any, to establish suitable investment objectives.[144] But the presence of intermediary fiduciaries having responsibility for assuring adequate funding also distinguishes investment managers of pension funds from officers of and advisers to investment companies in three critical respects, all of which are known to investment managers of pension funds and each of which makes the reliance of pension beneficiaries virtually unavoidable. Together, these distinctions render the investment company model inadequate for setting suitability standards for investment managers to pension funds.

First, the investment objectives of pension funds are much less visible to employees and other beneficiaries than those of investment companies

---

[143] ERISA §§ 302(c)(2)(A), 302(c)(3), 29 U.S.C. §§ 1082(c)(2)(A), 1082(c)(3). See also Black, "The Investment Policy Spectrum: Individuals, Endowment Funds and Pension Funds," 32 Fin. Anal. J. 23, 28-30 (Jan.-Feb. 1976). On the complexity of the funding problem, see Paul, "Can Private Pension Plans Deliver?" 52 Harv. Bus. Rev. 22 (Sept.-Oct. 1974); Faltermayer, "A Steeper Climb Up Pension Mountain," 91 Fortune 78 (Jan. 1975); Bauer, "Are Unfunded Pension Liabilities Getting Out of Hand?" 8 Institutional Investor 85 (April 1974).

[144] Compare Cant v. A.G. Becker & Co., 374 F. Supp. 36, 379 F. Supp. 972, and 384 F. Supp. 814 (N.D. Ill. 1974) (client's reliance establishes fiduciary obligation), with Gammage v. Roberts, Scott & Co., [1974-1975 Transfer Binder] CCH Fed. Sec. L. Rep. ¶ 94,760 (S.D. Cal. 1974) (no fiduciary relationship because plaintiff did not place great reliance on defendant).

are to shareholders. Investment companies state their investment objectives in their advertising and in their prospectuses; indeed, they base their selling appeal in large part on their stated objectives. The supervisory fiduciaries of pension funds, in contrast, set investment objectives on the basis of data and assumptions which it is highly unlikely most employees understand. As a consequence, even if most employees had the requisite financial sophistication—which they ordinarily do not—it does them little good to know what risk and return constraints are imposed on the investment manager because the appropriateness of those figures depends entirely on how the other factors of future claims, contributions, valuation, investment experience, and unfunded liabilities amortization have been established. For this reason, pension beneficiaries must rely on others to estimate those factors so as not to require hazarding pension assets by pursuing an unnecessarily risky investment program.

Second, employees have less practical recourse than shareholders of investment companies. In an important sense, pension beneficiaries are involuntary investors who, in accordance with their contract of employment, receive as a substitute for current wages payments to a trust fund designed to provide retirement benefits. Whether forced savings plans are good or bad may be a matter of personal philosophy, but the mandatory nature of the contribution is ordinarily complemented by the absence of choice on the part of the employee as to the trust fund which will receive his contribution. Unlike the investment company shareholder, who can select an investment company which meets his own objectives, the pension beneficiary is locked in to the trust named to receive his contributions or those made in his behalf, except to the extent the pension plan permits an employee to direct contributions to different assets in the fund's portfolio or to one or more multiple trusts designed to invest in different kinds of assets.[145] Furthermore, unlike the investment company shareholder who can redeem or sell his shares whenever his investment objectives change, the pension beneficiary again remains locked in to his fund except to the extent he can shift his interests among different assets in the fund's portfolio or among different trusts designed to invest in different kinds of assets.[146] For this reason,

---

[145] On such grounds, in part, participations in a union pension fund were held to be securities. See Daniel v. International Brotherhood of Teamsters, 410 F. Supp. 541 (N.D. Ill. 1976).

[146] For example, many university professors participate in a plan sponsored by Teachers Insurance and Annuity Association of America, Inc., which permits them to divide their pension contributions between a fund

pension beneficiaries rely on the establishment of investment objectives which have a high probability of being achieved, or at least are well known and remain constant, so that they can adapt their personal objectives in other investments to pension expectations which are reasonably accurate.[147]

Third, and most significant, is the comparatively unfettered discretion given pension supervisory fiduciaries to change investment objectives. The free hand that the Investment Company Act of 1940 and the regulations adopted pursuant to the statute afford management over the investment company's portfolio is tightly controlled by rules requiring that fundemental investment policies be disclosed, described in detail, and maintained without change unless shareholders agree otherwise. Under Section 8(b),[148] the registration statement of a management investment company must contain a description of its policy concerning its subclassification as either an open-end or closed-end company and as a diversified or nondiversified company. The registration statement must also detail the freedom of action the company reserves over borrowing money and issuing senior securities, underwriting the securities of other companies, concentrating investments, investing in real estate and commodities, making loans, and portfolio turnover.[149] In addition, the guidelines for preparation of the registration statement,[150] Form N-8B-1, in accordance with the statutory requirement that matters the registrant deems fundamental policy be disclosed,[151] provide that the regis-

---

of interest-bearing securities (TIAA) and a fund consisting of equity participations (CREF). The TIAA/CREF arrangement also permits participants to shift proportions between the two funds, but limits this power to shift in both frequency and percentage.

[147] The individual objectives of beneficiaries will differ, of course, but the point is that with respect to participations in pension plans, particularly fixed-benefit pension trusts, most beneficiaries will adapt their personal investment programs to the prospect of having virtually certain pension returns. Even when benefits are not fixed, as in profit-sharing plans and variable benefit plans, beneficiaries will orient their individual programs in large degree to the returns which can reasonably be expected from participation.

[148] Investment Company Act § 8(b), 15 U.S.C. § 80a-8(b).

[149] Investment Company Act § 8(b)(1), 15 U.S.C. § 80a-8(b)(1).

[150] SEC Investment Company Act Release No. 7221 (June 9, 1972), [1972-1973 Transfer Binder] CCH Fed. Sec. L. Rep. ¶ 78,835.

[151] Investment Company Act § 8(b)(3), 15 U.S.C. § 80a-8(b)(3). Fundamental policy might include, for example, an investment policy limiting the company to "socially responsible" investments. See, e.g., Shapiro, "Wall Street's New 'Social Responsibility' Funds," Saturday Review, Aug. 26, 1972,

tration statement set out the company's investment objectives, including the relative proportions to be invested in different types of securities.[152]

A similar inflexibility over changing investment objectives would be unwise in the case of pension funds. As claims, contributions, investment experience, and other variables change, the trustees must adapt investment policy. But the fact that the trustees have this power also

---

p. 43; Shapiro, "Trying to Do Well by Doing Good," 6 Institutional Investor 64 (Feb. 1972). Whether such a policy can be profitable for investors, however, is another question. See Gapay, "Do-Good Mutual Funds Fund Customers Rare, Profits Elusive Indeed," Wall Street J., Aug. 9, 1972, p. 1, col. 6.

[152] Guidelines for the preparation of Form N-8B-1, note 150 *supra*, Item 5. Item 4 of the guidelines requires the registration statement also to describe the company's intentions with respect to the policies listed in Investment Company Act § 8(b)(1) (15 U.S.C. § 80a-8(b)(1)), as set out in the text at note 149. The statute treats these policies as unchangeable absent voting approval of a majority of outstanding voting securities (see Investment Company Act § 13(a), 15 U.S.C. § 80a-13(a)), thus treating them just like policies the company lists in its organizational documents as unchangeable except by shareholder vote (see Investment Company Act § 8(b)(2), 15 U.S.C. § 80a-8(b)(2)).

Actually, the language of the statute is less demanding on disclosure of investment policy than it might have been. One of the bills submitted to the Senate in 1940 provided that an investment company specifically describe its investment objectives as income or growth, or whatever the objectives were. Thus, in its present form, the statute may permit investment companies more flexibility in shifting investment objectives to adapt to perceived market conditions.

Nonetheless, such flexibility as exists in this regard is limited by the name or title the company adopts. See Item 5(a) and the facing-page item of the guidelines. Section 8(b) is not the only source of investment policy regulation to be found in the statute. There are some investment restrictions contained in Section 12 (15 U.S.C. § 80a-12), including the prohibition of purchases on margin (§ 12(a)(1)); short sales, unless the company is a participant in an underwriting (§ 12(a)(3)); and the purchase of shares of other investment companies, with numerous qualifications (§ 12(d)). Additionally, an investment company is subject (1) to statutory classification in Section 4 (15 U.S.C. § 80a-4) as a face-amount certificate company, unit investment trust or management company, and, with respect to management companies, (2) to statutory subclassification in Section 5(a) (15 U.S.C. § 80a-5(a)) as an open-end company or a closed-end company and in Section 5(b) (15 U.S.C. § 80a-5(b)) as a diversified company or a nondiversified company.

Also relevant in this regard are state blue sky requirements, which in some jurisdictions restrict the investment discretion of investment companies. See, e.g., Cal. Reg. Admin. Code, Tit. 10, § 260.140.85, 1 CCH Blue Sky Law Rep. ¶ 8624.

expands the possibility of error and enlarges the opportunity for manipulation. Though inadvertent, error might arise from simple uneducated optimism about the level of return possible in the market at a given level of risk.[153] More likely, the willingness of trustees to undertake excessive risk is traceable to interests which may be adverse to those of the beneficiaries. Some employer-run funds succumb to the temptation of reducing current pension costs in order to enhance the company's reported earnings by establishing high-return investment objectives.[154] Some employee-run funds engage in risky investment programs in which the trustees or persons affiliated with them are interested.[155] In either event, the power the trustees have to vary investment objectives for the purpose of accommodating changed conditions makes it possible to mask unsuitable investment objectives until irrevocable damage to the pension fund has occurred. For this reason, a pension fund arrangement places beneficiaries beyond any practical power of contract or consent, and they must rely on the judgment and good faith of the pension trustees, supervisory fiduciaries, and investment managers.

[iii] *Investment Management Performed for Persons Having Authority to Set Risk-Return Constraints: The Pension Fund Model II:* Although it is possible to argue that the extra protection pension beneficiaries require does not justify shifting extensive suitability obligations onto investment managers who lack the authority to make changes in investment objectives, legal doctrine already has gone a long way toward making the shift. Indeed, it appears that investment managers, as the ones whose knowing or negligent final acquiescence is necessary to the execution of an unsuitable investment program, have suitability responsibilities almost as strict as those of the supervisory fiduciaries. Investment managers who accept pension accounts that have unsuitable

---

[153] See, e.g., J. Brooks, *Conflicts of Interest: Corporate Pension Fund Asset Management* 29-32 (Twentieth Century Fund 1975). Jansson, "Is Preservation of Capital Making a Comeback?" 8 Institutional Investor 55 (April 1974). Cf. Architectural League of N.Y. v. Bartos, CCH Fed. Sec. L. Rep. ¶ 95,329 (S.D.N.Y. 1975).

[154] J. Brooks, *Conflicts of Interest: Corporate Pension Fund Asset Management,* 27-34 (Twentieth Century Fund 1975).

[155] See, e.g., Kwitny, "Questions Are Raised by Loans and Benefits of Teamsters Fund," Wall Street J., July 22, 1975, p. 1, col. 6. See also BNA Daily Tax Report, No. 44, March 4, 1977, at G-4; *id.,* No. 50, March 14, 1977, at G-7; *id.,* No. 66, April 5, 1977, at G-7 (trustees resign pursuant to negotiations with government).

investment objectives, knowing that the reason for the unsuitability is to permit pension fund fiduciaries to breach their duty of loyalty to the fund, are answerable both at common law[156] and, in accordance with the aider and abettor doctrine, under the federal securities laws.[157] Moreover, in Section 405(a),[158] ERISA codifies the principle that knowing assistance of a breach of trust is an actionable wrong and extends that principle to apply to any fiduciary of a pension fund who knows of a breach of duty by another fiduciary and fails to make "reasonable efforts under the circumstances to remedy the breach." [159]

---

[156] *Restatement (Second) of Trusts* § 326 (1959).

[157] The aiding and abetting doctrine has been applied in numerous cases, with varying levels of "scienter" required. Woodward v. Metro Bank of Dallas, [1975-1976 Transfer Binder] CCH Fed. Sec. L. Rep. ¶ 95,351 (N.D. Tex. 1975), required a high level of scienter in refusing to find a bank liable as an aider and abettor under Exchange Act § 10(b) (actual awareness of a violation necessary). On the other hand, Bondy v. Chemical Bank, [1975-1976 Transfer Binder] CCH Fed. Sec. L. Rep. ¶ 95,360 (S.D.N.Y. 1975), seemed to uphold an action against a bank as an aider and abettor with little proof of actual knowledge of wrongdoing. While in Ernst & Ernst v. Hochfelder, 425 U.S. 185 (1976), an aiding and abetting charge based solely upon negligence was held not cognizable under Securities Exchange Act § 10(b), that case, discussed in detail in ¶ 6.01, note 5, dealt with an accountant's professional duties and not an investment manager's fiduciary duties. Given the separate duty owed beneficiaries of a pension plan by an investment manager, it would be difficult to argue that an investment manager making an ineffectual suitability inquiry in the face of orders to pursue an aggressive investment program could escape answerability under the statutory fraud provisions on the authority of *Hochfelder*. See Rolf v. Blyth Eastman Dillon & Co., [1976-1977 Transfer Binder] CCH Fed. Sec. L. Rep. ¶ 95,843 (S.D.N.Y. 1977).

[158] 29 U.S.C. § 1105(a).

[159] ERISA § 405(a)(3), 29 U.S.C. § 1105(a)(3). According to the conference report, H.R. Rep. No. 1280, ERISA, 93d Cong., 2d Sess. (Aug. 12, 1974), something less than actual knowledge constitutes a breach under Section 405(a)(3). The report gives the following example:

"A fiduciary also is to be liable for the loss caused by the breach of fiduciary responsibility by another fiduciary of the plan if he *enables* the other fiduciary to commit a breach through his failure to exercise prudence (or otherwise comply with the basic fiduciary rules of the bill) in carrying out his specific responsibilities. For example, A and B are co-trustees and are to jointly manage the plan assets. A improperly allows B to have the sole custody of the plan assets and makes no inquiry as to his conduct. B is therefore enabled to sell the property and to embezzle the proceeds. A is to be liable for a breach of fiduciary responsibility." [Emphasis added.]

Conference Report, *supra*, at 300.

The more subtle issue is how ERISA will be interpreted to deal with investment managers who fail to make suitability inquiries or who make inadequate suitability inquiries for pension accounts which turn out to have had unsuitable investment objectives. Pension beneficiaries are not totally without practical relief if an unsuitable investment program results in inadequate funding because ERISA created the Pension Benefit Guaranty Corporation (PBGC) to insure the payment of pension benefits in that event.[160] For that reason, from a pension beneficiary's point of view, there is less urgency about requiring the investment manager to make a suitability inquiry. But the PBGC does not insure the payment of all promised benefits, nor does it apply to all pension plans,[161] so the need of pension beneficiaries for suitability protection through the investment manager is still strong. Furthermore, the argument that an investment manager's suitability responsibility is limited to knowing violations is difficult to sustain against the fiduciary-duty provisions of the statute. Section 402(b)(1) of ERISA provides without qualification that funding be "consistent with the objectives of the plan and the requirements of this title." [162] Section 404(a)(1),[163] also without qualification, provides that a fiduciary, a classification applicable to investment managers,[164] "shall discharge his duties . . . (A) for the exclusive purpose of: (i) providing benefits to participants and

---

[160] ERISA, Title IV, Subtitle A—Pension Benefit Guaranty Corporation §§ 4001-4009, 29 U.S.C. §§ 1301-1309.

[161] ERISA, Title IV, Subtitle B—Coverage §§ 4021-4023, 29 U.S.C. §§ 1321-1323. See generally R. Bildersee, *Pension Regulation Manual* ¶¶ 6.2, 6.4 (1975).

[162] 29 U.S.C. § 1102(b)(1).

[163] 29 U.S.C. § 1104(a)(1).

[164] ERISA § 3(21)(A) (29 U.S.C. § 1002(21)(A)) classifies a person as a fiduciary "to the extent . . . (ii) he renders investment advice for a fee or other compensation, direct or indirect, with respect to any monies or other property of such plan, or has any authority or responsibility to do so. . . ." ERISA § 3(38) (29 U.S.C. § 1002(38)) defines investment manager as:

"any fiduciary (other than a trustee or named fiduciary . . .)—

"(A) who has the power to manage, acquire, or dispose of any asset of a plan;

"(B) who is (i) registered as an investment adviser under the Investment Advisers Act of 1940; (ii) is a bank, as defined in that Act; or (iii) is an insurance company qualified to perform services described in subparagraph (A) under the laws of more than one state; and

"(C) has acknowledged in writing that he is a fiduciary with respect to the plan."

their beneficiaries." For investment managers to escape liability for the failure at least to make an adequate suitability inquiry, particularly in light of the Conference Report's explanation of the knowledge requirement in Section 405(a),[165] these provisions will have to be interpreted as imposing less than the absolute duty ERISA imposes on all pension-fund fiduciaries.

The statutory provisions limiting the liability of fiduciaries are also instructive. Section 405 of ERISA,[166] which pertains to limitations on liability for breach of duty by a co-fiduciary, fails to describe any specific means by which an investment manager can avoid responsibility for the improper setting of a fund's investment objectives. In contrast, Section 405(d) expressly provides that trustees and other fiduciaries can limit their responsibility for the management of the fund's assets by appointing a statutorily defined investment manager to invest them.[167] The differences in treatment may well cause a court to conclude that Congress did not intend to relieve investment managers of liability for undertaking an unsuitable investment program at the direction of the fund supervisory fiduciaries.[168] Nor does it appear that in-

---

[165] See note 159 *supra*.

[166] 29 U.S.C. § 1105.

[167] 29 U.S.C. § 1105(d) provides:

"(1) If an investment manager or managers have been appointed under § 402(c)(3), then, notwithstanding subsection (a)(2) and (3) and subsection (b) [describing the liability of a trustee for a breach of trust by a co-trustee both where responsibility is held separately and jointly], no trustee shall be liable for the acts or omissions of such investment manager or managers, or be under an obligation to invest or otherwise manage any asset of the plan which is subject to the management of such investment manager."

A fiduciary may not register under the Investment Advisers Act for the sole purpose of insulating a trustee from investment management responsibility. See Investment Advisers Act Rule 202-1, 17 C.F.R. § 275.202-1.

[168] One might argue that the silence of Section 405 (29 U.S.C. § 1105) about means for investment managers to limit responsibility for suitability, in contrast to the extensive treatment given to how trustees can limit answerability for breaches of trust by co-trustees and other fiduciaries, should not be interpreted as placing an affirmative suitability obligation on the manager. Certainly, Congress did not intend to shift responsibility to the investment manager for every fiduciary duty imposed on pension trustees and fiduciaries. Additionally, the statutory prudent-man rule in Section 404(a)(1) (29 U.S.C. § 1104(a)(1)) cannot impose suitability on its own authority since it applies only to discharge of a fiduciary's "duties," and the question here is antecedent to that: Is there such a duty? See text at notes 169-170 *infra*.

Yet ERISA is equally silent on how investment managers can avoid

vestment managers can limit their responsibility for suitability contractually. Section 410(a) prohibits exculpatory provisions relieving fiduciaries from their statutory duties.[169] In addition to the statutory provisions discussed above, investment managers, like other fiduciaries, must comply with the prudent-man standard codified in Section 404 (a)(1)(B).[170] Application of that standard to investment managers would seem to hold them answerable for negligence in accepting investment objectives. Furthermore, an inadequate suitability inquiry may be held negligent even without reliance on a specific duty imposed by the statute. In accordance with standard negligence doctrine, evidence that some investment managers were making suitability inquiries as a matter of course would probably establish such a duty among investment managers generally.[171]

But it is not yet possible to detail exactly how suitability responsibilities will be imposed on investment managers of pension funds. Some of the problems arising out of the suitability issue have already received regulatory attention. For example, it is common, especially among large pension funds, to divide the assets among several investment managers, either to take advantage of different areas of expertise, to stimulate performance competition, or simply to refine the diversification principle by applying it to investment managers as well as to securities. Administrative costs, to say nothing of the proprietary interests of these investment managers, would be seriously affected if

---

answerability for any breach of trust by a trustee or other fiduciary. Moreover, a suitability breach of trust is more closely linked to an investment manager's area of expertise than most other trust matters that are not within the scope of the authority delegated to the investment manager. Whereas pension beneficiaries would probably rely on investment managers at least to make some effort to assure that the investment program being followed is suitable, it is doubtful that comparable expectations would be raised in the case of other administrative fiduciary responsibilities normally part of the trustees' or other fiduciaries' duties.

[169] 29 U.S.C. § 1110(a). Insurance and indemnification are permissible (ERISA § 410(b), 29 U.S.C. § 1110(b)), but this only emphasizes the point that Congress intended fiduciaries to be responsible for duties they assume.

[170] 29 U.S.C. § 1104(a)(1)(B). The standard adopted in the provision is "with the care, skill, prudence, and diligence under the circumstances then prevailing that a prudent man acting in a like capacity and familiar with such matters would use in the conduct of an enterprise of a like character and with like aims."

[171] The T.J. Hooper, 60 F.2d 737 (2d Cir. 1932) (per Learned Hand, J.).

each manager were required separately to take into account the investment policy of each other manager. Consequently, the regulations now provide that several investment managers for a single pension fund are not responsible for each other's investment program unless some form of collusion or knowing silence is involved.[172] Other accommodations to the practicalities of suitability inquiries by investment managers can be anticipated. There is as yet no sentiment to hold investment managers strictly liable for adhering to unsuitable investment objectives: The issue remains a negligence inquiry.

[iv] *The Lessons of the Models:* However the details of an investment manager's suitability responsibility to pension fund clients develop, either through regulation, adjudication, or business convention, it is plain that pension funds represent a different model for investment-manager suitability standards from that established for investment companies. Pension funds, because of the trust form and the need of the beneficiaries for aid and protection, place a heavy suitability responsibility on investment managers. Investment companies, because the service they offer would be unreasonably expensive otherwise and because they hew to preset, tightly controlled investment objectives, leave most suitability responsibility with the investor.

But even though neither is perfect as a model for every other type of investment management arrangement, together they illustrate how suitability obligations can vary despite an identical grant of investment authority to the investment managers of both. Ordinary trusts, for example, are structurally similar to pension funds in that the trustee as intermediary sets investment objectives for the trust. Yet one would expect that if the assets of the trust were invested in a common trust fund, the manager of the common fund would have suitability responsibilities similar to those of the officers and investment advisers of an investment company. Like an investment company, a common trust has investment objectives which are fixed in advance. In addition, the objectives of a common fund are visible to trustors, trustees, and beneficiaries, and those who become dissatisfied or change objectives can cease participating relatively easily. Thus, although the structural form of an investment management arrangement can indicate how suitability responsibility is to be allocated, the appropriate model for setting standards of suitability for investment managers in a given case also de-

---

[172] 29 U.S.C. § 1105 (a). See also 29 C.F.R. § 2510.3-21 and 26 C.F.R. § 54.4975-9.

pends on the three factors which distinguish the allocation of responsibility for suitability in the two models:

(1) The visibility of the process by which investment objectives are set;

(2) The recourse of beneficiaries; and

(3) The authority of the intermediary to change investment objectives.

[2] Factors Tending to Place Responsibility for Suitability on the Client

[a] Actual notice of risk

An investment manager has no significant suitability duty to a client who fully understands the risk and return constraints of the investment program the manager proposes. Presumably, if an investor knows what he wants and understands the possible consequences associated with different courses of action, he is entirely capable of choosing an investment program which best accommodates his attitude toward risk regardless of whether other investors in comparable financial circumstances would have responded in similar fashion. The only exception to allocating suitability responsibility in this way might occur if a client demonstrates himself to be incapable of responding rationally to the information he receives. For example, in *Powers v. Francis I. DuPont & Co.*,[173] the court exonerated a broker from liability on suitability grounds where the facts showed that the client, a business executive who lost a great deal in heavy trading, misrepresented his financial condition and ignored repeated warnings about speculative trading. But the court also observed that it may be the case that a broker must refuse the use of its trading facilities to a "compulsive investor" when it becomes clear that the client's activity has become "irrational gambling." [174] In a similar vein, the SEC Advisory Committee on Investment Management Services for Individual Investors[175] took the position that an investment manager must refuse accounts which are too small to justify the manage-

---

[173] 344 F. Supp. 429 (E.D. Pa. 1972).

[174] *Id.* at 433. The court analogized the broker's duty in these circumstances to that of bartenders subject to laws prohibiting them from selling liquor to drunks.

[175] SEC, *Report of the Advisory Comm. on Investment Management Services for Individual Investors, Small Account Investment Management Services,* CCH Fed. Sec. L. Rep. No. 465, Pt. III (1973).

ment fee in view of the services rendered[176] or to risk the type of investment program proposed.[177]

Since actual notice of risk to the client relieves an investment manager of further suitability responsibility—at least, if the client is not specially dependent on the manager either because of the client's legal status[178] or because of his obvious inability to control himself[179]—the question is when a client has actual notice of risk. Some cases seem to hold that notice merely of the transactions in an account constitutes sufficient notice to the client. In *Greenfeld v. D.H. Blair & Co.*,[180] for example, the court rejected a churning claim and granted a motion for summary judgment on the grounds that the plaintiff "received confirmation slips for every transaction so that she was continuously aware of what was being purchased and sold for her account. In addition she received monthly statements which reflected every transaction made during that particular month."[181]

Cases like *Greenfeld*[182] seem seriously misguided, however. Though

---

[176] Cf. Anderson Co. v. John P. Chase, Inc., [1974-1975 Transfer Binder] CCH Fed. Sec. L. Rep. ¶ 95,009 (S.D.N.Y. 1975), *cert. denied* 424 U.S. 969 (1976) (client promised manager that additional funds sufficient to reach manager's minimum account size would be forthcoming).

[177] Cf. John G. Kinnard & Co., Inc., [1973-1974 Transfer Binder] CCH Fed. Sec. L. Rep. ¶ 79,662 (1973) (staff doubtful that an investment program involving short selling and margin trading can be suitable for clients having a minimum account size of $15,000).

[178] If an investment manager knows that the client has no real appreciation of how to respond to investment risk—for example, a person or an institution managed by persons known to the manager to have no experience in investing, or a child presumed to lack such experience—it is unrealistic to expect the investor to realize the necessity of contracting for suitability assistance on the part of the manager. Actual notice of risk is also probably insufficient to relieve a manager of suitability responsibility also in cases where the client is a trust, unless the trustor has expressly authorized fair notice to the beneficiaries as a sufficient basis for approving the trustee's proposed investment program. The client of a trustee is the trust, and he must exercise independent judgment about how best to carry out the purposes of the trust. Beneficiaries, however, can consent to acts which might otherwise constitute a breach of trust so long as the consenting beneficiary is capable of exercising an informed consent and does not affect the interests of other nonconsenting beneficiaries. 3 Scott note 12 *supra*, § 216.

[179] See text at note 173 *supra*.

[180] [1975-1976 Transfer Binder] CCH Fed. Sec. L. Rep. ¶ 95,239 (S.D.N.Y. 1975).

[181] *Id.* p. 98,255.

[182] See, e.g., Landry v. Hemphill, Noyes & Co., [1972-1973 Transfer Binder] CCH Fed. Sec. L. Rep. ¶ 93,758 (1st Cir. 1973) (customer estopped

notice of transactions may be evidence of actual notice of risk, there still must be a showing that the information provided was sufficient for the client, or at least a reasonable person comparable in age and experience to the client, to understand how much risk was involved in the transactions at issue. Thus, in *Shearson, Hammill & Co.*,[183] a case which preceded *Greenfeld* by a decade, even though the respondent's brokerage clients were aware of the actual transactions taking place in their accounts, the Commission held that respondent induced excessive trading in accounts for which that activity was unsuitable and imposed heavy disciplinary sanctions.

If simple notification of the transactions executed for an account does not constitute actual notice of risk, *Architectural League of N.Y. v. Bartos*[184] is instructive as to what will. In 1969, the officers of the League decided to seek a higher return on the League's assets, which previously had been invested in a mutual fund and an interest-bearing bank account. The officers of the League retained Bartos, a stockbroker, to manage the League's account on a discretionary basis. Bartos pursued a highly speculative investment program, executing over 200 transactions in under three and one-half years. When the account was closed, it had fallen to less than one-sixth of its initial value. The League sued Bartos and his employers for investing in highly speculative securities contrary to its intentions or policy.

The court found as a fact that the League was aware of the speculative nature of the investment program in which it was engaging.[185] To reach this conclusion, the court relied in part on defendant's practice of sending plaintiff a written confirmation for each transaction carried out and a copy of the prospectus for each new issue purchased. But much more persuasive to the court were letters and verbal communications by Bartos to one or more of the officers of the League—usually, to whoever was treasurer at the time—informing them of the nature of particular investments, the progress of the program, and attendant risks.

---

from holding broker-dealer liable for excessive trading of account because customer failed to object to number of transactions).

[183] SEC Securities Exchange Act Release No. 7743 (Nov. 12, 1965), [1964-1966 Transfer Binder] CCH Fed. Sec. L. Rep. ¶ 77,306.

[184] 404 F. Supp. 304 (S.D.N.Y. 1975).

[185] *Id.* at 309. The court said:

"All of plaintiff's claims in the first category involve the one central issue in this case: was the League in fact aware of the speculative nature of the securities in which it was investing. This question must be answered in the affirmative."

Furthermore, the performance of the account amply indicated its risky character. When Bartos initially took control, its asset value was approximately $90,000. In less than a year, the portfolio declined in value to about $23,000. Ten months later, it had appreciated to about $80,000. At one point during his management, Bartos reported a value for the portfolio which differed substantially from a figure reached independently by the League. Bartos explained this by conceding the possibility of error, but he also stated that the portfolio consisted of a large number of volatile stocks which fluctuated so much that even in a brief period, such a discrepancy could occur. The court was not surprised that the League's treasurer accepted this explanation "because he knew at the time the League's investment policy pursued by Bartos was 'aggressive.' " [186]

Architectural League of N.Y. suggests that actual notice of risk to the client can eliminate much of an investment manager's suitability responsibility, even when the manager is granted discretionary authority to engage in a high-risk investment program. But the case also raises the question of whether, if an intermediary retains an investment manager and limits his responsibility to portfolio management, actual notice of risk to the intermediary satisfies the manager's suitability duty. Bartos never made any suitability inquiry to determine whether the officers of the League had reached a proper judgment concerning the suitability of a risky investment program, and the court made no mention of that fact.[187] Application of the pension fund model described in ¶ 4.03[1] [b][iii] would suggest that Bartos had an independent duty to the beneficiaries of the League's endowment. That issue cannot be determined in this case because the League's officers apparently had to adopt an unduly risky investment policy, and the court specifically found that the investment program adopted by Bartos was suitable for the League.[188] The League apparently desired to undertake projects requiring expen-

---

[186] *Id.* at 312.

[187] The court may simply have assumed from the facts that defendant Bartos was adequately informed. Bartos' father was an officer of the League during part of the period in question, and the evidence showed that father and son had frequent conversations about the performance of the League's portfolio. The family relationship may have been one of the reasons defendant was retained as investment manager for the League's portfolio, and the court seemed to regard the conversations between father and son as a positive contribution to the League's understanding of the investment program in which it was engaged. There is no indication that that relationship produced any investment interest adverse to the League.

[188] 404 F. Supp. at 314.

ditures far in excess of its existing assets and its prospects of obtaining additional assets from the membership. The report of the case suggests that circumstances were such that the League was in a position in which it would be no worse off it it suffered substantial losses but would be in a sharply improved position if it could obtain high gains. Bartos thus may have breached a suitability obligation by not making an independent inquiry, but his breach, if any, was not causally related to any harm the League suffered.

Furthermore, even assuming that the investment program Bartos carved out was unsuitable and that Bartos' failure even to make a suitability inquiry violated his duty to the League, the entire unsuitability claim is colored by the fact that the League initiated suit under the authority of its officers and without joining them as defendants. Whatever Bartos' independent responsibility for suitability to the League may have been, it is clear that the officers of the League had at least as great an obligation. Since the evidence shows that they were aware of the risk, they also should be answerable for any unsuitability involved. Yet instead of being joined as defendants, they and their successors brought suit in behalf of the League against Bartos. To hold Bartos answerable in such circumstances would have, in effect, permitted the officer-intermediaries to shift their own wrong entirely onto the shoulders of Bartos. Indeed, that circumstance gives added emphasis to the impression one gains from reading the case that the action resulted more from dissatisfaction with investment results than from unsuitability.[189] To the extent that reading is accurate, it only emphasizes the ease with which questions of competence in carrying out an investment program can be converted into suitability questions.

[b] Constructive notice of risk: The sophisticated-investor doctrine

There is extant a doctrine which deprives a certain class of investor of virtually all suitability protection. Sophisticated investors, apparently by virtue of their sophistication, are supposed to understand the risk incident to whatever investment program or security their investment managers suggest, or at least to know enough to ask, so long as no material facts are either misrepresented or omitted.

As a limit on an investment manager's responsibility for suitability, the sophisticated-investor doctrine probably traces its origins to the private placement exemption in the Securities Act of 1933. In Section

---

[189] See note 126 *supra*.

4(2),[190] the Act codifies the principle that investors able to finance nonpublic offerings are of sufficient wealth and investment experience to obtain all necessary information without the mandatory disclosure requirements imposed by the statute, and the courts and the SEC have interpreted that exemption as applying to such investors.[191] In fact, as initially proposed, the latest revision of Rule 146, the regulation implementing Section 4(2), expressly incorporated the term "sophisticated investor" to describe the essential qualifications of an investor eligible to participate in a private placement.[192] From the private placement rule, it is an easy step to the idea that a sophisticated investor is presumptively capable of evaluating the appropriateness of any investment opportunity he is afforded,[193] including a continuing program planned and carried out by an investment manager.

If the sophisticated-investor doctrine signifies an approach which relieves an investment manager of further responsibility after satisfying himself that an investor has sufficient experience to evaluate the manager's proposals, the doctrine is defensible. It requires at least that the manager make a suitability inquiry to determine the client's financial circumstances and investment experience for the purpose of determining whether the client is sophisticated, and it requires, therefore, that the manager make at least a rough suitability judgment. Furthermore, if, by actions or statements, a client indicates an ability to understand intricate investment matters, a manager should safely be able to assume that the client will reject proposals which are unsuitable. In *Anderson*

---

[190] 15 U.S.C. § 77d(2).

[191] See SEC Securities Act Release No. 5336 (Nov. 28, 1972), [1972-1973 Transfer Binder] CCH Fed. Sec. L. Rep. ¶ 79,108; SEC v. Ralston Purina Co., 346 U.S. 119, 125 (1953). Bayoud v. Ballard, [1975-1976 Transfer Binder] CCH Fed. Sec. L. Rep. ¶ 95,457 (N.D. Tex. 1975). For a fuller discussion of the sophisticated-investor concept, see Weinberg & McManus, "The Private Placement Exemption Under the Securities and Exchange Act of 1933 Revisited, and Rule 146," 27 Baylor L. Rev. 201 (1975). Green & Wittner, "Private Placements of Securities Under Rule 146," 21 Prac. Law. 9 (Jan. 1975). 1 L. Loss, *Securities Regulation* 3C2(d) (2d ed. 1961).

[192] If the investor were not sophisticated, his adviser was required to be. See Proposed Rule 146(d), SEC Securities Act Release No. 5336 (Nov. 28, 1972), [1972-1973 Transfer Binder] CCH Fed. Sec. L. Rep. ¶ 79,108. In the final version, the SEC decided not to invest the phrase "sophisticated investor" with status as a term of art. It did, however, retain the idea in different language. See note 109 *supra*.

[193] See, e.g., Gammage v. Roberts, Scott & Co., [1974-1975 Transfer Binder] CCH Fed. Sec. L. Rep. ¶ 94,760 (S.D. Cal. 1974).

Co. v. John P. Chase, Inc.,[194] for example, the evidence showed that plaintiff's managing general partner had been in corporate finance and investment banking for a decade prior to initiating the management arrangement with defendant. To the extent consistent with the partner's cooperation, the defendant-manager maintained records of plaintiff's financial position and continually advised the partner about the wisdom and prospects of various securities transactions. The partner maintained full working authority over investment decisions for plaintiff at all times. For these reasons and because of the client's extensive experience, the nature of which defendant was aware, the court held that the manager had no further duty of suitability.[195]

The problem with the sophisticated-investor doctrine is the ease with which it can be misapplied. Unlike *Anderson Co.*, in which there was ample evidence of experience in investing and understanding of investment risk, the court in *Greenfeld v. D.H. Blair & Co.*[196] found in favor of a broker on a churning charge in part on the grounds that the plaintiff was an intelligent college-educated person. Given the complexity of the investment process, the *Greenfeld* case seems to carry the sophisticated-investor doctrine well beyond its proper limits.

---

[194] [1974-1975 Transfer Binder] CCH Fed. Sec. L. Rep. ¶ 95,009 (S.D. N.J. 1975), *cert. denied* 424 U.S. 969 (1976).

[195] There were two plaintiffs in this case, the company and the mother of the managing partner. The company was a limited partnership with assets consisting of real estate, securities, and cash. The managing partner, in addition to being authorized to direct investments for the company, held a power of attorney from his mother for the management of her personal property. The court failed to consider the possibility that, despite the managing partner's sophistication, defendant owed at least the mother and perhaps also the limited partnership an independent duty of suitability. Mrs. Anderson was a widow, and she bore the full brunt of her son's miscalculations, a fact of which defendant was aware. It is possible that the reason the court gave no consideration to these circumstances is that the managing partner was not named a defendant in the case and stood to benefit from any recovery received from the defendant. Even if defendant owed an independent suitability duty to Mrs. Anderson, the failure to join the person most responsible for the investment program losses Mrs. Anderson experienced indicates that dissatisfaction with results, much more than unsuitability, was the basis for this lawsuit. Compare the discussion in the text at note 189 *supra*.

[196] [1975-1976 Transfer Binder] CCH Fed. Sec. L. Rep. ¶ 95,239 (S.D.N.Y. 1975).

Chapter 5

SPECIAL PROBLEMS IN STRUCTURING THE INVESTMENT MANAGEMENT AGREEMENT

¶ 5.01.   UNENFORCEABLE PROVISIONS GENERALLY

The record of the undertakings of an investment manager is the management contract or trust instrument.[1] Although investment management relationships vary considerably in form and substance, there are several provisions which are common in investment management agreements. Most important is the more or less detailed description of the investment, trading, and support services the manager will provide the client.[2] Often, these terms include language reminiscent of agency- and trust-law duties,[3] but they also set forth more specific management un-

---

[1] An explicit instrument would, of course, be a practical necessity in the case of a directory trust; that is, a trust in which control of various aspects of the trust, and especially the management of the trust portfolio, is vested in a person other than the trustee. Directory trusts are often formulated in order to place details of administration in expert hands and to receive an individual trustee of that burden. These trusts may also be used in situations where the ideal trustee does not meet the legal qualifications for the office. See generally Note, "Directory Trusts and the Exculpatory Clause," 65 Colum. L. Rev. 138 (1965).

[2] The standard form advisory agreement developed by the Investment Counsel Association of America, for example, contains provisions covering such details as adviser authority; services to clients; reports; relationship with clients other than contracting client; brokerage responsibilities; proxy responsibilities; portfolio valuation; investment restrictions; bond; termination; notice provisions; advisory fees; and representations of client authority. In addition, advisers may attach various orders or supplementary letters indicating compliance with applicable federal or state law.

[3] See generally ¶ 2.02. There is explicit recognition in the Employee Retirement Income Security Act of 1974 (ERISA), Pub. L. 93-406, 88

dertakings. Moreover, depending on the type of investment management relationship involved, they may extend or restrict the manager's discretion in various particulars. There may also be a number of administrative provisions establishing, among other things, responsibilities for making reports to the client or to public agencies, custodianship arrangements, bonding requirements, auditing requirements, and amendment, renewal, and removal procedures. Additionally, matters material to the investment management relationship not contained in the management agreement may be imposed by federal and state statutes or implied through reference to state agency or trust law.[4]

But apparent assent by the parties is not assurance of the validity of all the terms of the agreement. Notwithstanding express and precise language, provisions which are illegal or contrary to public policy under state or federal law are unenforceable.[5] Thus, for example, agreements binding investors to waive compliance with the federal securities laws are void.[6] Nor may a manager agree to obtain, or defend on grounds

---

Stat. 829 (Sept. 2, 1974), of this division of responsibilities between trustee and manager. Section 405(d) (29 U.S.C. § 1105(d)) permits trustees to avoid responsibility for acts and omissions of appointed investment managers (defined in Section 3(38), 29 U.S.C. § 1002(38)).

[4] E.g., *Restatement (Second) of Trusts* §§ 164(b), 169-196 (1959); *Restatement (Second) of Agency* § 376, Comment a (1958). The duties of a trustee are quite similar to those of an agent, but the former are imposed by the settlor in the trust instrument, with the trustee required to either accept the duties or not assume his post, while the latter arise from an agreement with the principal. Note that absent any "duties" provision in a trust instrument, or unless otherwise agreed upon in an agency relationship, Sections 169-196 of the *Restatement (Second) of Trusts* and Sections 377-398 of the *Restatement (Second) of Agency* impose a number of mandatory duties upon the fiduciary.

[5] *Restatement (Second) of Trusts* § 166 (1959); *Restatement (Second) of Agency* § 411 (1958). A trustee or agent cannot be required to perform an illegal act, and illegality is a defense to an action based on nonperformance. This rule applies in all cases, although an agent may be held liable for the separate violation of duty which results from failure to inform an unknowing principal that an act is unlawful, either because of a blanket prohibition or because the agent is not legally qualified to perform the act in question. As to an agent's accountability to his principal for money received from the principal to accomplish an unlawful purpose, see *Restatement (Second) of Agency* § 412 (1958).

[6] Securities Act of 1933 § 14, 15 U.S.C. § 77n; Securities Exchange Act of 1934 § 29(a), 15 U.S.C. § 78cc(a); Investment Company Act of 1940 § 47(a), 15 U.S.C. § 80a-46(a); Investment Advisers Act of 1940 § 215(a), 15 U.S.C. § 80b-15(a).

of fiduciary duty the use of, inside information.[7]

This limitation on the power of investment managers and investors to contract or structure trust obligations has special import for two additional provisions common to investment management agreements: exculpatory clauses and compensation arrangements. Exculpatory clauses, designed to relieve an investment manager of liability to the investor for duties otherwise imposed by law, are generally disfavored, and in some cases, absolutely prohibited. Similarly, compensation arrangements are suspect if they approve unusually high fees for standard services or unbalanced incentive fees for exceptional performance, or if they fail to disclose sources of indirect compensation or recipients of any part of the management fee. The balance of this chapter explores the limitations placed on exculpatory and compensation arrangement provisions.

¶ 5.02. EXCULPATORY CLAUSES

Exculpatory clauses explore the tension between two competing sets of values. Freedom of contract suggests that investment managers should be able to exact agreements immunizing themselves from civil liability to their clients for their defaults. But professional investment managers hold themselves out as experts willing to act in a fiduciary capacity. In circumstances such as these, the law often imposes duties arising out of the assumption of the office, and responsibility for these duties cannot be avoided regardless of contract. In its present state, the law sharply limits the effectiveness of exculpatory clauses in investment management agreements.[8]

[1] Bad Faith or Reckless Disregard of Fiduciary Duties

According to the *Restatement (Second) of Trusts*, trust doctrine rejects outright exculpatory provisions absolving trustees from acts com-

---

[7] Use of material inside information in the purchase or sale of securities is unlawful. SEC v. Texas Gulf Sulphur Co., 401 F.2d 833 (2d Cir. 1968), *cert. denied* 394 U.S. 976 (1969). The SEC has held that the fiduciary duty of investment managers does not extend to or validate the use of inside information for the benefit of client accounts. *In re* Investors Management Co., SEC Securities Exchange Act Release No. 9267 (1971), [1970-1971 Transfer Binder] CCH Fed. Sec. L. Rep. ¶ 78,163, at 80,522.

[8] See, e.g., Auchincloss & Lawrence Inc., [1973-1974 Transfer Binder] CCH Fed. Sec. L. Rep. ¶¶ 79,762, 79,686 (exculpatory clause suggesting waiver of legal rights violates Investment Advisors Act § 206).

mitted in bad faith or in reckless disregard of trustee obligations.[9] Agency law is not quite so specific,[10] though it is doubtful that the failure of the *Restatement (Second) of Agency* to speak squarely to exculpatory provisions excusing bad faith and reckless disregard of investment management obligations is intended as an admission of their validity. Comment a to Section 379 of the *Restatement (Second) of Agency* expressly refers to Section 574 of the *Restatement of Contracts* as limiting the scope of exculpatory provisions. Section 574 permits exculpation only for negligence "not falling greatly below the standard established by law. . . ." [11] Furthermore, the illustration in Section 574 describes an exculpatory clause in a fiduciary relationship and takes the position that the clause is unenforceable to the extent that it forgives "gross carelessness." Section 379 also invites comparison, for purposes of interpretation, with Section 222 of the *Restatement (Second) of Trusts*, which limits the effect of exculpatory clauses in trust documents to negligence.[12]

Even if trust or agency doctrine could be construed to permit exculpatory provisions affecting more than ordinary negligence, it is highly probable that the fraud provisions of the federal securities laws would intervene. Although there is no holding or ruling that bad faith or reckless disregard of duty is per se statutory fraud, there is no recent case in which such conduct in securities dealings has not been deemed fraudulent or deceptive, particularly under Rule 10b-5[13] or Section 206

---

[9] *Restatement (Second) of Trusts* § 222(2) (1959). The basis of this rule is public policy. A trust in which the trustee might commit willful breaches of the trust, conduct himself with reckless disregard for the interests of the beneficiary, or profit from his breach of trust, would not be a trust at all.

[10] *Restatement (Second) of Agency* § 379 (1958). Cf. *id.* §§ 438-440.

[11] *Restatement of Contracts* § 574 (1932) provides:

"A bargain for exemption from liability for the consequences of negligence not falling greatly below the standard established by law for the protection of others against unreasonable risk of harm, is legal except in the cases stated in Section 575."

Restatement of Contracts § 575 (1932) contains exceptions for willful breach of duty, injury to employees in the course of employment, and breach of duty to the public.

[12] See note 9 *supra.*

[13] E.g., Thomas v. Duralight Co., 524 F.2d 577 (3d Cir. 1975); Baker v. Bevan, 395 F. Supp. 192 (E.D. Pa. 1975); Beecher v. Able, [1975-1976 Transfer Binder] CCH Fed. Sec. L. Rep. ¶ 95,303 (S.D.N.Y. 1975). In Ernst & Ernst v. Hochfelder, 425 U.S. 185, the Supreme Court limited application of Rule 10b-5 in civil actions to breaches of duty involving

of the Investment Advisers Act.[14] Moreover, the SEC has issued a release dealing with the use of hedge clauses' by broker-dealers and investment advisers.[15] According to that release, clauses disclaiming responsibility for the accuracy of information supplied clients may violate the antifraud provisions of the securities laws if their language creates the impression that investors have waived any federal or common-law right of action. Certainly, if merely promoting the belief that rights of action may be lost is fraudulent, attempts to avoid liability for conduct amounting to statutory fraud would be so also.

[2] Negligence

Problems with the effectiveness of exculpatory clauses are not confined to instances of bad faith and reckless disregard of duty. There is also little basis for confidence that exculpatory clauses will permit investment managers to avoid the consequences of ordinary negligence. Despite the ostensible acquiescence of trust and agency doctrine in exculpatory provisions applying to negligence,[16] courts have a strong

---

scienter. The Court's discussion of the origins of Rule 10b-5 strongly implies that bad faith or deliberate misfeasance is always fraudulent. See ¶ 6.01 at note 5.

14 Angelakis v. Churchill Management Corp., [1975-1976 Transfer Binder] CCH Fed. Sec. L. Rep. ¶ 95,285 (N.D. Cal. 1975); *In re* Intersearch Technology, Inc., SEC Administrative Proceeding No. 3-2991 (Feb. 28, 1975), [1974-1975 Transfer Binder] CCH Fed. Sec. L. Rep. ¶ 80,139; *In re* Steadman Sec. Corp., SEC Administrative Proceeding No. 3-3101 (Dec. 20, 1974), [1974-1975 Transfer Binder] CCH Fed. Sec. L. Rep. ¶ 80,038.

15 SEC Securities Exchange Act Release No. 4593 (April 10, 1951), 2 CCH Fed. Sec. L. Rep. ¶ 25,095. See First Nat'l Bank of Akron, [1975-1976 Transfer Binder] CCH Fed. Sec. L. Rep. ¶ 80,441 (1976) (clause limiting liability to bad faith or willful misconduct may violate Investment Adviser's Act §§ 206, 215).

16 *Restatement (Second) of Trusts* § 222 (1959); *Restatement (Second) of Agency* § 379 (1958). See also *Restatement of Contracts* §§ 574-575 (1932). To be distinguished from provisions exculpating for negligence are provisions that expand an investment manager's authority. For example, many trust agreements include clauses authorizing the trustee to invest in investment companies, investments thought by some to violate the trustee's duty not to delegate (see, e.g., Langbein & Posner, "Market Funds and Trust-Investment Law," 1 Am. B. Foundation J. 1, 18-22 (1976), and Shattuck, "The Legal Propriety of Investment by American Fiduciaries in the Shares of Boston-Type Open-End Investment Trusts," 25 B.U.L. Rev. 1 (1945)); authorizing the purchase of stocks that pay no dividends, investments thought by some to violate the trustee's duty to serve the interests of

bias against them and rely on a variety of interpretation techniques to construe them narrowly.[17] Also, legislation, regulation, and learned commentary have taken an increasingly restrictive attitude toward exculpatory provisions for negligent investment management. In New York, trustees of testamentary trusts have been prohibited from relying on these provisions for almost forty years.[18] Federal law now prohibits qualified employee benefit plans from absolving fiduciaries from the consequences of negligent investment management.[19] And there is the possibility that, according to regulations issued under the Internal

---

the income beneficiaries (see, e.g., A. Loring, *A Trustee's Handbook* § 77 (Rev. Ed. 1962)); authorizing investments in companies of recent incorporation, thought by some to violate the trustee's duty to avoid securities of unseasoned companies (see, e.g., J. Farr, *An Estate Planner's Handbook* 596 (3d ed. 1966)); and, more important perhaps than most such provisions, clauses authorizing expansion of investment discretion to include investments not normally part of trust portfolios. This latter class of provision was developed primarily as a response to legal-list investment restrictions (see ¶ 1.02[2][c] at notes 95-96), but it often now appears also in instruments governed by the Massachusetts interpretation of the prudent-man rule, in part as a consequence of the efforts of some legal commentators to promote rules narrowing investment discretion of trustees, and in part out of apprehension that courts will not truly adhere to professional customs, conventions, and practices as the legal standard applicable to trust investment but will interpolate their own more restrictive notions of what those practices should be.

These kinds of clauses are not, in the strict sense, exculpatory, since they are not designed to forgive wrongful acts committed while engaging in authorized conduct. They are designed to permit trustees to avoid exposure to the consequences of misguided application of trust investment law. For example, a general prohibition against investment in investment companies would prevent small trust funds not being managed by a corporate trustee from diversifying adequately and would severely limit access to money-market funds and index funds for trusts which, though larger, are too small so to invest on their own. Similarly, were dividends mandatory for a trust investment, access to many stocks of low yield or stocks of companies which pass dividends from time to time would be jeopardized. Clauses authorizing such investment tactics head off challenges to trust investments on the ground that the investments were per se unlawful. They do not authorize the making of these investments without exercising ordinary skill and care.

[17] See *In re* Jarvis, 110 Misc. 5, 180 N.Y.S. 324 (1920); Smith v. Boyd, 119 Fla. 481, 161 So. 381 (1935). But see *In re* Mann's Will, 251 A.D. 759, 296 N.Y.S. 71 (1937).

[18] N.Y. Estates, Powers and Trusts Law § 11-1.7 (McKinney 1967).

[19] ERISA § 419(a), 29 U.S.C. § 110(a).

Revenue Code, private foundations risk their tax-exempt status by approving exculpatory provisions for investment managers.[20] If that is the case, a court might well hold such a provision invalid rather than injure the beneficiaries of the foundation.

One can, of course, take the position that these developments are merely exceptions from the general rule that agreements exculpating negligence are enforceable. The Investment Company Act of 1940, for example, can be interpreted as authority for that proposition. Section 17(h) prohibits only agreements protecting willful misfeasance, bad faith, gross negligence, or reckless disregard of duties assumed.[21] By implication, exculpatory provisions applying to ordinary negligence are valid. Moreover, the legislative history supports that interpretation of the Act.[22] Nonetheless, it would be shortsighted to rely on Section 17(h) to justify exculpatory clauses for negligence in managing the investments of investment companies or any other kind of investor. In contrast to the indirectness of Section 17(h), too many other statutory and regulatory developments are precise in their disapproval of contractual avoidance of liability for mismanagement. When different statutes dealing with connected problems adopt a common perspective, the legislative message eventually comes to be recognized as an expression of a societal judgment deserving of general application. This is probably what is happening in the case of exculpatory clauses excusing investment managers from the consequences of their negligence. As

---

[20] Reg. § 53.4944-1 (promulgated under I.R.C. § 4944) deals with the imposition of additional tax for investments which "jeopardize" a foundation's charitable purposes. Penalty taxes are imposed upon both the foundations and their managers, and Regulation § 53.4944-1(a)(2)(b) specifies that a tax imposed on the manager "shall be paid by" him.

[21] 15 U.S.C. § 80a-17(h).

[22] See the SEC Report to the 76th Congress, *Investment Trusts and Investment Companies*, Pt. III, H.R. Docket No. 279, 76th Cong., 2d Sess. (1939), where it is noted, without disapproval, that of sixty-eight investment management contracts in existence at the end of 1935 and reviewed in the study, twenty-two of them contained provisions exculpating the contract holder from all liability other than for willful misfeasance or bad faith. See also Hearings on S. 3580 Before a Subcomm. of the Senate Comm. on Banking and Currency, 76th Cong., 3d Sess. 262-263 (1940). In discussing the drafting of a fiduciary-duty provision for the Investment Company Act (Section 17(e)), the SEC stated that to impose liability for negligence, as distinguished from gross misconduct or abuse of trust, "was possibly too onerous an obligation to impose upon people who are managing investment companies," *id.* at 262. Thus, what was an existing practice in 1935 was allowed to continue.

Professor Scott has pointed out with respect to professional trustees,[23] an objective evaluation of the function filled by professional investment managers suggests that exculpatory clauses for negligence are contrary to public policy. The anomaly of permitting investment managers to avoid responsibility for unreasonable failure to provide expert investment management, the only service justifying their existence, may be more than the law will tolerate.

But it would be a serious mistake to assume that there is no room for contracting out of personal liability for the consequences of negligent investment management. The denial of the protection of exculpatory provisions for nonprofessional trustees, for example, would probably result in diminished willingness by such persons to accept trusteeship despite the desire of many settlors that they serve. In addition, courts would likely respond with inconsistent application of rules of law in order to avoid undue harshness of nonprofessional trustees acting without expectation of personal gain.[24]

Even where professional investment managers are involved, it seems excessively protective to prevent any investor, fully aware of what he is doing, from relieving those providing him with management services from some of the consequences of their negligence. In their proper place, exculpatory clauses perform the important function of allocating risk of loss. Holding investment managers accountable for all consequences of mismanagement does not necessarily reflect sensible risk allocation. Were all kinds of exculpatory provisions deemed invalid, investment managers would be forced to self-insure or to purchase liability insurance against all losses resulting from their mismanagement, even when less costly protection of comparable order would

---

[23] 3 A. Scott, *Law of Trusts* § 222.3 (3d ed. 1967). As Professor Scott indicates, a professional trustee who holds himself out as one skilled in his business or profession should not be relieved of liability for providing less than the standard of service normally expected of such a person.

[24] The Uniform Management of Institutional Funds Act (7 *U.L.A.*) § 6 (Supp. 1976) sets out what is essentially a business-judgment rule for the "standard of conduct" of institutional trustees. "[M]embers of a governing board shall exercise ordinary business care and prudence under the facts and circumstances prevailing at the time of the action or decision." The Commissioners' Prefatory Note to the Uniform Act (7 *U.L.A.* (Supp. 1976) at 291) indicates the drafters' sensitivity to the "debilitating effect" of placing a high standard of conduct and liability upon such trustees who are "often uncompensated public-spirited citizens." Hence, the less restrictive business-judgment rule, similar to that applicable to directors of a corporation, was adopted.

be available to investors if they would assume the risk of loss. This is often the case when the probability of loss is low, but the determination of the negligence question is expensive.

Thus, the issue with respect to exculpatory clauses for negligence should not be whether they are good or bad in themselves. That is an issue which is incapable of resolution. The relevant question is whether exculpatory provisions are the product of a process in which investors are made aware of their existence and are possessed of sufficient information to make a reasonable evaluation of the risks they would be required to bear. In practical terms, this means that broadly worded, indefinite, open-ended exculpatory clauses for negligence are suspect and that cautious investment managers and counsel will not rely on their protective power. The wiser course would be for the investment management agreement to identify the particular risks investors are to assume. There is excellent precedent for this type of approach. Prior to the adoption of the Trust Indenture Act of 1939,[25] indenture trustees for publicly corporate obligations developed exculpatory-clause draftsmanship into high art. With Hohfeldian precision, they carefully authorized themselves to exercise the powers of their office while declining responsibility for the corresponding duties.[26] Though courts initially were supportive of these kinds of provisions,[27] some rather astonishing derelictions by indenture trustees turned some courts decidedly hostile to a contract approach, and through complicated technical legal devices, they avoided the full thrust of the language contained

---

[25] 15 U.S.C. §§ 77aaa et seq.

[26] See Posner, "Liability of the Trustee Under the Corporate Indenture," 42 Harv. L. Rev. 198 (1928). The author points out that "The ordinary [trust] indenture is impregnated with negatives. Wherever a power is conferred, the draftsman hastens to add 'but the trustee shall be under no duty so to do.' . . . The modern indenture bristles with general and specific exculpations." (*Id*. at 240.) In addition to exculpatory provisions running to specific duties and powers, to cover inadvertent omissions the governing trust instrument would also typically contain a general exculpatory provision applying to gross negligence, or willful default, or some similar language.

[27] See, e.g., Hazzard v. Chase Nat'l Bank, 159 Misc. 57, 287 N.Y.S. 541 (Sup. Ct. 1936). In this case involving an exculpatory provision holding a corporate trustee answerable only for his "own gross negligence or bad faith," the court, citing the "general rule of exoneration of trustees in this State under similar indentures" (159 Misc. at 62, 287 N.Y.S. at 547), held that duties created under indenture trusts arise solely out of contract, and that so long as the trustee complied with all of the provisions of the contract, he was not liable for gross negligence.

in indentures.[28] A major effect of relying on technical pretense to sidestep contractual restrictions, however, was to promote uncertainty and increase the prospect of inconsistent results. The Trust Indenture Act reintroduced predictability into the treatment of exculpatory clauses by expressly imposing a nonavoidable duty of prudence[29] subject to specific exceptions.[30] This same strategy of not attempting to escape all accountability for negligent investment management but of limiting accountability by specifying risks to be borne by investors can enhance the effectiveness of exculpatory provisions.

While the Trust Indenture Act itself is limited in its application, its treatment of the exculpatory clause issue is instructive for another reason. Trust indentures subject to the statute commonly include all the provisions the statute permits. There is no real negotiation over them, and it is doubtful that purchasers of corporate obligations pay them much heed. That being the case, it is an heroic argument that these provisions reflect conscious risk allocation between investors and indenture trustees for management by the trustees. Indeed, the history of exculpatory provisions in trust indentures suggests that, in the absence of legislation, the exculpatory provisions in trust indentures would be more inclusive than they are. Indenture trustees have argued that in the absence of these exculpatory provisions, the cost of administering the office would be much higher.[31] But there was no attempt on the part of Congress before passage of the Act, nor has there been an attempt on the part of underwriters since passage of the Act, to determine the preference of investors as to the higher premium broader recourse against indenture trustees would involve. The likelihood is that investors have not been sufficiently well informed about the risks they have contracted to bear or, if adequately informed, that they are unable to evaluate the risks properly in order to reach a considered judgment

---

[28] For example, the application of exculpatory provisions has been avoided by treating the act of the trustee as beyond the power conferred by the governing instrument and therefore not protected by contractual immunity inserted in the instrument. See, e.g., Conover v. Guarantee Trust Co., 88 N.J.Eq. 450, 102 A. 844 (1917), aff'd 106 A. 890 (1918).

[29] Trust Indenture Act of 1939 § 315(d), 15 U.S.C. § 77ooo(d).

[30] Id. §§ 315(d)(1)-315(d)(3), 15 U.S.C. §§ 77ooo(d)(1)-77ooo(d)(3).

[31] See A.L.I. Federal Securities Code, Tentative Draft No. 4, p. xxvi (April 1, 1975): "The Reporter has been persuaded that extension of the 'prudent man' test for purposes of *ascertaining the occurrence of a default,* as proposed in early drafts, would be impracticable and prohibitively expensive in terms of increased trustee's fees." (Emphasis in original.)

about absolving indenture trustees from accountability for different types of management. It is in these very circumstances that the law enters, through decision, statute, or regulation, and rejects freedom-of-contract analysis in favor of duty analysis. In effect, lawmakers substitute for existing arrangements their judgment as to what investors would prefer if they were adequately informed and capable of evaluating the information in their possession.

[3] Drafting Effective Exculpatory Provisions

Assuming that exculpatory clauses for specific occurrences are enforceable, it is still difficult to determine the types of provisions that will be effective. Exculpatory clauses for conflict-of-interest situations, for example, are of doubtful value for transactions which are not fair and reasonable for investors.[32] Moreover, there is no assurance that a particular kind of exculpatory provision will be equally effective in all environments. Disclosure of exculpatory provisions must be detailed enough to satisfy the antifraud rules of the federal securities laws. But disclosure alone may not suffice. Given the risk allocation function of exculpatory clauses, the intended audience must be capable of making use of the disclosure.[33]

----

[32] In New England Trust Co. v. Triggs, 334 Mass. 324, 135 N.E.2d 541 (1956), a bank trustee, despite a provision holding trustees liable only for their "receipts, payments," and "wilful defaults," but not for "errors of judgment," was held accountable for profits which accrued to its commercial department as a result of the premature sale of trust securities and unreasonably long retention of the proceeds of sale in its commercial department. The court deemed a reading of the exculpatory provision which would allow the trustee to profit from trust transactions as against public policy. In O'Hayer v. de St. Aubin, 293 N.Y.S.2d 147, 30 A.D.2d 419 (1969), the court held that an exculpatory clause excusing trustee self-dealing still required the trustee to exercise "good faith" and that failure to do so was a breach of the trust.

[33] Thus, it may be the case that exculpatory provisions will be observed more strictly with respect to the accounts of those individual investors who understand the nature of such provisions and presumably can contract intelligently in their own interests, than with respect to many institutionalized arrangements. Illustrative of this view is the position taken in SEC, *Report of the Advisory Committee on Investment Management Services for Individual Investors, Small Account Investment Management Services*, CCH Fed. Sec. L. Rep. No. 465, Pt. III, 24-25 (1973):

"[W]here a person offers investment advice of an impersonal or general character to clients on a discretionary basis, the investor will not receive

As a pragmatic line of inquiry, it may be useful to seek to identify classes of exculpatory provisions which can be defended as means of furthering their function of allocating responsibility for risk. It is not always necessary to draft exculpatory provisions in the form of general disclaimers which give little information to investors about the particular risks they will be bearing in connection with the management of their accounts. It is also possible to contractually define terms or establish the propriety of certain procedures in ways that may achieve many of the same ends as simple disclaimers. In contrast to general disclaimers, contractual definitions and statements of procedure have the positive ring of express undertakings and give the impression of achieving a degree of precision in allocating responsibility for risk. For example, investment managers must diversify unless it would be imprudent to do so.[34] Even if they cannot generally disclaim liability for failure to diversify,[35] managers should be able to establish diversification criteria in a way which, if credible according to investment theory,[36] can prevent subsequent disputes over whether they have met their statutory obliga-

---

all of the benefits that usually attend a professional or fiduciary relationship, and thus should have all of the risks and other material information spelled out in a prospectus."

To apparently similar effect is a distinction between testamentary and inter vivos trusts. For example, under New York law, executors and testamentary trustees are subject to Section 11-1.7 of the Estates, Powers and Trusts Law (McKinney 1967), which provides that it is contrary to public policy to exonerate such trustees "from liability for failure to exercise reasonable care, diligence and prudence." There is no comparable statutory restriction with respect to inter vivos trustees. This may be attributable to the fact that every person who wishes to make a testamentary disposition must appoint an executor or trustee or rely upon the court to appoint an administrator, the alternative being intestacy. An inter vivos trust, however, involves less of an element of compulsion, particularly if it is revocable, as it is only one of many alternative methods of disposing of one's property. It is usually created by persons with definite objectives in mind and with at least a degree of understanding as to the risks involved and the functions of the trustee.

[34] *Restatement (Second) of Trusts* § 228 (1959); *Restatement (Second) of Agency* § 425, Comments a, c (1958). See generally ¶ 6.02[4].

[35] Cf. ERISA § 404(a)(1)(C), 29 U.S.C. § 1104(a)(1)(C) (establishing statutory duty to diversify), and *id.* § 410(a), 29 U.S.C. § 1110(a) (prohibiting provisions relieving fiduciaries from statutory duties).

[36] It is now known, for example, that a large number of common stocks must be included in a portfolio to elimnate nonmarket risk. See ¶ 7.08. Investment in fewer stocks may be indicated, however, in furtherance of a particular investment strategy or because of the investor's means.

tion.[37] Similar tactics might be useful in any situation in which the protective power of a mere general disclaimer is suspect, and the discussion which follows considers some types of narrow provisions, support for which is based on an allocation-of-risk analysis.

[a] Reliance on the opinions of experts

Agency doctrine imposes responsibility on investment managers for the negligence of subagents chosen by the manager.[38] Trust doctrine imposes liability on trustees for the negligence of agents employed by them if the agents are selected without reasonable care, are supervised inadequately, are directed or permitted to exercise improper authority, or are not compelled to redress their wrongs to the trust beneficiaries.[39] But carrying out management responsibilities, even within the manager's own area of expertise, including securities and market analysis, executions, and other elements of portfolio management, frequently requires the manager to rely on outside experts. In such cases, assuming there is no delegation-of-responsibility problem,[40] questions about adequacy of supervision, extent of authority, and so forth can be expensive to litigate. As a result, investment managers may wish to reserve the right

---

[37] For example, the settlor of a trust may confer authority or express preferences for retaining or maintaining particular holdings in a portfolio. See, e.g., Mazzola v. Myers, 363 Mass. 625, 296 N.E.2d 481 (1973); North Adams Nat'l Bank v. Curtiss, 278 Mass. 471, 180 N.E. 217 (1932).

[38] *Restatement (Second) of Agency* § 406 (1958). An example of this principle's operation is Christensen v. Pryor, 75 Ariz. 260, 255 P.2d 195 (1953), where a broker was held liable for his salesmen's deceit. Liability for failure to supervise employees can occur under the federal securities laws, particularly if the person having the duty to supervise carries it out negligently. See, e.g., Johns Hopkins Univ. v. Hutton, 297 F. Supp. 1165 (D. Md. 1968), *aff'd in part and remanded* 422 F.2d 1124 (4th Cir. 1970), and 343 F. Supp. 245 (D. Md. 1972), *aff'd in part and remanded* 488 F.2d 912 (4th Cir. 1973), *cert. denied* 416 U.S. 916 (1974). (Securities Act of 1933, Ch. 38, § 12(2), 48 Stat. 84 (May 27, 1933).)

[39] *Restatement (Second) of Trusts* § 225 (1959). For examples of imposition of liability upon executors or trustees, see *In re* Estate of Lohm, 440 Pa. 268, 269 A.2d 451 (1970), and *In re* Hartzell's Will, 43 Ill. App. 2d 118, 192 N.E.2d 697 (1963).

[40] *Restatement (Second) of Trusts* § 171 (1959); *Restatement (Second) of Agency* §§ 18, 78 (1958). See, e.g., *In re* Kohler's Estate, 348 Pa. 55, 33 A.2d 920 (1943) (power to invest funds of estate is "personal" and not to be delegated); *In re* Hartzell's Will, 43 Ill. App. 2d, 118, 192 N.E.2d 697 (1963) (trustee held liable for delegating the power to collect the unpaid balance of proceeds from a sale of real estate where the unsupervised agent converted the funds to his own use and purposes).

to rely on the opinions of experts whenever advisable without incurring possible liability for any negligence by the experts. Opinions of counsel and certifications by accountants are the most common types of expert opinion on which investment managers rely. Provisions for investment managers so to rely have the support of authority[41] and custom.[42] The same principle should extend to other experts on matters necessary to analysis of securities, quality of execution, portfolio valuation, and like matters with respect to which investment managers may have occasion to rely on outside experts.

[b] Responsibility for co-managers

An increasingly common phenomenon is the distribution of investment management responsibility for the portfolio of a single investor among a number of investment managers. The investor may regard such an arrangement as a way to foster greater attention to his account by virtue of the competition among managers, or to improve diversification or to obtain specialized management services. But whatever the investor's rationale, the diversion of the portfolio into separate investment compartments may not relieve a manager from all responsibility for investing so that the *entire* portfolio is suitable and adequately diversified.[43] If that is the case, co-managers, though unconnected in every way other than through their common client, would need to be

---

[41] Newhouse v. Canal Nat'l Bank of Portland, 124 F. Supp. 239 (D. Me. 1954) (upholding a clause exonerating trustees from the neglects and defaults of others, including mistake of fact or law, or loss not caused by the trustee's own willful default); Dill v. Boston Safe Deposit & Trust Co., 343 Mass. 97, 175 N.E.2d 911 (1961) (validating a clause entitling trustees to rely and act upon the opinion or advice of "any . . . attorney . . . selected with reasonable care"). See also Note, "Directory Trusts and the Exculpatory Clause," 65 Colum. L. Rev. 138 (1965).

[42] See American Bar Foundation, Model Debenture Indenture Provisions §§ 603(a)-603(d) (1967).

[43] *Restatement (Second) of Trusts* § 184 (1959) imposes upon co-trustees a duty "to participate in the administration of the trust and to use reasonable care to prevent a co-trustee from committing a breach of trust. . . ." *Restatement (Second) of Agency* § 405(2) (1958) imposes liability upon an agent who "directs, permits, or otherwise takes part in the improper conduct of other agents." It should be noted, though, that Section 405 does not impose on an agent liability "for the conduct of another agent merely because they are working together upon the principal's affairs. . . ." For further discussion of the duties of co-trustees, see Note, "Directory Trusts and the Exculpatory Clause," 65 Colum. L. Rev. 138 (1965).

aware of what is contained in the portions of the portfolio they do not manage.

Since the diversification of a single portfolio among several investment managers on a wide scale is a relatively recent phenomenon, it is unsurprising that the legal response has been modest. An instructive development has occurred, however, in connection with the definition of statutory fiduciary under the Employee Retirement Income Security Act of 1974 (ERISA).[44] The duties of co-fiduciaries are largely drawn from common-law principles,[45] but, if anything, are stricter than under the common law.[46] In apparent recognition of the effects of broad co-fiduciary responsibility on the practice of dividing a pension-plan portfolio among unaffiliated investment managers, the Department of Labor and the Internal Revenue Service have promulgated identically worded regulations defining investment advice (the giving of which triggers statutory fiduciary status) so that a fiduciary will not enjoy such status with respect to assets of the plan over which he lacks control and to which he provides no investment advice.[47] It would seem that a similar approach, carried out contractually, would be useful when an investment manager is made responsible for only a portion of a portfolio owned by an investor other than an employee benefit plan.

---

[44] ERISA § 3(21)(a) (29 U.S.C. § 1002(21)(A)) and § 2003(a) (I.R.C. § 4975(e)(3)).

[45] ERISA § 405 (29 U.S.C. § 1105) contains various provisions defining the responsibility of "co-fiduciaries" and, like Section 184 of the *Restatement (Second) of Trusts,* requires that where plan assets are held by co-trustees, "each shall use reasonable care to prevent a co-trustee from committing a breach." *Id.* § 405(b)(1)(A) (29 U.S.C. § 1105(b)(1)(A)). Section 405(d) relieves trustees, however, of liability for the acts and omissions of investment managers appointed pursuant to Section 402(c)(3) (29 U.S.C. § 1102(c)(3)).

[46] Section 405(a)(2) (29 U.S.C. § 1105(a)(2)) provides that a fiduciary is liable for a breach of fiduciary duty "if, by his failure to comply with § 404(a)(1) [which imposes general duties of acting solely in the interest of the beneficiaries, performing with skill and care of a prudent man, diversifying investments, and complying with the governing instruments] in the administration of his specific responsibilities which give rise to his status as a fiduciary, he has enabled such other fiduciary to commit a breach." There is no explicit knowledge or negligence requirement with respect to the connection between a fiduciary's breach of Section 404(a)(1) and the co-fiduciary's breach imposing joint liability under Section 405(a)(2).

[47] Labor Reg. § 2510.3-21(2) (29 C.F.R. § 2510.3-21(2)) and Reg. § 4975-9(2) (26 C.F.R. § 54.4975-9(2)).

[c] Responsibility for portfolio diversification

Although for certain investors, primarily individuals and investment companies, investment managers may adopt a policy of concentrating investments in a few securities in hopes of improving asset appreciation, in general, investment managers are under a duty to diversify the portfolios of their clients and may engage in a program of concentration only with the express concurrence of their clients. The law of trusts makes diversification mandatory except where diversification would be imprudent,[48] and agency doctrine makes it a factor to be considered in formulating an investment program.[49] A fuller discussion of the duty to diversify appears in Part III,[50] but for purposes of examining the effectiveness of exculpatory clauses, it is enough to make two observations:

(1) Under modern investment theory, the failure to diversify is an error of serious magnitude.

(2) Because proper diversification for a given investor depends on a number of variables, a precise definition of the concept is not possible.

In the past, certain broad exculpatory clauses have provided in-

---

[48] *Restatement (Second) of Trusts* § 228 (1959). The comments to Section 228 state that the trustee is not to invest a disproportionately large segment of the trust estate in any one security, and that "it is not enough that each of the investments is a proper investment under the rule stated in Section 227 [the general guideline provision for trustee investment]." After listing various factors to be considered, including purposes of the trust, type of investment, and distribution as to industries, the comments mention "special circumstances" in which diversification may not be prudent, such as the management of only a very small trust estate (one or two thousand dollars), or "times of crisis and general financial instability." Even with small estates. however, diversification is a ready option through common trust funds and investment companies.

[49] *Restatement (Second) of Agency* § 425(b) (1958). The section requires that an agent "invest only in such securities as would be obtained by a prudent investor for his own account, having in view both safety and income, in the light of the principal's means and purposes. . . ." The comment to Section 425(b) states, "it would be beyond the discretion of the agent . . . in the case of a large sum, to fail to diversify investments so as to minimize the risk of the loss of the whole." Exceptions to this rule have appeared, however. An agent may not be required to diversify where he follows the principal's earlier investment pattern in good faith. O'Connor v. Burns, Potter & Co., 151 Neb. 9, 36 N.W.2d 507 (1949).

[50] See ¶¶ 6.02[4], 7.02[4], 7.03[3][d], 7.08.

vestment managers with protection for nondiversification. One type of provision previously approved under state law empowers trustees to retain all or part of an existing portfolio when administration of the trust begins.[51] Such a provision might be useful today to protect investment managers who delay liquidating a portfolio while they bring it into conformity with investment programs of their own design. But the original function of these provisions was to avoid forcing trustees to dispose of investments that were otherwise prohibited for inclusion in trusts. This function has little to do with diversification as an investment policy. Moreover, it is a tenuous proposition that provisions simply authorizing investment managers to retain investments adequately inform investors of the risks of nondiversification. Consequently, if such provisions are intended to include protection for a deliberate decision not to diversify as a matter of investment policy, they should refer specifically to that fact.

A more common ground for absolving investment managers from accountability for failing to diversify has been the broad exculpatory clause applying to all negligence.[52] Whether such provisions will continue to protect investment managers against failures to diversify depends, of course, on how extensively broad exculpatory clauses will continue to be honored.[53] But to obtain protection for nondiversification, careful draftsmen should not rely only on such clauses, even assuming that the courts and regulatory authorities will continue to enforce them in some respects. The variety of collective investment vehicles available today makes diversification simple to achieve even for the smallest accounts. Even though the advisability of diversification for every investor and the type of diversification to be sought may still be a matter over which reasonable investment managers can disagree, diversification on some order has become so fundamental[54] that where concentration is the investment manager's policy, the investment management agreement should spell that out with care.

Where federal law displaces state law on this issue, it may be impossible to draft exculpatory provisions protecting the manager against liability for failing to diversify. Federal law has already expressly im-

---

[51] See, e.g., Baldus v. Bank of Calif., 12 Wash. App. 621, 530 P.2d 1350 (1975).

[52] New England Trust Co. v. Paine, 317 Mass. 542, 59 N.E.2d 263 (1945).

[53] See ¶ 5.02[2] *supra*.

[54] See note 50 *supra*.

posed a diversification duty on managers of employee benefit plans.[55] It may also have done so by implication, at least by setting minimum diversification standards, for such other institutional investors as investment companies[56] and private foundations.[57] If accountability for non-diversification is unavoidable, it is advisable for the investment management agreement to define diversification in order to avoid later dispute. The need for a contractual definition of diversification can be especially important when more than one investment manager is servicing an investor's portfolio. In any event, by adapting a contractual definition to the risk profile of the investor, an investment manager can set a base beneath a portfolio to establish compliance with the duty to diversify. Should the investment manager deem it wise, he can also prescribe conditions and procedures for dipping below the base.

¶ 5.03.   MANAGEMENT COMPENSATION ARRANGEMENTS

Compensation arrangements between investment managers and their clients raise two legal questions: (1) how much may be charged

---

[55] ERISA § 404(a)(1)(C) (29 U.S.C. § 1104(a)(1)(C)). According to Section 410 (29 U.S.C. § 1110), exculpatory clauses are restricted to those provided for in Section 405(b)(1) (29 U.S.C. § 1105(b)(1)) and Section 405(d) (29 U.S.C. § 1105(d)). Section 405 only relieves trustees of liability for certain acts of co-trustees and investment managers.

[56] Investment Company Act § 5(b)(1) (15 U.S.C. § 80a-5(b)(1)), defines a "diversified company" as

"[A] management company which meets the following requirements: At least 75 per centum of the value of its total assets is represented by cash and cash items (including receivables), Government securities, securities of other investment companies, and other securities for the purposes of this calculation limited in respect of any one issuer to an amount not greater in value than 5 per centum of the value of the total assets of such management company and to not more than 10 per centum of the outstanding voting securities of such issuer."

Also, Section 851 of the Internal Revenue Code provides that a corporation shall not be considered a regulated investment company unless, among other things, its investments are diversified according to a formula set forth in the Code. Thus, an "investment company," here meaning a mutual fund, will lose its advantageous tax treatment under Section 852 of the Code if it does not meet the diversification requirements. Diversification to meet either the Code or the Act requirements would not establish a portfolio as diversified. See ¶ 6.02[4]. Failure to meet such requirements, however, might establish a level of nondiversification beyond which exculpation is impermissible because of the resulting statutory consequences.

[57] See Reg. § 53.4944-1, discussed in note 20 *supra*.

for investment management services; and (2) what is to be classified as compensation. The array of services a number of investment managers provide to and obtain for their clients often makes it difficult to identify the purposes for which payments are made by investors and to determine who the beneficiaries of those payments really are. Unartful drafting of compensation provisions can have adverse consequences for investment managers because most forms of management compensation are subject to state and federal law. Direct compensation in the form of management fees and "performance" fees are the most apparent objects of regulation. But also of serious regulatory concern are indirect benefits which, though not specified in the investment management agreement and consented to by the client, flow back to the investment manager or to designated but undisclosed third parties.

Because of the fiduciary capacity in which investment managers act, contractual provisions which attempt to justify receipt of benefits to management through various avenues not fully disclosed to the investor are suspect. At least in the abstract, the duty of loyalty requires investment managers to act solely for the benefit of their clients unless there is prior agreement otherwise on the basis of adequate disclosure. Furthermore, the federal securities laws reinforce this common-law duty by regulating the degree of disclosure necessary to substantiate any prior agreement.

Actually, insofar as drafting an investment management agreement is concerned, it is confusing to rely on the term "compensation" to describe benefits to management. Because compensation arrangements are so highly regulated, compensation has developed a rather inclusive meaning as a legal concept. Referred to expressly as compensation or in some related phraseology, it has been applied, for example, to the return of brokerage and other commissions to management and its affiliates,[58] the overly high valuation of assets,[59] the power to direct the amount or determine the recipient of brokerage commissions,[60] the

---

[58] See *In re* Winfield & Co., SEC Securities Exchange Act Release No. 9478 (Feb. 9, 1972), [1971-1972 Transfer Binder] CCH Fed. Sec. L. Rep. ¶ 78,530.

[59] *Id.*

[60] See, e.g., *In re* Cornfeld, SEC Securities Exchange Act Release No. 9094 (March 1, 1971), [1970-1971 Transfer Binder] CCH Fed. Sec. L. Rep. ¶ 77,963; Hubshman Management Corp., SEC Securities Exchange Act Release No. 8557 (March 20, 1969); *In re* Managed Funds, Inc., SEC Securities Exchange Act Release No. 4122 (July 30, 1959), [1957-1961 Transfer Binder] CCH Fed. Sec. L. Rep. ¶ 76,662.

failure to recapture brokerage commissions,[61] fees received by an affiliated tender agent during a tender offer,[62] the offer of a note at a price reduced from a public offering price,[63] and a variety of reciprocal practices designed to reward third parties for doing business with the investment manager.[64]

Some of these practices, such as overvaluing assets to increase management compensation, are simply unlawful, a circumstance no amount of skill in drafting can change.[65] Some, on the other hand,

---

[61] Moses v. Burgin, 445 F.2d 369 (1st Cir.), cert. denied sub nom. Johnson v. Moses, 404 U.S. 994 (1971).

[62] See In re Provident Management Corp., SEC Securities Act Release No. 5115 (Dec. 1, 1970), [1970-1971 Transfer Binder] CCH Fed. Sec. L. Rep. ¶ 77,937 ("personal enrichment").

[63] E.g., United States v. Deutsch, 451 F.2d 98 (2d Cir.), aff'g 321 F. Supp. 1356 (S.D.N.Y. 1971), cert. denied 404 U.S. 1019 (1972).

[64] E.g., Frooks v. Barnett, [1974-1975 Transfer Binder] CCH Fed. Sec. L. Rep. ¶ 94,903 (S.D.N.Y. 1974) (purchase of certificates of deposit in return for loan to affiliates of an officer of the fund); In re Continental Inv. Corp., SEC Securities Act Release No. 5318 (Oct. 11, 1972), [1972-1973 Transfer Binder] CCH Fed. Sec. L. Rep. ¶ 79,024 (purchase of unnecessary services; failure to negotiate favorable execution price; special arrangements with custodian); In re Provident Management Corp., Securities Act Release No. 5115 (Dec. 1, 1970), [1970-1971 Transfer Binder] CCH Fed. Sec. L. Rep. ¶ 77,937 (brokerage used to obtain sales brochures, sales lectures, and other selling aids). See also Wynn v. Heller, 391 F. Supp. 507 (S.D.N.Y. 1975) (unlawful receipt of fees to administer pension trust).

[65] E.g., Investment Company Act Release No. 5847 (Oct. 21, 1969), 5 CCH Fed. Sec. L. Rep. ¶ 72,135. In In re Mates Fin. Serv., SEC Securities Exchange Act Release No. 8836 (March 9, 1970), [1969-1970 Transfer Binder] CCH Fed. Sec. L. Rep. ¶ 77,790, an investment company investment adviser was held liable for overvaluing restricted securities in order to inflate the fund's asset value. See generally Gottleib, "Guidelines for Mutual Fund Valuation of Portfolio Securities," P-H Sec. Reg. Rep. ¶ 1103.

There are some common-law protections against overvaluation of assets, also. A trustee has a duty to render a proper accounting, and failure to do so is a breach of trust. Restatement (Second) of Trusts § 172 (1959). It has been held that provisions dispensing with judicial accounting when otherwise required by law are void as against public policy. See Application of Burden, 5 Misc. 2d 558, 160 N.Y.S.2d 372 (Sup. Ct. N.Y. Co. 1957). Also, agency law provides for a similar duty to account. See, e.g., Clark v. Greenberg, 296 N.Y. 146, 71 N.E.2d 443 (1947); Restatement (Second) of Agency § 382 (1958). An agent may forfeit all compensation for failure properly to account. See, e.g., Lamdin v. Broadway Surface Advertising Corp., 272 N.Y. 133, 5 N.E.2d 66 (1936). Based on the duty of loyalty, an action in equity will lie for the recovery of excessive compensation. See, e.g., In re Di Filippo's Estate, 162 Misc. 423, 294 N.Y.S. 802 (Sur. Ct. 1937).

which would otherwise raise serious duty-of-loyalty questions, may be made effective by proper drafting and disclosure. Cautious practice suggests that an investment management agreement acknowledge explicitly, or incorporate by reference to extrinsic documents, all direct and indirect sources of substantial pecuniary benefit to management which otherwise would appear as separate expenses to investors. That will at least prevent any claim that the agreement failed to describe management compensation accurately.

The discussion which follows considers management compensation problems based on the assumption that there has been adequate disclosure to clients of indirect benefits to management.

[1]　The Management Fee

The management fee, also called the advisory fee, represents the principal expense to an investor for obtaining the professional services described or implied in the management agreement. Both trust law[66] and agency law[67] entitle investment managers to reasonable compensation for their efforts. The significant difference between trust doctrine and agency doctrine is that trustees are under tighter legal controls than agency managers if the details of payment of the management fee are not precisely set out. Although the rule for both is reasonableness,

---

[66] Although the law as to compensation varies among the states, it is generally true that a trustee is entitled to compensation for his performance of duties unless he commits a breach of trust, or the trust instrument provides otherwise, or the trustee voluntarily waives compensation. The amount may be prescribed or limited by statute or by the will or trust instrument, and in many states a court may vary an amount that is unreasonably high or low. *Restatement (Second) of Trusts* § 242 (1959). In New York, for example, testamentary trustees are compensated at a statutory rate, based upon the total principal and the amount of principal paid out, payable one-half from income and one-half from principal unless the will provides otherwise. Separate rules apply to charitable trusts, situations involving multiple trustees, and trusts where the trustee is required to manage real property or to accumulate income. N.Y. Surr. Ct. Proc. Act § 2309 (McKinney 1967). This is contrary to the law of England, where a trustee is not entitled to compensation unless it is authorized in the governing instrument; see 3 A. Scott, *Law of Trusts* § 242 (3d ed. 1967).

[67] Where an agent's contract provides for compensation, he is entitled only to the definite amount set forth in the instrument or, if no figure is stated, to the fair value of his actual services. *Restatement (Second) of Agency* § 443 (1958). A rate of compensation may be inferred from custom or usage in a particular trade or profession, and compensation may be made conditional upon a certain occurrence or result. *Id.* §§ 445-446.

many states determine reasonableness legislatively for trustees through statutory schedules of trustee fees.[68] Furthermore, trust-law constraints extend beyond concern only with the amount of compensation to be paid. Also important are the sources within a trust estate from which compensation may be paid. In some states, annual or periodic trustee compensation may be drawn only from income or from a specific portion of income and principal.[69]

But this difference between agency law and trust law is not of major significance. It is generally the case that statutory restrictions on trustee fees can be avoided by prior agreement between the trustee and the trustor[70] or by subsequent agreement between the trustee and the beneficiaries.[71] As a practical matter, the rate of compensation is the provision least likely to be glossed over in an agreement between a professional investment manager and a client. Moreover, it is fairly common practice for trustee investment managers to set the management fee by incorporating by reference into the document establishing the trust a renewable contract specifying compensation arrangements. This avoids the necessity of having to amend the trust should a change

---

[68] See note 66 *supra* and note 70 *infra*.

[69] See note 66 *supra*. See also Uniform Principal and Income Act (7 U.L.A.) §§ 3, 13 (1970).

[70] *Restatement (Second) of Trusts* § 242, Comment i (1959); 3 A. Scott, *Law of Trusts* § 242.6 (3d ed. 1967). In New York, a testamentary trustee is not entitled to compensation in excess of that provided in the will, N.Y. Surr. Ct. Proc. Act § 2309(10) (McKinney 1967), and an inter vivos trustee is entitled only to the compensation or commission agreed upon or provided in the trust instrument, e.g. *In re* Bostwick's Trust, 189 Misc. 331, 70 N.Y.S.2d 352 (Sup. Ct. N.Y. Co. 1947); *In re* Irving Trust Co., 65 N.Y.S.2d 824 (Sup. Ct. N.Y. Co. 1946). Courts have, in unusual situations, changed the stated compensation, especially where the compensation has been set so low that no competent trustee will undertake to administer the trust. See, e.g., Oregon Bank v. Hendricksen, 267 Ore. 138, 515 P.2d 1328 (1973); *In re* Estate of Taylor, 6 Cal. App. 3d 16, 85 Cal. Rptr. 474 (1970) (statutory grounds); *In re* Coleman's Estate, 12 Pa. D. & C. 548, 7 Fiduc. 580 (Pa. Orphans' Ct. 1957). Also, courts have on occasion reduced unreasonably high rates. See, e.g., *In re* Trust Estate of Powell, 68 Wash. 2d 38, 411 P.2d 162 (1966). For a discussion of the effects of limiting provisions in contracts, wills, and trust instruments, see Annotation, "Limiting Effect of Contract, Will, or Trust Instrument Fixing Trustee's or Executor's Fees," 19 A.L.R.3d 520 (1968), and Annotation, "Validity and Effect of Provision of Contract of Trust Instrument Limiting Amount of Fees of Trustee," 161 A.L.R. 860 (1946).

[71] *Restatement (Second) of Trusts* § 242, Comment i (1959); 3 A. Scott, *Law of Trusts* § 242.7 (3d ed. 1967).

in rate of compensation be negotiated. More important, in establishing the management fee by contract outside the trust instrument, the investment manager avoids being forced to serve for a fee which subsequently becomes too low; for if a trustee cannot obtain amendment to the trust, the trustee is nonetheless required to serve in accordance with the terms of the trust, at least until judicial relief can be obtained.[72] If, on the other hand, the trustee and the investor cannot renew the compensation contract because of disagreement over the rate of compensation, the trustee would nonetheless be entitled to reasonable compensation.

But management fees which are too low are ordinarily not the problem. Most of the disagreement over management fees comes from investor complaints that they are too high. Normally, the reasonableness standard would deny relief to investors attacking management fees as excessive, unless the fees were so high that no reasonable person would have agreed to them.[73] Particularly where investment management agreements are negotiated between individual investors and professional investment managers, the reasonableness standard has been quite effective in protecting the fees to which the parties have agreed, unless there is evidence of undue influence or overreaching on the part of the investment manager in promoting the relationship in the first place.[74]

---

[72] Once a trustee accepts a trust, he may not resign unless the court so orders, or the trust instrument permits, or all beneficiaries consent. *Restatement (Second) of Trusts* § 106 (1959). Resignation or transfer of the trust res under other circumstances constitutes a breach of trust.

A common practice is the inclusion in trust agreements of a cancellation clause whereby either party may terminate the trustee's tenure on sixty days' notice or after some definite period. Even if such a termination is effected, however, the familiar principle that a trust will not fail for want of a trustee is applicable. *Restatement (Second) of Trusts* § 101 (1959). Although a trustee who withdraws under a cancellation clause might be entitled to expenses if forced to serve after the notice period, the trustee may nonetheless be required to remain in office and to refrain from transferring trust property until a successor trustee has assumed office voluntarily or by order of the court. In view of these restrictions on trustee resignation, an investment manager trustee looking directly to the trust as a source of such compensation would be better off having the rate of compensation determined by contractual arrangements extrinsic to the trust instrument.

[73] See, e.g., Saxe v. Brady, 40 Del. Ch. 474, 184 A.2d 602 (1962).

[74] If unreasonably high compensation is provided for because of an initial "abuse of a fiduciary or confidential relationship existing between the trustee and the settlor at the time of the creation of the trust," the trustee is entitled only to reasonable compensation. *Restatement (Second) of Trusts* § 242, Comment f (1959); 3 A. Scott, *Law of Trusts* § 242.4 (3d ed. 1967). Otherwise, absent statutory limitations, the trustee is entitled to the full

Recently, however, the reasonableness standard has been giving way to other standards. On the grounds that many investors do not fully appreciate the services their payments for investment management fees are underwriting, the SEC has been using the statutory fraud rules as a weapon against high management fees. The Commission staff now takes the position that failure to disclose departures from typical fee schedules is a deceptive practice violative of the statutory fraud provisions.[75] The staff also has concluded that fee-sharing arrangements, if not unlawful entirely, at least must be fully disclosed to investors.[76] These developments may be unexplainable as refinements of the common-law fiduciary principle which prohibits secret diversion of property from a beneficiary or principal to the use of a trustee or agent, and, though the perceived need for refinement can be traced to the Commission's concern for protecting individual investors,[77] there is no reason to believe that the disclosure requirements will not be applied to institutional investor accounts as well.

---

amount provided for. See, e.g., Lederman v. Lisinsky, 112 N.Y.S.2d 203 (Sup. Ct. N.Y. Co. 1952). Fiduciary abuse in setting high management fees applies to agency relationships also. See, e.g., Hurt v. Cotton States Fertilizer Co., 159 F.2d 52 (5th Cir.), cert. denied 331 U.S. 828 (1947); Williams v. Schatz Manufacturing Co., Sec. Reg. L. Rep. No. 309, July 2, 1957, Sec. Reg. L. Rep., Aug. 2, 1975, at A-14 (S.D.N.Y., May 23, 1975). For a useful discussion of management fees, especially in comparing the opportunities different types of managers have to profit from the management relationship, see Welles, "How Profitable Is Managing Money?" 9 Institutional Investor 39 (Sept. 1975).

[75] See, e.g., John G. Kinnard, [1973-1974 Transfer Binder] CCH Fed. Sec. L. Rep. ¶ 79,662; Rotan Mosle Inc., [1973-1976 Transfer Binder] CCH Mutual Funds Guide ¶ 10,070 (1974); Commodity Management Serv. Corp., [1973-1976 Transfer Binder] CCH Mutual Funds Guide ¶ 10,035 (1974). See also Mexico Fund, Sec. Reg. L. Rep., July 30, 1975, at C-1 (1975) (fee of 1.5 percent of net asset value raises questions under Investment Company Act § 36(b)); Edward D. Jones & Co., [1975-1976 Transfer Binder] CCH Fed. Sec. L. Rep. ¶ 80,391 (1975) (fee for advising mutual fund shareholders exchanging shares within fund complexes).

[76] See Casey, " 'Finders Fee' Compensation to Brokers and Others," 31 Bus. Law. 707 (1976); Bines, "Regulating Discretionary Management: Broker-Dealers as Catalysts for Reform," 16 B.C. Ind. & Com. L. Rev. 347, 374-378 (1975).

[77] SEC, Report of Advisory Committee on Investment Management Services for Individual Investors, Small Account Investment Management Services, reprinted in CCH Fed. Sec. L. Rep. No. 465, at 39-41; Freidman, "Problems Involving Investment Advisers and Broker-Dealers Serving Individual Accounts," in A. Fleischer & R. Mundheim, Fourth Annual Institute on Securities Regulation 297-308 (PLI 1973).

The growing institutionalization of the investor community has also led to another subtle but very perceptible shift in the application of the reasonableness standard. The adversary context in which management fees are negotiated where individual investors are concerned can be blurred in negotiations over fees for managing institutional accounts. Although there are important distinctions, of course, virtually all institutional accounts are characterized by an organizational structure which delegates to certain surrogates the authority for obtaining investment management services. Moreover, it is commonly the case that the persons to whom this authority is delegated have little or no personal financial stake in the success of the investment venture.

The practical impossibility of collecting all those having a direct financial stake and explaining to them the details of the proposed agreement obviously requires delegation of negotiating responsibility to some select group. Nonetheless, the insertion of intermediaries in the negotiating process, particularly with respect to setting fees for management, produces an unstated but distinct reluctance on the part of courts and regulatory authorities to accept as enforceable all fees not demonstrably unreasonable. One sees, rather, a disposition to replace the passive test that management fees not be so excessive as to be unreasonable with the positive requirement that management fees be reasonable and fair. This dual test of fairness and reasonableness is said to stem from the fiduciary nature of the relationship between the investment manager and the client. What this really means is that if the facts surrounding the establishment of the management agreement indicate that the manager is in effect setting his own fees, those facts raise questions involving the duty of loyalty and hence undermine the justification for a passive approach to attacks on management fees for excessiveness.

A case in point is the treatment of management fees received by investment advisers to investment companies. Under the original conception of the Investment Company Act of 1940, the unaffiliated directors or trustee of statutory investment companies were supposed to represent the interests of the shareholders to the extent they came into conflict with the interest of the investment advisers.[78] The size of

---

78 See, e.g., Brown v. Bullock, 194 F. Supp. 207 (S.D.N.Y. 1961). Investment Company Act §§ 10(a)-10(c) (15 U.S.C. §§ 80a-10(a) to 80a-10(c)) limit the affiliation of investment company directors with officers and affiliates of the adviser brokers, underwriters, and banks. Section 10(a), requiring 60 percent of the board to consist of outside directors, was amended by Section 5(a) of the Investment Company Act Amendments of 1970 (Pub. L. 91-547, 84 Stat. 1413 (Dec. 14, 1970)) to narrow the

advisory fees, however, apparently has not been a matter of major concern to these shareholder representatives. Extensive study and documentation by the SEC in the 1960s failed to reveal any instance in which unaffiliated directors attempted to reduce advisory fees charged to large investment companies despite the economies of scale associated with managing the companies.[79] Nor were there recorded instances of unaffiliated directors attempting to reduce fees or seek the services of competing investment advisers as a result of a record of consistently poor investment performance.[80] On the issue of fees, at least, the unaffiliated directors appeared to be the captives of the investment managers. In effect, investment advisers to investment companies were determining the reasonableness of their own fees,[81] and so severely straining the duty of loyalty thereby that the contractual facade constructed for their management fees ultimately crumbled.

The first signal that a passive reasonableness standard would not suffice to vindicate management fees charged investment companies came in a series of lawsuits attacking the size of the fees. Initially, the inroads were modest. Many of these lawsuits were settled by agreements to scale down management fees slightly as the size of investment companies increased.[82] Indeed, in the cases which were actually litigated, the investment advisers were able successfully to defend their manage-

---

pool of eligible directors from statutory "affiliates" (§ 2(a)(3), 15 U.S.C. § 80a-2(a)(3)) to statutory "interested persons" (§ 2(a)(19), 15 U.S.C. § 80a-2(a)(19)).

[79] See SEC, *Report of the Wharton School of Finance and Commerce: A Study of Mutual Funds,* H.R. Rep. No. 2274, 87th Cong., 2d Sess. 28-29 (1962) (hereinafter cited as *Wharton Report*); SEC, *Report on the Public Policy Implications of Investment Company Growth,* H.R. Rep. No. 2337, 89th Cong., 2d Sess. 94-96 (1966) (hereinafter cited as *PPI Report*); Note, "The Mutual Fund Industry: A Legal Survey," 44 Notre Dame Law. 732, 886-955 (1969) (hereinafter cited as Notre Dame Survey); Manges, "The Investment Company Amendments Act of 1970," 26 Bus. Law. 1311, 1314-1319 (1971).

[80] *Wharton Report,* note 79 *supra,* at 30; *PPI Report,* note 79 *supra,* at 126-127, 130-131.

[81] *PPI Report,* note 79 *supra,* at 131. The chairman of the SEC repeatedly made this point during the hearings leading up to the Investment Company Act Amendments of 1970 (Pub. L. 91-547 (Dec. 14, 1970)). Cf. Kauffman v. Dreyfus Fund, Inc., 434 F.2d 727 (3d Cir. 1970), *cert. denied* 401 U.S. 974 (1971).

[82] *PPI Report,* note 79 *supra,* at 102, 138-143; Notre Dame Survey, note 79 *supra,* at 917-930.

ment fees.[83] But even these cases further weakened the management position, since they were based not on fiduciary principle, but on the doctrine of ratification. The courts took the position that the un-affiliated director approval of management fees followed by shareholder ratification precluded further inquiry into the question of excessiveness, so long as the fees did not amount to a waste of corporate assets.[84]

Inevitably, the ratification doctrine destroyed the very thing it was designed to protect. Ratification may have been an appropriate basis for dispostion of the management fee issue under state corporation law,[85] but in being reduced to reliance on ratification by shareholders to protect management fees established by contract, the investment company industry was tacitly admitting that the unaffiliated directors were incapable of performing the watchdog function which the drafters of the Investment Company Act had purportedly assigned them.[86] The

---

[83] Hearings on S. 1659 Before the Senate Comm. on Banking and Currency, 90th Cong., 1st Sess., 20-21 (1967); (hereinafter cited as 1967 Senate Hearings); *PPI Report,* note 79 *supra,* at 132-138; Notre Dame Survey, note 79 *supra,* at 916-944.

In Saxe v. Brady, 40 Del. Ch. 474, 184 A.2d 602 (1962), the court held that fees paid to an investment adviser by a registered fund were not excessive. Of the shareholders participating, 99.1 percent ratified the payments after disclosure, and the court decided that where ratification has taken place the defendants need not show fairness since the transaction is governed by the business-judgment rule. Later, in Kleinman v. Saminsky, 41 Del. Ch. 572, 200 A.2d 572 (*aff'g* Saminsky v. Abbott, 41 Del. Ch. 320, 194 A.2d 549 (1963), *cert. denied* 379 U.S. 900 (1964)), the Delaware Supreme Court approved a settlement establishing fees found to be fair, the participants having ratified the prior payments after being fully informed of the earlier fee structure.

[84] E.g., Kleinman v. Saminsky, discussed at note 83 *supra.* Continual shareholder ratification is not required. After majority shareholder approval, annual approval by the board of directors validates the management contract. Investment Company Act § 15(a)(2), 15 U.S.C. § 80a-15(a)(2).

[85] For example, although violations of the Investment Company Act were alleged in Kleinman v. Saminsky, note 83 *supra,* it was held, in effect, that plaintiffs' federal claims were frivolous, and the case was decided under state law. Under Delaware law, e.g., Saxe v. Brady, note 83 *supra,* it was proper for the court to use the ratification principle to bring the payments under the business judgment rule.

[86] Investment Company Act § 1(b)(2), 15 U.S.C. § 80a-1(b)(2); Hearings on H.R. 10065 Before a Subcomm. of the House Comm. on Interstate and Foreign Commerce, 76th Cong., 3d Sess. 109-110 (1940); Hearings on S. 3580 Before a Subcomm. of the Senate Comm. on Banking and Currency, 76th Cong., 3d Sess. 1113 (1940); *PPI Report,* note 79 *supra,* at 69, 332-334.

ratification doctrine simply turned the management-fee issue into a contest between the philosophy of freedom of contract and the practical need to establish a mandatory duty of care.[87]

As a basis for shielding management fees from attacks on the grounds of excessiveness, ratification assumes that shareholders are capable of controlling management discretion through the ratification process. Various studies by and for the SEC, however, demonstrated that to be a doubtful proposition in the case of investment company shareholders.[88] Not only was the Commission unable to find any instance in which shareholders or outside directors had rejected a proposed management contract on the grounds of excessiveness of the management fee,[89] the Commission found that investment company management fees were high relative to other institutional investors[90]; that there were significant economies of scale in the management of large investment companies[91]; that even though there was fierce competition in the sale of investment company participations, there was no significant competition for the management of established companies[92]; and that because of the great dispersion of ownership of investment companies, the control of the proxy machinery by the investment adviser effectively foreclosed serious internal review of management fees by shareholders.[93]

The SEC recommended that Congress impose a positive duty of reasonableness on investment advisers in setting management fees for investment companies, and that reasonableness be determined according to several factors: the nature and extent of the services provided; the quality of the services rendered; economies of scale attributable to growth; economies of scale attributable to operation of other investment companies under common management; the value of benefits received by the investment adviser in addition to the compensation provided for

---

[87] See ¶ 5.01 *supra*.

[88] *PPI Report*, note 79 *supra*, at 128-130; *Wharton Report*, note 79 *supra*, at 66-73; 1967 Senate Hearings, note 83 *supra*, at 18, 20, 112; Question 14.

[89] Hearings on H.R. 9510 and H.R. 9511 Before the Subcomm. of Commerce and Finance of the House Comm. on Interstate and Foreign Commerce, 90th Cong., 1st Sess., 42, 696-697 (1967) (hereinafter cited as 1967 House Hearings).

[90] See *PPI Report*, note 79 *supra*, 114-121.

[91] See *PPI Report*, note 79 *supra*, at 94-96.

[92] *PPI Report*, note 79 *supra*, at 125-127; 1967 House Hearings, note 89 *supra*, at 41.

[93] *PPI Report*, note 79 *supra*, at 130.

in the contract as a result of the management arrangement; and any other factors appropriate for consideration.[94] The investment company

---

[94] See S. 1659 § 8(d), *amending* Act § 15, 1967 Senate Hearings, note 83 *supra*, at 915; 1967 House Hearings, note 89 *supra*, Pt. I, at 8. The original SEC proposal appears in H.R. 9510 § 8(d), 90th Cong., 1st Sess. (1967) and *id.* S. 1659:

"(d) Section 15 of said Act is further amended by striking subsection (d) thereof and inserting immediately after subsection (c) a new subsection (d) to read as follows:

"(d)(1) All compensation for services to a registered investment company received by an investment adviser, officer, director, or controlling person of or principal underwriter for such company and any affiliated person of such investment adviser, officer, director, controlling person, or principal underwriter shall be reasonable. This subsection shall not apply to sales loads for the acquisition of any security issued by a registered investment company.

"(2) In determining whether the compensation provided for in a contract whereby any person undertakes to serve or act as investment adviser of a registered investment company is reasonable, the factors considered shall include but not be limited to the following:

"(A) The nature and extent of the services to be provided pursuant to such contract, including separate evaluations of the compensation to be received for investment advisory services and of the compensation to be received for other services;

"(B) The quality of the services theretofore rendered to such investment company by the person undertaking to serve or act as investment adviser, or, if no such services have been theretofore rendered, the quality of the services rendered to other investment clients, if any, by such person;

"(C) The extent to which the compensation provided for in such contract takes into account economies attributable to the growth and size of such investment company and any such economies attributable to the operation of other investment companies under common management with such company, giving due consideration to the extent to which such economies are reflected in the charges made or compensation received for investment advisory services and other services provided to investment companies having no investment adviser, other clients of investment advisers and other financial institutions, but with due allowances for any relevant differences in the nature and extent of the services provided;

"(D) The value of all benefits, in addition to compensation provided for in such contract, directly or indirectly received or receivable by the person undertaking to serve or act as investment adviser by reason of his relationship to such investment company;

"(E) Such other factors as are appropriate and material.

"(3) In any action pursuant to this subsection, no finding shall be made that any compensation provided for in a contract or other arrange-

industry strongly resisted the Commission proposal on the grounds that it was tantamount to setting rates by regulation.[95] After extended debate, Congress adopted a compromise position. It amended the Investment Company Act to impose an explicit fiduciary duty for investment advisers with respect to compensation.[96] Additionally, in order to reemphasize the watchdog function of the outside directors, Congress

---

ment approved or otherwise authorized in compliance with the provisions of this title (other than the requirement of reasonableness in paragraph (1) of this subsection (d)) is unreasonable unless the party seeking such finding sustains the burden of proving by a preponderance of evidence that such compensation is unreasonable.

"(4) No action shall be maintained pursuant to this subsection to recover compensation paid more than two years prior to the date on which such action was instituted.

"(5) No person shall be held liable in any action pursuant to this subsection for damages in excess of the difference between the amount of compensation actually received by such person and the amount determined to be reasonable compensation for the period for which the action is brought and the interest on the difference between such amounts.

"(6) A finding that any compensation subject to the provisions of this subsection is unreasonable shall not be deemed to be a finding of a violation of this title for purposes of sections 9 and 49 of this title, section 15 of the Securities Exchange Act of 1934 and section 203 of title II of this Act."

See also S. 3724, 90th Cong., 2d Sess. (1968); S. 34, 91st Cong., 1st Sess. (1969); H.R. 14742, 90th Cong., 2d Sess. (1968).

[95] E.g., 1967 Senate Hearings, note 83 *supra,* at 186-269.

[96] Pub. L. 91-547 § 20, 89 Stat. 97 (Dec. 14, 1970), *amending* 15 U.S.C. § 80a-35 (1970) (codified at 15 U.S.C. § 80a-35(b)). See Mexico Fund, Sec. Reg. L. Rep., July 30, 1975, at C-1 (1975) (fee of 1.5 percent of net asset value raises questions under Investment Company Act § 36(b)). It is a relatively simple matter to initiate litigation under Section 36(b) since it appears that no demand on directors is necessary prior to commencing derivative litigation. Boyko v. Reserve Fund, Inc., [1975-1976 Transfer Binder] CCH Fed. Sec. L. Rep. ¶ 95,304 (S.D.N.Y. 1975).

Related to the question of compensation consistent with the statutory fiduciary-duty standard is the question of who will bear certain fees and expenses. For example, the SEC staff has declined to take a definitive position on the degree to which promotional expenses may properly be borne by a no-load fund. Compare Steadman Security Corp., [1975-1976 Transfer Binder] CCH Fed. Sec. L. Rep. ¶ 80,252 (1975) (internal adviser), with Carl L. Shipley, [1975-1976 Transfer Binder] CCH Fed. Sec. L. Rep. ¶ 80,253 (1975) (external adviser). See also Galfand v. Chestnutt, [1975-1976 Transfer Binder] CCH Fed. Sec. L. Rep. ¶ 95,248 (S.D.N.Y. 1975) (increase in expense ratio for mutual fund adviser inadequately disclosed to shareholders).

required greater independence of outside directors,[97] increased their proportionate representation on the boards of investment companies,[98] and required a majority of disinterested directors, on the basis of information they must request and evaluate, to approve the commencement and renewal of the advisory contract.[99]

The lesson of the investment company experience should not be lost on investment managers handling other types of institutional clients. The interest investment managers have in charging fees as high as their clients are willing to pay or are capable of paying is in direct conflict with duty of investment managers to act solely for the benefit of their clients. So long as fees are to be charged, this conflict cannot be avoided. It is necessary, therefore, that someone be capable of fairly representing the interests of the investor. It was the inability of the outside directors and trustees of investment companies to act as a counterforce to the divided loyalties of the investment manager with respect to the management fee which led to closer judicial and regulatory scrutiny of the fee. Similar concerns explain legislative regulation of trustee fees.[100] The same analysis should obtain, therefore, in the case of other institutional and individual investors, and there is every indication that the investment company experience will be mirrored in the treatment of management fees charged other types of investors.[101]

Nor is it possible to distinguish the investment company experience as unique simply on the grounds that the outside directors and trustees were chosen by the investment managers. While it is true that the Investment Company Act was amended to increase the independence and authority of the outside directors, none of the studies leading to amendment of the Act on the issue of compensation seriously contended that the outside directors and trustees had been personally profiting from their approval of the management fees charged the companies they served or that they were otherwise serving their own interests.[102] The most that was said was that their judgment may have been affected by

---

[97] *Id.* § 2(a)(2), *amending* 15 U.S.C. § 80a-2(a) (codified at 15 U.S.C. § 80a-2(a)(19)). See note 78 *supra*.

[98] *Id.* § 5(a), *amending* 15 U.S.C. § 80a-10(a) (codified at 15 U.S.C. § 80a-10(a)).

[99] *Id.* § 8(c), *amending* 15 U.S.C. § 80a-15(c) (codified at 15 U.S.C. § 80a-15(c)).

[100] See notes 66 and 70 *supra*.

[101] Mayer v. Chase Manhattan Bank N.A., [1974-1975 Transfer Binder] CCH Fed. Sec. L. Rep. ¶ 94,936 (S.D.N.Y. 1974).

[102] *Wharton Report*, note 79 *supra*, at 34; *PPI Report*, note 79 *supra*, at 130-132.

the possibility that their directorships depended upon their supporting the position of the investment adviser in setting the management fee.[103] Thus, it was not so much divided loyalties on the part of the outside directors as it was their ineffectiveness as a control on the investment adviser in fee-setting which produced stricter review of the size of management fees. What this implies with respect to management fees charged other types of institutional clients is that courts and regulatory authorities are unlikely to rely on a passive reasonableness test if the client has not been adequately represented in fee negotiations with the investment manager, especially if the management fee is significantly higher than fees for comparable services charged others who are knowledgeable and for whose accounts there is serious competition among investment managers.

It is also worth pointing out that, to the extent sentiment affects judicial and regulatory action, many institutional clients are appealing parties. The beneficiaries of a pension fund, a foundation, or a college endowment, for example, are not investors in the true sense. They cannot, like shareholders in an investment company, shift their accounts when they are dissatisfied with the investment management they are receiving, to the extent they know anything about it in the first place. They are effectively locked in, and they require the directors or trustees of their organizations to represent their interests adequately. It is quite unlikely that in such an environment, the law will permit investment managers to charge management fees which are disproportionate to the services they are providing. There now exists a considerable body of literature comparing management fees charged different types of investors.[104] Therefore, investment managers should be prepared to defend, by more than reliance on contractual provisions, differentials in

---

[103] *PPI Report*, note 79 *supra*, at 130-132; *Wharton Report*, note 79 *supra*, at 465-466; 1967 House Hearings, note 89 *supra*, at 40, 41; Notre Dame Survey, note 79 *supra*, at 909-916.

[104] See note 30 *supra*. In SEC, *Institutional Investor Study*, H.R. Doc. No. 64, 92d Cong., 1st Sess. 364 (1971) (hereinafter cited as *Institutional Investor Study*), there appears a regression analysis of the principal variables affecting the size of management fees. According to the *Study*, these variables are: (1) newness of account; (2) frequency of account valuation; (3) growth of account asset value; (4) aggressiveness of investment objectives; (5) discretionary character of account; (6) tax bracket of client; (7) affiliation with broker-dealer; (8) adviser execution authority; (9) client authority over execution; (10) association with fund complexes; and (11) turnover. Obviously, these variables overlap considerably.

fees between their clients and the clients of other investment managers, as well as among their own clients having accounts of comparable size.

[2] Performance and Incentive Fees

Performance-related fees can be a source of additional direct compensation to investment managers. Most investment management agreements providing for performance fees charge those fees as a supplementary expense to investors beyond the basic management fee. Only rarely is compensation for management tied entirely to performance. Normally, performance fees are calculated in one of two ways: (1) as a fixed percentage of either the capital appreciation or income or both of a portfolio; or (2) as a variation in the rate of the basic management fee measured by comparing the total return of the portfolio against an agreed-upon market index for a sepcified period of time.

Performance fees have been a feature of investment management arrangements for some time, but their emergence as a phenomenon of significance is comparatively recent. Performance fees and other incentive schemes were well-known, if not common, in agency investment management relationships prior to passage of the Investment Advisers Act of 1940.[105] Based on its study of investment trusts and investment companies,[106] the SEC recommended that Congress prohibit compensation based on a share of capital gains to registered investment advisers and investment advisers to investment companies.[107] Advisers to investment companies objected to the Commission's position,[108] but others

---

[105] A discussion of performance fees and the response to them in the Investment Advisers Act of 1940 appears in the *Institutional Investor Study*, note 104 *supra*, at 256-262. See also Spiegel v. Beacon Participations Inc., 297 Mass. 398, 8 N.E.2d 895 (1937).

[106] SEC, *Report on Investment Trusts and Investment Companies* (1939-1942) (hereinafter cited as *Report on Investment Trusts*). The Report, in five parts and six supplemental reports, was transmitted to Congress piecemeal, some sections not being submitted until after the bill became law. Most sections of the Report are listed by House document number in Hearings on S. 3580 Before a Subcomm. of the Senate Comm. on Banking and Currency, 76th Cong., 3d Sess. Pt. 1, at 307 (1940) (hereinafter cited as 1940 Senate Hearings). The portions of the Report printed after the Act was passed were printed as H.R. Doc. Nos. 136, 246, and 279, 77th Cong., 1st Sess. (1942). See North, "A Brief History of Federal Investment Company Legislation," 44 Notre Dame Law. 677, 678 n.7 (1969).

[107] S. 3580, 76th Cong., 3d Sess., Title I, § 15(a), and Title II, § 205 (1940).

[108] 1940 Senate Hearings, note 106 *supra*, at 664, 1055.

supported it[109]; as a compromise, Congress adopted the Commission's recommendation for all registered investment advisers, but released investment advisers to investment companies from the registration provisions of the Act.[110]

Despite the exclusion from regulation of performance fees handed investment advisers to investment companies by the Investment Advisers Act, performance fees stayed an unimportant issue for some time. It was not until the performance cult of the late 1960s that these fees once again came to the attention of regulators. According to the *Institutional Investor Study,* only four mutual funds had performance-fee arrangements in 1966,[111] whereas by mid-1970, one hundred and twenty-eight mutual funds had them, and fifty-two other mutual funds proposed to add them.[112] Moreover, though the public record is sparse for trust and agency accounts handled by investment managers who are not required to register under the Investment Advisers Act, there is evidence that they too have been tending toward performance fees.[113]

The drafting of performance-fee provisions raises a number of problems uniquely associated with leveraging the compensation of investment managers against the investment results they achieve. Like the basic management fee, a performance fee must be reasonably related to services provided the investor. But more so than for the basic management fee, a performance fee can pit the interests of an investment manager against those of his client[114]: The leveraging feature of performance

---

[109] Hearings on H.R. 10065 Before a Subcomm. of the House Comm. on Interstate and Foreign Commerce, 76th Cong., 3d Sess. 92 (1940) (hereinafter cited as 1940 House Hearings); 1940 Senate Hearings, note 106 *supra,* at 319; *Report on Investment Trusts,* note 106 *supra, Supp. Report on Investment Counsel, Investment Management, Investment Supervisory, and Investment Advisory Services,* H.R. Doc. No. 477, 76th Cong., 2d Sess. 30 (1939).

[110] Compare H.R. 10065, 76th Cong., 3d Sess., Title I, § 15(a), and Title II, § 205 (1940), with S. 3580, note 107 *supra.*

[111] *Institutional Investor Study,* note 104 *supra,* at 254.

[112] *Id.*

[113] Mayer v. Chase Manhattan Bank, N.A., [1974-1975 Transfer Binder] CCH Fed. Sec. L. Rep. ¶ 94,936 (S.D.N.Y. 1974); Hearings on H.R. 11995, S. 2224, H.R. 13754, and H.R. 14737 Before the Subcomm. on Commerce and Finance of the House Comm. on Interstate and Foreign Commerce, 91st Cong., 1st. Sess. 656 (1969) (hereinafter cited as 1969 House Hearings).

[114] Investment Company Act § 36(b) (15 U.S.C. § 80a-35(b)), which imposes a fiduciary duty on investment advisers to investment companies,

fees accelerates the rate of compensation the more an investment manager can show a statistical superiority over the standard chosen to measure performance—whether or not the investor's portfolio is in fact improved by the manager's program.

Perhaps the extra incentive performance fees are thought to give investment managers to cheat (by overvaluing letter stock, for example), to adopt favorable standards of comparison, or to engage in excessive risk-taking explains the suspicion with which this means of compensation is viewed. Performance fees are supposed to encourage investment managers to provide superior performance of their duties and to reward them for doing so, but, despite the label, there is no demonstrated connection between performance fees charged by investment managers and superior investment performance. On the contrary, the record suggests that performance fees have been largely a device for raising total management fees. The rapid growth in performance-fee arrangements in the mutual fund industry occurred on the heels of the reductions in basic management fees, reductions made in part because of the severe attacks on the basic fees for excessiveness.[115] Many of the performance-fee arrangements which were adopted provided little or no penalty for inferior performance.[116] Moreover, even where penalties for inferior performance were included in the management agreement, frequently no provision was made for paying them, except as charges against future fees.[117]

[a] The controversy surrounding performance-fee arrangements

Defenders of performance fees claim that such fees provide other advantages to investors besides the incentive to produce better investment results. Properly drafted performance fees, they say, can reduce total management fees during periods of market decline when investors are not well disposed towards sizable fees and, conversely, increase fees during periods of rising returns when investors' attitudes are quite dif-

---

applies to performance fees. SEC Investment Company Act Release No. 7113 (April 6, 1972), [1971-1972 Transfer Binder] CCH Fed. Sec. L. Rep. ¶ 78,694.

[115] See text at notes 82-84 and 112 *supra*.

[116] 1969 House Hearings, note 113 *supra*, at 870.

[117] *Id*. See also *Institutional Investor Study*, note 104 *supra* at 262.

ferent.[118] They argue, too, that performance fees reward performance rather than sales, in that investment managers can realize high income even though assets under management are not large.[119] Investors serviced by small organizations are supposed to benefit because the higher income attainable through performance fees attracts the management talent necessary to produce superior results.[120]

These defenses are not persuasive. Although performance fees may reduce total management fees during periods of declining securities values, these fees can still be very large relative to standard management-fee arrangements, particularly if the performance fee is superimposed on the basic management fee. Those investment management agreements which calculate performance fees on the basis of the total returns on a portfolio will have interest and dividend income against which to levy fees in a falling market. Moreover, performance fees tied to a market index are even less likely to reduce total management fees during periods of declining market values. So long as a portfolio's performance exceeds that of the index, which is the whole idea in the first place, performance fees must be paid even though the asset value of the portfolio may have diminished substantially.

Nor is there much substance to the argument that performance fees are necessary so that good management organizations can compete with good sales organizations for personnel. That argument has merit only if it would be possible to prevent sales-oriented investment managers from charging the performance fees permitted to other investment managers. Otherwise, talented investment managers would affiliate with organizations which possess effective sales operations and charge performance fees too. Furthermore, even assuming some limitation on performance fees could be imposed on sales-oriented organizations, it seems unlikely that good sales can exist for long with a product of markedly inferior quality to sell. For their own long-term survival, they must hire and pay competent management at competitive rates.

Admittedly, where unsophisticated investors are concerned, referrals supported through undisclosed fee-sharing arrangements, though

---

[118] 1969 House Hearings, note 113 *supra,* at 649-680; *Institutional Investor Study,* note 104 *supra,* at 255; Augenblick, "Compensation of Investment Managers," in M. Cohen & K. Bialkin, *Institutional Investors in a Changing Economy* 72-82 (PLI 1970) (hereinafter cited as 1970 PLI Institutional Conference).

[119] *Id.*

[120] See, e.g., 1970 PLI Institutional Conference, note 118 *supra,* at 76.

unlawful,[121] can reward a good sales effort without a strong management record behind it. But, questions of legality aside, it is doubtful that the mere blandishments of sales personnel would be sufficient to attract many institutional clients or individual investors with substantial estates. To the extent a sales versus management dichotomy has existed, it has been a feature of the investment company industry during the period that investment managers could reward brokers selling mutual fund shares with substantial commissions on portfolio transactions without disclosing that fact to purchasers of mutual fund shares. The abolition of give-ups and the regulation of other types of reciprocal arrangements between investment company advisers and brokers, however, has substantially reduced the incentive for sales organizations to support investment managers who have undistinguished performance records.[122] If there remains any value to performance fees as a means of boosting management-oriented organizations to a position of competition with sales-oriented organizations, it is marginal at best.

On the other hand, criticism of performance fees has been more emotive than substantive, with the consequence that it is difficult to respond constructively in drafting performance-fee provisions. For example, it is claimed that performance fees lead only to higher management expenses for investors.[123] While this may be accurate as an historical observation, it is compelled by no law of finance. It assumes that investment managers will receive a basic management fee large enough to represent the usual amount charged for managing a portfolio, and that the performance fee represents an additional charge. But performance fees can be useful where clients want the basic management fee to be low or investment managers offer to keep it low. If the total fee—that is, the basic fee plus the performance fee—compensates the manager at a level reasonably related to that customary under ordinary arrangements, it is difficult to agree that excessive fees are inevitable.

Nor, as it is also claimed, need performance fees lead investment managers unnecessarily to take high risks,[124] though even if they did,

---

[121] See ¶ 3.02[2][b].

[122] See ¶ 8.02.

[123] E.g., *Institutional Investor Study,* note 104 *supra,* at 254; Lipper, "Fund Distribution," in 1970 PLI Institutional Conference, note 118 *supra,* at 50-51.

[124] *Id.* See also Testimony of David Schenker, Chief Counsel of the SEC Investment Trust Study, in 1940 Senate Hearings, note 106 *supra,* at 320 ("Heads I win, tails you lose"). See also S. Rep. No. 1775, 76th Cong., 3d Sess. 22 (1940).

high risk is by no means inappropriate for all investors. The point is, however, that the use of contractual risk-control devices can eliminate an investment manager's incentive to entertain excessive risk. By relating the size of performance fees to the risk level of an investor's portfolio as well as to the returns on the portfolio, the investment management agreement can remove any advantage an investment manager might achieve for himself by taking on risk beyond that appropriate for his client.[125]

As for the contention that performance fees lead to favoritism among clients, which is also commonly heard,[126] it is difficult to understand the grounds for this complaint, even if it is accurate. Certainly, preference given to accounts managed under performance-fee arrangements is no cause for concern for those clients. Moreover, if other clients are not being led to believe they are receiving the same services as the performance-fee accounts, and if such differences in treatment are fully disclosed, clients receiving lesser services should have no grounds for complaint.[127]

So long as performance fees are constructed to avoid exacerbating the division of interest between investors and investment managers in determining the level of compensation, and so long as performance fees can exist in harmony with a suitable design and execution of an investor's program of investment, they need not be rejected as inherently corrosive of an investment management relationship. But the fact that they are not necessarily an unmitigated evil does not really resolve the issue of their legitimacy. More telling than the attacks on performance fees as inevitably harmful to investors is the claim that they are unnecessary, and, therefore, in view of their potential for abuse, to be avoided. For even assuming performance fees represent a good-faith fee arrangement rather than an attempt to gouge unsuspecting investors, the question still remains what thing of value the payment of performance fees provides to investors. If indeed performance fees reflect little of value, that fact tends to substantiate the suspicion that they exist only to serve the interests of the managers. Moreover, as a matter of technical analysis, a performance fee which does not represent payment for something more than the benefits and burdens comprehended by the basic management fee would be unsupported by consideration—

---

[125] *Institutional Investor Study,* note 104 *supra,* at 264-265. See also ¶ 7.03[2].

[126] *Institutional Investor Study,* note 104 *supra,* at 254-255.

[127] For an extended treatment of allocating management costs among accounts fairly, see ¶ 9.06[4].

to say nothing of the breach of fiduciary duty involved in accepting additional compensation with nothing of value being provided.

There are two principal arguments made in support of the claim that performance fees are unnecessary. An investment manager's interest in preserving and expanding his clientele is said to provide sufficient motivation to carry out his responsibilities without the added incentive of performance fees.[128] Also, the standard management fee arrangements, calculated as a percentage of a portfolio under management, are said to offer investment managers an adequate basis for sharing in the fruits of superior investment results without also having to leverage management fees with a performance kicker.[129]

Taken literally, these arguments fall wide of the mark. Fear of losing accounts is hardly the incentive it is made out to be, except perhaps for investment managers specializing in managing accounts for individuals. Trust accounts tend to remain with the same corporate trustee, and institutional accounts in particular do not lightly change investment managers.[130] Finding and developing a relationship with a new investment manager is expensive, and trustees and directors generally prefer avoiding the documentation necessary to justify such a shift. Moreover, unless an investment manager's performance has been consistently poor, changing managers is no sure way to achieve better results. Too, some institutional investors are immobile for all practical purposes. Investment companies, for example, change advisers only on the rarest occasions.[131]

The argument that the basic management fee provides a sufficient means for investment managers to share in superior performance fails to recognize the importance performance can have in declining markets.

---

[128] *Institutional Investor Study,* note 104 *supra,* at 254-255; Bernstein, "In-House Asset Management," in 1970 PLI Institutional Conference, note 118 *supra,* at 228-229.

[129] Notre Dame Survey, note 79 *supra,* at 886-891.

[130] A 1975 survey of one hundred and sixty-four Taft-Hartley pension funds indicated that approximately one-fourth of the funds surveyed made some shift in investment managers. The larger funds reported using more than one investment manager; 4 CCH Pension Plan Guide ¶ 25,009. See also *Institutional Investor Study,* note 104 *supra,* at 194, which finds an 18 percent annual movement "surprising."

[131] There is no record of investment companies shifting management until fairly recently. In part, this is because the incentive of the outside directors to cause a shift on performance grounds is small. See Notre Dame Survey, note 79 *supra,* at 916 n.1175. With institutional accounts, performance records tend to affect the flow of additional investable funds from the client. Outright terminations are not common.

In such circumstances, the basic fee only falls less fast with superior performance than it would otherwise. But index-based performance fees generate additional income so long as clients' portfolios outperform the index, regardless of the condition of the market.[132]

But behind the claim that performance fees are unnecessary is the unstated premise that performance fees have, at best, a marginal capacity to produce superior investment management. Whether or not other incentives are sufficient to cause investment managers to do their best work, it is far from clear what investment managers can do to produce better results with performance fees than they would without them.

In other contexts, the consideration for which performance fees are paid is readily identifiable.[133] Time may be purchased, for example, through early delivery of goods or rapid completion of construction.[134] Continuity of service is another example. As an incentive not to change jobs, employees may receive pay raises in accordance with schedules based on longevity alone; similarly, after a period of service, employees may become eligible for pension benefits. Both these forms of compensation are in addition to salary and reflect the value to employers of retaining experienced personnel or maintaining low employee turnover, or the like.[135]

But what is it that investment managers bring to their office in return for performance fees? What variable affecting investment results can they control according to the amount of compensation they receive? Do they spend more hours analyzing data? Do they hire bigger staffs or purchase more outside research? What, in short, can investment managers, already committed to exercise ordinary skill and care, do in addition in order to enhance the likelihood that they will increase the returns of their clients beyond what they would have been with only a standard management fee arrangement?

Yet investors place great stock in performance records. For many investors, a performance record is the only attribute permitting ready

---

[132] Indeed, it may be that the ability to make good defensive moves during hard times is the best test of investment acumen, and hence most deserving of a performance award.

[133] See generally S. Williston, *Treatise on the Law of Contracts* §§ 952 D, 1019, 1019A (3d ed. 1957); A. Corbin, *Contracts* § 153 (1952); 17 Am. Jur. 2d *Contracts* §§ 122, 343-354 (1964).

[134] See A. Corbin, *Contracts* § 720 (1952).

[135] E.g., Rogers v. Hill, 289 U.S. 582 (1933). See also E.F. Hutton & Co., [1975-1976 Transfer Binder] CCH Fed. Sec. L. Rep. ¶ 80,249 (1975) (mutual fund underwriter compensation based on Consumer Price Index rejected as unrelated to services rendered).

comparison among investment managers. Moreover, there is a strong belief that an investment manager's performance record is a valid basis for determining management fees. During the hearings leading to the 1970 amendments to the Investment Company Act, the SEC argued that past performance was a relevant factor in determining the reasonableness of management fees.[136] If hindsight concerning the performance of a portfolio really is a reliable factor in evaluating a management fee, it should follow that performance is also useful in setting management fees.[137]

The judgment that performance fees are not an incentive to superior performance but that records of performance are a basis for evaluating management quality is not as paradoxical as it seems. Consistently poor performance, adjusted for risk, is strong evidence that an investment manager does not possess or has not exercised the ordinary skills incident to his profession. It also is the case that a properly diversified portfolio should produce close to average returns for the level of risk assumed.[138] The probabilities are such that investment managers who consistently fail to achieve at least average results have either not diversified properly or have engaged in an investment program based on postulates that do not accurately describe market events. In either case, it is entirely reasonable to conclude that if such investment managers are being compensated at customary rates, they are not providing services commensurate with their fees.

In contrast, future performance is by its very nature unknowable, and hence performance fees can provide no obvious insight into the care and skill an investment manager will exercise. Moreover, for performance fees to offer investment managers incentives to produce superior results, at least insofar as the selection of investments is concerned, one must assume that there is some variable which investment managers can control to produce superior investment results and that the degree of control they have over that variable depends on the rate of compensation they receive. No such variable has yet been identified. On the

---

[136] See, e.g., 1967 House Hearings, note 89 *supra,* at 44. The SEC proposed to make performance an element of its "reasonableness" standard for calculating the basic fee. See H.R. 9510 § 8(d)(2)(B), 90th Cong., 1st Sess. (1967) (quoted in full at note 94 *supra*), to amend Investment Company Act § 15.

[137] Nonetheless, in his testimony, SEC Chairman Cohen tried to distinguish past performance from future performance as a criterion. 1967 Senate Hearings, note 83 *supra,* at 111.

[138] See generally ¶¶ 7.03[1], 7.03[2], 7.08.

contrary, performance is in reality a measure of an investment manager's ability relative to other investment managers, and is far more dependent on their collective efforts than on any faculty he can control and vary according to his level of compensation.

[b] Bases for effective performance-fee provisions: Risk-sharing, cost control, superior managerial talent

Although pegging management compensation to a performance record may not be more effective an incentive than adjustments of a standard management fee as a result of a performance record would be,[139] performance fees can enable management fees continuously to reflect the level of services actually being provided. Viewed from this perspective, the principal justification for performance fees tied to the returns on a portfolio would be the mutual understanding that the uncertainty in the quality of the product purchased—the management of the portfolio—is being shared. Based on the investment manager's previous record and the risk appropriate to the investor, both parties expect returns at a certain level. The returns may be better or worse because of market conditions and because of the manager's ability to deal with them. If, after discounting that part of the investment results reflecting market conditions, the portfolio does worse despite the best efforts of the investment manager, the investor pays lower fees because the manager failed to produce results consistent with reasonable expectations. If the portfolio does better, the converse is true. In either event, the investor is paying a total fee which more accurately reflects the level of services actually being provided than would be the case with a constant fee fixed solely on the basis of past performance.

Performance fees can also be justified somewhat less forcefully on two other grounds, both more related to the incentive philosophy so often cited in favor of such a method of compensation. When some quantification of the variables affecting costs is possible, but precision in predicting costs is beyond reach, performance fees can be an incentive encouraging cost control. An investment program may involve substantial administrative expenses, particularly with respect to brokerage and outside support services, which, though estimable, are potentially highly variable. Assuming investment managers can identify less costly alternatives better on a day-to-day basis than by trying in advance to fix expenses for extended periods, tying compensation to total costs may

---

[139] See note 137 *supra*.

provide a useful incentive to minimize expenses. This technique is often used in government defense contracts where it is difficult to determine with specificity the costs of developing new technology and new production facilities. The government compensates contractors in part by permitting them to share in the savings if actual costs are below estimated costs.[140]

In investment management, incentives to control costs will occur if performance fees are calculated on the basis of portfolio results, net of expenses paid by the account.[141] Then, superior investment selection is necessary to offset expenditures for brokerage, outside research, and other expenses, for the investment manager to obtain a performance fee. Indeed, performance fees fashioned to encourage investment managers to control expenses may well offer protection to those managers paying more than best price for brokerage to obtain outside support services. Since performance fees calculated net of expenses penalize investment managers who pay higher brokerage than necessary, those who do have a strong argument that their brokerage decisions are made only in their clients' interest.[142]

The other purpose performance fees can serve is to permit the genuinely superior investment manager to obtain higher compensation than is customary. Because of the fiduciary relationship between investment managers and their clients, performance fees may not push total compensation above levels reasonable for the services provided any more than standard management fees may be raised above such levels. The few investment managers who possess market insights regularly capable of producing above-average returns, adjusted for risk, are still subject to the constraints against excessive fees, even if such persons are worth more than other investment managers. Fixed management fees at higher levels than customary may be vulnerable, especially if the manager subsequently produces only average or inferior investment results. Performance fees, on the other hand, would tie higher compensation to an actual display of talent rather than an historical record of talent and thus substantiate the basis for charging high fees.[143]

If performance fees are to be incorporated into investment management agreements on the grounds that total compensation greater than

---

140 Nash, "Pricing Policies in Government Contracts," 29 L. & Contemp. Prob. 361, 366-367 (1964). Cf. Rogers v. Hill, 289 U.S. 582 (1933).

141 See note 165 *infra.*

142 The right of investment managers to execute above lowest price is discussed extensively in Chapter 9.

143 See ¶ 5.03[2][c][v] *infra.*

usual is justified because of the manager's quality, it might add to the credibility of such a provision if the fixed portion of the management fee were somewhat lower than is customary in comparable investment management relationships not involving performance-based compensation. Since performance fees are leveraged against investment results, the genuinely superior investment manager can anticipate higher total fees anyway. And the lower fixed fee supports the fact that the higher total fees are based on the manager's right to greater than usual compensation because of his talent in selecting investments. Conversely, the investment manager charging performance fees on the grounds of his superior talent should be entitled to leverage his fees more steeply than is customary. Obtaining a manager who is likely to achieve better-than-average results is sufficiently unusual an opportunity to justify recognition that his services, if in fact of better quality than usual, will be correspondingly more expensive.

[c] Standards for measuring the effectiveness of performance-fee provisions

Both the level of the fixed fee portion of a performance-based management fee and the degree of leverage contained in the variable portion of the fee are more business-judgment problems than drafting problems. Assuming that there is adequate disclosure to clients able to evaluate management fees responsibly and that total fees are reasonably related to services provided, management fees which include a performance-based feature ought to be able to withstand attack on grounds of excessiveness or as violative of statutory fraud rules. The more immediate concern is to draft performance-fee provisions which (1) as required by the fiduciary relationship between manager and client, fairly reflect the influence of the manager on the client's portfolio, and (2) avoid all incentive to the manager to undertake excessive risk. Recent official and quasi-official studies have idenitfied seven considerations important to determining whether performance fees meet these goals.[144]

---

[144] *Institutional Investor Study*, note 104 *supra*, at 254-256; Bank Administration Institute, *Measuring the Investment Performance of Pension Funds* (1968); J. Lorie & M. Hamilton, *The Stock Market: Theories and Evidence* 228-247 (1973) (hereinafter cited as Lorie & Hamilton). These studies all consider performance measurement subject to the assumption that the value of the portfolio, the performance of which is to be measured, is a known or easily established quantity. This is plainly not always the case since a portfolio may hold specific securities which are not traded sufficiently often to establish an objective market price. In some cases, this can lead to

[i] *Comparison of Returns With an Unmanaged Portfolio:* An unmanaged portfolio is a fully diversified portfolio, the returns of which are entirely dependent on the movement of the market. By definition, its returns are equivalent to market returns. As a practical matter, how-

---

an overvaluation of portfolio assets, particularly where the person whose compensation depends on performance is permitted to make the valuation. See note 65 *supra*. For this reason, many institutional investors obtain performance measurement through an independent service or through analysis of their account performed by their custodians. This only shifts the burden of fairly valuing the holdings in a portfolio, however, and does not guarantee that the valuations performed will be accurate and in accord with generally accepted accounting principles. See Patocka, "Custodian Banks: The Next Pension Battleground?" 9 Institutional Investor 87 (Sept. 1975).

One particularly vexing valuation problem, for example, occurs in connection with liquid asset mutual funds. Mutual funds ordinarily are valued according to the aggregate market values of the component securities of the portfolio, since these securities are generally not held until maturity, redemption, call, or liquidation by the issuer and are traded frequently enough to have reliable market quotations. (These securities must be valued according to the quoted market value. Investment Company Act § 2(a)(41)(B)(i), 15 U.S.C. § 80a-2(a)(41)(B)(i).) Liquid asset funds, in contrast, purchase short-term obligations which such funds hold to maturity and which are not regularly accorded reported market quotations. (These kinds of securities may be valued according to "fair value as determined in good faith by the board of directors," Investment Company Act § 2(a)(41)(B)(ii), 15 U.S.C. § 80a-2(a)(41)(B)(ii), subject to rules established by the Commission. *Id.* § 2(a)(41).) It has been argued that pricing to cost stabilizes valuation and yield quotes. It has also been argued that cost pricing deprives investors of fair valuation when interest rates fall and masks risk when interest rates rise. See Glenn, "Safety, Liquidity and Yield: Money Market Funds Are Here to Stay," Barron's, Oct. 6, 1975, pp. 3, 8. Responding to industry pressure to standardize valuation methods (see Securities Week, Aug. 11, 1975, p. 9), the SEC proposed valuation guidelines under which it would be misleading to report current return on investment without also stating the rate of return on the "yield to average life" of the portfolio. SEC Securities Act Release No. 5589 (June 12, 1975), [1975-1976 Transfer Binder] CCH Fed. Sec. L. Rep. ¶ 80,210.

Another difficult valuation problem, also first spotlighted by the mutual fund industry, is the value of insurance guaranteeing securities held in fund portfolios. Various conditions attach to insurance payments, thus complicating the valuation problem. See Glenn, "Guarantee Against Loss," Barron's, June 30, 1975, p. 5; Bronson, "Here's Another Way to Play the Market: an 'Insured' Fund," Wall Street J., June 24, 1975, p. 13, col. 2. The SEC staff has taken the position that the directors of a municipal bond trust owning insurance guaranteeing payment of interest and principal must fairly value that insurance is an asset of the trust. Wauterlek & Brown, Inc., and Van Kampern, Sauerman, Inc., Sec. Reg. L. Rep., April 21, 1976, p. C-1.

ever, an unmanaged portfolio must be approximated by a market index.[145] One element of performance measurement is the difference in investment returns of a managed portfolio compared to the returns of the index or unmanaged portfolio.[146]

A necessary consequence of measuring performance by comparing a managed portfolio with an unmanaged portfolio is that the technique of calculating performance fees as a portion of total return cannot be accommodated. There are two reasons for this. Performance fees based on total returns would depend on broad market movements as well as the decisions of an investment manager. To the extent performance fees include recognition of market movements, they do not reflect the ability of the investment manager, and hence would compensate him, in violation of his fiduciary duty, for something over which he had no control.[147] Furthermore, a total-return approach to performance fees can encourage investment managers to take undue risks since, in a rising market, risky assets as a class offer the highest rewards.

For these reasons, investment managers registered under the Investment Advisers Act of 1940 may not set fees as a percentage of total returns to a portfolio (though fees may be based on the total *value* of the portfolio). Section 205 of the Act prohibits registered investment advisers from charging fees tied to capital gains unless they are based on comparisons to an unmanaged portfolio. Even with this restriction, they are permitted only in the case of investment companies and other clients (except certain trusts) investing assets in excess of $1,000,000.[148]

---

[145] Lorie & Hamilton, note 144 *supra,* at 174-183, 198-200, 241-245.
[146] *Id.* at 242.
[147] See text following note 127 *supra.*
[148] Investment Advisers Act § 205, 15 U.S.C. § 80b-5, provides:

"No investment adviser, unless exempt from registration pursuant to section 80b—3(b) of this title, shall make use of the mails or any means or instrumentality of interstate commerce, directly or indirectly, to enter into, extend, or renew any investment advisory contract, or in any way to perform any investment advisory contract entered into, extended, or renewed on or after November 1, 1940, if such contract—

"(1) provides for compensation to the investment adviser on the basis of a share of capital gains upon or capital appreciation of the funds or any portion of the funds of the client;

"(2) fails to provide, in substance, that no assignment of such contract shall be made by the investment adviser without the consent of the other party to the contract; or

"(3) fails to provide, in substance, that the investment adviser, if a partnership, will notify the other party to the contract of any

The assumption that broad market movements have a dominant effect on total returns, however, is accurate only for portfolios which are highly correlated with the market.[149] This would not be the case for undiversified portfolios, particularly if they are concentrated in volatile securities. In that event, nondiversifiable risk or idiosyncratic risk—risk unque to that security alone and unaffected by market movement—would ordinarily control investment results. Nonetheless, even

---

change in the membership of such partnership within a reasonable time after such change.

"Paragraph (1) of this section shall not (A) be construed to prohibit an investment advisory contract which provides for compensation based upon the total value of a fund averaged over a definite period, or as of definite dates, or taken as of a definite date, or (B) apply to an investment advisory contract with—

"(i) an investment company registered under subchapter I of this chapter, or

"(ii) any other person (except a trust, collective trust fund or separate account referred to in section 80a—3(c)(11) of this title), provided that the contract relates to the investment of assets in excess of $1 million,

"which contract provides for compensation based on the asset value of the company or fund under management averaged over a specified period and increasing and decreasing proportionately with the investment performance of the company or fund over a specified period in relation to the investment record of an appropriate index of securities prices or such other measure of investment performance as the Commission by rule, regulation, or order may specify. For purposes of clause (B) of the preceding sentence, the point from which increases and decreases in compensation are measured shall be the fee which is paid or earned when the investment performance of such company or fund is equivalent to that of the index or other measure of performance, and an index of securities prices shall be deemed appropriate unless the Commission by order shall determine otherwise. As used in paragraphs (2) and (3) of this section, 'investment advisory contract' means any contract or agreement whereby a person agrees to act as investment adviser or to manage any investment or trading account of another person other than an investment company registered under subchapter I of this chapter."

Thus, an investment adviser may not waive his fees for failure of an investment to appreciate because that would entail profit-sharing in capital gains, V.L. McKenzie, [1975-1976 Transfer Binder] CCH Fed. Sec. L. Rep. ¶ 80,386 (1975). See also Lynn Wood Hall, Sec. Reg. L. Rep., Feb. 11, 1976, p. C-1 (1976) (performance fees for employee benefit plans and personal accounts under $1 million not permitted).

[149] The *Institutional Investor Study,* note 104 *supra,* at 400, asserts that, for an "average" security, the return on the market index will explain about 50 percent of that security's monthly rate of return.

with a deliberate policy of concentration, a total-return type of provision would still suffer from its inability to exclude market influence, and hence would not be an appropriate basis for setting a fee. Nor would reliance on a hypothetical portfolio as a standard against which to measure performance be satisfactory. Such a comparison portfolio would be vulnerable to statutory fraud claims because of its limited accuracy as a measure of the risk of the managed portfolio.[150] If a performance fee is to be included as part of the total management fee where concentration is a deliberate strategy, the standard of comparison still must be, as is generally the case, a broad market index, and the investor should be capable of evaluating the appropriateness of the index.

[ii] *Identity of Risk Between the Managed and Unmanaged Portfolios:* The second element of performance measurement is risk.[151] For a comparison between an unmanaged portfolio and a managed portfolio to be useful, both must reflect or be adjusted to the same level of risk. Broad market movements produce different returns in well-developed portfolios undertaking different levels of risk, regardless of the investment manager's contribution. Furthermore, failure to adjust properly for risk can create problems beyond merely introducing inaccuracies in measuring the investment manager's contribution to asset values. For example, if identity or adjustment of risk level is not required, an investment manager might be tempted to try to increase performance-based fees by assuming additional risk during periods of anticipated market appreciation.

For well-diversified portfolios, it is not difficult to construct an unmanaged portfolio reflecting the appropriate level of risk. Market risk can be expressed as a function of the rate at which securities move up or down relative to market movements. This rate of movement is called volatility. By adjusting the returns to the securities comprising any acceptable broad market index for the volatility relative to that index inherent in an investor's portfolio, it is possible to obtain a precise measure of the investor's market-related returns.[152]

---

[150] See Killgore Management, Inc., SEC Investment Advisers Act Release No. 332 (Aug. 25, 1972), [1972-1973 Transfer Binder] CCH Fed. Sec. L. Rep. ¶ 78,977; Jerry W. Smith, [1972-1973 Transfer Binder] CCH Fed. Sec. L. Rep. ¶ 78,856.

[151] Lorie & Hamilton, note 144 *supra,* at 234-235.

[152] See *Institutional Investor Study,* note 104 *supra,* at 400-410; Lorie & Hamilton, note 144 *supra,* at 235-245. See also ¶ 7.03.

But the choice of an appropriate index to represent an unmanaged portfolio can be a difficult problem.[153] Although the long-term movements of most widely used indexes are similar,[154] for short-term measurements, it is critical to know the basis on which securities are selected for an index and the weighting to be given the various component securities of the index.[155] The SEC, for example, has taken the position that an index should not be weighted according to the relative prices of its component securities because such an index may underemphasize the growth of certain component securities.[156]

[iii] *Accounting for Distributions and Other Returns:* Closely related to the problem of selecting an appropriate index is the necessity for taking into account all distributions and other returns to the securities in the index representing the unmanaged portfolio. Cash and non-cash distributions and capital gains together make up return on investment, at least before adjustments are made for taxes. For a realistic comparison between a managed portfolio and an unmanaged portfolio, it is essential to calculate the difference in return on investment both experience.[157]

A difficult question is whether distributions should be added to portfolio asset value as cash at the end of the evaluation period or whether they should be assumed to be reinvested as of the date of distribution. The *Institutional Investor Study* seems to prefer the approach of adding distributions as cash at the end of the evaluation period.[158]

---

[153] See Hyperion Fund, Inc., [1973 Transfer Binder] CCH Fed. Sec. L. Rep. ¶ 79,315 (1973 (Arthur Lipper Corp. average performance for all growth funds unacceptable; Arthur Lipper Growth Fund Index acceptable); Mexico Fund, Sec. Reg. L. Rep., July 30, 1975, p. C-1 (1975) (Wiesenberger indexes not appropriate for calculating performance fee).

[154] Lorie & Hamilton, note 144 *supra,* at 65-69.

[155] *Id.*

[156] SEC Investment Company Act Release No. 7113 (April 6, 1972), [1971-1972 Transfer Binder] CCH Fed. Sec. L. Rep. ¶ 78,694. It is worth noting that, although the SEC's position may be well taken, the Dow-Jones Industrial Index is price-weighted. Because it is calculated on the basis of the securities of companies which in 1970 constituted approximately 30 percent of the value of all of the stocks listed on the New York Stock Exchange, and because the volatility of the securities of such mature companies generally is low, the Dow-Jones industrials are reasonably representative of pure market factors in the advance and decline of securities. See Lorie & Hamilton, note 144 *supra,* at 60-62, 65-67.

[157] Lorie & Hamilton, note 144 *supra,* at 251; *Institutional Investor Study,* note 104 *supra,* at 265, 410.

[158] *Institutional Investor Study,* note 104 *supra,* at 409-410.

Nonetheless, either approach would seem to be acceptable so long as it is consistently applied both to the index and the managed portfolio.[159]

[iv] *Accounting for Receipts and Disbursements:* No useful comparison between a managed and unmanaged portfolio is possible unless there is an accounting for all receipts to and disbursements from the managed portfolio during the evaluation period. A portfolio worth ten dollars obviously has not experienced a 50 percent appreciation if the client entrusts his investment manager with another five dollars. In a more realistic sense, this means that portfolios must be adjusted to account for contributions and withdrawals before performance fees are calculated. The method adopted should be consistent with the purposes for which the portfolio is being managed, but, in general, it should be trying to achieve, to the extent feasible, the time-weighted rate of return.[160]

But adjusting for receipts and disbursements is not always a simple and inexpensive procedure. First, the portfolio must be valued accurately before there can be an adjustment for cash receipts or disbursals. Depending on the assets comprising the portfolio, the mechanics of portfolio valuation can be complex. Moreover, valuation can be costly. Because management fees are based on asset value, it can strain fiduciary responsibility if investment managers conduct the valuation themselves, particularly in the case of portfolios having significant amounts of non-liquid assets.[161] Investors, relying on assistance from independent or at least unaffiliated sources to carry out the valuation, add to the administrative costs of management.

Another serious portfolio valuation problem which results from cash inflows and outflows is pinpointing the period of investment. Undue delay in investing new cash or retention of excessive cash to cover anticipated disbursements at some point becomes an investment decision and represents the judgment of the manager that holding some cash is

---

[159] *Institutional Investor Study,* note 104 *supra,* at 265, 410; Lorie & Hamilton, note 144 *supra,* at 87.

[160] Bank Administration Institute, *Measuring the Investment Performance of Pension Funds* 73-88 (1968).

[161] Valuation of private placements, for example, has been a notorious source of fraud. See, e.g., *In re* Mates Fin. Servs., SEC Securities Exchange Act Release No. 8626 (June 12, 1969), [1969-1970 Transfer Binder] CCH Fed. Sec. L. Rep. ¶ 77,721, and SEC Securities Exchange Act Release No. 8836 (March 9, 1970), [1969-1970 Transfer Binder] CCH Fed. Sec. L. Rep. ¶ 77,790.

a good investment.[162] That cash is in reality a part of the portfolio and should be included in any performance measurement. To reduce problems here, it might be useful to decide contractually the period of time after which new cash held as cash is to be treated as an investment, how much notice the client must provide in advance of anticipated cash disbursements, and whether the excess cash held for this purpose should be treated as an investment.

[v] *Symmetrical Pricing of the Performance Fee:* The idea that performance fees mostly reflect the uncertainty of determining the appropriate level at which investment managers should be compensated suggests that, just as superior performance should increase the total management fee, inferior performance should result in a lower fee. It is the judgment of Congress that, for registered investment advisers at least, more is required than that performance fees be scaled down as well as up. Section 205 of the Investment Advisers Act also requires than any adjustment for performance rise and fall symmetrically about the basic management fee.[163] This "fulcrum fee" [164] is the sum to be paid for investment performance which is precisely equal to the performance of an unmanaged portfolio, net of expenses.[165]

In theory, other types of pricing performance fees besides symmetrical pricing can be fair to investors. If, for example, an investor

---

[162] See, e.g., Blankenship v. Boyle, 329 F. Supp. 1089 (D.D.C. 1971). See ¶ 6.02[3].

[163] See note 148 *supra.*

[164] See SEC Investment Company Act Release No. 7113 (April 6, 1972), [1971-1972 Transfer Binder] CCH Fed. Sec. L. Rep. ¶ 78,694.

[165] 17 C.F.R. § 275.205-1 provides:

"(a) 'Investment performance' of an investment company for any period shall mean the sum of:

"(1) The change in its net asset value per share during such period; and

"(2) The value of its cash distributions per share accumulated to the end of such period; and

"(3) The value of capital gains taxes per share paid or payable on undistributed realized long-term capital gains accumulated to the end of such period;

"expressed as a percentage of its net asset value per share at the beginning of such period. For this purpose, the value of distributions per share of realized capital gains, of dividends per share paid from investment income and of capital gains taxes per share paid or payable on undistributed realized long-term capital gains shall be treated as reinvested in shares of the investment company at the net asset value per share in

were charged a low basic management fee for performance identical to the unmanaged portfolio, an investor might very well be willing to assume more of the risk of uncertainty concerning the investment manager's performance than if the basic management fee were one customary for comparable services in a strict fixed fee regime. But as a practical matter, nonsymmetrical pricing may be too complex to arrive at a formula for computing investment results as an accurate reflection of that degree of uncertainty over an investment manager's performance investors would be willing to bear. Since an investment manager's duty of loyalty precludes taking advantage of client ignorance in setting fees, the potential for disagreement over the assumptions underlying nonsymmetrical pricing arrangements virtually dictates that they not be used except for highly sophisticated clients.

[vi] *Relating Performance Fees to Significant Differences in Result:* Most performance-fee arrangements provide for either step-rate performance fees or continuous-rate performance fees. Step-rate fees increase or decrease management fees for each full percent difference in result between the managed portfolio and the comparison unmanaged portfolio. Continuous fees reflect prorated adjustments for each percentage point difference in performance between the managed portfolio and the comparison unmanaged portfolio.

---

effect at the close of business on the record date for the payment of such distributions and dividends and the date on which provision is made for such taxes, after giving effect to such distributions, dividends and taxes.

"(b) 'Investment record' of an appropriate index of securities prices for any period shall mean the sum of:

"(1) the change in the level of the index during such period; and
"(2) the value, computed consistently with the index, of cash distributions made by companies whose securities comprise the index accumulated to the end of such period;

"expressed as a percentage of the index level at the beginning of such period. For this purpose cash distributions on the securities which comprise the index ˙shall be treated as reinvested in the index at least as frequently as the end of each calendar quarter following the payment of the dividend."

The *Institutional Investor Study,* note 104 *supra,* at 264 makes the point that performance should be calculated net of all expenses; but it is not costless to acquire a portfolio, and the initial costs of investment, including the costs of profiling the client, should not be netted out for purposes of calculating performance in the first investment period. Moreover, costs which the client would have to bear regardless of who manages the account (custodian fees and brokerage commissions, for example), should not be netted out. See Lorie & Hamilton, note 144 *supra,* at 257.

In either case, small differences in investment results between managed and unmanaged portfolios should not lead to large variations in management fees because of the great likelihood that random factors not associated with the efforts of investment managers would be responsible for the outcome.[166] The SEC takes the position that for maximum fee adjustments to be valid, there should be less than a 10 percent probability that they can occur as a result of random fluctuations in performance.[167] An example of a computational procedure the Commission rejects is a performance fee calculus based on the ratio between the returns of the managed portfolio and the returns on the unmanaged portfolio. With such a performance fee, a three percent return to a managed portfolio compared to a one percent return to an unmanaged portfolio would indicate performance by an investment manager three times that of the unmanaged portfolio, while corresponding 10 and 8 percent returns would indicate a performance only one-and-one-quarter times better.

A preferable performance fee arrangement would adjust compensation according to the *difference* between the percentage change in the managed and unmanaged portfolios. That way, a two percent difference in performance would produce the same fee adjustment whether the unmanaged portfolio changed by one or eight or any other percent during the period of evaluation.[168] Whatever the calculus adopted, however, performance fee arrangements producing proportionately greater fee adjustments for small performance differences than for large performance differences will be particularly suspect.

[vii] *Time Intervals for Evaluating Performance:* The generally recommended interval for measuring performance seems to be from one to three years.[169] A shorter time is not sufficient to average out short-run variations in performance not related to investment management input. Overly long evaluation periods, on the other hand, tend to produce performance measurements which mask recent performance. But choosing the right length of time over which to measure performance

---

[166] Lorie & Hamilton, note 144 *supra,* at 247.

[167] SEC Investment Company Act Release, No. 7113 (April 6, 1972), [1971-1972 Transfer Binder] CCH Fed. Sec. L. Rep. ¶ 78,694, at 81,467.

[168] *Id.* at 81,467 n.15.

[169] *Institutional Investor Study,* note 104, *supra,* at 265; Bank Administration Institute, *Measuring the Investment Performance of Pension Funds* (1968), recommends comparing performance records based on the time-weighted rate of return of a portfolio.

is not the only consideration. The method of determining when a particular interval should begin can also affect performance fee calculations.

First, if a portfolio is subject to infusions or withdrawals of funds, it is impossible to calculate the performance fee accurately as a percent of asset value unless the period for measuring asset value coincides with the interval over which performance is measured. This is the complement of the problem discussed above of valuing such a portfolio.[170] For reasons of convenience and expense, valuation may be determined through some form of averaging.[171] That period should be the same as the period in which the performance of those average assets is measured. For example, an investment company which calculated annual performance fees based on average asset values in the final quarter would reward good sales during a period of good performance and would inadequately penalize poor performance finally leading to net redemptions.[172]

Second, it is an obvious breach of the duty of loyalty for an investment manager to accept a performance fee for a period in which investment results are already known. Yet, precisely that problem can occur when initiating an investment management relationship or when introducing performance-fee arrangements into an existing relationship. Since it takes at least a year to develop a new performance profile, no performance fees can be charged until the end of the first year of a new regime, even if, as is ordinarily the case, management fees are to be levied more often. Similar considerations also apply to attempts to cancel performance-fee arrangements, especially after a period during which performance has been distinctly inferior. To remove any suggestion that an investment manager is engaged in a breach of the duty of loyalty to an investor, the SEC recommends that fees during transitional periods be the lesser of the fee that would have been charged under the outgoing arrangement and the fee charged under the incoming arrangement.[173] Presumably, with respect to newly initiated investment management arrangement, this recommendation means that only the fulcrum fee be charged until sufficient time has elapsed to make a reasonable evaluation of the investment manager's performance for the new client.

Finally, some of these problems of structuring the time interval for

---

[170] See ¶ 5.03[2][c][iv] *supra.*

[171] Lorie & Hamilton, note 144 *supra,* at 233.

[172] SEC Investment Company Act Release No. 7113 (April 6, 1972), [1971-1972 Transfer Binder] CCH Fed. Sec. L. Rep. ¶ 78,694, at 81,464 n.7.

[173] *Id.* at 81,466.

measuring performance properly can be reduced by adopting a rolling period as the standard interval, a technique generally supported by the SEC.[174] A rolling period is a moving average of the number of sub-periods included in the full interval over which performance is to be measured. The particular advantage of calculating performance fees over a rolling period is that it permits computation of interim management fees. Otherwise, performance cannot be measured until an entire interval has elapsed. Particularly in the case of mutual funds, which are required by law to redeem shares at net asset value, use of a rolling period is helpful because it permits greater accuracy in the calculation of net asset value where performance fees are involved. Without a rolling period calculation, performance fees to be charged against the fund would have to be deferred to the end of the full interval; hence, they would be expenses accrued against the fund, and if significant in amount, would affect net asset value figures.[175] But the same advantage applies to any client who adds to and subtracts from his assets during the full management period. The use of rolling periods reduces the need to accrue obligations between client and manager and thereby helps reduce potential strain on the fiduciary aspect of their relationship.

---

[174] *Id.* at 81,465.
[175] *Id.*

Part III

STRUCTURING THE PORTFOLIO

Chapter 6

PROFESSIONAL COMPETENCE IN PORTFOLIO SELECTION

¶ 6.01. PROFESSIONAL COMPETENCE AS A LEGAL DUTY

Investment managers owe their clients professional competence in the handling of client affairs.[1] The prudent-man rule of the law of

---

[1] See ¶ 1.02. An earlier and abbreviated version of Part III was published in article form in Bines, "Modern Portfolio Theory and Investment Management Law: Refinement of Legal Doctrine," 76 Colum. L. Rev. 721 (1976).

trusts[2] and of the law of agency,[3] the tort rule of ordinary skill and care for professionals,[4] the application of negligence concepts through the antifraud provisions of the federal securities laws,[5] and the imposi-

---

[2] *Restatement (Second) of Trusts* § 227 (1959).

[3] *Restatement (Second) of Agency* § 425 (1958).

[4] *Restatement (Second) of Torts* § 229A (1965); *Restatement (Second) of Agency* § 379 (1958).

[5] Negligence concepts have been developing under the antifraud provisions of the federal securities laws where the act in question could be connected with some failure of disclosure, though often the absence of adequate disclosure was a result of the negligence itself. See, e.g., Hiller v. SEC, 429 F.2d 856 (2d Cir. 1970) (broker-dealer must have reasonable basis for recommendations); Winfield & Co., SEC Securities Exchange Act Release No. 9478 (Feb. 9, 1972) (mutual fund adviser failed to determine securities purchased were restricted and relied too heavily on questionable research). But subsequent to these cases, the Supreme Court held that Rule 10b-5 (17 C.F.R. § 240.10b-5) is not grounds for civil damages on a pure negligence theory in Ernst & Ernst v. Hochfelder, 425 U.S. 185 (1976). According to the Court, there must be an "allegation of scienter—intent to deceive, manipulate, or defraud." *Id.* at 193. Even though Congress had recently completed a major overhaul of the federal securities laws (see Securities Acts Amendments of 1975, Pub. L. 94-29, 89 Stat. 97 (June 4, 1975)) without a hint of disapproval over the expansion of Rule 10b-5 by the federal courts and the SEC, the Court found that Congress intended a scienter requirement stricter than negligence. The Court reserved decision on whether recklessness amounted to scienter, and specifically refrained from interpreting Section 10(b) to prohibit the SEC from proceeding administratively on a negligence theory. 425 U.S. at 193 n.12.

The full impact of *Hochfelder* is as yet unclear. The lower federal courts seem to be interpreting the scienter requirement as meaning knowledge of the falsity or reckless disregard of the truth of material statements and omissions, and they are not requiring a showing of specific intent that the injured party be defrauded, or of actual knowledge that the making of such statements or omissions is in violation of law. See, e.g., Arthur Lipper Corp. v. SEC, [1976-1977 Transfer Binder] CCH Fed. Sec. L. Rep. ¶ 95,796 (2d Cir. 1976); Peltz v. Northern Ohio Bank, [1975-1976 Transfer Binder] CCH Fed. Sec. L. Rep. ¶ 95,905 (N.D. Ohio 1976); McLean v. Alexander, 420 F. Supp. 1057 (D. Del. 1976). See generally Haimoff, "Holmes Looks at Hochfelder and 10b-5," 32 Bus. Law. 147 (1976). If extended fully and simplistically to all allegations of negligence, *Hochfelder* would overturn, or at least severely limit, many branches of federal antifraud development, such as the reasonable-basis doctrine (see Manheim v. Wood, Walker & Co., [1976-1977 Transfer Binder] CCH Fed. Sec. L. Rep. ¶ 95,848 (D. Conn. 1976) (broker's failure to disclose that recommendation based on four-month-old report not scienter, but negligence; see generally

tion of a federal standard of reasonable care on pension management[6]

¶ 7.07[1]) and insider-trading rules. Furthermore, it could stunt the growth of federal antifraud remedies where duty-of-loyalty questions rather than mere professional-skill questions are raised. For example, in Sanders v. John Nuveen & Co., 524 F.2d 1064 (7th Cir. 1975), the court applied theretofore developed antifraud principles to hold, in essence, that an underwriter impliedly represents that it has made a reasonable investigation of an issuer. The Supreme Court reversed *Sanders* for further consideration in light of *Hochfelder* (425 U.S. 929 (1976)) without acknowledging than an underwriter is in the difficult *fiiduciary* position of marketing the issuer's securities at the same time as securities purchasers buying from the underwriter require assurance of the financial soundness and accuracy of information produced by the underwriter concerning the issuer.

Finally, the lower courts have split on whether *Hochfelder* also limits the SEC's enforcement authority. Compare SEC v. Geotek, [1976-1977 Transfer Binder] CCH Fed. Sec. L. Rep. ¶ 95,756 (N.D. Cal. 1976), and SEC v. American Realty Trust, [1976-1977 Transfer Binder] CCH Fed. Sec. L. Rep. ¶ 95,913 (E.D. Va. 1977), with SEC v. Bausch & Lomb, Inc., 420 F. Supp. 1226 (S.D.N.Y. 1976). The SEC takes the position that a showing of scienter is not necessary in enforcement actions. *In re* Irwin, SEC Admin. Proc. No. 3-4726 (Feb. 22, 1977), summarized in [1976-1977 Transfer Binder] CCH Fed. Sec. L. Rep. ¶ 80,893. While it is difficult to deny the simplistic logic which says that if Congress intended scienter as an element of statutory fraud, the statutory provisions on their face make no special allowance for the SEC, it is also the case that forcing the SEC to prove the equivalent of common-law fraud would deprive the Commission of jurisdiction over all but the most egregious securities practices and would restrict it in preventing and terminating schemes tending to work a fraud.

If one is willing to accept the possibility that the Court was being disingenuous with its statutory construction arguments, the explanation of the result in *Hochfelder* may be found in footnote 33 of the Court's opinion. Taking a note from Ultramares Corp. v. Touche, Niven & Co., 255 N.Y. 170, 174 N.E. 441 (1931), the Court argued that any lesser requirement than scienter would open the door to too many plaintiffs. Whatever may be said in defense of such an argument, it has little to do with "congressional intent" with respect to scienter, since Congress at any time could expand or contract the availability of civil-damage actions without disemboweling the federal antifraud jurisdiction by depriving the SEC of enforcement authority and private plaintiffs of equitable relief.

6 See Employee Retirement Income Security Act of 1974 (ERISA) § 404(a)(1)(B) (29 U.S.C. § 1104(a)(1)(B)), which restates the prudent-man rule of the law of trusts with slight modification ostensibly to narrow the legal standard to prudence as observed by pension managers. For an extensive discussion of the meaning of prudence under ERISA, see Hutchinson, "The Federal Prudent Man Rule Under ERISA," 22 Vill. L. Rev. 15 (1976) (by former Administrator of Pension and Welfare Benefit Programs, U.S. Dep't of Labor).

and foundation management[7] permit no other conclusion. But given the general statement of principle, the question is what the obligation to act with professional competence requires of investment managers.

The most important function of an investment manager—indeed, the fundamental service an investment manager offers—is expert assistance in the selection of investments through which clients can achieve their investment objectives. To an extent, existing case and statutory law already set some boundaries on the discretion of investment managers to choose investments for their clients. But those limits have been relatively crude, and insofar as the law has explicitly dealt with the question of professional competence in structuring a portfolio, the language of the law still lags greatly behind contemporary portfolio management practices. A brief but fairly thorough summary of the law would be as follows: An investment manager should not speculate[8]; should sell off assets unsuitable for an account[9]; should make an account productive[10]; and should diversify the portfolio.[11] And even this brief a recitation overstates the precision of the law. The *Restatement (Second) of Trusts*, for example, where the meaning of these rules is discussed as exhaustively as in any other source, is replete with the kind of vague generalities which make it virtually impossible to be confident about what is permitted and what forbidden.

Given the subjective nature of the applicable legal controls, it is hardly surprising that matters involving the exercise of judgment seldom have resulted in personal answerability for investment managers. That is not to say that there has been no answerability. On the contrary, it has been the practice in various jurisdictions specifically to forbid invest-

---

[7] According to I.R.C. § 4944(a)(2), as implemented in Reg. § 53.4944-1 (a)(2), investment managers employed by foundations are subject to tax sanctions for making investments without exercising ordinary business care and prudence.

[8] *Restatement (Second) of Trusts* § 227 (1959); *Restatement (Second) of Agency* § 425, Comment c (1958).

[9] *Restatement (Second) of Trusts* § 230 (1959); *Restatement (Second) of Agency* § 425(c) (1958). As defined in ¶ 4.02, a commitment is "suitable" if its inclusion in a portfolio accords with the investor's investment objectives. See also ¶ 7.06 and the brief summary of the authorities in note 24 *infra*.

[10] *Restatement (Second) of Trusts* § 181 (1959); *Restatement (Second) of Agency* § 425, Comment b (1958).

[11] *Restatement (Second) of Trusts* § 228 (1959); *Restatement (Second) of Agency* § 425, Comment c (1958).

ment managers to undertake certain types of commitments[12]—the rule against purchasing second mortgages for trusts, for example.[13] But for those types of commitments which are permissible, only in the most outrageous circumstances would a manager's decision result in personal liability.[14]

It is highly doubtful that enforcement of the investment manager's duty to exercise ordinary skill and care will remain so relaxed. For one thing, it is a contemporary phenomenon that professionals of all types are increasingly being required to conduct themselves competently, even in matters of judgment.[15] Furthermore, with the prohibition against

---

[12] See ¶ 6.02[1] at notes 25-33. The "legal list" is perhaps the most notorious example of the attempts to substitute a legal rule for the exercise of investment judgment of trustees. The legal-list approach categorizes securities, particularly common stock, as either appropriate or inappropriate for trust investment according to criteria that the drafters of such lists (typically lawyers) deem pertinent. Legal lists have become discredited and are on their way to extinction. See ¶ 1.02[2]. Equally simplistic in concept are the suggestions (again, typically advanced by lawyers) that there exist other legal criteria which, in and of themselves, disqualify securities for trust investment. Examples of such criteria include low yield, lack of seasoning, and lack of security for a loan. See, e.g., J. Farr, *An Estate Planner's Handbook* 573-603 (3d ed. 1966) (reprinting, in part, Shattuck, "The Massachusetts Prudent Man Rule in Trust Investments," 25 B.U.L. Rev. 307 (1945)).

[13] See 3 A. Scott, *Law of Trusts* § 227-7 (3d ed. 1967) (hereinafter cited as Scott). Massachusetts, which determines the standard of care applicable to trust investments by reference to professional practices (see ¶ 1.02[2]), has rejected the "absolute ironclad rule" of other jurisdictions condemning second mortgages. Taft v. Smith, 186 Mass. 31, 70 N.E. 1031 (1904).

[14] See, e.g., Spiegel v. Beacon Participations, Inc., 297 Mass. 398, 8 N.E.2d 895 (1937) (joint investment venture and purchase of high face-value demand note without recourse and without requiring payment seasonably both held negligent); *In re* Dickinson, 152 Mass. 184, 25 N.E. 99 (1890) (investment of over one-third of estate in stock of a new and untested railroad held inadequate diversification); Lare Estate, 436 Pa. 1, 257 A.2d 556 (1969) (trust assets held on deposit with commercial side of bank). See generally 3 Scott, note 13 *supra*, § 230.2.

[15] The growing impact on doctors of the duty to exercise ordinary care in their professional endeavors needs little comment. Although general negligence principles apply through state law to investment managers, there is growing interest in specific regulation of standards of competence for financial analysis and investment counseling at the state level. See, e.g., Securities Week, Jan. 19, 1976, p. 1 (N.Y.); Securities Week, Jan. 12, 1976, p. 9 (Mass.).

particular commitments for trustees falling away, with more and more professional investment management being carried out under arrangements not involving a formal trust,[16] and with the spread of a federal standard of professional competence developing,[17] it is inevitable that there will be legal pressure on investment managers to hew to stricter professional standards in structuring the portfolios of their clients. What this means to investment managers is that their discretion to select among different types of commitments is expanding, but at the same time the reasons for their investment decisions are becoming more testable. As a consequence, the generalized duties to avoid speculation, dispose of unsuitable commitments, make assets productive, and diversify the portfolio will become more specific in content, and thus permit more accurate measurement of whether they have been met.

This chapter begins the exploration of the considerations with which investment managers must now deal by reviewing existing law and the reasons for its inadequacy as an evaluative tool in an environment that is increasingly characterized by close scrutiny in the portfolio decisional process. The discussion then moves to a simplified nonrigorous exposition of modern portfolio theory. The concepts on which the theory is based permit a more highly refined analysis of the portfolio decisional process, and consequently are likely to become the basis of the professional standards against which the law will mature. Chapter 7 concludes the discussion of portfolio selection considerations by focusing on the practices on which investment managers rely in making portfolio decisions. The perspective there is on how modern portfolio theory applies to these practices and what it requires of them, and it should offer some guidance about how legal doctrine is likely to develop.

The speed with which federal law will fully extend the negligence principle to investment managers is not certain in view of the Supreme Court's restrictive interpretation of Rule 10b-5 in Ernst & Ernst v. Hochfelder, 425 U.S. 185 (1976) (discussed in note 5 *supra*), but extension has already occurred at least with respect to pension managers and foundation managers. See notes 6-7 *supra*. Moreover, there has been at least one serious move in Congress to establish minimum competence standards for statutory investment advisers by amending the Investment Advisers Act (15 U.S.C. §§ 80b-1 et seq.). See S. 2849, 94th Cong., 2d Sess. (1976).

[16] See, e.g., ERISA §§ 3(21) (defining fiduciary) and 3(38) (defining investment manager); 29 U.S.C. §§ 1002(21), 1002(38); Uniform Management of Institutional Funds Act (7 *U.L.A.*) § 5 (Supp. 1976) (permitting delegation by trustees of investment management authority).

[17] See ¶ 7.07[1] at notes 129-143.

¶ 6.02. THE IMPRECISE LEGAL PARAMETERS OF THE DUTY OF PROFESSIONAL COMPETENCE

[1] Avoiding Speculation

It is a commonplace of the law of trusts that a trustee must invest but may not speculate.[18] To remove all incentives from trustees to speculate, moreover, the law provides that losses from speculation may not be offset against gains from proper investments.[19] The rule is less fixed in agency law, but the bias is in the same direction. Absent express instructions authorizing speculative activity from the principal, an agent must act in a fashion very much like that of a trustee (though the range of investments an agent may consider may be much broader).[20] In effect, the legal definition of speculation limits an investment manager's discretion to carry out an investment program. No matter what the conviction of an investment manager concerning the safety and likely return of one or more opportunities for investment, the law must agree that investment rather than speculation is taking place, or else the manager proceeds at his own risk.

The federal securities laws also regard speculation as an investment activity subject to regulation. Though less judgmental than state law about the inclusion of speculative commitments in managed accounts, federal law requires that investors be given adequate disclosure of the speculative features of the arrangements to which they commit their assets. Thus, not only is it fraudulent to describe speculative securities as safe,[21] it may also be necessary to set forth speculative characteristics of an investment even when the level of risk involved is appropriate for the investor.[22] Although the full impact of this line of development on

---

[18] 3 Scott, note 13 *supra*, § 227.6; *Restatement (Second) of Trusts* § 227, Comments f-p (1959).

[19] *Restatement (Second) of Trusts* § 213, Comment b (1959). See *In re* Bank of N.Y., 35 N.Y.2d 512, 517, 323 N.E.2d 700, 703, 364 N.Y.S.2d 164, 168 (1974); Creed v. McAleer, 275 Mass. 353, 175 N.E. 761 (1931).

[20] *Restatement (Second) of Agency* § 425, Comment a (1958); *Seavey on Agency* ¶ 27 (1964).

[21] See, e.g., *In re* Isthmus S.S. & Salvage Co.; Robert Edelstein Co., SEC Securities Act Release No. 4716, SEC Securities Exchange Act Release No. 7400, [1964-1966 Transfer Binder] CCH Fed. Sec. L. Rep. ¶ 77,136 (1964).

[22] The S-1 registration statement requires, when applicable, that an offering involving a high degree of risk disclose that fact. See 1 CCH Fed. Sec. L. Rep. ¶ 3766. This requirement reflects a long-standing policy of the Commission. See, e.g., *In re* Doman Helicopter, Inc., 41 S.E.C. 431, 439

investment management practices is not yet clear, it is at least evident that, insofar as an investment manager's promotional efforts are concerned, there is a heavy duty of accurate disclosure of plans to engage in speculative activities.[23] Moreover, the suitability doctrine treats as a violation of the federal antifraud rules the recommendation or sale of speculative securities to investors who are not in a position to bear the risk involved.[24] A fortiori, therefore, it seems that engaging in speculative ventures in behalf of clients not suited to bear adverse consequences of speculation is violative of the antifraud provisions regardless of the degree of prior contractual authorization an investment manager may have obtained.

The difficulty with the common-law and federal law restrictions on speculation rests, in the first instance, with the imprecision of the term. To the extent there is common ground, two identifying features of a speculative commitment come to mind. On the one hand, speculation implies excessive risk of loss. Moreover, since investors do not expose

---

(1963); *In re* Universal Camera Corp., 19 S.E.C. 648, 652 (1945). Moreover, where an offering involves a high degree of risk, the particular speculative features of the offering should be set forth at least in summary fashion. See *In re* Woodland Oil & Gas Co., [1957-1961 Transfer Binder] CCH Fed. Sec. L. Rep. ¶ 76,598 (1958).

[23] See ¶ 3.03. See also Karp v. Kapchan, [1975-1976 Transfer Binder] CCH Fed. Sec. L. Rep. ¶ 95,477 (S.D.N.Y. 1976); Financial Programs, Inc., SEC Securities Exchange Act Release No. 11,312 (March 24, 1975), [1974-1975 Transfer Binder] CCH Fed. Sec. L. Rep. ¶ 80,146.

[24] The "suitability doctrine" is essentially a requirement that broker-dealers sell or recommend only securities that are suited to the particular investment needs of the individual customer. The doctrine arose in response to the high-pressure "boiler room" sales technique, which was designed to influence prospective investors to make on-the-spot decisions to buy instead of considering the advisability of the suggested purchases. 6 L. Loss, *Securities Regulation* 3708-3709 (2d ed., Supp. 1969). Various self-regulatory measures are designed to eliminate the problem (e.g., NYSE Rule 405 (the so-called know-your-customer rule); NASD Rules of Fair Practice, Art. III, § 2, CCH NASD Manual ¶ 2152, at 2051 (1974)), and the doctrine is not limited in its application to the classic "boiler room" (Gerald M. Greenberg, 40 S.E.C. 133, 137-138 (1960)). See generally Chapter 4.

The SEC's suitability rule for broker-dealers who are not members of national exchanges or the NASD is Rule 15b10-3 (17 C.F.R. § 240.15b 10-3), with reinforcing record-keeping requirements in Rule 15b10-6(a)(1) (B) (17 C.F.R. § 240.15b10-6(a)(1)(B)). Commentators have discussed the requirements at length. See Mundheim, "Responsibilities of Broker-Dealers: The Suitability Doctrine," 1965 Duke L.J. 445. See also Rice, "Recommendations by a Broker-Dealer: The Requirement for a Reasonable Basis," 25 Mercer L. Rev. 537 (1974).

themselves to unusual risks without reason, speculation also connotes opportunity for unusual gain. This is not to say that speculations are necessarily losers' bets—that is, the sum of all the returns of those who succeed is not necessarily less than the sum of all the returns of those who fail, as is the case in lotteries and pari-mutuel betting. Rather, there is a judgment that, whether the result of speculation is good or bad, it will have a major impact on the stake used to finance the venture.

For some time, the case law has recognized heavy risk and opportunity for unusual gain as the measure of a speculative commitment.[25] But the law has not advanced far beyond this relatively indefinite and therefore unhelpful categorization. Some cases have suggested also that permanent or long-term ownership indicates investment intent, whereas trading activity indicates speculative intent.[26] Other cases have focused only on the risk of loss, characterizing as speculations those commitments involving greater than ordinary risk.[27] Yet another hypothesis has been that speculative value depends on future prospects and contingencies, whereas investment value is a function of historical performance.[28] But, while these descriptions all contain an element of truth, they are neither accurate in every case, nor definite enough to suggest when the very criteria they set up are violated.

An interesting legislative effort to define speculation occurred during the initial development of the state blue-sky laws. Several states created regulatory authorities with the power to limit or even to deny access to public markets to issuers of speculative securities.[29] These statutes pro-

---

[25] See, e.g., Wild v. Brown, 120 N.J.Eq. 31, 33, 183 A. 899, 900 (1936); Arentsen v. Moreland, 122 Wis. 167, 184, 99 N.W. 790, 796 (1904).

[26] See, e.g., State v. Gibbs, 7 Ohio N.P. 371, 18 Ohio Dec. 694 (1908).

[27] See, e.g., Stewart v. Brady, 300 Ill. 425, 444, 133 N.E. 310, 317 (1921).

[28] Commonwealth v. Edgerton Coal Co., 164 Pa. 284, 30 A. 125 (1894).

[29] 1 L. Loss, *Securities Regulation* 23-30 (2d ed. 1961). See Ward v. Home Royalty Ass'n, 142 Kan. 546, 50 P.2d 992 (1935); State v. Welch, 42 N.D. 44, 172 N.W. 234 (1919). A classic statement of the purpose of the blue-sky statutes appears in Stewart v. Brady, 300 Ill. 425, 439, 133 N.E. 310, 315 (1921), where the court says:

"The purpose of the act is . . . not only to furnish information, to protect credulity and ignorance from deception and imposition and prevent fraudulent and deceitful sales of securities, but also to assure credit and freedom of commerce in such securities as, because of their character, the place and manner of their sale or the character of the seller, are not subject to the practices of deception and fraud to such a degree as in the judgment of the legislature to require legislation for the protection

hibited the sale of securities absent registration with and prior approval from a state securities commissioner. Some types of securities were excluded from the registration and prior-approval requirements of the statute, however, and thus were expressly or impliedly recognized as nonspeculative, apparently on the grounds either that the class of issuer involved tended to be responsible or that the type of security involved generally possessed a satisfactory degree of safety. Included among those issuing organizations not required to submit to regulation were governmental agencies, regulated industries, not-for-profit corporations, and corporations listed on certain national securities exchanges. Examples of securities generally regarded as safe included first mortgages on tangible property, short-term commercial paper, and certain kinds of promissory notes. On the other hand, all other securities not specifically excluded from regulation were regarded as speculative, although, in some cases, securities were classified in several gradations according to the degree of speculation thought to be characteristic of either the type of issuer or type of security in question.

In any event, the statutory definitions of factors rendering an issue more or less speculative were highly imprecise. One common test held that securities with an offering price reflecting a large element of future growth and accomplishment instead of equivalent value for tangible assets were speculative.[30] But there was no attempt to either identify or quantify the tangible features necessary to distinguish greater from lesser speculations. Another test for measuring the degree of speculation inherent in an issue, apparently on the theory that actions speak louder than words, focused on the size of the sales commission. Securities promotions involving unreasonably high commissions were sufficient to

---

of purchasers. Sales by unknown and non-resident vendors and sleek peripatetic salesmen, with glib tongues and indurated consciences, of stock or other securities for the purpose of developing wildcat oil fields in distant States, mythical rubber plantations in Guatemala, or imaginary copper mines in Mexico, for extracting gold from sea water and light from cucumbers and developing power from the rise and fall of the tides, and for the hundreds of visionary schemes, domestic and foreign, designed to secure a great return from a small investment in a short time, fall within the terms of the act. No one will question its application to such cases, even though eventually many of the enterprises may prove successful, because many people have been cheated and deceived by the statements made in such cases, have improvidently invested their money in worthless securities and are without remedy."

[30] See, e.g., Groskins v. State, 52 Okla. Crim. 197, 4 P.2d 117 (1931).

classify issues as speculative.[31] These attempts to define speculation were not terribly successful, and they occasionally fell to constitutional attack on ground of vagueness.[32] As a consequence, contemporary blue-sky laws have abandoned the search for a useful definition and even have largely withdrawn the authority of state securities commissioners to prevent an offering of regulated securities on ground that it involves speculative securities.[33]

Unable to create a workable definition of speculation, courts and legislatures fell to identifying categories of securities as either of investment grade or speculative without regard for the unique characteristics of a given commitment or the particular purpose for which a manager might desire to select it. Especially assiduous in this respect has been the law of trusts, both because of a perceived need to be especially protective of trust beneficiaries and because of the serious consequences for trustees of purchasing imprudent investments, of which speculations are a subclass. Examples of the types of commitments which have been condemned in this fashion are margin purchases, bonds selling at a large discount, junior mortgages on property, unsecured loans, new issues, purchases on margin, and short sales.[34]

But this technique of fixing categories has also proved an elusive method of defining speculation. Indeed, these kinds of absolute restrictions can force investment managers into making undesirable decisions which adversely affect the interests of their clients. For example, a prohibition on unsecured lending, long a common-law rule for trustees,[35] would prevent managed accounts from benefitting from modern cash-management techniques during periods when, for operational or investment reasons, they were not totally committed to long-term debt and equity positions. Even something as risky as short selling can

---

[31] Watters & Martin v. Homes Corp., Inc., 136 Va. 114, 116 S.E. 366 (1923).

[32] See Groskins v. State, 52 Okla. Crim. 197, 4 P.2d 117 (1931); State v. Skinner, 20 Ala. App. 204, 101 So. 327 (1924).

[33] Although Uniform Securities Act (7 *U.L.A.*) § 306(a)(2)(E) still permits state commissioners to withhold registration if an offering would tend to work a fraud upon purchases, the comments to that subsection make plain that the statutory meaning of fraud does not extend to a judgment that the venture may involve a highly risky undertaking.

[34] *Restatement of Trusts* § 227, Comments f-i (1935); see generally 3 Scott, note 13 *supra*, § 227.

[35] See, e.g., J. Tiffany & E. Bullard, *The Law of Trusts and Trustees* 588 (1862). Compare N.Y. Banking Law § 235(12-a) (McKinney 1971) (authority of trustees to invest in commercial paper).

have its sober advantage if it is not merely a bet on a market drop, but rather a hedge against loss on a portfolio security.[36] But the experience investment managers have had with common stocks as an investment vehicle best makes the point that fixed categories are a poor way to define speculation. The extended contest between the Massachusetts prudent-man rule, which left decisions as to common stock investments in the hands of trustees, and the New York rule, which, absent express authorization to the contrary, first absolutely prohibited common stock investments for trusts, and then created legal lists of approved securities, demonstrates the consequences of relying on fixed categories to define speculation.[37] While the original New York rule is now recognized as indefensible[38] and has been almost uniformly abandoned,[39] the damage

---

[36] See Dyl, "Negative Betas: The Attractions of Selling Short," 1 J. Portfolio Management 74 (1975); Note, "Prudence in Trust Investment," 3 U. Mich. J.L. Reform 491, 513-522 (1975); B. Graham, D. Dodd & S. Cottle, *Security Analysis* 625-626 (4th ed. 1962) (hereinafter cited as Graham, Dodd & Cottle); "Risk and Return on Short Positions in Common Stocks," 28 J. Fin. 97 (1973). While it may be persuasively argued that short selling should nonetheless be prohibited because too few investment managers are capable of engaging in it responsibly, that kind of policy justification merely concedes the point that it is not the commitment itself which is inherently speculative. Compare Sosnoff, "Hedge Fund Management," 22 Fin. Anal. J. 105 (1966), with Roscow, " 'Hedging': An Idea Whose Time Has Come," Fin. World, April 10, 1974, p. 141. Indeed, investment managers are coming to recognize the prudence of modulating the risk inherent in maintaining either short or long positions in securities through the use of options. See, e.g., "Paul Kolton Speaks Out," 114 Trusts & Estates 734, 736-737 (1975). See ¶ 7.05.

[37] See ¶ 1.02[2][c]. Ironically, the legal-list approach not only excludes securities which may be appropriate trust investments; it also may be used to make acceptable investments having speculative features but desired by the drafters of the legal list to be purchased by trust portfolios. See, e.g., Simpson v. Mitchell, Sec. Reg. L. Rep. No. 332, Dec. 17, 1975, at A-7 (N.Y. Co. Sup. Ct., Dec. 4, 1975), *aff'd* 53 App. Div. 2d 590, 386 N.Y.S. 2d 350 (1976) (teacher's petition to enjoin pension fund from investing in Municipal Assistance Corporation securities denied on grounds that state law specifies that securities of corporations are reasonable, prudent, proper, and legal investments). But see 3 Scott, note 13 *supra*, § 227.12 (in selecting among authorized investments, trustee must exercise skill and care).

[38] See, e.g., Note, "Prudence in Trust Investment," 3 U. Mich. J.L. Reform 491 (1975); Graham, Dodd & Cottle, note 36 *supra*, at 60-61; Elsom, "The Law of Trust Investment," 16 Fin. Anal. J. 27 (July-Aug. 1960); Shattuck, "The Massachusetts Prudent Man Rule in Trust Investments," 25 B.U.L. Rev. 307 (1945).

[39] See Torrance, "50 Years of Trust Investment," 93 Trusts & Estates 250, 252 (March 1954) (map of spread of Massachusetts rule).

it inflicted on managed portfolios is incalculable. Indeed, the major motivation for abandoning the New York rule came from the corporate trustee community, especially after the disastrous performance their accounts suffered during the depression years when they were denied access to common stocks and forced to invest in debt instruments of very low yield.[40]

It is significant that during this long period in the development of the law, the investment management community had little of value to offer the courts and legislatures in distinguishing investments from speculations. It may be a desirable goal that investment managers be given as much advance guidance as possible concerning their legal obligations, so long as their decisions are to be subject to review in a court of law on grounds of suitability or prudence or any similar standard. Nonetheless, it is evident that the power of legal institutions to accomplish that end is highly dependent on the ability of the investment management community itself to prescribe some basis for distinguishing between investments and speculation. A survey of the professional literature demonstrates that not only has no real convention existed among investment managers about how to make the distinction,[41] but also that there has been sharply varying opinion over the wisdom of adopting an investment policy oriented toward speculative commitments, especially if a manager's task is to preserve the purchasing power of an account and not simply its nominal value.[42]

In such an environment, it is hardly surprising that meanings became blurred and that rigid legal rules resistant to rational investment policy developed. The explanation for why speculation, despite its impact as a legal term of art, should have become so imprecise in application is simply that it was asked to do too much. In the nineteenth century, when investment management was largely personal trust management, it may well have been that a term such as speculation was useful as a description for investments which were inappropriate for

---

[40] *Id.*; see also Friedman, "The Dynastic Trust," 73 Yale L.J. 547, 568-571 (1964); 3 Scott, note 13 *supra*, § 230, at 1873 n. 6.

[41] See, e.g., Graham, "The Future of Financial Analysis," 19 Fin. Anal. J. 65 (May-June 1963); J. Lorie M. Hamilton, *The Stock Market: Theories and Evidence* 10-14 (1973) (hereinafter cited as Lorie & Hamilton); Graham, Dodd & Cottle,, note 36 *supra*, at 47-58; L. Engel, *How to Buy Stocks* 145-153 (1972); G. Loeb, *The Battle for Investment Survival* 19 (1965).

[42] Compare Graham, Dodd & Cottle, note 36 *supra,* at 60-61, with Loeb, note 41. *supra*, at 20-21. See ¶ 1.01[1] (discussion of the origins of the prudent-man rule). See 3 Scott, note 13 *supra,* § 227.6.

beneficiaries and remainderman receiving trust management services.[43] But it is mistaken to suggest that the same commitment is either speculative or of investment grade for every single investor or, assuming investors of like investment objectives, for every single portfolio. It ought to be plain that the character of a commitment can be determined only in relation to a set of investment objectives and, perhaps to a lesser extent, the purpose for its inclusion in a portfolio. Indeed, it is entirely reasonable to suggest that an investment manager could place each of three clients into the same commitment and have it characterized as speculative for one, adequate for the second, and incompetently conservative for the third. Speculation is a relative term only, referring to commitments which, given a specific portfolio, involve an unacceptable level of risk for the investor who is purchasing them.

[2] Disposing of Unsuitable Commitments

It is rare that an investment manager receives a totally uninvested portfolio to service. Almost all new accounts have existing commit-

---

[43] See Friedman, "The Dynastic Trust," 73 Yale L.J. 547 (1964). The inclination of the legal community to establish legal rules limiting the investment discretion of trustees is a danger which cannot be overstated. See ¶ 5.02[2], note 16. While it is understandable that courts and legal commentators prefer precise and objective rules for their own guidance and the guidance of nonprofessional trustees, such an attitude subverts the ability of professional investment managers to carry out their responsibilities properly. The bulwark of the Massachusetts approach to evaluation of trust investments has been an adamant refusal either to adopt absolute rules or to transpose decisions based on the facts of one case into a legal precedent in another. See, e.g., Kimball v. Whitney, 233 Mass. 321, 123 N.E. 665 (1919) (holding company in form of business trust for conglomeration of street, railway, and electric utility companies not improper investment even though trust was only four years old when bought and failed to pay dividends for five of the years held); Taft v. Smith, 186 Mass. 31, 70 N.E. 1031 (1904) ("absolute ironclad rule" of other jurisdictions that investment in second mortgage improper rejected); Thayer v. Dewey, 185 Mass. 68, 69 N.E. 1074 (1904) ("arbitrary, universal rule" of other jurisdictions that investment in foreign real estate improper rejected); In re Dickinson, 152 Mass. 184, 25 N.E. 99 (1890) (heavily indebted railroad being built in unsettled territory not improper investment); In re Hunt, 141 Mass. 515, 6 N.E. 554 (1886) (investment in certificates of deposit having substantially longer maturities than customary not improper); Bowker v. Pierce, 130 Mass. 262 (1881) (investment in stock of railroad company which ceased paying dividends and ultimately became worthless not improper); Brown v. French, 125 Mass. 410 (1878) (investment in bonds and promissory notes of an incomplete railroad where bond issue had not been fully sold out not improper).

ments undertaken either by a predecessor investment manager or by the investor. In either case, the manager must decide whether to continue those commitments or dispose of them. In the likely event that some adjustments are to be made, the manager must determine which commitments to sell, how much of each to sell, when to sell them, and the order in which to sell them. This process represents one of the most difficult problems for investment managers, particularly since commitments existing at the time the management relationship is initiated often are in securities not closely followed by the manager.[44] Furthermore, there is a definite psychological pressure on an investment manager when reconstituting a portfolio to make selections which outperform those disposed of.

The duty to dispose of unsuitable investments is closely related to two other duties investment managers must observe, both of which are based on a policy of reducing risk to an acceptable level. An existing portfolio may contain commitments which would be regarded as speculative, or it may be inadequately diversified.[45] In either event, the duty to avoid speculation and the duty to diversify would require the manager to make appropriate adjustments even without a separate duty to dispose of unsuitable investments. Furthermore, the question of what

---

[44] If it is the policy of an investment manager to liquidate commitments in securities not followed by the manager, he should disclose that fact in advance to a client. See ¶ 7.06, note 95. Contractual disclosure should suffice if it either leaves responsibility for continuing or liquidating such existing commitments with the client or if it states the outline of the sales program which the manager will use to dispose of such commitments. Cf. Angelakis v. Churchill Management Corp., [1975-1976 Transfer Binder] CCH Fed. Sec. L. Rep. ¶ 95,285 (N.D. Cal. 1975) (adviser recommended portfolio be liquidated and cash payment be made to initiate investment program).

[45] Conceptually, the duty to dispose of unsuitable investments could extend to two other situations often presented in newly acquired portfolios. Some portfolios contain commitments characterized by excessive safety of principal. Such commitments may deprive an investor of a full opportunity to achieve his investment goals. Some portfolios, though at a proper level of risk, are not well constructed to meet a client's goals. For example, a portfolio which is to produce income may be so heavily into low-yielding issues and so small in size that the deficiency in periodic income cannot be made up by selling part of existing commitments from time to time and taking capital gains as a substitute. Nonetheless, the duty to dispose of improper investments has traditionally been directed at unacceptably risky portfolios. To the extent unreasonable caution and imbalance in commitments have been a concern, they have been considered an aspect of the duty to make a portfolio productive.

action should be taken depends on the legal definitions of speculation[46] and diversification,[47] and the evaluation of an investment manager's judgment about what to sell and what to buy when adjusting a portfolio can be no more precise than the law would permit if those buy and sell decisions were being considered on their own merits. As discussed in ¶ 6.01, neither speculation nor diversification is defined precisely enough to provide a firm standard.

Beyond requiring workable definitions of speculation and diversification, however, the duty to dispose of unsuitable investments also creates special problems of selection and timing. An investment manager may be called upon to explain why he sold certain commitments rather than others, or why he chose the proportions he did in effecting adjustment, or why he did not act sooner, or why he acted as quickly as he did. Until now, however, the law has not been especially demanding on these points. A showing that the commitments sold were speculative or that they rendered a portfolio too concentrated,[48] along with a showing that the sales were effected in a reasonable time,[49] has been enough to insulate a manager from further review over the reconstitution of a portfolio.

But it is doubtful that such a tolerant attitude will continue. The law has been based on portfolio management concepts which are far too simplistic in view of contemporary theory and practice. At one time, it was easy to carry out the responsibility to dispose of unsuitable

---

[46] See 3 Scott, note 13 *supra,* § 230; *Restatement (Second) of Agency* § 70 (1958).

[47] 3 Scott, note 13 *supra,* § 230.3; *Restatement (Second) of Agency* § 70 (1958).

[48] See notes 46-47 *supra.*

[49] 3 Scott, note 13 *supra,* § 230.2. See Durscomb v. Durscomb, 1 Johns. Ch. 508 (1914) (money left dormant held negligent); *In re* Donohue, 88 Misc. 359, 151 N.Y.S. 1094 (1914) (executors and trustees liable upon failure of bank; funds deposited from time to time over ten-year period). But see Barney v. Saunders, 57 U.S. (16 How.) 535, 544-546 (1854) (proceeds of loans left on deposit in a passbook account more than seven months, held unreasonable delay; account held three months, held no unreasonable delay). Compare Jones Estate, 400 Pa. 545, 162 A.2d 408 (1960) (trust assets held on deposit with commercial side of bank for five years); Lare Estate, 436 Pa. 1, 257 A.2d 556 (1960) (investments held on deposit twenty years). See also Angelakis v. Churchill Management Corp., [1975-1976 Transfer Binder] CCH Fed. Sec. L. Rep. ¶ 95,285 (N.D. Cal. 1975) (two-month delay by investment adviser to liquidate account wrongful absent disclosure unless delay shown to be caused solely by client's former broker-dealer).

commitments, since legislation or case law had labeled securities either as speculative or as investment grade. Similarly, it was easy to achieve diversification. All one had to do was reduce the level of concentration in a portfolio to the point where one security or the securities of one issuer would not constitute a disproportionate segment of the portfolio. Moreover, the law has been quite generous in determining what level of concentration is permitted.[50] A statute once stricter than most other expressions of official policy, for example, tolerated commitments which accounted for up to 20 percent of total assets.[51] Nor has timing been a sticky legal problem. The only context in which it has been seriously raised is in the administration of estates where the rule is that, absent unusual circumstances, a year or more was reasonable to dispose of improper investments.[52]

Nowadays, however, the legal issues are far more complex. With reliance on rigid categories as a tool to define speculation diminishing, investment managers will have to be able to demonstrate that the securities they sold in fact reflected an unacceptable degree of risk. Diversification also has changed in concept. As is explained more fully in Chapter 7,[53] it no longer is simply the negative of concentration, but has acquired some highly quantitative features against which the action of investment managers can be measured. Finally, the understanding of the importance of timing to new portfolio adjustment decisions is also becoming more sophisticated.[54] Tax considerations and transaction costs, such as commissions, sources of information on portfolio securities not familiar to the manager, and the like, are all relevant to the decision when to sell and, insofar as review of a manager is concerned, are capable of fairly objective determination.

[3] Making a Portfolio Productive

The duty to make a portfolio productive tests the professional competence with which investment managers carry out an investment program. It is not enough merely to protect assets under management.

---

[50] 3 Scott, note 13 *supra,* § 228.1.

[51] Compare Wis. Stat. Ann. § 320.02 (1971) with 1935 Wis. Laws, Ch. 363.

[52] See note 49 *supra.*

[53] See ¶¶ 7.02[2], 7.03[3][b], 7.06.

[54] See, e.g., Chemical Bank & Trust Co. v. Ott, 248 App. Div. 406, 289 N.Y.S. 228 (1936) (Dore, J., dissenting in part), *rev'd* 274 N.Y. 572, 10 N.E.2d 557 (1937) (negligent failure to sell).

Unless a client is seeking only a custodianship arrangement, a manager must adopt an investment program likely to produce some returns, whether income or capital gains. Furthermore, the investments chosen for a client's portfolio must be of a type which characteristically provide a return likely to achieve the client's investment objectives. Even for clients for whom preservation of the nominal value of the principal is the overriding investment objective, achieving the highest return available without unreasonably increasing the risk of loss to the principal is the obligation of the manager.[55]

In practice, the failure to invest is a much rarer problem than the failure to invest competently.[56] A lack of ordinary skill and care in selecting investments for a portfolio in effect deprives a client of an opportunity for the full gain that could have been achieved. For this

---

[55] *Restatement (Second) of Trusts* § 227, Comment e (1959). See *In re* Talbot, 141 Cal. App. 2d 309, 296 P.2d 848 (1956).

[56] Sometimes, a failure to invest reflects inadvertence, neglect, or lack of ability on the part of the manager. In one case, the trustees of a charitable foundation were held in breach of duty for permitting the trustees' finance committee to maintain an excessive portion of the endowment in demand deposits and low-yielding securities. Stern v. Lucy Webb Hayes Nat'l Training School for Deaconesses & Missionaries, 381 F. Supp. 1003 (D.D.C. 1974); Annot., "Charitable Trusts: Liability of Trustee for Permitting Trust Income to Accumulate in Non Interest-Bearing Account," 51 A.L.R.3d 1293 (1973). (Accord, Manchester Bank of Pomo Indians, Inc. v. United States, 363 F. Supp. 1238 (N.D. Cal. 1973).) The record showed that the trustees gave unquestioning approval to the accounts presented and made no effort to evaluate them independently. 381 F. Supp. at 1008.

More often, however, a failure to invest assets under management is the result of a division of loyalties on the part of the manager. In Blankenship v. Boyle, 329 F. Supp. 1089 (D.D.C. 1971), for example, the trustees of the United Mine Workers pension fund maintained excessive demand and time deposits in a bank controlled by the union. The president of the union was also chairman of the trustees and a director of the bank. Other officers of the fund, including the comptroller, also served as directors of the bank. Much of the evidence adduced at trial demonstrated that the trustees were sacrificing the interest of the fund to enhance the position of the bank and the union. The court held that the trustees had violated their duty to make the pension assets productive. The division of loyalties causing delay in disposing of unsuitable commitments is usually not as blatant as that in *Blankenship*. For example, there is some question of how assiduously some banks invest the cash balances of trust accounts (see E. Herman, *Conflicts of Interest: Commercial Bank Trust Departments* 107-121 (1975)), or whether they cause managed accounts to invest in their own certificates of deposit at rates as high as may be available from others (see Wall Street J., April 2, 1976, p. 4, col. 3).

reason, trust law links the duty to make a portfolio productive with the duty to invest prudently,[57] and agency law takes a similar position.[58] Thus, not only does it violate the duty to make a portfolio productive to be overly conservative in selecting investments,[59] it also violates the duty to make a portfolio productive to construct a portfolio with investments of a type which are appropriate for the account, but which competent analysis would reject on the merits.[60]

But even though incompetent investing may be a more pervasive problem than a failure to invest at all, so far, the legal duty of an investment manager to select investments with ordinary skill and care has been treated more hypothetically than by any strict standard. In contrast to the attention the courts and legislatures have given to the undertaking of unduly risky commitments, the complementary problem that commitments be selected in a way reasonably likely to achieve the purposes for which they were chosen has not been an important legal issue. Moreover, even in those few cases in which a manager seemed to demonstrate professional negligence in selecting investments, undercurrents of conflict of interest affect the analysis. Typically, the facts indicate that although a manager may have acted out of negligence, he probably chose an inferior investment program deliberately because of divided loyalties. As a result, it is difficult to determine how much weight to give a court's conclusion that a particular practice was negligent in itself and how much of the conclusion to attribute to the context in which the transaction was conducted.[61]

---

[57] See *Restatement (Second) of Trusts* §§ 181, 227 (1959).

[58] *Restatement (Second) of Agency* § 425, Comment a (1958), adopts the trust analogy except to the extent an agent's duties are modified by the principal.

[59] See, e.g., Lynch v. John M. Redfield Foundation, 9 Cal. App. 3d 293, 88 Cal. Rptr. 86 (1970).

[60] See, e.g., Bishop v. People's Bank & Trust Co., 218 Ky. 508, 291 S.W. 718 (1927) (trustee may be liable for loan if there was a failure to exercise ordinary skill and care in making the loan).

[61] Spiegel v. Beacon Participations, Inc., 297 Mass. 398, 8 N.E.2d 895 (1937), provides an excellent illustration of how conflict-of-interest questions can cloud the professional-negligence issue. In that case, the directors of an investment company, among other things, approved the purchase of an overvalued note from a bank in which some of the directors were interested and entered into a joint stock account with a broker-dealer similarly connected to some of the directors. The court held that the directors' approval of these transactions was negligence. Nonetheless, although the court declined to base liability on a conflict-of-interest theory because various controlling documents extended authority to the directors to undertake the

The reason the duty to make a portfolio productive has lain so dormant with respect to the simple question of whether a portfolio has been structured competently is that until fairly recently, the element of judgment inherent in the process of selecting investments has been difficult to test. The *Restatement (Second) of Trusts*, for example, cites a number of considerations that can bear on the selection of authorized investments[62]: marketability, maturity and redemption dates of investments, duration of trust and needs of trust upon termination, present market conditions and estimation of future market conditions, total value of the portfolio, requirements of the trust beneficiaries, other assets of the beneficiaries, tax considerations, and the likelihood of inflation. Clearly, these factors are too general to be useful as a measure of professional competence except in the most egregious circumstances, nor are they satisfactory guides to investment managers of their legal responsibilities. Indeed, Professor Scott, who was the reporter for the *Second Restatement*, concedes in his treatise that the factors he identifies are only a limited aid in resolving actual cases, since their relative importance is so highly dependent on the facts of each case.[63] To make a more precise judgment in evaluating the decisional process, a methodology which is not so much a matter of opinion is necessary.

[4] Achieving Diversification

Because of its capacity for reducing risk of loss, diversification is important to proper management of a portfolio. It became an established practice among investment managers during the nineteenth century, and it first received legal endorsement from the Supreme Court of Massachusetts, in the case of *Dickinson's Appeal*, in 1890.[64] Moreover, the principle established in *Dickinson*, requiring a portfolio to be properly diversified, has been relatively uncontroversial. The major legal point of contention has been whether diversification is obligatory as a matter of law, or whether it is a fact to be taken into consideration in determining whether an investment manager has exhibited the

---

cross-directorships involved, when one reads *Spiegel*, there is the strong sense that the decision was affected by the existence of the divided loyalties on the part of the directors. That fact, at any rate, tends to undercut the strength of the court's statements about why the directors' actions were negligent. See also note 56 *supra*.

[62] *Restatement (Second) of Trusts* § 227, Comment o (1959).

[63] 3 Scott, note 13 *supra*, § 227.12, at 1840.

[64] 152 Mass. 184, 25 N.E. 99 (1890).

requisite degree of skill and care in structuring a portfolio.[65] The *Restatement (Second) of Trusts* has adopted the compromise position of imposing a duty to diversify, but qualifying that duty by recognizing nondiversification as an acceptable practice if "under the circumstances it is prudent not to [diversify]." [66] By reference to the trust analogy, the *Restatement (Second) of Agency* takes a similar position, though it affords broader discretion depending on the type of client.[67]

Like other restrictions on investment management discretion, the duty to diversify suffers from imprecise legal definition. Occasionally, based on cases in which courts have determined that a portfolio was inadequately diversified, some lawyers have apparently attempted to extrapolate a quantitative test of diversification from particularized holdings.[68] Such a simplistic method of defining diversification has not succeeded in attracting judicial support, however; nor are there such conventions among professional investment managers.[69] Consequently, the duty to diversify remains a general concept constrained only by the rule that the conduct of the investment manager be reasonable, given the time and circumstances. Indeed, in this area more than any other, the courts have looked to professional practices to set the standard of care against which a manager's conduct is to be measured. In this respect, the legal rule has not progressed much beyond that first announced in *Dickinson*, where, in support of its determination to impose liability for excessive concentration, the court pointed to the practices of trustees in Massachusetts to establish that the trustee invested too high a portion of the estate in a single issuer.[70]

The only significant refinement of the common-law rule appears in legislation which has adopted a fixed rule forbidding investment in any one security beyond a stated percentage either of assets under management or the float of the issuer. Wisconsin, for example, once prescribed limitations on concentration as a percentage of trust portfolios.[71] Presumably, that statute is intended to protect trust beneficiaries from being

---

[65] See Annot., "Duty of Trustee to Diversify Investments and Liability for Failure to Do So," 24 A.L.R.3d 730 (1969).

[66] *Restatement (Second) of Trusts* § 228 (1959).

[67] *Restatement (Second) of Agency* § 425, Comments a, c (1958).

[68] See Shattuck, "The Massachusetts Prudent Man Rule in Trust Investments," 25 B.U.L. Rev. 307, 324-325 (1945).

[69] See, e.g., Graham, Dodd & Cottle, note 36 *supra,* at 55, 465. But see ¶ 7.08, which discusses the number of stocks necessary to eliminate non-market risk.

[70] 152 Mass. at 185, 25 N.E. at 99-100.

[71] See note 51 *supra.*

exposed to excessive risk of loss by trustees who do not possess a level of skill sufficient to appreciate the importance of diversification, or at least how to achieve it.[72]

Having no quantitative test for diversification, the *Restatement (Second) of Trusts* cites several factors to be considered in determining whether a portfolio has been properly diversified:

(1) The purposes of the account;

(2) The size of the account;

(3) Investment conditions;

(4) The type of investment; and

(5) The geographical distribution, industry distribution, and maturity-date distribution of portfolio holdings.[73]

But while these factors may offer some insight into the kind of thinking investment managers might engage in when considering how to go about diversifying a portfolio, their usefulness as a basis for setting a legal standard is questionable. As has been the case in determining whether an investment manager has exercised ordinary skill and care in selecting among investments, the use of subjective factors to prescribe a legal standard to test the adequacy of diversification has made it very difficult to separate differences of opinion from unreasonable conduct.

---

[72] Statutes also define diversification for purposes other than distinguishing between the exercise of reasonable care in management and negligent management. Investment Company Act § 5(b) (15 U.S.C. § 80a-5(b)) defines a diversified company as one which has 75 percent or more of its total assets invested such that, for the 75-percent-of-assets amount, no more than 5 percent of the total assets is invested in any one company, and its holdings in any one issuer do not exceed more than 10 percent of the voting securities of that issuer. The purpose of this provision is to identify investment policy for the benefit of investors rather than to set quantitative criteria against which to measure the adequacy of diversification. A complementary tax provision, designed to encourage investment in diversified investment companies, applies a 5 percent-of-assets/10 percent-of-voting-securities test to 50 percent of an investment company's assets, and provides further that no more than 25 percent of total assets may be invested in any one issuer. I.R.C. § 851(b)(4). Any company so diversified can qualify, by satisfying certain other statutory requirements, for conduit tax treatment of its earnings. Such a disparity between the Investment Company Act and the Internal Revenue Code in defining diversification would be impossible if Congress were attempting to define diversification for the broader purpose of establishing a standard of care. It is doubtful, therefore, that any of these quantitative tests will be extended to portfolios not specifically governed by these statutes.

[73] *Restatement (Second) of Trusts* § 228, Comment b (1959).

To the extent a review of the authorities permits any refinement of the broad concept of diversification, the cases imposing liability in damages for a failure to diversify might be the best source. Since the damages rule holds the manager liable only for losses in that portion of the portfolio which was overly concentrated,[74] the portfolio losses for which the manager is relieved of responsibility would seem to indicate the outer limits on concentration that courts have been willing to allow. Unfortunately, authorities of this type are few, and their treatment of the diversification issue is so bound up in the facts that it is impossible to draw narrow rules from them.[75]

¶ 6.03. MODERN PORTFOLIO THEORY AS A MEASURE OF PROFESSIONAL COMPETENCE

Within the last twenty-five years, various observers have developed quantitative techniques which permit sharper insight into the concepts of speculation, unsuitability, investment productivity, and diversification. Of course, like any other analytic technique, portfolio theory is subject to the criticism that its assumptions and postulates are not perfectly verifiable and, hence, that its conclusions are not absolutely correct. That, however, is not the measure of the usefulness of an analytic method. If perfect precision were what the law required, legal doctrine applicable to investment managers would not have developed to its existing state. The advantage of the quantitative character of

---

[74] See, e.g., First Nat'l Bank v. Truesdale Hosp., 288 Mass. 35, 192 N.E. 150 (1934). See 3 Scott, note 13 *supra*, § 228.1. This rule follows, of course, from the torts principle that a wrongdoer may be held only for the harm his act or omission actually caused. W. Prosser, *Law of Torts* ¶ 41, at 236 (4th ed. 1971).

[75] In Steiner v. Hawaiian Trust Co., 47 Hawaii 548, 393 P.2d 96 (1964), for example, the court imposed liability on a trustee for retaining 1200 shares of stock, concluding that 300 shares should have been the limit. The record showed that the portfolio was concentrated in securities in one industry and that most of the portfolio companies were located in one geographic area. But the stock in question was also an issue by a company with a volatile earnings record. That fact tended to show that a large commitment was improper in any event. Moreover, the trustee did eventually suggest a diversification strategy long after acquiring the portfolio to manage. By the trustee's own admission, therefore, the portfolio was inadequately diversified. As a consequence, this case, like others dealing with the diversification issue, has little precedential value except as additional support for the proposition that diversification is a duty. See, e.g., Pennsylvania Co. for Ins. v. Gilmore, 142 N.J. Eq. 27, 59 A.2d 24 (1948); Davis' Appeal, 183 Mass. 499, 67 N.E. 604 (1903).

modern portfolio theory over the more subjective traditional approach is not that the exactitude on which it is based reflects the real world in all particulars, but that, properly limited, it offers a better test of whether an investment manager has met his professional duty to invest prudently than does traditional legal doctrine. In such case, the benefits to both reviewing authorities and investment managers are manifest. Those who sit in review can more accurately gauge the conduct of investment managers and thus reach fairer and more evenhanded decisions. And investment managers can determine in advance what is required of them with greater certainty.

As one might expect, modern portfolio theory is highly technical in structure. A rigorous presentation of the theory, however, is not necessary to an understanding of it.[76] The important point is that many of the implications of the theory are already making inroads into the legal literature.[77] One can expect this process to continue and to see the legal rules develop to accommodate generally agreed-upon applications of the theory.

[1] Measuring Possible Investments Against the Client's Objectives: Expected Value

It is basic that a principal function of an investment manager is to construct a portfolio having a return as close to a client's investment ob-

---

[76] For a rigorous proof of the elements of the theory, see, e.g., Markowitz, "Portfolio Selection," 7 J. Fin. 77 (March 1952); W. Sharpe, *Portfolio Theory and Capital Markets* (1970). For a quantitative but nonrigorous exposition of the theory, see, e.g., Lorie & Hamilton, note 41 *supra*; J. Lorie & R. Brealey, *Modern Developments in Investment Management* (1972); Bank Administration Institute, *Measuring the Investment Performance of Pension Funds* (1968).

[77] See, e.g., Langbein & Posner, "Market Funds and Trust-Investment Law," 1 Am. Bar Found. Research J. 1 (1976), and "Market Funds and Trust-Investment Law: II," 2 Am. Bar Found. Research J. 1 (1977); Pozen, "Money Managers and Securities Research," 51 N.Y.U. L. Rev. 923 (1976). Note, "The Regulation of Risky Investments," 83 Harv. L. Rev. 603 (1970); Note, "Prudence in Trust Investment," 3 U. Mich. J.L. Reform 491 (1975); Note, "Fiduciary Standards and the Prudent Man Rule Under the Employee Retirement Income Security Act of 1974," 88 Harv. L. Rev. 960 (1975); Cohen, "The Suitability Rule and Economic Theory," 80 Yale L.J. 1604 (1971); Note, "Regulating Risk-Taking by Mutual Funds," 82 Yale L.J. 1305 (1973); Barack, "Book Review of Malkiel, A Random Walk Down Wall Street," 83 Yale L.J. 1516 (1974); Note, "Trustee Investment Powers: Imprudent Application of the Prudent Man Rule," 50 N.D. Law. 519 (1975); Kassouf, "Towards a Legal Framework for Efficiency and Equity in the Securities Markets," 25 Hastings L.J. 417 (1974).

jectives as possible. But no portfolios have absolutely certain rates of return, and of those that have highly predictable rates of return, such as short-term obligations of the United States Government and insured time deposits, few precisely meet the investment objectives of most investors. Rather, nearly every portfolio, whether consisting of one, two, several, or many securities or other investments, must be viewed as having a probable return which is more likely than any other. In effect, the portfolio promises that if everything proceeds as expected, the investor will receive a return of some level for advancing his capital to the use of the venture or ventures under consideration. But realism dictates that investors recognize that events can occur which lead to an actual return which is different from that promised. Sometimes, these unanticipated events are disastrous for a venture; sometimes they bring unexpected rewards. The point is, however, that the price of a commitment includes some recognition on the part of an investor that one may experience an array of returns. The price of participating in a venture, therefore, reflects not the value an investor would receive only if it were to produce the most probable return, but rather its expected value—what the investor regards as the value of being able to participate in one of an array of possible returns without any power to know in advance which one will actually occur.

For simplicity, consider the example of parents who set aside a sum of money to defray college expenses for their child. Based on an appraisal of the parents' statement of how much of the college expenses they want the fund to meet, and based on the investment manager's assumption of the cost of college education at the time the child is graduated from high school, the investment manager concludes that it will be necessary to show the equivalent of an annual return of 8 percent uncompounded annually to achieve the parents' objectives. Assume that the manager knows all possible portfolios having some degree of probability of returning 8 percent per year over the life of the parents' investment program. Should the manager expect any of these portfolios actually to return 8 percent? No answer is possible without more information, for the manager knows that other outcomes are possible, and he can value each portfolio only by taking proper account of every possibility that might be associated with it.[78]

---

[78] Of course, it is impossible for an investment manager to identify every conceivable investment opportunity having a possible return of 8 percent, and even among those that the manager does identify, there is no way that he can determine in advance every possible event that can occur and affect the return of the security. Nonetheless, this does not mean that reasonable

This distinction between probable return and expected value can be illustrated very easily. Suppose the manager can buy at par a high quality corporate bond offering interest quarterly at an 8 percent annual rate. Suppose also that the bond matures in the same year that the child will enter college. In valuing this opportunity, the manager knows that the most probable outcome is that the issuer will meet all interest payments and that the principal will be returned on the maturity date of the bond. The most probable return, therefore, is in excess of 8 percent because the manager can reinvest the interest as it is received in virtually riskless investments such as insured time deposits or United States Government obligations.

But the issuer may default, in which case the actual return will probably be measurably less than an equivalent uncompounded 8 percent annual rate. The actual return in such event would consist of interest received and the return on reinvestment of that interest, adjusted for the loss of principal resulting from default and the return that can be obtained by reinvesting whatever remains of the principal after default. Another possibility is that the bond may be called. Typically, there is a premium associated with a call privilege, and this alone would tend to raise the actual return above the 8 percent annual interest plus return on reinvestment. On the other hand, a common reason for an issuer to exercise call privileges is that interest rates have dropped to a point making it advantageous to do so. Those circumstances tend to lower actual return, since any reinvestment after a call in the same quality security would also be offering interest well below an 8 percent annual rate.

There are other possible outcomes also.[79] For the sake of clarity, however, let us make some simplifying assumptions. Let us hypothesize that there are two possible outcomes for the portfolio: (1) If the issuer continues to make interest payments until maturity, the actual return will be the equivalent of an annual uncompounded rate of return of between 8½ percent and 9½ percent; (2) if any other event occurs, the actual return will be equivalent of a return of between 5½ percent and 6½ percent per year uncompounded. The probability of the first outcome is two chances out of three (i.e., two-thirds); the probability of all

estimates are impossible, and, in any event, the assumption of absolute precision only introduces the constraint that the predictions of the theory be tested under real-world conditions. In this regard, see ¶ 7.04.

[79] For example, if there is no call provision and the bond and interest rates drop far enough, the bonds may show a capital gain sufficient to justify sale of the bond and reinvestment in a less risky commitment.

other outcomes taken together is one chance out of three (i.e., one-third). Plainly, the value of the bond, measured by rate of return, is not the same as its most probable return. Since there is a good chance that its return will be much less than 8½ to 9½ percent, no rational investor would be willing to buy the bond for a price equivalent to that necessary to generate a guaranteed payout of 8 percent on investment. On the other hand, the bond is also worth more than an investment offering a guaranteed 5½ to 6½ percent return. No rational investor would turn down the opportunity to purchase the bond at a price equivalent to that necessary to generate a guaranteed annual payout of 5½ to 6½ percent, since there is such a significant chance that the actual results will be much better.

In order to value the bond properly, some system of averaging that takes into account each possible outcome is necessary. This can be accomplished by weighting each possible outcome according to the probability it will occur. If an investor bought this bond or one exactly like it and adopted precisely the same investment strategy over and over again, an inquiry into his investment experience eventually would show that two out of every three commitments returned between 8½ and 9½ percent, which for convenience of calculation, can be treated as 9 percent. One out of every three commitments, on the other hand, would have returned between 5½ and 6½ percent, which similarly can be treated as 6 percent. Thus, on the average, the return over time would be ⅔ (9 percent) + ⅓ (6 percent), or 8 percent. As a consequence, in advance of purchasing any identical new offering of this type, an investor would expect it to be priced at the return it shows on the average—8 percent.

This, then, is the idea underlying the concept of expected value. One weights each possible outcome according to the likelihood it will occur. An outcome of 6 percent with a probability of occurrence of one-third, therefore, would be 2 percent (.06 × ⅓ = .02). Similarly, an outcome of 9 percent with a probability of occurrence of two-thirds would be 6 percent (.09 × ⅔ = .06). The expected value is the sum of the outcomes weighted by probability, or 8 percent (.02 + .06 = .08). This figure informs one of the value of a portfolio measured by the average of the returns it may experience. It does not value the portfolio from any other perspective.

[2] Determining Relative Risk as a Deviation From Expected Return: Variance

Suppose the investment manager continues his search for portfolios which, measured by annual return, have an expected value of 8 percent, and he discovers two others. Table 6-1 lists the characteristics of each of the three portfolios. Figure 6-1 describes each graphically.

	Probability of Return	Return
Portfolio *A*		
	.33	6%
	.67	9%
Portfolio *B*		
	.05	10%
	.25	9%
	.50	8%
	.10	7%
	.05	6%
	.05	5%
Portfolio *C*		
	.35	9%
	.40	8%
	.15	7%
	.10	6%

Table 6-1

The manager knows that each of these portfolios will, on the average, show a return of 8 percent.[80] But with each, there is a degree of uncertainty about what the actual return will be. Portfolio *B* may experience a return from 5 percent to 10 percent. Portfolio *C* may vary between 6 percent and 9 percent. And portfolio *A* will never return

---

[80] The expected value of portfolio *A* is:

$(.33)(6\%) + (.67)(9\%) = 8\%$.

The expected value of portfolio *B* is:

$(.05)(10\%) + (.25)(9\%) + (.50)(8\%) + (.10)(7\%) +$
$(.05)(6\%) + (.05)(5\%) = 8\%$.

The expected value of portfolio *C* is:

$(.35)(9\%) + (.40)(8\%) + (.15)(7\%) + (.10)(6\%) = 8\%$.

Note that for each portfolio, the probability of all returns adds up to 1.00, thus indicating that no other return is possible.

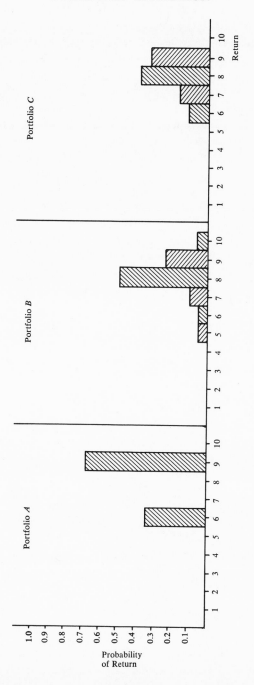

Fig. 6-1

8 percent. It will return either 6 percent or 9 percent. Being uncertain about what the actual experience of each of these portfolios will be, the manager is faced with the problem of deciding which of them is most likely to achieve the parents' investment objective of an 8 percent return. Furthermore, the manager is not simply uncertain about whether the actual return will be 8 percent. Otherwise, he would automatically choose portfolio *B*, which has the highest probability of actually returning 8 percent. He is also uncertain about how great a differential the account he chooses will experience from the stated goal of 8 percent.

This is a most important point. If the manager's task were only to select the portfolio of the three most likely to produce an actual return closest to 8 percent, his task would be easy. The manager knows that portfolio *A* will not return 8 percent, portfolio *B* has a 50 percent chance of returning 8 percent, and portfolio *C* has a 40 percent chance of returning 8 percent. But that information alone is insufficient for the manager to make an intelligent choice among the three portfolios. Investors are not only interested in constructing portfolios that are likely to achieve their objectives; they also want assurances that if their precise objectives are not met, the degree of disparity will be as small as possible.[81] An investment manager, therefore, also needs some way to compare the three portfolios for the strength of the tendency of each to diverge from the desired return.

For the manager to measure the degree to which he is uncertain about the range of returns each portfolio will show, the manager needs some system of averaging which takes into account the relative tendency of each portfolio to vary from its expected value. This can be accomplished by measuring the difference between each possible outcome and the expected value, and weighting that difference according to the probability it will occur. By summing these figures, one can obtain a measure of the tendency of each of these portfolios, relative to each other, to vary from their expected value of 8 percent. Actually, the statistical convention for measuring this tendency is to square the difference between each outcome and the expected value,[82] weight the

---

[81] Actually, this assertion reflects an assumption that investors are averse to risk. Whether or not this is true for all investors, the law makes it true for investment managers. The effects of the assumption of risk aversion and the related legal implications are discussed more fully in ¶ 7.03.

[82] The reasons for this convention are essentially practical, but since it is a convention and since its use should introduce no confusion, let us also observe it.

difference by the relevant probabilities, and sum the terms. The resulting figure is defined as the variance.[83]

It is now possible to determine the relative risk, measured by tendency to vary from expected value, of the three portfolios under consideration. Portfolio A has two possible outcomes, 9 percent and 6 percent. The difference between the possible 9 percent outcome and the expected value of 8 percent is 1 percent. One squared is one. And since the probability a return of 9 percent will occur is two-thirds, the contribution of that outcome to the variance of the portfolio is two-thirds. ((1) (1) $\times$ ⅔ = ⅔.) Similarly, since the difference between the possible 6 percent outcome and the 8 percent expected value of the portfolio is 2 percent, the contribution of that outcome to the variance of the portfolio is 4/3. ((2) (2) $\times$ ⅓ = 4/3.) The variance of portfolio A, therefore, is 2 percent. (⅔ + 4/3 = 2.) Through use of the same technique, the calculations for portfolio B yield a variance of 1.2 percent,[84] and for portfolio C, a variance of .9 percent.[85]

The parents and the investment manager now have enough information to choose a portfolio. Needing a return of 8 percent in order to achieve their investment objectives, the parents want the portfolio most likely to yield 8 percent in actual experience. On this basis, they would choose portfolio C because (1) the expected return of this portfolio is 8 percent; and (2) the chances that this portfolio would provide an actual return different from 8 percent are smaller than for either of the other two.

---

[83] There are other measures of dispersion besides variance. Skewness, for example, measures the degree to which a distribution is asymmetrical. See ¶ 7.03[1], note 25. Nonetheless, in most of the literature, risk is defined either in terms of the variance or the standard deviation, which is the square root of the variance. For a more extended discussion of why the measure of divergence from the mean is calculated in terms either of the variance or of the standard deviation, see Modigliani & Pogue, "An Introduction to Risk and Return," 30 Fin. Anal. J. 68, 70-72 (March-April 1974).

[84] The arithmetic is as follows:

(.05)[(10% − 8%)(10% − 8%)] + (.25)[(9% − 8%)(9% − 8%)]
+ (.50)[(8% − 8%)(8% − 8%)] + (.10)[(7% − 8%)(7% − 8%)]
+ (.05)[(6% − 8%)(6% − 8%)] + (.05)[(5% − 8%)(5% − 8%)]
= (.05)(4%) + (.25)(1%) + (.50)(0%) + (.10)(1%) + (.05)
(4%) + (.05)(9%) = .2% + .25% + 0% + .1% + .2% + .45%
= 1.2%.

[85] More briefly, the arithmetic is as follows:

(.35)(1%) + (.40)(0%) + (.15)(1%) + (.10)(4%) = .35% + .15% + .4% = .9%.

The choice of portfolio C permits an important observation: The portfolio that the theory recommends is not the one with the highest possible return; nor is it the portfolio with the greatest likelihood of returning precisely 8 percent. The theory says that less uncertainty as to the results likely to be experienced should be preferred, given an investment objective of a return at a predetermined level. But this raises the related question of whether portfolio C truly is the best portfolio for the parents. Even though a return of 8 percent would achieve their investment objectives, they would not be averse to achieving a higher return if they could do so safely. Might there not be a portfolio with a higher expected return, but having no greater risk, measured by variance from the expected value? That is, suppose the parents, having window-shopped the portfolios whose expected return is 8 percent, decide to look at some 8½ percent portfolios. Might it not be possible they ask their investment manager, that there is a portfolio returning 8½ percent, and having a variation pattern no worse than that of portfolio C? If there is such a portfolio, it is obvious that they would prefer it to portfolio C. For they could expect a higher return, and at the same time be no less confident of achieving that higher return than they are of achieving an 8 percent return with portfolio C.

The answer is that, in theory, no such portfolio exists. The explanation of why this is so must be deferred,[86] but the asking of the question, when taken in conjunction with the analysis is this section, spotlights the two principal postulates of modern portfolio theory:

(1) For a given level of return, the least risky portfolio, measured by its tendency to diverge from that level of return, is preferred to all other possible portfolios.

(2) For a given level of risk, the portfolio having the highest expected return, measured by average value, is preferred to all other possible portfolios.

[3] Measuring the Effects of Combinations of Securities on Risk and Return: Covariance

The discussion so far has assumed that portfolios come prepackaged with their vital statistics attached like a price tag. A more realistic model would recognize that portfolios can consist of commitments to more than one of the securities available in the marketplace and would

---

[86] See ¶ 7.03 at notes 21-23.

consider the effects of combining securities on risk and return. Plainly, the fact of combination produces a portfolio with an altered character if only as a result of differing expected values and variances among the component securities. But, as it turns out, the variance of a portfolio is not merely the weighted average of the variances of its components. Portfolio variance is also affected by the relationships of the component securities with each other.

Suppose the investment manager, in search of an 8 percent return, could choose from among four securities. Security *A* and security *B* each have an expected value of 8 percent. Security *C* has an expected value of 6 percent. Security *D* has an expected value of 10 percent. From this universe of securities, the manager may construct a number of different portfolios having an expected value of 8 percent. One possibility would be to invest in equal amounts of *C* and *D*. Still another possibility would be to invest in *A* and *B* in proportions determined by the preference of the investment manager. Other choices are available also.[87]

We know that the investment manager prefers the portfolio having the smallest variance for an 8 percent return. We also know that if the manager can construct a portfolio having a variance no worse than any of the 8 percent portfolios, the manager would prefer any portfolio offering a higher average return, and plainly prefer most the portfolio having the highest average return. Thus, a portfolio consisting of *A* and *D*, or *B* and *D*, or *A*, *B*, and *D* might be the portfolio desired most of all. Whether or not such outcomes are possible, the manager's task is to determine the components and proportions of the best portfolio, and, therefore, he needs some method of determining how combining the available securities would affect portfolio characteristics.

The first step in constructing the best portfolio is relatively simple. The manager chooses any portfolio with as few components as possible and having an expected value of 8 percent.[88] That portfolio has a

---

[87] For example, the manager could invest in *A* plus equal amounts of *C* and *D,* or *B* plus equal amounts of *C* and *D,* or *A* and *B* in any proportion plus equal amounts of *C* and *D.*

[88] It is not necessary to begin this way. The manager can start with any security in the universe of securities available to him so long as he adds securities to his portfolio only if he can reduce risk without reducing expected return or raise expected return without increasing risk. If there is only one best portfolio, the manager will always ultimately reach that portfolio, regardless of how he begins. If there are multiple solutions, it makes no difference which securities comprise the portfolio since, by definition, the risk and return characteristics will be the same. See note 91 *infra.*

probability distribution from which a variance can be calculated. The manager next determines to add securities to the portfolio only if doing so reduces the variance without reducing the expected value, or raises the expected value without raising the variance. Suppose he begins with a position in A, and wants to know whether adding some B will accomplish any reduction in the variance of the portfolio without affecting the expected return. Since A and B both have an expected return of 8 percent, no combination of the two will affect expected value.

Reduction in variance depends entirely on how, relative to each other, A and B react to events. Suppose A is a railroad and B is a trucking company. A railroad strike would hurt A but help B, and vice versa. Thus, holding both securities would have two effects. If A suffered a strike, a combination portfolio would reduce the impact on the actual results in comparison to a portfolio consisting exclusively of A. A combination portfolio would also mean that a strike in B would produce a worse result than would be experienced with a portfolio invested entirely in the securities of A.[89] Insofar as the variance is concerned, however, if the chance of strike is entirely fortuitous—that is, at the time of commitment the manager cannot know whether there is likely to be a strike in either company, or which company is more likely to experience one—an investment in both seems a sounder procedure than investing entirely in one or the other. For while the chance of gain above the expected value is reduced by purchasing commitments in both, the chance of experiencing a return below the expected value is also reduced because the portfolio will not be invested entirely in a company caught up in a strike.[90] This intuitive conclusion can be substantiated by analysis.

Suppose an investment manager wishes to know the expected value and the variance pattern for a portfolio consisting of more than one security. It is possible to gain a feeling for how expected value and variance may be affected as securities are added to a portfolio by considering the limiting case of the two-security portfolio. This simplifying assumption is not as unrealistic as it may seem. Any such portfolio will have an expected value and variation pattern which can be viewed as if belonging to a single security. By treating the two-security portfolio

---

[89] The analysis would be the same if the manager constructed the portfolio first with a commitment to B and wanted to determine whether adding A would be beneficial.

[90] Of course, it is possible that both A and B could suffer a strike. But then the portfolio would be no worse off than if the manager had invested in either A or B exclusively.

as a single security, the addition of a third security can be subjected to the two-security paradigm, and this process can be repeated for each security added to the portfolio.[91]

In the two-security portfolio case, if A and B respond identically to every event, no mixture of the two could affect the return to the portfolio. But in the more realistic case where a mixture of securities produces a response to events different from that which would have been experienced by investing in either A or B alone, it is reasonable to anticipate that the variance of the portfolio will depend in some way on contributions from the component securities. More precisely, the variance of the combination portfolio depends not only on the variance of the component securities, but also on the degree to which they covary. Like variance, covariance is a weighted average of deviations from expected value. But because it is a measure of the behavior of how two securities react to events in relation to each other, it is the average of the product of the deviations of each security from expected value of the portfolio, weighted by the probability that both those individual deviations will occur at the same time.

To demonstrate the dependency of the variance of the combination portfolio on the variance and covariance of its component securities satisfactorily, reference to an algebraic function is unavoidable, and the discussion which follows attempts to expose the interested reader to covariance analysis as applied to the simple case of a two-security universe. The discussion should make it easier to understand how combining securities can lower the variance of a portfolio below that of any of the component securities. This powerful principle makes it possible, at least in theory, to combine securities of high risk, measured by their individual variances, and yet produce a very safe portfolio. The reader

---

[91] It is not strictly accurate to suggest that the final results will aways be the same by adding securities one at a time under the constraints that expected return be maximized and variance be minimized. The characteristics of a portfolio will be affected by the proportion invested in each component security, and consequently, every time a commitment is added to a portfolio, the portfolio must be retested to see whether the concentration in one or more previously existing commitments should be reduced or even eliminated. The two-security paradigm, however, is at least useful for illustrating the criteria for expanding the number of commitments in a portfolio. Furthermore, as a practical matter, the capital-asset pricing model (which, with its focus on volatility relative to the market as the measure of risk, is discussed more fully in ¶ 7.03) offers a practical basis for measuring the contribution of a security to portfolio risk. See Lorie & Hamilton, note 41 *supra,* at 198-200.

willing to accept this conclusion without further demonstration may turn directly to ¶ 6.02[3][b], where the implications to be drawn from covariance analysis are discussed.

[a] Covariance analysis of a two-security portfolio

Let X be the proportion of the portfolio invested in a given security, V the variance of the security, and C the covariance of a security with any other security. The variance of a combination portfolio, V_P, can be expressed as a function of the variances of the two component securities, V_A and V_B, and their covariance, $C_{A,B}$[92]:

$$V_P = X_A{}^2 V_A + X_B{}^2 V_B + 2 X_A X_B C_{A,B}.$$

For simplicity of discussion, assume that V_A and V_B are known. In that event, V_B can be expressed as a multiple of V_A[93]:

$$V_B = k^2 V_A.$$

Thus, if V_B were twice as large as V_A, k^2 would equal two; if V_B were four times as large as V_A, k^2 would equal four, and so forth.

The assumption that V_A and V_B are known—by hypothesis, the investment manager knows the vital statistics of the component securities —also permits the covariance to be expressed as a proportion of V_A. But since, by definition, covariance includes the idea that knowing the effect of an event on A means that the effect of that event on B also can be determined, the covariance term is also affected by the degree to which movements in B correlate with movements in A. The conventional expression for this factor is the correlation coefficient. If we as-

---

[92] For a multisecurity portfolio, the variance can be expressed as follows:

$$V_P = \sum_{ij}^{NN} X_i X_j C_{ij}.$$

In the two-security portfolio, this formula reduces to the one stated in the text. A more extended and rigorous discussion of the probability theory involved here can be found in W. Sharpe, *Portfolio Theory and Capital Markets* 37-44 (1970).

[93] The constant representing the ratio between the variance of B and the variance of A—k^2—is expressed as a square for convenience of calculation. Otherwise, in order to express the covariance in terms of the variance of either component security, use of a square root of the constant would be necessary. See text at note 94 *infra*.

sign it the label R, covariance can be expressed in terms of V_A and R[94]:

$$C_{A,B} = kV_A R.$$

By expressing V_B and C in terms of V_A, V_P can also be expressed in terms of V_A:

$$V_P = X_A{}^2 V_A + k^2 X_B{}^2 V_A + 2kX_A X_B V_A R$$

or:

$$V_P = V_A (X^2{}_A + k^2 X_B{}^2 + 2kX_A X_B R).$$

The importance of the function in the parentheses is that whenever it totals less than one, V_P is less than V_A. If V_A is always taken as less than V_B ($k > 1$), the variance of the combination portfolio is less than the variance of a portfolio invested entirely in either component security. Let us investigate the power of this observation in some different contexts. The analysis which follows will apply to any set of variances assigned to component securities, but in order to keep the calculations simple, let k^2—the ratio of V_A to V_B—be 4; that is, security B has a variance of four times security A.

Suppose that A and B respond alike to events but with different intensities. Whenever A shows a 2 percent rise in price, measured by rate of return, B shows a 4 percent rise; whenever A shows a 3 percent decline in price, B shows a 6 percent decline. This means that that pattern will repeat itself across all price movements, such that both A and B move in exact cadence, but take steps of different size in response to every event that occurs. The price of A can always be determined by knowing the price of B, and vice versa.

Instances of perfect correlation between securities are difficult to imagine, but substantial correlation is reasonably common. An example of this might be a young company and an established company in the same industry.[95] In any event, on the facts presented ($R = 1.0$; $V_B = 4V_A$), the expression relating V_P to V_A reduces to:

---

[94] Technically, the covariance is defined as the correlation coefficient times the product of the standard deviation of the two securities. See Sharpe, *Portfolio Theory and Capital Markets* 42 (1970). Since the standard deviation is defined as the square root of the variance, this means that $C_{A,B} = R\sqrt{V_A V_B}$. Further, since $V_B = k^2 V_A$, substitution for V_B yields $C = R\sqrt{k^2 V_A{}^2} = kV_A R$, the equation cited in the text.

[95] The securities are not perfectly correlated for a variety of reasons. For example, if the companies are not in the same location, a natural disaster could strike one but not the other. Similarly, their labor relations

$$V_P = V_A(X^2_A + 4X^2_B + 4X_AX_B),$$

or:

$$V_P = V_A(X_A + 2X_B)^2.$$

No combination portfolio having a variation below that of security A is possible. If the portfolio consisted entirely of B, $X_A = 0$, $X_B = 1$, and $V_P = 4V_A$, which, not surprisingly, is V_B. If the portfolio were entirely invested in A, on the other hand, $X_A = 1$, $X_B = 0$, and $V_P = V_A$. Any combination of the two securities raises V_P above V_A. A portfolio invested half in A and half in B, for example, would have a variance 2¼ times as large as V_A.[96] This conclusion, of course, is precisely what one would expect if the two securities move in perfect cadence. The greater the proportion of B, the riskier security in the portfolio, the greater the impact of every event on the portfolio, since both A and B react in exactly the same way to events. Like the variance of the component securities, portfolio variance reflects the tendency of a portfolio to diverge from its expected value. Because a portfolio consisting of A and B responds more sharply to events the more B it contains, the variance of the portfolio increases and decreases according to the proportion of B.

Consider next the case in which A and B react to events in precisely the opposite direction. For a price rise of 2 percent in A, measured by rate of return, there is a price drop of 4 percent in B. For a price drop of 1 percent in A, there is a price rise of 2 percent in B. Here, A and B are entirely out of cadence. They are perfectly negatively correlated. Because their price movements also differ in degree, their variances differ as well. Once again, the price of A can always be determined by knowing the price of B.

Except for hedges in a single security (e.g., being long and short in one security at the same time), instances of perfect negative correlation are also difficult to imagine. For two companies to have substantial negative correlation, every change in the price of one must produce a change in the same proportion but in the opposite direction in the price of the other. Nonetheless, one can at least hypothesize cases of substantial negative correlation. For example, the rate of return on the soft-drink concession at a ballpark and the hot-coffee concession at the same ballpark might be highly negatively correlated. Assuming the fans are willing to spend the same amount of money on drinks at a

---

problems would not be the same. Nonetheless, for most purposes, the securities do react substantially alike.

[96] $V_P = V_A[1/2 + 2(1/2)][1/2 + 2(1/2)] = 9/4\ V_A.$

sporting event, the profits of each concession depend on the weather, more soft drinks being sold when it is warm, and more coffee when it is cold.[97]

On these facts $(R = -1, V_B = 4V_A)$, the expression relating V_P to V_A reduces to:

$$V_P = V_A(X_A{}^2 + 4X_B{}^2 - 4X_AX_B)$$

or:

$$V_P = V_A(X_A - 2X_B)^2.$$

Note that in this case, V_P equals V_A when the portfolio is invested entirely in A, and V_B when the portfolio is invested entirely in B. But unlike the previous case, there are some combinations of A and B which will produce a variance less than that possible from either alone. One can see from the equation above that $V_P = V_A$ in two cases: (1) When $(X_A - 2X_B) = 1$; and (2) when $(X_A - 2X_B) = -1$. In both cases, it is possible to solve for X_A because $X_A + X_B = 1$ by definition—the sum of the parts of the portfolio equals the whole. Thus, the variance of the combination portfolio is the same as that of one invested entirely in A when $X_A = 1$, or, as one would expect, when the portfolio in fact has only A in it. But $V_P = V_A$ also when $X_A = \frac{1}{3}$—that is, when one-third of the portfolio consists of A and two-thirds consists of B.

The phenomenon that A and B can be mixed to produce a portfolio variance no higher than that of A alone is of more than passing interest, for it marks the point at which portfolio variance can be reduced even below that of A. Indeed, suppose the investment manager desires a combination of A and B such that the variance of the portfolio is as small as possible. Let $V_P = 0$. Then, $X_A = 2X_B$; and, since $X_A + X_B = 1$, $X_A = \frac{2}{3}$ and $X_B = \frac{1}{3}$. In short, every combination portfolio invested more than one-third in A and consequently less than two-thirds in B will have a variance lower than that of A, which, by hypothesis, is lower than B. Moreover, a portfolio with no variance at all can be constructed by investing in precisely the right proportions of A and B, which, by virtue of the values hypothesized, is two-thirds and one-third, respectively.

The more common occurrence is that A and B will respond neither

---

[97] As in the example of positive correlation above, see note 95 *supra*, the negative correlation in this example is also less than perfect. The profits of both are dependent on the price of cups, the number of fans at the game, and so forth.

entirely in phase nor entirely out of phase to events. In the trucking and railroad example used above, it may be accurate to say that a labor shutdown of trucking would be good for railroads, and vice versa. But a labor shutdown of barge traffic or air freight traffic would benefit both truckers and railroads, whereas a rise in the price of steel might increase the price of vans and railroad cars and lower the profits of both. The important point is that as long as A and B do not act in perfect cadence or entirely out of cadence, their price movements are correlated to some degree and uncorrelated to some degree.

Suppose that 25 percent of the movement of B can be accounted for by a movement in A. Suppose also that A and B are positively correlated, that is, that events move their prices in the same direction. ($R = .25$; $V_B = 4V_A$.) To determine the points at which adding more B brings the variance of the portfolio down to and below the variance of A, we repeat the steps performed in the previous two examples. The expression relating V_P to V_A reduces to:

$$V_P = V_A(X_A{}^2 + 4X_B{}^2 + \tfrac{1}{2}X_AX_B).$$

Recalling that $X_A + X_B = 1$ and solving for X_A, $V_P = V_A$ in two cases: (1) $X_A = 1$; and (2) $X_A = \tfrac{2}{3}$.[98] Again, the variance of the portfolio is obviously the same as that of A whenever the portfolio consists exclusively of A. But also, whenever the proportion of the portfolio invested in A exceeds two-thirds, the variance is less than could be achieved by investing in either A or B alone. Moreover, this portfolio can be invested in A and B to achieve a lowest possible variance. But unlike the previous example, that figure will never reach zero. Under the facts hypothesized, the minimum variance occurs when five-sixths

---

[98] To solve for $V_P = V_A$, set the parenthetical expression equal to 1 as follows:

$X_A{}^2 + 4X_B{}^2 + 1/2X_AX_B = 1.$

Substituting for X_B, [$X_B = 1 - X_A$], the equation becomes:

$9/2X_A{}^2 - 15/2X_A + 3 = 0$

or:

$X_A{}^2 - 5/3X_A + 2/3 = 0$

or:

$(X_A - 1)(X_A - 2/3) = 0.$

The solution for X_A, therefore, is:

$X_A = 1; 2/3.$

of the portfolio is invested in A,[99] and the solution for V_P at $X_A = \frac{5}{6}$ is seven-eighths the variance of A.[100]

[b] Implications of the covariance analysis

In the general case for the two-security portfolio, if the covariance is less than the variance of the security possessing the smaller variance of the two component securities, there will always be a combination of the two which will produce a variance for the portfolio which is smaller than that of either of its components.[101] Once the vital statistics for the component securities are known, therefore, an investment manager can determine whether the addition of a security having relatively more risk

---

[99] To find the proportion of each component security so that portfolio variance can be minimized, it is necessary to express the rate of change of the variance of the portfolio as a function of concentration in one or the other of the component securities, and set the rate of change of the portfolio with respect to variance to zero. This can be accomplished by elementary differential calculus as follows:

Substituting for X_B [$X_B = 1 - X_A$],

$V_P = V_A(9/2X_A{}^2 - 15/2X_A + 4)$.

$\dfrac{dV_P}{dX_A} = V_A(9X_A - 15/2)$.

Setting $\dfrac{dV_P}{dX_A}$ to 0,

$9X_A - 15/2 = 0$

or:

$X_A = 5/6$.

[100] Substituting for the concentration in each component security where $X_A = 5/6$ and $X_B = 1/6$:

$V_P = V_A[(5/6)(5/6) + 4(1/6)(1/6) + 1/2(5/6)(1/6)]$

or:

$V_P = 7/8V_A$.

[101] Suppose $C_{A,B} = qV_A$, where $0 < q < 1$. Then:

$V_P = X_A{}^2V_A + X_B{}^2V_B + 2qX_AX_BV_A$ (See text at note 92 *supra*.)

Substituting for V_B [$V_B = k^2V_A$] and X_B [$X_B = 1 - X_A$]:

$V_P = V_A[X_A{}^2 + k^2(1 - X_A)(1 - X_A) + 2qX_A(1 - X_A)]$

or:

$V_P = V_A(X_A{}^2 + k^2X_A{}^2 - 2k^2X_A + k^2 + 2qX_A - 2qX_A{}^2)$.

Taking the rate of change of V_P as a function of the concentration of the portfolio in A:

than that contained in an existing portfolio can reduce the risk of the portfolio, and, if so, what range of proportions will achieve a reduction in the risk of the portfolio. In the special circumstances we have been considering, with the component securities A and B each having the same expected value, the correct mixture would be at the point providing the lowest possible variance for the combination portfolio. This conclusion follows from the postulate that investors prefer the lowest risk necessary to achieve a given expected value.[102]

But another considerable advantage of covariance analysis is that it applies regardless of the expected values of the component securities.

$$\frac{dV_P}{dX_A} = V_A(2X_A + 2k^2X_A - 2k^2 + 2q - 4qX_A).$$

Setting this function equal to zero in order to determine the concentration at which portfolio variance is at a minimum:

$$X_A + k^2X_A - 2qX_A - k^2 + q = 0$$

or:

$$X_A = \frac{(k^2 - q)}{(k^2 + 1 - 2q)}$$

Note that the denominator is larger than the numerator for all values of $q < 1$ since, by hypothesis, $k^2 > 1$. Thus, X_A will always be positive and less than 1.

Now, returning to the equation for V_P,
$$V_P = V_A[X_A^2(k^2 + 1 - 2q) - 2X_A(k^2 - q) + k^2].$$

Substituting for $(k^2 + 1 - 2q)$:

$$V_P = V_A[X_A(k^2 - q) - 2X_A(k^2 - q) + k^2]$$

or:

$$V_P = V_A[k^2 - X_A(k^2 - q)]$$

or:

$$V_P = V_A[k^2 - \frac{(k^2 - q)(k^2 - q)}{(k^2 + 1 - 2q)}]$$

or:

$$V_P = V_A\frac{(k^2 - q^2)}{(k^2 + 1 - 2q)}$$

Since $\frac{k^2 - q^2}{k^2 + 1 - 2q}$ is always positive, and since $(k^2 - q^2)$ must be less than $(k^2 - 2q + 1)$ [if $(k^2 - q^2)$ were greater than $k^2 - 2q + 1$, then $0 > q^2 - 2q + 1$, or $0 > (q - 1)^2$, which is impossible if q is not imaginary],

$$V_P < V_A$$

102 See ¶ 7.03 at notes 21-23.

If security D, with an expected value of 10 percent, were substituted for security B in each of the three examples analyzed in ¶ 6.02[3][a], the resulting variances for the combination portfolio would be precisely the same. This is because the variance of the combination portfolio does not depend on the expected value of the component securities, but rather on their variances and covariance and the proportions invested in each. Different expected values for the component securities, however, do affect the expected value of the combination portfolio. The new expected value is simply the sum of expected value of each component security, weighted by the proportion of the portfolio invested in it.

This aspect of covariance analysis provides another useful tool to investment managers. By changing the proportions of the component securities, the manager can raise or lower the expected value of the combination portfolio. If the manager has selected component securities having a covariance less than the variance of either, there is a range of portfolio mixes over which the manager can raise the expected value of the portfolio above that of the component security with the lesser expected value, and yet achieve a variance for the portfolio less than that possible by investing in either one alone.

An excellent way to illustrate this point is to reconsider the second example analyzed above, in which the component securities were perfectly negatively correlated.[103] There, the variance of the combination portfolio reached zero when it was two-thirds invested in A. Assuming D is subject to the same variance and covariance constraints as B, the expected value of a portfolio combining A and D and having zero variance would be 8.67 percent—($\frac{2}{3}$)(8) + ($\frac{1}{3}$)(10) = 8$\frac{2}{3}$. Similarly, if the investment manager were willing to maintain the same level of risk in a combination portfolio as would be experienced by a portfolio invested entirely in A, the manager could achieve a much higher return. At that level of risk, the combination portfolio would be one-third invested in A and two-thirds invested in D, and the expected value of the portfolio would be 9.33 percent—($\frac{1}{3}$)(8) + ($\frac{2}{3}$)(10) = 9$\frac{1}{3}$.

Covariance analysis thus adds a dimension to investment management. When covariance is less than the variance of either component security, a whole range of options opens up to the manager to raise expected value without affecting risk, or to lower risk without affecting expected value, or to raise expected value to some extent while still reducing risk below that possible by investing only in the one having

---

[103] See text at note 97 *supra*.

the lesser risk. This powerful insight also expands considerably the entire concept of suitability. Since the suitability of a commitment depends on its relation to the range of risk and return indicated by an investor's investment objectives,[104] covariance analysis demonstrates that unsuitable commitments are capable of creating a suitable portfolio. This does not mean that every commitment in a portfolio is suitable simply because the expected value and variance of a portfolio make the portfolio suitable. But covariance analysis does make it possible to justify a commitment which is unsuitable when analyzed solely on the basis of its own expected value and variance. So long as a security's inclusion does not push portfolio variance outside the range of risk which determines investor suitability, it is an appropriate addition to the portfolio.

---

[104] See ¶ 4.02.

Chapter 7

THE APPLICATION OF MODERN PORTFOLIO THEORY TO LEGAL STANDARDS OF PROFESSIONAL COMPETENCE

¶ 7.01.   THE IMPACT OF MODERN PORTFOLIO THEORY ON COMMON-LAW STANDARDS

Modern investment theory has introduced a profound shift in perspective into portfolio management. The traditional legal view placed securities in rigid categories and combined rather vague notions of the appropriateness of those categories for particular investors with an undifferentiated concept of diversification as the method of relating risk to return. Modern theory, as expressed in the capital asset pricing model and the efficient-market hypothesis, however, has identified and quantified the relationship between risk and return. In particular, the application of the covariance principle (that securities which are not highly correlated can be combined to reduce risk)[1] to securities selection and the distinction between systematic risk (risk which is an unavoidable part of market movement)[2] and unsystematic risk (risk which is uniquely attributable to a particular security)[3] are powerful insights which affect the entire process of structuring a portfolio. As with any departure of significance, modern investment theory brings with it both new opportunities and new responsibilities. It gives investment managers greater freedom to make commitments and adopt techniques that only a short time ago the law would have treated as a breach of duty. But, at the same time, it has deprived concepts such as reasonable care and prudence as applied to portfolio management of the broad scope with which they were formerly invested.

At this stage, it is difficult to foresee exactly the accommodation that will develop between law and theory. So far, the only real testing of the theory has focused on common stocks traded on the leading stock exchanges. Although investment managers are investing in common stocks traded in other markets, both domestic and foreign, and in other types of securities, such as debt instruments and options,[4] and although this kind of diversification appears to improve performance,[5] there is still no clear picture of how well price changes in these other markets accord with the predictions of the capital asset pricing model and the

---

[1] See ¶ 6.03[3].

[2] See ¶ 7.03[1] *infra*.

[3] See ¶ 7.03[1] *infra*.

[4] Connelly, "The New Emphasis on Portfolio Mix," 8 Institutional Investor 39 (August 1974).

[5] Bergstrom, "Spreading the Risk: Investors Do Better to Broaden Their Universe," Barron's, Feb. 24, 1975, p. 9.

efficient-market hypothesis.[6] Nonetheless, one can predict with assurance that as the testing of the theory proceeds and its limits are exposed, the law will take due account of what is learned. Enough is already known about covariance analysis to protect properly carried out hedging techniques. Enough is already known about listed common stocks to focus attention on the unsystematic risk to which an investment manager exposes a portfolio and his purpose in doing so. And enough is already known to test positive investment strategies for compliance with professional standards.

This chapter considers the application of portfolio theory, as explicated in Chapter 6, to law from three perspectives. First, it assumes that the vital statistics—the expected value and variance of every security, and the covariance of every pair of securities—are known precisely. Were this actually the case, only elementary mathematics would be necessary to select the "best" portfolio for any investor. Securities would be selected and portfolios adjusted to achieve the expected value and variance most consistent with the investor's investment objectives.[7] Even though such precision may be impossible to achieve in practice, the assumption that it exists permits a sharper view of what an investment manager should be seeking to accomplish in managing a portfolio.

Second, this chapter makes the application of portfolio theory to law more realistic by examining the pricing relationship between risk and reward.[8] The basic theory suggests a course of action for an investor who dislikes risk and is given, or can calculate, expected value, variance, and covariance for a set of securities. An extension of the theory postulates that most investors in fact dislike risk, and explains what that means for determining expected value, variance, and covariance. Although these values cannot be determined with certainty, extending the theory in this fashion is instructive for two reasons: It provides a measure of the cost of not acting in accordance with the basic theory; and, through its focus on the pricing mechanism, it provides a means by which investment managers can carry out the lessons of the basic theory.

Finally, this chapter recognizes and considers the effect on legal doc-

---

[6] Cf. Blume & Friend, "A New Look at the Capital Asset Pricing Model," 28 J. Fin. 19 (1973) (empirical testing of the capital asset pricing model in the bond market does not line up with theoretical predictions).

[7] For a discussion of the legal constraints on determining investment objectives, see Chapter 4.

[8] As the reader will recall, risk is measured by variance (see ¶ 6.03[2]) and reward is measured by expected value (see ¶ 6.03[1]).

trine of imperfect knowledge of expected value, variance, and covariance. Plainly, the law cannot insist on precision when the fundamental elements of the theory cannot be known precisely. But the absence of perfect knowledge should not permit behavior which does not take into account what can be known. To act with ordinary skill and care, investment managers must conduct themselves within the limits of the professional knowledge of which they are, or should be, aware. This means that errors are acceptable only if within the range of reasonable professional disagreement over matters of judgment and approach.[9] The failure to dispose of an unsuitable commitment, for example, is not forgivable if reasonable care on the part of an investment manager would have shown that the presence of the commitment, or the proportions in which it was present, kept a portfolio at an unnecessarily high level of risk. Security and portfolio analysis has matured sufficiently that the professional knowledge of which investment managers are capable allows them to make predictions about expected value and estimate measurements of variance such that the investment techniques indicated by pure portfolio theory, modified as appropriate, are highly useful.

¶ 7.02. THEORY IN A SINGLE-INVESTOR WORLD OF CERTAIN VALUES

The discussion that follows focuses on the behavior of a single investor and assumes that he knows the expected value, variance, and covariance of the securities in which he can invest. This kind of perfect knowledge would be possible if the history of a security were an exact predictor of the response of that security to events. Although unvarying consonance with history would not reveal the future, it would at least permit an investment manager to determine the limits on the ebb and flow of the return of a security, however the future unfolded.

[1] Speculation

The sole constant in the legal literature on speculation is that a speculation involves a high degree of risk borne in order to obtain unusual gains. Even conceding the essential accuracy of the definition, a notion of relativity is implicit in this concept. Risk can be high and gains can be unusual only in relation to some standard of measurement. Thus, a commitment may be a speculation for one investor and yet be

---

[9] See ¶ 1.02.

entirely proper for another, depending on the aims of each. In order to keep the analysis objective, therefore, let us treat the term speculation as descriptive not of an unvarying characteristic of a particular commitment, but of a commitment or group of commitments inappropriate for a given investor because risk is excessive and extent of gain unnecessary for achieving his investment objectives.

The gain an investor anticipates from a speculation, or any other commitment, for that matter, is its expected value. The risk it entails is its variance. For any investor, there is a proper expected value which his portfolio should be constructed to achieve. This expected value is determined entirely by the investor's investment objectives. After an investment management relationship is initiated and a client's investment objectives are identified, the manager's principal function is to construct a portfolio having the requisite expected value with as little variance as possible.

In its most rigid application, the rule of law prohibiting speculations says only that the manager must not include commitments having risk and reward characteristics that are extreme in relation to those of a properly structured portfolio. This does not mean, however, that all securities having an expected value above that appropriate for the client are not proper investments. Indeed, even the most simpleminded application of the legal rule would not preclude such commitments. If there were a prohibition against securities having an expected value in excess of that appropriate for the portfolio, the manager, paradoxically, could not include commitments in securities having a lower expected value than that indicated by his client's investment objectives; no combination of securities with expected values at the level set by the client's investment objectives and securities with lesser expected values can offer an expected value at the desired level.[10] Similarly, the legal rule cannot focus merely on the risk of a single commitment. Adding a commitment which raises the risk of a portfolio without also raising the expected value is certainly incompetent management and may be condemned also as speculative, but an absolute prohibition on adding a commitment merely because it raises the risk of a portfolio would lead to the absurd conclusion that the manager should construct his portfolio by making his most risky commitments first.

---

[10] If A represents securities having the expected value indicated by a client's investment objectives, B the securities having a lower expected value, X the proportion invested in each, and E the expected value, then:

$$X_A E_A + X_B E_B \neq E_A, \text{ unless } X_B = 0.$$

In order to understand the meaning of speculation, one must take into account all the relational characteristics of the commitment under consideration. Only the expected value and variance of a commitment and its covariance with an existing portfolio permit the kind of analysis which determines whether a commitment should be characterized as speculative. No rational investor can object to a commitment which raises the expected value of his portfolio without affecting risk or which lowers risk without affecting expected value. Moreover, depending on the covariance of a security with the rest of the portfolio, it may even be possible to reduce risk and raise expected value, although the commitment itself might have an expected value and variance outside the range appropriate for an account if it accounted for all, or too great a proportion of, the portfolio. A rule of law which prevented an investment manager from achieving a concurrent reduction of risk and increase in expected value would be totally indefensible.

The criteria for characterizing a commitment as speculative must test a commitment for its contribution to both expected value and variance. If it raises the expected value of a portfolio above that appropriate for the client and does not maintain or reduce the level of risk of the portfolio, it is speculative. In such a case, adding a security having an expected value exceeding that indicated by the investment objectives of the client and having a variance at a level unnecessary for the client to bear in order to achieve those investment objectives would be, in legal parlance, seeking an unusual gain by undertaking a high degree of risk of loss.

The important thing to note is that it is not enough to show that the commitment, taken by itself, may involve more risk than is appropriate for the client. It is the contribution of the commitment to the riskiness of the portfolio which is the vital question. This kind of analysis avoids the necessity of labeling commitments either as investment grade or speculative in advance of their inclusion in a portfolio. On the contrary, it postulates that the quality of a commitment for a given investor is entirely a function of that investor's proper investment goals. And, most important, it shifts the focus on surcharge of an investment manager for undertaking speculative commitments from a type of commitment to the conduct of the manager. By focusing on expected value, variance, and covariance, the relevant inquiry in reviewing a manager's investment decisions will be how the manager determined that the inclusion of the commitment under scrutiny was to contribute to the safety of the portfolio, or at least how including the commitment was to achieve a higher return without sacrificing safety. It will not be the arbitrary exercise of trying to classify a security in the abstract.

[2] Disposing of Unsuitable Commitments

The duty to dispose of unsuitable investments obliges an investment manager to eliminate speculative commitments from a newly acquired portfolio and to reduce or remove commitments rendering a newly acquired portfolio overly concentrated. In meeting this duty, the manager has the same point of view he would if he were adding commitments instead of considering terminating or modifying them. He wants a portfolio with an expected value as close as possible to that indicated by the client's investment objectives, and he wants that portfolio to have as little variance at the indicated expected value as he can accomplish. But, unlike the process of adding commitments, in disposing of unsuitable investments the manager needs some means of identifying candidates for elimination. He must ask the inverse of the question of whether a given security can reduce portfolio variance without affecting expected value excessively, or raise expected value without increasing variance unreasonably. Instead, he wants to know how removal or reduction of a commitment and possible substitution of one or more other commitments can achieve the same ends.

Reducing concentration is the easier task in evaluating a newly acquired portfolio. By calculating the covariances of every pair of securities in the portfolio, an investment manager can determine whether any pair are closely correlated. If so, the manager would want to eliminate every security which is closely correlated with and characterized by a greater variance than another security. The reason for this is that, because of the correlation, the presence of the security with the greater variance only inflates the variance of the portfolio. While it is true that the security with the greater variance may also have the higher expected value, the manager can reasonably expect to find another security with comparable expected value that is less closely correlated with the security retained in the portfolio. Indeed, if he can find one that will yield a covariance which is less than its variance or that of the security retained, the variance of the portfolio will be lowered. But even if they covary too closely to lower portfolio variance, so long as the new addition has a comparable variance to the commitment it is replacing and a covariance with the retained commitment less than that of the original pair, the variance of the portfolio would be reduced by making the switch.

The more difficult task is to identify securities which should be eliminated or reduced in concentration because they are too speculative, given the client's investment objectives. By determining the expected value of each commitment, the manager can determine the expected value of the portfolio placed under his control, and he can compare that figure with the expected value indicated by the client's objectives. If the calculations show that the portfolio has too high an expected value, action on the part of the manager is required unless no move toward the proper expected value can reduce the variance of the portfolio—a most unlikely event. (Intuitively, one would view an inability to reduce expected value without reducing variance as implausible, and the empirical evidence substantiates that conclusion, at least over the range of investments appropriate for most investors.[11] This point is considered in more detail below,[12] but for present purposes, assume that a greater risk in a security is generally associated with higher return.) Some adjustment of the existing portfolio, either in the number or proportion of high-expected-value securities, should produce a portfolio in consonance with the client's investment goals.

One approach the manager might take in restructuring the portfolio is to measure the variance of every commitment having an expected value above that appropriate for the portfolio.[13] For example, suppose the portfolio consists of five securities, A through E, having expected values of 6 percent, 8 percent, 8 percent, 10 percent, and 10 percent,

---

[11] Virtually all studies done, whether performed as a test of modern portfolio theory or as an attempt to measure the returns of various classes of securities, have shown that the returns on securities increase as the risk they entail goes up. See J. Lorie & M. Hamilton, *The Stock Market: Theories and Evidence* 211-227 (1973) (hereinafter cited as Lorie & Hamilton); J. Lorie & R. Brealey, *Modern Developments in Investment Management* 393-446 (1972). Of course, the empirical findings only support what all investors would claim to know anyway. On the average, holdings in currency return less than high-grade bonds, high-grade bonds less than low-grade bonds, bonds less than stock, and so forth. It is interesting to note, however, that apparently the expected value of a security begins to fall off when risk gets very high. The possibility of achieving unusually large returns seems to be an opportunity for which some investors will pay a premium, much in the fashion of persons who purchase lottery tickets. For a fuller discussion of this phenomenon, see Lorie & Hamilton, *supra,* at 217-218; Friedman & Savage, "The Utility Analysis of Choices Involving Risk," 56 J. Pol. Econ. 279 (1948).

[12] See ¶ 7.03 *infra.*

[13] This is not the only approach he might take. He might also measure the variance of all securities having an expected value either higher or lower than that indicated by the client's objective. He might then retain only those combinations of high- and low-expected-value securities which in combination reduce portfolio variance without affecting expected value. The inclusion of any low-expected-value securities in the portfolio dictates the inclusion of high-expected-value securities. See note 10 *supra.*

respectively. Suppose also that the client's investment objectives indicate 8 percent as the proper expected value for the portfolio. If the portfolio were comprised of equal proportions of each security, its expected value would be 8.4 percent.[14] In order to determine whether either D or E are contributing too much risk to the portfolio, the manager can consider the impact of removing either or both. More precisely, suppose the manager determines the variance of E, the variance of the remainder of the portfolio, and the covariance linking the two. The manager knows that if the covariance is greater than the variance of the remaining portfolio, there is no combination of E and the remaining portfolio that can lower the risk of the portfolio. Even if the covariance is less than the variance of the remaining portfolio, the manager may discover that the proportions of the commitment do not represent a proper mix for lowering risk. In either event, the manager can determine what adjustments are necessary in dealing with E. Furthermore, regardless of what the manager concludes with respect to E, he must repeat the process for D. In this way, he can evaluate the contribution of each security having a variance and expected value which taken alone would be excessive for the client.

As a theoretical matter, depending on the number of securities in a portfolio having high expected values and variances relative to client's investment objectives, multiple solutions are possible concerning which of these securities to retain and in what proportion to retain them. The final mix can depend on the order in which the securities are reviewed. But that fact is not significant because, whatever the final mix, the expected value and variance of the portfolio as a whole will be the same.[15] As a practical matter, therefore, an investment manager will want to isolate all securities which, taken alone, have unacceptably high expected values and variances. For any of them to be retained in the portfolio, the manager will have to find that their presence either reduces the variance of the portfolio, or at least provides an increase in expected value at no cost in variance.

But even if the investment manager cannot justify retention of some or all of the high-expected-value securities initially part of the portfolio,

---

[14] The arithmetic is as follows:

$$\frac{(6\% + 8\% + 8\% + 10\% + 10\%)}{5} = 8.4\%.$$

[15] Considering each of the high-expected-value securities separately against the remainder of the portfolio raises the same problem that occurs when a portfolio is constructed by means of the two-security paradigm. See ¶ 6.03[3], note 91.

that does not mean they should automatically be eliminated. If, without them, the expected value of the portfolio would fall below that indicated by the client's investment objectives, the manager must add high-expected-value securities or eliminate low-expected-value securities until the proper level is reached. If the best result is achieved through addition of high-expected-value securities, it may well be that the commitments initially part of the portfolio are better than any others. That is, although they raise portfolio variance in order to raise expected value, they may well raise variance less than any commitments that might be substituted for them. For example, calculations might show that no D or E can be combined with A, B, and C without raising the variance of the portfolio ABC. But the expected value of ABC is less than 8 percent, the return indicated by the client's investment objectives. Suppose F, G, and H, all with an expected value of 10 percent, were available, but all also covarying more closely with ABC than D and E and possessing comparable variances to D and E. In that event, D and E would be better choices for inclusion in the portfolio because, although they would raise the variance of the portfolio, they would raise it less than any combination of F, G, and H.

Thus, the process of testing high-expected-value/high-variance securities for suitability only identifies candidates for removal. For their removal to actually be essential, three conditions must be satisfied:

(1) Their presence in any proportion must raise the variance of the remaining portfolio;

(2) There must be no need to raise the expected value of the remaining portfolio; and

(3) If there is a need to raise expected value, one or more other high-expected-value securities must be capable of doing the job at less cost in increased portfolio variance.

But any analysis which shifts attention to securities outside those in the initial portfolio changes the legal question from disposing of unsuitable investments to making a portfolio productive.

[3] Making a Portfolio Productive

Once the manager has determined which securities should be disposed of, he is ready to structure the portfolio so that the client is most likely to achieve his investment objectives. When completed, the portfolio will probably consist of securities at different levels of expected value. Some will have the same expected value as that indicated by the client's investment objectives for the obvious purpose of providing the appropriate level of return. Some will have an expected value below that indicated by the client's investment objectives to reduce the risk of the portfolio. Finally, some will have an expected value exceeding that indicated by the client's investment objectives in order to counterbalance the impact of the low-expected-value securities in the portfolio and, if possible through covariance characteristics, to reduce the risk of the portfolio.

[a] Securities having a return at the expected value level indicated by the client's investment objectives

One possible method for an investment manager to construct a portfolio calculated to achieve a particular set of investment objectives is to purchase securities offering a return precisely at the level indicated. This approach without more, of course, would be far too simpleminded for it would permit an investment manager to include highly correlated commitments merely because they had the same expected value. A more sensible approach would be to identify groups of highly correlated securities and select the one with the lowest variance from each group. Each security selected would have less independent risk than any other member of its group, and together the securities so selected would be relatively uncorrelated. It would be possible then to combine these securities to construct a portfolio with a lower variance than any one of them. In accordance with the two-security paradigm, one might proceed by identifying a pair with a covariance capable of producing a two-security portfolio having a lower variance than any of the remaining securities. Each of the remaining securities would be added in proper proportion if its covariance with the portfolio was less than its own variance or that of the portfolio. In this fashion, the "best" portfolio having an expected value at the proper level and consisting only of securities with expected values at that level would be constructed.

[b] Securities having expected values lower than that indicated by the client's investment objectives

Securities having a lower expected value than that indicated by a client's investment objectives can be included in a portfolio to reduce the risk—but only if the reduction in risk is substantial. Since a low-expected-value security will usually have a lower variance than a higher-expected-value security, substituting some of the lower for some of the higher would reduce risk in any event. But mere reduction in risk is not the goal of the investment manager. If lower risk were the only concern, everyone would invest in risk-free securities. The manager is seeking to obtain the lowest risk possible consistent with achieving the client's investment objectives. Therefore, the inclusion of lower-expected-value securities in a portfolio is justifiable only if doing so offers an unusually great reduction in risk. This means that an investment manager is interested in only those low-expected-value securities which are highly uncorrelated or negatively correlated with the portfolio. In that case, a substantial reduction in the risk of the portfolio may be possible at a small cost in expected value.[16]

Incidentally, this test applies with equal force to low-expected-value securities initially part of the portfolio acquired by the manager. His duty to make the portfolio productive does not permit him to retain unduly safe commitments any more than his duty to dispose of unsuitable investments permits him to retain unduly speculative commitments. Existing low-expected-value commitments which are highly correlated with commitments closer to the expected value indicated by the client's investment objectives should be eliminated (unless retaining the low-expected-value securities and substituting other securities for those at the higher-expected-value level would substantially reduce risk).

[c] Securities having a higher expected value than that indicated by the client's investment objectives

An investment manager will always be willing to include high-expected-value securities in a portfolio if they do not increase its variance. If circumstances make this possible, an investment manager might identify candidates for inclusion in the portfolio by segregating high-expected-value securities into separate groups of highly correlated securities. The manager can then disregard all securities in groups closely correlated with the portfolio. In the other groups of securities, the manager will want to choose commitments having the highest expected value and smallest variance, since they will raise the expected value of the portfolio at the least cost in risk.[17]

---

[16] Although the point may seem repetitious, it cannot be overemphasized that an investment manager faces a conceptual problem having two variables in opposition to each other. The manager is trying to increase return at the least cost in risk and to reduce risk at the least cost in return. He is not trying merely to increase return or to reduce risk. Both must be considered simultaneously.

[17] As the reader can see, the conceptual problem is the same whether the manager is dealing with securities having an expected value higher than

The inclusion of high-expected-value securities can have an impact on a portfolio in two ways. First, the covariance may be such that inclusion can actually reduce portfolio variance. This will occur in the now-familiar case wherein the covariance is less than the variance of either the security under consideration or the portfolio.[18] But a more likely occurrence is that inclusion of a high-expected-value security would raise the portfolio variance somewhat. If the expected value of the portfolio is at the level indicated by the client's investment objectives, no such security should be added. To do so would increase risk and raise expected value above that necessary, the classic example of speculating by seeking an excessive gain at an unnecessary risk. On the other hand, if the expected value of a portfolio is below that indicated by the client's objectives because it includes some low-expected-value securities, the manager must add some high-expected-value securities in order to return the portfolio to the proper level of return. In these circumstances, it is the responsibility of the investment manager to raise the expected value of the portfolio at the least cost in risk. The determination of the securities best suited to achieve this depends on expected value, variance, and covariance. The higher the expected value of the security, the less of it that is required to raise the expected value of the portfolio to the proper level. And the smaller the variance of the security and covariance of it with the portfolio, the less the impact of the security on the variance of the portfolio.

[4] Diversification

Implicit in the entire discussion of covariance analysis is the concept of diversification. The whole idea behind diversification is to modulate the effect of unanticipated events on the performance of a portfolio. The common law has long recognized that the different reactions various securities experience to events reduce the effect of any particular event on a portfolio. Portfolio theory explains the advantage of diversification as lying in its power to reduce portfolio variance. But the message of both law and theory is the same. Highly correlated commitments involve unnecessary risk-taking on the part of an investor.

---

that indicated by the client's investment objectives, or the same or lower than those objectives. The two variables of expected value and variance must be considered together in order to achieve the best solution to the problem of structuring the portfolio. See note 16 *supra*.

[18] The judicious use of options is an example of how this can be accomplished. See ¶ 7.05 *infra*.

The more interesting question is what diversification means. The reader will recall that common-law development of the doctrine of diversification was highly qualitative.[19] In contrast, portfolio theory is quite precise in defining diversification, whether one is considering adding to or subtracting from a portfolio. Perfect diversification means that no addition to the portfolio can reduce risk without also lowering expected value nor increase expected value without also raising risk. Perfect diversification also implies that the removal of a security from a diversified portfolio or a change in the mix of the securities in the portfolio cannot reduce risk without lowering expected value nor raise expected value without increasing risk. When a portfolio has attained this level of diversification, it is called an efficient portfolio, a term of art used to describe members of the set of "best" portfolios that can be attained at every level of risk. There may be many different efficient portfolios at any level of risk, but their essential characteristic must be that no other mix of securities can expect to achieve a higher return at that level of risk.[20]

¶ 7.03. THEORY IN A MANY-INVESTOR WORLD OF CERTAIN VALUES

A tacit assumption in the preceding exposition of portfolio theory has been that the expected value and variance of individual securities are independent of each other. In a world of certain values, this assumption contains an unavoidable paradox if all investors prefer to bear as little risk as possible in order to achieve a given return. Assume, for example, that securities A and B each have an expected value of 8 percent, but B has four times the variance of A. All risk-averse investors seeking an 8 percent return would prefer A to B because B has a greater tendency to deviate from the 8 percent expected value and thus involves more risk than A. If most investors in fact seek to bear as little risk as they can at a given level of return,[21] for B to be marketable, either A must increase in price and thereby provide a lower return than 8 percent, or B must drop in price and thereby provide a higher return than 8 percent.[22]

---

[19] See ¶ 6.02[4].

[20] See, e.g., Lorie & Hamilton, note 11 *supra,* at 172-174, 270.

[21] See note 34 *infra.*

[22] The return on an asset consists of capital appreciation (or depreciation) plus every other source of income measured as a percentage of purchase price over a given time interval.

The same analysis applies in pricing portfolios consisting of more than one security. Suppose each of three securities, A, B, and C, has an expected value of 8 percent. Suppose also that the variance of A is three times that of C, and the variance of B is two times that of C. If expected value and variance were the only considerations, the three securities would change in price relative to each other such that, to be marketable, A would offer the highest return and C the lowest return. But suppose also that the correlation between A and B would permit those two securities to be combined into a portfolio with a lower variance than that of C. Plainly, the portfolio consisting of A and B would increase in price relative to C and thereby provide a lower return than C. Furthermore, if the correlation between C and the portfolio consisting of A and B is such that the inclusion of C would lower the variance of the portfolio still more, a portfolio consisting of A, B, and C would be priced the highest of all.[23]

The adjustment in price of A, B, and C that would occur in the marketplace permits an important extension of theory. Investors can only expect to be paid for risk they must bear, or, in other words, risk they cannot avoid. The obvious implication of this observation is that the market will not offer an investor a premium for risk which can be eliminated by diversification. But there is another implication which is more subtle, but potentially more far-reaching. Diversification need not be regarded merely as a defensive tactic to protect a portfolio by minimizing its variance. Diversification can also be the cornerstone of a positive strategy by which an investor, unable consistently to outguess the market, can put himself in the best position to achieve his investment objectives. To understand this strategy, one must become acquainted with two more quantitative concepts: volatility, which provides a more useful measurement of risk than variance; and capital asset pricing, which provides a means for determining the price of risk.

[1] Volatility

In keeping with the conventions of modern investment theory, let us call nondiversifiable risk "systematic risk," and diversifiable risk "unsystematic risk." Systematic risk is entirely market-related. This is the case because perfect diversification eliminates the effect on a portfolio of any event that does not affect all portfolios. Given this distinction with respect to risk, the return on any portfolio can be described

---

[23] That is, the return, measured as a percentage of purchase price, of a portfolio consisting of A, B, and C would be the lowest of all.

as consisting of two elements. One is its systematic return, that is, the return an investor receives for committing assets to the market; the other is its unsystematic return, that is, the return an investor receives from a portfolio which cannot be accounted for by market movements. For a perfectly diversified portfolio, unsystematic return would be zero. Unsystematic return may cause a portfolio to perform differently from a market portfolio over one or several investment periods. It is the expected return from unsystematic risk which will be zero.[24]

The systematic return for a portfolio is perfectly correlated with market return since it is the return achievable by perfect diversification. The systematic return from a portfolio may be more or less than that of the market, but because it is perfectly correlated with the market, the relationship between the systematic return of a portfolio and market return will always be the same. For example, if the systematic return of a portfolio were 1½ times that of the market, a 4 percent market gain would produce a systematic gain for the portfolio of 6 percent, and a 4 percent market drop would produce a systematic loss of 6 percent for the portfolio. The factor which describes the sensitivity of a portfolio's systematic return to market movement is called the beta factor (b), and the sensitivity, or beta, of a portfolio to the market is called its volatility. Since systematic risk is the only risk for which an investor can expect other investors to pay a premium over the risk-free rate,[25] volatility is an index of the compensable risk contained in a portfolio.

Total return of a portfolio which is not perfectly diversified is a

---

[24] See Modigliani & Pogue, "An Introduction to Risk and Return," Pt. I, 30 Fin. Anal. J. 68, 76-79 (March-April 1974), Pt. II, 30 Fin. Anal. J. 69, 83 (May-June 1974) (hereinafter cited as Modigliani & Pogue).

[25] This is not to say that systematic risk is the only characteristic of a security for which other investors will pay a premium. Securities also have a quality which is described as skewness. This term is used to describe the degree to which a distribution is asymmetrical. The returns from securities are generally positively skewed, since there is usually the possibility that they will increase in value by more than 100 percent. Few securities decrease in value by more than 100 percent, although it is theoretically possible through short selling or margin trading. Apparently, investors like the positive skewness associated with owning securities, since the evidence indicates that rates of return are inversely correlated with skewness. In any event, however, the skewness characteristic of securities does not affect the risk analysis essential to understanding the theory being explained in the text above since skewness appears to have a measurable impact only for the most volatile securities. See generally Lorie & Hamilton, note 11 *supra*, at 217-218.

function of both systematic and unsystematic return. Designating market return as R_M, and unsystematic return as R_U, portfolio return, R_P, can be expressed algebraically as:

$$R_P = bR_M + R_U.$$

There are two important lessons in this equation. An investor can affect his return by changing the volatility of the portfolio he constructs. Indeed, through perfect diversification, he can control his expected return entirely by selecting a volatility appropriate to the investment objectives because the expected value of unsystematic return would be zero. On the other hand, by foregoing perfect diversification, the investor can affect his return by the degree of accuracy with which he can determine the unsystematic return from his portfolio.

[2] Capital Asset Pricing

Since the market does not compensate for unsystematic risk, and since unsystematic risk always raises portfolio risk above systematic risk, an investor would want to construct a nondiversified portfolio only if his strategy would produce an expected return equal to or above what he could achieve simply by diversifying at a higher volatility level. This means that some method for pricing risk is necessary so that the investor can compare the amount of additional return he anticipates from his strategy with the return he could get simply by raising systematic risk. Fortunately, because the return on a portfolio can be expressed as a function of its volatility, the price of the risk of a portfolio can be determined as a function of market return.

Let us examine this relationship between risk and return. Suppose an investor holds a portfolio of risky assets having the same systematic risk as a market portfolio. By definition, the volatility of this portfolio is 1. If the portfolio is perfectly diversified, the investor should expect the same return as he would receive if he held a market portfolio. Suppose the investor now considers adding some risk-free assets, such as Treasury bills, to his portfolio. The volatility of the combination portfolio is simply the average of the volatility, or beta coefficient, of each component, weighted by the proportion invested in each. If X_F represents the proportion of the portfolio invested in risk-free assets and X_M represents the portion invested in the risky assets in the market-equivalent portfolio, the volatility index of the combination portfolio is:

$$b_P = X_F b_F + X_M b_M.$$

But $b_F = 0$ since, by definition, the return of risk-free assets is always the same regardless of what the market does, and $b_M = 1$ by hypothesis. Therefore:

$$b_P = X_M.$$

In other words, the volatility of the combination portfolio is equal to the fraction of the portfolio invested in the risky assets. Note that this analysis extends to investors who want to achieve a beta higher than the market, also. If the investor could borrow money at the risk-free rate, he could purchase greater amounts of each of the securities making up his market-equivalent portfolio, and thereby increase his volatility index above that of the market. For example, if he borrowed enough money at the risk-free rate to double his securities holdings, then $X_F = -1$, $X_M = 2$, and therefore $b_P = 2$; the leveraged portfolio is twice as volatile as the market-equivalent portfolio alone.

This analysis extends to all portfolios. Any portfolio consisting of assets of various volatilities can be expressed in terms of an equivalent portfolio consisting only of the proper proportion of risk-free and market-risk securities. Let us consider, therefore, the relationship between expected value and risk, or market volatility, as if a portfolio consisted only of some combination of risk-free assets and other assets which, taken together, are equivalent in risk to the market.

The expected value of the combination portfolio is the average of the expected returns on each of its components, weighted by the proportion invested in each.[26] If E_P is the expected value of the portfolio, E_F the expected value of the risk-free assets, and E_M the expected value of the market-equivalent portfolio, the expected value of the portfolio can be expressed as follows:

$$E_P = X_F E_F + X_M E_M.$$

This equation can be simplified significantly. Since $X_F + X_M = 1$, $X_F = 1 - X_M$. Also, the solution arrived at just above for the volatility factor of the combination portfolio was $b_P = X_M$. By substituting for X_F and X_M, the equation stating the expected value of the portfolio reduces to:

$$E_P = (1 - b_P) E_F + b_P E_M,$$

or:

$$E_P = E_F + b_P (E_M - E_F).$$

---

[26] See ¶ 6.03[1].

This equation means that the expected value of a portfolio is linearly related to the beta—that is, the volatility—of the portfolio. Therefore, recognizing that the expected value of risk-free assets is simply the stated return on those assets, and assuming that the expected value of market returns can be calculated, this equation generates the price of risk.

By plotting expected value against beta, as in Figure 7-1, one can see that the capital market line extends from the risk-free rate of return when $b = 0$, through the point determined by the market rate of return at beta $= 1$, and beyond. By determining the beta coefficient of a portfolio, an investor can determine the expected value of his portfolio. Since beta measures the risk for which an investor is compensated, the premium the investor receives for undertaking that level of risk is the difference between the indicated expected value and the risk-free rate of return. Furthermore, the investor can see how much additional return he can expect for each additional quantum of risk he takes on, or how much it costs in lowered return for seeking safety.

[3] The Legal Parameters Revisited

In a world of certain values, the capital asset pricing model is highly appealing. Investors either will hold perfectly diversified portfolios at the level of volatility necessary to achieve their investment objectives, or they must find a strategy that permits them to construct a portfolio which, through the use of unsystematic risk, equals or exceeds the return dictated by the model. Let us assume for the moment that no such strategy exists and consider the implications of the model on legal doctrine.

[a] Speculation

Because the capital asset pricing model makes the level of systematic risk the determining factor in the expected return of a portfolio, speculation becomes almost a trivial concept. Given a client's investment objectives, an investment manager can calculate precisely the level of risk, as measured by the beta coefficient of a fully diversified portfolio, that should be borne by the client. Any portfolio involving systematic risk above that indicated by the client's investment objectives would be speculative. The expected return would be more than necessary and the risk would be excessive. The model gives the manager no means of raising the return on the portfolio without also increasing the risk.

Another important implication of the capital asset pricing model for interpreting the legal duty forbidding speculation is that diversification which eliminates unsystematic risk also destroys all utility in labeling individual securities as either speculative or of investment grade. The risk associated with every type of commitment consists of systematic risk, represented by its beta coefficient, and unsystematic risk. Although it is generally the case that the systematic risk of an individual security accounts for a small proportion of its total risk,[27] diversification eliminates unsystematic risk and, consequently, makes the beta coefficient of the portfolio the pertinent inquiry. The beta coefficient for a portfolio is simply the average of the beta of each individual security, weighted by the proportion of each security in the portfolio.[28] It is quite possible, therefore, that some types of commitments traditionally regarded as speculative, such as warrants, options, convertibles, and so forth, could be fully justified as components of a diversified portfolio.

Furthermore, according to the capital asset pricing model, particular investment techniques, formerly labeled as speculative as a matter of law, can no longer be so regarded. The model shows that an increase in the beta of a market-equivalent portfolio can be accomplished as well by leveraging a market-equivalent portfolio as by constructing a more volatile portfolio with securities with high beta coefficients.[29] An investor requiring a higher rate of return than that offered by the market would theoretically be indifferent to the method chosen for meeting his investment objectives, and in fact may have reason to prefer leveraging to purchasing high beta securities.[30] But the important point is that,

---

[27] Lorie & Hamilton, note 11 *supra,* at 224.

[28] Let b_P be the beta coefficient for the portfolio and b_i be the coefficient for any security. Let X_i be the proportion of the portfolio invested in any security. Then:

$$b_P = X_a b_a + X_b b_b + \ldots + X_i b_i.$$

See Modigliani & Pogue, note 24 *supra,* Pt. I at 68, 78.

[29] See Lorie & Hamilton, note 11 *supra,* at 186-191.

[30] Studies show that, in the real world, diversified high-volatility portfolios return less than a diversified portfolio of lower-volatility securities leveraged to the level of volatility indicated by the investor's investment objectives. See Modigliani & Pogue, note 24 *supra,* Pt. II at 81-85. The explanation for the divergence between an investment strategy of leveraging low-volatility securities and diversifying in high-volatility securities may be that, in the case of high-volatility securities, the value investors place on skewness reduces average returns. See note 25 *supra.* It may also be that the simple one-factor model (i.e., where expected value is expressed as a function of the single variable, portfolio volatility) explaining the relationship between risk and return is inaccurate because unsystematic risk is,

in a world of certain values, whatever an individual's preference, the capital asset pricing model recognizes neither method as superior. An investment manager can achieve the expected return indicated by his client's investment objectives equally well constructing a diversified portfolio at the requisite beta level or by leveraging a market-equivalent portfolio up to the proper beta level.

[b] Disposing of unsuitable commitments

The capital asset pricing model also has enormous impact on the duty to dispose of unsuitable commitments. Because an investment manager can adjust the beta of the portfolio by diversifying with securities having beta coefficients of varying levels, there is no necessity for a manager to dispose of any part of a portfolio newly placed under his control simply because an existing commitment might traditionally have been regarded as speculative. According to the model, the manager needs merely to adjust the portfolio to the level of risk, measured by volatility, indicated by the client's investment objectives and, at the same time, eliminate unsystematic risk through full diversification.

This is not to say that the manager will not have cause to sell any of the assets placed under his control. For unless the portfolio is perfectly diversified at the proper level of volatility at the outset, some adjustments must be made. If the portfolio lacks the cash or cash-equivalents to purchase the securities necessary to create a diversified portfolio having the proper beta coefficient, the manager will have to sell some or all of the commitments initially a part of the portfolio. Nonetheless, even if this procedure is necessary, it would not be compelled on the grounds that the securities to be disposed of are inherently speculative, but to eliminate unsystematic risk. In short, the manager would have a duty to dispose of these assets only to diversify the portfolio, not to dispose of speculations.

---

in fact, valued to some extent by investors. There have been various attempts to expand the one-factor model (in other words, to include other variables besides portfolio volatility) to explain the results obtained through empirical testing of the capital asset pricing model (see Modigliani & Pogue, note 24 *supra,* Pt. II at 70-85), though attempts to preserve the one-factor model by explaining the discrepancy in terms of the difficulty of obtaining the true risk-free rate have also been suggested. See Editor's Comment, "Why the Beta Models Broke Down," 31 Fin. Anal. J. 6 (July- Aug. 1975). A fuller discussion of the legal implications of the results of the empirical tests of the capital asset pricing model appears in ¶ 7.07.

[c] Making a portfolio productive

The capital asset pricing model makes the analysis, if not the execution, of an investment manager's duty to make a portfolio productive straightforward. Once a manager translates a client's investment objectives into a figure representing the rate of return on investment necessary to achieve those objectives, the manager than consults a market-line diagram—Figure 7-1, for example. The point at which the expected value reflecting the desired return intercepts the capital market line determines the value of the beta coefficient—the volatility relative to the market—necessary. The manager than structures the client's portfolio to eliminate unsystematic risk through diversification and to mold the systematic risk to yield the designated beta. In effect, given a set of investment objectives, the capital asset pricing model reduces an investment manager's task to engineering instead of art.

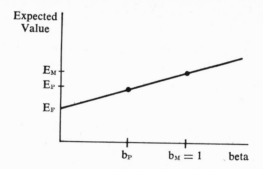

E_M = Expected value of market return

E_P = Expected value of portfolio return

E_F = Risk-free rate of return

b_M = Coefficient of market volatility

b_P = Coefficient of portfolio volatility

Fig. 7-1

[d] Diversification

The capital asset pricing model makes diversification not merely wise but mandatory. Unless an investment manager has a strategy for controlling unsystematic risk to provide consistently better returns over those provided by the capital asset pricing model (and we have assumed for purposes of this part of the discussion that no such strategy exists), an investment manager who fails to diversify introduces un-systematic risk into a portfolio for which his client receives no premium and from which a client can expect no return.[31] Even conceding that an investment strategy superior to the capital asset pricing model may exist, a failure to diversify reintroduces the problems of applying tradi-tional legal doctrine. For example, if an investment manager achieves 90 percent diversification in a portfolio under management, a deliberate policy of undertaking unsystematic risk means that the law must de-termine whether the amount of unsystematic risk being borne is proper, inadequate, or excessive, and whether the return expected by that strategy is below, equal to, or beyond that called for by any of the client's investment objectives. How the law could do this without resorting to the qualitative approach which marked an earlier time is difficult to see, since the only quantitative approach available is that derived from modern portfolio theory.

¶ 7.04. THEORY IN A MANY-INVESTOR WORLD OF UN-CERTAIN VALUES

In its pure form, the capital asset pricing model stands as both a bench mark for investment strategies and an obligatory strategy for in-vestment managers. It is a bench mark because it relates risk to return precisely. To be superior to the model, another strategy would have to offer an expected return greater than that of the model at an equivalent level of total risk. The model is obligatory on investment managers because it precludes the possibility of a greater expected re-turn for an equivalent total risk. In the model, total risk for a fully diversified portfolio equals systematic risk. Other strategies, by defini-tion, employ unsystematic risk either deliberately or inadvertently. Since unsystematic risk can easily be eliminated by full diversification, the market offers no premium for undertaking it, and therefore no strategy should expect returns based on it.

But the pure form of the model is possible only in a world of certain values, risk-averse investors, and no transaction costs.[32] The real world, on the other hand, needs no such assumptions to keep spinning on its

---

[31] This does not mean that there will, in fact, be no return. The un-systematic risk may produce above-average returns or below-average returns. The point is that the average returns from unsystematic risk are zero, and therefore an investor who introduces unsystematic risk into his portfolio is engaging in pure gambling, an improper activity for investment managers.

[32] More precisely, derivation of the capital asset pricing model assumes:
"(a) The market is composed of risk-averse investors who measure risk in terms of standard deviation of portfolio return. . . .

axis. Nonetheless, conceding that the assumptions underlying the pure form of the capital asset pricing model do not reflect conditions in the real world perfectly does not mean that the model is not useful. Restrictive assumptions underlying a theoretical model do not automatically disqualify it as a tool for explaining phenomena in the real world. For one thing, though restrictive, assumptions may be realistic in the sense that they account for behavior in most cases. Another possibility is that an assumption will be unrealistic as an explanation for most behavior, but realistic in the sense that it describes average behavior. In any event, the test of a theory is not the general accuracy of its assumptions, but the power of its predictions. If tests of a theoretical model show it to be a good predictor of events in the real world, its value is established. Indeed, to be useful, a model need not be precisely accurate in its predictions so long as a high degree of confidence can be reposed them.[33]

[1] Assumptions Underlying the Capital Asset Pricing Model

Let us examine the assumptions on which the model is based. They may not reflect the behavior of investors and markets with perfect accuracy, but none is outlandishly unrealistic. First, even though risk aversion may not characterize every investor, it certainly describes the attitude of professional investment managers whose clients, taken as a group, make up the greater part of the market. Indeed, if risk aversion

---

"(b) All investors have a common time horizon for investment decision-making (e.g., 1 month, 1 year, etc.). . . .

"(c) All investors are assumed to have the same expectations about future security returns and risks. . . .

"(d) Capital markets are perfect in the sense that all assets are completely divisible, there are no transactions costs or differential taxes, and borrowing and lending rates are equal to each other and the same for all investors. . . ."

Modigliani & Pogue, note 24 *supra,* Pt. II at 70. See also Lorie & Hamilton, note 11 *supra,* at 200.

[33] Conveniently, some of the very techniques of analysis underlying modern portfolio theory are useful in assessing the degree of confidence which should be placed in applications of a theoretical model. By comparing results with predictions, one can observe the correlation between the two, and thereby determine its statistically expected error. The lower the expected error, the more accurate is the model. For a fuller discussion of the measurement of expected error, see Milne, "Regression Analysis," in 1 S. Levine, *Financial Analyst's Handbook* 1064, 1071-1072 (1975).

for investors is defined as a preference for less risk over more at a given level of return, investment managers are legally obligated to be risk averse. It may be within the province of an individual investor to accept higher volatility than necessary in constructing his portfolio. The prospect of increasing his opportunity for fortuitous high gains may excite him enough to outweigh the fact that his portfolio will contain a greater than necessary risk of producing less than the return he is seeking to meet his investment objectives.[34] That attitude, however, is pure gambling, a luxury which is not permitted a professional managing someone else's assets. Plainly, if pure chance is to be an element of a person's investment policy, he requires no professional help to roll the dice.[35]

Second, the assumption of certain values is unrealistic only in the sense that it does not accurately describe the situation confronting individual investors. Simple observation of the amount of exchange which takes place in the marketplace amply demonstrates that uncertainty rather than certainty characterizes the pricing of individual securities. Basic research into the stability of systematic risk substantiates that instinctive impression. If investors were knowledgeable about the range of future experiences a company might expect, the volatility of its securities would be relatively fixed. Studies have shown, however, that the beta coefficients of individual securities are highly unstable.[36]

Nonetheless, on the average, the assumption of certain values should not introduce serious discrepancies into the expository power of the capital asset pricing model. Despite the instability associated with beta coefficients for individual securities, the beta coefficients for well-diver-

---

[34] This phenomenon reflects an observed aspect of human behavior. Purchasers of lottery tickets are the archetypal example. Indeed, in the case of most lotteries, the expected value of each individual commitment is less than zero, since the total amount of money paid in is typically less than the total value of the prizes paid out. The degree to which individual investors value opportunities for high gains associated with a particular commitment is represented by the skewness of the commitment. See note 25 *supra*. For a quantitative discussion of this phenomenon, see Friedman & Savage, "The Utility Analysis of Choices Involving Risk," 56 J. Pol. Econ. 279 (1948).

[35] The help of a professional adviser might be justifiable in one circumstance. An investor who values skewness (see note 25 *supra*) might not be able to identify securities having that characteristic to the degree the investor might desire. It might be worthwhile to such an investor, therefore, to purchase professional assistance in identifying opportunities having an appropriate level of skewness for the investor.

[36] See Lorie & Hamilton, note 11 *supra*, at 224.

sified portfolios are highly stable.[37] In effect, returns and losses from unsystematic risk tend to cancel in the face of large numbers. Moreover, even insofar as individual securities are concerned, action in the marketplace tends to show the degree of uncertainty over future prices to be relatively narrow. The disagreements investors have over the vital statistics of individual securities do not usually manifest themselves in abrupt or excessive changes in price. This indicates that most of the market at any time is in substantial agreement in evaluating a security, a conclusion supported by the efficient-market hypothesis, to be discussed below.[38] Of course, the degree of uncertainty over how much the actual return of a security will diverge from its expected return increases as the time over which estimates of future prices are made increases.[39] But the differences in time over which investors evaluate securities are small enough to eliminate them also as an unsettling influence on the stability of prices.[40]

The third assumption underlying the model is the absence of transaction costs associated with investment decisions and portfolio adjustments. Simple observation dispels any such notion.[41] Nonetheless, although the assumption of no transaction costs is unrealistic and cannot be averaged out like the consequences of uncertainty in the pricing of

---

[37] *Id.*; see also ¶ 7.08 *infra.*

[38] In its semi-strong form, the efficient-market hypothesis says that current prices fully reflect what the public knows about a security. See Lorie & Hamilton, note 11 *supra,* at 71, 83-87. See also ¶ 7.07 at notes 103-106, *infra.*

[39] The statistical expression for this phenomenon is that the standard deviation of possible portfolio returns after a number of investment periods is equal to the square root of the number of periods times the standard deviation for a single period. See Modigliani, note 24 *supra,* Pt. I at 73.

[40] Investors tend to adjust estimates quarterly in conjunction with quarterly reports of companies and annually in conjunction with the annual reports of companies. Predictions for a longer term are also made, of course, but even for highly stable companies, the degree of confidence which can be placed in such estimates is limited, and consequently, it is reasonable to assume that such time intervals are not deemed significant by investors.

[41] Transaction costs are of many kinds and can be large in amount. The purchase and sale of securities involves commission expenses; holding securities involves custodianship expenses; differential tax rates apply to investors; lending rates and borrowing rates differ from the risk-free rate; such rates also are set at different levels for different kinds of investors; access to information is costly; investors do not all gain access to information capable of causing them to revise their estimates at the same time; and so forth.

securities, the principal effect of introducing transaction costs as a factor is to make time a variable in the pricing model. Because it costs money to carry out investment decisions, because the information leading to changes in position is not disseminated to everyone at the same rate, because tax considerations cause investors to put off or hasten decisions about changing position, there is an element of delay in the market's reaching the position posited by the capital asset pricing model. In effect, the model represents an equilibrium that can never be reached because, even as prices adjust as the model postulates, the new information leads to new evaluations and new forces for adjustment.

The question is whether the time element introduces a significant distortion in the model. The answer depends mostly on the turnover rate associated with the management of a portfolio, since transaction costs in the form of commissions and payments for early dissemination of information rise rapidly as the turnover rate increases.[42] But at least for well-diversified portfolios having relatively low portfolio turnover, the transaction-cost effects would be relatively small. Indeed, this is exactly the investment approach the capital asset pricing model would demand. For investors seeking to rely on the model as a strategy, the principal reasons for adjusting a portfolio would be to control its volatility and to meet a need to liquidate some assets because of current expenses. Since well-diversified portfolios tend to have a stable beta coefficient, the need to maintain volatility at a predetermined level would justify only a low turnover. Also, cash needs ordinarily do not stimulate high turnover. On the contrary, they typically account for only a small percentage of a portfolio's market value, since investors faced with substantial cash needs would be unlikely to overcommit themselves to equity and long-term and medium-term holdings in the first place.

[2] The Capital Asset Pricing Model Tested

Even if the three assumptions—risk aversion, general agreement on the value of individual securities, and low transaction costs—do not characterize most investors, they are at least characteristic of the conduct of a good part of the investment management community. Theoretically, then, at least for most investors, the theory would predict an average return equal to market return adjusted for the volatility of a portfolio less transaction costs. Much of the research done to test the

---

[42] For further discussion of how transaction costs associated with turnover affect the standard of care, see ¶ 7.07 at notes 178-181, *infra*.

capital asset pricing model tends to substantiate the theoretical claims. The most significant finding is the existence of a positive linear relationship between realized return and systematic risk.[43] On the other hand, studies also have shown that portfolio return is not strictly proportional to volatility.[44] One major study found that high beta coefficients lead to somewhat lower returns than the model would have predicted, and that low beta coefficients lead to somewhat higher returns than the model would have predicted.[45] The plain implication of these findings is that unsystematic risk does, on the average, have an impact on expected return. Other studies confirm that the simple one-factor model, the pure capital asset pricing model (i.e., expected return expressed as a function of a single variable, portfolio volatility), does not fully explain the relationship between risk and return.[46]

There have, of course, been attempts to explain the discrepancy between predictions and observations.[47] But in practice, the discrepancy between theory and evidence turns out to be tolerable to theoreticians and reassuring to investment managers. To the satisfaction of the theoreticians, the evidence indicates that the volatility of a portfolio relative to the market dominates actual returns to a portfolio. This is in accord with the model. But if the theory were entirely accurate, the level of professional expertise required to structure portfolios would be modest. One would simply subscribe to a beta-coefficient calculating service, make the appropriate combinations of commitments, and put the portfolio away, except for occasional readjustments whenever the beta coefficients of the component securities shifted enough to change portfolio volatility. To the satisfaction of investment managers, the evidence also shows that some actual returns are unsystematic. In other words, portfolios for which average unsystematic risk is set to zero through full diversification will not show zero average returns in addition to the returns accounted for by the level of systematic risk undertaken.[48]

---

[43] Several studies have made this finding. For a summary of the more significant contributions, see Modigliani & Pogue, note 24 *supra,* Pt. II at 78-82. See also J. Lorie & R. Brealey, *Modern Development in Investment Management* 393 (1972).

[44] Modigliani & Pogue, note 24 *supra,* Pt. II at 78-82.

[45] Modigliani & Pogue, note 24 *supra,* Pt. II at 84-85. See also Lorie & Hamilton, note 11 *supra,* at 223-227.

[46] See, e.g., Blume & Friend, "A New Look at the Capital Asset Pricing Model," 28 J. Fin. 19 (1973).

[47] See, e.g., Editor's Comment, "Why the Beta Models Broke Down," 31 Fin. Anal. J. 9 (July-Aug. 1975).

[48] See notes 44-46 *supra.*

The importance of these findings is thus twofold. First, the beta coefficient in fact attains the bench-mark quality attributed to it by the model. Returns measured by level of volatility set the standard against which various investment strategies can be tested. Those strategies are suspect which fail by a wide margin to produce the returns that investment in accordance with the model would have yielded. Absent some explanation by an investment manager of why the actual results led to such a gap, the existence of disproportionate losses in an inadequately diversified portfolio would be strong evidence that the manager had adopted an investment strategy involving unsystematic risk either unnecessarily or erroneously and has thus failed to comport with standards of ordinary skill and care.

Second, the modified model is also important because it establishes that there are investment strategies capable of taking advantage of unsystematic risk to produce returns higher than the pure model would predict. This is important because the traditional article of faith of the investment management community—that professional investment management produces greater gains than management services cost—has come under severe attack from another quarter in the guise of the efficient-market hypothesis. In its semi-strong form, this hypothesis asserts that current prices fully reflect everything publicly known about securities issuers and that analysis of such data is a futile means of trying to beat the market.[49] This argument parallels the implication of the pure capital asset pricing model that no strategy is superior to simple full diversification at the appropriate level of risk: Both cast doubt on the utility of many of the investment strategies in which professional investment managers engage. But the modified model is an excellent rejoinder to these contentions. It says that unsystematic returns different from zero, on the average, are possible even with full diversification. It does not identify strategies by which to accomplish this, and indeed, in its bench-mark capacity, the model might punish someone who attempted a faulty strategy. Nonetheless, for the manager who diversifies his portfolio fully, but selectively, superior returns measured by systematic risk are possible.

[3] Application of the Capital Asset Pricing Model to the Reasonable-Care Standard

It would be foolish to ask the law to follow theory closely before theory is adequately tested. If for this reason alone, the capital asset

---

[49] Lorie & Hamilton, note 11 *supra,* at 71, 83-87.

pricing model cannot command a total commitment from the law. But, more important, while empirical research continues to substantiate the basic thrust of the model, puzzling inconsistencies defy full accommodation to the theory.[50] Additionally, although there is substantial movement toward investment strategies based on the model,[51] those who have forged ahead have yet to show that they can in fact consistently produce returns in accordance with theoretical predictions.[52]

But by the same token, in its ordinary growth, the law will recognize the lessons which have been learned well enough to set standards of ordinary skill and care. In this regard, the theory should have two immediate and important effects on the development of legal doctrine. First, the theory has withstood enough testing to render doubtful certain legal prescriptions which grew out of an earlier era. And second, the state of the theory should permit tighter limits to be imposed on the assessment of portfolio management under a reasonable-care standard.

[a] Consideration of the entire portfolio as a unit

The most critical step in accommodating law to theory is expanding the focus of legal doctrine to the characteristics of a portfolio in full. The common law has traditionally limited consideration to the characteristics of individual securities to determine whether investment managers have performed their duties with prudence or ordinary skill and care. The view has been that the investment decision underlying each commitment in a portfolio must be evaluated on its own merit[53]—as if a portfolio were only the sum of its parts, a collection of separate and independent investment decisions, and not a discrete entity to be considered on its own merit.

----

[50] See, e.g., Blume & Friend, "A New Look at the Capital Asset Pricing Model," 28 J. Fin. 19 (1973).

[51] News reports indicate that institutional assets in rapidly increasing amounts are being invested in accordance with the passive strategy indicated by the capital asset pricing model. See, e.g., Belliveau, "Will Pension Officers Stop Trying to Beat the Market," 10 Institutional Investor 18 (Feb. 1976); Laing, "More Pension Funds Try to Tie the Market Instead of Beating It," Wall Street J., Nov. 12, 1975, p. 1, col. 6.

[52] For a close account of how one of the earliest management entries into application of the capital asset pricing model has fared, see Black & Scholes, "From Theory to a New Financial Product," 29 J. Fin. 399 (1974). See also Shapiro, "How Do You Really Run One of Those Index Funds," 10 Institutional Investor 24 (Feb. 1976).

[53] E.g., In re Bank of New York, 35 N.Y.2d 512, 517, 323 N.E.2d 700, 703, 364 N.Y.S.2d 164, 168 (1974).

The source of the rule is not entirely clear: It may have developed out of the trust principle that a trustee cannot offset losses from a breach of trust with gains to the trust.[54] In any event, the law has never truly gone to the extreme of concentrating only on each investment decision separately. Were that the case, the doctrine of diversification would have been impossible to develop. Even without modern quantitative techniques based on covariance (i.e., the degree to which movement in one security can be explained by movement in another), the law has long recognized the need for determining diversification by examining each commitment relative to all other commitments making up an entire portfolio.[55] It would be impossible, for example, even from a qualitative perspective, to determine whether the addition of securities issued by *B* company significantly adds to the diversification of a portfolio consisting of *A* company without knowledge of such details as geographic location, market, suppliers, and so forth.[56] Furthermore, without considering a portfolio as a whole, it is impossible to tell whether the portfolio has been structured properly with respect to a client's investment objectives.[57]

Nonetheless, the resilience of the policy of focusing on each commitment separately except in regard to diversification cannot be ignored.[58] There is every indication that the individual evaluation of each commitment continues to characterize the legal approach up to the present time. In *Trustees of Hanover College v. Donaldson, Lufkin & Jenrette, Inc.*,[59] a case which was a source of concern throughout the

---

[54] E.g., Creed v. McAleer, 275 Mass. 353, 175 N.E. 761 (1931); King v. Talbot, 40 N.Y. 76, 90-91 (1869). A trustee may, however, offset losses against gains if investments constituting breaches of trust cannot be distinguished as separate breaches. See *Restatement (Second) of Trusts* § 213 (1959).

[55] Professor Scott emphasizes this point in his treatise. See 3 Scott, *Law of Trusts* § 227, at 1809 (3d ed. 1967) (hereinafter cited as Scott). See also Langbein & Posner, "Market Funds and Trust-Investment Law," 1 Am. Bar Found. Research J. 1, 24-26 (1976) (hereinafter cited as Langbein & Posner).

[56] See *Restatement (Second) of Trusts* § 228 (1959).

[57] Professor Scott makes this point also. See 3 Scott, note 55 *supra*, § 227 at 1809, § 227.12.

[58] See Langbein & Posner, note 55 *supra*, at 24-26; Williams, "The Prudent Man Rule of ERISA," 31 Bus. Law. 99 (1975).

[59] Civil No. 71-C686 (S.D. Ind. 1971). This case is unreported. A summary appears in Belliveau, "Discretion or Indiscretion," 16 Institutional Investor 65 (Aug. 1972). See also Lipton, "The Customer Suitability Doctrine," in R. Mundheim, A. Fleischer & J. Shupper, *Fourth Annual Institute*

investment management community, the court refused to take a full portfolio perspective in reviewing an investment manager's investment program. Plaintiffs alleged, among other things, that the manager had selected unsuitable securities. Defendants moved to dismiss partly on the grounds that the commitments in question should be judged in light of the performance of the entire portfolio. The court denied the motion even though the overall management of the portfolio had produced positive returns, and the parties settled.

The result in *Hanover College* was apparently a reflection of the reluctance of courts to adopt a rule which would exonerate any incompetent manager whose accounts were lucky enough to realize positive returns. The law has long held that how a manager carries out his obligations in this regard depends on conditions existing at the outset of an investment program.[60] But on the basis of *Hanover College* and other statements of authority concerning the legal rule to be applied to the evaluation of the separate components of a portfolio,[61] one could easily conclude that the law diverges sharply from modern investment theory on this point. Certainly, a good case can be made for the proposition that a security which is not of investment grade when considered on its own merit cannot be regarded otherwise by taking a full portfolio perspective. But that would be too narrow a reading of the present legal rule. The reason for classifying commitments as unsuitable is to protect a portfolio from exposure to excessive risk. It would make no sense to proscribe commitments which could render a portfolio safer simply because, considered in isolation, they would not be acceptable. Indeed, the common-law rule of diversification amply demonstrates that no security, except possibly an issue of the United States, is sufficiently safe to be considered in isolation from the rest of the portfolio. The diversification rule holds that virtually no security is sufficiently safe on its own merit to constitute all, or even a large part, of a portfolio.[62]

---

on Securities Regulation 273, 278-280 (PLI 1973) (hereinafter cited as *Fourth Annual Institute on Securities Regulation*); Gillis & Weld, "The Money Manager as Fiduciary," 28 Fin. Anal. J. 10 (March-April 1972).

[60] See 3 Scott, note 55 *supra*, § 227.

[61] See, e.g., Gillis, "Securities Law and Regulation: Professional Fiduciaries Under Fire," 28 Fin. Anal. J. 10, 14 (Sept.-Oct. 1972); Williams, "The Prudent Man Rule of ERISA," 31 Bus. Law. 99 (1975).

[62] See ¶ 6.02[4]. But see Baldus v. Bank of Cal., 12 Wash. App. 621, 530 P.2d 1350 (1975), holding that almost total concentration in the securities of one issuer was not a breach of duty, on the grounds that the rule of diversification is only a rule of general application and is not absolute in every case.

[b]   Limitations on the consideration of the entire portfolio as a unit

On the other hand, it is doubtful the law will ever presume a commitment suitable simply from the fact that it is one of a number of elements of a portfolio or that the entire portfolio taken as a whole has shown a net gain or better overall performance than a market-related bench mark. For the law to take into account the relationship between two or more commitments in a portfolio as a factor in judging suitability, there must be a showing that, on the average, the commitment contributes to safety. This can be done either presumptively or by affirmative proof. Some commitments, generally regarded as safe when combined in a diversified portfolio, may be established as presumptively suitable. This, in essence, is one of the functions of a legal list. Other commitments not meeting this standard require proof that they contribute to safety. In effect, the burden of proof lies with the manager to show that such commitments are a defensible way of carrying out a client's investment objectives. In that event, the relationship of a security to the remainder of a portfolio is relevant only on a showing, either through rebuttable rule or on proof of fact, that a challenged commitment makes a reasonable contribution to the achievement of the client's investment objectives. This means that, judging a commitment at the time it is made, it must raise the expected value of a portfolio without rendering the portfolio unsuitably risky.

Another way to understand the common-law rule is to recognize that a challenge to component securities in a portfolio on grounds of suitability is actually a challenge to professional competence demonstrated by the underlying investment strategy. By permitting particular securities to be challenged separately, the law forces the manager to explain the rationale for including them in the portfolio. No reasonable investment manager would add risk to a portfolio if he could achieve the client's objectives with less risk. As a result of years of experience, the law has set as the standard investment strategy for achieving the indicated level of return without undertaking excessive risk the approach of constructing a diversified portfolio consisting of securities close to or below the average level of risk appropriate for the particular client. Although modern investment theory says that some kinds of risky commitments, judiciously used, can increase the chances of accomplishing a client's investment objectives without raising risk, it does not say that all undertakings involving unusual risk have that capability. Given the degree of expertise required to carry out the lessons of modern theory, it is expected that managers who invest accordingly should have the burden of demonstrating that they have done so properly.

The possibility of improving on the investment approach heretofore adopted by the law as the standard is simply not widely enough practiced to abrogate the need for showing that what is done tends to produce better results.[63]

Seen in this light, the *Hanover College* case can be analyzed as an example of the defendant-manager's failure to demonstrate that the challenged investments contributed to the safe achievement of the client's investment objectives. To a mild extent, the court's failure to enter summary judgment in favor of the plaintiffs on the issue of suitability supports this position. If the court were not willing to take into account the relationship between the challenged securities and the remainder of the portfolio, it might have ruled as a matter of law that they were excessively risky.

Much stronger support for the proposition that the law will take into account the relationship of an individual commitment to the remainder of a portfolio can be found in *In re Bank of New York*.[64] There, the guardian ad litem of a common trust fund challenged four investments by the trustee. The appellate division had held for the trustee on the ground, among others, that the portfolio showed an increase in total value over the period in question.[65] The court of appeals rejected this theory on the sensible ground that a rising market would virtually assure fiduciary immunity, and held instead that each of the four investments was not imprudent even though losses in each had occurred. While acknowledging the necessity of examining each commitment separately, the court of appeals made several observations highly important to the question of whether full portfolio perspective is acceptable as a rule of law:

---

[63] There is also a practical reason for requiring that each commitment be justified separately, at least insofar as Securities Exchange Act § 10(b), 15 U.S.C. 78j(b), is to have an impact on the standard of care to be demanded of an investment manager in structuring and maintaining a client's portfolio. The "in connection with the purchase or sale" language of Section 10(b) requires a challenge to one or more separate transactions and will not support a claim of general mismanagement. See Blue Chip Stamps v. Manor Drug Stores, 421 U.S. 723, *reh. denied* 423 U.S. 884 (1975). To the extent it remains good law after Ernst & Ernst v. Hochfelder, 425 U.S. 185 (1976), the most significant development affecting portfolio management to arise out of the antifraud provisions of the federal securities law, the reasonable-basis doctrine (discussed at ¶ 7.07, notes 141-143 *infra*), focuses on recommendations leading to the purchase or sale of a particular security. *Hochfelder* is discussed in detail in ¶ 6.01, note 5.

[64] 35 N.Y.2d 512, 323 N.E.2d 700, 364 N.Y.S.2d 164 (1974).

[65] 43 App. Div. 2d 105, 349 N.Y.S.2d 747 (1973).

"The record of any individual investment is not to be viewed exclusively, of course, as though it were in its own water-tight compartment, since to some extent individual investment decisions may properly be affected by considerations of the performance of the fund as an entity, as in the instance, for example, of individual security decisions based in part on considerations of diversification of the fund or of capital transactions to achieve sound tax planning for the fund as a whole. The focus of inquiry, however, is nonetheless on the individual security as such and factors relating to the entire portfolio are to be weighed only along with others in reviewing the prudence of the particular investment decisions." [66]

This statement of the court explains the balance to be struck in the evaluation of how a portfolio has been structured. It denies investment managers the opportunity of justifying the inclusion of unduly risky investments either out of incompetence or a misguided desire to improve a mediocre performance or for any other reason by simply laying out an entire portfolio before a tribunal and saying that the whole is the sum of its parts. But is does permit an investment manager to demonstrate that a commitment reflects a professionally defensible effort to carry out a program reasonably related to a client's investment objectives. With this appreciation of how the law will accommodate the lessons of modern investment theory, let us reconsider the controlling legal doctrine one last time.

¶ 7.05.　SPECULATION

The impact of modern investment theory on the legal analysis for determining the distinction between investment and speculation does not change significantly by taking real-world conditions into account. The question is still whether a commitment subjects a client to more risk than is necessary to achieve his investment objectives. Modern theory shows that some commitments which, taken alone, might be regarded as speculative, can be proper investments when considered in the context of an integrated investment strategy.

[1]　Traditional Speculations and Modern Portfolio Theory

[a]　High-volatility securities

As a general rule, the types of commitments which the common law has traditionally regarded as speculative have been determined by

---

[66] 35 N.Y.2d at 517, 323 N.E.2d at 703, 364 N.Y.S.2d at 164. See also Langbein & Posner, note 55 *supra,* at 24-26.

measuring them against the standard investment strategy of holding interests in a group of seasoned companies, with the portfolio adjusted to reflect immediate income needs of the client. Modern investment theory demonstrates, however, that greater safety is possible through strategies not quite so venerated by the law. Studies show, for example, that the benefits of diversification are more rapidly achieved the greater the volatility of the securities making up the portfolio mix.[67] This empirical conclusion makes intuitive sense when one recognizes that low-volatility securities are more likely to be correlated with each other than high-volatility securities. The former represent large established companies whose short-term price levels tend to be relatively stable and, in large part, similarly responsive to major events. This is not to say, of course, that a portfolio should consist only of high-volatility securities. Too great a concentration on high-volatility securities would produce too risky a portfolio for many investors. The point is that the use of some high-volatility securities may produce better diversification (that is, more effective reduction of unsystematic risk) with fewer issues than is possible in a portfolio restricted to low-volatility securities alone.

[b] Leveraging

Another practice which the law has labeled speculative is leveraging a portfolio. The legislative history of the Investment Company Act of 1940 and various provisions of the statute limiting the borrowing power of investment companies amply demonstrate the official view of leveraging tactics.[68] Actually, the margining of individual securities has been

---

[67] For a summary of the findings and a discussion of the results of these studies, see Modigliani & Pogue, note 24 *supra*.

[68] Investment Company Act § (1)(b) (15 U.S.C. § 80a-1(b)) states that the public and investor interests "are adversely affected . . . (7) when investment companies by excessive borrowing and the issuance of excessive amounts of senior securities increase unduly the speculative character of their junior securities. . . ." To effectuate this policy, Congress limited the power of closed-end investment companies to issue senior securities by requiring asset coverage of 300 percent for debt instruments and 200 percent for senior equity, and, in the event either was issued, by prohibiting the establishment of more than one class of senior debt or equity. Congress prohibited open-end companies from issuing any class of senior securities, except that an open-end company could borrow from a bank subject to 300 percent asset coverage. Investment Company Act § 18, 15 U.S.C. § 80a-18. The legislative history shows the depth of SEC concern over the leveraging tactics of investment companies, tactics which were especially

a matter of greater concern than the leveraging of an entire portfolio.[69] Only a few years ago, it was virtually inconceivable that an investment manager might want to use borrowed funds to duplicate the commitments in an overly safe portfolio on a pro rata basis in order to raise the risk of the portfolio to the level necessary to achieve the expected return indicated by a client's investment objectives. Nonetheless, the problem is the same whether margining a particular security or leveraging an entire portfolio is at issue. The use of borrowed funds intensifies a portfolio's reaction to events, and for that reason, leveraging has always been viewed as the tool of the speculator, intent on obtaining large gains at the risk of substantial loss. But in theory, the capital asset pricing model suggests that leveraging is a good means of raising the volatility level of portfolio. More significant, empirical tests of the model have shown that leveraging may well be a better strategy for raising the volatility level of a portfolio than purchasing outright greater numbers of high-volatility securities.[70] Thus, contrary to the implications of traditional doctrine, leveraging may be the safest way of increasing expected return when a client's investment objectives call for undertaking additional risk.[71]

[c] Options

Yet another questionable practice under the traditional legal view of speculation is dealing in options.[72] On the surface, options transactions appear to have all the attributes of a gamble. The entire purchase price of an option can be lost in a relatively short period of time if the price of the underlying security does not pass the striking price[73] by a sufficient amount. Moreover, the market value of an option depends on both the difference between the price of the underlying security and the striking price and also on the time remaining until the date on which the option expires. Successful options purchases thus depend on a correct judgment not only as to the price movement of a security,

---

common in the period before the Great Crash. See, e.g., Statement of L.M.C. Smith, Associate Counsel, SEC Investment Trust Study, in Hearings on S. 3580 Before a Subcomm. of the Senate Comm. on Banking and Currency, 76th Cong., 3d Sess. 265-275 (1940).

[69] See *Restatement (Second) of Trusts* § 227, Comment f (1959).

[70] See Modigliani & Pogue, note 24 *supra*, Pt. II at 82-85.

[71] Love, "The Use and Abuse of Leverage," 31 Fin. Anal. J. 51 (March-April 1975).

[72] See, e.g., Comment, "SEC and FRB Treatment of Options: An Experiment in Market Regulation," 53 Tex. L. Rev. 1243, 1247 (1975).

[73] The striking price is the price at which the option may be exercised.

but also as to the degree of movement and the period of time within which it will take place. Also indicative of the speculative character of options is the chance for large gains. Any change in the price of an underlying security obviously causes a change in the market value of the option. Since the option purchase price is only a fraction of the price of the underlying security, however, the percentage change in value of the option will be much greater. In effect, options dealings permit investors to leverage the price movements of the optioned securities.

But this view of options dealing completely ignores the relationship between an options commitment and the remainder of a portfolio. An investment manager who is convinced that a market change is imminent may well conclude that it would be a defensive and conservative step to hedge against an erroneous appraisal of market movement.[74] If a manager anticipates a market decline, for example, he could close all or part of his client's position in various portfolio securities and forego additional purchases until his sense of the market changed. But in order to protect the portfolio against his being wrong, the manager might sell off fewer commitments so that he would not forego all benefits of a market rise. Hedging in this fashion would be expensive if his initial prediction of a market decline were correct, however, so instead of making fewer adjustments to the portfolio, the manager might decide that committing a small portion of the assets under his control to a diversified set of calls,[75] or selling a modest number of puts[76] on existing portfolio securities, will better cushion the effects of closing positions in securities or withholding the purchase of additional securities should the market actually move up. The same analysis applies to the use of calls on existing portfolio securities and puts in anticipation of a market rise. In both cases, the options commitments are negatively correlated with the primary investment action the manager intends to take. Although the use of options in this fashion will reduce returns if the manager's judgment about the movement of the market is correct, they also reduce the extent of loss in the event his judgment proves incorrect.[77] More important, if used correctly, options can modulate the effects of market movements on a portfolio at less expense than the continual

---

[74] See Brody, "Options and the Mathematics of Defense," 1 J. Portfolio Management 35 (Winter 1975); B. Malkiel & R. Quandt, *Strategies and Rational Decisions in the Securities Options Market* (1969).

[75] Calls are options to buy.

[76] Puts are options to sell.

[77] See note 74 *supra*.

purchase and sale of stocks and debt securities.[78] This modulation means that, without sacrificing expected return, a portfolio obtains a reduction in volatility, and hence, in risk.

The essentially defensive nature of options dealing is now widely recognized, at least insofar as writing options against existing holdings is concerned.[79] Indeed, the concept of using options as one of an array of hedging techniques for obtaining portfolio protection and for improving return have been known for some time.[80] The general acceptance of options dealing simply awaited the creation of a central marketplace, like the Chicago Board of Options Exchange, that could accommodate extensive options trading. In view of the growing reliance by investment managers on writing options against portfolio securities,[81] it is doubtful that options writing can still be presumed speculative for investment managers. Banking[82] and insurance regulators,[83] for example, are be-

---

[78] See, e.g., Trauer, "Call Options After ERISA," 114 Trust & Estates 618 (1975); "Weighing the Option," 114 Trusts & Estates 806 (1975) (panel discussion); Black, "Fact or Fantasy in the Use of Options," 31 Fin. Anal. J. 36 (July-Aug. 1975); Raback, "Risk and Return in CBOE and AMEX Options Trading," 31 Fin. Anal. J. 42 (July-Aug. 1975).

[79] Id. As an illustration of how respectable options dealing has become, the colloquy reported in "Weighing the Options," note 78 supra, came from a panel comprised of a trust investment officer of a leading bank, an officer in a major brokerage house, and a leading investment counselor. A survey of the major banks showed most either engaging in or planning to engage in options writing. Securities Week, April 26, 1976, p. 6. A good objective indicator of the extent to which options dealing has spread is their volume on the Chicago Board of Options Exchange and the American Stock Exchange. For example, for the week ending July 16, 1976, contracts representing calls on 88 million shares of stock were traded.

[80] See, e.g., Transcript, "Managing Investment Partnerships," in Investment Partnerships and "Off Shore" Investment Funds 73-90 (PLI 1969).

[81] See Stabler, "Hedging Your Bets: More Investors Using Options as Way to Cut Stock-Ownership Risk," Wall Street J., Aug. 15, 1975, p. 1, col. 6. See also Securities Week, July 28, 1975, p. 4 (description of options program of Continental Illinois Bank); Wall Street Letter, Aug. 4, 1975, p. 10 (description of Bank of Commerce (Fort Worth) options dealings). But cf. Securities Week, Nov. 10, 1975, p. 10 (growth of institutional interests in options dealing meeting resistance because of trust law and tax law restriction), Securities Week, Jan. 21, 1974, p. 6 (Central States Security Council considering limit on options dealing by closed-end investment companies). As additional evidence of the growth of interest in options, the Chicago Board of Options Exchange has proposed to expand into puts. See Wall Street Letter, Nov. 3, 1975, p. 1.

[82] See Trust Banking Circular No. 2, CCH Fed. Bank. L. Rep. ¶ 96,295 (1974) (national banks authorized to deal in options).

[83] See, e.g., 11 New York Code, Rules & Regs., Pt. 174 (1975).

ginning to authorize limited options writing for their constituencies.

The lawfulness of the purchase of options and the sale of naked options as a tool of ordinary investment management, on the other hand, is far more doubtful. The reason is not that these kinds of options transactions cannot, in fact, be used properly,[84] but that, at this stage of industry development, the skill required to handle safely the full range of options dealing cannot yet be said to be possessed by most investment managers.[85] Just as the legal-list approach to distinguishing between investment and speculation was designed in large part to protect beneficiaries from trustees who either could not satisfactorily evaluate individual securities on their own merit or would not do so, one should anticipate a cautious extension of the privilege of options dealing to investment managers in order to prevent this investment tool from falling into the hands of the many who do not yet know how to use it. Indeed, in conjunction with official authorizations for institutions to engage in options dealing have come also official admonitions not to speculate.[86]

[d] Other traditional speculations

Many other investments and investment techniques, though relatively risky in themselves, can be adapted to an overall portfolio strategy capable of reducing risk from that of a comparable portfolio restricted to more traditional investments. Warrants, convertible securities, gold stocks and gold bullion, and foreign securities are among the many diversification approaches which are being used to stabilize return at the appropriate level of risk.[87] In fact, as experience with nontraditional investment alternatives broadens and as these new diversification techniques mature, it is possible that the risk inherent in more traditional portfolios will become partially uncompensated since, according to modern portfolio theory, investors cannot expect to be compensated for risk they can reasonably avoid.

---

[84] On the contrary, purchases and sales of this type can be highly defensive in nature. See Brody, "Options and the Mathematics of Defense," J. Portfolio Management 35 (Winter 1975).

[85] See, e.g., Securities Week, Nov. 10, 1975, p. 10.

[86] See notes 82 and 83 *supra.* See also Wall Street Letter, Aug. 4, 1975, p. 10 (describing SEC attitude towards options dealing as one of suspicion).

[87] See, e.g., Klein, "The Convertible Bond: A Peculiar Package," 123 U. Pa. L. Rev. 547 (1975); Shishko, "Why Gold?" 3 J. Portfolio Management 34 (Spring 1977); Welles, "Modern Portfolio Theory 2: How the New Technology Will Change the Business," 11 Institutional Investor 44 (April 1977). For an extended discussion of the limits legal doctrine places on investment strategies, see ¶ 7.07 *infra.*

[2] Impediments to the Use of Traditional Speculations

[a] Proving reduction in risk

Investment managers desirous of utilizing investment techniques drawn from modern theory but regarded with suspicion by traditional legal doctrine—purchasing high-volatility securities, leveraging a portfolio, options dealing, and so forth—should recognize that, until experience broadens understanding, the burden will fall on them to justify the propriety of their actions. Certainly, the manager will have to show at the very least that the strategy motivating these kinds of commitments was designed with the client's investment objectives clearly in mind. Only in the context of an acceptable investment strategy will it be possible to show how reliance on apparently risky undertakings can be a reasonable means of achieving those objectives. Plainly, the less well tested the method of selecting securities for the portfolio, the greater will be the burden on the manager to demonstrate a factual foundation justifying his action; and, the more substantial the authorities in support of the method at issue, the easier it will be to justify it. Recognition by the investment management community of an investment strategy as a valid means for accomplishing a given set of investment objectives is virtually conclusive as a matter of law that such a strategy is a reasonable means of carrying out such investment objectives. This has been the rule at least since the Supreme Judicial Court of Massachusetts set standards for diversification by reference to ordinary investment management practices,[88] and it reflects the long-standing tort principle that business custom sets the standard of care for business practices unless the custom itself is unreasonable.[89]

Even after a manager has met the burden of showing that he has an accurate picture of the client's investment objectives and that the investment strategy he has chosen is a reasonable means of accomplishing those objectives, the manager still must be prepared to demonstrate professional competence in carrying out the techniques he has chosen. That the purchase of high-volatility stocks, or the leveraging of a portfolio, or the use of options, for example, may be tools appropriate for use in managing a portfolio, does not establish that they have been used properly. On the contrary, the effective application of these kinds of investment management techniques is advanced enough in theory and complex enough in application that, in an extreme case, portfolio losses

---

[88] *In re* Dickinson's Appeal, 152 Mass. 184, 25 N.E. 99 (1890).

[89] The T.J. Hooper, 60 F.2d 737 (2d Cir. 1932) (per Learned Hand, C.J.); Mayhew v. Sullivan Mining Co., 76 Me. 100 (1884).

attributable to reliance on these techniques might be sufficient to make out a prima facie case that a manager has acted imprudently.

But the question of whether the commitments investment managers make reflect proper execution of complex investment strategies is different from the question of whether the strategies should be labeled speculative so that, as a consequence, investment discretion is circumscribed by denying managers full opportunity to utilize them. To the extent a distinction between speculation and investment is to continue to have legal effect, it should not be construed to preclude reliance on investment strategies which reduce risk and improve a manager's ability to achieve the return indicated by his client's investment objectives. Rather, it makes more sense to treat the failure to apply such strategies properly as professional negligence.[90]

[b] Obtaining contractual protection

The importance of not adding specific types of securities or investment categories to a binding legal classification as speculations cannot be overemphasized. While it is true that investment managers can usually avoid the restrictions of legal lists through appropriate contractual provisions, no contract can successfully anticipate by name every kind of investment opportunity which might subsequently be labeled speculative by a court, legislature, or administrative body. Certainly, it would be highly impolitic, if not impractical, to get advance contractual authorization to engage in investing in all "legal speculations." The most that can be expected is that the parties will agree that investments which the law presumes to be speculative at the time of contract are to be authorized—for example, common stocks of all types may be stated in the controlling instrument to be acceptable.

The problem for the investment manager is to develop a method for getting the kind of protection that explicit contractual authorization would provide. In principle, an extension of the contract model points to disclosure as the most effective means of avoiding answerability for losses stemming from reliance on advanced and esoteric investment strategies. Just as, at common law, trustees have been able to avoid the

---

[90] For example, although earlier doctrine indicated that unsecured lending should be regarded as a breach of trust (see ¶ 6.02[1], note 35, and 3 Scott, note 55 *supra*, § 227.8), it seems apparent now that the failure to invest idle funds in interest-bearing cash equivalents without excuse is a failure to exercise ordinary skill and care. See Stern v. Lucy Webb Hayes Nat'l Training School for Deaconnesses & Missionaries, 381 F. Supp. 1003 (D.D.C. 1974); Blankenship v. Boyle, 329 F. Supp. 1089 (D.D.C. 1971).

legal limitations on common stock investment by including express authorization to invest in common stocks in the trust agreement,[91] informed agreement by clients should normally be sufficient to expand management discretion beyond the restrictions otherwise imposed by the law. This conclusion is supported by developments at the federal level. Under the federal securities antifraud provisions, adequate disclosure by investment managers is normally the only barrier to the full exercise of investment discretion. Indeed, the SEC seems to be taking the position that, for the most part, sanctions can be imposed only in the event of nondisclosure even in the case of apparently very risky ventures.[92]

If disclosure in fact will temper problems in utilizing advanced investment strategies, the critical inquiry is what must be disclosed. By hypothesis, these strategies can be defended as safer than more traditional approaches to portfolio management. What, then, explains the sentiment that their use is so risky as to require express informed agreement under conditions of full disclosure? The answer is not that they are inherently risky, but that they are highly risky if not carried out properly. Errors from inexperience or incorrect application of theory can be very costly even if the overriding methodology is demonstrably sound. Furthermore, the less well tested the strategy, the greater is the

---

[91] See, e.g., Annotation, "Authorization by Trust Instrument of Investment of Trust Funds in Non-Legal Investments," 78 A.L.R.2d 7, 50 (1961).

[92] Even where it is doubtful that investors are actually aware of the types of investment strategies their managers are engaging in, disclosure normally insulates the manager from liability. Consider, for example, the information conveyed by an aggressive mutual fund to its shareholders through its registration statement, Form N-8B-1 (SEC Investment Company Act Release No. 1932 (Dec. 15, 1953)). In the *Guidelines for Preparing Form N-8B-1* (SEC Investment Company Act Release No. 7221 (June 9, 1972), 4 CCH Fed. Sec. L. Rep. ¶ 51,301), the SEC asks registrants to disclose the types of securities it will buy and sell, whether it will borrow and lend, trade short, purchase on margin, write options, and underwrite other securities, and what its policies with respect to concentration and diversification and portfolio turnover are. *Id.* items 4, 5, at 39,273-39,289. So long as an investment company provides the information required accurately, an investment company with an investment policy of seeking high risk may enter the capital markets. Compare *Guides for Preparation and Filing of Registration Statements* (SEC Securities Act Release No. 4936 (Dec. 9, 1968)), which requires an introductory statement summarizing the factors which make an offering of high risk. 1 CCH Fed. Sec. L. Rep. ¶ 3766. See, e.g., Shearson, Hammill & Co., SEC Securities Exchange Act Release No. 7743 (Nov. 12, 1965), [1964-1966 Transfer Binder] CCH Fed. Sec. L. Rep. ¶ 77,306.

risk that the theory and its application will not produce results in accord with expectations. Consequently, full disclosure in this context means more than describing the strategy or strategies the client's portfolio is to follow. Also required is a description of how well proven the strategy is and how familiar the management personnel are with its application. This is not to say that every manager lacking practical exposure to new approaches cannot use them. But his clients ought to know about his inexperience so that they can give an informed consent, under limiting conditions satisfactory to them,[93] before new departures in management are undertaken. Although there are no authorities yet interpreting common-law trust and agency principles to this degree of refinement, recent SEC action indicates that the federal securities antifraud provisions are being interpreted to regard nondisclosure of management qualifications as fraudulent.[94]

¶ 7.06. DISPOSING OF UNSUITABLE COMMITMENTS

An investment manager's task upon receiving an existing portfolio is to restructure it so that, at the least risk possible, its expected return will be that indicated by the client's investment objectives. Capital market theory identifies reasonably accurately the level of systematic risk the portfolio must bear in order to achieve that return. By taking into account the expected value of the original securities, their volatility, the degree of unsystematic risk still in the portfolio, and the amount of cash and cash equivalents available to make adjustments without selling off existing commitments, the manager can come up with a reasonable plan

---

[93] There is the added problem that the investment manager must be dealing with a client capable of consenting to such management strategies. If the client is not positioned to evaluate the risk that the theory will be misapplied or that the theory is wrong, client consent may be meaningless.

[94] See, e.g., In re Financial Programs, Inc., SEC Securities Exchange Act Release No. 11,312 (March 24, 1975), [1974-1975 Transfer Binder] CCH Fed. Sec. L. Rep. ¶ 80,146 (mutual fund prospectus represents fund managed by competent personnel). Unquestionably, sophisticated investors may authorize greater experimentation than unsophisticated investors (see, e.g., Anderson Co. v. John P. Chase, Inc., [1974-1975 Transfer Binder] CCH Fed. Sec. L. Rep. ¶ 95,009 (S.D.N.Y. 1975)). But the degree of sophistication a client possesses ought to be something a manager assures himself of at the outset of an investment management relationship. See SEC Investment Advisers Act Release No. 442 (March 5, 1975), [1974-1975 Transfer Binder] CCH Fed. Sec. L. Rep. ¶ 80,128, proposing Rule 206(4)-d, requiring statutory investment advisers to set out policies, practices, and other details of their operations in a disclosure document to be given prospective clients. See generally ¶ 4.01.

for determining the amount and types of securities which must be bought and sold to bring the portfolio into line with the client's investment objectives.

The principal problem in meeting the duty to dispose of unsuitable commitments is the time allowed for formulation and execution of a readjustment plan.[95] The manager must carry the plan out within a reasonable time.[96] To the extent it is practical, the manager will want to use the existing commitments as part of the restructured portfolio. This reduces the costs of adjustment since there are substantial commission expenses and other transfer costs associated with restructuring a portfolio. Thus, the manager needs time to evaluate the existing commitments for their possible inclusion in the restructured portfolio. Another important constraint on the adjustment process is the tax position of the investor. The types of gains that would be involved, the availability of offsetting tax losses, and so forth, may well dictate some of the details of carrying out a restructuring strategy. But whatever the

---

[95] It is worth noting also that one does not satisfy the duty to dispose of unsuitable investments by selling off an entire portfolio immediately without investigating the client's situation or without regard to the suitability of existing commitments for inclusion in the restructured portfolio. The client is hiring investment management expertise, and a manager has a duty of inquiry with respect to the portfolio's contents. See 3 Scott, note 55 *supra*, § 223. The deliberate refusal to exercise expert judgment is no more acceptable when a portfolio is totally liquidated without regard to its contents, except perhaps for securities the new manager has been following, than it is when a portfolio remains unadjusted for too long a period because of the manager's incompetence or neglect. In either case, there is an absence of the considered judgment which the client expected as a result of entering the management relationship. As one authority put it over a century ago:

> "It has been held, that an express power for the trustees to vary the securities will not authorize a change to be made without any apparent object or prospect of benefiting the trust estate; and should the trustees dispose of existing securities without having in contemplation an immediate reinvestment, they will be responsible for any losses which might occur."

J. Tiffany & E. Bullard, *The Law of Trusts and Trustees* 615 (1862). If a manager intends to liquidate blindly, he should at least disclose that fact to a prospective client.

[96] See, e.g., Estate of Stetson, 463 Pa. 64, 345 A.2d 679 (1975) (trustee not liable for loss in value of stock having no effective market where trustee diligently attempted to arrange private sale). For a more extended discussion on the authorities dealing with the meaning of a reasonable time, see ¶ 6.02[2].

reasons for delaying action, the important point is that once the manager has had a reasonable time to take them into account, he must act.

For analytic purposes, one should recognize that the duty to dispose of unsuitable commitments is actually a legal incentive to engage in positive management practices which will improve a client's chances of accomplishing his investment objectives. This incentive forces an investment manager to compare the characteristics of a portfolio newly placed under his control with those he should be seeking in order to accomplish his client's investment objectives. The manager may want to dispose of some commitments because the portfolio should be seeking a lower level of systematic risk, or because the portfolio has too much unsystematic risk, or because it is difficult to obtain an accurate appraisal of the vital statistics of one or more of the commitments initially in the portfolio.[97] These kinds of considerations are aspects of positive management—steps taken because the result will be better for the client. Delays for reasons which are not equally compelling, or worse, for no reason at all, are sure to be regarded as unreasonable.[98]

The major practical problems that an investment manager faces when making adjustments in an existing portfolio are that: (1) The portfolio will suffer avoidable losses as a result of delay; or (2) the commitments the manager closes will show better performance than the ones substituted for them. In the face of these conflicting possibilities, the manager should be prepared to show that he acted in accordance with accepted investment management principles. That is, measured against the bounds of reasonable disagreement among professional investment managers, and considered from the perspective of the time at which the decision to delay or to restructure was made, one should be able to conclude that it was reasonable for the manager to expect his decision to be a better means of accomplishing the client's investment objectives than would have been the case otherwise. If loss from delay is the issue, the manager should be able to establish that, having exercised due diligence in attempting to determine the advisabil-

---

[97] This is not to say that every investment manager will analyze portfolios by reference to systematic risk, unsystematic risk, and so forth, in those specific terms. A manager who determines that a portfolio contains the securities of too many unseasoned companies may not say that he is reducing the level of systematic risk of the portfolio; or when he determines to achieve greater diversification, that he is reducing unsystematic risk. These, however, are the terms derived from modern portfolio theory and developed in this chapter, and they are adequate to describe such portfolio adjustments.

[98] See ¶ 6.02[2].

ity of retaining the questioned securities initially placed under his control, he reasonably believed that earlier action could have involved greater costs than the apparent benefit. If loss from restructuring is the issue, the manager should be able to defend his actions on the ground that, based on a reasonable evaluation of the securities initially placed under his control, his actions were called for (1) to improve portfolio diversification (reduce the unsystematic risk); (2) to bring the portfolio into closer conformity with the client's investment objectives (achieve the proper systematic risk); or (3) to conform with the manager's chosen investment approach (obtain unsystematic returns the substituted commitments being more likely to produce unsystematic returns than those disposed of). In that event, upon a proper showing through documentary evidence, expert testimony, and the like, the mere fact of loss would remain as the sole basis for imposing liability. The reasonable but erroneous exercise of judgment has never been held grounds for so doing.[99]

¶ 7.07. MAKING A PORTFOLIO PRODUCTIVE

Pure investment theory postulates that expected return on a portfolio is directly proportional to the systematic risk of the portfolio.[100] Empirical testing of the theory shows that, on the average, a portfolio will experience unsystematic returns or losses.[101] If, as modified to accommodate empirical findings, the theoretical model is an accurate statement of the investment opportunities facing an investment manager, the duty to make a portfolio productive consists of three elements:

(1) Structuring the portfolio to contain the level of systematic risk indicated by the client's investment objectives;

---

[99] This is not to say that no one has ever been held liable for an error of judgment which, under the circumstances, was not unreasonable. The administration of justice occasionally miscarries, and one must protect himself as much as possible against such an event. In a case severely criticized by Professor Scott, for example, a New Jersey court reduced the compensation due the executors of an estate because they had not anticipated the stock market crash of 1929. *In re* Chamberlain, 9 N.J. Misc. 809, 156 A. 42 (1931). See 3 Scott, note 55 *supra,* § 227. But even in this extreme example, the point of law was not that the executors had reached a wrong judgment, but that their exercise of judgment was unreasonable. As Professor Scott also points out, the prescience demanded in the *Chamberlain* case was later rejected by a different New Jersey court. People's Nat'l Bank & Trust Co. of Pemberton v. Bichler, 115 N.J.Eq. 617, 172 A. 207 (1934).

[100] See ¶ 7.03[2] *supra.*
[101] See ¶ 7.04, notes 43-46 *supra.*

(2) Minimizing unsystematic risk; and

(3) Adopting strategies intended to provide unsystematic returns to the extent possible.

Even under real-world conditions, the first element of the duty to make a portfolio productive, achieving a proper level of systematic risk, is a relatively easy task once a client's investment objectives are determined and quantified. Systematic risk is determined by the beta coefficient of a portfolio, which, in turn, is simply the average, weighted by concentration, of the beta coefficients of the constituent securities. The second element, minimization of unsystematic risk, is also relatively uncomplicated. Unsystematic risk can be eliminated through diversification. The actual degree of diversification needed to reduce unsystematic risk satisfactorily is discussed more fully below,[102] but for present purposes it is enough to say that, as a practical matter, full diversification can be achieved by holding a sufficient number of different securities which are not highly correlated. The difficult problem in structuring a portfolio is adopting a strategy which satisfies the third element of the duty to make a portfolio productive.

Investment strategies consistently capable of providing unsystematic returns are hard to find. Virtually all recent studies of investment management performance indicate that no investment strategy consistently provides better than average returns.[103] The significance of this finding is that, even though testing of the capital asset pricing model indicates that, on the average, achieving unsystematic returns may be possible, no generally known investment strategies seem capable of consistently doing so.

Since this is a rather striking conclusion, let us identify its source in greater detail. During the 1960s, evidence began to mount that secu-

---

[102] See ¶ 7.08 *infra*.

[103] See Lorie & Hamilton, note 11 *supra*, at 105-110, 141; Langbein & Posner, note 55 *supra*, at 6-18; Elia, "Institutions Find It Tough to Outperform Index Regardless of the Market's Direction," Wall Street J., Nov. 14, 1975, p. 37, col. 3 (study of bank-managed funds, insurance equity funds, independent advisory portfolios, and mutual funds showing no special ability regularly to exceed average market performance); Laing, "On the Average: More Pension Funds Try to Tie the Market Instead of Beating It," Wall Street J., Nov. 12, 1975, p. 1, col. 6 (report on investment managers adopting passive investment strategies because of apparent futility of applying positive investment strategies to achieve superior returns). But cf. "How Tweedy, Browne Does It," 93 Fortune 94 (March 1976) (investment partnership reported to outperform market for fifteen out of sixteen years).

rities prices move in a "random walk"—that is, that movement in the price of a security is independent of its previous price. This evidence became the foundation of the efficient-market hypothesis, and the random-walk assertion became the statement of the hypothesis in its weak form.[104] Additional investigation led to two other statements of the efficient-market hypothesis: (1) the semi-strong form, which asserts that current prices of securities have fully discounted the value of all public information and that above-average returns cannot be obtained by the acquisition and analysis of such information; and (2) the strong form, which asserts that even those with inside information cannot consistently make use of it profitably.[105]

The obvious question raised by the efficient-market hypothesis is how legal doctrine should respond. Certainly, strategies that deliber-

---

[104] A statement of the conditions required to create an efficient market appear in Kuehner, "Efficient Markets and Random Walk," in S. Levine, *Financial Analyst's Handbook* 1226, 1227-1228 (1975) (hereinafter cited as *Financial Analyst's Handbook*). They include:

(1) Rapid and free dissemination of news among actual and potential investors;

(2) Rational investors who will choose assets offering the greatest return at any level of risk and the lowest risk at any level of return;

(3) The potential for prices to change rapidly without the intercession of devices to resist such changes;

(4) Low transaction costs, meaning that commission, taxes, the cost of acquiring information not be so great as to impede investors from implementing their investment decisions; and

(5) Continuous trading allowing all transactions, whether large or small, to be executed rapidly.

Compare Kuehner's statement of the conditions necessary for an efficient market with the assumptions on which the capital asset pricing model is based, note 32 *supra*.

[105] For a full discussion of the efficient-market hypothesis and the evidence to support it, see Lorie & Hamilton, note 11 *supra*, at 70-110. The authors offer the strong form tentatively, conceding that unlike institutional investors, corporate insiders can use inside information profitably. Their reluctance is understandable, since it seems clear that true inside information —i.e., information which the general market has not had time to digest, evaluate, and discount—presents genuine opportunities for unusual returns. Other interpretations of the evidence cited by the authors include the possibilities (1) that the legal definition of materiality of inside information is overinclusive in that most such information cannot provide unusual returns, and (2) that investment managers do not receive such information with a frequency or in a degree sufficient to affect overall performance significantly. See note 144 *infra*.

ately undertake unsystematic risk but are demonstrably incapable of producing unsystematic returns on the average are professionally indefensible and hence do not satisfy the requirements of ordinary skill and care as a matter of law, whatever the accuracy of the efficient-market hypothesis.[106] But the plain implication of the hypothesis is that unsystematic returns are not obtainable on any regular basis. If the hypothesis is accurate, it seems that no investment strategy designed to obtain unsystematic returns would be legally permissible since, according to the hypothesis, no strategy will provide better than average performance over time. In view of the evidence in support of the hypothesis, one might conclude that if unsystematic risk is deliberately undertaken, a manager faces a heavy burden of showing that his strategy is at least as capable of meeting a client's objectives as would be a bench-mark portfolio derived from the capital asset pricing model.

Nonetheless, despite the implications of the efficient-market hypothesis, efforts to achieve unsystematic returns are appropriate and, in most cases, probably required by law. As the discussion below will show,[107] the diversification necessary to carry out a passive strategy derived from the capital asset pricing model and concentrating on common stocks can reach two hundred stocks. Few investors are in a position to buy so extensively. Furthermore, at this stage of development, such strategies have been studied extensively only for common stocks—and for the most well-known, highly traded and visible common stocks at that —because a passive strategy depends on there being a highly efficient market. Most portfolios are far more broadly based.[108] But most important, for a strategy based only on systematic risk, which is by

---

[106] The studies of professional investors and academicians have undercut more than one plausible investment strategy through testing of the available data. A good illustration of an investment strategy contradicted in this fashion is reliance on reported earnings to evaluate growth rates. In the 1960s, it became a matter of conviction in some quarters that firms which could report higher earnings by accounting gimmickry short of fraud would be more highly valued by the market than if generally accepted accounting principles had been applied in a fashion showing a reasonably accurate picture of company progress from accounting period to accounting period, and some investors made commitments in this belief. The evidence now indicates that the market has been fairly effective in discriminating between earnings supported by accounting manipulation and earnings resulting from real growth. See Lorie & Hamilton, note 11 *supra,* at 154-155.

[107] See ¶ 7.08 *infra.*

[108] See, e.g., Connelly, "The New Emphasis on Portfolio Mix," 8 Institutional Investor 39 (Aug. 1974).

definition capable of achieving only average returns,[109] to displace all positive investment strategies, which the evidence shows tend mostly to achieve average returns, there would have to be a showing either that no positive strategy could do better, or that the pursuit of such a strategy would ordinarily be too expensive to clients to justify developing and applying. But neither showing is likely to be made. For one thing, tests of the capital asset pricing model already demonstrate that unsystematic returns are possible.[110] Even assuming that no consistently superior investment strategy has yet been discovered by the researchers, the most this implies is that such a strategy is still awaiting discovery. Moreover, even assuming further that most investment managers are unlikely to discover such a strategy, there is still no convincing demonstration that the purely passive investment strategy, as indicated by the capital asset pricing model and as carried out by index fund investors, produces measurably greater investment returns than are produced by positive strategies, taking into account all management costs and adjusting for differences in risk undertaken.[111]

But this kind of reaction to the passive investment approach indi-

------

[109] See Laing, "On the Average: More Pension Funds Try to Tie the Market Instead of Beating It," Wall Street J., Nov. 12, 1975, p. 1, col. 6; Black & Scholes, "From Theory to a New Financial Product," 29 J. Fin. 399 (1974) (discussion of one bank's experience with managing a portfolio based on an investment strategy derived from the capital asset pricing model).

[110] See ¶ 7.04, at notes 43-46 *supra*.

[111] The principal saving available from pursuing a strategy based on the capital asset pricing model is lower commission expenses. Positive strategies can lead to heavy trading, and the evidence is that some institutional investors were turning over their portfolios 50 percent, 100 percent, and even more in the recent past. See SEC, *Institutional Investor Study,* H.R. Doc. No. 64, 92d Cong., 1st Sess., Ch. IV at 189, Ch. V at 464, Ch. VI at 736-737 (1971). Trading volume is almost entirely related to the belief that superior timing is capable of producing above-average returns. But while timing is certainly an element of investment decision-making, the evidence indicates that attempts to time the market do not lead to superior results. See Sharpe, "Likely Gains from Market Timing," 31 Fin. Anal. J. 60 (March-April 1975). But see Gray, "Index Funds and Market Timing: Harris Trust's Approach," 115 Trusts & Estates 314 (1976). On the contrary, the efficiency of the market makes it as difficult to call market turns in a fashion one can take advantage of as it does to pick individual securities that will perform well or poorly. All this only suggests that the expense of timing strategies makes them inferior to other positive investment strategies. It does not mean that all positive strategies are necessarily much more expensive than the passive approach based on the capital asset pricing model.

cated by the capital asset pricing model and reinforced by the efficient market hypothesis is essentially a burden-of-proof argument. The fact is that, in a highly efficient market, average performance seems to be the only constant observed among professional investment managers,[112] and the implication seems to be—indeed, it is already being argued with respect to pension managers—that investors should not try so hard when the rewards of trying are predictable and the cost of trying may be high.[113] Certainly, at some point, absent some justification, the law will begin to frown on attempts at investing according to positive strategies which produce below-average returns.

Such a justification exists, however; indeed, it virtually requires investment managers to pursue positive strategies in attempting to meet their clients' investment objectives. To see why this is so, one must understand why there is no such thing as an investment strategy which is capable of producing above-average returns consistently. Suppose it were the case that over a given period a particular strategy provided above-average returns. Assuming pure luck is not the explanation for these results, continuing success for that investment strategy would depend on two circumstances: It would have to remain secret, or at least generally unrecognized; and the conditions that made it successful would have to remain unchanged. Neither of these circumstances is likely over a long period.

The reason that lack of recognition is required is that general knowledge and use destroy the effectiveness of a strategy. If everyone is doing the same thing, everyone is obviously accomplishing the same results. For only a few to achieve results better than others, therefore, the many must remain in ignorance of the superior methods. But even with the most diligent efforts at maintaining secrecy, general recognition will ultimately prevail. As other investors discover that one of their number has developed a method of achieving above-average returns, they will study his actions to learn his strategy. At some point, others will learn the method and will copy it. After a time, it will become one

---

[112] See, e.g., Lorie & Hamilton, note 11 *supra,* at 70-97.

[113] See Langbein & Posner, note 55 *supra,* at 30, in which the authors ask, almost rhetorically, whether there might be a duty for pension trustees to invest in a fully diversified market fund as a strategy based on the capital asset pricing model would require. They have retreated from this position somewhat, however, though they have extended their basis arguments to apply to all trustees. Langbein & Posner, "Market Funds and Trust-Investment Law: II," 2 Am. Bar Found. Research J. 1, 9, 21-24 (1977).

more strategy which too many people use at the same time to guarantee consistently superior performance.[114]

The second and more critical reason why no investment strategy is capable of consistently producing above-average returns is that conditions change too rapidly in the real world for it to be otherwise. Even if a given strategy were capable of regularly producing above-average returns under a given set of conditions, other strategies would be required during periods when different conditions prevailed. These other strategies would generally have to provide at least average returns if the overall record were to remain above average. As a practical matter, therefore, superior investment management requires familiarity with a set of investment strategies, each proper in different investment environments, and each applied at the proper time.

The rub is that, in the professional investment management community, which controls most of the assets making up the market and, hence, effectively is the market,[115] knowledge of which strategies to use under varying investment conditions is general. Such disagreement as occurs focuses on what conditions are prevailing rather than on what to do in the face of a particular set of conditions. This means that for an investment manager to produce above-average returns consistently, he must be capable of shifting investment strategies in anticipation of changing conditions in advance of the remainder of the investment community. Given the level of talent and ability generally possessed by professional investment managers, it is unreasonable for their clients to expect consistently above-average returns on that ground. At best, only a few managers can apply conventional investment strategies more effectively than other managers—and then, only for a small portion of the market.

But it is a treacherous step to go from the observation that professional investment managers provide average returns, adjusted for risk undertaken, to the conclusion that the strategies they utilize provide

---

114 See Lorie & Hamilton, note 11 *supra,* at 103. For a well-written explanation of how widespread discovery of an investment strategy soon ruins its effectiveness, see Rozeff, "The Money Supply and the Stock Market: The Demise of a Leading Indicator," 31 Fin. Anal. J. 18 (Sept.-Oct. 1975). Of course, a great deal is written touting various kinds of investment strategies, but as is commonly noted, one indicator that a previously successful investment strategy has become part of the public domain, and is therefore no longer useful, is the fact that someone has written about it. Otherwise, he would continue to use it for his own benefit.

115 Schotland, "Bank Trust Departments and Public Policy Today," 4 Sec. Reg. L.J. 389 (1977).

no benefit and therefore are unnecessary. For one thing, an inadequately informed application of positive investment strategies is almost certain to produce below-average returns. Consider what is likely to happen to an investor, or investment manager, for that matter, unfamiliar with the full range and application of generally recognized investment strategies. Since such an investor, by definition, does not know as well as most of the rest of the market what to do as conditions change, or at least is slower than most to respond properly to changed conditions, he will be unable to select securities and adjust his portfolio before most others have already begun responding to changes he has failed to perceive. Only good fortune can protect such an investor from experiencing lower returns over time than otherwise might be expected for the level of risk undertaken. Thus, it is no coincidence that, as a class, individual investors fare the worst in the securities markets.[116]

But there are two more fundamental reasons for pursuing positive investment strategies than simply avoiding below-average returns. First, a passive strategy derived from the capital asset pricing model depends on the use of positive investment strategies and the existence of a highly efficient market. Presumably, the approach suggested by the model and implied in the efficient-market hypothesis will provide average returns. Unfortunately, like other investment strategies, it will work only for so long as most investors eschew it.[117] The strategy dictated by the model

---

[116] In other words, much of the expertise of a professional investment manager is directed at insuring that the expected return of a portfolio is in fact realized.

[117] Even the strongest proponents of an investment strategy based on the capital asset pricing model admit this. See, e.g., Lorie & Hamilton, note 11 *supra,* at 98; Langbein & Posner, note 55 *supra,* at 18. Professors Langbein and Posner argue, however, that it is not likely that all trustees will adopt a " 'buy the market and hold' " strategy and that, in any event, other investors will continue to search out advantageous investment opportunities in stocks. But their contention that not all trustees will follow the passive strategy dictated by the capital asset pricing model is puzzling in view of the position they later take that, as market-investment vehicles become available, trustees may have a duty to buy the market. *Id.* at 30. Furthermore, if they are correct that trustees will or should be obliged to buy the market, their contention that the passive strategy they advocate will remain effective also is difficult to understand. The efficiency of the market in valuing securities is a function, among other things, of the energy all investors expend in analyzing information pertinent to evaluating them. See note 104 *supra.* Trustees for pensions, foundations, common trust funds, and the like account for a large proportion of the market. According to the SEC (SEC, *Institutional Investor Study,* H.R. Doc. No. 64, 92d Cong., 1st

requires a manager to maintain the proper level of risk, measured by volatility, and to adjust the portfolio only as the volatility of constituent securities changes enough to affect the volatility of the portfolio. Since the volatility of component securities is measured by the band of historical price movement,[118] execution of the strategy would take place without any reference to current public information about the accomplishments and prospects of the companies concerned.[119] But if everyone began investing this way, volatility calculations for individual securities, and consequently for portfolios, would become worthless. Investing without regard to available information means that prices would move independently of changing conditions since no one would be taking such conditions into account in buying or selling a security. In other words, it would make no difference whether a company were large or small, profitable or unprofitable, well-managed or poorly managed, or any other such thing. Price movements would be determined by some irrational process, and, paradoxically, the condition necessarily for the capital asset pricing model to function, the existence of an efficient market, would disappear.[120]

Second, extensive reliance on passive investment strategies would offer some investors an unwarranted competitive advantage, and as a practical matter, therefore, widespread adoption of totally passive investment strategies could never happen. Serious investors would like nothing better than to have everyone else adopt a purely agnostic attitude toward using available information to predict prices in the capital markets. The opportunities for profit in such circumstances would be enormous because all the conventional strategies would still anticipate

---

Sess., Summary Vol., Ch. V, at 34), commercial bank trust departments administered $280 billion in assets, of which $180 billion was in common stock. In contrast, investment advisory complexes managed $130 billion, and only $54 billion of that was held by mutual funds (*id*. Ch. IV, at 19. If a large segment of the investor community were, in effect, to drop out of the process of valuing securities, the result for the passive investors would be to increase the instability of the individual betas of all securities and hence the volatility of the portfolio as a whole. There would surely come a point at which these trustees would recognize that the cost of research and securities analysis would pay for itself by improving predictability of portfolio return—i.e., reducing risk.

[118] Modigliani & Pogue, note 24 *supra*, Pt. II at 70-77.

[119] Not only is taking current information into account useless, according to the theory, to acquire information and to evaluate it would cost money. In short, it would be subversive of the strategy to attempt to use such information.

[120] See note 104 *supra*.

price movements, but with few people utilizing those strategies, the need to be correct early in order to profit would not be as great. Indeed, if one could be certain that other investors would forego all attempts to predict securities prices and market movements, an investor could wait until he was virtually positive about what was likely to happen before making any commitment. Consequently, absent a perfectly enforced agreement among investment managers to ignore investment data, simple competition to achieve better profits provides an irresistible incentive to identify and apply the investment strategies which seem to be called for under the circumstances.

Furthermore, as additional incentive for pursuing positive strategies in managing portfolios, a competitive advantage can be gained through the discovery of new insights into pricing relationships in the marketplace. Although the reference in this discussion to generally accepted investment strategies may seem to imply that such strategies are static— that is, that they exist in the same form and the same diversity in each successive investment period—associations between phenomena in the marketplace are discovered regularly, and they remain effective in providing above-average returns for so long as those associations remain strong.[121] On the other hand, these associations do not offer a permanent means for obtaining unusual gains. As pointed out above, success breeds imitators and imitation undermines success. Strategies capable of producing above-average returns for a time are doomed ultimately to become part of the stock of generally held professional knowledge. As more and more investors apply them, prices in the marketplace will respond more rapidly and the opportunity for individual investors to take advantage of the association will disappear. Nonetheless, the fact that a strategy can remain effective in producing above-average returns only while it enjoys its moment of comparative secrecy simply makes the drive for new discoveries relentless. Investors know that, however well their portfolios are performing, continued success depends on further advances in knowledge.

[1] Capital Asset Pricing and the Productive Portfolio: Legal Standards

If legal doctrine should to any extent denominate the capital asset pricing model as the standard investment strategy for investment managers, it should require no more than that the less capable a manager is

---

[121] See, e.g., White, "Is Credit Analysis a Growth Industry?" 10 Institutional Investor 57 (Jan. 1976); Rozeff, "The Money Supply: The Demise of a Leading Indicator," 31 Fin. Anal. J. 18 (Sept.-Oct. 1975).

in remaining familiar with the substance and execution of generally accepted investment strategies, the more he should adopt the passive approach suggested by the capital asset pricing model. In effect, such an investment strategy is parasitic to ordinary security and market analysis. It concedes that conventional investment strategies cannot outperform the market, but that the competent and diligent application of such strategies by others keeps the market efficient—that is, prices change rapidly to reflect changes in conditions accurately and too rapidly for most investors to profit on those changes.[122] By seeking full diversification at the proper level of risk, a manager can buy average returns, adjusted for risk, for so long as the market continues to maintain its efficiency.

But even if the capital asset pricing model cannot establish a mandatory strategy for investment managers,[123] that does not mean its teachings are irrelevant to the law. Investment managers must make a portfolio productive. They must do so with ordinary skill and care. The capital asset pricing model raises serious questions about strategies which are expensive to carry out—for example, the once popular strategies involving heavy turnover.[124] Furthermore, the model acts as a bench mark for positive investment strategies. The further the actual performance of a portfolio deliberately exposed to unsystematic risk diverges from the return achievable from a fully diversified portfolio at the same level of systematic risk, the greater will be the burden on the manager to defend his strategy. In cases where the divergence is especially great, a diligent client or regulator is almost sure to find something the manager neglected or ignored on which to base a case of professional negligence. Finally, the model and the testing of it demonstrate that the competitive edge in pursuit of unsystematic gains, if available at all, is small. This suggests that the legal standard applied to the portfolios of most investors will comprehend, absent an informed client consent to the contrary, strategies mixing the passive approach indicated by the model with one or more positive strategies. Most of a portfolio will consist of a well-diversified base of securities, with managers' activism generally reserved for a relatively few securities.[125]

---

122 See note 104 *supra.*

123 But cf. Langbein & Posner, note 55 *supra,* at 30.

124 See note 111 *supra.*

125 See, e.g., Graham, "The Future of Common Stocks," 30 Fin. Anal. J. 20 (Sept.-Oct. 1974). But see Belliveau, "Will Pension Officers Stop Trying to Beat the Market?" 10 Institutional Investor 18, 19 (Feb. 1976), in which Professor Posner reportedly took the position, since abandoned (see

As this standard develops, investment managers claiming strategies capable of significant departures from average, adjusted for risk, will become virtual warrantors of their performance because of the doubtful validity of such claims.[126]

If these speculations correctly anticipate the probable impact of modern portfolio theory on the law, they raise a related issue. There will be a need to set standards against which to measure strategies designed to obtain unsystematic returns. Until now, the law has gauged investment strategies against a generous negligence standard: So long as there was no violation of a statute circumscribing investment discre-

---

Langbein & Posner, "Market Funds and Trust-Investment Law," 2 Am. Bar Found. J. 1, 22-23 (1977)), that such an approach is "highly illogical" in that it involves two inconsistent strategies. But even theoretically, it is not illogical for every well-diversified portfolio which possesses fewer than every security available in the market to seek some unsystematic returns through a positive investment strategy. The return on each security consists of its systematic return and its unsystematic return (see ¶ 7.03[1] *supra*). Since the market does not value unsystematic risk, the expected value of unsystematic return is zero. But that does not mean there will be no unsystematic return in a given investment period or in a series of investment periods. An expected value of zero means only that, over the time, the return will average zero.

Now consider what happens in a well-diversified portfolio. Each security contributes both systematic and unsystematic return. If all securities in the portfolio are selected randomly and only for the purpose of achieving the proper beta coefficient for the investor, one would expect the unsystematic returns—the total of the unexpected gains added to unexpected losses (actual dollar losses plus gains less than expected returns) for all component securities—to cancel each other out because of the large numbers involved. If an investment manager could find a strategy that would force the unsystematic returns on component securities to complement each other over an investment period instead of canceling each other out, he could enhance actual portfolio return (or, if he successfully lines up the unsystematic returns of component securities but adopts an erroneous strategy, he would cut into portfolio return). The critical question in determining whether to seek and apply positive strategies, and, unfortunately, a question which ordinarily cannot be answered in advance, is whether the cost of finding and relying on positive strategies which successfully take advantage of unsystematic returns will be less or greater than the additional returns generated thereby.

[126] See, e.g., Trustees of Hanover College v. Donaldson, Lufkin & Jenrette, Inc., Civil No. 71-C686 (S.D. Ind. 1971), in which a broker-dealer manager allegedly represented it would achieve a 12 percent return a year, but actually achieved only about half that figure. The case, discussed more fully at ¶ 7.04[2] at note 59 *supra*, was ultimately settled.

tion, only the most egregious conduct has led to liability.[127] One can see the limited development of means to measure the adequacy of an investment strategy in the current state of trust law and agency law. Although the negligence principle has been applicable for many years to the design and execution of investment strategies by investment managers, neither agency nor trust law has gone much beyond a generalized statement of the manager to investigate investment opportunities, to secure information from available sources, and to exercise at least average skill in evaluating what he has learned.[128]

But the efficient-market hypothesis and the capital asset pricing model place a great deal of pressure on investment strategies seeking unsystematic returns. Accordingly, one can expect more penetrating inquiry into these strategies and a greater demand that they justify themselves. It is possible, of course, that any increase in legal scrutiny will progress in common-law fashion through refinements in trust and agency doctrine, supplemented by expansion of state securities regulation. Already, however, two important developments at the federal level foreshadow both the location and direction of most of the growth of the law. Although it is too early to tell what the final scheme will be, federal legislation is becoming more and more concerned with setting standards of management.

The first real sign of this concern appeared in the Investment Company Amendments Act of 1970, in which Congress authorized the SEC to issue rules defining, and thereby rendering unlawful, "fraudulent, deceptive or manipulative" practices.[129] The significant thing about this antifraud provision is that Congress expressly authorized the Commission to include "requirements for the adoption of codes of ethics" for investment companies and their advisers.[130] Shortly thereafter, Congress expressly adopted a negligence standard for the management

---

127 See, e.g., Spiegel v. Beacon Participations, Inc., 297 Mass. 398, 8 N.E.2d 895 (1937). See also ¶ 6.01.

128 See *Restatement (Second) of Trusts* § 227, Comments b, c (1959); 3 Scott, note 11 *supra*, §§ 227.1-227.2; *Restatement (Second) of Agency* § 425, Comment a (1958).

129 Investment Company Amendments Act of 1970, Pub. L. 91-547 § 9(c), 84 Stat. 1421 (Dec. 14, 1970). See also note 17.

130 15 U.S.C. § 80a-17(j). The section was directed more at personal and institutional trading practices of investment company advisers than at negligence, and despite apparent early interest, the SEC has, for the time being, no plans to issue ethical codes. Nonetheless, Section 17(j) is the first general antifraud provision in the Act, and the degree to which it will parallel the growth of the other federal securities antifraud provisions remains to be seen.

of employee benefit plans by incorporating the prudent-man rule of the law of trusts into the Employee Retirement Income Security Act of 1974[131] and imposing personal liability on plan fiduciaries.[132] Indeed, Congress went further than the common law of trusts. It also prohibited plan fiduciaries from exculpating themselves for their negligence.[133] Since most standard trust agreements contain provisions exculpating trustees for negligent mismanagement, and since the validity of such provisions at common law, though growing increasingly doubtful,[134] has support in precedent, the federal rule virtually guarantees that aggrieved plaintiffs will choose a federal forum and federal law. Furthermore, interest in direct federal regulation of the investment practices of investment managers on grounds of competence seems to be growing. Commissioners of the SEC and spokesmen for the investment management community have been arguing for tighter regulation of the profession.[135] Even while Congress was considering the Securities Acts Amendments of 1975,[136] the chairman of the House subcommittee responsible for that legislation suggested that the Investment Advisers Act of 1940 was ripe for reconsideration.[137] Partly in response to this interest and partly in response to its own concern with management practices, the SEC submitted late in 1975 a bill to amend the Act to authorize, among other things, the setting of standards of competence for investment advisers.[138]

The second important development concerning application of a federal negligence standard to the investment practices of investment

---

[131] ERISA § 404(a)(1)(B), 29 U.S.C. § 1104(a)(1)(B).

[132] Id. § 409, 29 U.S.C. § 1109.

[133] Id. § 410, 29 U.S.C. § 1110.

[134] See ¶ 5.02[2].

[135] Two Commissioners spoke out on the issue well in advance of the SEC's introduction of a bill (see note 138 *infra*) to amend the Investment Advisers Act to permit the SEC to set standards of professional qualifications. See Owens, "Investment Adviser Regulation: A Subject Too Long Neglected," 29 Fin. Anal. J. 12 (Jan.-Feb. 1973); Commissioner Sommer's call for federal regulation is reported in the Wall Street Letter, Feb. 11, 1974, p. 5. For a sampling of industry sentiment, see Hedberg, "Let's Regulate Investment Advice," 29 Fin. Anal. J. 24 (May-June 1973); Nelson, "Let's Make Investment Advisers Accountable," 29 Fin. Anal. J. 19 (Jan.-Feb. 1973).

[136] Pub. L. 94-29, 89 Stat. 97 (June 4, 1975).

[137] While he was still Chairman, Congressman Moss said that his Subcommittee's next project would be an inquiry into the need for legislative changes in the Investment Advisers Act. See Wall Street Letter, Sept. 16, 1974, p. 1.

[138] S. 2849, 94th Cong., 2d Sess. (1976).

managers has occurred through the extension of the existing statutory fraud provisions of the federal securities laws. This extension has proceeded on two fronts. First, the SEC has been taking the position that it is fraudulent to fail to perform competently when there has been a representation of competence. In *Financial Programs, Inc.*,[139] the SEC accepted an offer of settlement from a mutual fund and two portfolio managers on the grounds that through the portfolio managers, the fund had invested in unseasoned, limited-float securities largely on the recommendations of an institutional salesman. The prospectuses of the fund had represented that it was managed by competent persons. Other enforcement actions have been introducing the negligence standard in similar fashion.[140]

Second, the Commission has begun extending the reasonable-basis doctrine to securities analysis, the cornerstone of most investment strategies. Although the reasonable-basis doctrine grew out of the boiler-room cases in which broker-dealers combined optimistic predictions with high-pressure sales tactics to solicit orders,[141] it now seems evident that, before recommending the purchase of a security, a broker-dealer must have determined reasonably ascertainable facts.[142] Since investment managers generally have more influence on their clients' portfolios than broker-dealers do on the portfolios of their customers, it seems that, as the reasonable-basis doctrine is applied to managers, their obligations can only be greater. Thus, in *Winfield & Co.*,[143] the

---

[139] *In re* Financial Programs, Inc., SEC Securities Exchange Act Release No. 11,312 (March 24, 1975), [1974-1975 Transfer Binder] CCH Fed. Sec. L. Rep. ¶ 80,146. Another enforcement action arising out of the same incident is Thomas J. Herbert, d/b/a Pembroke Management Co., SEC Securities Exchange Act Release No. 11,496 (June 26, 1975).

[140] See, e.g., Ralph T. Lachman, SEC Securities Exchange Act Release No. 11,569 (Aug. 1, 1975); SEC v. Seaboard Corp., SEC Litigation Release No. 6269 (C.D. Cal. March 5, 1974). But see Ernst & Ernst v. Hochfelder, 425 U.S. 185 (1976), discussed in detail in ¶ 6.01, note 5 *supra*.

[141] See, e.g., Brudney, "Origins and Applicability of the 'Reasonable Basis' or 'Know Your Merchandise' Doctrine," in *Fourth Annual Institute on Securities Regulation*, note 59 *supra*, at 239-243.

[142] See Hiller v. SEC, 429 F.2d 856 (2d Cir. 1970); Hanly v. SEC, 415 F.2d 589 (2d Cir. 1969); Dlugash v. SEC, 373 F.2d 107 (2d Cir. 1967); R. A. Holman & Co. v. SEC, 366 F.2d 446 (2d Cir. 1966), *cert. denied* 389 U.S. 991 (1967).

[143] SEC Securities Exchange Act Release No. 9478 (Feb. 9, 1972). Professor Brudney suggests that the result in this case be considered in light of the special obligations created by the Investment Company Act. See Brudney, note 141 *supra*, at 245. Nonetheless, the SEC handled *Winfield* as a case involving statutory fraud and not simply a violation of the Invest-

SEC imposed disciplinary sanctions on the grounds that the advisers to a mutual fund unreasonably failed to determine that some of the securities they selected were restricted, they did not secure "pertinent information" about the securities they had placed in the fund's portfolio, and they relied too heavily on questionable research provided by others.

One can argue that the SEC's reliance on representations of competence on the one hand and the reasonable-basis doctrine on the other are really two sides of the same coin. After all, the authority to recommend a security to or include a security in the portfolio of a client derives from the unstated assumption on the client's part that the manager has the expertise to make such a judgment and that he has exercised that expertise. In any event, given the movement toward development of an all-encompassing federal standard of negligence applicable to investment managers and the already established negligence principle under state law, a more important question than where the law stands today is how the law of negligence is likely to impact on the use of positive investment strategies by investment managers.

[2] Positive Investment Strategies and the Productive Portfolio: Legal Standards

The general problem facing an investment manager desirous of applying positive investment strategies is how to obtain unsystematic returns. This can be accomplished only if the market price of a security does not accurately discount the probable impact of all events which can cause changes in it. A successful investment strategy, therefore, will have one of two characteristics: Either it will anticipate, better than the marketplace, price changes in an individual security as a result of events specifically associated with that security; or it will anticipate, better than the market, price movements of the entire market. If an investment manager can anticipate ahead of the great mass of other investors either price movement independent of market movement or general market movements, he can obtain higher returns for any given level of systematic risk in his portfolio.

For purposes of analysis, it is helpful to classify investment strategies as either conventional or unconventional. Conventional strategies are those generally known or available to professional investment managers; unconventional strategies are those that are either in the process of

---

ment Company Act. See also Blakely v. Lisac, 357 F. Supp. 255 (D. Ore. 1972), 357 F. Supp. 267 (D. Ore. 1973) (person represented in prospectus as financial consultant must make minimal investigation into accuracy of prospectus).

development and testing or, if of proven worth, known only to a few. It is also useful to classify investment strategies according to one of two principal schools of investment philosophy. One, fundamental analysis, evaluates available public data and applies its conclusions to different pricing models in order to increase the predictive power of those models. Most conventions associated with fundamental analysis are normally expressed algebraically. The other, technical analysis, focuses on securities price and volume data to discover historical trading patterns repeated with enough consistency to permit favorable forecasts of price and market movements. Relationships analyzed technically are normally expressed graphically.[144]

[a] Conventional strategies

The application of a negligence standard to investment strategies which are generally known raises a straightforward issue: Was the strategy a reasonable one to utilize under the circumstances? The legal issue involved in determining whether a manager's use of a conventional strategy is defensible is not whether he is right, but whether, based on information that he knew or should have known, his conclusion and the actions based thereon are reasonable.

As a simple example, consider interest rate projections, which can be an important factor in total portfolio management. Such projections may aid managers in deciding between commitments in stocks and bonds, particularly in industries which are sensitive to changes in in-

---

[144] Another means of improving portfolio returns, sometimes discussed as if it were a distinct investment approach, is the collection and use of material inside information. There is nothing distinctive about investment strategies which rely on inside information except that they tend to make conventional investment strategies more effective. By definition, material inside information concerns events about which the general market is unaware and, consequently, over which price remains to be affected. Inside information can be of a type likely to affect the price of the security on an individual company, as, for example, when secret explorations uncover rich mineral finds (see SEC v. Texas Gulf Sulphur Co., 401 F.2d 833 (2d Cir. 1968), *cert. denied* 404 U.S. 1005, *rehearing denied* 404 U.S. 1064 (1971)), or inside information can concern the market broadly, as would be the case if one had access in advance of the general public to plans of the Federal Reserve Board with respect to the money supply (cf. Rozeff, "The Money Supply and the Stock Market: The Demise of a Leading Indicator," 31 Fin. Anal. J. 18 (Sept.-Oct. 1975)). Investing in publicly traded issues on the basis of inside information is illegal, however, and will not be considered further in this section.

terest rates.[145] Furthermore, interest rate projections have a direct bearing both on the amount of cash reserves to be held away from longer-term commitments, and on the form in which such reserves will be held.[146] Whatever strategy an investment manager adopts based on his own interest rate projection, and how vigorously he acts on it, should depend upon the degree to which he believes that future interest rate changes have been properly discounted in the marketplace.[147] Thus, if the manager's projections are later proven wrong because of an abrupt shift in monetary policy by the Federal Reserve, there would be no grounds for attacking the strategy he adopted on the basis of those projections. But if his strategy was not suited to the conditions his projections indicated—as, for example, if he made a series of heavy commitments to long-term debt when the facts indicated the chance of a sharp rise in interest rates and consequently suggested caution in making such commitments—it is entirely possible that the manager could be held to answer for his actions, particularly if those instruments were purchased for investors unable to hold them to full term.

[b] Unconventional strategies

The utilization of investment strategies that purport to be new departures invokes a slightly different analysis of reasonableness and negligence. Plainly, some proof of the theoretical basis of a new strategy is required before a manager can fully rely on it. For example, during the 1960s, growth through regular increases in reported earnings seemed to some to have an excessive impact on the price movements of common stock. This seemed to indicate that there might be opportunities for profit by those particularly able in spotting accounting gimmickry used to inflate reported earnings. Some analysts apparently believed that inventory accounting offered one such opportunity since companies using the first-in, first-out (FIFO) system rather than the last-in, first-out (LIFO) system to account for their inventory reported higher earnings, other things being equal. The theory was that such companies were being priced higher in the marketplace. Though plausible, this theory would not have been a proper portfolio management tool, at least to justify substantial commitments, without first having been tested adequately. Indeed, as subsequent studies showed, the idea was highly

---

[145] See, e.g., Mennis, "An Integrated Approach to Portfolio Management," in *Financial Analyst's Handbook,* note 104 *supra,* 1207, 1210.
   [146] *Id.*
   [147] See, e.g., Lorie & Hamilton, note 11 *supra,* at 100.

simplistic and consequently erroneous.[148] Prices in the market generally showed that investors had properly discounted for the different inventory accounting systems.[149]

In contrast to the facile theoretical underpinnings of a model based on the FIFO/LIFO distinction is a stock valuation model which attempts to identify undervalued and overvalued stocks based on an unlimited-horizon forecast of earnings.[150] The forecast depends on several independent variables, ostensibly useful in calculating a price-earnings ratio reflecting the intrinsic worth of a common stock. The principle on which the model is based and which is supposed to identify opportunities for profit is that the intrinsic price-earnings ratio for all common stocks is determined in the same way, and that any divergence between an intrinsic price-earnings ratio and a market price-earnings ratio appearing in a particular issue would represent a disequilibrium that would tend to disappear over time. Whenever the disequilibrium is great enough, the theory posits, investors can profit by anticipating an inevitable move toward intrinsic value. This kind of thinking about pricing relationships in the capital markets is far more sophisticated than the FIFO/LIFO theory described above. Furthermore, the authors of this theory engaged in serious testing to prove its worth. Taking a large sample of common stocks, they produced data which indicated that the performance of portfolios could be improved slightly by application of the model. In this case, therefore, some positive action based

---

148 See Editorial, "The Market, Smart or Dumb?" Wall Street J., Oct. 1, 1974, p. 20, col. 1. In any event, it is doubtful that many investors will rely on the FIFO/LIFO distinction as an investment strategy in view of the widespread publicity given to the consequences of adopting one rather than the other. See, e.g., Bray, "New Sets of Books: More Companies Alter Accounting Methods to Neutralize Inflation," Wall Street J., Oct. 7, 1974, p. 1, col. 6. The SEC also requires that any method of inventory accounting shift from one to the other be fully disclosed in a company's annual report to stockholders. See SEC Accounting Series Release No. 169 (Jan. 23, 1975), CCH Fed. Sec. L. Rep. ¶ 72,191.

149 For another example of the market's effectiveness in discerning accounting gimmickry, see Lorie & Hamilton, note 11 supra, at 155, describing a study of mergers in which the assets of acquired firms were paid for by securities having an actual value which was difficult to determine because of deliberately complex financial arrangements. The study showed that after the merger, the risk-adjusted rate of return on these securities was comparable to the rate of return of the Standard & Poor's Composite Index. Lorie & Halpern, "Conglomerates: The Rhetoric and the Evidence," 13 J. Law & Econ. 149 (1970).

150 See Lorie & Hamilton, note 11 supra, at 129-131.

on the strategy derived from the theoretical insight would have been reasonable under the circumstances.[151]

But the reasonableness of reliance on unconventional strategies depends on more than the adequacy of pre-use testing. As with conventional strategies, reasonableness depends not only on the justifiability of the conclusion, but also on the action taken on the basis of the conclusion. The correlation between test results and future performance is never perfect, and overexuberant application of new discoveries can amount to professional negligence. Indeed, when one recognizes that litigation typically follows only when an account has suffered losses, one can appreciate the burden an investment manager would face in defending excessive application of a new strategy against application of a negligence standard. His claim of justification would be his certainty, based on his evaluation of existing data, of the success of the strategy. And yet, his very failure to produce unusual gains would probably be proof enough to a lay jury or a nonexpert judge of how misplaced his confidence was.

[c] Fundamental analysis

Fundamental analysis reflects the philosophy that the performance of a firm determines the price of its securities, and that the performance of the economy determines the level of prices in the market. By means of conventions drawn principally from accounting and corporate finance,[152] fundamental security analysis is supposed to sharpen the predictions of various valuation models of individual securities. Fundamental market analysis, less well developed than fundamental security analysis, is based on market valuation models drawn largely from economic theory.[153] Both fundamental security analysis and fundamental market analysis have in common an important idea: The evaluation of historical data permits one to project future performance, and the better the evaluation, the better the prediction.

This is not to indicate that security analysis and market analysis are

---

[151] With publication of the model, however, its utility probably declined to the point where it lost any usefulness it might have had in providing above-average returns.

[152] See generally B. Graham, D. Dodd & S. Cottle, *Security Analysis* (4th ed. 1962) (hereinafter cited as Graham, Dodd & Cottle); Stewart, "Corporate Forecasting," in *Financial Analyst's Handbook,* note 104 *supra,* at 907. See generally *id.* Pts. II-IV.

[153] See, e.g., Kavesh & Platt, "Economic Forecasting," in *Financial Analyst's Handbook,* note 104 *supra,* at 928.

unrelated to or proceed in ignorance of each other.[154] It might not make sense, for example, to buy shares in a company with good long-term prospects just as the market was about to slide, assuming both those conclusions can be determined with greater accuracy than is reflected in existing price levels. But distinguishing between security analysis and market analysis is useful because they rely on different sets of conventions and are designed for different purposes. Superior security analysis tells an investor which of a set of securities of a given type to prefer or avoid, assuming that type of security is worthy of a commitment. Superior market analysis tells an investor which markets to prefer or avoid under a given set of economic conditions.[155] Both are necessary to a successful investment program based on strategies characterized by fundamental analysis.

In theory, one should expect fundamental analysts possessing the same data and applying those data to a given valuation model[156] to reach the same estimates. But this would be the case only if all public data were totally accurate and there were perfect agreement about what would happen in the future.[157] In a world of uncertainty, analysts' conclusions about identical quantities will differ markedly. Consider, for example, the independent variable thought critical to virtually all common stock valuation models—the growth of earnings.[158] The reason

---

154 See Graham, Dodd & Cottle, note 152 *supra,* at 711.

155 No matter how one maintains his holdings, it is impossible to avoid being an investor in some kind of market. Even holding assets in cash is a form of investment. The function of market analysis is to assist an investor in identifying the investment medium that offers the best opportunity for appreciation in value, given reasonably foreseeable economic conditions and the investor's investment objectives and income requirements.

156 Often, the valuation model is not explicit. Many analysts will evaluate a company without seeming to follow any scheme save that of judging whether, based on the analytic conventions applied, the current market price of the company's securities reflect their intrinsic value. After assessing a number of factors, the analyst will reach a conclusion as to whether the securities offer acceptable returns with a tolerable cushion of safety. See, e.g., Graham, Dodd & Cottle, note 152 *supra.* Nonetheless, even this apparently intuitive process is based on an implied valuation model. The analyst is simply weighting the factors he scrutinizes, and the worth of his model merely depends on how accurate the weighting system is and how consistently the analyst applies it.

157 See ¶ 7.03 *supra.*

158 See, e.g., Lorie & Hamilton, note 11 *supra,* at 125-141; Cohen, "Analysis of Common Stock," in *Financial Analyst's Handbook,* note 104 *supra,* at 134, 171.

earnings growth is so important is that in principle, the value of a company's earnings stream discounted to present worth represents the actual value of its common stock. Thus, the better one knows how a company's earnings will change, the more accurately one can use the current earnings figure to evaluate the accuracy of the current price of a stock.[159]

There are a number of ways competent analysts could disagree in calculating earnings growth. In most cases, the period of estimate of an earnings stream is indefinite, since corporations have no set life span. Moreover, as a practical matter, no real precision in calculating future earnings is possible except in the near term, since the reliability of current information as a predictor of future performance attenuates rapidly. A figure calculated to represent the earnings growth rate, therefore, consists of two elements: (1) future earnings for the period during which extrapolations from the company's current record and business prospects are practicable; and (2) future earnings in the period beyond which extrapolation from current data is practicable.

Suppose, for the moment, that analysts would agree on an estimate for the first period. One would still expect them to reach different but reasonable conclusions about the value of the earnings stream. Estimates for the second period depend on important assumptions about how the earning power of a corporation changes over its life. Simple extrapolation of present growth rates, for example, would be too simplistic an approach, since that would predict that all companies temporarily having rapidly growing earnings will grow to infinite value, while all companies temporarily losing money will disappear. In the end, analysts have to adopt some convention for estimating earnings growth for periods too far in the future to relate reliably to existing data. So long as different analysts favor different conventions for making this estimate, their conclusions will differ.[160]

But it is the evaluation of current data to predict earnings growth in the near term which provides most of the potential for professional disagreement. Predictions of earnings growth based on the evaluation of current data usually begin with analysis of the historical earnings record, which is the bench mark against which the earnings growth rate is calculated. One might expect that, since the historical record has been completely written, it would be subject to uniform interpretation. But the primary sources of a company's historical record are its financial statements and reports to public agencies. Even where there is

---

[159] See, e.g., Lorie & Hamilton, note 11 *supra,* at 113-124.
[160] *Id.* at 134-136.

no hint of fraud,[161] accounting data are notorious for being more precise in appearance than in fact.[162] Those data are themselves gathered according to certain assumptions.[163] Reasonable professional competence for a securities analyst begins with an ability to recognize the play involved in the values assigned to stated assets, liabilities, and capital on a balance sheet, and stated revenues, expenses, and costs on an income statement and, where applicable, on a funds-flow statement.

Even assuming substantial agreement on a single way to interpret a company's historical record and a single convention to be used for

---

[161] Normally, analysts are entitled to rely on the accuracy of the information they receive from standard sources. But if an analyst has access to information which, in the exercise of reasonable care, would alert him to the existence of important misrepresentations, a failure to take those misrepresentations into account may subject him to liability. See, e.g., Levine v. SEC, 436 F.2d 88 (2d Cir. 1971). Furthermore, even where an analyst does not have access to special information, facts in the public record may create an obligation to make a more penetrating investigation. The head of the Auditing Standards Division of the American Institute of Certified Public Accountants, for example, has listed five situations signaling a need for closer attention to the possibility of fraud: "(1) lack of sufficient working capital or credit to continue operations; (2) extremely rapid expansion through new business or product lines; (3) an urgent need for a continued favorable earnings record to support the price of stock; (4) dependency on a single or relatively few products; and (5) operating in an industry experiencing a large number of business failures." See Sec. Reg. L. Rep. No. 302, May 14, 1975, at D-2.

[162] See, e.g., L. Friedman, *Financial Statement Analysis: Theory, Application, and Interpretation* 5-8, 574 (1974); Lorie & Hamilton, note 11 *supra*, at 144-150. Sensitive to this problem, the American Institute of Certified Public Accountants attempted to clarify the meaning of "generally accepted accounting principles" in its fifth Statement on Auditing Standards, as follows.

"(a) [T]he accounting principles selected and applied have general acceptance; (b) the accounting principles are appropriate in the circumstances; (c) the financial statements, including the related notes, are informative of matters that may affect their use, understanding, and interpretation; (d) the information presented in the financial statements is classified and summarized in a reasonable manner, that is neither too detailed nor too condensed; and (e) the financial statements reflect the underlying events and transactions in a manner that presents the financial position, results of operations, and changes in financial position stated within a range of acceptable limits, that is, limits that are reasonable and practicable to attain in financial statements."

Sec. Reg. L. Rep., No. 315, Aug. 13, 1975, at D-4.

[163] See, e.g., Friedman, note 162 *supra,* Ch. 2.

estimating its long-term earnings, however, mere extrapolation of a historical earnings record, according to the evidence, offers no significant advantage in predicting earnings growth over the near term.[164] Thus, there are yet other factors influencing changes in the rate of growth of earnings over the near term which virtually guarantee that analysts' final estimates of future earnings will differ. Relevant also are correct determinations of such things as availability and cost of required materials, customer demand, labor conditions, management quality, contingent liabilities, and so forth.[165] Plainly, these kinds of inputs are sufficiently subjective to influence analysis and produce different estimates by different analysts.

Thus, the negligence standard must deal with the phenomenon of professionally competent analysts, having access to the same data and familiar with the same conventions, arriving at different, yet entirely defensible, estimates for the same variable. The ambiguities of the estimating process typical in evaluating a company's earnings prospects extend to most of the conditions to which fundamental securities analysis and fundamental market analysis are applied. Nonetheless, the negligence standard is not a meaningless control in this context. In accordance with long-standing negligence principles, ignorance of important publicly available information is probably inexcusable.[166] Taking earnings growth as the example once again, no analyst can properly evaluate a historical record, much less estimate a company's future performance, without considering the available data, even if only to reject its relevancy. But those same negligence principles dictate that the mere existence of professional differences over how available information should be evaluated ought not to be the basis for concluding that there has been a failure to exercise ordinary skill and care. If, given a defensible valuation model,[167] an analyst has made a reasonable investiga-

---

[164] Much of the evidence is summarized in Lorie & Hamilton, note 11 *supra,* at 158-163.

[165] See, e.g., Cohen, "Analysis of Common Stock," in *Financial Analyst's Handbook*, note 104 *supra*, at 134.

[166] See the speech by the Chairman of the SEC to the Financial Analysts Federation, "Improved Disclosure—Opportunity and Responsibility for Financial Analysis," [1973-1974 Transfer Binder] CCH Fed. Sec. L. Rep. ¶ 79,776 (1974). Cf. Levine v. SEC, 436 F.2d 88 (2d Cir. 1971). In this connection, it is important to recognize that an investment manager's obligation to keep abreast of important public information includes detailed knowledge of unusual conditions attaching to the particular security held, as, for example, call provisions. Cf. Van Gemert v. Boeing Co., 520 F.2d 1373 (2d Cir.), *cert. denied* 423 U.S. 947 (1975).

[167] See ¶¶ 7.07[2]-7.07[2][a] at notes 144-146 *supra.*

tion into available information, the estimates determined for the independent variables of the model must be open to a reasonable band of professional disagreement.

Strict application of negligence principles also demands mastery of the conventions comprising the body of fundamental analysis. A securities analyst must know accounting and finance, and a market analyst must know economics. But here again, the law must tolerate a range of professional opinion about the conventions to be used in different circumstances and the weight to be afforded the conclusions such conventions yield. All conventions, whether those applicable to security analysis or those applicable to market analysis, are based on a set of assumptions which are less than perfect restatements of conditions in the real world. Moreover, analysts rarely state their conclusions with positive assurance. Rather, they qualify the confidence they have in their analyses by identifying the principal assumptions they have made to arrive at their opinions. It is really differences over the degree of confidence which should be placed in these assumptions which accounts for differences in conclusions in the forecasts of knowledgeable analysts.[168] Again, the law must accommodate differences in professional opinion. It is an unjustifiable lack of awareness of available information, or the mistaken application or negligent ignorance of generally accepted principles of analysis, that is a failure to exercise ordinary skill and care, and not mere differences based on professional judgment.[169]

---

[168] Forecasts of professional analysts will not ordinarily differ sharply. On the contrary, with most analysts relying on the same data, using the same conventions, and applying similar valuation models, the range of professional disagreement over the results produced by fundamental analysis normally will not be large. Indeed, it would be disturbing if it were otherwise, for if wide differences in opinion regularly occurred, it would raise serious doubts about the reliability of fundamental analysis as an investment approach.

[169] Paradoxically, application of the negligence standard to fundamental analysis reinforces the observed phenomenon that professional analysts produce forecasts which offer opportunity only for average returns, at least in those cases in which the valuation models at issue are not significantly different from those being used by most other investors. Where the valuation models from which the forecasts are made are widely known, opportunities for above-average returns through fundamental analysis are possible only if an analyst's forecasts differ measurably from the forecasts others are making. The mere existence of such a difference, however, does not establish superior estimating. Indeed, it is more likely in such a case that the analyst has missed something. For a divergent forecast to comport with the standard of ordinary skill and care, the telling point is the analyst's assump-

[d] Technical analysis

Like fundamental analysis, technical analysis can focus on the securities of individual companies or on the market as a whole. The principal hypothesis of technical analysis is that, largely because of investor psychology, buying and selling patterns recur.[170] If these patterns can be identified, knowledgeable investors can profit by anticipating positions forecast as inevitable but not yet priced in the marketplace. Ordinarily, charts or graphs of securities statistics deemed relevant are the medium through which technical analysts attempt to identify recurrent patterns, and hence technical analysts are also called chartists. Once a pattern is perceived, however, its message is often incorporated into ratios of the variables being charted. These ratios, usually referred to as indicators, are assigned critical values which, when approached or exceeded, are supposed to alert the analyst to unusual opportunities or hazards.

For a technical indicator to provide a useful means of achieving above-average returns, there must be a substantial correlation between it and future price levels not fully reflected in current price.[171] The ev-

---

tions. Forecasts that stray from the pack are defensible only if they have taken into account the assumptions of others and rejected or modified them on solid grounds. But herein lies the paradox: The more intuitive the grounds for the differing assumptions, the more difficult it is to defend them or for others to have confidence in them.

On the other hand, where assumptions are derived more objectively and their validity can be supported through documentation and calculation, it is highly likely that other analysts will reach similar conclusions and hence leave little opportunity for profit. See Lorie & Hamilton, note 11 *supra,* Chs. 6-9. This does not mean that there are no opportunities for profit. Occasionally, through a combination of hard digging and good fortune, an analyst will put diverse publicly available facts together in a way which leads to a conclusion not yet reached by others in the market. See, e.g., "A Superior Performance," 7 Institutional Investor 62 (Jan. 1973), a report about how one analyst, through hard digging and expert sleuthing, uncovered an oil stock which was seriously undervalued. But these occasions are rare, and neither investors nor their managers should expect them to happen often.

[170] See, e.g., Shaw, "Technical Analysis," in *Financial Analyst's Handbook,* note 104 *supra,* at 944; Stewart, "Corporate Forecasting," *id.* at 907, 908-911; Keuhner, "Efficient Markets and Random Walk," *id.* at 1226, 1229-1231; Black, "Implications of the Random Walk Hypothesis for Portfolio Management," 27 Fin. Anal. J. 16 (March-April 1971). For a popular discussion of technical analysis, its assumptions and its usefulness, see Ehrbar, "Technical Analysis Refuses to Die," 92 Fortune 99 (Aug. 1975).

[171] This is true for any method of investment aimed at achieving above-average returns. See, e.g., Lorie & Hamilton, note 11 *supra,* at 100.

idence, however, is that technical analysis does not do so with a frequency superior to that of any other system. In its weak form, the efficient-market hypothesis states that no information about future price useful for enhancing profits is contained in a historical sequence of prices. Current prices reflect everything implied in previous price movements.[172] Since technical analysis is based on price and volume figures for transactions already executed, it is obviously fundamentally at odds with the central tenet of the efficient-market hypothesis.

To help in prognosticating about the likely legal response to the use of technical analysis by investment managers, let us examine in closer detail some of the reasons that technical analysis ordinarily does not provide above-average returns. It is basic that, to hold promise as a device for enhancing profits, technical analysis must forecast events correctly. Yet correctness cannot be measured merely by whether a technical indicator leads an event more often than not. To be correct, an indicator must not only predict price movement accurately; it must also predict the timing of the movement and the degree of the movement. Even if a predicted move were inevitable, an untimely anticipation of it could be more costly than failing to respond to the move at all. Similarly, even if a predicted move were both inevitable and timed perfectly, costly errors could occur as a result of overreaction or underreaction to the change. The ability of a technical indicator to enhance profits thus depends directly on how much the benefits that accrue from responding to it outweigh the costs of responding mistakenly.

But the problem is even more difficult than deciding what to do when alerted by a technical indicator. Other investors are faced with similar decisions. At least in the case of an indicator which is generally known, investors will revalue their own holdings according to the confidence they place in the correctness of the indicator. Above-average profits, therefore, would be possible only if everyone else—that is, the market—were discounting the prediction of the indicator incorrectly, a most unlikely event.

Consider, for example, how investors might react to changes in the short-interest ratio, a technical indicator which is both well-known and widely believed accurate in anticipating stock market movement.[173] Studies have shown that the future direction of market movement cor-

---

[172] See text at notes 103-106 *supra*.

[173] The ratio is computed by dividing the average daily volume for the month (measured from the fifteenth to the fifteenth) into the number of shares sold short on the New York Stock Exchange (as of the fifteenth).

relates with movement in the short-interest ratio.[174] Suppose the correlation were perfect. Plainly, nothing could be gained if every investor changed his valuation of common stocks instantly and exactly in tune with movement in the short-interest ratio. The same analysis holds in the more realistic case of less than perfect correlation. Investors would still change their bids as the ratio changes. The only difference would be the degree to which they would let their bids be affected by movement of the ratio, and that would depend on the correlation between changes in the ratio and market movement. The greater the correlation, the greater the effect on prices. Moreover, it would not be necessary for every investor to be aware of the precise degree of correlation. All that is required is that the decisions of all investors, taken together, discount the correlation accurately. Nor is it necessary that most investors be using the short-interest ratio. If they are basing their investment decisions on factors that are highly correlated with the short-interest ratio, the market will reflect their actions just as if they were in fact relying on the ratio. Even assuming the statistical significance of the correlation will continue unchanged into the future, therefore, it seems doubtful that it can offer an opportunity for enhancing profits.

Now let us extend this analysis to technical indicators that are not generally known and are not highly correlated with other indicators which are generally known. Such conditions are unlikely, but even if they occur, above-average returns would be far from guaranteed. The analyst must still decide what action to take based on the indicator. Suppose, for example, that the short-interest ratio were not widely known or highly correlated with other indicators, and that it forecast an impending market drop. The immediate question facing the analyst would be whether to liquidate all common stock holdings, or only some portion of them. The correct decision depends on how much the market will move and how long the move will persist. Also important is the question of when to initiate the liquidation program and how to carry it out. That depends on the time relationship between the change in the ratio and the market move. The ratio itself gives no clue as to the answer to either, except *perhaps* that the greater the drift from average, the more imminent may be the move. Furthermore, the success of the analyst's decision is affected by what is done with the assets removed or withheld from the stock market. One cannot avoid selecting some

---

[174] Kerrigan, "The Short-Interest Ratio and Its Component Parts," 30 Fin. Anal. J. 45 (Nov.-Dec. 1974).

investment medium for his assets; even cash is a form of investment. If the medium selected by the investor sustains sharper losses or realizes smaller profits than the stock market for the period under scrutiny, even well-placed reliance on the ratio will have had a perverse effect on investment performance.

In view of these kinds of considerations, skepticism about the validity of the claims that technical analysis can enhance profits is understandable.[175] But doubtful as technical analysis may be as an independent strategy for obtaining above-average returns, it would be a mistake to conclude that it is without value. The government, for example, has various leading indicators on which many rely to predict the drift of the national economy. With varying degrees of accuracy, technical indicators do forecast the future, but in most cases, by the time an individual investor has digested the message contained in technical indicators, virtually all the opportunity to obtain better-than-average profits will have evaporated. The market simply corrects too fast for the advantages gained by following the predictions of technical indicators to offset the trading and other transaction costs involved.

But just because the market "knows" to adjust quickly to information about the future provided through leading indicators, individual investors do not always understand the reasons for price adjustments. The real utility of technical analysis is to reveal or, perhaps more accurately, to alert investors to the principal buying and selling pressures operating on securities prices at any given time. When technical indicators depart sharply from their average values, they focus attention on their constituent variables, and to that extent may be an aid to investors. An unusual movement in the short-interest ratio, for example, may indicate that, if the market begins a price rise, many short sellers will give prices an added boost as they cover their positions. The analyst still must determine from other sources whether the market will rise and, if so, how substantial a rise to expect, issues of obvious complexity not examined by the indicator. Technical analysis thus plays a subsidiary role in the investment process. Prudent consideration of the forecasts of technical indicators may aid the execution of investment decisions

---

175 See Black, "Implications of the Random Walk Hypothesis for Portfolio Management," 27 Fin. Anal. J. 16 (March-April 1971); J. Train, *Dance of the Money Bees* 241-243 (1974). Despite Train's professed attitude, however, he admits to at least one favorite technical indicator. *Id.* at 67. See also Ehrbar, "Technical Analysis Refuses to Die," 92 Fortune 99 (Aug. 1975).

arrived at on fundamentals by suggesting delay, reduced exposure, and so forth.[176]

The development of legal doctrine with respect to technical analysis will almost surely take into account both its limitations as an independent strategy and its use as a supplement to a full investment program. Ordinarily, it would not be defensible to rely on technical analysis alone to produce above-average returns. The necessary conditions for technical analysis to be capable of enhancing profits are that the relevant indicators not be generally known, that they not be highly correlated with indicators that are, and that, in the range they suggest action, they be highly correlated with movement in price. Those conditions are rare enough that an investment manager will probably have the burden of proving their existence if technical analysis comes to dominate his investment strategy. Moreover, even in the event those conditions are satisfied, it is not the indicator itself which is responsible. The indicator is simply a convenient expression of an underlying pricing relationship described in terms of the variables constituting the indicator. As a consequence, defense of an investment strategy based on technical analysis will probably require also that a manager identify and justify the relationships purportedly described by the indicators.

One can already see in the SEC's attitude toward the marketing of formula investment plans signs of special regulatory concern in connection with the capabilities of technical analysis. In enforcement proceedings and no-action letters, the SEC is taking the position that there must be full disclosure of the assumptions underlying any formula plan being sold to investors.[177] Since such disclosure destroys any effectiveness a formula might have in enhancing profits, a fact of which the SEC must be aware, the insistence on disclosure demonstrates a conviction that no amount of skill can promote reliance on a technical device into a successful strategy for realizing above-average returns, adjusted for risk undertaken. Furthermore, if it is true that disclosure is being

---

[176] As if in emphasis of this point, it is often said that a good technical analyst must first be a good fundamentalist. See, e.g., Ehrbar, note 175 *supra*.

[177] See Investment Advisers Act Rule 206(4)-1(a)(3), 17 C.F.R. § 275.206(4)-1(a)(3); *In re* Sackville-Pickard, SEC Securities Exchange Act Release No. 8433, (Oct. 24, 1968), [1967-1969 Transfer Binder] CCH Fed. Sec. L. Rep. ¶ 77,620; Security Evaluation, Inc., [1971-1972 Transfer Binder] CCH Fed. Sec. L. Rep. ¶ 78,786 (1972); Alphadex Corp., [1971-1972 Transfer Binder] CCH Fed. Sec. L. Rep. ¶ 78,624 (1972); Investment Quality Measurement Serv., Sec. Reg. L. Rep. No. 309 (July 2, 1975), at C-2.

used in this context as much to discredit formula plans as to inform investors, close regulation of investment managers who concentrate on technical strategies cannot be far behind, for these initial excursions by the SEC into regulating formula plans have focused on the marketing phase. If technical devices require regulation during the marketing phase simply because they are technical, the need is surely greater when actual management is involved.

Of course, formula investment plans represent the most rudimentary kind of technical analysis: They substitute mechanical devices having the appearance of objectivity for the exercise of judgment, the very antithesis of competent investment management. As a consequence, one should not extrapolate too readily from the regulatory response to formula plans to conclusions about the relationship between legal doctrine and all technical analysis. Moreover, the regulatory activity to this point has restricted itself to marketing efforts involving claims of superior investment returns. Few investment managers would make such claims in behalf of the technical indicators on which they rely, since those indicators only contribute part of the information on which an investment decision is based. Nonetheless, the distinction between support and dependency implied in the formula-plan cases is too important to ignore. The law may not yet be willing to conclude that the subordination of judgment to technical devices is presumptively professionally negligent, but the greater the dependency of a manager on technical analysis, the greater seems his obligation at least to disclose that fact.

Another problem looming for technical analysis is more subtle, but also seems bound to become involved in the development of the legal standard of care. Most technical analysis deals with questions of timing. The figures reported in the indicators tell the analyst how fast or slow to proceed with executing an investment decision already reached, or whether some opportunity or hazard suggests action of some sort. But although timing considerations are highly relevant to investment decisions, above-average results, adjusted for risk, as the efficient-market hypothesis postulates and the evidence indicates,[178] are not likely to be achieved by an investment program that concentrates on timing market turns or short-term price swings in an individual security. Unfortunately, strategies that overemphasize timing as a means to obtain above-average returns are likely to be costly. Far more than strategies based on the capital asset pricing model or on fundamental-valuation models, strat-

---

[178] See Sharpe, "Likely Gains for Market Timing," 31 Fin. Anal. J. 60 (March-April 1975).

egies based on timing involve heavy commission expenses. Obviously, the question of when portfolio readjustments based on timing considerations become excessive is a matter of degree, but it is doubtful that the turnover rate that characterized many stock portfolios during the 1960s[179] could be justified today.[180]

It is difficult to predict precisely how legal doctrine will respond to portfolio turnover as a deliberate investment strategy beyond saying that the heavier turnover is, the greater will be the burden on an investment manager to defend it. The issue is complicated by the fact that portfolio turnover seldom can be treated simply as a professional-negligence question. Often, portfolio turnover can provide indirect benefits to an investment manager or to an affiliated party. When this is the case, duty-of-loyalty questions arise, and the burden of justifying turnover practices expands considerably.[181]

¶ 7.08. DIVERSIFICATION

As should be apparent by this point, the most powerful device for reducing risk in a portfolio is diversification. This fact is neither a secret, nor a new discovery, and indeed its long-standing attractiveness to investors is what gave major impetus to modern portfolio theory.[182]

---

[179] See note 111 *supra*.

[180] Thus, for example, professors at the University of Pennsylvania advised the trustees of the school's endowment fund to reduce turnover sharply from previous levels which apparently went as high as 100 percent per year. Wall Street Letter, Nov. 18, 1974 p. 9.

[181] There are situations in which duty-of-loyalty questions arise pointedly: where an investment manager is affiliated with a broker (see Bines, "Regulating Discretionary Management: Broker-Dealers as Catalyst for Reform," 16 B.C. Ind. & Com. L. Rev. 347, 379 (1975)), where brokers are referring clients to a manager (see *id.* at 374), and where brokers are providing a manager with supplementary services (see Jorden, "Paying Up for Research: A Regulatory and Legislative Analysis," 1975 Duke L.J. 1103), the manager may be tempted to over-trade (churn) or sacrifice best execution to reward the broker. The affiliation problem was the subject of the 1975 amendments to the Securities Exchange Act, Pub. L. 94-29, 89 Stat. 111, § 7A (codified as 15 U.S.C. § 78k(a)). With respect to the paying-up problem, see *id.* § 28(e). For a fuller discussion of the effect of these statutory provisions, neither of which entirely resolves the duty-of-loyalty issue, see ¶¶ 9.06, 10.02.

[182] See Markowitz, "Portfolio Selection," 7 J. Fin. 77 (1952). From the observed phenomenon that investors diversify, the author postulated that most investors are averse to risk and that, as a consequence, at any level of return, investors will prefer the least risky security. From that postulate, he was able to define the risk-reward frontier for all portfolios.

But, as a result of modern portfolio theory, the duty to diversify has taken on new meaning. The former intuitive guides to diversification, such as the rule of thumb that investments be spread among different industries,[183] have given way to a contemporary emphasis on variance and systematic and unsystematic risk. Diversification can be understood as using the covariance of securities to reduce the variance of a portfolio, and it can be measured by the degree of unsystematic risk eliminated.

The duty to diversify raises two separate questions:

(1) To what extent must an investment manager diversify his client's portfolio holdings?

(2) What are the limits of professional competence in carrying out the duty to diversify?

Plainly, the duty to diversify does not mean that an investment manager must achieve the total elimination of unsystematic risk in a portfolio. If that were the case, no positive investment strategy seeking enhanced profits from the identification of undervalued securities would be permissible, and no account possessing insufficient assets to diversify fully could avail itself of investment management services. But some diversification is necessary, the amount depending on the investment objectives of the client. Even the most aggressive of investors is likely to require that some portion of his estate be put in a highly diversified medium. On the other hand, because of the potential for loss in exposing an account to a high level of unsystematic risk, strategies which utilize unnecessary unsystematic risk are unsuitable for most investors who require a solid foundation of diversified holdings.

The more serious problem is how to achieve the level of diversification required by the client. Studies show that the reduction in unsystematic risk proceeds very rapidly for the first several commitments placed in a portfolio, and that the reduction can be accelerated by including securities of relatively high volatility.[184] Simple quantitative rules, however, such as those appearing in the Investment Company Act, defining diversification in terms of concentration in a given percentage of securities of a single issuer,[185] are not particularly useful in setting the standard of care. The evidence also shows that even with a portfolio having a volatility equal to that of the market, holdings of

---

[183] See ¶ 6.02[4].

[184] See Modigliani & Pogue, note 24 *supra*, Pt. I at 73-76.

[185] 15 U.S.C. § 80a-5(b)(1). See ¶ 6.02[4], note 72.

fifty stocks may still produce returns that may differ from market returns by more than 4 percentage points per year.[186] Indeed, a portfolio consisting of over 200 stocks bought in proportion to market value would be necessary to reduce the standard error to less than 1 percent compared to the returns on the Standard & Poor's 500.[187]

On first impression, such extensive holdings appear to be a bludgeon system for eliminating unsystematic risk. It is obvious that one effective way to obtain market performance is to buy the market. But in principle, the fact that the ebb and flow of the market influences price changes in individual securities does not mean that it is necessary to purchase the market in order to eliminate nonmarket, or unsystematic, risk. The crucial variables in a multiple-security portfolio are the covariances of the component securities with respect to each other. If a portfolio bearing the level of risk indicated by a client's investment objectives consists of securities no rearrangement of, addition to, or removal of which from the portfolio can reduce the variance of the portfolio, the portfolio is perfectly diversified by definition.[188]

The problem with covariance analysis as a practical matter, however, is that the calculations necessary to make such a determination can be extensive. For example, if the investment universe consisted of only 1,000 securities, an investment manager would need to calculate 1,000 values for the variances of each security and 499,500 covariances for each security with each other security.[189] The capital asset pricing model, on the other hand, measures the risk of a portfolio by its volatility relative to the market. In effect, the model substitutes the relationship of each security to the market for the relationship of each security to each other. This represents an important simplification of the calculating process, but, by the same token, it requires that the relevant market be highly efficient and that a large number of commitments be made in order to eliminate the variance in security prices which is not related to market movement; that is, the unsystematic risk. Since the beta coefficients of individual securities are highly unstable, a fairly substantial number of securities must be included to maintain the volatility of a portfolio at a constant level.[190]

---

[186] See Lorie, "Diversification: Old and New," 1 J. Portfolio Management 25, 27 (Winter 1975).

[187] Id. at 28.

[188] See ¶ 7.02[4] supra. See also Lorie & Hamilton, note 11 supra, at 198-199.

[189] Id. at 198.

[190] Id. at 227. Those committed to passive investing (e.g., Langbein & Posner, note 55 supra, and "Market Funds and Trust-Investment Law: II,"

To a large extent, the skill and care with which an investment manager diversifies a portfolio must depend on the choices available to him. Until participations in pools of securities which have eliminated unsystematic risk become widely available, only the most substantial clients will be able to acquire a sufficient number of securities to reduce unsystematic risk into negligible proportions. Clients of smaller means will have to rely on mutual funds and commingled trusts in the interim. But investment managers will surely develop other approaches to diversification. Professor Lorie reports, for example, that one group of managers has developed a method for adjusting the proportions invested in the fifty stocks having the largest market value to reduce unsystematic risk. This method has halved the standard error of return of the

---

2 Am. Bar Found. Research J. 1 (1977)) may not fully appreciate the degree to which concentration on such a strategy can deprive a portfolio of effective risk reduction through diversification. Beta analysis is necessary as a surrogate for covariance analysis because analysis of individual securities is too unrefined to avoid the necessity of relying on volatility relative to the market as a substitute for covariance of component securities relative to each other. See text at note 189 *supra*. But reliance on volatility relative to the market as the cornerstone of an investment strategy designed to reduce unsystematic risk makes it absolutely essential that the market be highly efficient. This explains why supporters of passive investing restrict their attention to the New York Stock Exchange or a market index such as the Standard & Poor's Index of 500 Industrials to the exclusion of equity securities in other markets such as the American Stock Exchange, regional stock exchanges, the over-the-counter market, the private-placement market, and foreign stock markets.

Modern portfolio theory provides a far more powerful insight than the important lesson that an investor may successfully adopt a passive investment strategy parasitic to a highly efficient market. Indeed, it reaches no conclusions based on the efficiency of the market as to whether one strategy is preferable to another except that the more efficient the market, the less able are conventional strategies to provide unusual returns. The covariance principle, however, establishes that investing in different kinds of commitments, especially in the face of inefficiency in the relevant markets, can reduce portfolio risk. See ¶ 6.03[3]. Thus, while passive investing may have received most of the early headlines, the more significant development in the professional investment management community is the expanded reliance, whether expressly or impliedly, on the covariance principle, as demonstrated by the diversification of managed portfolios into options, foreign securities, real estate, gold, debt instruments, private placements, and so forth. To the degree these kinds of commitments are made in markets which are inefficient relative to the New York Stock Exchange, they simply place a greater premium on active management to assure that they are fairly priced when purchased.

portfolio relative to the market without affecting the volatility of the portfolio.[191] With computer services readily available, other innovations in resolving the problem of reducing unsystematic risk seem likely.[192]

The immediate effects of these developments on the duty to diversify are twofold. First, the law is bound to recognize the distinction between systematic risk and unsystematic risk as a bench mark for diversification. Furthermore, because measurement of unsystematic risk in a highly efficient market is relatively easy, and because it takes a relatively few securities to achieve a high degree of diversification, investment managers can expect that bench mark to result in a strict standard. By taking into account the means of the client, and thus the number of commitments the client reasonably can make, it is possible to determine the level of unsystematic risk his account need bear. Unless a manager can explain a substantial departure from a proper level of unsystematic risk, either by pointing to client direction[193] or by showing a defensible positive investment strategy,[194] diversification will not have been adequate. Moreover, the duty to diversify may soon open in another direction. As more and more vehicles diversified over the market become open to investors lacking the means to diversify their own portfolios fully, investment managers can expect an obligation to develop and use such services, as a standard professional practice, to expand the duty to diversify to the extent it does not conflict with defensible positive investment strategies.[195]

---

[191] Lorie, "Diversification: Old and New," 1 J. Portfolio Management 25, 27 (Winter 1975).

[192] An additional and important benefit of reducing the number of securities without affecting degree of diversification is that it permits an investment manager to concentrate his efforts and thereby to improve his chances of identifying securities which, in his judgment, offer opportunities for unsystematic returns.

[193] A client can relieve an investment manager from an obligation to diversify fully, at least if the client understands what he is doing. It has been held, for example, in both trust and agency relationships, that a manager may take guidance from an established pattern of investment by the trustor or principal even if greater diversification would have been possible. See, e.g., Steiner v. Hawaiian Trust Co., 47 Hawaii 548, 393 P.2d 96 (1964); O'Connor v. Burns, Potter & Co., 151 Neb. 9, 36 N.W.2d 507 (1949).

[194] See note 190 *supra*.

[195] For example, cash management is being assisted by the use of collective investment vehicles which concentrate their investments in the money market and thus enable investors to improve return on idle funds above

Second, the impact of the duty to diversify on investment managers pursuing an investment strategy based on the capital asset pricing model will be especially strong. The only strategic consideration in such a policy is diversification, once the proper level of volatility, or risk, is determined. Where full diversification takes on such importance in the management of an account, the burden on the manager to diversify fully will be heavy. Moreover, it is difficult for a manager who fails to achieve full diversification to hide that fact. The performance of accounts managed according to a strategy derived from the capital asset pricing model should be the average performance of the market during the same period, adjusted for the volatility of the portfolio. Significant departures from average value, so adjusted, virtually prove inadequate diversification.

---

what would be possible by relying only on demand and savings deposits in banks. The importance of this particular development was not immediately recognized in all quarters, however. The Comptroller of the Currency at first prohibited the investment of trust assets in money market funds on the ground that such investment represented an improper delegation of trustee responsibility. Trust Banking Circular No. 4 (Dec. 23, 1975), CCH Fed. Banking L. Rep. ¶ 97,786. But, once properly informed that such funds offered trustees a diversified participation in money market instruments, the Comptroller revised Circular No. 4 to permit investment in money market funds unless specifically prohibited by local law. CCH Fed. Banking L. Rep. ¶ 96,941 (1976).

The SEC has also felt it necessary to respond to these new funds. Recognizing that they offered investors an opportunity to diversify an investment in liquid assets, but that the range of such investments was relatively narrow, consisting primarily of short-term securities issued by the United States, bank instruments, and commercial paper, the Commission was forced to confront its traditional view that investment of more than 25 percent in assets in a single industry represents an investment policy of concentrating in that industry. The Commission concluded, in essence, that a fund's investment policy with respect to concentration in an industry would not be affected by reservation of freedom of action to invest in government securities and bank instruments. The traditional view on concentration, however, applies to the commercial paper of issuers in any one industry. SEC Securities Act Release No. 5639 (Oct. 30, 1975), 4 CCH Fed. Sec. L. Rep. ¶ 47,781.

Part IV

ONGOING MANAGEMENT: EXECUTIONS

Chapter 8

EXECUTING INVESTMENT DECISIONS AS A LEGAL DUTY

¶ 8.01. THE DUTY OF BEST EXECUTION

Although executions are probably the least glamorous and certainly the most suspect of all investment management activities, competent executions are essential to the success of an investment program. In an increasingly complex securities marketing system, the process of transposing ideas into investments can mean the difference between mediocre and superior returns.[1] In a relatively brief period, trading techniques have become more sophisticated, multiple markets have evolved, and service competition among broker-dealers has given much ground to price competition. Moreover, the trading process still shows little sign of stabilizing. Adaptation to fully negotiated commissions shows no sign of abating, and even if that were not the case, Congress and the SEC are pressing for brisk movement toward a central marketing and execution reporting system. Because of this unsettled state of affairs, investment managers are unsure about the legal obligations associated with executing investment decisions for their accounts.

Much confusion surrounds the term of art, "best execution." That confusion stems from concern over the legal consequences of the definition which is adopted. Since an investment manager is supposed to have a duty of best execution when trading for a client's account,[2] the fear is that established trading practices may fall outside the legal definition and hence be deemed breaches of a manager's duty. Also of concern to investment managers is the stringency with which the final definition of best execution will be applied as a standard of care. In particular, many managers worry about the legal consequences of subsequent discovery that a transaction could have been executed more cheaply and with comparable services through another route.

Since there is no agreed-upon legal definition of best execution as yet, it is obviously impossible to evaluate trading practices in light of

---

[1] As the head trader at a leading brokerage house is quoted as saying, "a good trader at an institution can be responsible for a substantial incremental improvement in portfolio performance; if a portfolio is up 20 per cent, then 10 to 30 per cent of that gain could be the result of a trader whose responsibility goes far beyond mere execution." White, "The Two-Tier Market in Traders' Compensation," 8 Institutional Investor 25 (Sept. 1974). Also on the importance of effective executions, see Mennis, "An Integrated Approach to Portfolio Management," in S. Levine, *Financial Analyst's Handbook* 1207, 1222 (1975).

[2] See, e.g., Arleen W. Hughes, 27 S.E.C. 629, 636 (1948), *aff'd* Hughes v. SEC, 174 F.2d 969 (D.C. Cir. 1949); *Restatement of Agency* § 424 (1933); SEC, *Policy Statement on the Structure of a Central Market System* CCH Fed. Sec. L. Rep. No. 473, at 46-47 (1973).

any such standard. Nor does it seem profitable to examine the possible impact of the various legal standards which have been proposed so far. Until some standard is actually adopted, the policies underlying their differences are better considered on their own merit. There is, however, a practical definition of best execution on which most traders would agree—best net price. Therefore, instead of examining the merits of the different suggested legal definitions for best execution, let us begin with that practical definition on the theory that proof of compliance with it will prima facie satisfy any duty imposed by the legal standard which ultimately is adopted. Furthermore, with such a definition as a base, it may then be possible to examine trading practices which depart from it and thereby anticipate some of the legal complications which might arise.

[1] Best Execution as Best Net Price: The Analytic Base for Professional Competence

Suppose an investment manager were to inform a client of a decision either to take a new position in a security, add to a position, or close out all or part of a position. If the manager were also to ask the client how much to pay for a purchase or what price to ask for a sale, the client would surely say that he would prefer to pay as little as possible for a purchase and to obtain as much as possible in a sale. That obvious conclusion is shared by institutional traders. Absent other considerations, a trader will describe the execution in any given transaction as "best" if it is for the best net price.[3]

While transactions in listed securities on stock exchanges in the United States have a great deal of visibility, the goal of best net price is not easily accomplished. For one thing, it is often impossible to say whether a trade has been executed at the best net price. Negotiated commission rates, fragmented markets, and the enormous variance in the size at which trades take place make the proof of best net price difficult when the only standard of measurement is a contemporaneous trade on a stock exchange or a quote from a dealer. Furthermore, an isolated focus on the net price of each separate trade can blind one to the effective accomplishment of the primary objective: the maximization of net

---

[3] Mattlin, "The Quest for a Definition of 'Best Execution,'" 9 Institutional Investor 60 (April 1975). Indeed, best execution is often used synonymously in the industry for best net price. See, e.g., Wall Street Letter, Jan. 6, 1975, p. 2, summarizing a survey response from broker-dealers to this question: "Do you expect to receive a higher than best execution rate for your research services?"

investment return. Even though an inferior trading system is bound to achieve fewer best-net-price executions than more sophisticated trading systems, for example, it may be uneconomic for some investors to support expensive trading networks with contacts in all markets and with many brokers in the same market if trading volume is too low to justify such practices.[4] A package of slightly inferior trades may cost less overall if the expense of obtaining marginal improvement in trading capability exceeds the resulting savings. Moreover, some accounts may be able to use brokerage to purchase advisory or other support services which are more valuable than the savings involved in obtaining best net price on a particular trade. The important issue for an investor is the risk-adjusted return his account realizes. It makes no sense to minimize execution costs if increases in advisory fees or costs for other support services increase disproportionately.

Another obstacle in the way of strictly defining best execution as best net price is the possibility that public-policy considerations will force investment managers to trade in markets or with brokerage houses which, in the manager's judgment, may not be able to provide best net price. The SEC is anxious to progress to a central market system without adversely affecting the existing brokerage-industry structure, except to the extent price competition adjusts the balance. As a consequence, the Commission is considering rules and guidelines which place an additional burden on investment managers to prove that the executions they obtained at other than best listed price actually were for the best net price.[5]

---

4 See Weisner, "Will the Small Institutions Grow Up?" 9 Institutional Investor 35 (June 1975).

5 The ostensible purpose behind this proposal is to reduce incentives for broker-dealers to withdraw from exchange memberships, to protect the business of regional exchanges, and to encourage the development of communications equipment to achieve a composite quotation and executions reporting system. See Statement of SEC Commissioner Evans in Securities Week, Feb. 3, 1975; Statement of SEC Commissioner Sommers in Wall Street Letter, Jan. 10, 1975. Apparently, the SEC Advisory Committee on the Central Market System has had some difficulty in accommodating these policy considerations with the duty of investment managers to seek best net price. Initially, the Committee adopted a proposal requiring broker-dealers to go to the market offering the best price. The proposed rule stated:

"All member broker/dealers shall have an affirmative obligation to execute orders at the best possible price. When the size of the order is smaller than or equal to the size of the best bid or offering shown in system, the broker/dealer shall be required to go first to that market."

[2] The Analytic Structure for Departures From Best Net Price: The Interplay Between the Legal Duties of Reasonable Care and Loyalty

Let us assume, therefore, that because of either business-judgment reasons or policy goals of the type just described, the law will not absolutely oblige an investment manager to obtain best net price on every trade. Still, the legal analysis is complicated because trading practices which yield less than best net price frequently involve application of two

---

Securities Week, Feb. 10, 1975; Wall Street Letter, Feb. 10, 1975. A month later, on the grounds that this could lead to greater cost for customers, the Committee reversed itself and proposed a rule which would allow a broker to bypass the market offering best possible price if "he has sound reason for believing that he can obtain better execution in another market." Wall Street Letter, March 3, 1975. This change also was not satisfactory, and the Committee began working toward a compromise position (see Securities Week, April 7, 1975, p. 1), which it tentatively adopted. The compromise requires a broker-dealer acting as agent to execute at the "best possible price," unless the broker-dealer can show "reasonable justification." Its proposed effective date is after introduction of a national system of quote dissemination, communication, and settlement. This "Best Execution Procedure" reads in full:

"a) A broker-dealer acting as agent has an affirmative obligation to execute orders at the best possible price for its customers.

"b) A broker-dealer who does not execute an order at the best possible price for a customer must be able to show reasonable justification.

Guidelines

"1. Best execution requires that the best possible price be obtained for the customer in the execution of an order under all circumstances and the broker-dealer should have access to facilities necessary to accomplish this objective.

"2. When the size of an order is a unit of trade or smaller, a broker-dealer shall, absent reasonable justification applicable to the particular order, execute the order in the market reflecting the best quotation (i.e., best bid or best offer).

"3. When the size of an order is larger than one unit of trade, a broker-dealer shall, absent reasonable justification applicable to the particular order, execute the order in the market or markets where in its judgment there is the greatest likelihood to obtain the best possible price for the entire order. In making such determinations, the broker-dealer should consider, among others, the following factors:

"(a) The size and type of transaction involved;

"(b) The character of the total market for the security (e.g., price, volatility [sic], and liquidity);

distinct legal principles. One, the manager's duty of competence, suggests that reasonable departures from best net price are justifiable. But the other, the manager's duty of loyalty, can call into question executions which, measured by a standard of ordinary skill and care, would be reasonable. Duty-of-loyalty considerations may preclude an investment manager from executing trade by a route which would be defensible if taken by a different investment manager, or they may shift the burden of proof to an investment manager to justify either that a trade was executed at best net price or that the client gave an informed consent to execution at less than best net price. Unfortunately, discussion of the validity of various trading practices often proceeds without apparent acknowledgment that the duty of ordinary skill and care and the duty of undivided loyalty may both be at issue. The effect is to cloud the analysis and miss significant factual distinctions which can determine when and how, consistent with legal doctrine, an investment manager may deliberately or inadvertently depart from best-net-price executions.[6]

Perhaps the best way to illustrate the importance of separating the influence of effectiveness-of-execution considerations from conflict-of-interest considerations for purposes of analyzing the legal constraints on an investment manager's execution discretion is to review the history of the transformation of the brokerage industry from a fixed-rate commission system to a regime of negotiated rates. Much of the impetus for change arose from a desire to make executions more efficient from the investor's point of view and from concern over the strains the fixed-rate system was placing on fiduciary relationships. Furthermore, many of

---

"(c) The quotations for the security;

"(d) The quantity which each market can be expected to accept at its quoted price and other prices; and

"(e) The importance to the customer of factors other than price, such as speed and certainty of execution."

B.N.A. No. 298, Sec. Reg. L. Rep., April 16, 1975, at H-1.

[6] If the legal definition of best execution finally adopted forces an investment manager to forego best net price on public policy grounds (see note 5 *supra*), the effect is actually to immunize the manager from answerability for executions known by the manager to be inferior. For this reason, it is likely that formal adoption of a rule expressly requiring executions to be carried out in that fashion will be necessary to provide such immunity. A manager will not be able to justify an inferior execution, for example, on the ground that he was acting for the general welfare of investors by supporting regional exchanges if a NYSE or over-the-counter trade would have been less costly.

the practices which are the subject of debate today are direct consequences of arrangements which developed under the fixed-rate system.
An historical perspective, therefore, should illustrate the interplay between effectiveness-of-execution considerations and conflict-of-interest
considerations in explaining why trading practices may fail to achieve
best net price, and, at the same time, offer some insights into the treatment departures from best net price can expect in a negotiated-rate era.

¶ 8.02. THE EFFECT OF COMMISSION RATE STRUCTURE ON BEST-EXECUTION STANDARDS

[1] Securities Transactions Before 1960: The Fixed-Rate System

In years past, it may have been the case that making a trade effectively was a relatively simple affair. Since brokerage fees were fixed
according to a published schedule, a trade in securities listed on an
exchange required only a reputable house of sufficient financial soundness to make it reasonably likely that an order would be carried out
properly either by that house, if it were a member of the exchange, or
by its correspondent. For unlisted securities, a customer needed only to
find, either on his own or through his broker, the house making the best
and most reliable market in the security which was the object of trade.
A regime of fixed commission rates established fairly stringent limits on
customers' ability to affect the cost of trades, and once one was assured
that he was dealing with a responsible house, the decision of which
broker or brokers to use really depended on nonprice factors such as
research assistance, participations in favorable new offerings, portfolio
valuation and custodianship services, personal relationships, and so
forth.

But, beginning in the 1950s, changing circumstances began to add
dramatically to the demands placed on investors in achieving favorable
executions. The complicating agent in this previously simple process
came in the form of a rapid rise in institutional and large-block trading.
Such trading was lucrative for brokers because, even though the cost
to a broker of executing a transaction was not directly proportional to
the number of shares traded, the fixed-rate commission system operated
almost exactly on that premise. The commission for trading 10,000
shares of a stock, for example, would be one hundred times the commission for trading one hundred shares of the same stock. As a result,
the nominal cost of a trade ceased to be a useful index of a fair return
to brokers, and economic pressure began to develop to permit customers to reduce costs on large trades.

Because the brokerage community strove, with SEC support of differing conviction, to preserve this system for as long as possible, the economic pressure caused by the excess price of executions over their actual costs manifested itself in two ways. The more notorious was the pervasive combination by the investment management community with broker-dealers to engage in practices which were either outright violations or severe tests of the duty of loyalty. Also significant, and, in the end, probably more responsible for the death of the fixed-rate system, was the emergence of competing markets designed to offer investors the opportunity of executing transactions at reduced cost—principally a "third market" consisting of nonmember dealers trading off an exchange in securities listed on that exchange, a "fourth market" of direct dealing between investors and indirect dealing through computer services and nonmember brokers, and regional exchanges offering investors opportunities either to affiliate with or become members of these exchanges and thereby recapture part of commission expenses.

[2] 1960 Through 1970: Identification of Conflict-of-Interest Problems and Public-Policy Considerations

The first indication that the institutional trading environment was changing appeared in the *Wharton Study of Mutual Funds*,[7] which reported that factors other than mere execution capability were accounting for the allocation of mutual fund brokerage, and that conflicts of interest of varying intensity might have been responsible for determining which brokerage houses either carried out trades or participated in commissions generated by mutual funds. Also material to the selection of a broker was whether a house was selling shares in the fund or otherwise assisting in promoting the fund, or providing research and statistical information, or providing daily quotation and wire services for portfolio valuation and transmission of orders.[8] Furthermore, the *Study* reported that "7 out of the 83 groups . . . acknowledged that affiliations influenced the flow of brokerage," [9] and it found that increased brokerage to affiliates was a general phenomenon whenever there was affiliation between mutual fund advisers and broker-dealers.[10]

---

[7] SEC, *Report of the Wharton School of Finance and Commerce: A Study of Mutual Funds,* H.R. Rep. No. 2274, 87th Cong., 2d Sess. (1962) (hereinafter cited as *Wharton Report*).

[8] *Id.* at 527-530.

[9] *Id.* at 530.

[10] *Id.* at 32, 473-475.

But the *Wharton Study* ventured only muted criticism of the fixed-rate commission system on policy grounds. Although the penultimate sentence of the report mentioned that "competitive prices for brokerage services . . . would allow adequate compensation to the executing broker and would leave what was formerly surplus brokerage to the free use of the fund," [11] the *Study* did not recommend abandonment or major change in the fixed-rate system. It came closer to urging reform where it exposed the connection between the sale of mutual fund shares and the allocation of brokerage. The *Study* made a matter of public record for the first time the practice of "give-ups," by which mutual fund advisers ordered executing brokers to give a portfolio of the commissions due them to houses selling fund shares.[12] The *Study* conceded that these excess commissions could not be recaptured because of stock-exchange anti-rebate rules,[13] but it did query whether shareholders were getting full value for brokerage allocated on the basis of share sales, since the excess brokerage could have been used to purchase research assistance and other support services.[14] For the same reason, the *Study* expressed reservations about the practice of allocating brokerage to affiliated houses.[15] It suggested that an affiliated fund might have been foregoing valuable services by not conducting more of its trading with other houses.[16]

Nonetheless, the prescience of the *Wharton Study* makes it a watershed in the history of the change from fixed to competitive commission rates. It identified the economic inefficiencies of the fixed-rate commission system and the extra costs it imposed on mutual fund investors, the conflict-of-interest problems associated with commission give-ups and affiliated brokerage, and even anticipated the move by institutional investors to join stock exchanges to recapture part of the excess com-

---

[11] *Id.* at 539.

[12] *Id.* at 537-539.

[13] *Id.* at 539 n.60. Though these same rules prohibited sharing commissions with nonmembers, there were indirect joint transactions through which excess commissions could be transferred, such as with over-the-counter business. *Id.* at 538 n.58.

[14] *Id.* at 33.

[15] *Id.*

[16] The *Wharton Report* did not find excessive trading by an investment company through an affiliated brokerage house to be a serious problem, although many broker-dealers were reportedly turning fund portfolios over at a higher rate than the industry average. The pattern was not even, some broker-affiliated funds trading at a relatively moderate rate and others at a distinctly high rate. *Id.* at 224-226.

mission expenses imposed by the fixed-rate system.[17] The lack of urgency in the *Study*'s conclusions is a consequence of its mission, which was more one of inquiry than one of reform. Moreover, it would have been beyond the competence of the *Study* to have recommended structural changes such as competitive commission rates and the separation of brokerage and money management—changes which, of course, ultimately occurred—on the basis of an inquiry only into the mutual fund industry. Though more public in their affairs than most other investors, mutual funds represented only a small segment of the money-management industry, and their holdings accounted for only a small portion of publicly owned securities.[18]

The first major movement toward reform of the brokerage industry because of practices arising out of the fixed-rate commission system came from the SEC's *Special Study of the Securities Markets*,[19] an investigation commissioned pursuant to Section 19(d) of the Securities Exchange Act.[20] The *Special Study* exposed the vulnerability of the fixed-rate system on two fronts. It described an intensifying price competition with fixed rates in the form of various developing brokerage arrangements designed to reduce the real cost of commissions. Such competition focused attention on the question of what commission rate structure best served public policy. It also reported on spreading conflicts of interest arising out of the allocation of brokerage. This phenomenon increased pressure to find ways to minimize such conflicts, and reform of the commission rate structure began to emerge as the chief candidate.

With respect to the question of how commission rates should be structured, the *Special Study* observed that execution costs could not justify the fixed-rate schedules under which the brokerage industry was operating,[21] and that investor resistance to established rates was manifesting itself in several ways. A third market involving over-the-counter trading in listed securities was growing.[22] Reciprocal business arrange-

---

17 *Id.* at 36 n.159.

18 Total assets under mutual-fund management just before the *Study* was submitted were only $23 billion. *Id.* at 4. Though perhaps large in absolute terms, these holdings were only a small force in the marketplace. Direct holdings of corporate securities at this time were in excess of $450 billion. See SEC, *Statistical Bulletin* 13 (April 1962).

19 SEC, *Report of Special Study of Securities Markets,* H.R. Doc. No. 95, 88th Cong., 1st Sess. (1963) (hereinafter cited as *Special Study*).

20 The Mack Resolution, H.J. Res. 438, 87th Cong., 1st Sess., Pub. L. 87-196, 75 Stat. 465 (Sept. 5, 1961).

21 *Special Study,* note 19 *supra,* Pt. 5, at 103-104.

22 *Id.* Pt. 5, at 138-144.

ments designed either to recapture excess brokerage or redirect it to purposes other than execution services were evolving.[23] There was also some evidence that most of the business of regional stock exchanges was competition with the primary markets through easily obtained SEC approval of dual listing.[24] But the *Special Study* was highly tentative about suggesting that full-price competition was desirable public policy simply because commissions under the fixed-rate system may have been economically unjustifiable. The approving observations about the competition offered by the third market, for example, were not without qualification. The newness of the third market and the lack of regulatory familiarity with transactions conducted in it left the SEC with mild concern over the possible impairment of liquidity in the primary market.[25] Consequently, the SEC recommended further study of the rate structure of the brokerage industry, with particular emphasis on variable commission rates depending on ancillary services provided and volume discounts for large trades.[26]

[a] Reciprocal practices

The more immediate contribution of the *Special Study* to the demise of the fixed-rate commission system was its uncompromising rejection on conflict-of-interest grounds of the reciprocal practices spawned by the fixed-rate system. Particularly criticized were give-ups[27] and interpositioning.[28] The *Special Study* found that these devices were typically used, mostly by investment advisers to mutual funds, for one of two purposes: either to reward brokers for selling mutual fund shares or to purchase advisory support services to assist the investment advisers. Fund sales tended to increase advisory fees, which are a percentage of net asset value, and support services tended to reduce management costs which otherwise would have to have been performed in-house.

---

[23] *Id.* Pt. 2, at 302-309; Pt. 5 at 136.

[24] *Id.* Pt. 2, at 949.

[25] *Id.* Pt. 5, at 142-143.

[26] *Id.* Pt. 5, at 105-107.

[27] *Id.* Pt. 4, at 215-223; Pt. 5 at 173.

[28] Interpositioning is a practice in which a broker-dealer is included as intermediary in a transaction between the retail customer and the market maker in an over-the-counter execution. It is, in effect, an over-the-counter give-up. Since there was no minimum rate structure in the over-the-counter markets, interpositioning would result in a higher cost to the customer than would have been the case if the retail broker had gone directly to the market-maker. The usual purpose of interposing a broker-dealer was to reward him for services rendered. See *id.* Pt. 4, at 223-229, 620-623.

These were both obvious benefits to fund managers, and there was no evidence that a significant share of these benefits were flowing to the funds, for instance, in the form of reductions in advisory fees. On the contrary, there was some indication that reciprocal practices were having pernicious effects. The evidence showed that many funds appeared to be experiencing high portfolio turnover rates and deliberate sacrifice of best execution in the over-the-counter markets, seemingly to generate more commission dollars for fund managers to allocate.[29] Furthermore, complementing the attitude toward give-ups and interpositioning, the *Special Study* generally disapproved of all reciprocal practices even though, as the SEC recognized,[30] such practices were indirect means by which investors could theoretically reduce commission expenses. Reciprocal practices were too well submerged to allay concern that most of the money channeled away from the executing broker was not being used to benefit the accounts making the trades.[31] The *Special Study* concluded, therefore, that the spread of reciprocal practices underlined the need for a review of the commission rate structure with an eye to achieving direct reductions in execution costs, either through rebates and volume discounts[32] or through some form of associate membership on exchanges.[33] Even without change in the commission rate structure, however, the *Special Study* labeled interpositioning as a flagrant breach of duty.[34]

Although the *Special Study* did not make an outright attack on all forms of the fixed-rate commission system, it made major change in the commission rate structure inevitable. The illogic of the arrangements which sprang up to sidestep full payment of commissions shifted the burden of proof to the brokerage industry to justify continuation of the traditional regime. This it did for a time with arguments such as the need for maintaining liquidity in the marketplace, the importance of using institutional commission dollars to underwrite services for small investors, and so forth.[35] But events kept conspiring to make support

---

[29] *Id.* Pt. 4, at 213-235.

[30] *Id.* Pt. 2, at 309.

[31] *Id.* Pt. 5, at 171-173.

[32] *Id.* Pt. 5, at 173.

[33] *Id.* Pt. 2, at 310.

[34] *Id.* Pt. 5, at 173.

[35] The various arguments mustered in support of preservation of fixed rates are summarized in the *Securities Industry Study,* Report of the Subcomm. on Commerce and Finance of the House Comm. on Interstate and Foreign Commerce, H.R. Rep. No. 1519, 92d Cong., 2d Sess. 135-136 (1972). Industry representatives contended also that competitive rates

for the fixed-rate system increasingly tenuous. For one thing, reciprocal arrangements, some of which had names strongly suggestive of sacrifice of fiduciary duty to achieve best execution, became more imaginative. In addition to the notorious give-up, and variations on the give-up,[36] there was the end run,[37] the reverse,[38] the double-reverse,[39] and later,

---

would mean that a dealer market would replace the auction market, regional brokers and underwriters would disappear, and primary exchange membership would eventually die out.

[36] Not all broker-dealers are members of the NYSE and the AMEX, yet a substantial number of these small houses were handling the bulk of broker sales of mutual funds. Some means, therefore, was necessary to get excess commissions to them. The easiest way to do this was to find a NYSE house which was a member of the same regional exchange as the broker to be rewarded. The NYSE house would then arrange the trade in the normal fashion but execute it on the regional exchange, since NYSE rules permitted dual-member houses to trade in NYSE-listed stocks on any other exchange on which those stocks were also listed. By executing on the regional exchange, the excess commissions became available for give-up to the regional-only houses.

[37] This device was another means for getting excess commissions to nonmembers of the major exchanges. Not all listed stocks are traded on the regional exchanges, and often regional-only members are forced to get execution through a NYSE or AMEX member firm. When this happens, the anti-rebate rules would prevent any sharing of commissions with the regional member firm that initiated the transaction. But the executing firm can reciprocate with commissions from other trades involving securities having a dual listing. Thus, even though a NYSE-exchange firm may have been able to execute an order on the Big Board, it would actually execute on a regional exchange through the regional firm. These kinds of transactions promoted form over substance since they are obvious means of avoiding the anti-rebate rules. The NYSE, however, took the position that there was no impermissible reciprocity as long as these arrangements did not represent actual commitments to reciprocate, but only the regional member's hope that he would get return business. Similar dealings occurred with respect to NASD-only firms. Even though they had departments perfectly capable of executing over-the-counter trades themselves, NYSE firms would direct over-the-counter business to designated NASD brokers. For a general discussion of the end run and associated practices, see Jennings, "The New York Stock Exchange and the Commission Rate Struggle," 53 Cal. L. Rev. 1119, 1121-1123 (1965).

[38] The reverse involved an order placed by a regional-exchange member with a NYSE member who purchased for his own account and immediately sold the same order at a markup on the regional exchange. The effect of the markup was to reduce the regional member's commission cost from what it would have been if he had purchased directly on the NYSE.

[39] This device took advantage of rules of regional exchanges permitting commission-splitting with nonmember broker-dealers. At the direction of a

the four-way (eight-way, etc.) ticket,[40] the mirror trade,[41] the step-out,[42] and others. Indeed, the deterioration in fiduciary responsibility appeared to be so serious that in 1966, the SEC *Report on the Public Policy Implications of Investment Company Growth*[43] finally concluded that reciprocal practices placed too much strain on the relationship between mutual funds and their investment advisers, and that the commission rate structure had, therefore, to be modified. The *Report* concluded that the exchanges and the NASD must make rule changes to eliminate the customer-directed give-up, that the effects of other reciprocal practices would have to be mitigated through discounts on large transactions,

---

customer, some NYSE member firms which were also members of these regionals would divert trades in NYSE-listed stocks to a regional in order to share commissions with an NASD firm. See Jennings, "The New York Stock Exchange and the Commission Rate Struggle," 53 Cal. L. Rev. 1119, 1141-1142 (1965).

[40] Also called the yellow ticket and the clearing-liability ticket, the four- (or more) way ticket was much akin to the give-up. It simply added some largely hypothetical service performed by sharing brokers as garnish. The member arranging the trade might have another member named as executing or clearing broker, for example. Once the trade had been arranged, however, the executing or clearing duties were largely nonexistent since the exchanges themselves maintained a clearing house. Thus, in exchange for assuming a meaningless responsibility, the clearing broker would receive up to 50 percent of the commission on the trade. The eight-way ticket and other variations were four-way trades sent through the clearing house several times in various guises. See Welles, "The War Between the Big Board and the Regionals: What It Means to Business," 4 Institutional Investor 21, 26 (Dec. 1970).

[41] The mirror trade was a device to create brokerage for regional members for trades which had to be consummated on the NYSE. In essence, the same trade was conducted in the opposite way on both the NYSE and a regional exchange. The broker moving the securities from the NYSE to the regional (or vice versa) absorbed the entire cost of the commission on the regional by himself. But although the customer bore none of this extra cost, the mirror transaction made it possible for the dual-member firm to pay back the regional firm any debts it may have owed for earlier services.

[42] If, in a block trade generated by a NYSE member firm, an affiliate of the customer were a member of a regional exchange, the NYSE house would meet the affiliate on the regional floor. It would then step out of one side of the transaction to permit the affiliate either to recapture commissions or to compensate it for NYSE business.

[43] SEC, *Report on the Public Policy Implications of Investment Company Growth*, H.R. Rep. No. 2337, 89th Cong., 2d Sess. (1966) (hereinafter cited as *PPI Report*).

and that if these steps were not largely successful, further action would have to be taken.[44]

The end of the SEC's tolerance of the effects of reciprocal practices on fiduciary relationships marked the first regulatory inroad into the traditional fixed-rate commission system. In early 1968, the SEC requested comment on proposed Rule 10b-10, designed to prohibit directed give-ups by investment companies unless the benefits accrued to the companies, and on a proposal by the NYSE to introduce volume discounts and limit give-ups to a fixed percentage of commission dollars, among other things.[45] Shortly thereafter, the SEC announced hearings on the commission rate structure and expressed an intent to move to negotiated rates on trades over $50,000.[46] Under such pressure, the NYSE gave in, and on December 5, 1968, it, and at or about the same time, all other exchanges, amended their constitutions to ban customer-directed give-ups and to adopt a volume discount.[47]

[b] Commission recapture

The period between the *Special Study* and the abolition of the give-up saw development of another condition which was more corrosive of the fixed-rate system than the conflicts of interest associated with reciprocal practices, although it too, because of its effect on mutual funds, was initially perceived as a conflict-of-interest issue. Succumbing to the attraction of increasing their business, the regional stock exchanges began adopting rules changes permitting institutional customers to recapture a portion of the fixed-rate commission. The *Special Study* had observed that the three regional exchanges granted discounts to certain

---

[44] *Id.* at 15-16, 187-188. The alternative the Commission was considering was to prohibit broker-dealers selling mutual fund shares from executing fund executions. Thus, even at this stage, though frustrated in its attempts to curb the adverse consequences of reciprocal practices, the Commission was still not prepared to consider publicly total abolition of fixed rates.

[45] SEC Securities Exchange Act Release No. 8239 (Jan. 26, 1968), [1967-1969 Transfer Binder] CCH Fed. Sec. L. Rep. ¶ 77,523.

[46] SEC Securities Exchange Act Release No. 8324 (May 28, 1968), [1967-1969 Transfer Binder] CCH Fed. Sec. L. Rep. ¶ 77,557.

[47] See SEC Securities Exchange Act Release No. 8399 (Sept. 4, 1968), [1967-1969 Transfer Binder] CCH Fed. Sec. L. Rep. ¶ 77,599. For a detailed review of the last stages of the proceedings leading to abolition of the give-up, see Independent Broker-Dealers' Trade Ass'n v. SEC, 442 F.2d 132 (D.C. Cir. 1971).

nonmembers, including firms which were only members of the NASD.[48] One consequence of these rules was development of the double-reverse reciprocal practice through which brokerage could be directed to NASD firms.[49] But these rules also made possible the return of brokerage to the mutual funds themselves. The reason for this is that the principal underwriters for most mutual funds are NASD members. They also are affiliates of the funds.[50] Thus, a mutual fund could direct a NYSE member firm to trade on a regional exchange and share part of those commissions with its own NASD member firm, the fund's principal underwriter. The principal underwriter could then either return the recaptured brokerage directly to the fund, or, through the affiliated investment adviser, credit the recaptured commissions against the advisory fee.[51]

Since commission splits between regional exchange members and NASD members did little good for mutual funds with captive sales

---

[48] *Special Study,* note 19 *supra,* Pt. 2, at 299-300. By 1966, six of the seven regional exchanges had adopted such a rule. *PPI Report,* note 43 *supra,* at 171.

[49] See note 39 *supra.*

[50] The principal underwriter would be an affiliate both in fact and in law. Ordinarily, it would be a subsidiary of, or under common control with, the investment adviser. The investment adviser is defined as an affiliate of any mutual fund it advises. The Investment Company Act of 1940 establishes such a relationship as technical affiliation. Investment Company Act § 2(a)(3) (15 U.S.C. § 80a-2(a)(3)), defines affiliated person as:

"(C) any person directly or indirectly controlling, controlled by, or under common control with, such other person; . . . (E) if such other person is an investment company, any investment adviser thereof. . . ."

Under Investment Company Act § 2(a)(9) (15 U.S.C. § 80a-2(a)(9)), control "means power to exercise a controlling influence over the management or policies of a company," and is presumed to exist through ownership of more than 25 percent of a company's (defined in Investment Company Act § 2(a)(8), 15 U.S.C. § 80a-2(a)(8)) voting securities and is presumed not to exist otherwise. The presumptions are rebuttable.

[51] Some form of credit was a legal obligation of the principal underwriter-investment adviser. As a fiduciary to the fund, it could not use its position to profit from use of the fund's assets unless it rendered services justifying the consideration received and such services were part of the management agreement. Since recaptured commissions would represent no service on the part of the principal underwriter other than use of its status, they would belong to the fund. See Fogel v. Chesnutt, 533 F.2d 731 (2d Cir. 1975); *In re* Arthur Lipper Corp., SEC Securities Exchange Act Release No. 11,773 (Oct. 24, 1975); *In re* Consumer-Investor Planning Corp., SEC Securities Exchange Act Release No. 8542 (Feb. 20, 1969), [1967-1969 Transfer Binder] CCH Fed. Sec. L. Rep. ¶ 77,677.

forces, however, and since they desired to obtain recapture privileges also, they required their own means of circumventing the rules against recapture. When it became apparent that recapture of commissions was available to mutual funds affiliated with NASD members, therefore, the management of large mutual fund complexes with captive sales forces began to press for membership on regional exchanges to gain for themselves the commission reductions mutual funds which relied on broker-dealers to sell their shares were obtaining. By 1966, four such complexes were members of the Pacific Coast Stock Exchange.[52]

The reason these changes in the rules of the regional exchanges were perceived as conflict-of-interest issues is that they placed mutual fund managers in the position of deciding whether to recapture brokerage or to allocate it to purchase other services. When fixed rates were protected by anti-rebate rules not subject to breach, it was possible to argue that the excess commission dollars had to be spent somewhere, and that so long as mutual fund managers made the allocation determination in good faith, no regulatory changes were necessary. Once it became possible actually to recapture portions of commission expenses, however, mutual fund managers had to justify continued purchase of such services as being of greater benefit to the fund than a straight return of cash to the fund's treasury. The recapture issue ultimately led to litigation in a series of cases which established that the conflict facing investment advisers to mutual funds was too severe for them or their affiliates to resolve without the independent and detached advice and approval of the fund's outside directors.[53]

But although the immediate effect of mutual fund membership on or affiliation with regional exchanges was to create a new and serious conflict-of-interest question for the mutual fund industry, the major consequence of those arrangements was to breach the fixed-rate commission system for all institutional investors. The economic advantage to institutions in bypassing the commission rate schedule of the NYSE

---

[52] *PPI Report,* note 43 *supra,* at 172-173. See also Jennings, "The New York Stock Exchange and the Commission Rate Struggle," 53 Cal. L. Rev. 1119, 1142-1143 (1965).

[53] Moses v. Burgin, 445 F.2d 369 (1st Cir.), *cert. denied sub nom.* Johnson v. Moses, 404 U.S. 994 (1971), was the first case to deal with the failure of mutual fund managers to recapture commissions. In holding that defendants violated their duty to disclose to the outside directors the possibility of recapture, the court raised a host of questions about whether there was an actual duty of recapture, and if so, how it was to be accomplished. The *Moses* line of cases is discussed more fully below (see ¶ 9.07[2] at notes 249-258).

simply meant that institutions would do so and that the NYSE would have to choose between preserving its rate structure and losing business to regional exchanges and other markets, or changing its rate structure and remaining competitive.[54] The SEC noted early the implications for other institutions of membership on regional exchanges by mutual funds,[55] and by 1970, many institutional investors had joined regional exchanges through brokerage affiliates. Once they became members, they took advantage of the reciprocal practices then characterizing the industry and also shifted a significant proportion of their block-trading business to the floor of these exchanges.[56] Moreover, the trend toward institutional membership gave every indication of accelerating.[57]

[3] 1970 Through April 30, 1975: The Move Toward Abolition of the Fixed-Rate System

The year 1970 marked a profound shift in perception by all parties concerning the viability of the traditional fixed-rate commission system. The third and fourth markets had become important competitors of the NYSE.[58] Institutions were receiving de facto commission reductions through affiliations with regional exchanges. The primary markets had already yielded the fundamental point that commissions

---

[54] For many institutions and managers, this was a grudging decision. Forming or operating a brokerage affiliate merely to reduce commissions was perceived as a questionable business decision, and some simply refused to engage in recapture as a matter of policy. See Tannenbaum v. Zeller, 399 F. Supp. 945 (S.D.N.Y. 1975), aff'd in part and rev'd in part [1976-1977 Transfer Binder] CCH Fed. Sec. L. Rep. ¶ 95,900 (2d Cir. 1977). For many, however, the savings were too great to decline, particularly when the NYSE began offering a 40 percent discount to NASD members.

[55] In its study of investment company growth, the SEC observed:

"Widespread emulation by institutional investors of the precedent set by these four complexes [joining a regional exchange] could have a marked effect on the economics of the securities industry."

PPI Report, note 43 supra, at 173.

[56] See Welles, "The War Between the Big Board and the Regionals: What It Means to the Business," 4 Institutional Investor 21 (Dec. 1970).

[57] See SEC, Institutional Investor Study, H.R. Doc. No. 64, 92d Cong., 1st Sess. Ch. XIII, at 2296-2322 (1971) (hereinafter cited as Institutional Investor Study).

[58] The growth of these markets can be traced through reference to the Special Study, note 19 supra, Pt. 2, at 716, 870; the PPI Report, note 43 supra, at 159-161; and the Institutional Investor Study, note 57 supra, Pt. 4, Ch. XI, at 1622-1630.

for executions should reasonably reflect the cost of executions by virtue of the introduction, albeit under regulatory pressure,[59] of the volume discount. Congress, having completed its work on reform of the investment company industry with passage of the Investment Company Amendments Act of 1970,[60] and having responded to the inadequacy of financial-responsibility rules to protect brokerage customers by passing the Securities Investor Protection Act of 1970,[61] was ready to consider the commission rate issue. Furthermore, the drafting and passage of these statutes exposed Congress to and educated it in practices of the securities industry, and led to a decision in both Houses to study the industry.[62] There was no longer any question that the traditional fixed-rate system was coming to an end: The only question was what would succeed it.

Early in 1971, the SEC published its *Institutional Investor Study*, an exhaustive investigation into the economics of institutional securities dealing and portfolio management.[63] The publication of the *Study* marked the beginning of the final drive to a regime of fully competitive commission rates. Theretofore, the SEC had pushed negotiated commission rates on institutional trades both as a threat and as a device to cope with the conflicts of interest it observed growing out of the use of excess commission dollars under the fixed-rate system. With publica-

---

[59] When the SEC proposed Rule 10b-10 to ban customer-directed give-ups (SEC Securities Exchange Act Release No. 8239 (Jan. 26, 1968), [1967-1969 Transfer Binder] CCH Fed. Sec. L. Rep. ¶ 77,523), and the NYSE offered its counterproposal, the SEC ordered public hearings on the commission-rate structure of registered national securities exchanges. SEC Securities Exchange Act Release No. 8324 (May 28, 1968), [1967-1969 Transfer Binder] CCH Fed. Sec. L. Rep. ¶ 77,557. Because "present commission rate structure rules, practices and policies do not, in fact, provide for fixed minimum commission charges," the SEC wrote to the NYSE "specifically requesting it to adopt a revised commission rate schedule which would, among other things, provide for reduced rates for that portion of an order involving round lots in excess of 400 shares or, alternatively, to eliminate requirements for minimum rates of commission for all orders in excess of $50,000."

[60] Pub. L. 91-547, 84 Stat. 1413 (Dec. 14, 1970).

[61] Pub. L. 91-598, 84 Stat. 1636 (Dec. 30 ,1970).

[62] S. Res. 109, 92d Cong., 1st Sess. (June 21, 1971); Letter of Transmittal, Report of the Subcomm. on Commerce and Finance of the Comm. on Interstate and Foreign Commerce, *Securities Industry Study*, H.R. Rep. No. 1519, 92d Cong., 2 Sess., III (1972) (hereinafter cited as *House Securities Industry Study*).

[63] The *Institutional Investor Study*, note 57 *supra*, comprised five principal volumes, a summary volume, and two supplementary volumes.

tion of the *Study*, however, the policy emphasis began to shift. In the letter of transmittal of the *Study*, the SEC recommended elimination of fixed commission rates, at least for institutional-sized transactions, for three reasons: (1) Relationships between institutions and broker-dealers aggravate potential conflicts of interest; (2) such relationships are anticompetitive; and (3) they impede the development of a central market system for securities trading.[64] The latter two, of course, identify price competition and efficient marketing as distinct values, and thus raise the question of whether, irrespective of conflict-of-interest issues, investors are better served by deemphasizing the service competition which had characterized the fixed-rate system and by reversing of the fragmentation of the securities markets which resulted from the institutional investors' practice of reducing commissions costs by trading away from the primary markets.[65]

---

[64]*Id*. Summary Vol., at XXII. See also *id*. at VII:

"[T]he Commission regards non-competitive fixed minimum commission rates on securities transactions of institutional size as the source of a number of difficulties in the development of institutional investing and the trading markets for equity securities. The clear conclusion from the Study Report is that competitive brokerage rates should be required at least on such transactions."

[65] In response to the SEC's release requesting comment on Proposed Rule 10b-10 (SEC Securities Exchange Act Release No. 8239 (Jan. 26, 1968), [1967-1969 Transfer Binder] CCH Fed. Sec. L. Rep. ¶ 77,523), and in the hearings on the commission rate structure (SEC Securities Exchange Act Release No. 8324 (May 28, 1968), [1967-1969 Transfer Binder] CCH Fed. Sec. L. Rep. ¶ 77,557), the Department of Justice took the position that fixed rates were unjustified violations of the antitrust laws unless they were "necessary to make the Securities Exchange Act work" (quoting Silver v. NYSE, 373 U.S. 341, 359 (1963)). *Institutional Investor Study*, note 57 *supra*, at 2199. Also prior to the preparation of the *Institutional Investor Study*, there was extended litigation in the case of Thill Secs. Corp. v. NYSE, 433 F.2d 264 (7th Cir. 1970), *cert. denied* 401 U.S. 994 (1971), which attacked the NYSE rules prohibiting the splitting of commissions with nonmember brokers initiating trades carried out on the exchange. Nonetheless, recognition of price competition as a separate virtue began to come to the SEC only as the *Institutional Investor Study* was being published. The decision to require the introduction of negotiated commission rates on trades above $500,000, for example, came only a month before the *Study* was formally published (SEC Securities Exchange Act Release No. 9079 (Feb. 11, 1971), [1970-1971 Transfer Binder] CCH Fed. Sec. L. Rep. ¶ 77,955), and the request of the SEC that the NYSE permit access to it by nonmember broker-dealers only three months before that. SEC Securities Exchange Act Release No. 9007 (Oct. 22, 1970), [1970-1971 Transfer Binder] CCH Fed. Sec. L. Rep. ¶ 77,918. Compare SEC Securities Exchange Act

The final stages of the transition from fixed commission rates to fully competitive rates can be traced to the securities industry studies conducted in both Houses of Congress. Although after publication of the *Institutional Investor Study*, the SEC had finally concluded that some form of rate competition was in order, it is plain that the Commission, even then, was not prepared to resolve the rate issue by pushing the brokerage industry to fully competitive rates. In its statement of policy on the future structure of the securities markets, the Commission ordered the breakpoint for negotiated commissions reduced to $300,000 from $500,000, but it also stated its determination to introduce competitive rates gradually and not in contravention of its policy to upgrade standards of brokerage service.[66] The Commission seemed married to the idea that competitive rates were appropriate only for substantial institutional business. Consequently, Congress, although willing to tolerate an amount of gradualism, had to establish its rejection of perpetuation of the fixed-rate commission system in any form. In the letter of transmittal of the House of Representatives *Securities Industry Study*, the Subcommittee chairman stated:

> "The Subcommittee finds that fixed minimum commission rates are not in the public interest. We have reviewed our own record, the relevant portions of the SEC's record and that of the Senate Study. On the basis of that review the Subcommittee finds that the fixed minimum commission rate system should be replaced by one where commission rates are determined by the forces of competition. We find further that competitively determined rates should apply to all transactions regardless of size, and that a competitive commission rate system should be phased in without excessive delay." [67]

The Senate study, albeit in somewhat less compelling language, took a similar position.[68]

Release No. 8791 (Dec. 31, 1969), [1969-1970 Transfer Binder] CCH Fed. Sec. L. Rep. ¶ 77,771, in which the SEC requested argument on eight questions, each of which involved, either expressly or implicitly, the issue of how much of an enforced subsidy above execution costs was advisable for various brokerage services.

[66] SEC *Policy Statement on the Future Structure of the Securities Markets* [Special Studies Transfer Binder] CCH Fed. Sec. L. Rep. ¶ 74,811 at 65,619 (Feb. 2, 1972) (hereinafter cited as *Policy Statement*).

[67] *House Securities Industry Study*, note 62 *supra*, Letter of Transmittal, at XIV.

[68] Report of the Subcomm. on Securities of the Senate Comm. on Banking, Housing and Urban Affairs, *Securities Industry Study*, S. Doc. No. 13, 93d Cong., 1st Sess. 43-47 (1973) (hereinafter cited as *Senate Securities Industry Study*). It is clear that the Senate Subcommittee on Securities

Early in 1973, H.R. 5050,[69] an omnibus bill dealing with a variety of securities matters, was introduced. The bill would have amended Section 6(b) of the Securities Exchange Act[70] to provide for the elimination of fixed rates by February 1, 1975.[71] The SEC at first continued to take the position that a fixed legislative timetable was bad policy and that the Commission should retain control over the elimination of fixed rates,[72] a position for which it received some support from the Senate Subcommittee on Securities.[73] Apparently recognizing that its best chance for maintaining control over the elimination of fixed rates was to exercise control, however, that September the Commission issued its own schedule for the introduction of fully negotiated rates.[74]

---

had little faith in the SEC's effectiveness in keeping fixed rates at appropriate levels. In its interim report, relying on a letter of the Chairman of the SEC, among other things, the Subcommittee concluded that the SEC exercised virtually no practical control over the setting of rates. See Report of the Senate Comm. on Banking, Housing and Urban Affairs, containing a Report of the Subcomm. on Securities, *Securities Industry Study*, 92d Cong., 2d Sess. 58 (1972) (hereinafter cited as *Interim Senate Study*).

[69] 93d Cong., 1st Sess. (March 1, 1973).

[70] 15 U.S.C. § 78f(b).

[71] H.R. 5050, 93d Cong., 1st Sess. § 202 (March 1, 1973). The bill authorized the SEC to extend fixed rates on transactions under $100,000 until February 1, 1976, if the Commission found such an extension necessary in the public interest. The Senate Subcommittee on Securities maintained its attitude, as expressed in the *Senate Securities Industry Study,* that further legislation to implement the termination of fixed rates was unnecessary. See *Senate Securities Industry Study,* note 68 *supra,* at 44. But in legislation the Subcommittee was considering, it did tie the termination of institutional membership on an exchange for the purposes of conducting its own brokerage to the elimination of fixed rates. See S. 470, 93d Cong., 1st Sess. § 2 (Jan. 18, 1973).

[72] See Testimony of SEC Commissioner Loomis, in Hearings on H.R. 5050 and H.R. 340 Before the Subcomm. on Commerce and Finance of the Comm. on Interstate and Foreign Commerce, 93d Cong., 1st Sess. Pt. 2, at 430, 446-447 (1973).

[73] See Summary of Principal Provisions of Securities Acts Amendments of 1975, S. 249, for the Senate Comm. on Banking, Housing and Urban Affairs, 94th Cong., 1st Sess. at 1-2 (Jan. 1975). See note 71 *supra.*

[74] SEC Securities Exchange Act Release No. 10383 (Sept. 11, 1973), [1973 Transfer Binder] CCH Fed. Sec. L. Rep. ¶ 79,511, decreed the end of all fixed rates by April 30, 1975. The release actually dealt with a proposed rate rise which the SEC approved subject to elimination of exchange rules prohibiting members from charging above the fixed minimum rate and subject to the introduction of competitive rates on some transactions below the $300,000 breakpoint. In SEC Securities Exchange Act Release No. 10560 (Dec. 14, 1973), the Commission ordered production of a plan to

Sixteen months later, the SEC carried out its promise and adopted Rule 19b-3[75] abolishing fixed commission rates as of May 1, 1975. On June 4, 1975, the President signed into law the Securities Act Amendments of 1975,[76] also abolishing fixed commission rates.[77]

[4] The Impact of Negotiated Commission Rates on the Structure of the Securities Industry

Depending on one's point of view, the establishment of fully competitive commission rates was to be either a boon or a disaster. The

---

introduce "limited price competition." The NYSE complied by letter of February 7, 1974 (see SEC, *Annual Report* 5 (1974)), suggesting interim price competition on transactions of $2,000 or less. The SEC accepted the proposal. SEC Securities Exchange Act Release No. 10,670 (March 7, 1974), [1973-1974 Transfer Binder] CCH Fed. Sec. L. Rep. ¶ 79,696. The NYSE maintained its truculence to a degree, however, first by refusing to extend negotiation to floor-brokerage rates (see SEC Securities Exchange Act Release No. 10670 (March 7, 1974), [1973-1974 Transfer Binder] CCH Fed. Sec. L. Rep. ¶ 79,696), and later by refusing to abandon fixed commission rates of its own accord (see Rustin, "Big Board Refuses to Heed SEC Order on Negotiated Rates," Wall Street J., Oct. 17, 1974, p. 2, col. 2). The NYSE's attitude caused the SEC to hold hearings on both issues. See SEC Securities Exchange Act Release No. 10751 (April 23, 1974), [1973-1974 Transfer Binder] CCH Fed. Sec. L. Rep. ¶ 79,764; SEC Securities Exchange Act Release No. 11073 (Oct. 24, 1974), [1974-1975 Transfer Binder] CCH Fed. Sec. L. Rep. ¶ 79,991. The Commission decided to terminate fixed commission rates by rule, but to permit fixed floor-brokerage rates to remain in effect for a year beyond the introduction of fully competitive rates for customers. See SEC Securities Exchange Act Release No. 11203 (Jan. 23, 1975), [1974-1975 Transfer Binder] CCH Fed. Sec. L. Rep. ¶ 80,067.

[75] SEC Securities Exchange Act Release No. 11203 (Jan. 23, 1975), note 74 *supra*.

[76] Pub. L. 94-29, 89 Stat. 97 (June 4, 1975).

[77] Act § 4 amended Section 6(e) of the Securities Exchange Act of 1934 to adopt the position of the House of Representatives that the authority of the SEC to return to partially fixed rates be tightly circumscribed. Consequently, the SEC was given limited authority to reinstitute fixed rates until November 1, 1976, on a finding that such fees are "in the public interest" (§ 6(e)(1)(A)), and after November 1, 1976, through highly formal administrative proceedings, on findings that such fees "(i) are reasonable in relation to the costs of providing the service for which such fees are charged . . . and (ii) do not impose any burden on competition not necessary or appropriate in furtherance of the purposes of this title. . . ."

The countdown to the passing of the Act was marked by much jockeying for political position, a phenomenon associated with any piece of major legislation. Although the NYSE had long since given up hope of preserving

Senate and House studies of the securities industry both set out the arguments for and against fully competitive rates,[78] and prior to adoption of Rule 19b-3 abolishing fixed rates, the SEC held hearings of the proposed rule[79] during which the contending positions were aired one final time. But by the time of the hearings, the outcome was no longer in doubt,[80] and debate turned to how the securities industry would restructure itself. The chief counsel to the Senate Subcommittee on Securities for most of the period of its investigation of the securities industry, for example, offered his view that "the NYSE in its present form will not long survive the elimination of fixed rates. The plain fact of the matter is that the NYSE has outlived its usefulness." [81] Either with resignation or anticipation, the securities industry turned to preparations for the new regime.[82]

---

fixed commissions, it used the overturning of that nearly 200-year-old prerogative to strengthen its claims on domination of the planned national marketing system. See, e.g., Wall Street Letter, Aug. 12, 1974, pp. 1, 3; Wall Street Letter, July 15, 1974, p. 6; Wall Street Letter, June 10, 1974, p. 1. An excellent summary both of the chronology of the legislation and of some of the political maneuvering it engendered appears in Rowen, "The Securities Acts Amendments of 1975: A Legislative History," 3 Sec. Reg. L.J. 329 (1976).

[78] Senate Securities Industry Study, note 68 supra, at 43-63; House Securities Industry Study, note 62 supra, at 131-146.

[79] SEC Securities Exchange Act Release No. 11073 (Oct. 24, 1974), [1974-1975 Transfer Binder] CCH Fed. Sec. L. Rep. ¶ 79,991. See also SEC Securities Exchange Act Release No. 11019 (Sept. 19, 1974) (requesting rule changes to unfix commission rate); SEC Securities Exchange Act Release No. 10986 (Aug. 27, 1974) [1974-1975 Transfer Binder] CCH Fed. Sec. L. Rep. ¶ 79, 944 (procedural explanation of SEC's approach to introduction of competitive rates).

[80] See, e.g., Securities Week, Nov. 25, 1974 (first week of hearings: Garrett Commission committed to Mayday). For an extended discussion and analysis of the principal arguments in the negotiated-rate debate, see Pozen, "Competition and Regulation in the Stock Markets," 73 Mich. L. Rev. 317 (1974).

[81] Ratner, "The NYSE's Day of Judgment," Wall Street J., Oct. 19, 1974, p. 27, col. 3. The country's largest broker-dealer apparently agrees. See Bacon & Rustin, "Merrill Proposes Central, Electronic Mart With Rival Market Makers for Securities," Wall Street J., Oct. 17, 1975, p. 4, col. 1.

[82] Some firms began constructing new rate plans for both individuals and institutions; some strengthened trading departments; some expected to become dealers; opinions differed on how they would continue to support their research activities. See Wall Street Letter, Jan. 6, 1975, p. 1. There were plans to negotiate requirements contracts on easy executions with institutions (Wall Street Letter, April 28, 1975, p. 11; Wall Street Letter, Feb. 3, 1975; Securities Week, Jan. 27, 1975, p. 1) and introduce round-

The first few days after May 1 were marked by nervousness but little fundamental change. Institutions and brokers began feeling each other out,[83] and commission rates for institutions dipped about 8 per-

---

turn discounts (Securities Week, April 28, 1975, p. 2a). The sensible attitude began to develop that brokerage commissions should reflect difficulty of execution. See, e.g., Wall Street Letter, Feb. 24, 1975; Securities Week, Feb. 24, 1975, p. 2a. Some firms decided that each customer's rates would depend on the quality of business the customer was providing. See, e.g., Wall Street Letter, April 7, 1975, p. 1.

Institutional managers began reassessing their record-keeping procedures with an eye to documenting quality of execution, although some apparently felt that maintaining records would simplify proof of failure to obtain best execution. See, e.g., Welles, "Are the Lawyers Taking Over the Business?" 9 Institutional Investor 77, 81 (March 1975). The source of most of the anxiety about quality of execution stemmed from extra commission charges to pay for research services, a topic discussed extensively in Chapter 9. Some institutions simply concluded that they would make no such payments as part of commissions on trades. See, e.g., Securities Week, March 24, 1975, p. 3. Many at first believed that the actual reduction in commissions would be modest—on the order of 15 percent—and that rates would return to fixed-rate levels within a few years. See Bacon & Rustin, "Brokers Admit That End of Rate Fixing Isn't End of World," Wall Street J., April 28, 1975, p. 1, col. 6; Wall Street Letter, April 7, 1975, p. 2. But as May 1 drew near, expectations in some quarters about the size of rate reductions began to grow. For easy trades, the talk was of up to 50 percent off the old rates, and on larger trades, up to 25 percent. See Wall Street Letter, April 28, 1975. p. 1; Securities Week, April 28, 1975, pp. 1, 3.

Because of the uncertainty surrounding the immediate effects of introducing fully negotiated rates (see, e.g., Shakin, "Comes the Revolution," Barron's April 28, 1975, p. 5), the SEC proposed to follow a monitoring program. The Securities Acts Amendments of 1975 later made that a statutory obligation of the Commission. Pub. L. 94-29 § 4, 89 Stat. 97 (June 4, 1975), 15 U.S.C. § 78f(e)(3). The program consisted of measuring industry trends, self-regulatory agency trends, and quality of the market. Securities Week, March 24, 1975, p. 1. The SEC's first quarterly report stated that institutions were enjoying measurably lower execution costs, but that the securities industry was remaining healthy. The Commission concluded there were no grounds for returning to fixed rates. See Sec. Reg. L. Rep. No. 331, Dec. 10, 1975, at A-13.

[83] An excellent report on the pattern of negotiations in these first days appears in the Wall Street Letter, May 5, 1975, p. 3, which recorded not only the results of some actual trades, but also the kinds of conversations going on between brokerage firm traders and institutional traders. The following is representative:

Broker: "What do you want to pay?"
Institution: "You tell me."
B: "33¢ a share."

cent to 15 percent, except on easy trades where the reduction was 30 percent and more.[84] Many broker-dealers began to put into effect the strategies they had devised during the last week of fixed rates.[85] But even at the outset, there were signs that the initial stability would give way. Reports indicated a measurable expansion in trading on the fourth market.[86] Also, in transactions on the primary markets, some firms were offering much larger discounts than those prevailing among other elements of the brokerage industry.[87] In short order, broker-dealers became engaged in a full-scale rate war,[88] and the deterioration of the

---

I: "How can I tell? Let's just print and see how you do."

B: "My head trader . . . wants to negotiate first."

I: "We can talk about it later, whether it's 35¢ or 30¢. Are you going to stay hard and fast?"

[84] See *id*. See also Securities Week, May 5, 1975, pp. 1, 3.

[85] An account of the plans of a number of different broker-dealers appears in Securities Week, May 5, 1975, pp. 3-6. According to the report, firms considered moving into market making; posting rate guidelines, either on retail business, or institutional business, or both; offering round-turn discounts; offering variable discounts, depending on whether an order came before or after the opening of the market. Other proposals abounded also.

[86] Wall Street J., May 5, 1975, p. 5, col. 1.

[87] The same issue of *Securities Week* which reported mostly mild adjustments to negotiated rates (see note 85 *supra*) also described "chinks in the armor" (Securities Week, May 5, 1975, p. 1), including at least one instance of a block trade at 40 percent to 50 percent of the old fixed rate. Furthermore, the announced strategy of some broker-dealers was simply to undercut the old fixed-rate schedule by a substantial margin. The reports identified firms willing to do business at 15 cents a share for orders under 1,000 shares, and offers to do business with selected customers for over 40 percent off the old rates (*id*. at 4). A few firms admitted to being under heavy economic pressure from others offering larger discounts. *Id*. at 3, 5. By the end of the first week, it was clear that rate erosion was progressing rapidly. See generally Securities Week, May 7, 1975.

[88] The rate of acceleration into heavy discounting seemed to catch many in the securities industry by surprise. See Rustin, "Some Brokers Say Impact of New Rates on Revenue Proves Surprisingly Severe," Wall Street J., May 8, 1975, p. 4, col. 3. See also Wall Street Letter, May 12, 1975, pp. 3-4. Within three weeks, there was no longer any doubt that discounting from the old fixed-rate schedule had left both the schedule and plans to support it in a shambles. See Securities Week, May 22, 1975 (institutional rate war: "firms are cutting each other to shreds"); Elia, "Cutting of Brokerage Rates on Big Trades Escalates Into All-Out War Among Firms," Wall Street J., May 23, 1975, p. 30, col. 1. By the end of May, the Chairman of the SEC was giving a pep talk to the securities analysts, the group which seemed the most exposed by the rapid break in price levels. See Securities Week, May 29, 1976. In addition to simple price-cutting, some brokerage firms came

old rate structure proceeded so rapidly that the Deputy Assistant Attorney General for Antitrust felt constrained to warn institutions against colluding in forcing commission rates down.[89]

But within several weeks, securities purchase and sale patterns began to emerge. The purchase of research and other services with commissions diminished substantially. Hardest hit were the research houses which, in the fixed-rate era, had made it quite plain that the execution aspect of transactions carried out through them was ancillary to the provision of high-quality examinations of companies, industries, markets, and so forth.[90] But the long delay in introducing competitive commission rates prevented major dislocations among research-oriented firms. Most, anticipating reduced business as a result of the introduction of competitive commission rates, improved their trading capabilities

---

up with imaginative devices to offer large discounts. One example was the introduction of a brokerage cooperative. See Securities Week, May 26, 1975, p. 10; Wall Street J., May 27, 1975, p. 33, col. 3. The large full-service firms tried as hard as possible to resist the pressure of the discounters (see Wall Street Letter, Oct. 27, 1975, p. 7), and another on the complaint 1975, pp. 4-5), and received some support in this from institutional traders ("I won't do business with cutthroats"). Id. at 5. But by June, even those houses were lowering their fees (see "Research Firms Regain Market Share by Lowering Rates—But Can They Make Money at Those Levels?" Wall Street Letter, June 2, 1975, pp. 1-2), and the institutions which had supported them in the beginning began to view the large discounts as an industry standard they had to observe. See Securities Week, June 2, 1975, p. 10. Within two months, even Autex, the computerized communication network for broker-dealers doing block trading, found itself forced to consider rate reductions. See Securities Week, July 14, 1975, p. 3.

[89] Wall Street Letter, May 26, 1975, p. 5. He also warned brokerage firms about the antitrust implications of attempting to force customers to purchase service packages, especially research support, as a condition to transacting any business with the firm. Wall Street J., June 19, 1975, p. 5, col. 2. Eventually, the division did launch some antitrust investigations, one apparently precipitated by the closing of a small firm offering deep discounts (see Wall Street Letter, Oct. 27, 1975, p. 7), and another on the complaint of a deep-discount house that institutions were boycotting it (see Securities Week, March 15, 1976).

[90] See Wall Street Letter, June 9, 1974, p. 4; Securities Week, July 28, 1975, p. 5; Wall Street Letter, Aug. 4, 1975, p. 8; Securities Week, Aug. 18, 1975, p. 9; Wall Street Letter, Aug. 25, 1975, p. 3; Wall Street J., Sept. 19, 1975, p. 36, col. 1; Securities Week, Feb. 2, 1976. See also "Trading," Institutional Investor 65 (Aug. 1975) (declining importance of institutional salesman and increasing importance of trader); "Trading," Institutional Investor 23, 27 (Aug. 1974) (research firms must provide both quality trading and execution to survive).

prior to the end of fixed rates. Once they adjusted to the heavy rate reductions that occurred during the first month of the new regime, they were able to reclaim much of the business they initially lost.[91] In a relatively brief period, arrangements between institutional investment managers and full-service brokerage firms seemed to stabilize at a point where traditional services, particularly research, were again being supplied in exchange for brokerage business so long as the commission rates charged were in line with the rates of brokerage firms providing execution services only.[92] Still, it is impossible to gauge the durability of this condition. Reports indicate that some institutions are paying in cash for services formerly received in connection with brokerage business.[93] Perhaps the most portentous indicator that relationships between institutional managers and full-service brokerage firms will enter a new stage is the developing practice of some managers to pay for research assistance in cash instead of brokerage business.[94]

Another pattern which seems to have emerged is a three-tiered commission rate structure. To be sure, commission rates are nowhere near as predictable as they were in the fixed-rate era. But out of the commission rate war there evolved a set of rates describable at least within reasonable range and showing signs of initial stability. As might have been expected, rates depend on the difficulty of the trade, with easy executions ("no-brainers") executed at about one-half the old rate; trades requiring time and effort, but within the capabilities of most brokers, executed at about three-quarters of the old rate, and unusually difficult trades executed up to and beyond the old rates.[95] This is not to say that most firms would have charged identical commission rates on a particular trade or that rates have not been adjusting down and up to reflect shifts in market volume, elimination of unprofitable activities, and other factors which any competitive business must take into

---

[91] See Securities Week, July 7, 1975, pp. 4-6 (research brokers report business lost in May returning in June, including a partial return on easy trades, as a result of their rates becoming more competitive). See also Securities Week, July 28, 1975, p. 5; Securities Week, Aug. 11, 1975, p. 8; Securities Week, Aug. 18, 1975, p. 9.

[92] See Wall Street Letter, Aug. 25, 1975, p. 3 (major cuts in research broker lists over).

[93] See Wall Street Letter, July 14, 1975, p. 6 (pension management performance measurement service).

[94] See Wall Street Letter, Aug. 4, 1975; Wall Street Letter, Nov. 17, 1975, p. 3; Securities Week, Nov. 17, 1975, p. 10.

[95] See Securities Week, July 7, 1975, pp. 4-6; Securities Week, July 28, 1975, p. 5; Securities Week, Aug. 11, 1975, p. 8.

account in pricing its product. It is simply that commission rates found their own level after a period of adjustment to the elimination of fixed rates, a development which should surprise no one.

With the development of a reasonably stable rate structure in response to competitive forces, the major change which can be expected is a drift away from the old fixed-rate schedule as the yardstick for commission rates. Although there was no early consensus on the kind of commission rate format the industry should adopt, professional traders quickly began discussing alternatives to the percent-discount method.[96] At least initially, debate seemed to focus on a cost-of-trade approach against a system permitting the inclusion of cost of services.[97] Much of the support for continuation of calculating execution costs as a percentage of the old fixed rates comes from institutional managers who believe that they can document quality of execution better using the fixed-rate schedule as a standard. As anxiety over the legal consequences of trading decisions diminishes,[98] and as market making by broker-dealers becomes a more significant phenomenon,[99] this support will erode.

Worthy of mention also are several other developments resulting from the introduction of negotiated commission rates. Investment managers are bunching orders to take advantage of the lower average commission ordinarily available on a single large transaction.[100] Some banks, in fact, have made the advantages of bunching available to individual investors who are customers of the bank.[101] Retail brokerage has also become a more important factor in the business of regional brokerage firms. Normally, institutions can get better rates on easy executions from the major firms, and since most regional firms do not have the block capability institutions require, institutions have reduced their business with the regional firms.[102] Another factor affecting re-

---

[96] See Securities Week, Oct. 13, 1976, p. 2b (report on discussions at National Securities Traders Association meeting).

[97] Id.

[98] See ¶¶ 8.03, 8.04 infra.

[99] See note 81 supra. See also Wall Street Letter, July 7, 1975, p. 3 (firms increase positioning and dealer-market activity). A market maker, as owner of the securities, trades on a net price basis.

[100] See, e.g., Reich, "Games People Are Playing with Fully Negotiated Rates," 9 Institutional Investor 29, 30 (July 1975).

[101] See Cole, "Should Banks Be Allowed a Stockbroker Role?" New York Times, Oct. 28, 1974, p. 49, col. 1; Securities Week, June 2, 1975, p. 2n; Securities Week, Nov. 3, 1975, p. 2a; Securities Week, March 15, 1976.

[102] See Wall Street J., Sept. 19, 1975, p. 36, col. 2.

gional firms has been the opportunity to enter into advantageous correspondent relationships with the major houses. This has resulted in the termination by some regional firms of their membership on regional exchanges.[103] While these developments indicate structural changes still to come in the securities industry, the extent to which they take on importance for an investment manager's duty of best execution depends too much on regulatory matters, especially the eventual form of and investor access to a national marketing system, to predict the effect they will have.[104]

¶ 8.03. THE DUTY OF BEST EXECUTION IN A NEGOTIATED-COMMISSION-RATE ENVIRONMENT: GENERAL OBSERVATIONS

Departures from best net price may be either inadvertent or deliberate. A manager seeking the least expensive execution obtainable may mistakenly fail in that goal. He may choose a broker whose commission charges exceed those otherwise available; or he may execute in a market in which the securities desired are priced higher than in another market at the same moment. A manager may also knowingly or purposefully depart from best net price. He may use commissions to pay for services in addition to those necessary in executing a trade; he may be directed by a client to use a particular broker, even though less expensive services are available from other brokers known to the manager; or an investment manager, either affiliated or having a continuing relationship with a brokerage firm, may choose to transact business with that firm in preference to other less expensive brokers. In all these situations and others like them, the manager is said to have a duty of best execution. The legal question raised in connection with an investment manager's duty of best execution is the degree to which he may transact business at other than best net price.[105]

---

103 See Securities Week, July 14, 1975, p. 1.

104 Banks bunching orders might find themselves obliged to register as brokers, for example. Although Securities Exchange Act § 3(a)(4) (15 U.S.C. § 78c(a)(4)) excludes banks from the definition of broker, by analogy to the ectoplasmic theory of investment companies (see ¶ 3.04, note 250) it can colorably be argued that the entity within the bank acting as introducing broker and providing confirmations must be treated as a broker.

105 Best net price is measured for an entire contemplated transaction and not merely for one or several of a related series of trades. Trading strategy,

For the most part, inadvertent departures from best net price raise only effectiveness-of-execution questions. Without some reason to do so, few persons will spend more on a service than is necessary. The only likely explanation for an inadvertent departure from best net price, therefore, is that the manager was not aware of how or where to carry out one or more of a series of transactions at less expense. In such cases, the scope of the duty of best execution is determined by the standard of reasonable care. A legal challenge to an investment manager's compliance with his duty of best execution on effectiveness-of-execution grounds must show not just that one or more of a series of tranactions occurred at other than best net price, but that the departure from best net price was unreasonable under the circumstances.[106]

Intentional departures from best net price, on the other hand, generally raise conflict-of-interest questions. Deliberate decisions to pay more than necessary for a service rarely can be explained except by reference to some competing interest to be served by such action. This is not to say that an investment manager's business judgment exercised solely for the client's benefit may not be the motivating force behind the manager's decision to sacrifice best net price. But, at least in the case of executions, such decisions almost always can serve the manager's interest also. For that reason, the analysis of intentional departures from best net price is different from that governing inadvertent departures. Not only must the execution be effective—that is, reasonable under the circumstances—but where conflict of interest is in issue, no departure from best net price is acceptable unless there has been some resolution of the conflict.[107]

The difference between the effectiveness-of-execution question and the conflict-of-interest question can be illustrated by analyzing a contemporary execution problem. With many listed securities, investment managers have the choice of executing on a commission basis by trading on an exchange or on a net-price basis by trading with a nonexchange market maker. Suppose a manager is offered a 50 percent discount from the fixed-rate schedule previously in force on a 1,000-share trade, and chooses to execute immediately for that commission. If, given the size of the discount, that trade accords with general business custom in the negotiated-rate environment (as would apparently have been the case during the period shortly after the introduction of negotiated

---

especially including testing the market, must be taken into account. See ¶ 8.01[1] *supra*.

[106] See ¶ 8.04 *infra*.

[107] See Chapters 9 and 10.

commission rates), it is virtually certain that the trade would satisfy the manager's duty of best execution, even if it could later be shown that direct dealing with a market maker would have yielded lower net cost. The possibility of greater cost through price fluctuation and the knowledge on the part of the manager that the commission rate he paid accorded with the lowest rates then generally available for a trade of that type establish his decision as reasonable.

But some investment managers apparently are sacrificing best net price to improve documentation of execution. Instead of trading on a net-price basis, they are purchasing and selling securities on a commission basis in order to establish a record of discounts from the former fixed-rate commission levels.[108] They fear that if a transaction is consummated on a net-price basis, there will be no way to show the execution cost involved, and the likelihood of a suit or an administrative investigation for failure to achieve best execution will be increased. Ironically, this practice of sacrificing best net price in order to make a record tending to show a satisfactory quality of execution, if it could be proved, would itself probably be treated as a breach of duty of best execution as a matter of law. Even though the commission charges might be shown to be reasonable given the nature of the trade, the reason for sacrificing best net price would be solely to serve the self-interest of the manager in avoiding a lawsuit or regulatory action.[109] It is doubtful that any client or person authorized to act for the client would give an informed consent to greater execution expenses for such a purpose. The conflict would therefore remain unresolved and render the sacrifice of best net price a breach of duty.

In addition to affecting the analysis of the duty of best execution, the distinction between effectiveness-of-execution questions and conflict-of-interest questions controls the context in which challenges to

---

[108] See Reich, "Games People Are Playing With Fully Negotiated Rates," 9 Institutional Investor 29, 30 (July 1975). In all probability, this practice will rapidly diminish in frequency. As traders become more acclimated to a negotiated-rate environment, they will be less compulsive about having to prove the quality of every transaction. Also, the growth of market making (see note 99 *supra*) will force more trades to be executed at net price.

[109] Not every transaction executed on a commission rather than net price basis is a sacrifice of best net price. The total cost of a trade may be the same whichever way it is carried out. Indeed, trading at net price makes it easier to hide inflated commission costs, and all other things being equal, a manager can justifiably prefer to trade on a commission basis. Nonetheless, to the extent trading on a market-price-plus-commission basis instead of on a net price basis imposes additional costs on a client solely to protect the manager, it violates the duty of best execution.

compliance with the duty of best execution are raised. Where the question is only one of effectiveness of execution, the burden remains with the challenging party to show that one or more of a series of transactions was carried out unreasonably. The existence of conflicts of interest, on the other hand, requires the challenging party only to show that best net price was not obtained. The manager then has the burden of proof either that the conflict was satisfactorily resolved or that best net price was not intentionally sacrificed.[110]

Distinguishing between effectiveness of execution and conflict of interest is important also in analyzing the authorities on best execution which originated in the fixed-rate era. As discussed in ¶ 8.02, the collapse of the fixed-rate system became inevitable for two reasons. With fixed rates, execution prices came greatly to exceed execution costs, thereby encouraging investors to improve the effectiveness of execution by circumventing the established brokerage system and reducing brokerage fees. Furthermore, in the process of establishing these outside routes to lower rates, the interests of brokers and investment managers became strongly tied into the system of distribution of the extra money generated under the fixed-rate structure. Far more than today, execution practices in the fixed-rate era involved overlapping effectiveness-of-execution considerations and conflict-of-interest considerations. To understand the proper scope of the authorities on best execution developed during this period, one must remain aware of the degree to which official tolerance of conflicts of interest reflected a practical compromise not necessary under a system of negotiated rates. In order to improve effectiveness of execution for investors under fixed rates, at least if effectiveness is to be measured on a cost-of-execution basis, it was necessary to suffer arrangements which introduced new conflicts of interest and exacerbated old ones.

¶ 8.04. INADVERTENT SACRIFICE OF BEST EXECUTION: STANDARDS OF REASONABLE CARE

Not every transaction is executed at best net price despite an investment manager's determination to do so. An investment manager purchasing or selling securities may be unaware that he can obtain identical services from another broker-dealer for a lower commission rate or markup. Or he may place a trade with a firm which appears fully competitive on a commission basis, but which inadvertently executes the transaction in an inferior market. Or the manager may rely

---

[110] 3 C.J.S. *Agency* §§ 503-507 (1973); 90 C.J.S. *Trusts* § 467 (1955).

on a firm offering fully competitive commissions and having access to a broad range of markets, but the firm may err in its trading strategy and fail to accumulate or distribute the order as effectively as another firm might have done. The question is what an investment manager's duty is in the event any of these or other comparable set of circumstances occur.

So long as the manager cannot profit from his failure to obtain best net price, there are no conflict-of-interest issues raised. The applicable principle, therefore, governing the duty relationship between manager and client is not loyalty but reasonable care. In general, this means that an investment manager's trading practices are not subject to challenge unless they so depart from professional standards of skill and care that no reasonable investment manager would have conducted himself similarly. In this regard, the failure to achieve best net price is not a prima facie violation of duty as it is when conflict of interest is at issue, and the burden remains on the client to prove that the manager's professional conduct was unreasonable, rather than on the manager to disprove lack of reasonable care.

But, although the general principle may be clear, its application to the contemporary trading activities of investment managers is difficult to determine. During most of the long experience with fixed commission rates, the trading function was a relatively simple affair. Only as markets became fragmented and prices became subject to wide variation in response to the economic pressure of institutional investors did serious differences about standards of care applicable to the trading function began to emerge. Coincident with the rise in institutional trading, and, of course, because of that rise, execution techniques entered a period of rapid change and development. Moreover, frequent change has remained the rule as traders adjust to the opportunities of a negotiated-rate regime and the industry progresses toward a central market system.

It is thus unsurprising that there is no real consensus about the meaning of professional skill and care with regard to the trading function. Furthermore, whatever opportunity there may have been to develop objective criteria for trading into rules of law has simply been overwhelmed by other concerns with the trading function. Except for discussions of institutional trading appearing from time to time in the securities industries studies, beginning with the *Wharton Report*,[111]

---

[111] See *Wharton Report*, note 7 *supra*, at 525-539; *Special Study*, note 19 *supra*, Pt. 2, at 838-870; *PPI Report*, note 43 *supra*, at 155-200.

until the *Institutional Investor Study*[112] official attention focused primarily on remedying deliberate trading abuses and rectifying market discontinuities operating to the general disadvantage of investors. Nor was institutional trading the object of much serious exposition by members of the industry. Perhaps because of temperament, traders treated their profession as unquantifiable art, and made few attempts to set forth statements of basic principles.[113] Finally, whether the amount of damages in instances of trading misfeasance tended to be small, or because client attention was held by duty-of-loyalty questions, or because clients were inadequately versed in the mechanics of trading, or because it was just simpler for dissatisfied clients to shift to some other investment manager, aggrieved clients failed to press their claims. Consequently, this potential source of developmental law with regard to the trading function also went untapped.

But the facts of ongoing change notwithstanding, official and client inattention to such a void in the law cannot reasonably be expected to continue. When trades follow a course of conduct of questionable professional validity and the losses are sufficient to warrant a lawsuit or an administrative proceeding, clients will begin to sue and administrative authorities will begin to investigate. Moreover, as managers' responses to conflict-of-interest situations become more refined and more sophisticated, one can expect to see plaintiffs tying negligence allegations into their duty-of-loyalty claims.[114] So long as they can find professionals willing to testify that a manager's trading practices did not rise to a professional standard of skill and care, aggrieved clients will be able to withstand summary judgment and provoke trial on the merits. Perhaps more important, state and federal regulatory authorities are presumed to have expertise in these matters, and courts can be expected to defer to their judgment, particularly as they establish definitional tables for best execution.[115]

---

[112] *Institutional Investor Study,* note 57 *supra,* Pt. 4, Chs. 10-13.

[113] One reasonably good, though somewhat out-of-date, presentation, however, appears in Geyer, "A Primer on Institutional Trading," 25 Fin. Anal. J. 16 (March-April 1969).

[114] See *In re* Flint's Will, 148 Misc. 474, 485, 266 N.Y.S. 392, 405 (1933) ("an investment for which there is no market except the corporate fiduciary is improvident"). Compare ¶ 10.06[2][b], note 328 *infra.* See also Weiser, "Will the Small Institution Grow Up?" 9 Institutional Investor 35, 36 (June 1975) (small trust institutions regularly receive poor block executions, in part because of need to buy research).

[115] See note 5 *supra.*

One situation with excellent prospects for early administrative proceedings, if not litigation, for example, is the practice described above,[116] of some institutional traders who, in hopes of making a record of effective execution performance, practice "defensive trading" by seeking the lowest rate of commission, even though to do so may entail sacrifice of a market price which would have produced a lower net cost to the client.[117] Another solid candidate for refinement under rules of law based on negligence principles stems from the emerging recognition that investment managers have a right to make reasonable inquiry into the financial responsibility of the brokerage firms on whose execution services they rely. Complementing the opportunity the introduction of negotiated rates has given managers to obtain large commission discounts is an increased need to exercise due care to assure that the executing brokers and clearing brokers a manager selects are not only capable, but trustworthy and creditworthy.[118] Considerations of financial stability, net worth of partners, net capital ratio of the firm, back-office capabilities, record of deliveries, and the like are all factors that inform a manager as to the risk involved in dealing with a particular firm. Since such information is readily available through financial statements and personal inquiry,[119] ignorance of it may well result in negligence liability for a manager if a brokerage firm's insolvency causes losses to his clients.

Too, as experience with the negotiated-commission-rate system increases, some features of the trading function will become sufficiently crystallized to set legal standards. Presently, the criteria for selecting one brokerage firm over others are relatively subjective. But since, on many transactions, the only material variable is the commission rate, attention will intensify on the criteria on which a manager relies when departing from the lowest rates generally available. Moreover, the fact

---

[116] See text at note 108 *supra*.

[117] See, e.g., Reich, "Games People Are Playing With Fully Negotiated Rates," 9 Institutional Investor 29, 30 (July 1975); Mattlin, "The Quest for a Definition of 'Best Execution,'" 9 Institutional Investor 60, 64 (April 1975); Wall Street J., Nov. 7, 1975, p. 40, col. 3; Securities Week, July 14, 1975, p. 10; Wall Street Letter, Sept. 30, 1974, p. 1.

[118] See, e.g., Mattlin, "The Quest for a Definition of 'Best Execution,'" 9 Institutional Investor 60, 68 (April 1975); Wall Street Letter, June 9, 1975, p. 1 (institutions intensifying scrutiny of brokerage firms' financial condition).

[119] See *id.*; Securities Week, May 19, 1975, p. 3 (questionnaire sent to brokers).

that commission rates are variable will not affect the analysis. Although commission rates are no longer as precise as they were when they were fixed, and can be expected to shift in response to changes in economic conditions, the securities industry has settled into identifiable patterns for determining commission rates, and rates can be expected to rise and fall across the industry at the same time.[120] In this connection, the introduction of negotiated rates has seen the development of commercially available trader-rating services,[121] and many investment managers have put together their own rating systems.[122] While agreement over the validity of the assumptions underlying these systems is yet lacking,[123] they are developing a following and their conclusions are influencing the allocation of brokerage business.[124] From beginnings like these are likely to evolve most of the substance of the standards under which the industry will operate.

Probably least adaptable to the kinds of objective criteria of performance which must exist before negligence principles can have much of an impact are those transactions in which security price considerations, far more than commission rates, determine the cost of execution. But even though execution costs are not as precisely measurable in this context, reconstruction of conditions that determine net price can be done effectively enough to identify significant departures from a reasonable net price.[125] Transactions of this type mostly involve large blocks of securities, although relatively small transactions in unlisted securities having small floats can have similar execution characteristics. At any rate, the cost of moving large blocks of securities depends principally on market phase and size of transaction. In an active improving market, most blocks can be executed on an agency basis and brokerage firms with block capabilities seek selling opportunities. Thus, a seller

---

120 See ¶ 8.02[4].

121 See Wall Street Letter, June 2, 1975, p. 12; Wall Street Letter, April 21, 1975, p. 7; Securities Week, April 7, 1975, p. 3; Wall Street Letter, Jan. 6, 1975.

122 See, e.g., Securities Week, July 7, 1975, p. 7; "Some Criteria for Evaluation of Brokerage Research," 7 Institutional Investor 72 (March 1973).

123 See Trading, "Rating the Trader 'Raters,' " 9 Institutional Investor 65 (Dec. 1975).

124 See Securities Week, Jan. 5, 1976, p. 6; Securities Week, July 28, 1975, p. 8; Wall Street Letter, Feb. 17, 1975, p. 6.

125 See, e.g., Wall Street Letter, Oct. 7, 1974, p. 5; Wall Street Letter, Sept. 30, 1974, p. 3 (sale of $80 million in equities in four days by a single seller).

who initiates an order can expect a better price relative to current market than a customer offered the opportunity to participate as a purchaser.[126] When trading is less active and brokerage firms must position part of an order and hence risk their own capital, execution costs are more substantial and, in some cases, may well exceed brokerage fees charged under the fixed-rate system.[127] But it is not a complicated affair to determine after the fact what the conditions were at a given time in the market generally and for a particular stock. Thus, although the number of brokerage firms capable of handling large block transactions may be small, and although many block transactions may have unique features which affect execution price from trade to trade, the prices associated with block transactions are not necessarily so uncertain as to preclude a useful evaluation of the quality of execution.

Presently, competition in the market for investment management services is the only significant control on the quality of execution clients receive. But the discipline of the marketplace will be joined progressively by standards of conduct enforceable at law. The rate of this progress depends on many factors, not the least of which are growth of investor sophistication in trading matters and resolution of political conflicts over whether to protect or restrict this or that element of the securities industry.[128] The initial reaction of many investment managers to the new environment has been to expand record-keeping. Some records can be useful, of course, but more relevant to the duty question than stated reasons for selecting a particular broker-dealer on a given trade will be records of commitment lists, research chits, ticket codes,

---

[126] See, e.g., Reich, "Games People Are Playing With Fully Negotiated Rates," 9 Institutional Investor 29 (July 1975); Wall Street Letter, Dec. 22, 1975, p. 7 (large institution informs brokers it will insist on flat rate at high discount on orders it initiates, but will maintain flexibility on response orders; brokers say institution's posture is in line with industry practices); Wall Street Letter, Sept. 6, 1975, p. 4.

[127] See, e.g., Du Bois, "Upstairs, Downstairs," Barron's Oct. 20, 1975, p. 11.

[128] For example, during the markup of H.R. 5050 (93d Cong., 1st Sess. (March 1, 1973)), a member of the House Subcommittee proposed an amendment to require managers to negotiate commissions before a transaction. See Securities Week, Aug. 24, 1974, p. 3. The purpose of the amendment was to prevent institutions from dictating commissions to brokers. Not only is it doubtful the amendment would have done anything to undercut the economic power of institutions, the attempted ban on post-transaction negotiations showed a notable ignorance of how institutional traders frequently decide on a fair commission. Most factors—difficulty of trade and quality of execution, for example—cannot be quantified until after the transaction is completed.

and so forth. Certainly, attempts by brokers and managers to preserve old, comfortable arrangements will be the first to fall.[129] A byproduct of the increasing attention trading can expect to see will be increased research into the trading function.[130] To some extent, that also will influence the development of standards of care. But, in the final analysis and without prior agreement, the community of traders will set their own standards for trading competence, and the law of negligence will ultimately endorse their product.

---

[129] There have been some abbreviated attempts by brokers to enter into retainer and guaranteed-commission arrangements. See, e.g., Wall Street Letter, March 3, 1975, p. 8. Because of the obvious self-dealing potential and the difficulty of assessing in advance of an investment period the amount and type of business to be executed, few institutions have contracted to do this. There are also reports that institutions have been squeezing certain broker-dealers to include full-service firms in their trades so that the institutions can pay off obligations to the larger firms. See, e.g., Securities Week, Feb. 2, 1976, p. 2a. This almost certainly results in higher cost to the client, and if not a breach of the duty of loyalty, still is of doubtful validity under negligence principles.

[130] See, e.g., Cuneo & Wagner, "Reducing the Cost of Stock Trading," 31 Fin. Anal. J. 35 (Nov.-Dec. 1975); Barnea & Logue, "The Effect of Risk on the Market Maker's Spread," *id.* at 45.

Chapter 9

USE OF COMMISSIONS TO PURCHASE SUPPLEMENTARY SERVICES

¶ **9.01.   CONFLICTS OF INTEREST SURROUNDING THE IN-
        TENTIONAL SACRIFICE OF BEST NET PRICE IN
        ORDER TO PURCHASE SUPPLEMENTARY SERVICES**

On first impression, it may seem surprising that there would be any
question about an investment manager's authority to use brokerage fees

to purchase services beyond pure execution. For one thing, the services purchased in that fashion ostensibly inure to the benefit of the client. Full-service brokerage firms provide research assistance, portfolio valuation, and performance measurement, and make many other services available to customers, depending on the amout of business transacted. Furthermore, the purchase of services with brokerage fees is a long-established practice and has been a matter of public record at least since publication of the *Wharton Report*.[1] Finally, the extent to which the purchase of supplementary services through the use of commissions goes on today is markedly diminished from what it was prior to the introduction of negotiated commission rates.[2] That fact would seem to indicate that competitive commissions have caused the market to price combinations of execution and other services so that the costs to investors are now reasonably related to the value they receive.

But there are at least four conflicts of interest that can operate on an investment manager who purchases supplementary services with brokerage fees. First, many of the services provided in exchange for additional commissions are services the manager has contracted to provide for a set management fee. To the extent a manager uses commissions to obtain services he is under contract to provide, the client pays for those services more than once. Furthermore, to the extent a manager can obtain, without expense to himself, client services he otherwise would have to provide, he can enhance management profits. Since commissions are paid by the client, the use of commissions to purchase supplementary services places a manager in the position of deciding not only whether a service is valuable to a client, but also whether the manager or the client should pay for it.

Second, the purchase of services with commissions can induce a manager to engage in heavier trading than is appropriate for an account. By increasing portfolio turnover, a manager generates more commissions. The greater the amount of commissions, the more extensive is the ability of the manager to purchase services. By purchasing more services from brokerage firms, a manager can cut back on his own management costs. The incentive to excessive turnover can be particularly acute if the executing broker provides services which are useful not only for management of client accounts, but also

---

[1] SEC, *Report of the Wharton School of Finance and Commerce: A Study of Mutual Funds,* H.R. Rep. No. 2274, 87th Cong., 2d Sess. (1962) (hereinafter cited as *Wharton Report*). See ¶ 8.02[2].

[2] See ¶ 8.02[4].

to promotion of the manager's business. This would be the case if an executing broker referred clients to the manager, for example.

Third, the purchase of services with commissions may lead a manager to risk poorer execution than he ought to, even though there is no apparent sacrifice of best net price. The executing broker may be less financially stable or more likely to produce a failed transaction than another broker. Or the executing broker may be less capable of providing as attractive a price for securities the manager wants to buy or sell than a different firm. For example, the broker may not have the capital to position a block as well, should that be necessary; or he may not have as extensive communications to all markets; or he may not have developed contacts as thoroughly with other investors who might be willing to make the other side of the trade. In such circumstances, the client risks higher net cost despite the apparent refusal of the manager to pay higher brokerage fees for supplementary services. It is only ready proof that execution has been more costly than necessary which is absent.

Finally, the purchase of supplementary services with commissions forces a manager to choose some system of allocating the extra costs among his clients. However objective the system of allocation a manager devises, it is virtually certain that the cost to each client will not reflect the proportional value of the service obtained. For example, executing immediately for discretionary accounts upon receipt of important research prefers them to the nondiscretionary accounts having similar investment objectives. Waiting until the nondiscretionary accounts decide what to do, on the other hand, would deprive the discretionary accounts of the advantage they were positioned to obtain by acting rapidly upon receipt of the information. Moreover, even if it were possible to allocate extra commission expenses proportional to benefits received, a conflict of interest still is present. There is always the danger that the manager will prefer one set of accounts over another because they represent a greater source of profit to him or because they are more closely watched by the client.

Given the seriousness of these conflicts of interest, one might expect most conscientious investment managers not to compromise their operations, but to pay outright for these services or to provide them themselves and to charge clients directly for the costs. The general practice, however, is to the contrary. The most important reason why investment managers continue to desire supplementary services from brokers, and that brokers package other services with their execution services to sell them as a unit, is that such arrangements are a product of the fixed-rate era, and an established structure is slow to change. But this is not the only reason. Otherwise, the end of purchasing supplementary services with commissions would be inevitable, as competitive pressures forced managers to respond to the interest of clients in identifying separate management costs as precisely as possible. Although the probability is high that the securities industry will move toward substantial separation of charges of broker-supplier services and toward internalization of many of these services by investment managers, there are reasons to expect at least some combinations of broker-supplied services to continue to be provided under a single charge for executions, especially in the case of research. But before considering why commissions are likely to continue to be used to purchase supplementary services in a negotiated-rate environment, let us analyze the duty of best execution as applied to the practice of purchasing such services in the fixed-rate era. In that way, the discussion of best execution as applied to the practice of purchasing supplementary services with commissions under negotiated rates can proceed with a properly developed framework for analysis.

¶ 9.02. THE DEVELOPMENT OF BEST-EXECUTION STANDARDS DURING THE FIXED-RATE ERA

[1] Best Net Price and the Duty to Recapture Excess Commissions

The starting point for analysis of the use of commissions to purchase supplementary services in the fixed-rate era is the *Delaware Management Co.* case.[3] Many of the trading practices the SEC criticized in its *Special Study*[4] were involved in *Delaware Management Co.*, and the case gave the Commission its first opportunity to speak about them in an adjudicatory setting. The evidence showed that an investment adviser to two mutual funds had regularly interposed a broker-dealer selling fund shares between the two funds and other broker-dealers making markets in or handling block trading in securities which the two funds purchased and sold. The adviser could have dealt directly with the same market makers and block traders used by the interposed broker-dealer. Interposing the broker-dealer thus caused the two funds to bear commissions paid to the interposed broker-dealer as additional, unnecessary execution expenses. Stating that the adviser "had a fiduciary responsibility . . . to seek the most favorable execution of port-

---

[3] Delaware Management Co., SEC Securities Exchange Act Release No. 8128 (July 19, 1967), [1966-1967 Transfer Binder] CCH Fed. Sec. L. Rep. ¶ 77,458.

[4] SEC, *Report of Special Study of Securities Markets*, H.R. Doc. No. 95, 88th Cong., 1st Sess. (1963) (hereinafter cited as *Special Study*).

folio transactions," [5] and finding that the purpose of engaging in interpositioning was to compensate the interposed broker-dealer beyond the underwriting commission obtainable for the sale of fund shares, the Commission concluded that the adviser had violated its duty to secure best execution.

The evidence also showed that the adviser had caused one of the funds to sell a large block of stock at $13.50 per share through one brokerage firm, even though the fund had been offered $14.00 per share by another firm and could have received the $14.00 price on the day the transaction occurred. The adviser selected the broker offering execution at $13.50, despite the lower price, because that firm had been providing the adviser with research and statistical services for both funds, whereas the other firm had not. Although recognizing as widespread the practice of transacting business through brokerage firms providing research and other support services, the Commission held that paying for such services through higher than necessary brokerage fees was unlawful on three grounds: The practice violated the adviser's contractual obligation to provide such services in exchange for the advisory fees it received; it violated the adviser's duty to obtain the best price for portfolio transactions; and it constituted a fraud upon a fund and its shareholders. [6]

The effect of *Delaware Management Co.* was to threaten established securities industry execution practices. The fixed-rate commission system had led to a business environment in which broker-dealers competed on the basis of services rendered, the costs of which were included in the established commission. When *Delaware Management Co.* was decided, however, partial negotiation of commission expenses was already a fact, both in large transactions off the New York Stock Exchange (NYSE) and, to a lesser extent, on it. [7] Moreover, pressure

---

[5] Delaware Management Co., SEC Securities Exchange Act Release No. 8128 (July 19, 1967), [1966-1967 Transfer Binder] CCH Fed. Sec. L. Rep. ¶ 77,458, at 82,885.

[6] *Id.* ¶ 77,458, at 82,886.

[7] Over-the-counter and third and fourth market transactions were being carried out on a net-price basis. Moreover, on some block trades executed on the New York Stock Exchange, member firms would negotiate a block price at other than the then-existing market price and pay the commission on that. Although the commission rates ostensibly remained fixed, in actuality the size of the fixed commission was one of the factors taken into account in setting the block price. See SEC, *Institutional Investor Study* Ch. XI ("Characteristics and Price Impacts of Block Trading in Common Stock Listed on NYSE"), H.R. Doc. No. 64, 92d Cong., 1st Sess. (1971) (hereinafter cited as *Institutional Investor Study*).

from both the SEC[8] and other sources[9] for the introduction of negotiated commission rates on large transactions was gathering momentum.
If best price meant lowest price, as seemed to be implied from the
facts of *Delaware Management Co.*, compensation for services through
the use of brokerage commissions under negotiated rates was in doubt.

Left by itself, *Delaware Management Co.* might have been limited
to its facts. The adviser had purchased services valuable to itself by
causing its clients to pay execution expenses above standard fees. So
long as managers did not exceed standard fees, the argument might
have gone, the duty of best execution did not necessarily preclude the
use of commissions to purchase services valuable to the client. Because
the fixed-rate system generated broker revenue greatly above actual
execution costs, the question after *Delaware Management Co.* was what
the Commission would require with respect to those excess funds. If
the duty of best execution really meant "a bona fide effort . . . to execute
transactions at the lowest cost," [10] investment managers would be
obliged to avail themselves of opportunities to recover excess brokerage
fees for their clients or at least to apply the recoverable portion of
brokerage fees to a dollar-for-dollar reduction of some other cash expense paid by the client.[11]

First indications were that the legal standard for best execution
would indeed be lowest cost. Six months after *Delaware Management
Co.*, the SEC proposed Rule 10b-10 to "prohibit investment company
managers from directing brokers executing transactions for an investment company to divide their compensation in any way with other
brokers unless the benefits of such division accrue to the investment
company and its shareholders." [12] For support, the release accompanying the proposed rule referred to the SEC's *Report on the Public
Policy Implications of Investment Company Growth*,[13] and concluded

---

[8] See ¶ 8.02[2][a], note 44.

[9] See ¶8.02[3], note 65.

[10] Delaware Management Co., SEC Securities Exchange Act Release No.
8128 (July 19, 1967), [1966-1967 Transfer Binder] CCH Fed. Sec. L. Rep.
¶ 77,458, at 82,886.

[11] It was the case at that time that mutual fund complexes with broker-
affiliates on regional exchanges and in the National Association of Stock
Dealers were returning at least a portion of the commission expenses recovered to their client funds or applying some of the recovery to reductions in
advisory fees. See ¶ 8.02[2][b], notes 50-52.

[12] SEC Securities Exchange Act Release No. 8239 (Jan. 26, 1968),
[1967-1969 Transfer Binder] CCH Fed. Sec. L. Rep. ¶ 77,523.

[13] SEC, *Report on the Public Policy Implications of Investment Com-*

that if the means exist to recapture commissions, a mutual fund manager "is under a fiduciary duty to do so." [14] Although Proposed Rule 10b-10 was withdrawn after the NYSE abolished the give-up and introduced volume discounts,[15] the SEC's stance seemed to indicate that investment managers had to expend at least reasonable effort to recapture commissions. This would have meant that best execution was to be equated with lowest cost since, if a manager were under a duty to recapture excess commissions, *a fortiori,* his duty would be to minimize commission costs.

The duty-of-recapture question raised by the proposed Rule 10b-10 proceedings was sharpened by the decision in *Consumer-Investor Planning Corp.* (CIPCO).[16] In that case, a mutual fund organized as a common-law trust was advised and managed by respondent CIPCO, a registered broker-dealer. CIPCO, which was not a member of the NYSE, chose as executing brokers member firms which would either porvide CIPCO with reciprocal brokerage in unrelated transactions on exchanges, permitting CIPCO to share in commissions generated by the transactions on those exchanges or share commissions with CIPCO on over-the-counter transactions, even though CIPCO performed no significant function. Holding that CIPCO was responsible for executing the fund's securities transactions "in such a manner that the result for the investment company was the most favorable under the circumstances," and citing the *Delaware Management Co.* case as authority for this proposition,[17] the Commission concluded that CIPCO had violated its fiduciary duty by applying the recaptured brokerage to its own use.

The only question apparently left open by *CIPCO* was whether investment company advisers were obliged to recapture excess commissions by all means possible. Together with *Delaware Management Co.,* *CIPCO* seemed solid authority that if excess commissions generated by an investment company's portfolio transactions were available to the adviser, they belonged to the fund. Although the two cases could be distinguished and limited on the grounds that in both the investment advisers were operating under severe conflicts of interest which led to actual injury to their clients, the Commission based its conclusions on

---

pany Growth, H.R. Rep. No. 2337, 89th Cong., 2d Sess. 173 (1966) (hereinafter cited as *PPI Report*).

[14] See note 12 *supra.*

[15] See ¶ 8.02[2][a], note 45.

[16] Consumer-Investor Planning Corp., SEC Securities Exchange Act Release No. 8542 (Feb. 20, 1969), [1967-1969 Transfer Binder] CCH Fed. Sec. L. Rep. ¶ 77,677.

[17] *Id.* at 83,528.

investment advisers' knowledge of the extra costs to the mutual funds instead of on their failure to adequately resolve the conflicts. If, in the Commission's view, a manager could intentionally sacrifice best net price, the circumstances permitting it were not made clear in these cases.

The possibility that the duty of best execution would include an obligation to take all steps necessary to participate in reciprocal brokerage arrangements for the purpose of returning excess commissions to mutual funds led to great concern in the industry and caused the Commission to release an opinion of its general counsel offering reassurances that recapture obligations were subject to the exercise of reasonable business judgment.[18] While qualifying his opinion in accordance with developments arising from the Commission's rate study, the General Counsel stated that there is no duty for mutual fund management to acquire a stock-exchange seat to recapture brokerage if, as a matter of business judgment, management concludes that it is not in the best interest of the fund to do so.[19] He explained statements by the Commission to stock exchanges directing that the abolition of give-ups not terminate arrangements permitting recapture of commissions as reflecting the Commission's intent not to preclude recapture by those institutional investment managers then able to use reciprocal practices to recapture commissions and interested in doing so. But he also took the position that, where a management affiliate was a member of a stock exchange, it might not be free to retain revenues derived from its membership, especially if "the affiliate on the exchange does not execute or clear transactions for the account of the fund, but merely receives revenue from other brokers, which revenue is attributable to transactions executed for the account of the fund by such other brokers." [20]

Although the General Counsel's letter provided some breathing space to investment managers concerned about the extent to which their duty of best execution comprehended an obligation to attempt recapture, much confusion remained over the issue of what a manager could do with excess brokerage either capable of recapture but not recovered or incapable of recapture but available for different purposes according to the determination of the manager. Particularly revealing of the depth of the concern and the extent of the confusion is the amount of energy spent on the institutional trading question at securities industry con-

---

[18] SEC Securities Exchange Act Release No. 8746 (Nov. 10, 1969), [1969-1970 Transfer Binder] CCH Fed. Sec. L. Rep. ¶ 77,761.

[19] *Id.* ¶ 77,761, at 83,747. He referred to the withdrawal of proposed Rule 10b-10 in support of his position.

[20] *Id.*

ferences in 1970. At three PLI conferences, for example, the trading obligations of institutional investment managers were the subject of extensive analysis and discussion.[21] Moreover, in addition to demonstrating the timeliness of the topic,[22] the proceedings of these conferences also indicated that investment managers already were adapting their trading techniques in ways they hoped would permit them to continue to purchase supplementary services with commissions. One panelist reported, for example, that many management companies were splitting up orders, presumably to remain within the fixed-rate schedule and thus generate excess commissions with which to purchase supplementary services.[23]

[2] The Manager's Discretion to Incur Supplementary Service Costs

The imminence of negotiated commissions[24] and the growth of administrative adjudications consistent with a lowest-price interpretation of *Delaware Management Co.* and CIPCO[25] increased the anxiety of the

---

[21] R. Mundheim & W. Werner, *Mutual Funds* (PLI 1970); A. Sommer, Jr., *New Trends and Special Problems Under the Securities Laws* (PLI 1970); M. Cohen & K. Bialkin, *Institutional Investors in a Changing Economy* (PLI 1970). See also Wells, "Negotiated Rates and the SEC's Institutional Investor Study," in *Proceedings of the Fourth Annual Institutional Investor Conference* 164, 173-174 (PLI 1971).

[22] See, e.g., Rotberg, "An Evaluation of Practices and Problems," in R. Mundheim & W. Werner, *Mutual Funds* 173, 181-182 (PLI 1970).

[23] *Id.* at 179. Such a bizzare method of executing portfolio transactions would be a plain breach of the duty of best execution, since its only purpose would be to mask the manager's decision to commit extra client funds to the purchase of supplementary services. Compare the analysis of the analogous practice of some managers operating under negotiated rates to execute on a market-price-plus-commission basis rather than on a net price basis to protect themselves against lawsuits (see ¶ 8.03 at note 108-109). Illustrative of how confusing the meaning of best execution was during this period is the panelist's analysis of this practice. To the question of whether splitting orders hurts the client he said, "it is doubtful whether the new system is really hurting the shareholders. Obviously, however, the new system is resulting in some poor executions." Neither the panelist nor the editors seemed to recognize how remarkable that statement is.

[24] See ¶ 8.02[3] at notes 58-65.

[25] See *In re* Provident Management Corp., SEC Securities Act Release No. 5115 (Dec. 1, 1970), [1970-1971 Transfer Binder] CCH Fed. Sec. L. Rep. ¶ 77,937 (retention of reciprocal commissions by broker-affiliate of mutual fund investment adviser); Mates Fin. Servs., SEC Securities Exchange Act Release No. 8836 (March 9, 1970), [1969-1970 Transfer Binder] CCH Fed. Sec. L. Rep. ¶ 77,790 (mutual fund adviser selling worthless advisory letter to executing brokers); Folger, Nolan, Fleming & Co.,

securities industry[26] to the point that the SEC felt constrained to offer further reassurances that best execution did not necessarily mean lowest price. In its *Policy Statement on the Future Structure of the Securities Markets*,[27] the Commission took the position that "broad-based securities research . . . is indispensable to an efficient system of securities markets" and that "the viability of the process by which research is produced and disseminated [should] not be impaired." [28] Based on that premise, the Commission concluded that "the bona fide expenditure of the beneficiary's funds is completely appropriate, whether in the form of higher commissions or outright cash payments." [29]

But the Commission's apparent rejection of best execution as lowest price was far more grudging than first appeared. The *Policy Statement* spoke only to research. Perhaps its silence about other services implied that they could not be carried through commission payments. The statement also mentioned the likelihood that "unbundling" [30]

SEC Securities Exchange Act Release No. 8489 (Jan. 8, 1969), [1967-1969 Transfer Binder] CCH Fed. Sec. L. Rep. ¶ 77,646 (interpositioning); Kidder, Peabody & Co., SEC Securities Exchange Act Release No. 8426 (Oct. 16, 1968), [1967-1969 Transfer Binder] CCH Fed. Sec. L. Rep. ¶ 77,618 (broker charging discretionary accounts markup as principal greater than commission as agent); Thomson & McKinnon, SEC Securities Exchange Act Release No. 8310 (May 8, 1968), [1967-1969 Transfer Binder] CCH Fed. Sec. L. Rep. ¶ 77,572 (interpositioning); Insurance Secs., Inc., SEC Securities Exchange Act Release No. 8226 (Jan. 11, 1968) (accepting brokerage for investment-company client without performing substantial service). See also Kurach v. Weissman, 49 F.R.D. 304 (S.D.N.Y. 1970), in which the court approved as a settlement to a claim of excessive management fees the application of the profits of a broker-affiliate of a mutual fund investment adviser to the fund's advisory fees. The SEC opposed the settlement on the grounds that the adviser was obliged to do so anyway. The case is discussed extensively in Eisenberg, "Disposition of Mutual Fund Brokerage," in M. Cohen & K. Bialkin, *Institutional Investors in a Changing Economy* 285, 286-299 (PLI 1970). The SEC consistently took this position in civil litigation raising the recapture question during this period. See Note, "Settlement Standards for Mutual Fund Shareholder Litigation Involving the Fiduciary Obligation to Recapture," 13 B.C. Ind. & Com. L. Rev. 1039 (1972).

[26] See, e.g., Brunke, "A New Strategy for Allocating Commissions," 6 Institutional Investor 52 (May 1972).

[27] (Feb. 2, 1972), [Special Studies Transfer Binder] CCH Fed. Sec. L. Rep. ¶ 74,811.

[28] *Id.* ¶ 74,811, at 65,620.

[29] *Id.*

[30] This has been the industry term describing the separation of multiple services under a single fee into separate services each having its own fee.

of services would eventually take place, and seemed to approve higher commissions for brokers preferring to charge for research through commissions. Finally, the Commission placed a heavy burden on the investment manager not only to make adequate disclosure (without detailing what that disclosure might be) to clients of his willingness to purchase research by foregoing "the cheapest execution regardless of qualitative consideration," but also to "stand ready to demonstrate that such expenditures were bona fide." 31

That the securities industry was left less than satisfied with the position of the *Policy Statement* is not surprising. Consequently, the Commission tried once more, issuing a release expanding on the statement.32 Although the Commission reiterated that it would "not sanction a disregard of either the obligation to seek best price and execution or of commission costs," it also took the position that the duty of best execution allowed "consideration of quality and reliability of brokerage services including the availability and value of research. . . ." 33 Seeking competitive bids or pursuing lowest price was not required if that would interfere with the obligation of investment managers to attempt to achieve best performance "by excluding the accounts they manage from information, analysis and services which may be of value to them." 34 *Delaware Management Co.* was reaffirmed but not to be distinguished, according to the Commission, by extending its policy to the introduction of negotiated commission rates. A manager's duty was "to obtain the best security price," but not the cheapest service, "so long as the difference in cost is reasonably justified by the quality of the service offered." 35

Plainly, this release demonstrated a greater willingness to accommodate the purchase of supplementary services through the use of commissions than did the *Policy Statement*. The Commission did not restrict the protective scope of the release to research, but extended it to all services of value to the client. More important, for purposes of

---

31 SEC, *Policy Statement on the Future Structure of the Securities Markets* (Feb. 2, 1972), [Special Studies Transfer Binder] CCH Fed. Sec. L. Rep. ¶ 74,811, at 65,620.

32 "Applicability of the Commission's Policy Statement on the Future Structure of the Securities Markets to Selection of Brokers and Payment of Commissions by Institutional Managers," SEC Securities Exchange Act Release No. 9598 (May 9, 1972), [1971-1972 Transfer Binder] CCH Fed. Sec. L. Rep. ¶ 78,776.

33 *Id.*

34 *Id.*

35 *Id.*

analyzing the duty of best execution, the Commission seemed to be dividing the price paid for the purchase or sale of securities into two elements: (1) the actual market price of the security; and (2) the charge levied by the executing broker in exchange for services rendered. In the Commission's view, apparently, best price meant maximum dollar return to and minimum dollar payout by the client only as applied to the market price of a security. With respect to the executing broker's own charge for carrying out the transaction, the manager retained discretion to pay higher fees if, in the exercise of his business judgment, he concluded that the services provided justified the additional cost.

But in most respects, the release fell far short of dispelling the uncertainty of the securities industry. For one thing, it gave no examples of other services that might be purchased as a commission expense. Furthermore, it did not express any opinion on whether the existence of comparable services on an unbundled basis would impose a restriction on a manager's discretion to pay higher commission costs. Most difficult of all, however, was its treatment of the conflict-of-interest issue. The release stated that "the selection of a broker and the determination of the rate to be paid should, of course, never be influenced by the adviser's self-interest in any manner." [36] But the purchase of services through the use of commissions invariably raises questions of whether the manager's self-interest influenced his judgment. Indeed, the Commission explicitly pointed out one particularly dangerous situation in the release. It warned of the heavy burden of justifying a commission rate above the lowest rate available when "the adviser is affiliated with or has a relationship with the brokerage firm executing the transaction. . . ." [37] The meaning of the term "relationship" was not explained.

[3] Congressional Attempts to Clarify the Rules: S. 470 and H.R. 5050

With the SEC unable to provide sufficiently clear guidelines concerning the authority of investment managers to purchase supplementary services through the use of commissions, and with Congress' studies of the securities industry approaching completion, industry efforts

---

[36] *Id.* Compare Continental Inv. Corp., SEC Securities Exchange Act Release No. 11072 (Oct. 24, 1974).

[37] *Id.* The Commission stated that in such a case, the commission rate should not exceed that charged the broker's most favored, but unaffiliated customers; that it should take into account other "posted" commission rates as guidelines; and that in any event, no excess commissions would be permitted for services the affiliated manager had contracted to provide.

shifted to obtaining remedial legislation. The Senate study, in particular, noted the depth of industry concern and recommended making a response.[38] It distinguished *Delaware Management Co.* as a case of fraudulent breach of contract, pointed to state laws and advisory contract provisions limiting fiduciary compensation in part because of the practice of using commissions to purchase broker-supplied research, noted the uncertainty remaining despite the SEC's attempt to clarify management obligations with respect to the use of commissions, and concluded that the Investment Company Act of 1940 and the Investment Advisers Act of 1940 "should be amended to make it more clear that institutional managers may incur additional commissions on portfolio transactions for the purpose of obtaining research which they determine to be of value to the institutions which they manage."[39] On January 18, 1973, the chairman of the Senate Subcommittee on Securities introduced S. 470, Section 3 of which would have amended Section 36 of the Investment Company Act and Section 4 of which would have amended Section 206 of the Investment Advisers Act along the lines recommended in the Senate study.[40] Six months after it was introduced, S. 470 passed the Senate.[41]

But although S. 470 explicitly endorsed the authority of investment managers "to pay a commission to a broker for effecting a transaction . . . in excess of commissions then being charged by other brokers for effecting similar transactions,"[42] the protection it extended was rather limited. It apparently excluded the trust departments of banks since they were not statutory investment advisers under either the Investment Company Act or the Investment Advisers Act. Moreover, S. 470 approved excess commissions only for research services, and not even then if the broker were affiliated with the adviser. Finally, S. 470 imposed general disclosure obligations on investment advisers choosing to pay excess commissions for research subject to rules and regulations issued by the SEC, but the version of the bill which was adopted provided no detailed guidelines as to the type of disclosure re-

---

[38] Report of the Subcomm. on Securities of the Senate Comm. on Banking, Housing and Urban Affairs, *Securities Industry Study*, S. Doc. No. 13, 93d Cong., 1st Sess. 61 (1973) (hereinafter cited as *Senate Securities Industry Study*).

[39] *Id.* at 62.

[40] 93d Cong., 1st Sess. (1973).

[41] 119 Cong. Rec. 20024-20025, 20026-20044 (June 18, 1973).

[42] Sections 3, 4, 93d Cong., 1st Sess. (1973).

quired.[43] This limited protection accorded with the views expressed by the Subcommittee in its *Securities Industry Study*, however, which acceded to the payment of commissions for research less out of a concern for the health of the industry[44] than for the political reason that, on this ground, the industry "not be allowed to hinder the movement towards competitive rates. . . ." [45]

Unlike S. 470, H.R. 5050,[46] the securities bill introduced in the House of Representatives, did not initially contain a provision dealing with the use of commissions to purchase supplementary services. In fact, Section 209 of the original draft required the SEC to adopt rules

---

[43] The original version of the bill had provided for disclosure of "the policy with respect to such payments, the amount of such payments, the identity of the recipients, and the nature of the research services provided. . . ." S. 470 §§ 3, 4 (Jan. 18, 1973). The final version only required "appropriate disclosure . . . of policies and practices. . . ." S. 470 §§ 3, 4 (May 31, 1973). It is not clear from the record whether the original draft was changed because it was regarded as being too restrictive of managerial discretion, too restrictive of regulatory discretion, or inadequate for some other reason.

[44] The *Study* noted that a transition to actual cash outlays from advisory fees was probably inevitable but would be slow. *Senate Securities Industry Study,* note 38 *supra,* at 61. Implicit in the making of this observation is the notion that once the transition occurs, investment managers would (and therefore should) be paying for broker-supplied research directly.

[45] *Senate Securities Industry Study,* note 38 *supra,* at 62. To the same effect, see Report of the Comm. on Banking, Housing and Urban Affairs to Accompany S. 470, *Regulation of Securities Trading by Members of National Securities Exchanges and the Sale of Investment Advisers of Registered Investment Companies,* S. Rep. No. 187, 93d Cong., 1st Sess. 18-19 (1973).

[46] 93d Cong., 1st Sess. (March 1, 1973). H.R. 5050 was an omnibus securities bill designed to deal with most of the problems identified previously in the hearings leading to the *Securities Industry Study* (Report of the Subcomm. on Commerce and Finance of the House Comm. on Interstate and Foreign Commerce, H.R. Rep. No. 1519, 92 Cong., 2d Sess. (1972)) (hereinafter cited as *House Securities Industry Study*). See Hearings Before the Subcomm. on Commerce and Finance of the House Comm. on Interstate and Foreign Commerce, Study of the Securities Industry, 92d Cong., 1st Sess., Ser. Nos. 37-37d, Pts. 1-5 (1971), 92d Cong., 2d Sess., Ser. Nos. 37e-37h, Pts. 6-9 (1972). In the Senate, on the other hand, separate bills were designed to deal with different sets of problems, S. 470 being the first bill disposed of by the Senate Subcommittee on Securities. For an excellent chronological review of the hearings, reports, principal documents, and events leading to passage of this legislation, see Rowen, "The Securities Acts Amendments of 1975: A Legislative History," 3 Sec. Reg. L.J. 329 (1976).

assuring that broker-dealers would execute at best net price.[47] The purpose of that provision was to override stock-exchange rules requiring member firms to obtain exchange permission before effecting a transaction in a listed security off the exchange,[48] not to restrict brokers from packaging execution and other services under one fee. Indeed, the House *Securities Industry Study* expressly acknowledged that brokerage firms would not shift to total separation of charges for services with the advent of negotiated rates.[49] But, as witnesses pointed out at the hearings on H.R. 5050,[50] the effect was to throw into doubt the authority of investment managers to pay anything above lowest brokerage fees. The drafters of the original bill seem simply not to have recognized that the question of purchasing services in addition to execution with brokerage commissions must be examined from the viewpoint not only of brokers but also of their customers.[51]

In November 1974, a revised version of H.R. 5050 was reported out of the full Committee on Interstate and Foreign Commerce. The provision in Section 209 designed to eliminate anticompetitive restrictions on a brokerage firm's ability to execute transactions in the best market for its customers had sensibly been changed from imposing a duty on broker-dealers to seek best net price to a prohibition against the adoption of rules by national securities exchanges limiting member access to other markets.[52] In addition, the revised bill added two new sections to amend the Investment Company Act of 1940 and the Invest-

---

[47] Section 209 would have added Section 20A to the Securities Exchange Act to provide:

"(b) The Commission shall adopt rules which assure that any transaction by any registered broker or dealer or member of an exchange is executed at a net price to such member's customer which is better than or equivalent to the net price which would have been obtainable if such transaction were to have been executed (in any unit of trading) on any other exchange (or otherwise than on an exchange)."

[48] See *House Securities Industry Study*, note 46 *supra*, at 126-128.

[49] See *House Securities Industry Study*, note 46 *supra*, at 145.

[50] See, e.g., Testimony of Bernard H. Garil, in Hearings on H.R. 5050 and H.R. 340 Before the Subcomm. on Commerce and Finance of the House Comm. on Interstate and Foreign Commerce, 93d Cong., 1st Sess., Ser. No. 53, Pt. 4, at 1576, 1580, 1587-1588, 1591-1596 (1973).

[51] The *House Securities Industry Study* focused on unbundling only as a practical issue of whether brokerage firms would continue to find "bundling" a profitable marketing technique. It recommended no legislation on this point. See note 49 *supra*.

[52] See H.R. 5050 § 602, 93d Cong., 2d Sess. (Nov. 19, 1974), *adding* Section 20B to the Securities Exchange Act.

ment Advisers Act of 1940 permitting investment managers to purchase supplementary services for commissions.[53] But it differed from S. 470 in several respects. It extended protection to banks.[54] It explicitly preempted all state and federal law which would treat the payment of higher commissions for additional services as a breach of fiduciary duty.[55] It did not prohibit such payments to affiliated brokers. It did not limit its protection to research services, but also included "brokerage" services.[56] And it imposed a standard of reasonableness, which the Committee regarded as more consonant with the exercise of reasonable business judgment than the good-faith test found in S. 470.[57]

For reasons having nothing to do with the question of commissions for supplementary services, H.R. 5050 did not reach the floor of the House.[58] Nonetheless, resolution of the matter was acquiring a degree of urgency. For one thing, investment managers, after having lived with negotiated rates above the $300,000 breakpoint for a number of months, were tilting, albeit reluctantly, toward a lowest-price standard in the absence of legislation permitting them broader discretion.[59] This is not

---

[53] See H.R. 5050 §§ 603, 604, 93d Cong., 2d Sess. (Nov. 19, 1974).

[54] Specifically, Sections 603 and 604 applied to statutory investment advisers and persons who would be so classified "except for the exemption contained in § 202(a)(11)(A)" of the Investment Advisers Act (15 U.S.C. § 80b-2(a)(11)(A)), which applies to "a bank, or any bank holding company as defined in the Bank Holding Company Act of 1956 which is not an investment company." Although the House Banking Committee stated a preference for relying entirely on the SEC (see Securities Week, Sept. 2, 1975, p. 3), the bill allowed banks to look to banking regulatory agencies rather than the SEC for disclosure rules and compliance oversight.

[55] The preemption could be overridden, however, if a state or federal statute "expressly provided to the contrary."

[56] Higher commissions than the cheapest available were to be based on "the quality and reliability of the brokerage services, including the availability and value of research or execution services." What other services might be covered is difficult to say. The Committee report on the bill referred only to "research and other services related to the execution of securities transactions." See *Report of the Committee on Interstate and Foreign Commerce on H.R. 5050, the Securities Acts Amendments of 1974*, H.R. Rep. No. 1476, 93d Cong., 2d Sess. 94 (1974).

[57] *Id.* at 93.

[58] The bill died in the Rules Committee, apparently in response to a strong lobbying effort of elements of the securities industry. See Rowen, "The Securities Acts Amendments of 1975: A Legislative History," 3 Sec. Reg. L.J. 329, 342-343 (1976).

[59] See, e.g., Research, "Can Banks Pay 'Up'—Or Can't They?" 8 Institutional Investor 15 (Sept. 1974); Securities Week, Nov. 25, 1974; Wall

to say that most institutional managers were refusing to pay higher negotiated commissions at all during this period.[60] But they were cutting back on the amount they were prepared to spend and the number of brokerage firms they were willing to deal with.[61] Furthermore, institutional managers were betraying their attitude toward their legal authority by their actions. One common practice, for example, was to split orders, a deliberate subterfuge to reduce the size of a transaction below the $300,000 breakpoint so that full fixed rates could be paid.[62] At an SEC conference in the fall of 1974 on the question of commissions for research, all these matters were discussed,[63] including some possible regulatory consequences under the Investment Company Act and the Investment Advisers Act.[64]

Street Letter, Nov. 11, 1974, p. 6 (manager of mutual fund complex); Securities Week, Oct. 7, 1974, p. 5; Wall Street Letter, May 27, 1974, p. 5. In part, the attitude of the securities industry was affected by the views of some officials. The Comptroller of the Currency's staff, for example, expressed doubts about excess commissions for supplementary service. See Securities Week, Dec. 9, 1974, p. 2.

[60] See, e.g., "Interview with Chairman of the SEC," Securities Week, Sept. 16, 1974, p. 5; Wall Street Letter, Nov. 11, 1973; Wall Street Letter, May 27, 1974, p. 4.

[61] See, e.g, Wall Street Letter, Nov. 18, 1974 (institutions lag in paying research debts); Wall Street Letter, Sept. 16, 1974, p. 3 (sharp cuts in broker payout lists). See also "Trading Desks at Research Firms: The Jury Is Still Out," 8 Institutional Investor 23 (Aug. 1974).

[62] See, e.g., Wall Street Letter, May 13, 1974, p. 3. That some institutional managers actually believed that deliberately splitting orders to avoid the negotiated-rates breakpoint and pay higher commissions left them in compliance with the law if they would not have been in compliance by paying higher commissions above the breakpoint is simply remarkable. See note 23 *supra*.

[63] A summary of the conference appears in Wall Street Letter, Oct. 30, 1974, pp. 1-4. See also Securities Week, Nov. 11, 1974, p. 2b.

[64] Wall Street Letter, Oct. 30, 1974. One witness questioned whether pooled research for a mutual fund complex might violate the joint transaction prohibition of Investment Company Act § 17(d) (15 U.S.C. § 80a-17(d)). Another witness claimed (correctly) that unbundling could require brokerage firms to register as statutory investment advisers. This point is discussed more fully in ¶ 10.06[2][b] at notes 318-324.

Actually, problems of interpretation and construction abound with respect to these statutes when statutory investment advisers purchase supplementary services with commissions. Investment Company Act § 15(a) (15 U.S.C. § 80a-15(a)) requires that the advisory contract precisely describe "all compensation to be paid thereunder," and Section 17(e) (15 U.S.C. § 80a-17(e)) makes it unlawful for any investment company affiliate "acting as agent, to accept from any source any compensation" other than wages

¶ 9.03. FEDERALLY LEGISLATED STANDARDS

[1] The Employee Retirement Income Security Act of 1974: Commission-Purchased Supplementary Services as a Prohibited Transaction

Another reason for resolving the question of use of commissions for supplementary services was the passage of pension reform legislation in September 1974.[65] Section 406 of the Employee Retirement Income Security Act (ERISA) prohibits a fiduciary to an "employee benefit plan" [66] from causing a plan to engage in a transaction constituting a direct or indirect "furnishing of . . . services . . . between the plan and a party in interest" [67] or "transfer to, or use by or for the benefit of, a party in interest, of any assets of the plan. . . ." [68] The definition of party in interest includes plan fiduciaries and persons providing services to a plan.[69] A defensible interpretation of these statutory provisions might make a brokerage firm a party in interest and commissions for supple-

---

for disposing of company property, unless the affiliate is acting as broker or underwriter. It has been held that use of commissions to pay for services can be compensation where the benefits to management are substantial. See Lutz v. Boas, 39 Del. Ch. 585, 171 A.2d 381 (1961) (contract between broker and mutual fund investment adviser whereby broker was exercising discretion in selecting and purchasing fund securities; broker held to be investment adviser and commissions held undisclosed compensation); Consumer-Investor Planning corp., SEC Securities Act Release No. 8542 (Feb. 20, 1969), [1967-1969 Transfer Binder] CCH Fed. Sec. L. Rep. ¶ 77,677 (commissions recaptured by broker affiliated with investment company and not providing services to company held undisclosed compensation); Provident Management Corp., SEC Securities Exchange Act Release No. 8790 (Jan. 5, 1970), 1 CCH Fed. Sec. L. Rep. ¶¶ 4845.6292, 4845.75, 4845.827 (brokerage for selling mutual fund shares held undisclosed compensation to manager); but see Moses v. Burgin, 316 F. Supp. 31 (D. Mass.), *rev'd on other grounds* 445 F.2d 369 (1st Cir. 1970), *cert. denied sub nom.* Johnson v. Moses, 404 U.S. 994 (1971). If this interpretation of compensation is valid, these authorities have implications for a similar interpretation of compensation under the Investment Advisers Act. See Section 202(a) (11), 15 U.S.C. § 80b-2(a)(11); Section 203(c)(1)(E), 15 U.S.C. § 80b-3(c)(1)(E); Section 205, 15 U.S.C. § 80b-5; cf. Proposed Rule 206(4)-4, SEC Investment Advisers Act Release No. 442 (March 5, 1975), [1974-1975 Transfer Binder] CCH Fed. Sec. L. Rep. ¶ 80,128.

[65] Employee Retirement Income Security Act of 1974 (ERISA), Pub. L. 93-406 (Sept. 2, 1974).

[66] *Id.* § 3(3), 29 U.S.C. § 1002(3).

[67] *Id.* § 406(a)(1)(C), 29 U.S.C. § 1106(a)(1)(C).

[68] *Id.* § 406(a)(1)(D), 29 U.S.C. § 1106(a)(1)(D).

[69] *Id.* §§ 3(14)(A), 3(14)(B), 29 U.S.C. §§ 1002(14)(A), 1002(14)(B).

mentary services an indirect furnishing of such services, or it might treat excess commissions as a transfer of plan assets for the benefit of the investment manager, who would be a statutory fiduciary[70] and hence a party in interest. Under either interpretation, paying commissions for supplementary services would be a prohibited transaction. Section 406 also prohibits a fiduciary from dealing with plan assets "for his own account." [71] Since the purchase of most broker-supplied services other than execution arguably relieves a manager of furnishing those same services at his own expense, this provision also can be interpreted to prohibit pension managers from paying brokerage fees except for executions.

Other sections of the statute can be interpreted to similar effect.[72] Indeed, the tax provisions of the statute, though similar to the labor provisions, are, if anything, more stringent with respect to prohibited transactions.[73] Whereas Section 406 imposes a duty on plan fiduciaries only for transactions which they know or ought to know are prohibited, Section 2003, the corresponding tax provision, levies an excise tax irrespective of the awareness of plan fiduciaries. Nor was there any significant indication of a congressional intent to exempt the purchase of supplementary services with brokerage paid for with plan assets. Section 408[74] lists exemptions from application of Section 406, and although it includes, for example, ancillary bank services,[75] there is no mention of services other than execution paid through brokerage fees. The conference report which accompanied the bill also omits discussion of payment for such services with the commission expenses of employee benefit plans.[76] Because the effective date of the prohibited-transaction

---

[70] See *id.* § 3(21), 29 U.S.C. § 1002(21).

[71] *Id.* § 406(b)(1), 29 U.S.C. § 1106(b)(1).

[72] One commentator points out that Section 406 can be construed in conjunction with Section 404, which requires plan fiduciaries to carry out their responsibilities for the exclusive benefit of plan beneficiaries. See Section 404(a)(1)(A)(i), 29 U.S.C. § 1104(a)(1)(A)(i), and Jorden, " 'Paying Up' for Research: A Regulatory and Legislative Analysis," 1975 Duke L.J. 1103, 1115.

[73] See Section 2003 (26 U.S.C. § 4975), which imposes an excise tax on disqualified persons, a term of art essentially the same as party in interest (see note 69 *supra*), for engaging in prohibited transactions, defined to correspond to Section 406 (see note 67 *supra*).

[74] 29 U.S.C. § 1108.

[75] Section 408(b)(6), 29 U.S.C. § 1108(b)(6).

[76] See Conference Report on H.R. 2, ERISA, 93d Cong., 2d Sess. (1974). In contrast, the Report took explicit note of the problem of investment management of a plan by a broker, but left it with the Secretary of

provisions was January 1, 1975,[77] and because Congress had failed to provide express relief through amendments to the securities laws,[78] the Secretaries of Labor and the Treasury granted interim and then permanent exemptions to plan managers purchasing supplementary services with commissions.[79]

[2] The Securities Acts Amendments of 1975: Protections Provided by Section 28(e) of the Securities Exchange Act

When the Ninety-Fourth Congress convened, securities legislation was immediately introduced in both houses. Offered in the Senate was S. 249,[80] essentially a compromise of the draft legislation of the previous Congress. Section 24 of the original draft of S. 249 followed the model of S. 470 in providing protection for the use by investment managers of commissions for research services, the principal difference being that S. 249, in language closely tracking the definition of investment adviser in the Investment Advisers Act, defined "research services." [81] For po-

---

Labor and Secretary of the Treasury to grant an appropriately limited exemption, if feasible. *Id.* at 309-310.

[77] Section 414(a), 29 U.S.C. § 1114(a); Section 2003(c), 26 U.S.C. § 4975, note. The effective date of these sections was delayed until June 30, 1977, if the party in interest (or disqualified person) "ordinarily and customarily furnished such services on June 30, 1974" and "if such provision of services remains at least as favorable to the plan as an arm's-length transaction with an unrelated party. . . ." Sections 414(c)(4)(B), 2003(c)(2)(D)(ii). Both qualifications made any delay in application of the prohibited-transaction provisions to brokerage transactions doubtful. The grandfather clause meant that a firm would have to have had an established relationship with a plan, which meant, in turn, that plan managers could not use new firms. And the arm's-length-unrelated-party requirement could easily be interpreted to focus on commission price levels generally available as the legal standard. With so many firms offering and able to carry out transactions at reduced cost, plan managers paying higher commissions might have lost the protection of these provisions.

[78] See note 58 *supra*. But see ¶ 9.03[2] *infra*.

[79] The exemptions were granted retroactive to January 1, 1975. See 40 Fed. Reg. 5201 (Feb. 4, 1975). They were extended three times at regular intervals (see 40 Fed. Reg. 17,861 (April 23, 1975); 40 Fed. Reg. 24,578 (June 9, 1975); 40 Fed. Reg. 43,785 (Sept. 23, 1975)) until permanent exemptions could be adopted. Prohibited Transaction Exemption 75-1, 40 Fed. Reg. 50,842 (Oct. 31, 1975).

[80] 94th Cong., 1st Sess. (Jan. 17, 1975).

[81] " '[R]esearch services' means advice, either directly or through publications or writings, as to the value of securities or as to the advisability of investing in, purchasing, or selling securities, and analyses and reports con-

litical and procedural reasons, the House bill, H.R. 10, was identical to H.R. 5050.[82] Investment managers and broker-dealers felt both to be unsatisfactory.[83]

At the hearings on S. 249, witnesses made a number of points about the shortcomings of previous drafts,[84] principally of the need to provide that bank trust departments be covered,[85] that the imputed value of broker-supplied services not be required to be traced to particular accounts,[86] that the provision apply to services beyond pure research, and that there be a clearer statement of preemption of federal and state law. Contemporaneous with the hearings, the Chairman of the Securities Subcommittee introduced Amendment No. 16 to S. 249, which re-

---

cerning securities." Compare Investment Advisers Act § 202(a)(11), 15 U.S.C. § 80b-2(a)(11), quoted in note 90 infra.

[82] 94th Cong., 1st Sess. (Jan. 14, 1975). The purpose of introducing the same bill was to avoid the necessity of additional hearings. Since Title I seemed to be generating opposition, H.R. 10 was divided into H.R. 2548, embodying Title I, and H.R. 4111, embodying Titles II-VI. See Rowen, "The Securities Acts Amendments of 1975: A Legislative History," 3 Sec. Reg. L.J. 329, 344-345 (1976).

[83] See, e.g., Securities Week, Dec. 2, 1974, p. 2a.

[84] Hearings on S. 249 Before the Subcomm. on Securities of the Senate Comm. on Banking, Housing and Urban Affairs, 94th Cong., 1st Sess. 202-203, 321-324, 351, 456-457, 460, 474 (1975).

[85] Like its predecessor, S. 470, the original version of S. 249 still did not reach bank trust departments.

[86] The report accompanying H.R. 5050 (see *Report of the Comm. on Interstate and Foreign Commerce on H.R. 5050, the Securities Acts Amendments of 1974*, H.R. Rep. No. 1476, 93d Cong., 2d Sess. (1974)) seemed to take quite the opposite position. It stated at 93-94:

"The Committee has rejected a suggested amendment to these sections which would have given unqualified license to use the assets of one beneficiary to compensate for research which may inure to the benefit of another. There may be circumstances where a fiduciary can successfully defend the reasonableness of his business judgment in evaluating and compensating for research without the necessity of demonstrating a direct benefit to the portfolio whose assets are used for compensation. On the other hand, there may be cases where, because of the nature of the research service or advice rendered and the investment objectives of the beneficiary, it would be inappropriate to use commission dollars for such investor research. The reasonableness of the business judgment of the fiduciary will, of necessity, turn on considerations related to the nature of the research service provided, the investment objectives of the beneficiary and the disclosed practices and policies of the money manager."

sponded to these points[87] and which, with slight modification, became the provision ultimately adopted.[88] In addition to its substantive content, it represented a major jurisdictional shift from parallel provisions in the Investment Company Act and Investment Advisers Act to a single provision in the Securities Exchange Act. Finally adopted as Section 28(e) of the Act, it provides:

> "(1) No person using the mails, or any means or instrumentality of interstate commerce, in the exercise of investment discretion with respect to an account shall be deemed to have acted unlawfully or to have breached a fiduciary duty under State or Federal law unless expressly provided to the contrary by a law enacted by the Congress or any State subsequent to the date of enactment of the Securities Acts Amendments in 1975 solely by reason of his having caused the account to pay a member of an exchange, broker, or dealer an amount of commission for effecting a securities transaction in excess of the amount of commission another member of an exchange, broker, or dealer would have charged for effecting that transaction, if such person determined in good faith that such amount of commission was reasonable in relation to the value of the brokerage and research services provided by such member, broker, or dealer, viewed in terms of either that particular transaction or his overall responsibilities with respect to the accounts as to which he exercises investment discretion. This subsection is exclusive and plenary insofar as conduct is covered by the foregoing, unless otherwise expressly provided by contract: Provided, however, That nothing in this subsection shall be construed to impair or limit the power of the Commission under any other provision of this title or otherwise.

> "(2) A person exercising investment discretion with respect to an account shall make such disclosure of his policies and practices with respect to commissions that will be paid for effecting securities transactions, at such times and in such manner, as the appropriate regulatory agency, by rule, may prescribe as necessary or appropriate in the public interest or for the protection of investors.

---

[87] Amendment No. 16 generally received praise from members of the securities industry and officials. See Wall Street Letter, March 3, 1975, p. 1; Wall Street Letter, Feb. 24, 1975; Securities Week. Feb. 24, 1975, p. 5.

[88] The version of the bill reported out of committee and passed by the Senate, S. 249, 94th Cong., 1st Sess. (April 18, 1975), made it clearer than Amendment No. 16 that it was to preempt all law, including statutes to be adopted in the future, which did not expressly reject it. The bill reported out of conference (see Conference Report on S. 249 of the House Comm. on Interstate and Foreign Commerce, Securities Acts Amendments of 1975, H.R. Rep. No. 229, 94th Cong., 1st Sess. (May 19, 1975)), added "member of an exchange" (see Securities Exchange Act § 3(a)(3)(A), 15 U.S.C. § 78c(a)(3)(A)) to brokers and dealers as parties eligible to receive excess commissions.

"(3) For purposes of this subsection a person provides brokerage and research services insofar as he—

"(A) furnishes advice, either directly or through publications or writings, as to the value of securities, the advisability of investing in, purchasing, or selling securities, and the availability of securities or purchasers or sellers of securities;

"(B) furnishes analyses and reports concerning issuers, industries, securities, economic factors and trends, portfolio strategy, and the performance of accounts; or

"(C) effects securities transactions and performs functions incidental thereto (such as clearance, settlement, and custody) or required in connection therewith by rules of the Commission or a self-regulatory organization of which such person is a member or person associated with a member or in which such person is a participant."

[a] Good faith and reasonableness as a defense to challenged conduct: Section 28(e)(1)

Subsection (1), the operational portion of Section 28(e), extends its protection to all persons exercising "investment discretion with respect to an account." Investment discretion is defined in Section 3 of the Securities Exchange Act, as amended by Section 3 of the Securities Acts Amendments of 1975, to include both actual authority to make investment decisions and the power to influence the investment decisions of persons possessing such authority.[89] This construction makes Section 28(e) less generally available than its draft legislative antecedents in S. 470, H.R. 5050 (and H.R. 10), and S. 249. The provisions in those bills applied statutory investment advisers under the Investment Company Act and the Investment Advisers Act, and, in the latter two bills, to banks fitting the statutory definitions but granted statutory exclu-

---

[89] See ¶ 9.02[3]. Securities Exchange Act § 3(a)(35) (15 U.S.C. § 78c(a)(35)) provides:

"A person exercises 'investment discretion' with respect to an account if, directly or indirectly, such person (A) is authorized to determine what securities or other property shall be purchased or sold by or for the account, (B) makes decisions as to what securities or other property shall be purchased or sold by or for the account even though some other person may have responsibility for such investment decisions, or (C) otherwise exercises such influence with respect to the purchase and sale of securities or other property by or for the account as the Commission, by rule, determines, in the public interest or for the protection of investors, should be subject to the operation of the provisions of this title and the rules and regulations thereunder."

sions.[90] The practical significance of this distinction does not seem great except possibly in regard to persons acting as agents for investment managers in executing transactions. If a broker handling a block transaction for an investment manager found it necessary to approach a market maker to complete the trade, for example, the broker could not avail himself of Section 28(e) by paying a markup higher than otherwise available in consideration of research services from the market maker even if the research were intended solely for the benefit of the client. Such a broker would not be exercising investment discretion even though, if he were receiving a commission above a bare execution fee, he might be a statutory investment adviser.[91]

The subsection is not an enabling provision, nor does it establish a legal standard the violation of which is a breach of fiduciary duty. It is remedial in character, providing a defense for investment managers whose conduct in paying brokerage fees[92] is challenged in some judicial

---

[90] Investment Company Act § 2(a)(20) (15 U.S.C. § 80a-2(a)(20)) provides:

" 'Investment adviser' of an investment company means (A) any person (other than a bona fide officer, director, trustee, member of an advisory board, or employee of such company, as such) who pursuant to contract with such company regularly furnishes advice to such company with respect to the desirability of investing in, purchasing or selling securities or other property, or is empowered to determine what securities or other property shall be purchased or sold by such company, and (B) any other person who pursuant to contract with a person described in clause (A) of this paragraph regularly performs substantially all of the duties undertaken by such person described in said clause (A). . . ."

Investment Advisers Act § 202(a)(11) (15 U.S.C. § 80b-2(a)(11)) provides:

" 'Investment adviser' means any person who, for compensation, engages in the business of advising others, either directly or through publications or writings, as to the value of securities or as to the advisability of investing in, purchasing, or selling securities, or who, for compensation and as part of a regular business, issues or promulgates analyses or reports concerning securities; but does not include (A) a bank, or any bank holding company, as defined in the Bank Holding Company Act of 1956, which is not an investment company. . . ."

[91] See Bines, "Regulating Discretionary Management: Broker-Dealers as Catalysts for Reform," 16 B.C. Ind. & Com. L. Rev. 347, 362-374 (1975).

[92] There is a question whether Section 28(e) applies to a higher markup than necessary paid to a dealer in consideration of brokerage or research services. Some take the position that since Section 28(e) uses the term "commissions," it applies only to agency transactions. See Stark, "Problems

or administrative proceeding. It is important, therefore, to recognize the scope of the defense. It does not make paying excess commissions irrelevant to the question of whether a manager has breached his fiduciary duty. It merely precludes answerability based solely on proof that the manager has caused an account to pay "an amount of commission for effecting a securities transaction in excess of the amount of commission another member of an exchange, broker, or dealer would have charged for effecting that transaction." As a practical matter, actions against investment managers for commission expenditures would never have been limited to such proof anyway. The material considerations are such factors as the amount and frequency of excess brokerage fees, comparisons between broker-supplied services received and advisory services the manager obliged himself contractually to provide, the availability of such services on a cash basis and the practice of other investment managers in purchasing them, and so forth. The real protection provided by Section 28(e) derives from the language "if such person determined in good faith that such amount of commissions was reasonable in relation to the value of the brokerage and research services provided." This means either that the complaining party must prove both that the excess brokerage fees paid were un-

---

of Institutions Under Competitive Rates: 'Paying-Up' for Research," in R. Mundheim, A. Fleischer & B. Vandegrift, *Seventh Annual Institute on Securities Regulation* (PLI 1976). Such an interpretation would seem overly narrow in view of the statutory purpose of permitting investment managers to pay with client funds for such services as superior securities analysis and willingness to take risk by positioning as part of the cost of trading. Moreover, such an interpretation might have a mildly depressing effect on the willingness of brokerage firms to make a market in securities and thereby improve liquidity. Nothing in the legislative history indicates that a distinction was to be made between agency and principal transactions, and indeed, the prohibition against application of the section to transactions with affiliated brokers indicates that the legislative purpose was to the contrary. Compare Section 11(a) (15 U.S.C. § 78k(a)), amended in the same legislation to separate investment management from brokerage. It specifically excepts from its application transactions by a dealer acting in the capacity of a market maker. *Id.* § 11(a)(1)(A), 15 U.S.C. § 78k(a)(1)(a). There is plainly a lot more potential for abuse in a transaction between a manager and an affiliated dealer than between a manager and an unaffiliated dealer. Finally, and perhaps most important, the language of Section 28(e) suggests that "commission" was not intended to exclude a dealer's markup. It applies to "an amount of commission" paid to "a member of an exchange, broker, or dealer." The ordinary practice for a dealer, as defined in Section 3(a)(5) of the Act (15 U.S.C. § 78c(a)(5)), is to charge a markup as his brokerage fee.

reasonable and that the manager was in fact aware he was paying too much, or that the manager may show that he was in fact unaware that the excess commissions were unreasonable.[93] This statutory protection is in sharp contrast with the typical approach of holding professionals to execution of their duties under the entirely objective duty standard that they exercise ordinary skill and care in carrying out their responsibilities.

The subsection also tries to deal with the problem of attribution of benefits to and allocation of costs for the services provided through the expenditure of excess brokerage fees. In response to concern that the fiduciary prohibition against commingling of assets precluded the use of excess brokerage fees from the account to purchase broker-supplied services benefitting other accounts,[94] Section 28(e) permits an investment manager to determine the reasonableness of excess brokerage fees for a given transaction "in terms of either that particular transaction or his overall responsibilities with respect to the accounts as to which he exercises investment discretion." For reasons discussed below,[95] the allocation problem is much less serious than the energy expended on it would indicate. Nonetheless, to the extent it is a problem, both the statutory language and the legislative history[96] make it clear that no direct accounting for expenditures and benefits need be made from client to client.

---

[93] The burden of proof on this question is left unresolved by the statute and the legislative history. At least as regards investment companies, the SEC had initially adopted a more stringent standard for the use by investment managers of commissions to purchase supplementary services than the good faith/reasonableness standard of Section 28(e). The Commission felt a need to develop guidelines of its own because federal legislation was being delayed beyond the date of introduction of fully negotiated commission rates. But instead of restating the standard in proposed Section 28(e) pending in S. 249, it chose to impose a standard of essentiality by requiring investment company advisers to disclose whether the adviser considered the availability of the services essential to its ability to perform their contractual and fiduciary duty. See Securities Week, Aug. 4, 1975, p. 5. Even after Section 28(e) became law, however, the Commission persisted in this standard until forced to drop it under pressure from the Chairman of the Senate Subcommittee on Securities. See Wall Street Letter, Sept. 22, 1975, p. 10.

[94] See, e.g., Teberg & Cane, "Paying Up for Research," 115 Trusts & Estates 4, 58 (Jan. 1976); Wall Street Letter, March 3, 1975, p. 8.

[95] See ¶ 9.05[2] infra.

[96] See Report on S. 249 of the Senate Comm. on Banking, Housing and Urban Affairs, S. Rep. No. 75, 94th Cong., 1st Sess. 70 (1975).

[b] Disclosure requirements: Section 28(e)(2)

Subsection (2) of Section 28(e) requires investment managers to make disclosure of "policies and practices with respect to commissions that will be paid for effecting securities transactions" as are prescribed by the Comptroller of the Currency, Federal Reserve Board, Federal Deposit Insurance Corporation, or SEC, as appropriate.[97] This regulatory authority is not an exclusive statement of disclosure obligations, but only an enabling provision for the proper federal regulatory agency to impose such disclosure obligations as it sees fit.[98] Thus, full compliance with such disclosure regulations as are issued does not relieve an investment manager of additional disclosure obligations that are or might be required to make the payment of commissions for supplementary services fair in every set of circumstances. Proposed Rule 206(4)-4 of the Investment Advisers Act,[99] for example, requires statutory investment advisers to disclose to clients other than investment companies, prior to the initiation, extension, or renewal of an advisory contract, sources of information relied on for any investment advice[100]; and if the adviser provides investment supervisory services,[101] to disclose the extent of his discretion to select broker-dealers and the factors considered in making such selections.[102]

The SEC has issued Proposed Rule 28e2-1 to help implement Section 28(e).[103] The proposed rule provides, in substance, that persons subject to SEC jurisdiction in connection with Section 28(e) are to describe (1) how brokers are selected and how the reasonableness of

---

[97] See Section 3(a)(34) (15 U.S.C. § 78c(a)(34)), defining "appropriate regulatory agency."

[98] This is a fact not recognized by some. See Teberg & Cane, "Paying Up for Research," 115 Trusts & Estates 4, 62 (Jan. 1976).

[99] SEC Investment Advisers Act Release No. 442 (March 5, 1975), 4 CCH Fed. Sec. L. Rep. ¶ 56,383B.

[100] Proposed Rule 206(4)-4(b)(5).

[101] See Investment Advisers Act § 202(a)(13), 15 U.S.C. 80b-2(a)(13).

[102] Proposed Rule 206(4)-4(c)(3).

[103] SEC Securities Act Release No. 5772 (Nov. 30, 1976), 3 CCH Fed. Sec. L. Rep. ¶ 26,578A. The SEC, which did not favor Section 28(e) (see note 93 *supra* and notes 103-106 *infra*) and remains hostile to it (see Securities Week, March 14, 1977, p. 1), issued Proposed Rule 28e2-1 only under great pressure from the Chairman of the Senate Subcommittee on Securities and other members of Congress. Securities Week, Oct. 25, 1976, p. 7; *id.*, Oct. 20, 1975, p. 2a. Initial reaction to the Proposed Rule was unfavorable both from the Chairman of the Senate Subcommittee (Securities Week, March 21, 1977, p. 2) and from investment managers (Securities Week, Jan. 10, 1977, p. 2a; *id.*, Feb. 21, 1977, p. 10).

commissions is determined; (2) what research services are obtained and how the benefits of those services are allocated among clients; (3) what other services are obtained and their estimated fair market value; and (4) classified according to various particulars, including assets, affiliation, and other executions, what brokerage commissions were paid during the previous year. As such regulations are adopted, compliance will be mandatory, of course, in order to come within the safe-harbor protection of Section 28(e)(1). But it is doubtful that compliance will always provide sufficient disclosure to insulate investment managers from subsequent judicial or administrative action. No set of disclosure rules can sufficiently inform all clients, nor can any set of disclosure rules avoid providing more information than is necessary for some clients. Such regulations as are adopted, therefore, will reflect a compromise in administrative judgment about whether additional disclosure would benefit too few investors to justify making such disclosure mandatory in every case. This compromise, however, is not an endorsement of the notion that an investment manager may forgo disclosure to investors who are not sufficiently informed to make an intelligent decision about how much discretion to give their investment managers in using commissions for more than execution services. Particularly in cases in which a manager is aware that a client requires additional facts is a manager's appeal to his compliance with the disclosure regulations likely to fail to protect him from answerability.

In this connection, prior to issuance of Proposed Rule 28e2-1, the SEC had one instructive brush with an informal set of disclosure guidelines. During the spring of 1975, it became apparent that Congress was not going to complete its securities legislation in time for the introduction of fully negotiated commission rates on May 1 in accordance with Rule 19b-3. This hiatus between full negotiation and the adoption of Section 28(e) was to have an enormous impact on the entire controversy over services for commissions,[104] but because some mutual fund investment advisers began changing fund prospectus, advisory contract, and proxy language to tell prospective customers, existing shareholders, and outside directors of their intention to pay higher commissions, the SEC decided to draft a set of informal guidelines. Far more restrictive than the pending provision in S. 249, they required disclosure as to whether the services purchased were "essential" to the adviser's performance of duty; whether they increased the fund's expenses while decreasing the adviser's expenses; whether there was any contractual or statutory prerequisite to such purchases; and, if the adviser managed other clients,

---

[104] See ¶ 9.06[3][c] at notes 196-199 *infra*.

how such costs were allocated.[105] Once S. 249 became law, the effect of these guidelines was unclear since they were not formal rules; and since they applied only to investment companies, they did not satisfy Section 28(e)(2). Moreover, even if they could somehow have been interpolated into Section 28(e)(2), they seemed to impose a narrower legal standard than the reasonable/good-faith standard in Section 28 (e)(1). In addition, the disclosure provision concerning allocation policy seemed a good deal more demanding than Section 28(e)(1). For these reasons, the chairman of the Senate Subcommittee on Securities objected vigorously to these guidelines, and after some pressure from him, the Commission revised them.[106]

[c] Definition of brokerage and research services: Section 28(e)(3)

Subsection (3) of Section 28(e) defines "brokerage and research services." A constant issue in the legislative process out of which Section 28(e) evolved was the kind of services an investment manager could purchase with commissions. S. 470 referred to "research services," [107] H.R. 5050 to "brokerage services, including the availability and value of research or execution services." [108] The legislative history of both bills is vague on the meaning of the quoted phrases, however, and outside of what is facially implied, neither the hearings nor the reports accompanying the bills give much guidance, either by way of exclusion or inclusion, as to the particular services a manager may purchase through expenditure of client funds on brokerage fees.

The first serious attempt to describe the limits of an investment manager's discretion to purchase supplementary services with commissions appeared in Amendment No. 16 to S. 249, the provision which, with minor modifications, eventually became Section 28(e).[109] Subsection (3) describes three types of "brokerage and research services":

---

[105] See Securities Week, Aug. 4, 1975, p. 5.

[106] Securities Week, Aug. 4, 1975, p. 1. The Commission dropped the "essential" standard and the requirement that allocation policy be disclosed. See Securities Week, Sept. 22, 1975, p. 1; Wall Street Letter, Sept. 22, 1975, p. 10.

[107] See text following note 42 *supra*. The original version of S. 249 also referred to research services.

[108] See note 56 *supra*. The Treasury Department submitted a draft provision proposed as an amendment H.R. 10 § 604. It also, without amplification, used the same phrasing as H.R. 5050 and H.R. 10 to describe the services covered (see note 82 *supra*). See Wall Street Letter, Feb. 17, 1975, p. 2.

[109] See notes 86-87 *supra*.

(1) Advice;

(2) Analysis;

(3) Execution.

This statutory definition is broadly inclusive in character, and it is intended to avoid depriving an investment manager access to a service he believes in good faith offers his client a reasonable value in consideration of the additional commission expense incurred. The only well-known broker-supplied service plainly missing is sales support, which is understandable in view of the SEC's treatment of give-ups to promote mutual fund sales. But it is important also to recognize that a service which falls within the statutory definition is not protected merely because of that fact. It still must satisfy the reasonable/good-faith standard of Section 28(e)(1) when purchased.

From a regulatory perspective, it would be possible to set by rule services which no manager could reasonably and in good faith claim to be of value principally to an account rather than to himself. Purchasing broker assistance in selling mutual fund shares is an obvious example.[110] A more convenient regulatory approach to limiting the services a manager can purchase with commissions, because the authorities are willing to say as a matter of law that such services do not provide reasonable value to the client given the expenditure, is to refine the statutory definition of brokerage and research services. This is precisely what the SEC has done. In an administrative interpretation of Section 28(e)(3),[111] the Commission took the position that Congress did not intend Section 28(e) to extend to items such as entertainment, transportation, furniture, and like products. Nor, in the Commission's judgment, may an investment manager purchase periodicals or advisory services "which are readily and customarily available and offered to the general public on a commercial basis." The Commission also warned brokers that cooperation with fiduciaries acting in violation of Section 28(e) in attempting to purchase supplementary services could involve them in violations of the antifraud provisions of the federal securities laws.

-----

110 See ¶ 8.02[2][a] at notes 45-47.

111 SEC Securities Exchange Act Release No. 12251 (March 24, 1976), [1974-1975 Transfer Binder] CCH Fed. Sec. L. Rep. ¶ 80,407. For a dissenting view about the wisdom of defining research by rule, see Jorden, " 'Paying Up' for Research: A Regulatory and Legislative Analysis," 1975 Duke L.J. 1103, 1123-1124.

¶ 9.04.　DETERMINING THE LIMITS OF AN INVESTMENT MANAGER'S DISCRETION TO PURCHASE SUPPLEMENTARY SERVICES WITH COMMISSIONS

No understanding of the commissions-for-supplementary-services issue is possible without recognizing that the problem is not one of exercise of business judgment. Absent any duty-of-loyalty questions, no one would suggest that any standard stricter than business judgment should apply to an investment manager's selection of a broker for execution services for which no excess commissions are paid or to the employment of staff analysts at high salaries to provide research services. The problem is that, for the most part, broker-supplied services, though valuable to both the client and the manager, are paid for only by the client when purchased with commissions. If competitive forces are of insufficient strength to cause an investment manager to take into account the benefits he receives from controlling his client's brokerage in setting his management fee, the manager, in effect, has discretion over how much his clients will pay him for managing their accounts. He receives the base fee listed in the management contract plus the value to him of all supplementary services bought with his clients' commissions.

In a world of perfect knowledge, it would make no difference whether the charge for supplementary services were assumed by the client or the manager. The client, concerned only with the net return on his investment, would insist that the combined figure for management fees plus commissions be at a level which would maximize his net return. But in the world as it actually is, investors have imperfect knowledge and therefore face two difficulties, only one of which presents a legal problem. First, a client cannot determine whether his manager has accurately calculated that the value of the benefit accruing though the expenditure of additional funds on commissions is at least as great as the extra funds expended. A manager's decision about whether the purchase of a supplementary service is worth the cost is, however, precisely the kind of business judgment a manager is retained to exercise. But secondly, even conceding the accuracy of the manager's determination about the value of such supplementary services, the client's imperfect knowledge permits the manager to arrogate all or part of the value received to himself. Indeed, if the client is sufficiently uninformed, the manager may forego the best use of the client's commissions and choose to spend them in other ways that provide management with particularly significant benefits. It is this discretion to decide how to split up the value of the services purchased which creates legal problems for a manager.

[1] Deciding Which Services to Purchase

Consider the example of the discredited give-up for the sale of mutual fund shares.[112] Management's argument in support of this practice was that fund shareholders benefited because the higher cash inflow thus stimulated would reduce the possibility that redemptions would force liquidation of portfolio positions contrary to sound investment judgment. Expenditures for this purpose were, in a sense, premiums for an insurance program to protect the accomplishment of management's investment objectives.

It is doubtful that the excess commissions expended in this fashion really provided any such benefit to the fund shareholders. The amount of the excess retained as a cash asset of the fund would in most cases probably have exceeded the total of uninvested cash introduced by the acquisition of new shareholders (whose contributions rapidly were turned into securities holdings and not kept as cash), and, if so, the give-up practice was, for shareholders, a costly use of commissions. Nonetheless, assume for the sake of argument that shareholders obtained a positive benefit of the type management claimed. The total benefit of the give-up practice contained another factor in addition to the insurance value to the shareholders. Since advisory fees were calculated as a fixed percentage of asset value, all increases in shareholder contributions produced higher fees for management. Thus, the total benefit from using commissions to stimulate sales was the insurance value (I) plus the increase in advisory fees (F_1).[113]

---

112 The Commission has also given a qualified warning against engaging in other give-up practices. SEC Securities Exchange Act Release No. 12251 (March 24, 1976), [1975-1976 Transfer Binder] CCH Fed. Sec. L. Rep. ¶ 80,407. The use of give-ups under negotiated rates is discussed more fully in 9.06[2] infra.

113 The use of commissions to reward sales could prove costly to shareholders in other ways also. For simplicity, however, this analysis ignores the tendency of mutual fund advisers to turn fund portfolios over more rapidly to generate additional commissions and thereby encourage more sales. It also ignores the tendency to sacrifice best execution by selecting inferior executing brokers or more costly execution techniques to ease the flow of commissions to the selling brokers. But cf. Heritage Fund, Inc., [1974-1975 Transfer Binder] CCH Fed. Sec. L. Rep. ¶ 80,073 (1974) (decline in fund's portfolio value resulted in insufficient asset coverage of borrowings).

On the other hand, it is not necessary that the larger management fees generated through extra sales based on commission allocation be pocketed by management. It is conceivable that at least some of the higher fees

If the excess commissions were applied to purchase research instead of to stimulate sales efforts,[114] one can assume that the additional research would improve investment performance (P) to some degree, and that this improvement would increase advisory fees, either by attracting new shareholders and additional contributions from existing shareholders or by reducing the manager's need to generate such research through his own operation and, therefore, his internal research costs (F_P). In most cases, the improvement in performance would not attract as much additional money as would use of commissions to stimulate sales, since a shift of emphasis from sales to research will cause many selling brokers to lose some of their enthusiasm for selling fund shares and consequently to shift attention to mutual funds which pay for sales or to exert more effort in selling other investment products. For present purposes, assume that to be so. Which use of excess commissions would a mutual fund adviser choose—commissions for research or commissions for sales?

The total benefit if commissions are used for sales is $I + F_I$, and if they are used for research, it is $P + F_P$. Logically, the preferable approach is to maximize the total benefit. But suppose that $P + F_P > I + F_I$. It does not follow that an investment manager would choose research over sales. If $F_I > F_P$, the manager might choose to use commissions for sales, because that way he obtains the greatest profit even though he is sacrificing the total benefit. So long as the shareholders are not aware of the relative values of sales and research, they would not know to object. But suppose that $P + F_P < I + F_I$. It still does not follow that the manager may, without doing anything else, choose sales over research. If $P > I$, the shareholders of the fund would prefer research to sales, regardless of which use of commissions provides the

---

would be expended for better analysts and more research. This argument in support of using commissions for sales does not appear to have been seriously advanced in the litigation over the give-up question, however.

114 "Research" is a highly imprecise term, including, as it does, information at various stages in process as well as final conclusions. Furthermore, the discussion in the text makes the assumptions that the value of research can be quantified and that this value can be realized without additional expense to management. Finally, it should be noted that broker-generated research can differ from management-generated research in that the former tends to be transaction-oriented to encourage purchases and sales whereas the latter tends to emphasize protection of an existing portfolio. For the view that the expenditure of commissions for research has little effect on performance, see Pozen, "Money Managers and Securities Research," 51 N.Y.U. L. Rev. 923 (1976).

greatest total benefit, since they bear the entire expense of the commissions in either event. Of course, if management can persuade the shareholders to choose sales simply by paying the fund something in excess of the difference between P and I (as, for instance, by reducing advisory fees), both parties would be better off by choosing sales. The manager would simply be sharing enough of the benefit he got from sales to make it worthwhile for the shareholders, who are paying the costs of generating the benefits of each, to go along with the expenditure of commissions, which maximizes total benefit.

Suppose we extend this analysis to the period when reciprocity made it possible to reduce the level of excess commissions. Assume for simplicity that commissions could be spent entirely for brokerage services as well as for sales and research. In that event, the value of recapture would depend on how the excess commissions (C) necessary for research or sales compared to the benefits received from expending excess commissions. For example, supposing research to be more valuable overall than sales, it would be worthwhile to continue purchasing research if $P + F_P > C$. But from the shareholders' point of view, it would be worthwhile only if $P > C$, since the fund receives no benefit from F_P. As above, if the purchase of research provided a greater total benefit than the recapture of commissions, the manager could persuade the shareholders to purchase research by paying the fund something in excess of the difference between P and C. But if the shareholders were not aware of the relative values of P, C, and I, the manager could choose research or sales regardless of whether either provided the maximum total benefit, and would have an incentive to exercise his choice so as to obtain F_P or F_I, whichever were greater.

There is yet a final point to this analysis. Implicit in the discussion of whether the mutual fund shareholders would prefer recapture, research, or sales is the notion that the shareholders would be willing to bear the total cost of the approach that would increase their net return the most. But this is not necessarily the case. Suppose the manager set his advisory fee at his reservation price—that is, the price below which he would not go to provide management services. If the shareholders knew that the purchase of research or of sales would increase the manager's advisory fee, they might refuse to permit commissions to be expended for that purpose, even though they were costing themselves additional return, until the manager agreed to cut the shareholders in for a portion of the management fee increase. If buying research, for example, would cost $1 in excess commissions ($C = \$1$), improve investment performance by $2 ($P = \$2$), and increase advisory fees by $10 ($F_P = \$10$), this would produce a total net benefit of $11. The shareholders, assuming they were adequately informed and able to act as a unit, might nonetheless turn down their $1 net increase in return until management contracted to pay over some of the $10. The final split would depend on the relative bargaining power and negotiating ability of the parties, but without affecting total net benefit, the shareholders could increase their portion above the mere increase in portfolio performance.

Thus, there are three ways in which a manager's discretion to spend extra commissions paid by the client to purchase supplementary services may fail to serve the client's interest fully:

(1) In the worst case, a manager may choose not to maximize total benefits in order to maximize the benefit he receives from the transaction. This would be the case, for example, if a manager purchased sales instead of research to maximize his advisory fees, even though the combination of research plus increased advisory fees was greater than the combination of benefits resulting from purchasing sales $(P + F_P > I + F_I$; but $F_I > F_P)$. This would also be the case if the manager spent extra commissions even though no purchase of supplementary services could increase total benefits. Plainly, forgoing all such expenditures deprives the manager of any fee increase $(C > P + F_P$ and $C > I + F_I$; but $F_P > 0$ and $F_I > 0)$.

(2) Less bad, but also costly from the client's point of view, is an expenditure on extra commissions which increases total benefit but decreases the net return to the client. This would be the case if purchasing sales produced a better overall result but purchasing research produced a better investment return $(I + F_I > P + F_P$; but $P > I)$. The same effect would result if forgoing extra commissions saved more than purchasing research (or sales) would return to the client, even if the increase in management fees were to make such a purchase a better overall value $(P + F_P > C$; but $C > P)$.

(3) The best case, but still not entirely satisfactory from the client's point of view, is the one in which the expenditure of extra commissions benefits both the client and the manager, as, for instance, if the purchase of research improves both the client's investment return and the manager's advisory fees $(P + F_P > C; P > C)$. Even here, the client's power to deny the manager any increase in fee through the expenditure of extra commissions by denying the manager discretion to make such expendi-

tures places the client in a position to pressure the manager into sharing part of the advisory-fee gain (or its equivalent, the savings realized through reducing the internal operating costs of management).

Now the problem associated with the use of commissions can be put into sharper relief. So long as the client lacks perfect knowledge, he may not know whether the manager's choice of how to spend extra commissions, or whether to spend them at all, is achieving either the maximum total benefit or the proper share of the total benefit for the client. The failure to achieve the maximum total benefit may reflect an error in business judgment or it may reflect a deliberate decision by the manager to improve his own position at the expense of his clients. But regardless of whether, in the exercise of his business judgment, the manager correctly determines the strategy which maximizes total benefit, he still must decide how to allocate that benefit between himself and his client.

[2] Allocating the Benefits of Purchased Services Between Manager and Client

Section 28(e) of the Securities Exchange Act reaffirms the manager's power to decide which approach represents the best strategy for using commissions, as well as his right to be wrong within the scope of reasonable business judgment.[115] The good-faith requirement, again reaffirming the traditional rule, denies him the power to make his choice motivated by a purpose of enhancing his own profits regardless of

---

[115] The fact that, in this respect, Section 28(e) reaffirms common-law principle is reflected in the legislative history. The position taken initially was that no legislation along the lines of Section 28(e) was necessary because investment managers already had authority to exercise business judgment in determining where and how to spend commissions. See *Senate Securities Industry Study,* note 38 *supra,* at 60-62; *House Securities Industry Study,* note 46 *supra,* at 145. Even as late as publication of the Conference Report on S. 249, the drafters were taking the position that Section 28(e) did not really change anything. The Report on H.R. 4111 of the Comm. on Interstate and Foreign Commerce, H.R. Rep. No. 123, 94th Cong., 1st Sess. 95 (1975), stated:

"Some institutional money managers have expressed the feeling that, with the advent of competitive rates, they must direct a payment of no more than the lowest commission obtainable for a transaction, or else they will be subject to suit for violation of their fiduciary obligations. This result will occur, they contend, without regard for the quality of the broker's execution and settlement service or the research information

whether that choice can be defended as maximizing total benefit or as being within the scope of reasonable business judgment.

But the manager's decision as to the allocation of the benefits received through the expenditure of extra commissions between himself and his client is not protected by Section 28(e). As the discussion above has shown, it is possible for a manager to maximize total benefit through the expenditure of extra commissions and yet leave a client worse off than had no such expenditure been made. Whether or not the client enjoys a net benefit, however, the manager must decide how much, if any, of the benefit he receives he will share with the client. To do this, he must in effect negotiate with himself to determine the allocation to which he and the client would have agreed had both parties had perfect knowledge. Of course, since the manager also has less than perfect knowledge, he cannot calculate precisely the actual total and separate benefits from a given commission strategy. The question, however, is not whether his calculations are absolutely accurate, but whether the discretion to make the allocation will cause him either deliberately or inadvertently to err in his own favor.[116] Perhaps the most telling blow to the practice by mutual fund advisers of using give-ups to reward sales was the general reluctance of management to adjust advisory fees

---

which he may provide. *The Committee does not believe that general fiduciary principles necessitate this result,* but accepts responsibility to clarify the law in this respect." [Emphasis added.]

And the Conference Report, note 88 *supra,* at 108, took the position that the only substantive difference of note between the House and Senate versions was that the latter more clearly preempted state and federal law.

116 In the release accompanying the adoption of Rule 19b-3, SEC Securities Exchange Act Release No. 11203 (Jan. 23, 1975), [1974-1975 Transfer Binder] CCH Fed. Sec. L. Rep. ¶ 80,067, at 84,976 n.42, the Commission argued that fixed commission rates were bad policy because, among other things:

"[I]nvestment managers may be inclined to seek services in exchange for brokerage since the cost of such services may be buried in the carrying value of the portfolio securities rather than charged to the beneficiaries as an expense of administration. The tendency . . . to corrupt fiduciary relationships is not the least of the evils. . . . Even where no misconduct is present, the situation leads to inefficiency in the management of assets. The foregoing does not mean that fiduciaries may not utilize commissions on transactions for beneficiaries to obtain for their beneficiaries research and other valuable services."

This statement by the Commission exposes the unavoidable dichotomy dominating the controversy over commissions for supplementary services. The Commission is worried lest managers try to use commission strategies

significantly as the size of a fund increased.[117] Had they made a fairer allocation of the benefits accruing from use of commissions to stimulate sales, assuming there were such benefits, it is possible that the regulatory[118] and judicial[119] activity stemming from reliance on give-ups would have been less unrelenting. It would probably be useful for contemporary investment managers to keep that lesson in mind in evaluating the commission expenditure practices they follow today.

There are two ways to solve the problem of allocating the benefits of broker-supplied services. The easier is for the manager to pay the premium those services cost out of his own pocket and to adjust his advisory fee accordingly. This approach is useful for two reasons. First, direct payment from the manager discourages overspending on broker-supplied services because the manager knows his own revenues for an investment period in advance (a fixed percentage of total assets under management), and he knows his overhead costs for that period. The amount he pays, therefore, must return him enough, either through retention and expansion of existing business or attraction of new business, or through control of his internal costs, to justify the expenditure.[120] Direct payment from the manager also gives an investor more accurate information about his actual costs of management than is pos-

---

to hide benefits to themselves from their clients, and is further concerned that even where a manager acts in good faith, there is a tendency toward overpurchase of supplementary services if the manager benefits thereby. But, at the same time, the Commission does not want managers to cause their clients to forego additional benefits they could receive by correct commission strategies.

[117] See *PPI Report,* note 13 *supra,* at 16, 97-102.

[118] See, e.g., ¶ 8.02[2], notes 12, 27, 45.

[119] E.g., Fogel v. Chestnutt, 533 F.2d 731 (2d Cir. 1975); Moses v. Burgin, 445 F.2d 369 (1st Cir. 1970), *cert. denied sub nom.* Johnson v. Moses, 404 U.S. 994 (1971).

[120] See, e.g., Statement of Alliance One, Institutional Services, Inc., in Hearings on S. 249 Before the Subcomm. on Securities of the Senate Comm. on Banking, Housing and Urban Affairs, 94th Cong., 1st Sess. 288 (1975):

> "If our clients [investment managers] were required to pay for our services only in hard dollars [i.e., at their own expense], we're told that their budgets would, of necessity be quite small for a variety of reasons. The principal reason given is the negative impact it would have upon their own profitability."

To similar effect, but from the viewpoint of the manager, is a statement by a trust officer of a commercial bank which pays for research itself, rather than through client commissions:

sible if his own commissions pay the premium.[121] This is important because the investor can make no possible claim later that, as between himself and the manager, the allocation of benefits was unfair to him.[122] His share is included in the management fee where the cost of outside services is just another expense item for the manager, such as salaries for in-house analysts and rent. The only conceivable complaint on the part of a client might be that the advisory fee, said by the manager to include the client's share of the cost of broker-supplied services, is excessive.[123] But it is doubtful that a management fee would be held excessive because it included the cost of purchasing outside services. Moreover, given the small cost of broker-supplied services as a percentage of total management costs,[124] it is doubtful many managers would want to raise the cost of outside services as a serious defense to an excessive fee claim.

The second way to allocate the benefits of broker-supplied services is to adopt some mechanism that tests the fairness of the manager's allocation policy with respect to the excess commissions the client is

---

"We're getting less research now [but] we're using the research we get more, and we're getting more out of it. . . . We're forced to make decisions, to ask ourselves, how much is it really worth?"

Wall Street Letter, Nov. 17, 1975, p. 3. See also Hearings on S. 470 and S. 488 Before the Subcomm. on Securities of the Senate Comm. on Banking, Housing and Urban Affairs, 93d Cong., 1st Sess. 308 (1973).

121 Management fees are so important in conveying information about management services that the Commission staff takes the position that it is fraudulent not to disclose management fees that are substantially higher than necessary. See, e.g., Rotan Mosle, Inc. [1974-1975 Transfer Binder] CCH Fed. Sec. L. Rep. ¶ 79,961 (1974).

122 See, e.g., Securities Week, April 19, 1976, p. 5 (trust division of bank avoids allocation problem by paying hard dollars).

123 Cf. Kurach v. Weissman, 49 F.R.D. 304 (S.D.N.Y. 1970). In a settlement of an excessive-management-fee claim against a mutual fund adviser, the SEC took the position that recaptured brokerage should be applied against the management fee. See note 25 supra. For a discussion of the problem of excessive management fees, see ¶ 5.03[1].

124 See SEC Securities Exchange Act Release No. 11203 (Jan. 23, 1975, [1974-1975 Transfer Binder] CCH Fed. Sec. L. Rep. ¶ 80,067, at 84,992 n.73, the release accompanying adoption of Rule 19b-3, in which the SEC said: "[T]he cost of research does not appear to be so large a part of the expense incurred by brokerage firms as to make it impossible for them to supply it in reasonable quantity if their customers desire it." The SEC reported that only four of 235 firms estimated research expenses as more than 25 percent of total expenses, and that about three-quarters of brokerage firms reported such expenses as 10 percent or less of total expenses.

paying. In principle, when the client pays for supplementary services with commissions, his total management costs should not exceed his costs when the manager purchases such services out of his own pocket. In other words, when the client pays, the base management fee plus the cost of excess commissions should, on the average, not exceed what the base management fee would be if the manager paid. The problem is that, as a practical matter, it is impossible to make this determination directly, even where the service purchased is available either through a cash payment or through increased commissions. Instead, the ordinary practice is for the manager to disclose what he plans to do and to propose some oversight mechanism, such as regular reports to the client or to a set of outside directors, for example.[125] Consent by the client then authorizes the manager to proceed, but it does not permit the manager to arrogate to himself a disproportionate share of the benefits from purchasing broker-supplied services. It only shifts the burden back to the client to show that the consent was fraudulently obtained or that the authority to pay excess commissions, though properly obtained, was abused. Fraud in obtaining consent would be shown through the traditional proof of misrepresentations or material omissions. Abuse of authority might be shown through evidence of excessive turnover of an account in light of its investment objectives, high account-manager ratios, size, education, and experience of in-house staff, referral of accounts by executing broker-dealers, and other such factors which tend to indicate that a manager is succumbing to the use of commissions in a way which benefits him excessively.

In view of the hazards attendant to the use of excess commissions to purchase supplementary services, it is unsurprising that many investment managers have been taking the position that they will not pay higher commissions for research and that they will pay for broker-supplied services with their own funds.[126] Nonetheless, it is clear that

---

[125] The importance of having an objective oversight mechanism for investment companies has manifested itself in the practice of providing independent counsel for the outside directors. Much more unusual, but potentially useful for resolving the problem of allocating benefits between client and manager, is the practice of relating part of the management fee to a percentage of commissions paid. See, e.g., Securities Week, Jan. 19, 1976, p. 2a (brokerage firm offering to credit customer commissions toward purchase of its research products).

[126] See, e.g., Securities Week, Feb. 9, 1976, p. 13; Securities Week, Nov. 17, 1975, p. 10; Wall Street Letter, Nov. 17, 1975, p. 3; Wall Street Letter, Aug. 4, 1975, p. 8; Wall Street Letter, July 14, 1975, p. 6; Wall Street Letter, April 21, 1975, p. 4; Securities Week, March 17, 1975, p. 2;

many, if not most, investment managers are using client commissions to purchase broker-supplied services.[127] As Section 28(e) confirms, such purchases are not a breach of duty solely on the ground that another brokerage firm was offering pure execution (or even execution plus research) for a lower price. Yet, as the discussion above shows, Section 28(e) does little to help managers resolve the fundamental conflict of interest which comes of having to allocate the benefits of broker-supplied services between themselves and their clients. Moreover, matters have been made more complex than necessary because of the tendency to treat extra commissions for brokerage services and extra commissions for research alike. Consequently, the remainder of the discussion in this chapter explores in more detail the limits on an investment manager's discretion to pay for supplementary services with commissions in light of the conflict-of-interest problem and, because of the distinct issues present, analyzes "brokerage" services and "research" services separately.

¶ 9.05. CONFLICT-OF-INTEREST PROBLEMS IN THE USE OF EXCESS COMMISSIONS TO PURCHASE BROKERAGE SERVICES

Over the last decade, the idea has developed that an investment manager is paying an excess commission if he executes with a brokerage firm at a higher commission rate than another firm is charging, or if he purchases at a higher market price or sells at a lower market price than another firm is quoting. If the manager chooses an ostensibly higher-priced broker or dealer purely for execution services and not to mask the purchase of other services, he is paying no excess commission and the apparent difference in price is illusory. The SEC's interpretative release[128] expanding on its position in the *Policy Statement on the Future*

Securities Week, Sept. 30, 1974, p. 7. See also the summary of testimony at the SEC's conference on the use of commissions to purchase research (see note 63 *supra*) in Wall Street Letter, Oct. 30, 1974, pp. 1-4. Not all managers claiming that they refuse to pay excess commissions for research are being completely forthright, however. Some decline to do business with pure execution firms on grounds of concern over quality of execution, so they do business with full-service firms and receive research anyway. See, e.g., Securities Week, Feb. 9, 1976, p. 13; Securities Week, Sept. 1, 1975, p. 8.

[127] See, e.g., Securities Week, March 15, 1976, p. 4; Securities Week, Feb. 9, 1976, p. 13; Securities Week, Nov. 17, 1975, p. 6; Securities Week, Oct. 27, 1975, p. 11; Securities Week, Sept. 22, 1975, p. 9; Securities Week, Sept. 1, 1975, pp. 1, 8; Wall Street Letter, Aug. 11, 1975, p. 4; Wall Street Letter, July 21, 1975, p. 7.

[128] Note 32 *supra*.

Structure of the Securities Markets[129] separated the price paid for the purchase or sale of a security into two elements:

(1) The actual market price of the security; and

(2) The service charge levied by the executing firm for carrying out the transaction.

In choosing a firm for execution, an investment manager must keep both elements in mind, and insofar as he is trying to minimize the costs of execution, the manager cannot allow pursuit of the best price for one to cause the price of the other to deteriorate beyond the savings he obtained. From a manager's perspective, this ordinarily means that he will pay a higher commission or markup on a transaction than appears to be available because he believes that the market price thus received is sufficiently superior to that obtainable through the firms charging lower commission or markup rates to justify bypassing them.

On any rational analysis, it would be ridiculous for the rule of law to look solely to the size of the commission or markup to determine the scope of an investment manager's authority to select a brokerage firm, unless there were some greater evil to be prevented by such a rule. The most likely source of concern that the law would adopt a smallest-commission bias is the *Delaware Management Co.* case.[130] One of the principal issues in that case was the practice of the respondent, an invest-ment adviser to a mutual fund, of interposing brokers between the fund and market makers the fund could have approached itself, thus causing the fund to pay the broker's commission as well as the market maker's markup. If the SEC's holding that the respondent breached its fiduciary duty in this regard had been based on the practice of interpositioning rather than on the purpose behind it, the decision would have meant that investment managers could not pay a higher price for execution services than the lowest available. Right up through the enactment of Section 28(e), many persons in the securities industry regarded this interpretation of the *Delaware Management Co.* case as a serious pos-sibility.[131]

---

[129] Note 27 *supra.*

[130] See text at notes 3-11 *supra.*

[131] See, e.g., Testimony of Bernard H. Garil, in Hearings on H.R. 5050 and H.R. 340 Before the Subcomm. on Commerce and Finance of the House Comm. on Interstate and Foreign Commerce, 93d Cong., 1st Sess., Ser. No. 53, Pt. 4 at 1594 (hereinafter cited as Hearings on H.R. 5050):

"Mr. [Cong.] Young: . . . Don't you think that the fiduciary law re-

But actually, the interpositioning issue illustrates very nicely when an investment manager can pay a higher price for execution services and when he cannot, at least without the informed consent of his client (or his client's representative). In *Delaware Management Co.*, the manager was not interposing brokers to assist in carrying out transactions at the best price for the mutual fund clients. Indeed, the report of the case provides no evidence that any of the interposed brokers ever produced a difference in the market price of the security involved or a reduction in the markup charged by the market maker sufficient to offset the commission of the interposed broker. The purpose of interposing these brokers was to compensate them beyond the underwriting commission for the sale of fund shares and, to a much lesser extent, for research. If the purpose had been to improve the net price at which the mutual funds' purchases and sales were carried out, there is little doubt that the case would have turned out differently, at least with regard to the interpositioning issue.[132] *Delaware Management Co.* was authority, at best, for when an investment manager was operating in a conflict-of-interest environment, not for when he was seeking to maximize profits for his client.

Obviously, when pure execution is an investment manager's purpose, there is no conflict of interest present which would lead him to sacrifice the best price he can gain for his accounts. To pay a higher commission

---

quires the fiduciary to get the best price not only on the stock but also on the commission?

"Mr. Garil: This is the area of great confusion. The SEC itself has come out with almost two different opinions over time. There was a *Delaware Management* case which basically said that you should get the lowest commission."

[132] Bahn, "Two Current Broker-Dealer Problems," in R. Mundheim & A. Fleischer, *First Annual Institute on Securities Regulation* 341 (PLI 1970). To the question of Professor Mundheim of whether the Enforcement Division's position was that mutual funds must always go to the market-maker, Director (now Commissioner) Pollack referred to the NASD rule permitting interpositioning "where the member can demonstrate that . . . the total cost . . . of the transaction . . . was better than the prevailing inter-dealer market for the security," quoting NASD Rules of Fair Practice, Art. III, § 1 (CCH NASD Manual ¶ 2151.03). Bahn, *supra,* at 344. To the same effect, see the extensive discussion of interpositioning in Schwartz, "Execution of Portfolio Transactions—Legal Aspects," in R. Mundheim & W. Werner, *Mutual Funds* 129, 131-137 (PLI 1970). See also *PPI Report,* note 13 *supra,* at 179, which criticized interpositioning only as it enabled broker-dealers providing no substantial service on the transaction to obtain a commission.

or markup than necessary without obtaining at least an equivalent shift in market price only costs the client money and profits the manager not at all. Few managers are in the habit of making a gift of their clients' assets to executing broker-dealers, if for no other reason than that it reduces the net return of their accounts, affecting them adversely in their competition with other investment managers. This is precisely the situation in which the business-judgment rule is supposed to operate. Because their own self-interest suggests that managers will pay no more for pure execution services than they must, the law permits them to be wrong up to the point that no reasonable investment manager would have carried out the transaction in the same way.

To this point, the analysis of execution services has been oversimplified for purposes of explanation. The cost of a transaction consists not only of the market price of the security plus the cost of execution, but also the cost of the risk that the transaction will not take place as promised by the executing broker—that it will fail or, because clearance and settlement will not be handled expeditiously, that it will be delayed. Moreover, even if one could eliminate the cost of the risk of a failed or delayed transaction from consideration, the market price and the commission or markup may be indeterminable in advance of the transaction. An investment manager, still determined to achieve best net price for his client, must somehow quantify each of those elements of the total price for the transaction such that his client nets as much as possible. Obviously, a manager's ability to quantify costs is quite different for a small trade, where the market price cannot be affected and where a large number of brokerage firms can execute at modest cost and with virtually no risk of failure or delay, from what it would be on a large trade, where skills in accumulation or distribution and a willingness on the part of the broker to risk his own capital are involved. In a block transaction, for example, a manager's attitude might vary from insistence on a net price in advance of a transaction to a willingness to accept variable market prices and to negotiate commissions, depending on the actual difficulty of the transaction and the skill demonstrated by the executing firm. Any suggestion that such transactions ordinarily permit a meaningful determination of whether a better net price was obtainable is unrealistic.[133] In fact, attempts by managers to

---

[133] This is a point made persuasively by a number of authorities. See, e.g., Stark, "Problems of Institutions Under Competitive Rates: 'Paying-Up' for Research," in R. Mundheim, A. Fleischer & B. Vandegrift, *Seventh Annual Institute on Securities Regulation* (PLI 1976); Testimony of Bernard H. Garil, in Hearings on H.R. 5050, note 131 *supra*, at 1596; Kay, "Block Trading for Best Execution," 114 Trusts & Estates 738 (Oct. 1975).

solicit competing bids on block transactions or to force down the commission price alone in advance of a trade are often counterproductive, resulting in higher prices to an account.[134]

The limits the business-judgment rule places on investment managers to choose brokers have been explored above.[135] For present purposes, it is enough to establish that, where pure execution is the only service an investment manager seeks, he satisfies his duty of best execution by carrying out portfolio transactions within the scope of the business-judgment rule. The special problems facing investment managers who seek only execution services arise in two contexts: (1) proving that execution services were all he was seeking when executing with a firm which provides him with other services as well or when executing with a firm with which he is affiliated; and (2) properly allocating execution costs among his accounts.

[1] Proving Pure Execution

Suppose an investment manager executes a transaction with a brokerage firm which provides him with research services for which he insists he does not pay excess commissions. Or suppose a manager executes with an affiliated firm or a firm which has referred clients to him. The manager may honestly have selected the firm because of its execution capabilities, and yet, because of the conflict of interest, he may find himself in the position of having to prove that he was not motivated by that conflict.

In such circumstances, it is impossible for a manager to demonstrate conclusively that he was not motivated by the conflict. In principle, that should make no difference, since the client has suffered no injury and therefore there are no damages. But if, in a subsequent lawsuit, a client can satisfy a court that the conflict of interest motivated both the choice of executing broker and the price paid, the burden may shift to the manager to show that the client was not damaged. If that happens, and the facts would support a reasonable conclusion that a better net price was in fact available, the manager might find himself answerable even though his choice was within the scope of reasonable business judgment. Speculation and lack of precision about actual cost differentials will be no aid to the manager. As Judge Friendly said in

---

134 See, e.g., Reich, "Games People Are Playing With Negotiated Rates," 9 Institutional Investor 29, 30 (July 1975); Securities Week, July 14, 1975, p. 10; Wall Street Letter, Sept. 30, 1974, p. 1; Testimony of Bernard H. Garil, in Hearings on H.R. 5050, note 131 *supra*.

135 See ¶ 8.04.

a case involving a mutual fund adviser's failure to resolve the conflict over the direction of mutual fund brokerage: "If this [resolution of the damages issue] should seem a departure from strict logic, it would not be the first time this has occurred in a law of damages." [136] In addition to exposure to private litigation, there is the possibility of administrative action which is, at best, inconvenient, and may lead to imposition of sanctions.

Plainly, the most important step to take where conflict-of-interest questions may arise is to resolve the conflict by obtaining the informed consent of the client.[137] But client consent does not free the manager to act in his own interest at the expense of the client. It only permits him to engage in a course of dealing which, because of the conflict, might otherwise hold the manager absolutely accountable for his profits and the client's expenses.[138] Therefore, the prudent manager, executing portfolio transactions in a conflict-of-interest context, should avoid practices which are difficult to justify as fairly allocating the benefits they produce between manager and client, particularly if such practices might well be characterized as lying close to the limits of business judgment.

Again, the interpositioning issue is instructive here. One can make a case that interpositioning is a valid execution practice in pursuit of best net price.[139] Nonetheless, it would be dangerous for an investment manager to interpose an affiliated broker or a broker providing services other than executions without direct compensation from the manager, at least if the client is not fully informed about and capable of understanding what has transpired. Because interpositioning was used so extensively by mutual fund advisers, it has acquired a reputation as being a device primarily useful for paying off brokers to whom favors are owed. The *Special Study*,[140] the *Report on Public Policy Implica-*

---

[136] Fogel v. Chestnutt, 533 F.2d 731, 756-757 (2d Cir. 1975).

[137] For a detailed discussion of how to resolve a conflict-of-interest through informed client consent, see ¶ 9.07 *infra*.

[138] See, e.g., Fogel v. Chestnutt, note 136 *supra*. There, the manager failed adequately to inform the outside directors of the mutual fund it advised of the possibility of recapture of commissions on regional exchanges. The court held that the adviser was answerable not only for the recapturable brokerage from those transactions executed on the regionals, but also, depending on plaintiffs' proof, for the recapturable brokerage with respect to transactions which could have been executed on the regionals.

[139] See note 132 *supra*.

[140] *Special Study*, note 4 *supra*, Pt. 2, at 620-623.

tions of Investment Company Growth,[141] and the *Institutional Investor Study*[142] were all critical of it. Even the National Association of Stock Dealers (NASD) placed the burden on the executing broker to show that it was justifiable under the circumstances.[143] Thus, in view of the not wholly undeserved reputation interpositioning has acquired, caution would suggest that an investment manager interpose only those brokerage firms with which he does only an execution business.

Another dangerous practice is trading with firms which refer business to an investment manager if the brokerage fees they charge are not highly competitive. Furthermore, even where the trades are small enough to demonstrate that the commissions charged are in line with the lowest rates of competing brokers and that market prices plus markups are in line with competing dealers, hazards remain for a manager. An overly aggressive investment program relying on high turnover, for example, may raise a suggestion of trading to generate brokerage fees. Certainly there can be no question about the sensitivity of the SEC to connections between referring brokers and investment managers, especially with regard to the management of the accounts of unsophisticated investors. For a period, the staff was taking the position that compensation arrangements between investment advisers and broker-dealers for referral business is inherently fraudulent and deceptive.[144] In a similar development, the SEC first forced the NASD to adopt a so-called antireciprocal rule to regulate execution business between mutual funds and brokers selling their shares,[145] and then adopted

---

141 *PPI Report,* note 13 *supra,* at 179.

142 *Institutional Investor Study,* note 7 *supra,* Ch. XIII, at 2256.

143 NASD Rules of Fair Practice, Art. III, § 1, CCH NASD Manual ¶ 2151.03.

144 See, e.g., John C. Tead Co., [1973 Transfer Binder] CCH Fed. Sec. L. Rep. ¶ 79,557 (1973). For a fuller discussion of the problems raised by referrals from broker-dealers, see ¶ 3.02[2][b]. See also Casey, " 'Finders Fee' Compensation to Brokers and Others," 31 Bus. Law. 707 (1976); Bines, "Regulating Discretionary Management: Broker-Dealers as Catalysts for Reform," 16 B.C. Ind. & Com. L. Rev. 347, 374-378 (1975).

145 In the Policy Statement on the Future Structure of the Securities Markets, (Feb. 2, 1972), [Special Studies Transfer Binder] CCH Fed. Sec. L. Rep. ¶ 74,811, at 65,621, the Commission warned the NASD to adopt its own rule requiring its members to discontinue reciprocal brokerage for the sale of investment company shares or "the Commission will then consider rulemaking to accomplish the desired result." The NASD proposed such a rule July 31, 1972 (see [1969-1973 Transfer Binder] CCH Mutual Funds Guide ¶ 9511), and amended the Rules of Fair Practice, Art. III, § 26, on May 25, 1973, by adding new subsection (k) (see CCH NASD Manual ¶ 2176, at 2105-5).

Rule 15b10-10, paralleling the NASD rule and applying to brokers not belonging to the NASD.[146] The rules provide in substance that brokers may not show favor or disfavor in the distribution of mutual fund shares on the basis of brokerage commissions received or expected; solicit a promise for brokerage from a mutual fund; arrange with other broker-dealers for commission splits; or circulate information about the level of commissions received in connection with such distribution.[147]

These illustrations are not meant to indicate that an investment manager cannot rely on an execution device which in his judgment is best for the client at the time, or that a manager cannot deal with a firm which is providing it other services. They are only meant to suggest

---

[146] SEC Securities Exchange Act Release No. 10439 (Oct. 19, 1973), [1973 Transfer Binder] CCH Fed. Sec. L. Rep. ¶ 79,536. See also SEC Securities Exchange Act Release No. 10246 (June 27, 1973), [1973 Transfer Binder] CCH Fed. Sec. L. Rep. ¶ 79,414 (Rule 15b10-10 proposed).

[147] The rules also expressly provide that they are not intended "to prohibit the execution of portfolio transactions of any investment company . . . by members [nonmembers] who also sell shares of the investment company; provided, however, that members [nonmembers] shall seek orders for execution on the basis of the value and quality of their brokerage services. . . ." NASD Rules of Fair Practice, Art. III, § 26(k)(5), CCH NASD Manual ¶ 2176, at 2105-5.

From the outset, these antireciprocal rules came under fire (see, e.g., Wall Street Letter, May 20, 1974, p. 2) because neither mutual fund managers nor brokers were sure of what they had to demonstrate in order not to be held in violation of the rules. As a consequence, mutual fund managers tried to avoid all indications of impropriety. See Securities Week, June 3, 1974, p. 6. Mutual fund managers complained that the rules seemed to bar execution business with selling brokers to reward their sales efforts even if their execution prices were consistent with best execution. See, e.g., Wall Street Letter, Aug. 26, 1974, p. 3; Securities Week, Aug. 26, 1974, p. 8. (No one seemed willing to acknowledge the policing problem of how to be sure that most managers would in fact seek best execution, however.) Issuance of the rules also reportedly caused brokers to cease selling fund shares as aggressively as before. See Securities Week, Sept. 2, 1974, p. 7; Wall Street Letter, Sept. 2, 1974, p. 8.

The NASD proposed to amend the rule by eliminating the second clause of Section 26(k)(5), beginning with "provided, however," and adding a new clause permitting a broker to sell shares of a fund which, with appropriate disclosure in its prospectus, were executed with selling brokers "qualified to provide best execution." See Securities Week, Sept. 9, 1974, p. 8. (The Antitrust Division of the Justice Department opposed any change in the rules. Id. at 3.) The NASD further revised its proposal in response to the reaction its proposed amendment received at SEC staff-conducted hearings. Securities Week, Nov. 11, 1974, p. 4. No new changes were approved, however.

that, to the extent a question of compromise can arise after the fact, an investment manager should exercise care to assure that the transaction appears entirely aboveboard. Thus, for example, on easy executions where rates are fairly standardized, investment managers should anticipate no problems in using a referring or affiliated broker-dealer[148] who charges competitive rates or makes a competitive market. Similarly, executions with full-service firms from which the manager is receiving research should present no special problem so long as the conflict arising out of the purchase of research with commissions is properly resolved. The important point is that, in principle, if an investment manager is truly seeking pure execution on one or more of a series of trades, or if the portion of the commissions paid for research can be reasonably identified, there is no excess commission associated with the execution services themselves. To the extent brokerage fees differ from the lowest prices quoted, they reflect a premium not for the manager's own benefit, but for the account's benefit to assure greater certainty that the trade will be completed, that the market price will be right, or both.

[2] Allocating Execution Costs Among Multiple Accounts

Since most investment managers handle more than one account, they require a system of allocating execution costs fairly among those accounts. There is a strong policy in the law against a fiduciary's commingling the assets of one beneficiary with those of another, lest one obtain assets belonging to the other or it become impossible to separate the assets of one from the other.[149] Additionally, a fiduciary managing separate accounts must justify a transaction involving each as being

---

148 Dealings with affiliated brokers present special problems under Securities Exchange Act § 11(a) (15 U.S.C. § 78ka), as discussed in ¶ 10.02.

149 See, e.g., *Restatement (Second) of Trusts* § 179 (1959); *Restatement (Second) of Agency* §§ 398, 426 (1958). The rule against commingling is not practical in all instances, of course, and there are numerous exceptions to it, including the right of a trustee to deposit the proceeds of separate trusts in a common bank account (see *Restatement (Second) of Trusts* § 179, Comment c) and of a bank to maintain a common trust fund in accordance with statutory restrictions (see *id.* § 227, Comment k). But these are exceptions developed for limited purposes, and a fiduciary looking to avoid liability for the general prohibition against commingling must similarly rely, absent established fiduciary practice, on Securities Exchange Act § 28(e) as an exception which frees a manager from the requirement of allocating excess commissions precisely from account to account if the procedure relied on is reasonable and if the allocation is made in good faith.

fair to each.¹⁵⁰ When an investment manager trades without regard to whether each account is paying for the quality of execution it obtains, but rather with concern only for satisfactory overall execution, he is in effect commingling the accounts he is managing for the purpose of sharing brokerage expenses. Furthermore, an unfair allocation of execution costs may be the product of the manager's own self-interest. Even though it may not be possible to show that a manager has received any services valuable to him as a result of his execution practices, he has breached his duty of loyalty if his system of allocation purposefully prefers one set of accounts over another. He might do this, for example, to improve the net investment return of accounts, such as pension accounts (which ordinarily are closely monitored by such clients), and thereby enhance his competitive ability to retain existing business and develop new business.

The allocation problem arises in two contexts:

(1) An investment manager may make an investment decision which affects a number of accounts he is managing, and the process of accumulating or disposing of the securities involved may extend over a period of time, with separate transactions executed at different market prices and for different brokerage fees.

(2) A manager may have an established course of dealing with various brokers such that some adjustments in execution costs are traceable to the continuing relationship and particular savings or additional expenses on a given trade cannot entirely be attributed to that one transaction.

In both cases, Section 28(e) relieves managers having reasonable systems of allocation from liability under a commingling theory on a showing solely that execution costs were not divided among accounts precisely in accordance with the execution services received by each individual account.¹⁵¹ Section 28(e) does not, however, relieve a manager from resolving the conflict of interest present in allocating

---

¹⁵⁰ See *Restatement (Second) of Trusts* § 170, Comment m (1959); *Restatement (Second) of Agency* § 387, Comment b, § 394, Comments b, c (1958).

¹⁵¹ See note 149 *supra.* In this respect, Section 28(e) is in accord with common-law principles which permit a fiduciary to transact business involving separate accounts if the transaction is fair to each. The burden is on the fiduciary to show that the transaction is fair. See note 150 *supra.*

execution costs among different types of accounts if preference of one type over another could inure to the manager's benefit.

In the case of executing a single investment decision for a number of accounts over a period of time, a developing practice is to average the costs of the entire series of trades and charge each account accordingly.[152] Although this is not the only way to allocate costs fairly, it does have the advantage of being objective, and since every account is treated alike, it seems also eminently fair.[153] But equal treatment for different types of accounts is not always a virtue. If, as a general rule, early execution is preferable to later execution once an investment decision has been reached, prorating the costs equally between discretionary and nondiscretionary accounts, for example, deprives the discretionary accounts of an important advantage they were positioned to take and the nondiscretionary accounts deliberately forwent. Thus, it would be reasonable for a manager to adopt an objective procedure that has the effect of distinguishing between discretionary and nondiscretionary accounts,[154] for example, by prorating execution expenses for

---

[152] See, e.g., Stark, "Problems of Institutions Under Competitive Rates: 'Paying-Up' for Research," in R. Mundheim, A. Fleischer & B. Vandegrift, *Seventh Annual Institute on Securities Law* (PLI 1976).

[153] It is not entirely correct to say that each account is being treated fairly. In a series of transactions in an issue having a large float, for example, large orders could, on their own, command a substantial reduction in commission rates. Much of the commission savings the small accounts enjoy, they owe to the bargaining power of the large accounts. On the other hand, in an issue having a small float, substantial transactions are likely to affect the market price. In such cases, the small accounts would be subject to a drag on price they could have avoided if they were executing for themselves alone.

[154] It has been suggested that Section 28(e) does not apply to allocation decisions with respect to nondiscretionary accounts because Section 28(e) (1) refers to a person acting "in the exercise of investment discretion with respect to an account. . . ." See Stark, "Problems of Institutions Under Competitive Rates: 'Paying-Up' for Research," in R. Mundheim, A. Fleischer & B. Vandegrift, *Seventh Annual Institute on Securities Law* (PLI 1976). That analysis, however, fails to adequately take into account the statutory definition of investment discretion in Act § 3(a)(35), quoted at note 89 *supra,* which extends to accounts over which a manager has substantial influence. "Investment discretion" is not restricted to the conventional discretionary account over which the manager has actual contractual authority to invest without consulting the client. Even if protection for a good faith exercise of reasonable business judgment does not apply to the allocation decisions of investment managers at common law, it applies to all managers having statutory investment discretion. In almost all cases in

nondiscretionary accounts over which he had custody, or at least execution responsibility, only as those clients communicated an intention to follow his investment recommendations. The point is that not all distinctions among types of accounts in allocating brokerage costs are unjustifiable. Investment managers can remain fully within the protection of the business-judgment rule of Section 28(e) in their allocation decisions by avoiding, to the extent practicable, allocation arrangements which give the appearance of preferring one type of account over another where the preference cannot ordinarily be explained without implicating the manager's own interests. If arrangements involving such preferences are unavoidable, the manager must take steps to resolve the conflict of interest.

Brokerage fees may also include an element of cost not directly attributable to the transaction for which they are paid, if the investment manager has established a course of dealing to gain a preferred position with brokerage firms of high quality. Establishing such a position can promote early opportunities for the manager's accounts to buy attractive merchandise, can make it easier for them to buy or sell blocks of securities, and can enable them to obtain other benefits which may well be worth the cost in extra brokerage on certain transactions. But allocating brokerage fees generated through different transactions to support an established relationship can be a more complex problem than allocating execution costs among clients when carrying out a particular investment decision, because it is more difficult to determine who is benefiting at the expense of whom. A client with a small account, for example, may question whether he should pay higher brokerage fees to a firm for the purpose of supporting that firm's willingness to risk its capital through positioning, to recompense that firm for a difficult block trade previously executed, or for any other purpose that tends to benefit the executions of large clients. On the other hand, it is not necessarily the case that using small trades to cushion large ones prefers large accounts over small ones. An execution system in which small accounts participate along with large accounts and share brokerage expenses would obviate any contention that discriminatory benefits were flowing to the larger accounts. The basic issue in any event is not whether different accounts are paying different prices on different trades, but whether allocation practices appear to prefer one set of accounts over another to the benefit of the manager. If they do not, there is no con-

---

which that authority is lacking, the client will be responsible for his own executions because of the degree of control he is retaining over his account.

flict of interest to be resolved, and the manager has the full protection of the business-judgment rule of Section 28(e).

¶ 9.06. CONFLICT-OF-INTEREST PROBLEMS IN THE USE OF EXCESS COMMISSIONS TO PURCHASE RESEARCH SERVICES

[1] Identifying Breaches of Fiduciary Duty

Unlike commissions for brokerage services, commissions for research unavoidably involve a conflict of interest. Outside research serves a client's interest because it aids his investment manager in making investment decisions. But research is also at the heart of the manager's own responsibilities, and the management fee is in large part compensation to the manager for producing reliable research. This the manager may do through his own staff or through an outside source. If the client is paying both a management fee and excess commissions to purchase research, it is in the manager's interest to rely more on the outside source and less on his own staff because he increases his profits[155] in that fashion, at least until he reaches the point where the client becomes aware that an excessive amount of commission money is paying for research to satisfy the manager's advisory responsibility.

A manager's interest in maximizing profits may cause him to purchase outside research with commissions in derogation of his client's interest in three cases[156]:

(1) Where the value of the research is less than the excess commissions expended.

(2) Where the value of the research is greater than the excess commissions, but the improvement in performance the client enjoys is less than the amount he spends on excess commissions.

(3) Where the research improves the client's performance beyond his excess commissions costs, but also so substantially enhances the manager's profits as to suggest that the manager's share of the total benefit is disproportionate.

Each of these cases serves a manager's own interest over his client's in a relationship which, by definition, is based on precisely the opposite premise.

---

155 See note 120 *supra*.
156 See ¶ 9.04[1] at notes 113-115 *supra*.

[2] The Limited Protective Scope of Section 28(e) of the Securities Exchange Act

There is sentiment, in many cases bordering on conviction,[157] that Section 28(e) effectively declares paying excess commissions for supplementary research not to be a breach of duty even when the consequences described in ¶ 9.06[1] follow; such an interpretation of Section 28(e), however, aside from the policy questions it raises, imputes a great deal to the phrasing "No person . . . shall be deemed to have breached a fiduciary duty . . . *solely* by reason of his having caused the account to pay . . . an amount of commission for effecting a securities transaction in excess of the amount of commission another . . . would have charged. . . ." (Emphasis added.) A more realistic reading of the phrase beginning with "solely" would conclude that Section 28(e) is directed at a problem of proof: A client cannot show that his manager succumbed to the conflict of interest inherent in paying excess commissions for research merely by proof that excess commissions were paid. But it is an entirely different matter if the proof proffered shows that the excess commission costs benefited the manager in derogation of his client's interests. For the manager to escape a trial on the question of breach of fiduciary duty, in the event that an aggrieved client alleges and proves that any of the three circumstances listed in ¶ 9.06[1] occurred without his informed consent, a court would have to rule as a matter of law that no reasonable trier of fact could infer from such proof that the manager more probably than not succumbed to the conflict of interest. There are several reasons such a holding is unlikely.

First, there are a number of services arguably classifiable as research-related which virtually everyone concerned agrees are beyond the scope of Section 28(e). As one might expect, there is disagreement over the particulars of what is in and what is out. But less important than what educated opinion regards as unprotected is the fact that everyone concerned agrees that some things are beyond the protection of Section 28(e) as a matter of law. If such a rule of exclusion applicable to some research services exists, it is not traceable to any statutory language. Section 28(e) reaches all research services purchased

---

[157] See, e.g., "The Use of Commission Assets to Acquire Investment-Related Services," 115 Trusts & Estates 101 (Feb. 1976) (memorandum of law interpreting Section 28(e) by counsel to NASD member firm); Securities Week, June 16, 1975, p. 8 (Director of Capital Markets Office of Treasury Department says institutions safe if they pay commissions up to old fixed rates). See also Teberg & Cane, "Paying Up for Research," 115 Trusts & Estates 4 (Jan. 1976); Securities Week, July 7, 1975, p. 7.

for "an amount of commission . . . reasonable in relation to [their] value." Unless one were prepared to say that no excluded services can be purchased for "an amount of commission . . . reasonable in relation to [their] value," one would have to conclude that a rule of exclusion is based on the judgment that, whatever the net benefit of an excluded service, its purchase would usually represent a preference by the manager for his own interests over those of his client.[158] As if in emphasis of this point, argument over whether a particular service is protected under Section 28(e) typically proceeds without reference to price. That can only mean that observers are convinced that, whatever is to be excluded as a matter of law, the reason for doing so is that most of the value would flow to the manager and that therefore he has chosen his own interests over those of his client.

Consider, for example, the purchase of a subscription to the *Wall Street Journal*. Suppose a broker offered to buy a manager a subscription to the *Journal* for an excess commission amounting to less than the subscription price.[159] It seems difficult to argue that, in such case, the excess commission is not reasonable in relation to the research service purchased. It seems difficult also to argue that the *Journal* is not a valuable research tool. Yet the *Journal* is apparently to be excluded from Section 28(e) in all events.[160] The only explanation for

---

[158] It is possible to construe the "good faith" requirement of Section 28(e) as the basis of a rule of exclusion, but to do so would strain the statutory phrasing. A manager must determine in good faith that the amount of commission is reasonable in view of the research services provided. To say that a manager who honestly believes that the services he purchases with excess commissions are more valuable than the amount of the excess is to interpret good faith as meaning more than honest belief. It is also possible to add as a gloss to the "reasonable value" standard a requirement that the value be reasonable solely from the point of view of the client. This again takes the statutory language quite a distance. In any event, construing good faith or reasonable value as suggested here only leads to substantially the same analysis of the protection available from Section 28(e) as appears in the text.

[159] Rejection of the *Journal* and other such publications does not appear to change even if a broker can provide subscriptions at less than the publicly available rate (as, for example, might be the case if he obtains a given number of subscriptions for the publisher) and the broker passes that saving on to the manager. Indeed, in the general case, the availability of a research product in the open market for the same price in cash as it is in excess commissions is a serious evidentiary problem, which is considered more fully in ¶ 9.06[1][3][e] *infra*.

[160] See, e.g., Jorden, " 'Paying Up' for Research: A Regulatory and Legislative Analysis," 1975 Duke L. J. 1103, 1123-1124 ("a prudent adviser

such a conclusion is a belief that the benefit to the manager so out-weighs the benefit to the client as to be conclusive on whether the manager has given in to conflict of interest.

Second, the conceptual basis on which those concerned are attempt-ing to distinguish protected research services from unprotected re-search services demonstrates the importance of the allocation of benefits between manager and client to determining the protective scope of Section 28(e). At the Seventh Annual Institute on Securities Regula-tion, the panel considering the problem of commissions for research took the position that Section 28(e) excludes practices which involve rebates. It is plain that the term rebate, in the context it is used, con-notes pecuniary benefit for the manager. Three of the factors charac-terizing a rebate, it was said, are whether the service is available for cash, whether purchasing it reduces the fiduciary's costs, and whether the fiduciary is being paid to render the services purchased. All of these factors are neutral on the question of reasonable value for the amount of commission paid.[161] Measurable pecuniary benefit to the manager can be a danger signal only because it suggests that a manager may be preferring his own interests above those of his clients.

Finally, and perhaps most instructive, is the treatment of the give-up by the Congress and the SEC. The Conference Committee Report on S. 249 seems unequivocally to take the position that Section 28(e) is designed deliberately to exclude give-ups because they are inherently a breach of fiduciary duty.[162] But the language of Section 28(e) and

---

. . . cannot use brokerage to purchase . . . a subscription to the Wall Street Journal"); Securities Week, May 19, 1975, p. 14 (SEC Commissioner says "Wall Street Journal . . . is not the 'research' which [a manager] can law-fully buy with his beneficiary's dollars"); Stark, "Problems of Institutions Under Competitive Rates: 'Paying-Up' for Research," in R. Mundheim, A. Fleischer & B. Vandegrift, *Seventh Annual Institute on Securities Regula-tion* (PLI 1976).

[161] Stark, note 160 *supra*.

[162] The Conference Committee Report (see note 88 *supra*) stated at 108:

"The conferees analyzed the possibility that the fiduciary provision would be asserted as a shield behind which the give-ups and reciprocal prac-tices which were so notorious during the late 1960's could be reinstituted. The conferees believed the new language would not permit such a result. The provision agreed to provide that a money manager may pay *a* broker or dealer an amount of commission, for *that* broker or dealer's executing a transaction, if the money manager determines that the services it receives from *that* broker or dealer justify the payment. The provisions have no application whatsoever to a situation in which pay-

the Committee's interpretation of it, on closer reading, are not entirely exclusionary of give-ups. For one thing, Section 28(e) does not by its own terms directly prohibit give-ups. It merely fails to protect them and thus, at most, throws fiduciaries back onto common-law rules. Moreover, the House Report on H.R. 4111 takes the position that Section 28(e) does not contravene common-law fiduciary principles, but rather has as its purpose the prevention of a restrictive interpretation of the common law to permit a finding of breach of fiduciary duty solely on grounds of failure to pay lowest commission.[163] It is difficult to imagine that if a manager directed an executing broker to share part of his commission with another broker providing services solely for the benefit of the client and outside the responsibility of the manager— custodianship or performance evaluation, for example—the common law would regard that as a breach of fiduciary duty.

Furthermore, Section 28(e), taken on its own terms, does extend to commission splits between executing brokers and research houses. So long as the research is provided by the executing broker, the manager may pay excess commissions reasonably related to the value of the research. The only way Section 28(e) could be interpreted to exclude commission splits for research would be to construe "brokerage and research services provided by" the executing broker as meaning brokerage and research services having originated with the executing broker.[164] But such an interpretation would strain the section to the breaking point. First, the definition of brokerage and research services in Section 28(e) comprehends items such as publications, analyses and reports, and clearance, settlement and custody, which do not necessarily, either in ordinary understanding or in typical practice,[165] always originate

---

ment is made by a money manager to one broker or dealer for services rendered by another broker or dealer. The give-up was a regrettable chapter in the history of the securities industry and the limited definition of fiduciary responsibility added to the law by this bill will in no way permit its return." [Emphasis by Committee.]

[163] Report on H.R. 4111 of the Committee on Interstate and Foreign Commerce, H.R. Rep. No. 123, 94th Cong., 1st Sess. 95 (1975). Compare note 115 *supra*.

[164] Some believe "provided" should be so interpreted. See Securities Week, July 7, 1975, pp. 7, 9.

[165] The Chairman of the Senate Subcommittee on Securities indicated that the term "services" in Section 28(e) was to be construed in light of ordinary practice. Responding to a statement of the Chairman of the SEC that the Commission would not "open the door to such services as weekends at resort areas," the Subcommittee Chairman said: "I thought we had

with executing brokers. Second, if "provided by" were interpreted to mean having originated with the executing broker with respect to research services, it would be difficult to interpret that phrase more broadly with respect to brokerage services. Yet, as investment managers well know, and have a duty to know in view of their obligation to obtain best execution for their accounts, many of the executing brokers with whom they deal must maintain correspondent relationships to have practical access to various markets.[166] Also, many executing brokers carry out clearance and settlement through the facilities of other houses, even in markets in which they are members.[167] Since to interpret "provided" restrictively with respect to research would throw sound executions relationships into useless uncertainty, one can seriously doubt that will happen.

There is also the possibility that "provided" may be interpreted to include commission splits only if the services from the third party are the result of the executing broker's own initiative. In other words, perhaps Section 28(e) does not exclude all commission splits, just customer-directed commission splits. But that interpretation would deprive investment managers of all access to houses they wanted to include in a transaction because of the quality of their services and permit only the third-party services marketed by executing brokers or the in-house services marketed by full-service firms. Aside from the questionable policy this represents, the SEC has already rejected such an interpretation of Section 28(e) in an interpretative release.[168] Responding to the concern of investment managers that prohibiting customer-directed commission splits would deprive them of access to valuable services,[169] and of execution houses and research houses that such a prohibition would give full-service houses an unfair competitive ad-

---

embraced [in Section 28(e)] that area of services that logically and historically should be considered in this context." Hearings on S. 249 Before the Subcomm. on Securities of the Senate Comm. on Banking, Housing and Urban Affairs, 94th Cong., 1st Sess. 205 (1975).

[166] See, e.g., Securities Week, April 21, 1975, p. 1 (customer can contact correspondent directly and correspondent will split commission).

[167] See, e.g., Wall Street Letter, April 14, 1975, p. 5 (regional exchange seeking rule permitting floor broker to divide bunched orders).

[168] SEC Securities Exchange Act Release No. 12251 (March 24, 1976), [1975-1976 Transfer Binder] CCH Fed. Sec. L. Rep. ¶ 80,407.

[169] In the weeks prior to issuance of the release, a number of investment managers, especially those handling relatively small accounts, urged that research purchased with commissions not be limited to the in-house products of executing brokers. See, e.g., Securities Week, Feb. 9, 1976, p. 13.

vantage,[170] the Commission concluded that, "under appropriate circumstances," Section 28(e) might apply to "situations where a broker provides a money manager with research produced by third parties."

This concession by the Commission, particularly because it is made so grudgingly, is very illuminating about the protective scope of Section 28(e). Like the Conference Committee Report, which was highly condemnatory of give-ups,[171] the Commission takes an apparently uncompromising attitude toward give-ups: "Nor may money managers, under the authority of § 28(e), direct brokers employed by them to make 'give up' payments." Yet, in the very next sentence of the release, the Commission recognizes at least a limited legitimacy for commission payments to executing brokers for research services provided by third parties.[172] The question is what is implied in the term give-ups which, though they are a subset of commission splits, makes them ineligible for protection under Section 28(e). The answer, of course, is that give-ups bring to mind the commission splits which either transferred the excess over pure execution services to persons providing services principally of benefit to the manager or, through an affiliate or association with a regional exchange, transferred it back to the manager in cash.[173] With that background, the source of Congress's concern and the SEC's caution with respect to commission splits is that there will not be a fair allocation of benefits between manager and client where a third party is providing (directly or indirectly) a service useful to the manager.[174]

---

[170] See, e.g., Securities Week, Feb. 23, 1976, p. 8; Securities Week, Feb. 2, 1976, p. 6. Unsurprisingly, full-service firms objected to commission splits for research originating away from the executing broker as creating too great a strain on fiduciary responsibility. See, e.g., Securities Week, Dec. 1, 1976, p. 2. Whether or not such a ruling would strengthen fiduciary responsibility, it improves the competitive position of full-service firms.

[171] See note 162 *supra*.

[172] Even this concession is hedged, however. Where such payments are made, "the money manager should be prepared to demonstrate the required good faith determination in connection with the transaction." SEC Securities Exchange Act Release No. 12251 (March 24, 1976), [1975-1976 Transfer Binder] CCH Fed. Sec. L. Rep. ¶ 80,407.

[173] See ¶¶ 8.02[2], 9.02[1], 9.02[2].

[174] Almost a year before issuance of the release interpreting Section 28(e) (note 172 *supra*), Commissioner Sommer observed that use of the give-up for paying small or regional research houses might be consistent with fiduciary duty. He also suggested, however, that it would probably be the better practice for the executing broker to buy the service and then charge the customer a higher commission. See Wall Street Letter, March 3, 1975, p. 5. Commissioner Evans was less sanguine about the legitimacy of the

The analysis above suggests that, even if an investment manager can show that he believed in good faith that the economic value of the research services he purchased with excess commissions was reasonably related to the amount of the excess, Section 28(e) will not necessarily offer him the protection of a directed verdict. A client in a damages action or regulatory authorities in an enforcement action can make out a triable claim of breach of fiduciary duty by alleging and proving that, without the client's informed consent, the manager used excess commissions to purchase research services in any of three circumstances: (1) when such commissions benefited the manager but were not economically justified in view of the research services obtained; (2) when such commissions, though economically justified, did not benefit the

---

give-up. See Securities Week, April 21, 1975, p. 2a; Wall Street Letter, April 21, 1975, p. 3.

But as interesting as are the speculations of the regulators about what kinds of customer-directed business are permissible and what kinds are not, the more important issue for investment managers is how to analyze new customer-directed arrangements, since the imagination of the investment management community and the securities industry generally outstrips the ability of the regulators to anticipate developments. Two practices which are at least first cousins to the give-up come to mind in this context. Institutional managers have rediscovered the underwriting commission as a means of directing funds to firms providing them with services (rediscovered because, during the height of reciprocity in the fixed-rate era, some mutual funds were directing members of an underwriting syndicate to split underwriting commissions with other syndicate members who were either affiliated brokerage firms of the funds or were providing services to the funds). See 10 Institutional Investor 29 (April 1976). Cf. Papilsky v. Berndt, [1976-1977 Transfer Binder] CCH Fed. Sec. L. Rep. ¶ 95,627 (S.D.N.Y. 1976). The opportunity for directing money (called "syndicate dollars") to firms providing services comes about because of the contractually fixed underwriting commission which must be paid by purchasers of new issues and can be shared by members of the underwriting syndicate. Thus, an institutional manager, desirous of participating in a new issue, can direct the managing underwriter to have the selling syndicate member share commissions generated by the manager's clients with other members of the syndicate even though those firms had nothing to do with the sale or even with stimulating interest in the purchase.

Although this practice may be objectionable to the underwriters, on first impression, it appears that clients can only benefit. So long as fixed underwriting commissions remain the rule, they must pay the underwriting commission in any event, and they benefit, at least to some extent, from the manager's access to supplementary services. But, in fact, this practice raises all the old issues applicable to the give-up during the fixed-rate era. Even assuming that a manager will not be tempted to purchase new issues unnecessarily, or worse, purchase unsuitable new issues, in order to generate

client as much as the cash value of the excess commissions; or (3) when such commissions, though economically justified and beneficial to the client, provided a disproportionate benefit to the manager. Thus, under this analysis, the critical inquiry in evaluating an investment manager's compliance with his fiduciary duty when he pays excess commissions for research is to determine whether the benefits of research purchased with excess commissions are being allocated fairly between manager and client. This determination depends on what the evidence shows was the manager's purpose in making such expenditures.

[3] Allocating Benefits Between Client and Manager: The Relevant Factors

[a] Congressional purpose behind enactment of Section 28(e)

The long legislative and regulatory debate over the need for and proper form of a rule recognizing the authority of investment managers to pay excess commissions for supplementary research generated many different arguments in support of such a rule. If state law were interpreted to oblige an investment manager to execute at the lowest

---

funds to buy supplementary services, there is still the question of whether the total benefit from the supplementary services is being allocated fairly between manager and client. Should, for example, there be a reduction in management fee reflecting lower research costs to the manager? Should a manager have an affiliated brokerage firm join the underwriting syndicate and either return excess commissions or credit them against the advisory fee? (In passing, it should be noted that ironically, ERISA § 406, the prohibited-transactions section, can be literally read to ban any arrangement by which excess commissions are either to be used to purchase supplementary services or to be returned directly or indirectly to the pension fund client. See ¶ 10.03[3][c]. Moreover, it is not even certain that the contractually fixed rate set as the underwriting commission is really fixed, since it appears that participations in new underwritings are being set off against transactions in other securities. Belleveau, *supra*, at 32-33. Such practices sound very much like the reciprocal arrangements which characterized an earlier era and raise the question whether the client is benefiting at all when both transactions—the new issue and the subsequent trade—are considered together.

Another practice which has evolved is for a manager to omit actually to direct a commission split, but to place the firm he wishes to reward into a trade constructed by another broker-dealer. Suppose, for example, a broker calls an institution with 50,000 shares of U.S. Widget. The manager wants all 50,000 shares, but he buys only 25,000. Then, to pay off a research or other service debt, he calls the second house and tells it where to go to buy the other 25,000. See Securities Week, Feb. 2, 1976, pp. 11-12. This dis-

commission rate he could get (consistent with assuring himself that the transaction would be executed effectively), that would preclude investment managers from purchasing outside research except through the expenditure of their own funds. Such a result, it was said, would have four adverse consequences. First, research brokers would lose a substantial portion of the market for their services and might even be forced out of business if they lacked competitive ability in handling pure execution business.[175] Second, small investment managers would no longer be able to purchase the research necessary for effective management of their accounts.[176] Third, both the quantity and quality of research would diminish, leading to increased volatility and lowered efficiency in the securities markets.[177] And finally, clients with accounts managed under fees set by law when commission rates were fixed would not obtain necessary research services since, because of the low fee levels, their managers would be able to afford neither the purchase of outside research nor an expansion of in-house research capability.[178]

To the extent the common law would have been interpreted to require investment managers to seek lowest price execution, there was good reason for Congress to have enacted a business-judgment rule to permit investment managers to pay excess commissions for outside research. But not to be found explicitly in any of the arguments recounted above is the reason that sound business judgment on a manager's part may lead him to conclude that the purchase of outside research can provide substantial benefits to his accounts and a fair allo-

---

reputable practice not only treats the original selling broker unfairly, it almost assuredly also deprives the manager's client of best execution because the second broker will have to pay a higher price to make up for the first broker's lowered profits, or because the first broker would have executed the entire transaction for a commission reduced close to the amount he was forced to share with the second broker.

[175] See, e.g., Report on S. 249 of the Senate Comm. on Banking, Housing and Urban Affairs, 94th Cong., 1st Sess. 69-70 (1975); Testimony of Chairman of the SEC, in Hearings on S. 249 Before the Subcomm. on Securities of the Senate Comm. on Banking, Housing and Urban Affairs, 94th Cong., 1st Sess. 202 (hereinafter cited as Hearings on S. 249); Testimony of President, Trust Division, American Bankers Association, id at 459.

[176] See, e.g., Testimony of Chairman of the SEC, in Hearings on S. 249, note 175 supra, at 201. See also id., at 285-289; Securities Week, Dec. 9, 1974, at p. 9.

[177] See, e.g., Testimony of four officers of leading brokerage firms, in Hearings on S. 249, note 175 supra, at 322-323. See also id. at 290-291.

[178] See, e.g., Report on S. 249, note 175 supra, at 70; Testimony of Chairman of the SEC, in Hearings on S. 249, note 175 supra, at 202.

cation of the total benefits between the manager and his accounts. Quite the contrary, the House and Senate subcommittees responsible for securities legislation supported Section 28(e) in order to undercut securities industry opposition to the introduction of fully negotiated rates.[179] For without the assurance of Section 28(e) or something like it, brokers, facing sharp reductions in revenues for execution services once fully negotiated rates became law, would face additional drops in revenues as caution led investment managers to disdain excess commissions for research also. The securities industry succeeded in sidetracking the Securities Acts Amendments of 1975 at least once for sure,[180] and no one can be certain how long the industry was able to delay the introduction of negotiated rates and the lowering of negotiated rate breakpoints.[181] But, even assuming that the political and practical arguments advanced in support of Section 28(e) explain the willingness of Congress and the SEC to adopt a federal rule, none of them relates to the duty-of-loyalty issue raised when an investment manager pays excess commissions for research.

Consider the argument emphasizing the ill effects on research-oriented brokerage firms of limitations on the use of excess commissions to purchase research. Suppose sound public policy mandates that research be a product of a well-diversified, highly competitive industry. Still, it is difficult to see how such a policy can justify a decision on the part of an investment manager to pay excess commissions from the accounts he manages to research firms. Excess commissions for the pur-

---

[179] The *Securities Industry Study* of the Senate Subcommittee was most frank on this point. See text at note 45 *supra*. The chairman of the Senate Subcommittee on Securities also made an especially revealing remark to similar effect at the outset of the hearings on S. 249:

". . . [A]n amendment which I will introduce today concerning the fiduciary principles applicable to the payment of 'soft dollars' for research must be enacted before the elimination of fixed rates if it is to provide the protections the industry wants and needs. Surely it would be irresponsible to tell securities research firms that we are going to wait and see whether their business is actually destroyed by competitive rates before we legislate protections."

Hearings on S. 249, note 175 *supra*, at 2. See also notes 105-106 *supra*, which discuss the exchanges between the Subcommittee Chairman and the SEC on the adoption of regulations to implement Section 28(e).

[180] See note 58 *supra*.

[181] For example, in 1968 the SEC took the position that negotiated rates down to $50,000 should be introduced (see ¶ 8.02[2][a], note 46), but the breakpoint prior to the effective date of Rule 19b-3 abolishing fixed rates was $300,000.

pose of maintaining the health of the research industry would, in effect, be a general subsidy. Investors would be purchasing research not needed to maintain portfolio performance only so that funds would be available to keep more people in the research business. While it may be true that investors as a class would be better off transferring money to the research industry, and that investors would be willing to do so according to some equitable formula which fairly allocates the costs of such a transfer among investors, there is little to be said for the proposition that an investment manager is the one to determine what the fair share is for each of the accounts he manages.[182] There is no way for him to tell whether his clients are paying too much measured by what their fair share should be and by what other investors are in fact contributing to research brokers. The problem is that, whereas the health and competitive character of the research industry may be a matter of general policy, the payment of excess commissions is highly individualized: Excess commissions must always come from a particular investor and go to a particular research broker. Without some coordinated means of collection and distribution specifically designed to preserve the health and competitive character of the research industry, there is no reason to expect excess commissions to serve that policy. Indeed, it seems more than possible that generating excess commissions might lead to greater rather than lesser concentration in the industry. If most rational investment managers will direct excess commissions to the houses providing the best research, investment managers will just pay more to the best houses.

Consider next the argument emphasizing the need to provide small investment managers with access to research. For one thing, it is limited since it applies only to small investment managers. But even in regard to small investment managers, though on first impression a need-for-access argument may seem sensible, on further reflection it turns out to be based on a highly questionable premise. It may well be true that small investment managers have not been able to afford to generate sufficient research out of their own operating funds, either by direct payments to research firms or through the strengthening of their own research staffs. But assuming that the accounts of such managers do not have management fees subject to ceilings set by law, this phenomenon would continue only if they could not raise advisory fees directly by contractual authorization, because by raising fees, they could

---

[182] But cf. Securities Week, Sept. 1, 1975, p. 1 (bank will cease insisting on lowest commission because of need to contribute to local business environment).

recoup the costs of outside research formerly paid with excess commissions. The barrier to raising management fees is that to do so would lose business, because other investment managers would be offering comparable performance for fees lower than those many small managers must charge to remain competitive. But that means that excess commissions are a subterfuge to obtain higher fees. They are paid not by design on the part of investors, but out of ignorance.

Again, it may be sound public policy to keep the investment management industry as competitive as possible at all levels. Some subsidy arrangement for doing so may also be desirable. But from the point of view of the individual investor, it would plainly be in derogation of the idea of fiduciary responsibility for Congress to select a few investors to bear the subsidy and, worse, to do so on the ground that such investors do not know any better. In view of the statements in the legislative history that Section 28(e) is intended to clarify fiduciary principle rather than to change it,[183] it is doubtful that an investment manager will be able to justify paying excess commissions for research on the ground that it was necessary in order to keep his business profitable. If there is any value at all in the need-for-access argument made in behalf of small investment managers, it is that, through Section 28(e), Congress has given them an opportunity to remain competitive during the period that the brokerage industry learns how to price its research products under negotiated rates. Had the rule applicable to fiduciaries been lowest-commission executions, large investment managers would have found it much easier than small investment managers to bolster their own research staffs and to absorb the costs of purchasing outside research directly until appropriate adjustments in management fees could be negotiated.

The other two arguments in support of Section 28(e) are similarly ineffective as justifications for an investment manager's decision to pay excess commissions for research on a particular transaction or series of transactions. If the quantity and quality of research demanded diminish, it is because managers have been overpurchasing research when paying for it with commissions, not because they will be underpurchasing it if they pay for it as one of their own expenses. Moreover, to make a public-policy issue out of the amount of research produced is to raise the same issue as is raised in appeals to policy to strengthen the research industry or the management industry: Some way is needed to decide

---

[183] See note 115 *supra*.

which investors are to be chosen to pay the subsidy and how much is to be their share of the load.[184]

The argument emphasizing legal limits on management fees offers the weakest defense of all for investment managers. It begins by conceding the basic point that the manager is using commissions as a hidden supplement to the management fee. Thus, at most, only managers of accounts which cannot agree contractually to higher advisory fees or higher expense limits[185] will be able to use such grounds to explain their excess-commission practices. Moreover, if state authorities really were taking into account, as proponents of this argument contend, the inherent subsidy implicit in the provision of research under the fixed-rate commission system, they should be equally visionary in setting legal limits on management fees now that negotiated rates are in effect, and consequently, they should make appropriate adjustments in the limits on fee levels. In any event, even during the period a manager is subject to legal limits on his management fee and decides to supplement it with excess commissions for research, Section 28(e) does not relieve him of his obligation to inform his clients of the fact that he is paying excess commission for the purpose of meeting his own research expenses.

In short, arguing the congressional purpose in adopting Section 28(e) will not be much help in a dispute over whether an investment manager has given in to a conflict of interest and breached his fiduciary duty through payment of excess commissions to purchase research services. If the evidence shows that the manager has succumbed to the conflict of interest inherent in using commissions for research, he will not be able to escape liability by contending that the research industry is better off or that some other managers have fees set too low by law, and so forth. Fiduciary responsibility requires not simply that a manager in good faith believe the research service purchased be worth the

---

[184] A particularly specious argument about the need for supporting a diverse research industry is that even poor research can be useful to acquire since it helps to tell what others are thinking. The use of poor research, if any, would seem to be quite the opposite.

[185] Section 28(e) might not even help managers subject to legal limits on fees and expenses. If state authorities hold excess commissions for research to be a management expense or a management fee instead of a client expense, a manager will not be able to evade the legal limits by purchasing research with commissions. Some state authorities are apparently inclining toward this very conclusion. See Securities Week, Oct. 13, 1975, p. 6 (state securities commissioners question whether excess commissions for research should be charged as separate expense of mutual funds instead of commission expense and thus subject to legal limit).

excess commissions paid, but also that the reasonable value received for the extra commission expenditures be allocated fairly between his client and himself. Thus, the problem a manager confronts is whether the evidence shows that he is fairly allocating the benefits between his client and himself, or whether the evidence can be interpreted by a reasonable trier of fact to show that his purpose in paying excess commissions was primarily to affect his own costs.

[b]   The value of the service purchased

In determining whether a manager's commission expenditures for research are motivated primarily by self-interest or by client interest, it is important not to confuse the question of value of the services purchased with the question of value of the services *to the client*. Arguments supporting a broadly protective scope of Section 28(e) typically emphasize the value of research without acknowledging this critical distinction. Some point, for example, to the inability of investment managers to provide as broad coverage of the securities markets with research produced only in-house as they can through broker-supplied research; or to the greater efficiency available through lodging certain research operations in the brokerage community instead of having a number of managers reproduce essentially the same research many times over; or to the fact that the brokerage industry has better analysts than many investment management operations; or to the fact that broker-supplied research gives an investment manager an opportunity to stay better informed about what others are thinking, which, in turn, both permits him to improve his feel for market psychology and gives him material against which he can test his own ideas.[186] But conceding the accuracy of these arguments,[187] they are still no answer to the question

---

[186] See, e.g., Teberg & Cane, "Paying Up for Research," 115 Trusts & Estates 4 (Jan. 1976); Stark, "Problems of Institutions Under Competitive Rates: 'Paying Up' for Research," in R. Mundheim, A Fleischer & B. Vandegrift, *Seventh Annual Institute on Securities Regulation* (PLI 1976); Hearings on S. 249, note 175 *supra,* at 285-291, 322-327; Wall Street Letter, Dec. 29, 1975, p. 9.

[187] The efficient-market hypothesis challenges the supposition that more research, even of high quality, is normally worth the cost of acquiring it. See Pozen, "Money Managers and Securities Research," 51 N.Y.U. L. Rev. 923 (1976); ¶ 7.07. But the challenge to fundamental analysis, which relies heavily on research, posed by the efficient-market hypothesis, which does not (or at least which points to research on volatility of price rather than to intrinsic value), only raises questions of business judgment, not conflict of interest. In any event, so long as one agrees that research is a product of

of why broker-supplied research should be paid for by the client out of his commissions instead of by the manager out of his operating funds.

The best evidence that self-interest is not motivating a manager in purchasing supplementary research services with excess commissions and that most of the value of such services is flowing to the client is that the desired services cannot be bought any other way. It may be, as some say, that a separate and stated charge for every broker-supplied service is the inevitable structure of the securities industry.[188] But, at least until then, an investment manager, desiring research assistance from a broker who ties research costs in with pure execution costs, must be able either to expend commissions for the service or to forgo it. Furthemore, there is reason to doubt that brokerage firms will ever be able to price research separately in every case. Block positioners, for example, might generate their own research on some of the securities they position so that they can improve their pricing capabilities. If they also make that research available to customers, especially those on the passive side of a transaction, they may find it not only convenient to charge for the research with the brokerage fee, but difficult to do otherwise.[189]

A more common reason why brokerage firms might not set a price for research derives from the nature of the product. Since the value of research is much more easily determined retrospectively than prospectively, an investment manager and a broker can better agree on a price after they see how well the broker's research product has performed. This is not to say that retrospective pricing is not possible with the manager making the requisite cash outlay himself, but since brokers and managers transact business when trades are executed, it is at least

---

value, it is clear that there are many circumstances in which research is more efficiently generated by outside sources than by a multiplicity of internal analysts.

[188] See Securities Week, Feb. 9, 1976, p. 3, where SEC Commissioner Pollack contended that Section 28(e) is merely a transitory provision designed to ease the establishment of negotiated commission rates while members of the securities industry adjust to pricing their services.

[189] Indeed, a strong argument can be made that such research is actually an execution cost since it is necessary, at least in part, to induce the passive customer to trade.

Another reason for higher commission costs derives from the public policy favoring suitability determinations and reasonable-basis recommendations by brokers. See ¶¶ 4.01[2], 7.07[1]. An important part of a broker's operations is to stimulate interest in purchases and sales. To meet reasonable-basis and suitability requirements, the broker must know his merchandise as well as his customer. Meeting these obligations, of course, raises the broker's costs and thereby increases commission costs.

convenient to include the price of proven research in one or more of a series of commissions. More important, the fact that extra payment is conditional on research's proving itself by the results realized by the manager's accounts is strong evidence that most of the benefit is flowing to the clients. In effect, the client pays for results. If the manager were forced to buy research at prices set in advance or by expanding his in-house research capabilities, clients might pay, through their management fees, for a good deal of research which turned out to be of little worth to them.

Reliance on subsequent transactions to pay for proven research necessarily introduces some imprecision into the process by which an investment manager and a broker determine its value.[190] But quantifying the value of research is necessarily a highly subjective process anyway. Only in the elemental case in which a broker recommends purchase of a security the manager was about to sell or had ignored, or sale of a security the manager would have held or bought, can a manager calculate the exact benefit to him, and even then, he must distinguish the portion of the gain attributable to general market movement from that attributable to the stock by itself. Much research is of a more general nature—analyzing conditions in the economy, for example—and the manager must devise his own strategy to take advantage of the research report's conclusions. Furthermore, the value even of highly sophisticated research services to a manager's accounts can depend on how high on the list of research recipients the manager is. In cases like these, the manager must make a fair judgment as to the worth of the research to the performance of his accounts and pay the broker accordingly.[191]

---

[190] Indeed, determining the value of research in advance can be so imprecise that commission negotiations may be the best forum for keeping both manager and broker satisfied. If a broker and manager disagree on the precise value of the research, they will also probably disagree on the value of the execution services. But in negotiating both costs as a package, the manager can conclude he has gotten a fair price because the execution services were of high quality. The broker can feel the same, knowing that, if pressed, he might have been willing to cut his commissions for execution services by a few cents. Because neither party had to set an exact price on either service, both can look back on the transaction satisfied that the total payment for the two services was fair.

[191] Although he retains a great deal of power in setting the value of research, a manager cannot simply dictate price. At some point, a broker will cut him off or, short of that, drop him several places in the line of customers called. See, e.g., Securities Week, May 19, 1975, p. 5 (broker will deny research to institutions seeking deep discounts).

[c] The execution price

Probably the single most important evidentiary fact determining whether an investment manager is paying excess commissions primarily to enhance his profits or primarily to enhance his clients' returns is the price at which the manager executes his transactions. It may not be possible to say on any given trade that a commission or markup was excessive in light of the research services or execution services provided. But testing a pattern of dealing against standard industry practices is a relatively uncomplicated affair. Since the introduction of negotiated commissions, the securities industry has settled into a structure of rates for execution services,[192] and although rates for pure execution services are not as easily determined as they were when commissions were fixed, a pattern of dealing which regularly pays in excess of standard levels will be readily detectable. An expert trader could look at market price, market activity, float, issuer, executing broker, size of trade, and so forth, and, whether a given trade was carried out on a commission or net-price basis, reconstruct reasonably circumscribed estimates of pure execution costs. Significant deviations from those boundaries would tend to cast suspicion on the motives of the manager.

The more difficult question is what size deviations in a pattern of trading would be indicative of breach of fiduciary duty on the grounds that the manager's purpose in purchasing research with excess commissions was primarily to defray his own operating costs. Since the research purchased virtually always confers some benefit on both client and manager, but the excess commission reflects only the direct cost to the client, it is impossible to determine directly from execution price alone how much of the benefit of the supplementary research is captured by the client and how much inures to the manager. The problem is complicated by the fact that the amount of excess commission paid is not a fully avoidable cost to the client, even if the manager were paying all the research expenses himself. At least part of the extra expense the manager must bear by forgoing the use of commissions to purchase research would be passed on to the client through higher management fees. Indeed, the whole thrust of the inquiry into the fairness of the allocation of benefits between manager and client when research is purchased with excess commissions is whether, by choosing to obtain outside research in that fashion, the manager is charging the client substantially more through direct management fees and excess commissions than he would

---

[192] See ¶ 8.02[4].

if he were buying the same research himself and charging for it through increased management fees.[193]

But on the assumption that most investment managers who purchase supplementary research with commissions are acting primarily in the interest of their clients, it is possible to relate an individual manager's practices to an industry standard to determine whether disproportionate benefits are flowing to the manager. One approach is to compare the amount a manager pays in excess commissions for research to the amount generally paid by investment managers. That is, if the total commission on a transaction consists of a commission for pure execution and a commission for research, the ratio of an investment manager's research expenditures to total commission costs should compare favorably to industry standards. This approach has certain limitations, of course. For one thing, it is impossible to say exactly how much of a commission is for research, since transactions are carried out at a price which includes both research and execution services. Also, the ratio will not be the same for all types of clients. One would expect, for example, that clients with relatively small accounts would have to bear a higher research cost in proportion to total assets than would be the case with large investors. Furthermore, for this simple ratio to provide a reliable basis for comparison with industry standards, it would have to be averaged over a substantial number of transactions, since the rate paid for research can vary from trade to trade.

There are other possible approaches to determining whether a manager is acting primarily in the interest of his clients when he purchases outside research. One could measure the amount of excess commissions against the manager's own expenditures on research and compare that figure to industry standards. Or, one could measure average excess commissions as a percentage of assets against the management fee (which is ordinarily determined as a percentage of assets) and compare that figure to industry standards. There is an advantage to using a ratio which relates commissions for research to total commissions because

---

[193] See ¶ 9.06[3][f] *infra*. Of course, a manager may be inclined to buy more research when paying with commissions instead of his own operating funds. The more distant the calculation of cost from the assessment of benefit, the greater is the tendency to underassess cost and overassess benefit. See text at note 120 *supra*. But this occurs subtly and not with purpose, knowledge, or reckless indifference to the interests of a client, states of mind which would have to be proven to establish a motive of self-interest on the part of a manager in purchasing research with commissions.

statistics on commissions paid are readily available.[194] But any figure which provides a reliable basis for comparison with industry standards is helpful. The important point is that excess commission expenses for research which are in essential conformance with the collective behavior of most other investment managers are likely to be good evidence that there has been no breach of fiduciary duty.[195]

While it is outside the scope of this work to attempt to calculate the range of excess commission expenses which comports with industry standards, it is worth noting that ordinarily the amount expended on research is relatively small compared to total commission expenditures. Apparently out of an abundance of caution after the introduction of negotiated commission rates, most investment managers initially refused to pay any extra for supplementary services.[196] Congress had been unable to finish work on the Securities Acts Amendments of 1975 until well after the effective date of Rule 19b-3[197] and, without the statutory protection ostensibly supplied by Section 28(e), managers were reluctant to expose themselves to the possibility that state law would be interpreted restrictively to impose a lowest-cost execution standard. The levels to which brokerage fees fell thus provide good standards for measurement of commission costs for pure execution, at least until the brokerage industry makes substantial structural changes in the way it does business. More important, however, by the time Section 28(e) became law, managers had become acclimated to the substantial reduction in execution costs which had occurred. Although with Section 28(e) they became more confident of the legitimacy of their authority to purchase research with excess commissions, they became unwilling to

---

[194] For example, the Comptroller requires banks periodically to publish figures for trades of equity securities in an amount of $500,000 or more or in volume of 10,000 shares, including:

(1) Trade or settlement date;
(2) Name of issuer, title, and class;
(3) Price at which purchased or sold;
(4) Number of shares;
(5) Market; and
(6) Name of executing broker-dealer.

12 C.F.R. § 9.102.

[195] Cf. Stillman v. Watkins, 325 N.E. 2d 295 (Mass. App. 1975) (trustees' expenditure of $2,600 for investment advice disallowed, in part because such an expense, in addition to trustee's fee, was not in accordance with prevailing practice in area).

[196] See ¶ 8.02[4].

[197] See ¶ 8.02[3] at notes 75-77.

pay a lot more than pure execution costs.[198] Published statements indicate that ordinarily the difference between the price for pure execution and for execution plus services was not exceeding 15 percent on the old commission rate scale.[199]

[d] Portfolio performance

If an investor is benefiting from research, it ought to show up in performance. This is especially the case with respect to outside research, since the major element affecting portfolio performance is ordinarily the quality of the manager. Moreover, the relationship between performance and research ought to be most observable with respect to the supplementary research a manager obtains from a broker. For one thing, in many cases, a manager can pay for supplementary research in proportion to how it proves itself. More important, however, with relative ease, a manager can construct a portfolio showing close to average return for the risk assumed.[200] In principle, if supplementary research purchased with commissions truly has value, it ought to make itself felt by helping to produce above-average return for the risk assumed.

But there is a problem with using performance to determine whether the client is getting value commensurate with the amount he is spending on excess commissions from the supplementary research his manager obtains. Reliable measurement of performance requires a long time—at least a year, and preferably more.[201] Much research is defensive in purpose. It is supposed to alert an investment manager to situations which require action to avoid losses and to prevent a manager from taking action which can incur losses. If research is successful as a defense against loss, its full value can show up only after enough time has passed that losses forgone can reflect themselves as better opportunities taken. Furthermore, even research suggesting positive action is not necessarily valuable unless it occurs regularly enough to push return above its average value for the risk undertaken.

Suppose, for example, a broker recommends three stocks, *A*, *B*, and *C*, each selling at $10 per share and each having the same volatility as

---

[198] See, e.g., Wall Street Letter, June 16, 1976, p. 2; Securities Week, June 2, 1976, p. 10.

[199] See, e.g., Securities Week, Sept. 1, 1975, pp. 1, 8.

[200] In an efficient market, a well-diversified portfolio will provide market return adjusted for the volatility of the portfolio relative to market volatility. See ¶ 7.04.

[201] See ¶ 5.03[2][c][viii].

the market. Based on the broker's analysis, the manager buys one share of each. Suppose that one year later A is selling at $20, B at $15, and C at $10. Even if the events, the prediction of which caused the broker to make his original recommendations, have come to pass, it may not be possible to credit the broker for the performance record. Although, on first impression, it appears that the broker's research has produced a $15 (150 percent) net gain, no such conclusion is possible until one knows how the market has behaved over the same period. If the market has advanced to 150 percent of its original value, the gain in portfolio ABC could be entirely attributable to that. Only if the market has arrived at substantially less than 150 percent of its original value can the manager reasonably attribute much of the difference in performance to the broker's analysis. Moreover, even in that event, it may be that other developments (such as an unexpected discovery of great value) account for the price appreciation. The point thus is not that performance is unimportant as a measure of the value of research, but that it is a highly imprecise index and therefore of utility only in clear cases.

[e] Published price (unbundled pricing)

The research service that is probably most problematic for an investment manager to justify purchasing with excess commissions is one which is available for a preset price. The SEC has taken the position that the purchase of research services for excess commissions is suspect if such services can be purchased directly for a set price. In its release interpreting Section 28(e),[202] the Commission said:

"Section 28(e) is not authority for the proposition that money managers may charge to beneficiaries' accounts brokerage commissions calculated so that the broker may directly or indirectly provide to the money manager products and services, such as those referred to above [newspapers, magazines and periodicals, computer services, quotation equipment, etc.], which are readily and customarily available and offered to the general public on a commercial basis."

Other nonofficial statements from the Commission have displayed an even firmer attitude,[203] and the staff's earliest investigations in connec-

---

[202] SEC Securities Exchange Act Release No. 12251 (March 24, 1976), [1975-1976 Transfer Binder] CCH Fed. Sec. L. Rep. ¶ 80,407.

[203] See, e.g., Securities Week, Feb. 9, 1976, p. 3 (two Commissioners regard Section 28(e) as transitory, prefer unbundling). See Securities Week, Aug. 4, 1975, p. 5 (original disclosure guidelines used by staff of SEC).

tion with Section 28(e) have been directed at brokerage firms selling commercially available services.[204]

This is not to say that, in the Commission's view, any availability at a set price is automatically a disqualifying feature for a research service. Otherwise, the Commission would not be willing to construe Section 28(e) to include commission splits for services originating with third parties and furnished through the executing broker.[205] Instead, the question raised is why the fact of availability for a set price is so significant a factor in assessing the legitimacy of purchasing research with excess commissions. Plainly, disapproval of the purchase with commissions of a subscription to the *Wall Street Journal*[206] is not based on a conviction that it is not worth the price, for if circulation is any indicator of quality, the *Journal* is one of the best research values around. Something else must explain this widely held attitude.

The explanation lies in a fundamental, though usually unstated, assumption about an investment management relationship in which a manager has the responsibility (though not necessarily the actual discretion) for organizing, structuring, and carrying out an investment program for a client. Implicit in a management arrangement is the assumption that the manager will exercise ordinary skill and care in meeting his management obligations. Even if the management contract exculpates the manager for negligence,[207] it does not relieve him of his contractual obligation to exert the amount of effort ordinarily required to perform consistent with professional standards. Furthermore, the idea of effort includes more than time expended in cerebration about the economy, the state of the market, the relative worth of different securities, and so forth. It also includes the accumulation of information which is necessary to make that cerebration worthwhile. In other words, there is a core investment in acquiring the information necessary to manage with ordinary skill and care, and it is the undertaking to make that investment which is implicit in and comprehended by every management agreement for which the contract does not indicate otherwise.[208]

Note that this assumption of a core investment by the manager says

---

[204] See Securities Week, April 5, 1976, p. 4 (firm provides subscriptions, quotation equipment, dues for professional society memberships, etc.).

[205] See ¶ 9.06[2] at notes 162-174 *supra*.

[206] See ¶ 9.06[2] at notes 159-160 *supra*.

[207] See ¶ 5.02.

[208] See, e.g., Fogel v. Chestnutt, 533 F.2d 735 (2d Cir. 1975), a case involving a mutual fund investment adviser's failure to recapture brokerage without adequate disclosure. The court said:

nothing about the source of the information a manager acquires. Although he will generate much of it through his own staff, he will also find it efficient to purchase it from outside his organization. In even the largest management complexes, for example, it would be wasteful to generate in-house most of the information contained in the *Wall Street Journal.* Nor does the assumption of a core investment by the manager suggest that any particular kinds of information must be included. One manager may be primarily a fundamentalist, another a technician, and another a capital-asset-pricing-model theorist. Whatever a manager's investment philosophy, however, by accepting his office, he represents that he will expend at least that amount necessary to acquire sufficient information to permit him to perform in accordance with general professional standards.

But if it is correct to say that an assumed part of most management agreements is a core investment in information on the part of the manager, it is also correct to classify generally available information as the primary constituent of the core. Generally available information is essential to successful performance within the bounds of professional standards. Without it, a manager will not ordinarily be able to achieve average performance, and superior performance would almost assuredly be a matter of pure luck. Consider again the example of the *Wall Street Journal.* For many investment managers, it is a rich educational tool and keeps them current with many financial, political, and social developments which may cause them to reassess elements of the investment programs they manage. But because the *Journal* provides that same service to so many investors, it has all the earmarks of a core research service on which investment managers build. Furthermore, again because it is a source of information common to so many investment managers, it is doubtful that the information the *Journal* contains offers much of an opportunity for superior performance. Its wide circulation means that markets adjust rapidly to the information it contains.

This point that the *Journal,* in conjunction with other generally available sources of information, is ordinarily a constituent element of a core research service can be made more succinctly by considering information requiring less extensive inference-drawing to be useful to a

---

"There was an obvious tension between the give-up and those representations made by the investment company in its prospectuses which investors would be likely to understand as meaning that the amounts paid to the investment adviser constituted the fund's cost for management and investment advice. . . ."

manager. Consider, for example, a computer service which generates beta coefficients (the index which measures volatility relative to the market) for common stocks. It is obviously core research to managers investing according to the passive approach dictated by the capital asset pricing model,[209] since an investment program based on the model is impossible to structure without calculating the coefficients for large numbers of securities. Furthermore, the link between publication of the data and portfolio adjustment is so close as to preclude any chance for superior action merely by altering a portfolio based on the published numbers. In the absence of explicit disclosure to the client, it would be difficult for a manager to contend that he was not obliged to furnish this information as a matter of contract.

In short, information that is fundamental to the execution of an investment philosophy is the type of information which ordinarily constitutes the core investment of the manager in research. Furthermore, information which is "readily and customarily available and offered to the general public on a commercial basis" [210] is usually of this very type. First, the fact that such information is available to any purchaser at a set price indicates that it has a broad enough market to justify gathering and disseminating it through one or more centralized outlets and, therefore, that it is a basic component of management strategies similar to the manager's own. Second, its availability at a set price also indicates that it is not of much use for achieving superior performance and, therefore, that it is a basic research service from which a manager's pursuit of superior performance must depart. If one assumes that a management agreement comprehends an investment by the manager into acquiring at least this kind of core information, the purchase of such information in any fashion inures primarily to the benefit of the manager.[211]

In principle, it is possible to argue that the purchase of core infor-

---

[209] See ¶ 7.04.

[210] SEC Securities Exchange Act Release No. 12251 (March 24, 1976), [1975-1976 Transfer Binder] CCH Fed. Sec. L. Rep. ¶ 80,407.

[211] This point about undertakings implicit in a management contract is even clearer where services other than research are concerned. It seems obvious that rent, limousines, office furniture, and the like are purchased primarily for the benefit of the manager. But the reason it seems so obvious is that in contracts for services, both parties characteristically expect that part of the purchase price will go toward paying the service provider's overhead. Rent and office furniture are simply more obvious overhead items than is all research. See note 202 *supra*.

mation does not necessarily benefit the manager unfairly. Suppose that, in order to meet his duty to manage up to professional standards, a manager would have to spend X dollars of his own acquiring core research. Suppose also that he is willing to spend Y dollars of commissions on sophisticated research to achieve superior performance. It would appear to make no difference how the manager purchases the total package of research so long as he spends $X + Y$ in combined funds, and at least X of his own. Indeed, so long as a manager spends at least X, it is arguable that there should be no ceiling on purchases through excess commissions. But the problem with this line of reasoning is that, as a practical matter, it is not possible to determine in advance how much X is. The best one can say is that X is the amount a manager should be spending to give his clients an expected return which is about average for the risk assumed.[212]

In the face of this uncertainty over what should be spent on core research, it is preferable to let the amount a manager *actually spends* on information fundamental to carrying out his investment philosophy determine what he *should spend* on such information. In other words, to keep the manager's estimate of X as accurate as possible, he should be forced to decide in a way that he must suffer the consequences of error. That is, if he overspends, his own profits are affected, and if he underspends, his performance (and hence the amount of funds under his management) is affected. This means he should pay for core research. In contrast, if the manager is purchasing sophisticated information, unusual in concept and available only to a select few, one would ordinarily conclude that the purpose of such purchases is to improve performance above average. Since superior performance is not an implicit representation of most management agreements[213] and therefore does not help satisfy a contractual obligation of the manager,[214] one could also conclude that such purchases are primarily for the benefit of the client.

---

[212] See ¶ 7.03[2].

[213] If for no other reason, this is so because it is virtually impossible for most investors to do better than average. Since in principle an average performance is the collective experience of all investors, many large investors would have to do worse than average for most other investors to be able to do better.

[214] This might not be so if the manager contracted to provide superior performance. Cf. Trustees of Hanover College v. Donaldson, Lufkin & Jenrette, Inc., Civ. No. 71-C686 (S.D. Ind. 1971), discussed in ¶¶ 4.03[1] [a][iv] and 7.04.

[f] Management fee

Ideally, it should make no difference in net cost to the client whether his manager pays for all research out of his own funds or whether he purchases supplementary research with excess commissions. In either case, the total cost of research paid for by the manager (R_M), supplementary research produced by executing brokers or third parties (R_B), and executions (C_E) should be the same. If the manager pays for all supplementary research with his own funds, the management fee (M) should be:

$$M = R_M + R_B + \text{(fixed expenses and profit)};$$

and the commission expenses (C) should be:

$$C = C_E.$$

If the manager purchases supplementary research with commissions, the management fee (M') should be:

$$M' = R_M + \text{(fixed expenses + profit)};$$

and the commission expense should be:

$$C' = R_B + C_E.$$

In either event, $M + C = M' + C'$.

If the net cost to a client is not identical irrespective of the way research is obtained, it would mean that the manager would be varying his conduct depending on the way he bought research.[215] In particular, if

---

[215] The broker might also be changing his conduct depending on how he was paid. Suppose, for example, a broker were charging seven dollars in cash for a service or ten dollars in commissions for a service. (See Wall Street Letter, July 14, 1975, p. 6.) If the cost of pure execution were other than three dollars and the service was essential to the client, the client's best deal would depend on the cost of pure execution. But in principle, the possibility that brokers will act differently depending on the currency in which they are paid should not change the analysis in the text. A rational manager should choose the less expensive method of acquiring the service and adjust the cost to the client accordingly. As a practical matter, however, since management fees are usually set in advance at a fixed level, a manager will not always choose the cheaper method of payment, because he might then bear too much of the cost. If, for example, the fee had been set at a level which contemplated purchasing research with commissions, it is highly probable that the manager will purchase in that fashion even though it might be cheaper to pay with his own funds, since the fee arrangement leaves the manager no opportunity to recoup his share of the benefit available. Note that this situation is the converse of a manager's

$M' + C' > M + C$, it follows that the manager has probably reduced R_M and filled the research gap by buying additional research with commissions—either at greater cost than if he had paid for it himself, or even at the same or lesser cost,[216] but, in any event, without reducing the management fee to reflect all or part of his own lower research expense.[217] Since it would be a breach of fiduciary duty for a manager deliberately to enhance his profits by cutting his own research cost and instead spend client funds,[218] all things being equal, one should expect to see managers who purchase much of their research with commissions charging lower management fees than managers paying for research primarily with their own money.

Admittedly, the qualifier "all things being equal" is a major limitation on the reliability of combinations of commissions and management fees as an indicator of whether the costs and benefits of outside research

---

paying excess commissions for research out of his own funds. Here the manager would be faced with whether to prefer his client's interest by purchasing supplementary research at his own expense.

[216] If $M + C = M' + C'$, so that the manager's profit would be unaffected by whether he spent his own funds or the commissions of his client to purchase research, it would ordinarily be the case that his choice between R_M and R_B would be determined by cost of production. If he could purchase the *Wall Street Journal*, for example, by paying an excess commission 10 percent under the equivalent cash subscription price to him, he would ordinarily do so. The critical cost is the total of $R_M + R_B$. So long as the manager's profit depends only on minimizing that total and not on paying for it one way or another, it should make no *regulatory* difference how research is purchased. Of course, in reality, because management fees are fixed in advance, the manager's profit would depend on the method of purchase. See note 215 *supra*.

[217] It is conceivable that the manager would simply raise M' without increasing R_M. But if the market for management services is not efficient enough to keep $M' + C' = M + C$, it is likely that potential clients will rely more heavily on management fees than commission expenditures, or, at least, on the sum of the two, to determine the relative prices of competing managers.

[218] See ¶ 9.04[1] *supra*. It is worth noting here that the SEC considers it fraudulent for a manager charging higher fees than those generally available not to disclose that fact. See ¶ 5.03[1] at note 75. It does not seem much of an extension of that principle, now that negotiated commission rates are operative, to suggest that a manager whose clients pay higher than usual total costs—that is, management fees plus commissions (plus, by analogy, custodian fees)—is also under a duty to disclose that fact. But even if the statutory fraud provisions of the federal securities laws are not extended this far, disclosure obligations still arise under common-law fiduciary principles. See ¶ 9.07 *infra*.

are being fairly allocated between manager and client. For one thing, administrative, regulatory, and structural distinctions cause the costs of managing a mutual fund, for example, to differ from the costs of managing a common trust fund of comparable size, and the costs of managing each to differ from the costs of managing a single charitable endowment of comparable size. Moreover, some managers are able to capitalize on their reputation, whether deserved or not, for providing superior performance. They make higher profits because investors are willing to pay more for their services. Finally, differences in investment philosophy can account for differences in net cost to similar clients. An investment program emphasizing high turnover, for example, can be more costly to an investor than a passive program following a buy-and-hold strategy.

Nonetheless, comparisons of management fees plus commission costs are far from valueless. There are enough investment managers around to arrive at standard fees for particular types of accounts managed in accordance with particular investment approaches.[219] Furthermore, comparisons between managers for similar types of clients also can be useful in evaluating the practices of managers who extensively purchase outside research. Indeed, such comparisons take on added importance in view of the stated policy of Section 28(e) to provide protection for small investment managers who rely heavily on support from outside research.[220] It should not be the case that clients of managers purchasing outside research with commissions are paying management fees comparable to those they would pay if their managers purchased research directly. It is the total cost of management fees plus commissions which should be comparable. This kind of comparison would be particularly useful where a manager uses excess commissions to purchase research from another manager who handles similar accounts but pays for almost all his research requirements himself.[221]

---

[219] For purposes of examining mutual fund fees, the *Wharton Report* (note 1 *supra,* at 475-494) reported on standard fee levels for different investment managers. The *PPI Report* (note 13 *supra,* at 114-125) did the same more extensively and more completely. And, of course, the *Institutional Investor Study* (note 7 *supra,* at 210-224 (investment advisory complexes), 476-486 (bank trust departments), 670-684 (life insurance companies)) provided extensive documentation of management fees for different types of managers.

[220] See ¶ 9.06[3][a] at note 176 *supra.*

[221] Some larger banks sell their research to other investment managers, most of which are smaller banks. Although the selling banks prefer to be paid in cash, they will accept as payment deposits in noninterest-bearing accounts and, apparently, rebates from brokers. See Wall Street Journal,

[g] Quality of execution

Suppose an investment manager purchases research with excess commissions from a broker who is not competitive in price on a pure execution basis; or who is less likely to achieve the lowest combination of market price plus brokerage cost, considering pure execution only; or who is more likely to produce a delay or a fail than other brokers willing to transact business for the manager. In principle, the additional brokerage costs are simply a part of the price of the research and could be treated like any other use of excess commissions to purchase research. That is, if a client's total brokerage costs are the commission for pure execution plus the commission for research, analysis of the general problem should not be affected by a disparity between pure execution commissions charged by different brokers so long as the total excess commission can be justified as reasonable in value and fair in allocating benefits between manager and client.

Nonetheless, as a practical matter, it will be difficult for an investment manager, in order to purchase research with excess commissions, to justify transacting business with brokers unable to offer competitive prices for pure execution services. The reason is the relative ease with which execution costs can be quantified compared to the difficulty involved in quantifying research benefits. Most investors would prefer the definite savings of a better execution to the indefinite return on a research product. This would be even more the case if comparable research could be purchased for a set price about equivalent in amount to the excess the research broker is charging. But the most important factor is the nature of the transaction in which the research is purchased. The primary function of an execution is the purchase and sale of securities. To choose an expensive executing broker in order to obtain research is an excellent example of letting the tail wag the dog, and it can render suspect the motives of an investment manager who does so. In practical terms, it is a dangerous situation if, in order to satisfy a commitment of the management committee or the research division, a trader finds himself forced to forgo the services of an executing broker he believes is well situated to carry out a transaction effectively in order

---

April 13, 1976, p. 41, col. 3. Such deposits and rebates raise the same issues analyzed in this chapter if the deposits are of client funds or the rebates are generated by client executions. On the cash management practices of banks and duty-of-loyalty questions generally, see E. Herman, *Conflicts of Interest: Commercial Bank Trust Departments* 107-119 (Twentieth Century Fund 1975).

to deal with a research broker he believes to have inferior execution capabilities, at least for that transaction.[222]

[4] Allocating Costs Among Multiple Accounts

The same policy against commingling which operates with respect to the allocation of pure execution costs among clients operates also with respect to the allocation of supplementary research costs.[223] Similarly, the conflict-of-interest problem arising when a manager prefers certain accounts over others for his own benefit is as much a problem in the context of research services as it is in the context of pure execution services.[224] But there is some concern that, unlike the allocation of pure execution costs, the purchase of research with excess commission inherently involves the use of the assets of one account for the benefit of another in violation of common-law fiduciary principles.[225] Assuming, however, that an investment manager is not deliberately favoring certain accounts in allocating excess commission costs and that the system by which he allocates the cost of purchasing research with commissions is reasonable—that is, to an average outside observer, it would appear fair to all clients—legal challenges to a manager's authority to allocate without precisely matching costs and benefits are without merit.

For one thing, if precise matching were required, it would be impossible for a manager with multiple accounts to purchase supplemen-

---

[222] This throws into serious question the practice of determining where to place brokerage business through the use of research chits. All things being equal on the execution side, a manager may prefer a research house in selecting a broker to execute. But the notion of being behind on one's research debts is the very type of practice which can indicate a manager is sacrificing best execution. See, e.g., Wall Street Letter, Dec. 16, 1974, p. 6; id., Nov. 18, 1974; id., May 13, 1974, p. 3. The better practice for managers purchasing research with excess commissions is to leave the trader with discretion to choose a broker based on execution capability, but to keep him informed of preferred brokers once the trader feels such brokers are competitive. But see Securities Week, May 29, 1976, p. 1 (SEC Commissioner Sommer believes that institutional managers should not let their traders determine commissions).

[223] See note 149 supra.

[224] See ¶ 9.05[2] supra.

[225] See, e.g., Stark, "Problems of Institutions Under Competitive Rates: 'Paying-Up' for Research," in R. Mundheim, A. Fleischer & B. Vandegrift, Seventh Annual Institute on Securities Regulation (PLI 1976), in which one panelist went so far as to contend that if Section 28(e) were construed to legitimize benefiting one account at the expense of another, the constitutionality of the statute might be questioned as a taking in violation of the due-process clause. See also Wall Street Letter, March 3, 1975, p. 6.

tary research with excess commissions. As a practical matter, he would not be able to ignore the research he purchased with the commissions from one account in dealing with his other accounts. As a matter of law, he probably could not ignore such research anyway.[226] But there is no way to quantify precisely the benefits of a particular research product and thus to allocate the costs for it among each participating account. Moreover, even if some form of quantification were possible, every method of allocation would have its inherent inequalities. Suppose, for example, a research report deals with a particular common stock. If costs are allocated on a per-share basis, various accounts will benefit in proportion to their commitment to that stock. On the other hand, if costs are allocated in proportion to each account's commitment to the stock, the per-share cost will differ from account to account. The only way the impact of the research product could be the same on every account is if every account had an identical portfolio.

But there is a more fundamental reason for concluding that a reasonably fair system of allocation of excess commision costs is fully consistent with common-law fiduciary principles against commingling and against benefiting one account at the expense of another. Suppose it were the case that an investment manager paid for all research he used with his own funds, either generating it in-house or purchasing it directly from outside organizations. He would still face allocation problems comparable to those associated with the use of commissions to purchase research. First, it is common practice to reduce management-fee rates as the size of an account under management increases. Even if the manager were distributing the benefits of his research equally, the larger accounts would be underwriting a proportionally smaller part of the manager's research expenses by virtue of their lower average management fee. Second, the concentration of effort a manager gives an account varies according to the type of account and the stage of development of the account's investment program. Account/manager ratios are much smaller for pension accounts, for example, than they are for individual trust accounts. In addition, a manager must attend

---

[226] The fiduciary duty to use information acquired in the management of one account for the benefit of another, of course, stops short of using information acquired unlawfully or, though acquired lawfully, not transmittable lawfully, as would be the case with respect to inside information. See, e.g., *In re* Investors Management Co., SEC Securities Exchange Act Release No. 9267 (July 29, 1971), [1970-1971 Transfer Binder] CCH Fed. Sec. L. Rep. ¶ 78,163 (fiduciary duty does not require investment manager to use for his accounts information which may be inside whether or not it later develops that the information is of such a nature).

much more closely to a new account for which portfolio changes are necessary or for an account experiencing shifts in investment objectives for which portfolio adjustments may be required. In cases such as these, it is plain that the less actively managed accounts are paying a higher share of the manager's research expenses.

It may be argued that, at least when a client pays a management fee, he knows in advance what his own costs will be, and, therefore, such inequalities as occur in the degree to which various accounts bear a manager's research costs differently is not important. But such an argument misses the essential point that no system is capable of exactly matching the costs and benefits of research. Moreover, it is difficult to believe that by paying a set management fee, a client gives his informed consent to such differences in allocation as go on, or that his consent is any more meaningful than it would be if given to a manager who purchased research with excess commissions.

Since there is no practical way to match costs and benefits of research, whether a manager purchases all research out of his own funds or purchases some with excess commissions, it makes no sense to distinguish one method from the other on the ground that purchases of research with excess commissions result in commingling or using one account to the benefit of another. It is not even known whether a system of purchasing research with excess commissions involves greater or lesser misallocations of costs and benefits than is the case where all research is purchased out of a manager's own funds. If the manager is not deliberately using one set of accounts to pay excess commissions to subsidize the research costs for other accounts, simple logic suggests that he will use all research, from whatever source derived, in proportion to the needs of each client, since it is in the manager's own interest to maximize the return of each client within the bounds of the client's investment objectives.[227]

Insofar as deliberate favoritism among accounts is concerned, little more need be said than to repeat that such a practice violates common-law fiduciary principles[228] and is not protected by Section 28(e).[229]

---

[227] Indeed, a case can be made that paying for research with commissions may be a fairer system in some respects. Where research is purchased with commissions, it is the accounts with higher turnover that pay the most. Yet such accounts are ordinarily being managed in connection with investment strategies that require more research than do strategies which are more passive. Thus, although they pay more, they also benefit more.

[228] See *Restatement (Second) of Trusts* § 170 (1959); *Restatement (Second) of Agency* § 387 (1958).

[229] See, e.g., Stark, "Problems of Institutions Under Competitive Rates:

But, like any other legal rule based on intent or knowledge, proof of whether, in paying excess commissions for research, a manager is favoring certain accounts over others will be based largely on an objective assessment of his management practices. In this regard, differences in treatment for different accounts can have a bearing. It is a common practice in management organizations, for example, for research and analysis to be generated and gathered centrally, and for different portfolio managers to use that research and analysis for the management of the accounts entrusted to them. But it is also common for investment management organizations to assign portfolio managers in a way that inherently leads to greater concentrations of management effort for certain accounts, a fact which can be demonstrated by comparing the number of accounts each portfolio manager handles. Obviously, a client sharing the services of a portfolio manager with nine other clients is receiving a proportionally greater advantage from centralized research than a client sharing a portfolio manager with 249 other clients. It is also a fact that small accounts generally pay proportionally higher management fees than large accounts. This means that not only are such accounts receiving less attention from their portfolio managers, and therefore less exposure to investment opportunities identified by the organization's research division, they are also paying a proportionally greater share of the cost of producing the research.

The question is whether facts such as these should be probative of a preference by a manager for one set of accounts over another. Although it is difficult to say they are irrelevant, these facts can only be evaluated by recognizing two counterbalancing facts. First, investment management is an activity in which economies of scale enter rapidly. If research motivates a portfolio manager to purchase a security, for example, the benefit of that decision has much greater dollar effect on large accounts than small. Yet the cost of generating that research is the same in either event. Second, the ability of timely research to be utilized by an account is much greater for such accounts as large pension funds than for small accounts. If a small account were to change its portfolio every time an interesting opportunity appeared, it would quickly be devoured by execution costs. Large pension funds, on the other hand, ordinarily have a regular flow of cash to be invested. Moreover, portfolio adjustments are relatively less costly for them than for

'Paying Up' for Research," in R. Mundheim, A. Fleischer & B. Vandegrift, *Seventh Annual Institute on Securities Regulation* (PLI 1976); Jorden, " 'Paying Up' for Research: A Regulatory and Legislative Analysis," 1975 Duke L. J. 1103, 1120-1121; Teberg & Cane, "Paying Up for Research," 115 Trusts & Estates 4, 58 (Jan. 1976).

small accounts, unless the small accounts are always able to participate on a bunched basis with the large accounts. Thus, differences in exposure to and relative cost of research among accounts, so long as such differences accord with general industry practices, should not of themselves be indicative of unlawful preferences by a manager.

¶ 9.07. DISCLOSURE AND INFORMED CONSENT: RESOLVING CONFLICTS OF INTEREST ARISING FROM USE OF COMMISSIONS TO PURCHASE SUPPLEMENTARY SERVICES

As the reader has surely noticed by this point, there is no litmus-paper test for determining whether conflict of interest has influenced the execution practices of an investment manager who pays excess commissions for brokerage and research services. It seems that a colorable case can always be made that a manager has chosen an executing broker to serve his own interests whenever any other relationship, direct or indirect, exists between the broker and the manager. In consequence, the question of whether a manager has succumbed to the opportunity to favor his own interests over his client's rapidly becomes transposed into a problem of proof: Is the evidence of such a nature that a reasonable trier of fact could conclude that service of the manager's interest explains the manager's conduct? Worse, from the manager's point of view, once the evidence is sufficient to permit a reasonable trier of fact so to conclude, the burden shifts to the manager to show that the conflict of interest was not responsible for the manager's conduct. Since, as a practical matter, disproving a conflict-of-interest explanation of events almost always involves demonstrating that the complainant has suffered no injury, the manager's proof, almost insidiously, concedes the major premise that a conflict of interest was operative by joining issue only on the degree to which the client was injured. And, still worse from the manager's point of view, the rule of law tends to regard any substantial collateral benefit a fiduciary receives from his position as belonging to the beneficiary, even absent a demonstrated breach of trust, the theory being that removing all chance of profit will dissuade a fiduciary from engaging in conflicts of interest.[230] As we have seen, everything a man-

---

[230] *Restatement (Second) of Trusts* § 203 (1959) states:

"The trustee is accountable for any profit made by him through or arising out of the administration of the trust, although the profit does not result from a breach of trust."

The comments explicitly state that lack of intent is irrelevant, *id.* Comment a. To the same effect is *Restatement (Second) of Agency* § 338 (1958).

ager obtains through commissions beyond pure execution involves benefit to himself as well as his client. Thus, if any substantial collateral benefit to an investment manager is treated as belonging to the beneficiary, a manager purchasing supplementary services with excess commissions would be in violation of his common-law fiduciary responsibility, and, since the proof would consist of more than payment of commissions in excess of those charged by others, Section 28(e) would be a questionable shield against that common-law violation.

This, then, is the tension created by execution practices involving a manager's use of commissions to purchase brokerage and research services. Congress has specifically determined that the mere fact of paying excess commissions is not sufficiently probative of benefit by an investment manager to permit a court or regulatory authority to conclude that the manager has breached his fiduciary duty. Yet, paying excess commissions ineluctably draws in other facts arising out of an investment management relationship which, in connection with proof of payment of excess commissions, tend to raise duty-of-loyalty questions. Should it be the case that these additional facts are regarded as sufficient to permit a reasonable trier of fact to conclude that the manager has received demonstrable economic benefit from administering to his accounts, or that he has favored his own interests against those of his clients, he will not be able to avoid defending his reasons for his execution practices and will likely find his entire case dependent on the degree to which he can show that his clients were not damaged.

Consider, for example, the case of *Fogel v. Chestnutt*.[231] A stockholder action brought in behalf of a mutual fund against its investment adviser, *Fogel* developed from the adviser's decision not to form a brokerage affiliate or seek a special membership on a regional exchange. By forming a brokerage affiliate or obtaining a special membership on a regional exchange, the adviser could have recaptured commissions for the benefit of the fund.[232] The adviser did not do so, but executed transactions with firms providing it with either or both research and sales assistance. Although the court agreed, at least for the sake of argument, that reasonable business judgment might have led to the conclusion that no affiliate should be formed and no special membership sought, the court took the position that the adviser could not

---

See, e.g., SEC Securities Exchange Act Release No. 10102 (April 12, 1973), [1973 Transfer Binder] CCH Fed. Sec. L. Rep. ¶ 79,327 (recaptured tender-offer fees belong to the managed companies).

[231] 533 F.2d 731 (2d Cir. 1975).
[232] See ¶ 8.02[2].

make that decision without having also to weigh his own interests against those of the fund. The striking thing is that the plaintiffs never proved that the defendants actually gave in to the conflict. They simply proved that the fund could have recaptured commissions and thus was forced to bear an apparently extra cost of operation. The plaintiffs also proved that the adviser benefited from purchasing research and sales assistance. Since the adviser did not disprove that the fund had suffered injury,[233] conflict of interest was presumed as the explanation for the adviser's decision. For failure to resolve the conflict of interest, the adviser[234] was held answerable for the unrecaptured business actually executed on regional exchanges of which the manager could have become a special member, and additionally, the court held that damages could include recapturable business which could have been executed on those exchanges.[235]

[1] The Informed-Consent Principle

In view of the way in which the rules of fiduciary responsibility operate against a fiduciary faced with conflicting interests between himself and his client, his most sensible course of action is to resolve the conflict before acting. With respect to paying excess commissions for research, an investment manager could simply refuse to expose himself to the conflict and decline to pay excess commissions for research services.[236] Another possibility is to adopt a structural from which fairly allocates the benefits from research services purchased with excess commissions.[237] But the best method of resolving the conflict of interest is for the manager to have the client agree to or acquiesce in the manager's execution practices. For it is also an established principle of the

---

[233] The adviser tried but failed to show absence of injury by contending that recapture would have been unlawful, or at least impossible. It did not attempt to argue that, if it could have recaptured, the allocation of costs and benefits between it and the fund absent recapture were fair.

[234] Affiliated directors were also defendants in the case.

[235] Damages also included unrecaptured tender-offer fees. See note 230 *supra*.

[236] See ¶ 9.04[2] at notes 120-121 *supra*.

[237] A manager might, for example, attempt to relate costs and benefits from research services to some formula allocation method which would, in effect, adjust management fees according to the amount of excess commissions actually expended to acquire research. Cf. Parthenon Fund, Inc., [1975-1976 Transfer Binder] CCH Fed. Sec. L. Rep. ¶ 80,451 (1976) (adviser and mutual fund may purchase errors-and-omissions policy and allocate coverage and payment).

common law of trusts and of agency that the consent of a beneficiary permits conduct by a fiduciary that might otherwise be regarded a breach of duty of loyalty.[238]

There are two principal limitations on a fiduciary's authority to act based on the consent of a beneficiary:

(1) The transaction must be otherwise reasonable and fair to the beneficiary.[239] This principle, of course, also finds expression in Section 28(e), which imposes a reasonable good-faith requirement on the payment of excess commissions for brokerage and research services.

(2) The beneficiary must be made aware of material facts which the fiduciary knows or ought to know, unless the fiduciary has grounds reasonably to believe that the beneficiary knows of such facts.[240] In other words, the fiduciary must have the informed consent of the beneficiary in order to proceed.

While the informed-consent principle and the rationale behind it are easy enough to understand, applying the principle is often problematic. In particular, in dealing with the issue of excess commission payments for brokerage and research services, the obvious impracticality of requiring an investment manager to assure himself prior to every transaction that his clients appreciate the full implications of what he plans to do would make complete disclosure so burdensome as effectively to eliminate the practice. The sensible procedure is to disclose to the client in advance what the manager proposes to do from time to time and why he proposes to do it. The previous understanding of the client of what is involved and the fact that the conflict-of-interest problem is virtually identical from transaction to transaction ought to provide adequate protection to any client who believes that his interests would be adversely affected by using his commissions in that fashion. Since the federal securities laws have historically and regularly taken the position that full disclosure of material information is usually sufficient protection for investors,[241] it is doubtful that an investment manager paying excess

---

[238] *Restatement (Second) of Trusts* § 216 (1959); *Rstatement (Second) of Agency* §§ 319, 390 (1958).

[239] *Id.*

[240] The common-law rule also denies the consent defense to a fiduciary obtaining consent from a beneficiary acting under an incapacity *(Restatement (Second) of Trusts* § 216(2)(a) (1959))* or induced by the improper conduct of the fiduciary *(id.* § 216(2)(c)).*

[241] See, e.g., SEC v. Capital Gains Research Bureau, Inc., 375 U.S. 180,

commissions for brokerage and research services will be obliged to do more absent legislation or regulations requiring it.

[2] Disclosure Obligations

As in other contexts, the meaning of full disclosure in connection with the purchase of supplementary services for excess commissions is not easy to determine. Indeed, the difficulty of determining disclosure requirements is illustrated by the SEC's experience with disclosure guidelines for mutual funds. Partly as a result of the introduction of negotiated rates under Rule 19b-3 and partly in anticipation of the adoption of Section 28(e), the SEC adopted a set of informal disclosure guidelines for mutual funds paying excess commissions for brokerage and research services.[242] These guidelines were strict, requiring management to explain why it regarded the services so purchased as essential and how it was allocating the excess commission costs. Ironically, although they made compliance difficult, and thus tended to discourage the purchase of supplementary services with excess commissions, the guidelines failed to explain to shareholders and unaffiliated directors the conflict of interest management was facing. In any event, after Section 28(e) became law, the chairman of the Senate Subcommittee on Securities forced the Commission to drop the guidelines on the grounds that they were inconsistent with the letter and the policy of the law.[243] He also urged the Commission then and regularly thereafter to adopt formal rules more closely related to his view of Section 28(e).[244] The Commission eventually abandoned its informal guidelines as requested,[245] and, after some

---

186 (1963), in which the Supreme Court, in an oft-quoted statement, described the fundamental purpose of the federal securities laws to be "to substitute a philosophy of full disclosure for the philosophy of caveat emptor, and thus to achieve a high standard of business ethics in the securities industry."

[242] See ¶ 9.03[2][b] at notes 104-105 *supra*.

[243] See *id*. at note 105 *supra*.

[244] From the time he first wrote the Commission complaining about the informal guidelines on disclosure it had adopted for prospectuses and advisory contracts of mutual funds (see Securities Week, Aug. 4, 1975, p. 5) through the time the Commission issued its release interpreting Section 28(e) (SEC Securities Exchange Act Release No. 12251 (March 24, 1976), [1975-1976 Transfer Binder] CCH Fed. Sec. L. Rep. ¶ 80,407), the Chairman of the Senate Subcommittee continued to urge the Commission to implement Section 28(e)(2). See Sec. Reg. L. Rep., Feb. 18, 1976, at A-11; Securities Week, Dec. 1, 1975, p. 2; Securities Week, Oct. 20, 1975, p. 2; Securities Week, Oct. 6, 1975, p. 1.

[245] See ¶ 9.03[2][b] at note 106 *supra*.

delay, it has proposed a set of disclosure regulations under Section 28(e)(2).[246]

Until implementing regulations under Section 28(e)(2) are adopted, investment managers must decide for themselves how much to disclose and to whom disclosure is to be made. Moreover, even after regulations are adopted, the question will remain for a manager complying with the regulations of when and under what circumstances he must make additional disclosures. To an extent, SEC decisions with respect to disclosure in other contexts may be helpful, by analogy, in answering these questions.[247] For example, disclosure will surely be limited, here as elsewhere, by the concept of materiality.[248] Additionally, the cases involving recapture of brokerage under the fixed-rate system offer much substantive guidance as to the particular disclosure problems raised in connection with excess commission payments for supplementary services.

Moses v. Burgin[249] was the first case to explore the limits of an investment manager's duty of disclosure when purchasing supplementary services with excess commissions. *Moses* was a derivative action against the investment adviser and directors of a mutual fund, and the theory on which the plaintiff proceeded has remained fundamentally unchanged in all the subsequent litigation challenging the practices of investment managers in disposing of excess commissions.[250] The plaintiff contended

---

[246] The Commission established a task force late in 1975 to deal especially with disclosure regulations for paying excess commissions for brokerage and research services. See Stark, "Problems of Institutions Under Competitive Rates: 'Paying Up' for Research," in R. Mundheim, A. Fleischer & B. Vandegrift, *Seventh Annual Institute on Securities Regulation* (PLI 1976). See also Wall Street Letter, Nov. 24, 1975, p. 3. About a year later, the Commission issued Proposed Rule 28e2-1. SEC Securities Act Release No. 5772 (Nov. 30, 1976), 3 CCH Fed. Sec. L. Rep. ¶ 26,578A, discussed at 9.03[2][b], *supra*.

[247] At the Seventh Annual PLI Conference on Securities Regulation (note 246 *supra*), the Director of the Division of Investment Management Regulation (as it then was) took the position that previous Commission decisions with respect to disclosure were obligatory where applicable to paying excess commissions for supplementary services.

[248] See, e.g., Intersearch Technology, Inc., SEC Admin. Proc. File No. 3-2991, [1974-1975 Transfer Binder] CCH Fed. Sec. L. Rep. ¶ 80,139, at 85,188 n.30. In TSC Indus., Inc. v. Northway, Inc., 426 U.S. 438, 449 (1976), the Court established as the standard of materiality in a proxy statement that there be "a substantial likelihood that a reasonable shareholder would consider [an omitted fact] important in deciding how to vote."

[249] 445 F.2d 369 (1st Cir.), *cert. denied sub nom.* Johnson v. Moses, 404 U.S. 994 (1971).

[250] A veritable flood of litigation followed *Moses*. See Butowsky, "Fiduciary Standards of Conduct Revisited—Moses v. Burgin and Rosenfeld v.

that the fund could have recaptured brokerage commissions if its affiliated underwriter had sought and obtained membership as an introducing broker on the NYSE, had joined regional exchanges, or had obtained give-ups directable to it by virtue of its NASD status. As in all these cases, the defendants were unsuccessful in arguing that they had no duty of recapture because recapture in any form would have been illegal. Various forms of recapture were too widely practiced with the full knowledge of the stock exchanges and the NASD for that argument to prevail.[251] In the view of the court of appeals, management had the alternatives of recapturing commissions, which would have benefited only the fund, or of directing commissions to brokers selling fund shares, which, in the court's view, benefited management as much as fund shareholders.[252] The problem for management was that its own interests depended on the choice it made between these alternatives.[253] Before it could choose the alternative which benefited it, it was obliged, under fiduciary principles, to resolve the conflict of interest.

Black Revisited," 17 N.Y. Law For. 735 (1971). Law review commentary was also extensive. See, e.g., Miller & Carlson, "Recapture of Brokerage Commissions by Mutual Funds," 46 N.Y.U.L. Rev. 35 (1971); Note, "Conflict of Interest in the Allocation of Mutual Fund Brokerage Business," 80 Yale L.J. 372 (1970); Comment, "Mutual Funds and Independent Directors: Can Moses Lead to Better Business Judgment," 1972 Duke L.J. 429.

[251] Although it seems that such a defense was bound to fail in view of the extensive and spreading recapture practices of the securities industry in the late sixties (see ¶ 8.02[2]), it did prevail in the *Moses* district court. 316 F. Supp. 31 (D. Mass. 1970).

[252] 445 F.2d at 374. In concluding that the shareholders benefited equally, the court was probably being excessively generous to management. The use of commissions to reward sales mostly expands management fees without significantly enhancing management costs; whereas, at least in the case of mutual funds, the shareholders get only a possible increase in liquidity to protect against excessive redemptions and the additional probability (unmentioned in *Moses*) that a larger and wealthier fund will attract better management. Nonetheless, the important point is that even if the shareholders did benefit equally, the services purchased only by the shareholders inured to the benefit of both management and shareholders. Recapture, on the other hand, would have benefited only the shareholders.

[253] Both management and the court recognized the fundamental nature of the point that management would be affected by how it decided what to do with the excess commissions of the fund. In its brief, management argued that management's commission practices created "a community, rather than a conflict of interests." But the court replied "the conflict, of course, was who was to pay for it." *Id.* at 374 n.8.

In view of the conflict of interest, the court said that management had a duty of disclosure to the unaffiliated directors. Although that holding has received a great deal of attention,[254] it really is not a major departure in the law. As this discussion has already noted, disclosure is a standard means for a fiduciary to resolve a conflict of interest. Indeed, the court made this point itself.[255] The holding is more significant for its conclusion that disclosure could have insulated management from liability, since the court could have concluded, as the SEC did subsequently,[256] that the conflict was so pervasive as to preclude any mutual fund adviser from directing brokerage for sales assistance.

Also significant is the court's position on the kind of disclosure which would have sufficed to protect management. The court rejected plaintiff's claim that the fund's affiliated underwriter should have sought membership on regional exchanges to recapture commissions because the record showed that the unaffiliated directors had learned of the opportunity to join a regional exchange and had decided against it. But the facts reported in the opinion raise real doubts about whether the unaffiliated directors realized the full extent to which fund commission expenses could be recaptured by affiliation.[257] If, when they approved management's recommendation not to join regional exchanges, the unaffiliated directors really did not know about the possibility of recapture, this would mean they had been apprised of only the detriments and not the advantages of affiliation. This would impose rather a modest disclosure obligation indeed. Perhaps the explanation for the court's attitude lies in the ground-breaking nature of the case: Although, in

---

[254] See note 250 *supra.*

[255] The court said:

"[T]his is a clear conflict of interest case that routinely calls for disclosure quite apart from any special burden that may be implicit in the Investment Company Act." 445 F.2d at 383.

[256] See ¶ 9.05[1] at notes 145-146 *supra.*

[257] The court said:

"[T]here is evidence that some of them did not consider, when deciding, the full possibility of thereby recapturing the broker's profits and give-ups accruing from trading with other houses. . . . We cannot find in the evidence, however, any reason to suppose that the difference would have swung the balance in the other direction."

Id. at 375. The court relied in part on the failure of the unaffiliated directors to testify that it would have made a difference to them. Compare this with Fogel v. Chestnutt, note 231 *supra,* in which the court refused to credit the proffered testimony of directors after the fact in order for the manager to establish that its decision not to recapture would have been approved.

conception, *Moses* was really only a straightforward application of fiduciary principle, in actuality, the case was an attack on the practices of an entire industry.

It is instructive also to consider the facts that the court regarded as significant in establishing management's liability arising out of the opportunity to recapture brokerage by virtue of the affiliated underwriter's NASD status. The court pointed to two visits, over a year apart, by representatives of the SEC who suggested to management the possibility of recapture of commissions by the affiliated underwriter. The court also pointed to publication of the SEC *Report on the Public Policy Implications of Investment Company Growth (PPI Report)*.[258] The evidence showed that management did not tell the unaffiliated directors of the substance of the meetings with the SEC representatives, and that, though management distributed the *PPI Report* to the unaffiliated directors, it did not spotlight the portion which dealt with NASD recapture.[259] In the court's view, no one of these facts triggered a disclosure obligation if management wanted to continue to reward sales services with directed brokerage. Rather, it was their cumulative effect which did so. Thus, the court established liability as beginning no later than three months after publication of the *PPI Report*, but authorized the district court to set the date earlier, depending on its findings of fact as to when management became alerted to the possibility of recapture.[260] This means that a disclosure obligation arises at least as soon as an investment manager becomes aware that he has a conflict of interest with regard to the disposition of excess brokerage, and it also suggests that the obligation arises when an investment manager *ought* to be aware he has a conflict.

Even though there has been extensive litigation since *Moses* raising essentially the same issue,[261] only two cases throw additional light on the nature of an investment manager's disclosure obligations in connection with the use of excess commissions to purchase supplementary ser-

---

[258] *PPI Report,* note 13 *supra.*

[259] The court also recounted management's reaction after the SEC promulgated Proposed Rule 10b-10 to abolish give-ups with its accompanying statement that mutual fund managers are obliged to recapture fixed brokerage to the extent possible. With the approval of the unaffiliated directors, the fund began banking commissions with executing broker-dealers on regional exchanges until it could get formal approval from these exchanges that the excess commissions were recapturable by the affiliated underwriter.

[260] 445 F.2d at 385.

[261] See note 250 *supra.*

vices. *Fogel v. Chestnutt*[262] held that the management of a no-load (shares sold at net asset value) mutual fund did not adequately inform the outside directors of the possibility of recapture. *Tannenbaum v. Zeller*[263] held that the management of a load (underwriting commission included in the sale price of shares) mutual fund had adequately informed the outside directors of the possibility of recapture. Since *Fogel* did not involve complete nondisclosure and *Tannenbaum* did not involve complete disclosure, it is instructive to read those cases against *Moses*.

Because the fund in *Fogel* was no-load, it had no affiliated underwriter member of NASD. Management would have had to form a brokerage affiliate to recapture commissions. This management declined to do because, according to the apparently unimpeached evidence of management, the brokerage business was something beyond its expertise, was fraught with opportunities for self-dealing, and would have diverted its attention from its advisory responsibilities. Although the *PPI Report* was distributed to each director, there had been no discussion of the possibility of recapture.

Fogel differs from *Moses* in two important respects. First, the reports of the two cases suggest that the outside directors in *Fogel* were at least as well informed of the reasons management did not want to form a brokerage affiliate as the outside directors in *Moses* were of why their management did not want to join a regional exchange. The testimony of the *Fogel* outside directors, supported by management's answer to interrogatories, establishes that, based on what they knew, they would have rejected the formation of an affiliated broker for largely the same reasons management was opposed. Also like the directors in *Moses*, they were unaware of the possibility and mechanics of recapture. Nonetheless, unlike *Moses*, management was held liable in *Fogel* on the grounds it failed effectively to communicate the nature of the "problem" to the outside directors.[264] This means that in the *Fogel* court's view, both the advantages as well as the disadvantages of denying management use of excess commissions to purchase supplementary services must be disclosed.

The second difference of significance is that, according to the evidence reported, the *Fogel* management was far less aware of the possibility of recapture than was the *Moses* management. One director tes-

---

[262] 533 F.2d 731 (2d Cir. 1975).

[263] 552 F.2d 402 (2d Cir. 1977), *aff'g in part and rev'g in part* 399 F. Supp. 945 (S.D.N.Y. 1975).

[264] 533 F.2d at 749-750.

tified that he did not realize a brokerage affiliate could be formed to act solely as a conduit back to the fund for excess brokerage.[265] Others testified that the *PPI Report* did not apply to them either because they believed they were ineligible to join the NASD or because they were structurally different from the load funds, which they believed were the objects of the *PPI Report* with regard to recapture.[266] Although the court said that there should have been further inquiries by management after publication of the *PPI Report* about the possibility of recapture, the court never concluded that management, or at least all affiliated officers and directors, were aware of what could be done. Certainly, there was far less awareness on management's part than was the case in *Moses*.

Nonetheless, adopting the *Moses* rule, the *Fogel* court held that, as of three months after publication of the report, management became liable as a matter of law for continuing to operate in the face of the conflict of interest created by the opportunity to recapture. Indeed, with respect to most of the affiliated officers and directors, the court rejected a defense of reliance on a lawyer-director, not because they were aware of the recapture possibility, but because he probably knew.[267] Unless, without saying so, the court was not crediting the testimony of these other affiliated officers and directors, it was implicitly adopting as the standard for requiring a manager to resolve a conflict of interest a test based not only on when a manager actually knows of a conflict, but also on when he should know of it. Although the common-law rule says that all profit from a fiduciary's administration of his beneficiary's interests belongs to the beneficiary,[268] as a general principle, this seems about as far as a disclosure obligation can be stretched. It is difficult to see how a manager can recognize a conflict of interest and act accordingly if he is not aware of the adverse interest of his client. With respect to use of commissions to purchase supplementary services, however, it is highly doubtful that any manager could still claim ignorance of the conflict.

In *Tannenbaum*, the court claimed, based on the analysis in *Fogel*, to be slightly at odds with *Moses*, and certainly, the result in both cases is different. Nonetheless, unless one reads *Moses* as imposing recapture as a duty, the cases are in harmony. The *Tannenbaum* court simply rejected on the facts any claim that the unaffiliated directors were not adequately informed about the possibility of recapture. The evidence showed that management summarized the *PPI Report* for the board of

---

[265] *Id.* at 749.
[266] *Id.* at 749-750.
[267] *Id.*
[268] See note 230 *supra*.

directors and made specific reference to the SEC's attitude favoring using brokerage business to reduce management costs.[269] When Proposed Rule 10b-10 was issued, the board received copies, and counsel to the fund issued an opinion letter which advised the board that, having considered the advantages and disadvantages of recapture, it could reach a reasonable business judgment not to change its execution practices.[270] At regular intervals thereafter, the board reconsidered and reaffirmed the brokerage practices of management. In the face of this policy of full disclosure to the entire board of directors, the plaintiff was compelled to argue that the directed brokerage practices of the fund were unlawful in themselves, and, like the *Moses* court, this the *Tannenbaum* court declined to hold.

These three cases are also interesting for what they say about another aspect of the disclosure question: to whom must disclosure be made. Each court made it a point of emphasis that the outside directors of mutual funds have a responsibility for protecting shareholder interests. It seems a reasonable conclusion that, in any investment management relationship which places a surrogate or intermediary between the manager and the ultimate beneficiaries, the manager must make full disclosure to the surrogate. But it is also likely that there are disclosure obligations to the beneficiaries themselves. For although the representatives of the ultimate beneficiaries may have the power to approve practices which, though involving conflicts of interest, are within the scope of reasonable business judgment, in some instances the beneficiaries also should have the information to evaluate the choices their representatives have made in their behalf. Furthermore, disclosure to the ultimate beneficiaries can provide an added degree of protection to management, especially where management has a degree of influence over the surrogate or intermediary. Although the plaintiffs in *Moses* and *Fogel* did not make an issue out of the adequacy of disclosure to the shareholders,[271] the plaintiff in *Tannenbaum* did argue that proxy statements and prospectuses and notices of annual meetings were false and mis-

---

[269] 552 F.2d at 419.

[270] *Id.* at 420. The fund's investment adviser was a subsidiary of a brokerage firm, but it was fund policy not to execute through the affiliated broker. *Id.* 412-413, 425-426.

[271] The *Moses* court did, however, recognize shareholder awareness as a basis for protecting management in conflict-of-interest situations. It rejected a claim by plaintiff that management was obliged to form a brokerage affiliate capable of executions so that the advisory fee could be reduced by profits from such an entity. The court said that plaintiff could have chosen an executing broker-affiliated fund if she wanted. 445 F.2d at 375.

leading.[272] The disclosures to shareholders were far less revealing than those made to the unaffiliated directors. The district court had rejected the claim on the grounds of full disclosure to the unaffiliated directors and on the grounds that the shareholders had been "informed" of the fund's policy of brokerage allocation.[273] Perhaps by this the court meant that documents sent to shareholders did describe the basis on which management was making brokerage allocations well enough to alert a concerned shareholder to further action. In any event, the court of appeals reversed on the ground that disclosure to shareholders was inadequate in that, though informed of the fund's brokerage practices, they were not told specifically of the possibility of recapture.[274] The position taken by the court of appeals is particularly significant since disclosure to shareholders comparable in quality to that in *Tannenbaum* with respect to the use of excess commissions to purchase research seems to be the practice now that negotiated rates have been introduced.[275]

The principal lesson of *Moses*, *Fogel*, and *Tannenbaum* is that investment managers should be disclosing the advantages to the manager that come from purchasing supplementary services with excess commissions, and the advantages that the client might realize if the manager does not. This does not mean that the manager cannot express a good-faith opinion as to which course of action will provide the maximum return to the client. The manager can, and surely will, describe the disadvantages the client may experience if the manager foregoes the use of excess commissions for that purpose. Disclosure having been made, either the client or his representative can approve the manager's recommendation as being within the realm of reasonable business judgment.

---

[272] *Id.* at 429 n.3.

[273] 399 F. Supp. at 953.

[274] 552 F.2d at 429-435. The court remanded for a determination of damages for material omissions during the period 1967-1971. The 1972 proxy statement had raised the possibility of recapture in discussing a proposed amendment to the fund's certificate of incorporation designed to make explicit the power of the board of directors to determine portfolio brokerage allocation. This, the court held, was adequate disclosure.

[275] See, e.g., Securities Week, April 26, 1976, p. 12 (mutual fund adviser adds authority to pay excess commissions for research to advisory contract); Securities Week, March 15. 1976, p. 4 (management of mutual fund describes to shareholders factors it relies on in selecting executing brokers); Securities Week, Sept. 22, 1975, p. 9 (investment manager tells clients it will take into consideration research and other investment services in selecting executing brokers).

Finally, it is worth observing that the greater the conflict, the greater the burden of disclosure. In *Tannenbaum,* for example, management argued, and the district court relied on management's statement in a prospectus that the services purchased with the fund's excess commissions did not materially reduce management's expenses to establish that disclosure to shareholders was adequate.[276] Of course, however, the failure to recapture increased the fund's expenses. If management had disclosed merely the payment of sales-related give-ups and the evidence had showed substantial benefit to management, it is doubtful the court's attitude would have been so accommodating. In the same vein, the *Moses* court stated that management's practice of awarding "reciprocals" to selling brokers was not absolutely a conflict of interest giving rise to liability. While this statement suggests less than full appreciation on the part of the court of what was involved in reciprocal practices,[277] it also makes the point that the less significant the conflict, the less extensive the disclosure must be. In light of this, it would be sound practice for managers whose excess commission practices raise serious conflict-of-interest questions to repeat disclosure at regular intervals, including facts and figures on payments made and goods and services received. For example, because of the ease with which they can reduce their own costs and because of the temptation to overtrade in order to generate commissions, managers who purchase virtually all services outside should have available quantitative data at least estimating the amount of excess commissions expended and perhaps also the approximate value of the services purchased to management.

---

[276] 399 F. Supp. at 953.
[277] See ¶ 9.02[2] *supra.*

Chapter 10

SPECIAL RELATIONS BETWEEN MANAGER AND BROKER

¶ **10.01. CONFLICTS OF INTEREST SURROUNDING THE INTENTIONAL SACRIFICE OF BEST NET PRICE WHEN MANAGER AND BROKER ARE CONNECTED**

Connections between investment managers and brokerage firms can raise serious duty-of-loyalty questions. When a brokerage firm acts as manager or is formally affiliated with a manager, the manager may be tempted to turn his accounts over for the purpose of increasing commission income to the brokerage arm or to use his accounts as repositories for overvalued securities which cannot be sold conveniently on the open market. Turning over a portfolio to generate commissions is called churning.[1] Selling overvalued securities to a client to remove them from inventory or from a more favored account is called dumping.[2] Both practices violate the antifraud provisions of the federal securities laws.[3]

Beyond these blatant examples of a manager's sacrificing his client's interests to serve his own are other arrangements which are less obvious reflections of the conflict of interest which arises out of combinations of brokerage and money management. Being more subtle conflicts of interest, they are also more insidious, since not even the manager may realize the extent to which they influence his conduct. Rather than deliberately creating trades which have no investment purpose, a manager may simply fail to obtain best execution by executing with the brokerage firm to which the manager is connected. In the fixed-rate era, this problem could manifest itself by executions made on an inferior market, or made to satisfy a reciprocity obligation, or made without taking advantage of reciprocal benefits.[4] Negotiated rates, though they eliminated much of the need to consider reciprocal benefits and the like,[5] only made the conflict-of-interest problem worse

---

[1] See 1 SEC, *Report of Special Study of Securities Markets,* H.R. Doc. No. 95, 88th Cong., 1st Sess. 297 (1963) (hereinafter cited as *Special Study*); Report of the Subcomm. on Securities of the Senate Comm. on Banking, Housing and Urban Affairs, *Securities Industry Study,* S. Doc. No. 13, 93d Cong., 1st Sess. 75 (1973) (hereinafter cited as *Senate Securities Industry Study*).

[2] See *Senate Securities Industry Study,* note 1 *supra,* at 76. Although the descriptive term "dumping" would no longer be accurate, the issue is the same when the manager buys undervalued securities from a managed account at an advantageous price. See SEC, *Institutional Investor Study,* H.R. Doc. No. 64, 92d Cong., 1st Sess. 1597 (1971) (hereinafter cited as *Institutional Investor Study*).

[3] See ¶¶ 10.06[1], 10.06[2], *infra.*

[4] See, e.g., *Senate Securities Industry Study,* note 1 *supra,* at 75-76; Report of the Subcomm. on Commerce and Finance of the House Comm. on Interstate and Foreign Commerce, *House Securities Industry Study,* H.R. Rep. No. 1519, 92d Cong., 2d Sess. 148-149 (1972) (hereinafter cited as *House Securities Industry Study*). See also Folk, "Restructuring the Securities Markets—The Martin Report: A Critique," 57 Va. L. Rev. 1315, 1362-1363 (1971).

[5] *Id.* The problem of reciprocal arrangements is not entirely eliminated by negotiated rates. Broker-managers can still execute with firms that also execute with them or provide them with other valuable services.

for managers executing through brokers to which they are connected. Where the broker is the manager, he may effectively be negotiating commissions with himself. Where there is more distance between the manager and the broker, it is more realistic to speak of negotiation. But even then, one cannot be sure how much the broker's demands for commission income control the negotiations. Consider, for example, an investment manager executing through a brokerage firm which refers clients to him. The price of executing could as well be set by what it takes to keep the referral business flowing as by anything else.

Ostensibly on conflict-of-interest grounds, Congress, in the Securities Acts Amendments of 1975, amended Section 11(a) of the Securities Exchange Act to restrict combined investment management and brokerage.[6] The amendment did not eliminate all such combinations, however, and, subject to a grandfather clause, it delayed its effective date until May 1, 1978. Moreover, there is growing question about the wisdom of an absolute prohibition on the combined management and brokerage arrangements affected by the statute, and the SEC and members of the securities industry are actively reconsidering the statute to determine whether to recommend that Congress either modify Section 11(a) again, or even repeal the 1975 amendment outright.[7] But whatever forms combinations of investment management and brokerage are ultimately permitted to take, analysis of the general problem must begin with a study of the genesis of Section 11(a) as amended. Because the public debate focused so heavily on the conflict-of-interest issue, it is easy to attribute much more serious consequence to it—almost a presumption against combinations of brokerage and management—than the issue deserves. As the discussion in ¶ 10.02 will show, arguments favoring the separation of brokerage and investment management on conflict-of-interest grounds were based almost entirely on invention. No regulatory studies recommended such action, and the evidence that these conflicts of interest were truly acting to the detriment of investors was scanty, at best. Moreover, to support its determination to restrict brokerage and money management activities on conflict-of-interest grounds, Congress lumped in conflicts which, though real in the sense that brokerage firms could engage in them, have little to do with the

---

6 Pub. L. 94-29 § 6(2), 89 Stat. 97 (June 4, 1975).

7 See SEC Securities Exchange Act Release No. 12055 (Jan. 27, 1976), [1975-1976 Transfer Binder] CCH Fed. Sec. L. Rep. ¶ 80,367; Nagdeman, "Free the Captives?" Barron's March 8, 1976, p. 3; Securities Week, Nov. 8, 1976, p. 1.

combination as a unique operational feature in an investment management relationship.[8]

The special case of employee benefit funds also requires consideration. The Employee Retirement Income Security Act of 1974 (ERISA) operates broadly on the general principle that a fiduciary to an employee benefit fund should not have a personal interest either in the assets the fund purchases or sells or in the expenditures of the fund to acquire and dispose of such assets. This general principle was enacted in the form of prohibited-transaction provisions in the statute, and its application necessarily sweeps in relationships between brokers and managers, going well beyond the separation of brokerage and management found in Section 11(a) of the Securities Exchange Act. In this case, however, the congressional decision to prohibit transactions between a fiduciary and an employee benefit fund developed from a record of abuses which had little to do with relationships between investment managers and brokerage firms, whether affiliated or not. The automatic inclusion of such relationships stemmed from what seemed a logical extension of the general principle underlying the prohibited-transactions provisions and from the neglect of brokers to respond to the pension legislation as it was incubating than it did from any demonstrated need to bear down on such relationships. Belatedly, the brokerage industry, in conjunction with others servicing pension plans, moved unsuccessfully to amend the Act.[9] But, however successful such efforts may eventually be, the burden is now on the brokers to defend previously standard relationships. Like new Section 11(a) of the Exchange Act, ERISA's prohibited-transactions provisions give sustenance to the conviction that combined brokerage and management involves conflicts of interest too dangerous to permit.

Thus, to analyze the special conflict-of-interest problems associated with combinations of brokerage and investment management, it is first necessary to put the conflict-of-interest issue in perspective by exploring the developments which led to amendment of Section 11(a) and analyzing its effects as enacted. For the same reason, but to a lesser extent, it is necessary to do the same for the prohibited-transactions provisions of ERISA. Once that is done, it is possible to consider the nature of these conflict-of-interest problems, how they might be affected under common-law principles and under the antifraud provisions of the federal securities laws to the degree they are not otherwise prohibited, and what might be done to resolve these conflict-of-interest problems.

---

[8] See ¶ 10.02[1] *infra*.
[9] See H.R. 7597, 94th Cong., 1st Sess. (1975).

¶ **10.02. THE SECURITIES ACTS AMENDMENTS OF 1975: RESTRICTIONS ON BROKER-MONEY MANAGER COMBINATIONS UNDER SECTION 11(a) OF THE SECURITIES EXCHANGE ACT**

[1] Conditions Leading to the Decision to Separate Brokerage and Management

If conflict of interest is the explanation for Congress's decision to separate brokerage from money management, one of the most puzzling aspects of that decision is the suddenness with which the need to make the separation was discovered. Brokerage firms had been providing customers with advisory services, including discretionary management services, for many years[10] without a murmur from Congress. Furthermore, the SEC kept Congress well informed on the nature of the conflicts of interest involved in combining brokerage and management. The *Report of the Wharton School of Finance and Commerce: A Study of Mutual Funds* (*Wharton Report*), prepared for the SEC, found a mild indication that portfolio turnover was higher for mutual funds affiliated with brokers, although the largest funds apparently experienced lower turnover than average.[11] The *Wharton Report* also speculated that the high concentration of executions with broker-affiliates[12] indicated that such mutual funds may have been sacrificing certain service benefits that could have been obtained by executing elsewhere.[13] The *Report of the Special Study of Securities Markets* found evidence of churning, dumping, sacrifice of best execution, and preferential treatment of customers, though it made no distinction between managed and nonmanaged accounts.[14] The SEC *Report on the Public Policy Implications of Investment Company Growth* (*PPI Report*) found, contrary to the *Wharton Report*, that median turnover rates for broker-affiliated investment companies were below industry averages.[15] The SEC speculated without evidence that broker affiliation might lead to

---

[10] See, e.g., *Institutional Investor Study*, note 2 *supra*, at 2296-2298.

[11] SEC, *Report of the Wharton School of Finance and Commerce: A Study of Mutual Funds*, H.R. Rep. No. 2274, 87th Cong., 2d Sess. 224-226 (1962) (hereinafter cited as *Wharton Report*).

[12] *Id.* at 473-475.

[13] *Id.* at 32.

[14] See 1 *Special Study*, note 1 *supra*, at 297-298, 371-374; *id.* Pt. 2, at 958-959.

[15] SEC, *Report on the Public Policy Implications of Investment Company Growth*, H.R. Rep. No. 2337, 89th Cong., 2d Sess. 189 (1966) (hereinafter cited as *PPI Report*).

sacrifice of best execution, but specifically declined to recommend legislation limiting such affiliations if commission income were a factor in setting advisory fees.[16]

After publication of the *PPI Report*, Congress undertook extensive legislative efforts to amend the Investment Company Act.[17] Throughout the entire four-year period preceding enactment of the Investment Company Amendments Act of 1970,[18] there was no sentiment expressed to change Section 17(e) of the Act,[19] which permits broker-affiliates of investment companies to receive normal commissions on executions for such companies. Shortly thereafter, the *Institutional Investor Study* examined affiliations between brokerage firms and investment managers.[20] The results of regression analysis of the collected data show a slightly higher turnover,[21] but lower advisory fees, for affiliated accounts.[22] The only conflict of interest identified as serious was the preferential treatment of certain accounts, although the data suggested that managed accounts were beneficiaries rather than victims.[23] The letter of transmittal accompanying the study explicitly asserted that the study had found no demonstrated need for separating brokerage and management.[24]

Early in 1972, the SEC published its *Policy Statement on the Future Structure of the Securities Markets (Policy Statement)*.[25] Although the Commission deferred to Congress on the decision whether brokerage and management should be separated,[26] it recommended against flatly prohibiting such affiliations on grounds of economic impact and fairness.[27]

---

[16] *Id.* at 190.

[17] See S. Rep. No. 184, 91st Cong., 1st Sess. (1969); H.R. Rep. Nos. 1382, 1631, 91st Cong., 2d Sess. (1970); Hearings on S. 34 and S. 296 Before the Senate Comm. on Banking and Currency, 91st Cong., 1st Sess. (1969); Hearings on S. 1659 Before the Senate Comm. on Banking and Currency, 90th Cong., 1st Sess. (1967); Hearings on H.R. 11995, 13754 and 14737 Before the Subcomm. on Commerce and Finance of the House Comm. on Interstate and Foreign Commerce, 91st Cong., 1st Sess. (1969).

[18] Pub. L. 91-547 (Dec. 14, 1970).

[19] 15 U.S.C. § 80a-17(e).

[20] See *Institutional Investor Study*, note 2 *supra*, at 2296-2311.

[21] *Id.* at 173, 191, 363.

[22] *Id.* at 213.

[23] *Id.* at 372-374.

[24] *Id.*, Summary Vol., at XX.

[25] SEC, *Statement on the Future Structure of the Securities Markets*, [Special Studies Transfer Binder] CCH Fed. Sec. L. Rep. ¶ 74,811 (1972) (hereinafter cited as *Policy Statement*).

[26] *Id.* ¶ 74,811, at 65,624.

[27] *Id.* ¶ 74,811, at 65,623.

Additionally, the Commission emphasized that Congress had not seen fit to alter affiliations between brokers and investment companies.[28] Right on the heels of the *Policy Statement*, the Senate Subcommittee on Securities filed an interim *Securities Industry Study (Interim Senate Study)*.[29] Conflict of interest was barely mentioned in the discussion of affiliation between brokerage firms and investment managers, and such mention as was made concluded only that whatever separation was mandated be applied equally to all investment managers.[30] Yet within half a year, the *House Securities Industry Study* concluded that brokerage and management should be separated,[31] and the Senate reached the same conclusion in its completed study, the *Senate Securities Industry Study*, published half a year later.[32] Both studies strongly argued that it was necessary to separate brokerage and management because of the serious conflicts of interest that result when those activities are combined.

[a] Congress's conflict-of-interest rationale

Since Congress was so well apprised of the conflicts resulting from the combination of brokerage and management, if the conflict-of-interest problem really was a strong motivating force behind the amendment of Section 11(a) of the Securities Exchange Act, there had to have been some precipitating factor which finally convinced Congress to act. One possibility is that broker expansion into investment management had become so great as to warrant remedial action. And, in fact, the Senate and House studies do suggest that the extent of broker expansion into management had alerted Congress to the need to act.[33] But both the figures these studies report and the casual way in which they were gathered belie the importance of the expansion point to the de-

---

[28] *Id.*

[29] Report of the Senate Comm. on Banking, Housing and Urban Affairs, containing a Report of the Subcomm. on Securities, *Securities Industry Study*, 92d Cong., 2d Sess. 60-69 (1972) (hereinafter cited as *Interim Senate Study*).

[30] *Id.* at 68. Several senators filed separate views, saying it was premature to express personal views about the policy conclusions of the report. One senator dissented from the rule of equal treatment, arguing that institutional investors should not be permitted to merge with member firms absent a showing that merger was in the public interest. *Id.* at 87-88.

[31] *House Securities Industry Study*, note 4 *supra*, at 147-154.

[32] *Senate Securities Industry Study*, note 1 *supra*, at 64-87.

[33] See *id.* at 67-68; *House Securities Industry Study*, note 4 *supra*, at 147.

cision to separate brokerage and management. According to the most optimistic estimate of the amount of actual management services being provided by brokerage firms at publication of the final Senate study, brokerage firms accounted for well under 10 percent of assets under management.[34] Based on some testimony and some imprecise figures, there was little evidence of a significant shift to broker-managers or growth in management opportunities except in the area of pension fund management.[35] But as far as pension funds were concerned, no additional legislation was necessary. Pension legislation under consideration by Congress at the same time as the Senate and House studies would have had precisely the effect of separating brokerage from management.[36]

Another possible explanation for congressional action against combined brokerage and management is the discovery of evidence that the conflicts of interest created when those two activities are connected were causing significant injury to investors. The evidence, recounted above,[37] which Congress already had when the Senate Subcommittee submitted its interim report, hardly makes a case that broker-managers were regularly violating their fiduciary obligations to their managed accounts in order to serve their own interests as brokers. In any event, that evidence was already available when the *Interim Senate Study* was published, and if it had been strong enough to justify legisla-

---

[34] The figures describing the growth of broker expansion into investment management have always been difficult to evaluate because the distinction between accounts vesting contractual discretion in brokerage firms and managed accounts—those in which the client retains discretion but largely follows the advice of a brokerage firm—have always been blurred. See *Senate Securities Industry Study*, note 1 *supra*, at 67-68.

[35] Although the dollar increase in assets under management by brokerage firms was substantial, much of that growth resulted from a general increase in investable funds and the general postwar rise in securities values rather than massive shift to brokerage firms as investment managers. *Institutional Investor Study*, note 2 *supra*, Chs. 3, 4. Most pension trustees were and have remained firmly disposed against broker-management. See, e.g., Patocka, "Will Broker-Affiliates Still Manage Money?" 9 Institutional Investor 67, 69 (July 1975).

[36] Although ERISA was still in Conference Committee at the time of publication of the Senate and House Studies, the bill was reported out on August 12, 1974 (see Conference Report, ERISA, H.R. Rep. No. 1280, 93d Cong., 2d Sess. (Aug. 12, 1974)), well in advance of the introduction of S. 249 and H.R. 10, the two bills which produced the Securities Acts Amendments of 1975. See S. 249, 94th Cong., 1st Sess. (Jan. 17, 1975), and H.R. 10, 94th Cong., 1st Sess. (Jan. 14, 1975).

[37] See notes 11-24 *supra*.

tive action, one would have thought an argument based on it would have appeared there. As a further indication that the evidence gathered by the SEC in its several studies was not the basis of congressional action, neither the House nor the Senate study referred back to them for much support for their conclusion that separation was necessary.[38]

Nor did either Subcommittee come up with any hard evidence of its own prior to publication of the two studies that the conflicts associated with combined brokerage and management were leading to overtrading, or producing questionable participations in block transactions, or resulting in inferior performance, adjusted for risk. The House study justified the House Subcommittee's position on the conflicts of interest involved in combining brokerage and management in only seven footnotes of citations to treatises and articles containing no new empirical information and to a few cases which were, at most, modestly supportive.[39] The Senate study, too, added no new information,[40] except perhaps a suggestion, but not proof, that dumping in block transactions was on the increase.[41] The two Subcommittees simply relied on testimony about

---

[38] The House study referred only to the *Special Study's* discussion of churning in its discussion of why conflicts of interest require separation of brokerage and management. See *House Securities Industry Study*, note 4 *supra*, at 148 ns.4, 5. The Senate study referred to the *Institutional Investor Study*'s findings with respect to portfolio turnover (note 1 *supra*, at 75 n.68), but those findings tended to show that broker-managers were not over-trading (see note 21 *supra*).

[39] *House Securities Industry Study*, note 4 *supra*, at 148-49 ns. 4-10.

[40] This is not to say that the Senate Subcommittee did not try. It sent out over one hundred questionnaires to investment managers, brokers, and others to inquire about institutional membership on exchanges and the effects of the conflict of interest where brokerage and management were combined. The overwhelming sentiment of the respondents was not to separate brokerage and management because, most respondents claimed, there was little evidence of a need to do so. See Hearings on S. 1164 and S. 3347 Before the Subcomm. on Securities of the Senate Comm. on Banking, Housing and Urban Affairs, Pt. II, 92d Cong., 2d Sess. (1972) (hereinafter cited as Senate Institutional Membership Hearings).

[41] See *Senate Securities Industry Study*, note 1 *supra*, at 76, in which it quoted the testimony of the director of the *Institutional Investor Study:*

"The Institutional Investor Study found trades between block positioners and managed accounts to be common during the 1968-69 period studied, absorbing on average three percent of the passive side of all NYSE block trades in excess of $1 million. Other portions of positioned blocks occasionally may find their way into the positioning dealer's managed portfolio(s) via intermediate broker-dealers. The potential for conflict of interest inherent in such practices is considerable and *may be* growing

the potential for abuse[42] to substantiate the need to deal with abuse.

If the justification for separation of brokerage and management on conflict-of-interest grounds was weak on the basis of the evidence the Subcommittees had before them when they published their studies, it was weaker still when one considers that separation reduces the effectiveness of brokers as competitors in the provision of investment management services against bank trust departments, insurance companies, and investment counselors, all of which, incidentally, suffer their own conflicts of interest in carrying out their management responsibilities. Indeed, as a result of the amendment of Section 11(a) to prohibit brokerage firms from executing transactions for managed accounts, the brokerage community reports being less able to market their management services, and a number of management firms have divested themselves of brokerage affiliates.[43] More important, there is no doubt that the Senate and House Subcommittees were aware that legislating a separation of brokerage and management would have anticompetitive consequences on the market for investment management services. The conclusion is thus irresistible that the conflict-of-interest issue was acting as a proxy for other considerations and that it was dressed up to justify action which seemed less demonstrably necessary without it.

Ironically, competition is the issue which explains Congress's decision to amend Section 11(a). But it was not the competition offered by the relatively modest entry of brokerage firms into the investment management business that interested Congress. Rather, the amendment of Section 11(a) was only one more consequence of the attempt by the brokerage firms to prevent full price competition in the provision of brokerage services. The conflict-of-interest issue became a useful tool for Congress to respond to the attack of the brokerage industry, with the support of the SEC, on institutional membership on stock exchanges

---

as some of the more active block positioners expand their management activities." [Emphasis added.]

[42] See id. at 75 ns.69, 70, and at 76 ns.71, 73, 74. It may be generous to say the *House Securities Industry Study*, note 4 *supra*, relied on testimony before the Subcommittee, since it referred to none of it. Nonetheless, witnesses in the House hearings did testify about the conflict-of-interest issue. See, e.g., Hearings on the Study of the Securities Industry Before the Subcomm. on Commerce and Finance of the House Comm. on Interstate and Foreign Commerce, 92d Cong., 2d Sess., Ser. No. 37g, Pt. 8, at 4271-4272, 4274 (1972) (churning); *id.* at 4281 (dumping).

[43] See, e.g., Nagdeman, "Free the Captives?" Barron's, March 8, 1976, p. 3; Wall Street J., Feb. 24, 1976, p. 8, col. 2; Securities Week, Nov. 24, 1975, p. 5.

without permitting that attack to succeed in slowing down institutional progress toward negotiated commission rates.

[b] The brokerage community's public-business argument for exclusion of institutions from the brokerage business

Institutional investors had begun forming brokerage affiliates and joining regional stock exchanges in the mid-1960s to recapture excess commissions otherwise unavailable because of the fixed-rate commission system and the stock exchange anti-rebate rules.[44] The pace of this process began accelerating in the early seventies, pushed along in part by spreading knowledge about how to form a brokerage affiliate,[45] in part by some aggressive marketing by some of the regionals, especially the PBW Stock Exchange,[46] and in part by the belief on the part of some mutual fund managers that they were under a fiduciary duty to recapture commissions as a result of *Moses v. Burgin*.[47] At least up through publication of the *Institutional Investor Study*, the SEC supported and, in many cases, actively encouraged institutional investors to recover commission costs by forming brokerage affiliates.[48] In fact, in the *Institutional Investor Study*, the Commission took the position that, in order to encourage the brokerage industry to adopt unfixed commission rates on institutional orders, barriers to institutional membership on exchanges should be removed.[49] In its interim report, the

---

44 See ¶ 8.02[2][b] at notes 52-57.

45 For example, the state of Connecticut formed a brokerage affiliate to recapture commissions for the state-administered pension funds. Testimony of Treasurer of the State of Connecticut, in Hearings on Fixed Rates and Institutional Membership Before the Subcomm. on Securities of the Senate Comm. on Banking, Housing and Urban Affairs, 93d Cong., 1st Sess. 262 (1973) (hereinafter cited as Senate Fixed-Rate Hearings).

46 See, e.g., Testimony of President of PBW Stock Exchange, Senate Institutional Membership Hearings, note 40 *supra*, at 236. The Exchange fought vigorously but unsuccessfully to prevent the SEC's restricting its membership policies. See PBW Stock Exch. v. SEC, 485 F.2d 718 (3d Cir. 1973), *cert. denied* 416 U.S. 969 (1974).

47 445 F.2d 369 (1st Cir.), *cert. denied sub nom.* Johnson v. Moses, 404 U.S. 994 (1971). This case is discussed extensively above. See ¶ 9.07[2].

48 For example, in *Moses,* the court held management liable because it failed to disclose the substance of meetings with staff members of the SEC who suggested ways in which the fund's underwriter affiliate could recapture brokerage. See *id.* See also *PPI Report,* note 15 *supra,* at 172-173.

49 See *Institutional Investor Study,* note 2 *supra,* Summary Vol., at XX.

Senate Subcommittee expressed itself as being "in full agreement" with the Commission's position.[50]

Having a brokerage affiliate makes commission savings possible only if an institution can execute through its affiliate or have reciprocals directed to it. Thus, the Commission was absolutely right in holding that institutional membership in stock exchanges would exert pressure for introduction of some form of negotiated rates and that the pressure would remain until all barriers to negotiation of commissions on institutional-sized transactions were removed.[51] But brokers were also aware of this fact, and, as the phenomenon of institutions forming their own brokerage firms spread, the traditional brokers became increasingly disquieted by the loss of commission revenues. Furthermore, the loss of institutionally generated commissions was paralleled by two other events which also depressed the revenues of the brokerage industry. The "paperwork crisis" of the late sixties had led to massive fails-to-deliver securities. Coupled with declining securities values, it produced severe strains on the capital position of many brokerage firms.[52] As if in conspiracy, the volume of trading fell off sharply at the same time.[53] Thus, while brokers were facing higher operational costs and experiencing fewer transactions, they were also watching some of their best customers leave them to conduct their own brokerage business.

Brokerage firms could do little about trading volume, and it would be a painful and slow process for them to improve operational efficiency, but they could regain some of the lost institutional business if they could force institutions out of exchange membership, or at least away from executing for their own accounts or recapturing commissions either directly or through reciprocals. With the New York Stock Exchange at the vanguard, the brokerage community began selling a theme which would remain essentially unchanged throughout the period the 1975 Securities Amendments Act was in gestation. The brokers argued that brokerage firms should be required to carry on primarily a "public" business to avoid disruption of established trading patterns and to preserve the fairness of and public confidence in the marketplace. More precisely, the brokers expressed concern that institutional exchange

---

[50] The report quoted the SEC's letter of transmittal in the *Institutional Investor Study,* note 2 *supra. Interim Senate Study,* note 29 *supra,* at 61.

[51] See note 49 *supra.*

[52] See, e.g., *House Securities Industry Study,* note 4 *supra,* at 9-12; *Senate Securities Industry Study,* note 1 *supra,* at 28-39; SEC, *Study of Unsafe and Unsound Practices of Brokers and Dealers,* H.R. Doc. No. 231, 92d Cong., 1st Sess. (1971).

[53] *Id.*

membership would lead to a deterioration of the auction market in favor of a dealer market and to unhealthy concentration of economic power in the market to the disadvantage of public investors and institutional customers without brokerage connections.

If the brokerage community succeeded in pressing this argument, it would regain a good deal of the revenue lost through institutional membership, particularly if some form of fixed rates could be preserved. Even in the event of fully negotiated rates, however, the traditional brokers would still have virtually all the institutional business since, with brokerage and management separated for institutions, the only reason an institutional manager would maintain a brokerage affiliate would be to compete actively as a broker for public business. But, as the brokers well knew, few institutions had formed brokerage affiliates for the purpose of diversifying into a separate profit-seeking activity. They had done so to recapture commissions.[54] If the brokerage community could obtain a rule requiring a significant proportion of a broker's business to be with unaffiliated customers, most institutions would disband or sell off their brokerage affiliates.

To appreciate fully why conflict of interest became such an issue, it is necessary to trace through some of the consequences of a public-business rule. To concede any validity at all to the position that widespread institutional membership on exchanges will act to the overall detriment of the investing public necessarily promotes an imbalance between the competitive position of brokers and that of other investment managers in seeking and maintaining investment management business. If brokers can credit a part of their commission income against advisory fees or charge lower advisory fees, they can attract clients by offering lower management costs. Institutions barred from exchange membership, on the other hand, cannot. Since brokers are not inherently more worthy investment managers than other types of managers, any form of public-business rule limiting institutional membership would provide an undeserved competitive advantage to broker-managers and would therefore necessitate a complementary reform for eliminating the disparity thus created in favor of brokers.

[c] Eliminating the broker-manager's competitive edge: The public-interest rationale

An excellent method for reaching a competitive balance, and one which events were then moving toward, is to adopt fully negotiated

---

[54] See, e.g., Testimony of Treasurer of the State of Connecticut, in Senate Fixed-Rate Hearings, note 45 *supra*.

rates and thus deprive brokerage firms of excess commissions to apply against advisory fees. But when the Senate and House Subcommittees began considering the institutional membership issue, it was not at all clear that fully negotiated rates would be introduced, at least within a reasonable period of time. The Studies of both Subcommittees agreed to defer legislative action pending rate developments at the industry and regulatory levels. Moreover, the two Studies differed on the urgency of going to fully negotiated rates. The Senate study took the position that elimination of fixed commissions on large transactions down to a $100,000 breakpoint "may ultimately lead to their elimination on all orders." [55] The House study was firm in insisting on passage to fully negotiated rates, but it offered no timetable for doing so, threatening legislation only if the industry did not "voluntarily continue to reduce the breakpoint until all fixed rates are abolished." [56]

Thus, at the time of publication of the congressional studies, a fully negotiated rate system was not certain enough to eliminate the need for a response to the competitive imbalance that would be created by restricting institutional membership. Some other means for responding had to be found. The NYSE, armed with a special report on the securities markets it had commissioned William McChesney Martin to write, offered a package proposition that would restrict institutional membership and forbid members from crediting commissions against management fees.[57] It must have taken some courage to make this proposal, since its most obvious effect would have been to increase the revenues of member firms without any apparent benefit to the investors who would suffer the increased costs. Nonetheless, the NYSE had no real alternative. The only way to remove the competitive advantage of broker-managers under any system of fixed rates was to prohibit executions for managed accounts. Since some of the most important members of the NYSE were offering investment management services, the Exchange would not want to support that solution, at least not initially.

Of course, Congress, not subject to the same constraints as the brokers, would have no problem with the device of separating brokerage from management if that were the most convenient means of dealing

---

[55] *Senate Securities Industry Study,* note 1 *supra,* at 62.

[56] *House Securities Industry Study,* note 4 *supra,* at 145.

[57] See Submission of the NYSE, in Senate Institutional Membership Hearings, note 40 *supra,* at 618, 626-627 (hereinafter cited as *Martin Report*). For tactical reasons, discussed at notes 61-65 *infra,* the *Martin Report* also recommended separation of control of investment companies by brokerage firms.

with the institutional membership issue. But if Congress was going to separate brokerage from management to deny brokers the strategic advantage of using commission income to offset management fees, it needed an excuse to do so. Thus enters the conflict-of-interest theory. If the conflict of interest inherent in combining brokerage and management could be elevated to a public danger warranting their separation, many of the complexities surrounding the institutional membership issue drop away. No manager would have an inherent advantage based on access to commission income. Institutional managers would be happy because most of them never wanted to be in the brokerage business in the first place. The separation of brokerage and management would also act to the competitive advantage of managers who were not brokers by making the management business less attractive to brokers. The only loss suffered by restricting institutional membership would be the pressure such membership exerted on the brokerage community to adapt to negotiated rates. But with the elimination of fixed rates on institutional-sized transactions, the value of institutional membership on exchanges would no longer be large enough to be much of an incentive to the brokerage community to move further. The total elimination of fixed rates would have to come from regulatory or legislative prodding, not from the threat of institutional membership. Moreover, the preservation of a low fixed-rate level was actually in the interest of many institutions which, relieved thereby of the burden of being at a competitive disadvantage for management services, could use excess commissions to purchase supplementary services.[58]

While this explanation of how the conflict-of-interest issue came to spawn amended Section 11(a) of the Exchange Act is plausible, until it is tested it cannot be accepted as accurate. If it is consistent with events, the record should show at least three things: (1) The timing of the entry into the legislative calculus of the conflict-of-interest issue as grounds for separating brokerage from management coincided with maturation of the public-business issue into a matter requiring a legislative response; (2) support for separation of brokerage and management on conflict-of-interest grounds came principally from those who had the most to gain by restricting broker access to the investment management business; and (3) the draft legislation proposed by Congress responded more to the issue of institutional business than it did to the conflict-of-interest problems associated with combinations of brokerage and management. On all three counts, the record is convincing

---

[58] See ¶ 9.02[1] at note 23 and ¶ 9.02[3] at note 62.

that the conflict-of-interest issue was more convenient than it was compelling.

[i] *Timing of the Conflict-of-Interest Theory:* About the time the *Institutional Investor Study* was published, the New York Stock Exchange commissioned the *Martin Report*,[59] a study intended to make a broad examination of the NYSE and its rules and procedures, and to recommend changes which, in the public interest, would enhance the capital-raising ability of the Exchange. The *Martin Report* was presented on August 5, 1971,[60] and, among other matters, it dealt directly with institutional membership and brokerage and money management. Making an issue of the public business theme for the first time, the report recommended three things with respect to the membership/management problem: (1) NYSE Rule 318, requiring the primary purpose of every member to be the "transaction of business as a broker or dealer in securities," should be preserved; (2) member firms should be required to divest themselves of control of investment companies; and (3) members should be prohibited from crediting commissions against advisory fees.[61]

If one's perspective is to preserve as much of the traditional prerogatives of the Exchange while appearing responsive to the public interest, the *Martin Report* recommendations made eminent good sense. Rule 318 became elevated from a refusal-to-deal rule having serious antitrust implications[62] to a rule protecting the investing public from the adverse consequences of institutional domination of the securities markets. Divestiture of investment company control was tactically sound because it would remove an obvious source of antagonism toward money management by brokers. Moreover, since investment companies were the only institutions with which NYSE brokers were affiliated, it gave the

---

[59] See note 57 *supra.*

[60] Although the Report initially established the basis for the NYSE's strategy in dealing with Congress and the SEC, it was roundly and effectively criticized on several of its major points very soon after it was published. See Folk, "Restructuring the Securities Markets—The Martin Report: A Critique," 57 Va. L. Rev. 1315 (1971). Particularly poorly received were its recommendations to retain a fixed-rate system and conditionally to limit institutional membership. The Senate study specifically rejected the *Martin Report* approach in these matters (see *Senate Securities Industry Study,* note 1 *supra,* at 78-80), and by 1973, the NYSE had shifted its strategy in recognition of this. See discussion *infra.*

[61] [1970-1971 Transfer Binder] CCH Fed. Sec. L. Rep. ¶ 78,184, at 80,562.

[62] See, e.g., *Senate Securities Industry Study,* note 1 *supra,* at 219-240.

NYSE membership the appearance of accommodation by demonstrating a willingness to surrender an apparently lucrative activity in the public interest. Actually, however, with the collapse of the performance cult of the sixties,[63] and the tightening of the Investment Company Act's demands on independent directors in 1970,[64] managing such companies was no longer the attraction it earlier had been. The growth area for broker-managers was pension management, and the *Martin Report*'s recommendations left pension clients untouched.[65]

Finally, the recommendation that members not be allowed to credit commissions against management fees was especially ingenious. In one swoop, it offered a way to remove the competitive advantage that restricting institutional membership afforded brokers; it eliminated the appearance of circumventing the anti-rebate rules created by crediting commissions against management fees; it permitted brokers to retain their competitive advantage stemming from the value some clients attached to the closeness of broker-managers to the market; and it enhanced broker revenues by forcing institutional investors to pay higher commissions.

The *Martin Report*'s recommendations with respect to the membership/management problem were simply too transparent to stand much chance of adoption, especially given its stand on fixed rates. As the *Senate Securities Industry Study* pointed out, with fixed commissions but unfixed management fees a broker-manager could still preserve his competitive advantage by taking anticipated commission income into account in setting his management fee.[66] Furthermore, the fixed-rate system was by then well recognized as the instigator of the push for institutions to seek exchange membership as well as the source of many of the conflicts of interest arising out of the reciprocal practices in which institutions had to engage to take advantage of the exchange memberships. By refusing to connect preservation of fixed rates with the problem of institutional membership, the *Martin Report*'s recommendations on institutional membership were doomed from the outset.[67]

---

[63] For an interesting, if somewhat narrow and unsympathetic, account of the fortunes of the mutual fund industry during the sixties, see J. Brooks, *The Go-Go Years* (1973).

[64] See Sections 10(a)-10(d), 15(a)-15(c), 15 U.S.C. §§ 80(a)-10(a) through 10(d), 80(a)-15(a) through 15(c).

[65] See, e.g., Mattlin, "Prospecting the Hottest Investment Frontier," 5 Institutional Investor 36 (Aug. 1971). See also *Senate Securities Industry Study*, note 1 *supra*, at 78 n.84.

[66] *Senate Securities Industry Study*, note 1 *supra*, at 80.

[67] See *id*. See also Folk, "Restructuring the Securities Markets—The Martin Report: A Critique," 57 Va. L. Rev. 1315 (1971).

But, despite the fate of its recommendations, the *Martin Report* did succeed in making a credible issue out of the public-business theme. The SEC *Policy Statement*, albeit without specifically mentioning the *Martin Report*, took the position that "membership in the market system should be confined to firms whose primary purpose is to serve the public as brokers or market makers." [68] Based on this, the Commission proposed to adopt uniform rules restricting exchange membership to firms doing a public business. Although the SEC tried to make it appear that this represented a normal evolution of regulatory policy,[69] it was, in fact, a new departure, placing the Commission for the first time behind an operating principle having an effect comparable to the NYSE's primary-purpose rule,[70] and doing so in large part by making the same public policy argument raised in the *Martin Report*.[71] That the SEC's position

---

[68] *Policy Statement*, note 25 *supra*, at 65,622.

[69] See Adoption of Rule 19b-2, SEC Securities Exchange Act Release No. 9950 (Jan. 16, 1973), [1972-1973 Transfer Binder] CCH Fed. Sec. L. Rep. ¶ 79,178, and Rep. No. 460, at ns.3, 92 (hereinafter cited as Adoption of Rule 19b-2).

[70] The mechanism by which the NYSE rule operated was a so-called parent test that excluded from membership firms which were subsidiaries of other entities. The SEC rejected this, since it was obviously discriminatory against institutional brokerage affiliates, and substituted an affiliate test which, on its face, seemed to apply to all equally. Measured by its effectiveness, however, the definition of affiliate was functionally equivalent to the parent test in excluding brokerage firms formed by institutional investors. See notes 77-79 *infra*.

[71] The Senate Subcommittee said that the SEC had proceeded from "premises quite different from those advanced by Martin." *Senate Securities Industry Study*, note 1 *supra*, at 80. The *Martin Report*, note 57 *supra*, had argued that institutional membership should be considered apart from the fixed-rate question, whereas the SEC had argued that they were connected. In this respect, the Subcommittee was correct, but the difference was irrelevant as far as the respective proposals of the *Martin Report* and the SEC on institutional membership were concerned. The premise from which both began was that management of institutional accounts, except investment companies, should not be restricted so long as the administrative control of brokerage firms was not reposed in any significant sense in institutional clients. The *Martin Report*'s contention that fixed rates and institutional membership be considered separately was a ploy made necessary by the report's determination to support a form of fixed rates. But it was also a ploy doomed to fail, something the SEC fully recognized. Since institutional membership could be attacked on the basis of the public-purpose theory without pretending that institutional membership was not intimately tied into the fixed-rate issue, and since the SEC was already committed to negotiated rates on institutional-sized transactions, the SEC had no need to follow the whole *Martin Report* line.

was new was noted in the Subcommittee's *Interim Senate Study*. Though issued only two days after the SEC *Policy Statement*, and therefore unable fully to respond to it, it described the Subcommittee's concern with the potential for unequal treatment contained in the Commission's position and it announced the Subcommittee's intention to conduct hearings on the Commission's proposal.[72]

It was in between publication of the *Policy Statement* and the House study that the critical events leading ultimately to the amendment of Section 11(a) occurred. In the spring of 1972, the SEC began moving to implement the conclusion it reached in the *Policy Statement* that institutional membership on exchanges be restricted. The chairman of the SEC wrote a series of letters to each national securities exchange requesting data and opinions on the institutional-membership question.[73] He presented a white paper on institutional membership to the House and Senate Subcommittees, significantly expanding on the public-purpose principle previously floated in the *Martin Report* and picked up in the *Policy Statement*.[74] In the *White Paper*, the chairman stated that the Commission was leaning toward a percentage test for exchange membership that would require 80 percent of all brokerage business to be executed with nonaffiliated accounts.[75] A month later, the Commission requested each national securities exchange to adopt the substance of a proposed rule limiting membership to those conducting business as suggested in the white paper.[76] Finally, on August 3, 1972, having orchestrated developments as much as possible, the Commission proposed Rule 19b-2, which would have restricted exchange membership on any national securities exchange to those firms doing at least 80 percent of their business with unaffiliated accounts.[77] As is relevant to this discussion, the Rule was adopted substantially as proposed.[78]

There could not have been any doubt that some congressional response to Rule 19b-2 would be forthcoming. Taking a cue from the *Martin Report*, the Commission had structured the Rule to make virtually every institution ineligible for membership on an exchange but to preserve the freedom of broker-managers to handle as many institutional clients as they could except for investment companies. Rule 19b-

---

72 See *Interim Senate Study*, note 29 *supra*, at 68.
73 See Adoption of Rule 19b-2, note 69 *supra*, at ns.105-108.
74 Senate Institutional Membership Hearings, note 40 *supra*, at 197-230.
75 *Id.* at 226.
76 SEC Securities Exchange Act Release No. 9623 (May 30, 1972).
77 SEC Securities Exchange Act Release No. 9716 (Aug. 3, 1972), [1972-1973 Transfer Binder] CCH Fed. Sec. L. Rep. ¶ 78,929.
78 See Adoption of Rule 19b-2, note 69 *supra*.

2 accomplished this by defining public business as unaffiliated business, by defining affiliated business not to include any person, except an investment company, not in a control relationship with the broker, and by defining control to mean only the right to participate in over 25 percent of the client's profits or the ownership of over 25 percent of the client's voting securities.[79] Thus, under Rule 19b-2, a member broker could act solely for a single pension fund or a single endowment fund or any other single client over which he had discretionary authority or substantial influence in portfolio selection so long as his relationship with the client did not fall within the Rule's technical definition of control. Yet a pension fund would not be permitted to form a brokerage affiliate and join an exchange, even though it might represent thousands of pensioners.

---

[79] As finally adopted in Rule 19b-2, the definition of "affiliated person" reads as follows:

"(b) For purposes of this Rule, an 'affiliated person' of a member shall include

"(1) any person directly or indirectly controlling, controlled by or under common control with such member, whether by contractual arrangement or otherwise, provided that the right to exercise investment discretion with respect to an account, without more, shall not constitute control;

"(2) any principal officer, stockholder or partner of such member or any person in whose account such person has a direct or material indirect beneficial interest; and

"(3) any investment company of which such member, or any person controlling, controlled by or under common control with such member, is an investment adviser within the meaning of the Investment Company Act of 1940.

"A person shall be presumed to control another person, for purposes of this Rule, if such person has a right to participate to the extent of more than 25 percent in the profits of such other person or owns beneficially, directly or indirectly, more than 25 percent of the outstanding voting securities of such person."

Adoption of Rule 19b-2, note 69 *supra*, at 190.

It was no accident that the rule had the effect of enacting the *Martin Report* recommendations. In the accompanying release, the SEC frankly and unabashedly acknowledged that Rule 19b-2 was intended to be protective of the brokerage community. It explicitly recognized the arguments against competitive advantage in favor of brokers, but instead of contesting those arguments on the merits, the Commission took the position that other institutional managers have their own tie-in arrangements between management services and other services, meaning, apparently, they had no standing for objection. See *id*. ns.441-447.

But if adverse reaction to Proposed Rule 19b-2 was inevitable, it nonetheless made some concession to the public-purpose issue difficult to avoid. The SEC had put its professional reputation behind the need for a public-business approach to membership on securities exchanges. Although the Commission's arguments in support of its position were hypothetical and doubtful—the chairman of the Senate Subcommittee debunked the arguments of the *White Paper* virtually line by line when it was presented at the Senate Institutional Membership Hearings[80]— the very fact the SEC was taking such a strong position on institutional membership meant that Congress would either have to acknowledge the validity of the public-business theme or implicitly declare that its expert agency in the area of securities regulation did not know what it was talking about. Moreover, Rule 19b-2 took the issue of institutional membership out of the realm of the abstract and put it into a particular context. For Congress to reject the underlying public-business premise of Rule 19b-2, it would have to fashion remedial legislation which did not create worse consequences than those traceable to the Rule.

The only practical way for Congress to accept the SEC's public-business theme without tolerating the favoritism shown by Rule 19b-2 for broker-managers was to eliminate all brokerage business for managed accounts. Such an approach would be responsive to public-business concerns because brokerage firms, whether affiliated with institutional investors or not, would be forced to transact all brokerage business with outsiders. Furthermore, such an approval would be re-

---

[80] The Subcommittee Chairman told the Chairman of the SEC that he had provided no concrete example of trading abuses such as short-swing speculation, delay of public executions, or interference with the specialist function; that the Subcommittee's evidence indicated that institutional membership had improved the regional markets; that the SEC's conception of public business permitted brokerage firms to serve nothing but institutional accounts, whereas an institutional member executing for thousands of beneficiaries of a pension fund or shareholders of a mutual fund would be regarded as doing a private business; that the Commission's position led inevitably to the conclusion that institutions had an obligation to subsidize the brokerage business since, without a bar to membership, they would be executing for their own accounts; that institutional interest in joining an exchange as demonstrated to that point belied any early rush by institutions to obtain exchange membership and that, on the contrary, most institutions would avoid doing their own brokerage as soon as fixed rates were removed. See Senate Institutional Membership Hearings, note 40 *supra,* at 141-144. The Chairman of the SEC responded to this criticism by saying that restrictions on trading for a member's own account were necessary to preserve the appearance of fairness as well as actual fairness in the execution of exchange transactions. *Id.* at 233-235.

sponsive to the favoritism problem by forcing all investment managers, brokers included, to buy execution services at the going rates.

The only problem with this approach is that it necessarily separates brokerage from management. Unless combining those services could be shown to be an evil in its own right, Congress would have been forced to prove that the danger from institutional membership was so great as to justify separating them anyway. This would have been a formidable task for Congress since neither Subcommittee really believed that institutional membership was much of a threat to fair and orderly functioning of exchange trading in the first place.[81] But if combined brokerage and management could be shown to be an evil, Congress could munificently eliminate two evils with one thrust. The timing of the entry of conflict of interest as an issue strongly suggests it was to serve this very purpose.

This is the chronology of key events:

(1) March 10, 1971—Publication of the *Institutional Investor Study*: insufficient evidence that the conflict of interest in combined brokerage and management warrants their separation.

(2) August 5, 1971—Publication of the *Martin Report*: brokerage and management should not be separated, but brokers should be required to do a public business.

(3) February 2, 1972—*Policy Statement*: SEC will not act to separate brokerage and management but will take steps to require brokers to do a public business.

(4) February 4, 1972—Senate Subcommittee *Interim Senate Study*: rules of access to exchange membership should apply equally and without anticompetitive effect; restrictions on access on conflict-of-interest grounds must take into account all accounts over which broker exercises investment discretion.

(5) March 14, 1972—S. 3347 introduced by chairman of Senate Subcommittee: SEC may not limit institutional access to membership on an exchange until one year after fixed commission rates drop below $100,000.

---

[81] When opening the Senate Institutional Membership Hearings, the Subcommittee Chairman said:

"Despite the substantial impact and fundamental policy implications of its assertions, the SEC has not shown a public interest or need which would justify the elimination of institutional membership at this time."

Id. at 2. See also *House Securities Industry Study,* note 4 *supra,* at 153-154.

(6) April 20, 1972—*White Paper* by chairman of SEC: membership on an exchange should be limited to firms doing at least 80 percent public business; conflict of interest not mentioned as an issue.

(7) August 3, 1973—Rule 19b-2 proposed: SEC formalizes 80 percent-20 percent test for membership on an exchange.

On August 23, 1972, when the House Subcommittee published its *Securities Industry Study*, full separation of brokerage and management on conflict-of-interest grounds became a matter of public policy for the first time. Significantly, in the very same section of the Study in which the Subcommittee concluded that the conflict-of-interest problem necessitated the separation of brokerage and management (without uncovering any materially new or different evidence justifying such action), it rejected the SEC's 80 percent-20 percent test, primarily because of its possible anticompetitive effects, though the possibility that brokers would churn unaffiliated accounts to meet the 80 percent figure was also mentioned.[82] This suggests that competition rather than conflict of interest was the principal motivating factor for the Subcommittee's position. Particularly in view of the substance of the Subcommittee's arguments on the conflict-of-interest issue, the discovery of the need to separate brokerage and management on conflict-of-interest grounds was simply too convenient to be believed unskeptically.

There are additional reasons for suspecting from the timing of the conflict-of-interest issue that it was tied more to the SEC's attempt through Rule 19b-2 to impede institutional incursions into the domain of the brokerage community than to a need to protect investors from a real danger from conflicts of interest. The SEC adopted Rule 19b-2 almost five months *after* the House Study.[83] Yet a two-hundred-page release accompanying adoption of the rule made no mention of conflict of interest as grounds for separating brokerage and management, except to reject recommendations for a 100 percent-0 percent test on those grounds.[84] Of course, the Commission could not adopt Rule 19b-2 if the conflict-of-interest problem really was severe, since the rule permitted brokers to do all their business for accounts over which they had investment discretion or substantial influence. On the contrary, the Commission specifically rejected investment discretion as a test of control to define affiliated status, and did so without referring to conflict

---

[82] See *id*. at 148-153.
[83] Adoption of Rule 19b-2, note 69 *supra*.
[84] *Id*. at 138.

of interest as a problem.[85] Thus, if one assumes the Commission was acting in good faith, it is not possible to believe that the Commission was suppressing or ignoring evidence that investors were actually being injured extensively through combinations of brokerage and management. Indeed, on the only occasion on which the release spoke of conflict of interest in a particular context, it summarily dismissed the House Study's stated concern that the 80 percent-20 percent rule would lead to churning.[86]

Nonetheless, despite the Commission's refusal to treat the conflict-of-interest issue as worthy of response, the Senate Subcommittee, reversing its earlier position, concluded that brokerage and management had to be entirely separated. Again, the timing of the decision colors the credibility of the conflict-of-interest rationale. The Commission's decision to adopt Rule 19b-2 came in the face of the direct opposition that the chairman of the Senate Subcommittee had expressed the previous spring.[87] It came also in the face of the House Study's explicit rejection of the proposed rule, and it made no attempt to reconcile either Subcommittee's stated concern with the competitive advantage it afforded broker-managers. Only after the Commission demonstrated its intent not to compromise on giving institutional managers equal opportunity to offset commissions against other management costs through exchange memberships did the Senate Subcommittee act to separate brokerage and management on conflict-of-interest grounds. Two days after the SEC adopted Rule 19b-2, the chairman of the Senate Subcommittee introduced S. 470, which would have prohibited a broker-dealer from executing a transaction on any exchange of which it was a member "for its own account, the account of any affiliate . . . or any managed institutional account." [88] Shortly thereafter, the Subcommittee issued its study recommending total separation of brokerage and management and the chairman of the House Subcommittee introduced H.R. 5050, which paralleled S. 470 in this respect.[89]

[ii] *Support for Separation of Brokerage and Management:* The question of whether to separate brokerage and management, though

---

85 *Id.* n.435.

86 *Id.* n.409.

87 See note 80 *supra.*

88 S. 470, 93d Cong., 1st Sess. § 2 (Jan. 18, 1973).

89 H.R. 5050, 93d Cong., 1st Sess. § 205 (March 1, 1973). Instead of reaching managed institution accounts directly, like S. 470, this bill defined affiliated person to include managed accounts and exempted natural persons from application of the section.

nominally a question directed at the public interest, plainly involves the private interest of all types of investment managers. The discussion to this point has already shown how the NYSE turned the public-business principle into an argument that, in the public interest, affiliated brokerage be separated from management. Whether or not the public interest would have been served, the NYSE position also promoted the private interests of many exchange members because it would have permitted them to continue their management activities unabated, except with respect to investment companies, while requiring institutional investors to use commercial brokers to execute transactions.[90] If the conflict-of-interest issue really was a mechanism of convenience rather than an evil requiring remedy, one should expect also that, like the NYSE, other parties to the controversy would argue conflict of interest mostly as it served their own purposes to do so.

Some investment managers had no intention of entering the brokerage business unless absolutely forced to do so. Bank trust departments, for example, would face serious practical, legal, and political problems

---

[90] It is an interesting sidelight to the brokerage-and-management issue that, once it became clear that the NYSE position and Rule 19b-2 were doomed, the Exchange did a complete reversal and came down foursquare against any brokerage for either affiliated *or* managed accounts. See, e.g., Testimony of NYSE Panel, in Hearings on H.R. 5050 and H.R. 340 Before the Subcomm. on Commerce and Finance of the House Comm. on Interstate and Foreign Commerce, 92d Cong., 1st Sess., Ser. No. 52, Pt. 3, at 889-890 (1973) (hereinafter cited as House 1973 Amendments Hearings). Having lost that battle, but recognizing that the public-purpose issue had been fashioned into something formidable, the NYSE moved behind the 100 percent-0 percent test coupled with a requirement that all transactions in listed stocks be executed on an exchange. The supposed public interest in having brokers do a public business, the NYSE contended, meant that the public should have a right to know about all business that was being transacted in listed securities, and the Exchange requested legislation to that effect. See Hearings on S. 2519 Before the Subcomm. on Securities of the Senate Comm. on Banking, Housing and Urban Affairs, 93d Cong., 1st Sess. (1973). Of course, that such a rule would have destroyed the third and fourth markets and most likely have made the NYSE the dominant force in a restructured national exchange did not escape the NYSE's attention. See, e.g., Welles, "The Big Board Takes the Offensive," 7 Institutional Investor 49 (March 1973). Nor did it escape Congress' (see Staff Report on Off-Exchange-Trading Amendment to S. 2519, reprinted in Securities Week, March 4, 1974, p. 2a), and this strategy ultimately failed also. See discussion of the reception given that amendment in Wall Street Letter, March 11, 1974, pp. 1-2.

In fairness to the NYSE, it is important to note that it was concerned over the possibility that institutional managers, particularly insurance com-

if they chose to form broker affiliates. Among other things, they have commercial relations with many broker-dealers; the Glass-Steagall Act is a possible bar to such activity[91]; and even if problems such as these could be brushed aside, there is little doubt that a move by banks into the brokerage business would raise strong political opposition, leading to legislative review of bank investment management activities, with possibly unpredictable consequences for banks beyond the brokerage question.[92] Professional investment counsel, chiefly characterized by their independence from all relationships which could complicate total concentration on portfolio management and financial advice, comprised another industry group that wanted no involvement in the brokerage

---

panies, would try to comply with the 80 percent-20 percent test by seeking nonaffiliated institutional business. This would have the effect of siphoning business away from the brokerage community. See Bleakley, "Institutional Membership: The Plot Continues to Thicken," 7 Institutional Investor 66 (March 1973). Because members of the securities industry were also fearful of entry into the brokerage business by banks (see, e.g., Cole, "Should Banks Be Allowed a Stockbroker Role," New York Times, Oct. 28, 1974, p. 49, col. 1), they came to support the 100 percent-0 percent test. After adoption of Section 11(a), the Securities Industry Association decided to support the 100 percent-0 percent test to inhibit growth of a dealer market, a phenomenon which obviously would cut back substantially on the revenues of smaller firms which do not engage in market making to a significant degree. See Securities Week, April 19, 1976, p. 1.

But though the NYSE was willing to sacrifice its members who were managers for the greater good of all, the members affected by separation of brokerage and management were not so accommodating. See, e.g., Testimony of Chairman of Donaldson, Lufkin & Jenrette, House 1973 Amendments Hearings, *supra,* Pt. 4, at 1738, 1742-1743. And, in contrast to its position after Section 11(a) was amended, the Securities Industry Association in particular argued for a primary-purpose test that would permit brokers to continue to manage institutional accounts. See *id.* Pt. 2, at 662, 699-670; Senate Fixed-Rate Hearings, note 45 *supra,* at 379-391.

[91] See House 1973 Amendments Hearings, note 90 *supra,* at 793, 794; Adoption of Rule 19b-2, note 69 *supra,* at n.445. Even if the Glass-Steagall Act were not applicable to bank brokerage activities, bankers would become subject to SEC jurisdiction, an unappealing consequence.

[92] Immediately upon completion of its work on the Securities Acts Amendments, the Senate Subcommittee on Securities turned to investigating the need for legislation dealing with the securities activities of banks. See Wall Street Letter, Oct. 6, 1975, p. 1; Hearings on Brokerage and Related Commercial Bank Services Before the Subcomm. on Securities of the Senate Comm. on Banking, Housing, and Urban Affairs, 94th Cong., 2d Sess. (1976). See also SEC, *Initial Report on Bank Securities Activities, Pursuant to Section 11A(e) of the Securities Exchange Act of 1934* (Jan. 3, 1977).

business. Their standards of practice explicitly exclude participation in profits arising from securities transactions carried out for clients.[93] It is in the interest of managers such as these to eliminate the competitive advantage brokers had in offsetting management fees with commission income. It is also in their interest to get a total separation of brokerage and management, since broker-managers are less effective competitors if they cannot use their execution capabilities to support management activities. While legislation to separate brokerage and management would be difficult to obtain on the grounds it improves the competitive position of banks and investment counsel, it could be supported by a public-interest rationale. It is not necessary to impugn the sincerity of the banks and investment counsel to note that they fully supported separation of brokerage and management on conflict-of-interest grounds.[94] That their own interests would be served thereby does suggest that their opinions about the degree of danger not be taken as the last word.

But other investment managers, mostly insurance companies anxious to expand management services to pension funds, were willing to operate brokerage affiliates if that was necessary to help them market their management services more effectively. The critical problem to be resolved from their point of view was the elimination of the competitive advantage broker-managers enjoyed, and they did not camouflage their concern. Thus, after the SEC proposed Rule 19b-2 but before S. 470 and H.R. 5050 were introduced, the American Insurance Association (AIA)[95] and the American Life Convention and Life Insurance Association of America (ALC-LIAA)[96] strongly took the position that their constituents should have access to exchange membership on an equiv-

---

[93] See Investment Counsel Association of America, Inc., "Standards of Practice for Member Firms" (Nov. 16, 1972), reprinted in House 1973 Amendments Hearings, note 90 *supra,* at 749-750. Not all investment counsel, as defined by the ICAA, adhere to the separation idea, however.

[94] See Testimony of the American Bankers Association, in Senate Fixed-Rate Hearings, note 45 *supra,* at 283-285; House 1973 Amendments Hearings, note 90 *supra,* Pt. 2, at 783, 788; Submission of American Bankers Association, in Senate Institutional Membership Hearings, note 40 *supra,* at 445; Testimony of Investment Counsel Association of America, in Senate Fixed-Rate Hearings, note 45 *supra,* at 567; House 1973 Amendments Hearings, note 90 *supra,* at 740-758; Submission of Investment Counsel Association of America, in Senate Institutional Membership Hearings, note 40 *supra,* at 694-696.

[95] See Testimony of AIA, in Senate Institutional Membership Hearings, note 40 *supra,* Pt. 1, at 9-16.

[96] Testimony of ALC and LIAA, *id.* at 87-96.

alent basis with commercial brokers. To the specific question of whether brokerage and management should be separated on conflict-of-interest grounds, the ALC and LIAA answered that disclosure and regulation were adequate to police such conflicts.[97] The response of the AIA was even more direct. It stated that, while it was more logical to deal with the conflict-of-interest problem through disclosure and thereby promote competition in the provision of investment management services, the Association would insist on separation of brokerage and management "if any restrictions are placed upon the development of our brokerage affiliates." [98]

After S. 470 and H.R. 5050 were proposed, the insurers shifted their position. It was plain that if those bills led to completed legislation, the competitive advantage brokers enjoyed from denying exchange membership to brokerage affiliates would largely disappear. Moreover, although it might not serve the public interest with respect to competition in the provision of investment management services, separation of brokerage and management would make brokers less capable competitors, to the benefit of the insurers and other investment managers. In any event, the AIA came out fully in support of Section 205 of H.R. 5050, designed to prevent brokers from executing for managed or controlled accounts on the exchanges of which they were members.[99] Indeed, the AIA proposed an antireciprocal provision to prevent brokers from entering into mutual arrangements to feed each other brokerage.[100] The American Life Insurance Association (successor to the ALC-LIAA) took the same position.[101] But again, the record shows that the concern of both organizations was to eliminate the competitive advantage of broker-managers. Each tied its support for the restriction on institutional membership in Section 205 of the bill to the implementation of Section 202, the provision restricting fixed rates. The insurers urged that both provisions take effect on the same date, a position which is obviously directed to competitive standing rather than conflict of interest.[102]

Finally, Congress also received opinions from those responsible to

---

[97] Submission of ALC and LIAA, *id.,* Pt. 2, at 474-475.

[98] Submission of AIA, *id.* at 447.

[99] See House 1973 Amendments Hearings, note 90 *supra,* at 718.

[100] *Id.* at 722.

[101] *Id.* at 768-769. See also Testimony of ALIA, in Senate Fixed-Rate Hearings, note 45 *supra,* at 288, 289-291.

[102] The AIA wanted any ban on institutional membership to be linked to total elimination of fixed rates. See House 1973 Amendments Hearings, note 90 *supra,* at 738-739. The ALIA would have been satisfied so long as fixed rates were limited to trades below a $100,000 breakpoint. *Id.* at 769.

certain institutional investors, such as trustees of pension funds and investment managers serving only mutual fund complexes. These managers are generally not in competition with other investment managers. The trustees of many pension funds, to a greater or lesser extent, make their own investment decisions, though many also rely extensively on other investment managers for support. The investment advisers to mutual fund complexes especially have to rely mostly on their own investment judgment, though even they may obtain supplementary research and advice from outside sources.[103]

The attitude of these institutional investor representatives toward the brokerage and management issue depended on how strongly they felt about operating a brokerage affiliate in order to save money for the pension funds and mutual funds for which they are responsible. If a brokerage affiliate had been formed solely to recapture commissions under fixed rates, the affiliated institution wanted equal access for institutions and no separation of brokerage and management, at least until the introduction of negotiated rates.[104] If an institution preferred using broker-managers, either because it believed brokers to be better managers or because it believed broker-managers had the ability to execute efficiently, it opposed separation of brokerage and management.[105] If an institution had no intention of forming a brokerage affiliate or trading through a broker-manager, it supported separation of brokerage and

---

[103] Any person contractually furnishing investment advisory services to an investment company via a person contractually obliged to provide such services to the company is a statutory investment adviser under Investment Company Act § 2(a)(20) (15 U.S.C. § 80a-2(a)(20)). Thus, in an extreme case, a person regularly rendering investment advice to an investment company for the purpose of influencing the investment decisions of the company may be deemed to be rendering such advice pursuant to a contract. It is unlawful to serve as investment adviser if an advisory contract has not been properly approved (see Investment Company Act § 15(a), 15 U.S.C. § 80(a)-15(a)) and may be an assignment of the primary advisory contract, in which case that contract terminates. Cf. Lutz v. Boas, 39 Del. Ch. 585, 171 A.2d 381 (1961).

[104] See, e.g., Testimony of the Treasurer of Connecticut, in Senate Fixed-Rate Hearings, note 45 *supra,* at 262-281. (The State of Connecticut had formed its own brokerage affiliate.) Submission of Secretary of Commerce of Ohio, in House 1973 Amendments Hearings, note 90 *supra,* Pt. 4, at 1736-1737.

[105] See, e.g., Testimony of Executive Director of New York City Teachers' Retirement Board, in House 1973 Amendments Hearings, note 90 *supra,* Pt. 4, at 1703-1707; Submission of Investors Diversified Services, Inc., in Senate Institutional Membership Hearings, note 40 *supra,* at 562, 578-581.

management.[106] Thus, the position of the institutions themselves on the issue was almost uniformly a function of their own plans and perceived interests.

[iii] *Client Interests Protected by the Separation of Brokerage and Management:* The most puzzling aspect of the conflict-of-interest explanation of the congressional decision to separate brokerage and management is the exclusion of individual accounts from the coverage of amended Section 11(a). Whereas the *Institutional Investor Study* found no significant evidence of churning or dumping with respect to institutional accounts,[107] the record is replete with examples of such conduct by brokers managing the accounts of individual investors.[108] Furthermore, even if one assumes that preferential treatment of clients is a special conflict problem of broker-managers which supports separating brokerage from management, the record shows that institutional accounts were usually the beneficiaries. The victims were individuals.[109] But, more to the point, it is difficult to see how separation of brokerage and management only for institutional clients adds any protection for individual accounts, since nothing about such separation prevents managers inclined to favor their institutional clients from executing for or providing research to them ahead of individuals anyway.[110]

Nor was it accidental that individual accounts were excluded from the scope of Section 11(a). S. 470 would have applied only to transactions on an exchange of which a broker-manager was a member executed for his own account, the account of an affiliate, or a "managed

---

[106] See, e.g., Testimony of Executive Officer of California State Public Employees' Retirement System, in House 1973 Amendments Hearings, note 90 *supra,* Pt. 4, at 1699, 1701, 1715-1717.

[107] See notes 20-24 *supra.*

[108] See, e.g., Hecht v. Harris, Upham & Co., 430 F.2d 1202 (9th Cir. 1970); Jenny v. Shearson, Hammill & Co., [1974-1975 Transfer Binder] CCH Fed. Sec. L. Rep. ¶ 95,021 (S.D.N.Y. 1975); Leonard v. Colton, [1967-1969 Transfer Binder] CCH Fed. Sec. L. Rep. ¶ 92,312 (E.D.N.Y. 1968).

[109] See note 23 *supra.*

[110] As a conflict-of-interest problem, preferential treatment of certain accounts over others has little to do with combining brokerage and management. Questions such as who will receive the benefit of research first, who will execute first, and how the costs of research and executions will be allocated are involved in every investment management operation irrespective of whether the manager also executes for his accounts. See ¶¶ 9.05[2] and 9.06[4].

institutional account." [111]   As originally proposed, H.R. 5050 would
have applied to exchange transactions[112] executed for a member's own
account or the account of an affiliate.[113] Affiliate was defined to include
accounts for which the broker-manager retained authority to choose
investments or for which he regularly furnished investment advice, but
transactions for the accounts of individuals not otherwise affiliated with
the broker-manager were expressly excluded.[114] As reported out of
Committee, H.R. 5050 was substantially redrafted,[115] though without
effect on individual accounts. It applied to a broker-manager's own
account, the account of an affiliated person, or "any managed account,"
but still expressly excluded a "managed account of a natural person." [116]
S. 249, the bill which amended Section 11(a) of the Securities Exchange
Act, adopted the House approach, specifically excluding "any transaction for the account of a natural person." [117]

Yet, if the exclusion for accounts of individuals was not accidental,
it also did not receive a great deal of attention. The Committee Report
accompanying H.R. 5050[118] only referred to exceptions "traditionally
recognized to serve a positive market function. . . ." Although it con-

---

111 S. 470, 93d Cong., 1st Sess. § 2 (1973). Individual accounts could
not have been included under the category of affiliated accounts. Otherwise,
the inclusion and definition of managed institutional accounts would have
been superfluous.

112 H.R. 5050, 93d Cong., 1st Sess. § 205 (1973), referred to transactions executed by a member on *an* exchange. S. 470, note 111 *supra,*
referred to executions on *such* exchange. It is thus possible that H.R. 5050
would have applied more broadly to transactions by a broker-manager than
S. 470. The question, however, is moot since Section 11(a), as amended,
applies only to transactions by a member on "such" exchange.

113 H.R. 5050, 93d Cong., 1st Sess. § 205 (1973).

114 *Id.*

115 The bill was changed to repose authority in the SEC to prescribe
rules to regulate or prevent trading for affiliates and managed accounts.
H.R. 5050, 93d Cong., 2d Sess. § 205 (1974). Presumably, this would
extend to all kinds of trading by broker-managers. The separation of brokerage and management was made mandatory, however, for defined accounts on all transactions on an exchange. The SEC was also given limited
authority to exempt transactions for the defined accounts.

116 *Id.*

117 Securities Exchange Act § 11(a)(1)(E), 15 U.S.C. § 78k(a)(1)(E).
See note 131 *infra.*

118 Report of the House Comm. on Interstate and Foreign Commerce,
Securities Acts Amendments of 1974, H.R. Rep. No. 1476, 93d Cong., 2d
Sess. 52 (1974) (hereinafter cited as *House 1974 Amendments Report*).

tinually emphasized the conflict-of-interest problem arising out of combined brokerage and management, the Senate report accompanying S. 470[119] also ignored the inconsistency of treating individual accounts differently from institutional accounts. Even the Committee report[120] and the Conference Committee report[121] for S. 249 merely acknowledged the exclusion of individual accounts from the amendment of Section 11(a) to separate brokerage from management. Indeed, if one wants any overt recognition that there is an inconsistency in the treatment of individual and institutional accounts, it is necessary to go all the way back to the *Senate Securities Industry Study.* It asserted that individuals, receiving more detailed reports of the transactions in their accounts, are better positioned to protect their interests than beneficiaries of pooled accounts.[122] This distinction, of course, badly ignores not only the presence of watchmen—the trustees and directors of pooled accounts, who receive at least as much information about their clients as individuals do about their accounts—but also the record which shows that beneficiaries of pooled accounts have fared far better than individuals in avoiding the consequences of the identical conflict-of-interest problems they both experience with combined broker-management.

[2] Analysis of Section 11(a): Prohibitions and Exemptions

Section 11(a) of the Securities Exchange Act of 1934 was amended by Section 6(2) of the Securities Acts Amendments of 1975 to deal with trading by a member of an exchange in behalf of an account in which it is interested. Subject to certain exceptions, Section 11(a)(1)[123] makes it unlawful for a member of an exchange to execute a transaction on that exchange "for its own account, the account of an associated person, or an account with respect to which it or an associated person thereof exercises investment discretion." Associated person is defined in Section 3(a)(21) to include officers of a member and per-

---

[119] Report of the Senate Committee on Banking, Housing and Urban Affairs, *Regulation of Securities Trading by Members of National Securities Exchanges,* S. Rep. No. 187, 93d Cong., 1st Sess. (1973).

[120] Report of the Senate Comm. on Banking, Housing and Urban Affairs, *Securities Acts Amendments of 1975,* S. Rep. No. 75, 94th Cong., 1st Sess. 63-65, 99-100 (1975).

[121] Conference Report, *Securities Acts Amendments of 1975,* H.R. Rep. No. 229, 94th Cong., 1st Sess. 105-107 (1975).

[122] See *Senate Securities Industry Study,* note 1 *supra,* at 87.

[123] 15 U.S.C. § 78k(a)(1).

sons in a control relationship with a member.[124] Investment discretion is defined in Section 3(a)(35) to include (1) actual authority to determine the securities to be purchased and sold by an account; (2) responsibility for deciding the securities to be purchased and sold for an account even though another person has actual responsibility for the investment decisions of that account; and (3) any other relationship involving influence with respect to the purchase and sale of securities as defined by rule of the Commission.[125]

In general, the exemptions from the prohibition in Section 11(a)(1) are exceptions applicable to "certain classes of transactions which have been traditionally recognized to serve a positive market function. . . ." [126] Thus, exemptions apply to transactions of odd-lot dealers,[127] stabilizing transactions,[128] arbitrage and hedge transactions,[129] and transactions

---

[124] "The term 'person associated with a member' or 'associated person of a member' when used with respect to a member of a national securities exchange or registered securities association means any partner, officer, director, or branch manager of such member (or any person occupying a similar status or performing similar functions), any person directly or indirectly controlling, controlled by, or under common control with such member, or any employee of such member." 15 U.S.C. § 78c(a)(21), *as amended by* Securities Acts Amendments of 1975 § 3(5).

Member is defined in Act § 3(a)(3) (15 U.S.C. § 78c(a)(3)), *as amended by* Securities Acts Amendments of 1975 § 3(1). The term "control" is undefined. H.R. 5050 had adopted the definition of control used by the SEC in Rule 19b-2, in which control is presumed when a person owns or has a beneficial interest in more than 25 percent of the voting securities or profits of another person. See note 79 *supra*; cf. Investment Company Act § 2(a)(9), 15 U.S.C. § 80a-2(a)(9).

[125] ¶ 9.03[2][a] at note 89.

[126] Report of the House Committee on Interstate and Foreign Commerce on H.R. 4111, *Securities Reform Act of 1975*, H.R. Rep. No. 123, 94th Cong., 1st Sess. 57 (1975). H.R. 4111 was identical to H.R. 5050 with respect to the amending of Section 11. See ¶¶ 9.02[3] note 58 and 9.03[2] note 82.

[127] Section 11(a)(1)(B), 15 U.S.C. § 78k(a)(1)(B), exempts:

"any transaction for the account of an odd-lot dealer in a security in which he is so registered."

[128] Section 11(a)(1)(C), 15 U.S.C. § 78k(a)(1)(C), exempts:

"any stabilizing transaction effected in compliance with rules under section 10(b) of this title to facilitate a distribution of a security in which the member effecting such transaction is participating."

[129] Section 11(a)(1)(D), 15 U.S.C. § 78k(a)(1)(D), exempts:

"any bona fide arbitrage transaction, any bona fide hedge transaction involving a long or short position in an equity security and a long or

offsetting transactions made in error.[130] But the exemptions also make large holes in the statutory prohibition, particularly when the conflict-of-interest explanation for Section 11(a)(1) is taken into account. Subsection 11(a)(1)(E) exempts transactions involving the accounts of natural persons,[131] which introduces a serious inconsistency into the conflict-of-interest explanation of why Section 11 was amended.[132] Subsection 11(a)(1)(A), which exempts "any transaction by a dealer acting in the capacity of market maker," [133] also reopens a conflict-of-interest problem the statutory prohibition was supposed to have resolved. Section 3(a)(38) of the Securities Exchange Act defines market maker to include "any dealer acting in the capacity of a block positioner." [134] This means that a broker-manager can purchase a block from or sell a block to a client so long as he is dealing for his own account, and thus has the curious effect of exempting principal transactions even though the incentives to self-dealing are often higher than in the case of agency transactions. This interpretation also yields the anomalous result of discouraging institutional clients from retaining block-positioning houses to act as their money managers. An institutional client relying on such a manager would be cut off from a substantial portion of market liquidity because only a few firms are well enough capitalized, at least in contemporary markets, to handle block trades,[135] and thus

---

short position in a security entitling the holder to acquire or sell such equity security, or any risk arbitrage transaction in connection with a merger, acquisition, tender offer, or similar transaction involving a recapitalization."

For an early interpretation of this provision, see Debevoise, Plimpton, Lyons & Gates, [1975-1976 Transfer Binder] CCH Fed. Sec. L. Rep. ¶ 80,418.

[130] Section 11(a)(1)(F), 15 U.S.C. § 78k(a)(1)(F), exempts "any transaction to offset a transaction made in error."

[131] Section 11(a)(1)(E), 15 U.S.C. § 78k(a)(1)(E), exempts

"any transaction for the account of a natural person, the estate of a natural person, or a trust (other than an investment company) created by a natural person for himself or another natural person."

[132] See ¶ 10.02[1][c][iii] *supra.*

[133] 15 U.S.C. § 78k(a)(1)(A).

[134] 15 U.S.C. § 78c(a)(38), *as amended by* Securities Acts Amendments of 1975 § 3(6).

[135] Block positioners prefer not to tie up their own capital when they handle orders for their customers. A price must be provided, however, within a brief period of time, which often precludes the collection of sufficient commitments on the other side of the order to match the initial customer's desires. The result is that a block positioner may have to inven-

the broker-manager would be unable to handle the institution's own block trades as agent. Moreover, because of Section 11(a)(1)(A), the institutional client would be a potential receptacle for trades the manager had positioned for other institutions.[136] Finally, the statute grants the SEC general exemptive power. Recognizing that its stated policies of equalizing competitive power, eliminating conflicts of interest, and promoting liquidity in the market would not necessarily lead to the same conclusion, Congress authorized the SEC in Section 11(a)(1)(H) to exempt by rule transactions it determines are "consistent with the purposes of this paragraph, the protection of investors, and the maintenance of fair and orderly markets." [137]

Congress was also faced with the problem of what to do about transactions on exchanges of which a broker-manager was not a member and

---

tory part of the position himself. Given the capital this requires, the number of block positioners has been small. For a discussion of the mechanics of block trading, see *Institutional Investor Study,* note 2 *supra,* Pt. 4, at 1584- 1720.

[136] The legislative history shows plainly that the purpose behind the block-positioning exemption was to improve the liquidity of the market and not to protect the interests of clients of broker-managers having block-positioning capabilities. The exemption first appeared in Rule 19b-2 as one of a group of exempted principal transactions which "contribute to depth, liquidity, stability and continuity." Adoption of Rule 19b-2, note 69 *supra,* at 146. S. 470 at first picked up the exemption verbatim from Rule 19b-2 (see S. 470, 93d Cong., 1st Sess. § 2 (Jan. 18, 1973)), but apparently the Subcommittee recognized the theoretical inconsistency of separating brokerage and management for institutions in one breath and allowing all block transactions to be exempted in the other. Consequently, as reported out of committee, S. 470 denied the block-positioning exemption to managed institutional accounts. See S. 470, 93d Cong., 1st Sess. § 2 (June 19, 1973). H.R. 5050, apparently recognizing the size of the hole in the original version of S. 470, approached block positioning from the opposite direction. Its block-positioning exemption initially did not apply to transactions for affiliated persons, which included managed institutional accounts. See H.R. 5050, 93d Cong., 1st Sess. § 205 (March 1, 1973), and note 89 *supra.* But by the time H.R. 5050 was reported out, it had modified its position to exempt all block transactions subject to criteria acceptable to the SEC. See H.R. 5050, 93d Cong., 2d Sess. § 205 (Nov. 19, 1974). S. 249 resolved the matter by specifically exempting block positioning by houses acting as dealers and by giving the SEC broad exemptive powers which presumably can apply to block transactions executed on an agency basis. See Securities Exchange Act §§ 11(a)(1)(A). 11(a)(1)(H), 15 U.S.C. §§ 78k(a)(1)(A), 78k(a)(1)(H).

[137] 15 U.S.C. § 78k(a)(1)(H).

about transactions conducted over the counter. Both types of execution involve conflict-of-interest problems analogous to those which supposedly justify the separation of brokerage and management for transactions on exchanges to which a broker-manager belongs. A broker can profit from overtrading in the over-the-counter market in the same fashion as he can by overtrading using exchange facilities.[138] Furthermore, a broker-manager inclined to dump overvalued securities into a managed account can do so effectively by executing over the counter or through an exchange of which he is not a member. On the other hand, if Congress had extended the prohibition on brokerage and management beyond the exchanges to which a broker-manager belonged, that action would have had a depressing effect on the competitive posture of regional exchanges listing securities traded on the NYSE and on the third and fourth markets. Furthermore, if the prohibition had been extended to the over-the-counter markets, it would have effectively ordered broker-managers to interposition other brokers because broker-managers would have to forgo direct contact with over-the-counter market makers in both listed and unlisted securities. As a practical matter, such action would virtually have eliminated the competitive posture of broker-managers with respect to institutional accounts in the over-the-counter market.

Congress resolved this problem by drafting Section 11(a)(2) to authorize the Commission to regulate or prohibit a member's execution on exchanges of transactions not made unlawful under Section 11(a)(1),[139] transactions effected other than on an exchange,[140] and transactions executed through the facilities of any exchange by nonmember brokers.[141] Congress also delayed the effective date of Section 11(a) until three years after the introduction of negotiated rates.[142]

---

[138] Cf. Securities Week, May 3, 1976, p. 1 (broker-manager reportedly being investigated by SEC for interpositioning affiliate and for trading to generate commissions for research).

[139] Section 11(a)(2)(A), 15 U.S.C. § 78k(a)(2)(A).

[140] Section 11(a)(2)(B), 15 U.S.C. § 78k(a)(2)(B).

[141] Section 11(a)(2)(C), 15 U.S.C. § 78k(a)(2)(C).

[142] Section 11(a)(3), 15 U.S.C. § 78k(a)(3). Other amendments of Section 11 by the Securities Acts Amendments of 1975 do not pertain to separation of brokerage and management. New Section 11(b) (15 U.S.C. § 78k(b)) deals with transactions by odd-lot dealers and specialists. Securities Acts Amendments of 1975 § 6(3) repealed Section 11(e), which authorized a study, to be completed in 1936, of the advisability of separating the functions of broker and dealer.

[3] SEC Implementation of Section 11(a)

In a combined release about eighteen months after passage of the Securities Acts Amendments of 1975,[143] the SEC rescinded Rule 19b-2, adopted one temporary rule, and proposed another rule to begin implementing Section 11(a).[144] In that same release, the Commission, looking toward the full implementation of Section 11(a), also requested descriptions of problems encountered or anticipated under Section 11(a) (1) and suggestions on how the Commission should exercise its power to exempt under Section 11(a)(1)(H) and its power under Section 11(a)(2) to control transactions not covered by Section 11(a)(1). In particular, the Commission sought responses to several specific questions of interpretation, including how "block positioner" should be defined[145] and whether and under what circumstances a member should be allowed to carry out transactions for his own account and for managed institutional accounts through the facilities of another member.[146]

---

[143] SEC Securities Exchange Act Release No. 12055 (Jan. 27, 1976), [1975-1976 Transfer Binder] CCH Fed. Sec. L. Rep. ¶ 80,367.

[144] The Commission adopted Temporary Rule 11a1-1(T) permitting members to execute for their own accounts so long as they yield "priority, parity and precedence." *Id.* The Commission also issued Proposed Rule 11a1-2 to permit members to execute transactions for customers of associated persons to the same extent as for customers of members. Finally, the Commission proposed an amendment to Rule 17a-3 to improve record-keeping for showing compliance with Section 11(a). *Id.*

[145] Regulation U (12 C.F.R. § 221.3(c)(2)), which applies to credit for purchasing or carrying stocks on margin, defines block positioner according to four criteria: (1) minimum net capital, as determined according to Rule 15c3-1 of the Securities Exchange Act, of $1 million; (2) a purchase long or sale short (subject to certain restrictions) as principal of blocks of stock having a current market value of $200,000 in a single transaction or in a related series of transactions; (3) a certification to the lending bank that the block could not have been sold to or purchased from others on equivalent or better terms; and (4) a disposition of the block as rapidly as possible according to the circumstances. The definition of block positioner in Rule 17a-17 of the Securities Exchange Act (see SEC Securities Exchange Act Release No. 9761 (Sept. 12, 1972), [1972-1973 Transfer Binder] CCH Fed. Sec. L. Rep. ¶ 78,985), dealing with reports by block positioners, is like that of Regulation U in principal effect. See also NYSE Rule 127, 2 CCH NYSE Guide ¶ 2127.10.

[146] Section 11(a)(1) (15 U.S.C. § 78k(a)(1)) makes it unlawful for a member "to effect any transaction" on an exchange of which it is a member for its own account, for the accounts of an associated person, or for a managed account. None of the eight exemptions expressly authorizes an exchange member to effect transactions through the facilities of another

The Commission also sought responses on questions involving the treatment of persons required to become members of an exchange as a consequence of Section 6(f) of the Act[147] and of foreign parents, subsidiaries, and associates of exchange members.[148]

The SEC release also raised some fundamental questions of policy with respect to the conflict-of-interest issue.[149] Furthermore, it raised them in a way that seriously questions the stated assumptions of Congress, which ostensibly argued for the separation of brokerage and management. First, the Commission, after noting the exemption for natural persons in Section 11(a)(1)(E), pointed out that no similar exemption applies to "pension funds or other aggregations of investments by small investors." [150] The Commission asked whether a broader exemption should be given to aggregated funds or whether individual investors should be afforded additional safeguards. In either event, these questions implicitly reject the basis on which the Senate distinguished individual and institutional accounts.[151] If aggregated funds of small investors should be treated more like accounts of individual investors,

---

member for accounts to which the statutory prohibition applies. The closest any provision comes to speaking to this issue is Section 11(a)(1)(G) (15 U.S.C. § 78k(a)(1)(G)), which authorizes a member engaged principally in a public brokerage business to execute transactions for the member's own account, but this provision is triggered only upon the adoption of rules by the Commission to assure fair and orderly markets and to require that the member yield "priority, parity and precedence to the orders of nonmembers."

[147] Securities Acts Amendments of 1975 § 4 amended Securities Exchange Act § 6 to aid the transition to a national market system. In amended Section 6(f), the Commission has the power to require nonmembers effecting transactions on an exchange without the services of another acting as broker and nonmember brokers regularly effecting transactions on an exchange to comply with whatever exchange rules the Commission may specify.

[148] The Commission had previously solicited comments on foreign access to United States exchanges. See SEC Securities Exchange Act Release No. 10634 (Feb. 8, 1974), [1973-1974 Transfer Binder] CCH Fed. Sec. L. Rep. ¶ 79,644. As is normally the case in matters involving equal regulation, questions of investor protection were inextricably interwoven with questions of competitive advantage.

[149] The Commission also asked two other questions: (1) What recordkeeping requirements are necessary to insure compliance with Section 11(a)(1); and (2) how the Commission should respond on the matter of floor trading which is not specifically exempted from application of the prohibition in Section 11(a)(1).

[150] SEC Securities Exchange Act Release No. 12055 (Jan. 27, 1976), [1975-1976 Transfer Binder] CCH Fed. Sec L. Rep. ¶ 80,367, at 85,978.

[151] See note 122 *supra*.

pooled accounts are not less capable of protecting themselves. If individual investors need more protection, the converse is true.

The Commission made an even more telling point by asking whether experience with the introduction of negotiated rates has "affected in any way the reasoning (and the factual predicates therefor) underlying the enactment of Section 11(a)." [152] Experience with negotiated rates could not have affected the "factual predicates" of Section 11(a) if conflict of interest was the justification for separating brokerage and management, since there never were any significant facts in the record of institutional accounts being hurt. The factual predicates the Commission was referring to involved the question of competitive advantage. As discussed in ¶ 10.02[1][c], the Senate and House Subcommittees were very upset with the thrust of the *Martin Report* recommendations and the effect of Rule 19b-2 that broker-managers be authorized to continue to manage institutional accounts but that institutions not be permitted to join exchanges. This system would have given broker-managers a measurable competitive advantage over institutional managers and it would have forced institutions to pay higher commissions for their transactions than would have been the case if they joined exchanges. Most persons recognized that the competitive advantage enjoyed by brokers and the incentive for exchange membership felt by institutions would disappear as soon as fixed rates were eliminated. Thus, the Commission was simply asking for evidence to confirm what everyone predicted. Furthermore, to emphasize that the real force behind the amendment of Section 11(a) was the problems of competitive advantage and the extra costs of fixed commissions, the Commission went on to ask whether Section 11(a) had actually become a disincentive to exchange membership and whether, as a consequence, the Commission should ask Congress to amend Section 11(a).

¶ 10.03. RESTRICTIONS ON BROKER-MONEY MANAGER COMBINATIONS UNDER THE EMPLOYEE RETIREMENT INCOME SECURITY ACT OF 1974

[1] The Prohibited-Transaction Provisions

However defensible the separation of brokerage and management may be as a general principle, with respect to employee benefit plans covered by the Employee Retirement Income Security Act of 1974

---

[152] SEC Securities Exchange Act Release No. 12055 (Jan. 27, 1976), note 150 *supra*, at 85,979.

(ERISA),[153] the carefully drafted language of Section 11(a) of the Securities Exchange Act and the timetable for its implementation as proposed in S. 249 was already preempted before enactment. ERISA § 406(a) prohibits a fiduciary from causing a plan to engage in a transaction constituting a direct or indirect "furnishing of . . . services . . . between the plan and a party in interest" [154] or "transfer to, or use by or for the benefit of, a party in interest, of any assets of the plan. . . ." [155] The definition of party in interest[156] includes plan fiduciaries, and fiduciary is defined to include any person rendering "investment advice . . . with respect to any monies or other property of . . . [a] plan, or . . . [having] any authority or responsibility to do so. . . ." [157] Additionally, ERISA § 2003 amended the Internal Revenue Code[158] to levy an excise tax on disqualified persons, a term of art essentially the same as party in interest, for engaging in prohibited transactions, defined in Section 2003 to correspond to Section 406.[159] Furthermore, Section 406 (b)[160] and Section 2003[161] also prohibit a fiduciary from dealing with plan assets "for his own account." Except for a grandfather clause in Section 414(c)(4)[162] and a corresponding provision in Section 2003 (c)(2)(D), which expired June 30, 1977, the prohibited-transactions provisions were to take effect on January 1, 1975. Thus, ERISA would have prohibited broker-managers from taking on new employee benefit plan accounts and would have terminated all such management relationships before application of the less sweeping restrictions of Section 11(a) even began.

The prohibited-transactions provisions of ERISA also apply to relationships between plan managers and brokers in addition to those in which the broker acts as investment manager. Again, Sections 406(a) (1)(C) and 406(a)(1)(D) prohibit a fiduciary from causing a plan

---

153 Pub. L. 93-406 (Sept. 2, 1974).

154 *Id.* § 406(a)(1)(C), 29 U.S.C. § 1106(a)(1)(C).

155 *Id.* § 406(a)(1)(D), 29 U.S.C. § 1106(a)(1)(D).

156 *Id.* §§ 3(14)(A), 3(14)(B), 29 U.S.C. §§ 1002(14)(A), 1002(14) (B).

157 *Id.* § 3(21)(A)(ii), 29 U.S.C. § 1002(21)(A)(ii).

158 26 U.S.C. § 4975.

159 The definitions of prohibited transactions in the labor provisions and tax provisions are not precisely the same. See ¶ 2.04[2]. As they affect brokerage for managed accounts, however, there is no apparent difference in scope.

160 ERISA § 406(b)(1), 29 U.S.C. § 1106(b)(1).

161 I.R.C. § 4975(c)(1)(E).

162 29 U.S.C. § 1114(c)(4).

to engage in a transaction constituting a "furnishing of goods, services, or facilities between the plan and a party in interest"; or a "transfer to, or use by or for the benefit of, a party in interest, of any assets of the plan." [163] A party in interest includes anyone "providing services to . . . [a] plan." [164] Since this renders a broker providing execution services a party in interest, taken literally, Section 406(a) can prevent a fiduciary from using that broker for any other purpose in servicing the fund's needs. That is, the broker could not execute ordinary agency transactions and still provide research services or custodian services, or act as principal, underwriter, or market maker.

Despite their obvious impact on relationships between brokers and investment managers serving pension funds, the prohibited-transactions provisions of ERISA are in no significant sense a response to a demonstrated problem requiring legislative remedy. By far, the major impetus for inclusion of the prohibited-transactions provisions in the Act was self-dealing by trustees, sponsoring companies, and sponsoring unions, particularly with respect to real estate purchases, loans, investment in company securities, and so forth.[165] At most, there was a suspicion, unsupported by substantial evidence, that conflicts of interest to which brokers were exposed were having consequences detrimental to pension funds.[166] But by the time the Act was reported out of conference, this

---

[163] See notes 154-156 *supra*.

[164] ERISA § 3(14)(B), 29 U.S.C. § 1002(14)(B).

[165] See, e.g., Interim Report of the Senate Subcommittee on Labor of the Committee on Labor and Public Welfare, *Private Welfare and Pension Plan Study*, S. Rep. No. 634, 92d Cong., 2d Sess. 85 (1972); Lurie, "Prohibited Transactions," 31 Bus. Law. 131, 134 (1975).

[166] As originally introduced, ERISA expressly authorized the provision of multiple services by a party in interest serving as a paid fiduciary. See S. 4, 93d Cong., 1st Sess. § 15(d) (Jan. 4, 1973). When S. 4 was reported out of committee on April 18, 1973, Section 15(d) was deleted. The original proposal was intended to recognize that fiduciaries, subject to regulation under state and federal laws affecting the banking, insurance, and securities industries, performed a variety of services and functions, many traditional in nature and some in response to contemporary competitive pressures. The Committee felt that, though traditional safeguards might suffice for investment management arrangements with respect to estates, mutual funds, endowment funds, variable annuities, and so forth, in the special case of pension funds there might be some difficulty in securing an adequate system of control over fiduciary-commercial relationships. The Committee feared that these relationships might cause some subordination of the strict professionalism expected of fund managers to business pressures, and that abuses of this kind are not often subject to early discovery. Consequently, the Committee took the position that the better way to pro-

suspicion had turned into a congressional recommendation that, consistent with pending securities reform legislation, the Secretaries of Labor and the Treasury grant variances to persons providing brokerage and management services.[167] Furthermore, because of the effect of ERISA on persons traditionally furnishing multiple services to employee benefit plans, there has been subsequent, though unsuccessful, legislative effort aimed at narrowing the scope of the prohibited-transactions provisions as originally enacted.[168]

For reasons that are not entirely clear, the securities industry did not take much note of the impact of ERISA on existing broker-management arrangements until the eve of the effective date of the statute's prohibited-transactions provisions.[169] Nonetheless, after prompting, the Department of Labor and the Internal Revenue Service recognized the potential effects of strict application of Sections 406 and 2003 and hastily granted appropriate exemptions retroactive to January 1, 1975.[170] These exemptions were extended three times[171] until permanent exemp-

---

ceed was to proscribe multiple functions and entrust the Secretary of Labor with broad exemptive power. Senate Committee on Labor and Public Welfare, *Report on S. 4*, 93d Cong., 1st Sess. (1973). That exemptive power may be exercised upon findings of administrative feasibility and protection of the interests and rights of the plan and its participants and beneficiaries. ERISA § 408(a), 29 U.S.C. § 1108(a).

[167] See Conference Report, ERISA, H.R. Rep. 1280, 93d Cong., 2d Sess. 309-310 (1974) (hereinafter cited as *ERISA Conference Report*).

[168] See H.R. 7597, 94th Cong., 1st Sess. (1975).

[169] Perhaps industry attention was tunneled toward progress of the securities legislation which, in the summer and fall of 1974, appeared to be a sound bet for enactment before Congress adjourned and a new crop of legislators unfamiliar with the proceedings on federal securities reform took office. Perhaps the industry was lulled by language in the Conference Report on ERISA which, recognizing the effect of Sections 406 and 2003 on brokerage and management, suggested that the Secretaries of Labor and the Treasury might grant appropriately safeguarded variances to broker-managers. See *ERISA Conference Report*, note 167 *supra*, at 309-310. In any event, few broker-managers came forward to defend combined brokerage and management for pension funds. But see Written Statements Submitted by Interested Organizations on H.R. 10470 to the House Comm. on Ways and Means, 93d Cong., 1st Sess. 564 (1973) (submission of leading broker-manager). It was not until December 12, 1974, that the Securities Industry Association filed with the Labor Department a brief seeking clarification of a host of questions relating to traditional relationships between brokers and pension funds and including the management of pension accounts by brokers. See Wall Street Letter, Dec. 23, 1974, pp. 1-2.

[170] See 40 Fed. Reg. 5201 (Feb. 4, 1975).

[171] See 40 Fed. Reg. 17,861 (April 23, 1975); 40 Fed. Reg. 24,578 (June 9, 1975); 40 Fed. Reg. 43,785 (Sept. 23, 1975).

tions could be adopted.[172] During this period, of course, the Securities Acts Amendments of 1975 were in the process of becoming law, and in the Conference report accompanying S. 249, the Conference Committee expressly enjoined the Department of Labor and the Internal Revenue Service to provide an exemption from the prohibited-transactions provisions of ERISA paralleling Section 11(a) of the Securities Exchange Act by suspending the separation of brokerage from management until May 1, 1978.[173] Responding to this congressional directive, but maintaining some important limitations, the Department of Labor and the Internal Revenue Service adopted Prohibited Transaction Exemption 75-1,[174] exempting broker-managers from application of the prohibited-transactions provisions until May 1, 1978 and implementing regulations defining fiduciary.

Before discussing Exemption 75-1 and the regulations in detail, it may be useful to make some preliminary observations. The statutory definitions of party in interest and disqualified person are so broad that they have a potential reach to anyone providing multiple services to an employee benefit plan. In explaining the exemption for ancillary bank services from the prohibited-transactions provisions,[175] the Conference Committee stated parenthetically that "the prohibition against providing multiple services is not to apply to parties-in-interest, who are not fiduciaries." [176] It has been argued that this statement means that multiple services are not, without more, prohibited transactions.[177] This argument seems mostly precatory in view of the plain sense of the statutory language, the location of the quoted qualification, and the specificity of the statute with respect to other exemptions. Indeed, the Department of Labor and the Internal Revenue Service took a distinctly safe-harbor approach in issuing Prohibited Transaction Exemption 75-1, stating expressly in the preamble that its applicability to a particular transaction "is not dispositive of whether the transaction would have been a prohibited transaction. . . ."

Additionally, ERISA presents fiduciaries with the prospects of heavy liability in the event of breach of duty, including a potentially

---

[172] See 40 Fed. Reg. 50,842 (Oct. 31, 1975).

[173] Conference Report, Securities Acts Amendments of 1975, H.R. Rep. No. 229, 94th Cong., 1st Sess. 107 (1975).

[174] See note 172 *supra.*

[175] ERISA § 408(b)(6), 29 U.S.C. § 1108(b)(6); ERISA § 2003, I.R.C. § 4975(d)(6).

[176] *ERISA Conference Report,* note 167 *supra,* at 314.

[177] See Gerard & Schreiber, "ERISA," 9 Rev. Sec. Reg. 943, 944 n.12 (1976).

broad reach with respect to vicarious liability of one fiduciary with respect to another. It extends the principle that knowing assistance of a breach of trust is an actionable wrong to apply to any fiduciary who knows of a breach of trust by another fiduciary and fails to make "reasonable efforts under the circumstances to remedy the breach." [178] The exemption generally responds to the concern that fiduciary status would be too inclusive by classifying persons as fiduciaries only with respect to the assets which gave them that status and by exempting persons reasonably unaware that they are serving covered plans from the prohibited-transactions provisions. This means, for example, that if a plan divided its assets among three separate managers, none would be a fiduciary except with respect to the assets entrusted to him unless he engaged in some other act with respect to the other assets, the performance of which satisfied the statutory or regulatory definition of fiduciary in its own right.

Finally, the exemption is not merely technical, but is conditioned on a general obligation of fairness. Agency and principal transactions must be at least as favorable to a covered plan "as an arm's length transaction with an unrelated party would be. . . ." [179] Transactions with a related market maker must be more favorable. Furthermore, agency and principal transactions and extensions of credit are subject to the prohibited-transactions provisions of Section 503(b) of the Internal Revenue Code, which generally requires that the consideration received for purchases and sales be proper.[180]

---

[178] ERISA § 405(a)(3), 29 U.S.C. § 1105(a)(3).

[179] This language, which is adopted for use in the Exemption, is taken from ERISA § 414 (29 U.S.C. § 1114).

[180] Section 503(b) reads:

"Prohibited Transactions—For purposes of this section, the term 'prohibited transaction' means any transaction in which an organization subject to the provisions of this section:

"(1) lends any part of its income or corpus, without the receipt of adequate security and a reasonable rate of interest, to;

"(2) pays any compensation, in excess of a reasonable allowance for salaries or other compensation for personal services actually rendered, to;

"(3) makes any part of its services available on a preferential basis, to;

"(4) makes any substantial purchase of securities or other property, for more than adequate consideration in money or money's worth, from:

"(5) sells any substantial part of its securities or other property, for less than an adequate consideration or money's worth, to; or

[2] Definition of a Statutory Fiduciary

The ERISA regulations defining fiduciary are of critical importance to a broker providing services to an employee benefit plan because the potential liability of a statutory fiduciary is greater than for a party in interest and because the scope of the regulations implementing the prohibited-transactions provisions depends on whether a broker is classified as a fiduciary or merely a party in interest. A fiduciary is answerable in damages for causing a prohibited transaction to be effected and may be held to a civil fine in accordance with Section 502(i)[181] as well as an excise tax.[182] Absent complicity with a fiduciary, however, a party in interest is not liable for civil damages. Section 3(21)(A) of ERISA and Section 4975(e)(3) of the Internal Revenue Code provide[183] that a person is a fiduciary with respect to an employee benefit plan to the extent[184] he exercises a discretionary managerial authority over the disposition of its assets, renders the plan investment advice for compensation in any form, or has discretionary administrative responsibility for the plan. Labor Regulation § 2510.3-21[185] and I.R.C. Regulation § 4975-9[186] are intended to clarify the definition of fiduciary in both sections of the statute with respect to persons who, rendering in-

---

"(6) engages in any other transaction which results in a substantial diversion of its income or corpus to;

"The creator of such organization (if a trust); a person who has made a substantial contribution to such organization; a member of the family (as defined in § 267(c)(4) of an individual who is the creator of such trust or who has made a substantial contribution to such organization; or a corporation controlled by such creator or person through the ownership, directly or indirectly, of 50 per cent or more of the total combined voting power of all classes of stock entitled to vote or 50 per cent or more of the total value of shares of all classes of stock of the corporation."

[181] 29 U.S.C. § 1132(i).

[182] I.R.C. § 4975(a).

[183] 29 U.S.C. § 1002(21)(A)(ii); I.R.C. § 4975(e)(3).

[184] Actually, only Section 3(21)(A) says "to the extent." Section 4975(e)(3) is drafted slightly differently, but no practical difference seems to be intended. See Gerard & Schreiber, "ERISA," 9 Rev. Sec. Reg. 943, 944 n.11 (1976).

[185] 29 C.F.R. §§ 2510.3-21(c), 2510.3-21(d). Counsel to the congressional task force appointed, pursuant to ERISA § 3031, to government and municipal pension plans, has reportedly warned that the regulatory interpretation of the Department of Labor of "fiduciary" may be rejected by the courts. Securities Week, March 15, 1976, p. 7.

[186] 26 C.F.R. §§ 54.4975-9(c), 54.4975-9(d).

vestment advice to employee benefit plans, execute securities transactions on behalf of such plans. The regulations are structured to define "investment advice" inclusively and "execution of securities transactions" exclusively. One who gives investment advice as defined in the regulations is deemed to be a statutory fiduciary. One who merely executes securities transactions as defined in the regulations is deemed not to be a statutory fiduciary.

[a] Rendering investment advice for compensation

Labor Regulation § 2510.3-21(c) and I.R.C. Regulation § 4975-9(c) define investment advice.[187] The thrust of the regulations is to place

---

[187] The definition as adopted reads:

"*Investment advice.* (1) A person shall be deemed to be rendering 'investment advice' to an employee benefit plan, within the meaning of § 3(21)(A)(ii) of the Employee Retirement Income Security Act of 1974 (the Act) [§ 4975(e)(3)] and this paragraph, only if:

"(i) Such person renders advice to the plan as to the value of securities or other property, or makes recommendations as to the advisability of investing in, purchasing, or selling securities or other property; and

"(ii) Such person either directly or indirectly (e.g., through or together with any affiliate)—

"(A) Has discretionary authority or control, whether or not pursuant to agreement, arrangement or understanding, with respect to purchasing or selling securities or other property for the plan; or

"(B) Renders any advice described in paragraph (c)(1)(i) of this section on a regular basis to the plan pursuant to a mutual agreement, arrangement or understanding, written or otherwise, between such person and the plan or a fiduciary with respect to the plan, that such services will serve as a primary basis for investment decisions with respect to plan assets, and that such person will render individualized investment advice to the plan based on the particular needs of the plan regarding such matters as, among other things, investment policies or strategy, overall portfolio composition, or diversification of plan investments.

"(2) A person who is a fiduciary with respect to a plan by reason of rendering investment advice (as defined in paragraph (c)(1) of this section) for a fee or other compensation, direct or indirect, with respect to any moneys or other property of such plan, or having any authority or responsibility to do so, shall not be deemed to be fiduciary regarding any assets of the plan with respect to which such person does not have any discretionary authority, discretionary control or discretionary responsibility, does not exercise any authority or control, does not render investment advice (as defined in paragraph (c)(1) of this section) for a fee or other compensation, and does not have any authority or responsi-

one who provides investment advice in the category of statutory fiduciary only if he has actual discretionary authority to invest plan assets or if, having in mind particular investment needs of a plan and maintaining the expectation that his advice will strongly influence the investment of plan assets, he provides advisory assistance pursuant to a regularized arrangement. To make the definition of investment advice more concrete in cases where actual discretionary authority is not present, the regulations suggest a number of factors material in determining whether the requisite degree of influence is present. These factors include:

(1) Advice on a regular basis;

(2) A mutual understanding (although not necessarily in writing) between representatives of the plan and someone providing investment advice;

(3) The expectation that the advice will serve as a "primary basis" for investment decisions; and

(4) Individualized investment advice pertaining to such matters as investment policy and strategy, portfolio composition, or diversification.

On any reasonable interpretation of these provisions, a broker advising a plan and responsible for fomulating investment strategy would be classified as a fiduciary.

To be a statutory fiduciary, it is not sufficient that a person render investment advice. He must also be compensated for that advice. The Department of Labor and the Internal Revenue Service expressly declined to define compensation in the regulations on the grounds that additional consideration of the issue was necessary. The preamble to the regulations, however, states that compensation should be deemed to include all fees incident to particular transactions in which investment advice is rendered, including by way of example, brokerage commis-

---

bility to render such investment advice, provided that nothing in this paragraph shall be deemed to:

"(i) Exempt such person from the provisions of section 405(a) of the Employee Retirement Income Security Act of 1974 concerning liability for fiduciary breaches by other fiduciaries with respect to any assets of the plan; or

"(ii) Exclude such person from the definition of the term 'disqualified person' (as set forth in section 4975(e)(2)) with respect to any assets of the plan."

sions, mutual fund sales commissions, and insurance sales commissions. Read in connection with the statutory language, "direct or indirect," this certainly means that payment of a stated management fee is not a prerequisite to fiduciary status, and until some limiting regulation is adopted, compensation should be treated as extending to any pecuniary benefit received in connection with a plan transaction.

Finally, the regulations as issued differ in some material respects from those originally proposed,[188] the final version responding to several concerns voiced by the securities industry. As issued, the regulations made clearer that one would not be deemed to be rendering investment advice absent a mutual understanding to that effect.[189] In other words, a person would not become a fiduciary without reason to know that an employee benefit plan was relying on his advice. The final version also tightened the language so that a broker-dealer would not be classified as a fiduciary merely by offering advice on the availability of securities[190] and so that a person actually rendering investment advice to some plan assets would not be classified a fiduciary with respect to the plan's remaining assets.[191]

[b] Executing securities transactions

Whereas the regulations define investment advice inclusively—that it, by identifying the conduct which will cause a person to fall within the statutory definition of fiduciary—the regulatory definition of "execution of securities transactions" is exclusionary. It specifies conduct which falls outside the statutory definition of fiduciary.[192] The regula-

---

[188] See 40 Fed. Reg. 33564 (Aug. 8, 1975).

[189] 29 C.F.R. § 2510.3-21(c)(1)(ii)(B); 26 C.F.R. § 54.4975-9(c)(1)(ii)(B).

[190] The earlier version (see note 188 *supra*) had encompassed investment advice more broadly along the lines of the statutory definition of investment adviser in Section 202(a)(11) of the Investment Advisers Act (15 U.S.C. § 80b-2(a)(11)). This language was removed from the final version of the regulation.

[191] 29 C.F.R. § 2510.3-21(c)(2); 26 C.F.R. § 54.4975-9(c)(2). Such a person retains his status as party in interest or a disqualified person, however.

[192] The definition as adopted (29 C.F.R. § 2510.3-21(d)) reads:

"Execution of securities transactions. (1) A person who is a broker or dealer registered under the Securities Exchange Act of 1934, a reporting dealer who makes primary markets in securities of the United States Government or of an agency of the United States Government and reports daily to the Federal Reserve Bank of New York its positions

tions provide that a registered broker-dealer shall not be deemed a statutory fiduciary "solely because such person executes transactions for

with respect to such securities and borrowings thereon, or a bank supervised by the United States or a State, shall not be deemed to be a fiduciary, within the meaning of § 3(21)(A) of the Act [§ 4975(e)(3)], with respect to an employee benefit plan solely because such person executes transactions for the purchase or sale of securities on behalf of such plan in the ordinary course of its business as a broker, dealer, or bank, pursuant to instructions of a fiduciary with respect to such plan, if:

"(i) Neither the fiduciary nor any affiliate of such fiduciary is such broker, dealer, or bank; and

"(ii) The instructions specify (A) the security to be purchased or sold, (B) a price range within which such security is to be purchased or sold, or, if such security is issued by an open-end investment company registered under the Investment Company Act of 1940 (15 U.S.C. 80a-1, et seq.), a price which is determined in accordance with Rule 22c-1 under the Investment Company Act of 1940 (17 CFR 270.22c-1), (C) a time span during which such security may be purchased or sold (not to exceed five business days), and (D) the minimum or maximum quantity of such security which may be purchased or sold within such price range, or, in the case of a security issued by an open-end investment company registered under the Investment Company Act of 1940, the minimum or maximum quantity of such security which may be purchased or sold, or the value of such security in dollar amount which may be purchased or sold, at the price referred to in paragraph (d)(1)(ii)(B) of this section.

"(2) A person who is a broker-dealer, reporting dealer, or bank which is a fiduciary with respect to an employee benefit plan solely by reason of the possession or exercise of discretionary authority or discretionary control in the management of the plan or the management or disposition of plan assets in connection with the execution of a transaction or transactions for the purchase or sale of securities on behalf of such plan which fails to comply with the provisions of paragraph (d)(1) of this section, shall not be deemed to be a fiduciary regarding any assets of the plan with respect to which such broker-dealer, reporting dealer or bank does not have any discretionary authority, discretionary control or discretionary responsibility, does not exercise any authority or control, does not render investment advice (as defined in paragraph (c)(1) of this section) for a fee or other compensation, and does not have any authority or responsibility to render such investment advice, provided that nothing in this paragraph shall be deemed to:

"(i) Exempt such broker-dealer, reporting dealer, or bank from the provisions of section 405(a) of the Employee Retirement Income Security Act of 1974 concerning liability for fiduciary breaches by other fiduciaries with respect to any assets of the plan; or

"(ii) Exclude such broker-dealer, reporting dealer, or bank from the definition of the term 'disqualified person' (as set forth in section 4975 (e)(2)) with respect to any assets of the plan."

the purchase or sale of securities on behalf of . . . [a] plan in the ordinary course of its business. . . ." [193] The exclusion is subject to important limitations, however:

(1) The broker-dealer may not otherwise be a fiduciary to the plan or affiliated with a fiduciary to the plan.

(2) Additionally, the execution must be pursuant to instructions of a plan fiduciary and they must specify four things:

    (a) The securities which are the subject of the transactions;

    (b) The price range in which the transaction is to be carried out;

    (c) The time span for the transactions, not in any case to exceed five business days; and

    (d) The quantity of securities to be purchased or sold.

Thus, although a plan manager may confer some discretion on an executing broker to buy or sell securities, a broker can easily enter fiduciary status by exercising too much discretion even though he is pursuing best execution in good faith.

A program of accumulation or disposition of a block of securities presents particularly difficult problems of interpretation, including the width of the price range which can be authorized, the degree to which the broker can be permitted to stray from initial market price, the extent to which he may be allowed to depart from a fixed quantity, and so forth. Moreover, it is not clear from the language of the regulation when and under what circumstances a series of transactions will be considered sufficiently related to treat them as a single execution for purposes of determining fiduciary status. Indeed, considering the quality of these regulations and the treatment block positioning receives in the market-making section of Prohibited Transaction Exemption 75-1,[194] the Department of Labor and the Internal Revenue Service seem to have taken a relatively elementary position with respect to the mechanics of block trading.

During the comment period, before the regulations were adopted, broker-dealers raised several other matters pertinent to fiduciary status arising out of execution discretion including when fiduciary status terminates; whether a broker-dealer will be deemed a fiduciary if, though exceeding the authority allowable, he is unaware that he is transacting

---

[193] 29 C.F.R. § 2510.3-21(d)(1); 26 C.F.R. § 54.4975-9(d)(1).
[194] See ¶ 10.03[3][d] at notes 226-231 *infra*.

business for a covered plan; and whether a fiduciary executing securities transactions would be deemed a fiduciary only with respect to those assets which are the subject of a transaction, or whether his fiduciary status would apply to the plan's other assets as well. The Department of Labor and the Internal Revenue Service took accommodating positions on these matters:

(1) The preamble to the regulations states that fiduciary status continues only until a transaction or related series of transactions is completed.

(2) The preamble also states that, although it is unlawful for a fiduciary to delegate enough discretionary authority to a broker-dealer in the execution of securities transactions to make him a fiduciary without disclosing that fact, a justifiable lack of knowledge on the part of a broker-dealer that the client is a covered plan will prevent him from being classified as a fiduciary.

(3) Finally, the regulations expressly provide that, if a broker-dealer acquires fiduciary status in the execution of securities transactions because he exercises discretion in excess of that allowable, he will be deemed a fiduciary only with respect to those assets which are the subject of the securities transactions in which he is involved.[195]

[3] Prohibited Transaction Exemption 75-1

Pursuant to their authority to grant variances from ERISA's prohibited-transactions provisions,[196] the Department of Labor and the Internal Revenue Service issued Prohibited Transaction Exemption 75-1, dealing, among other things, with relationships between broker-dealers and employee benefit plan managers. By and large, Exemption 75-1 permits broker-dealers to carry on multiple-service relationships with a plan except with respect to services which render a broker-dealer a fiduciary. This means, of course, that investment management of covered plans by brokerage firms is highly problematic unless the firm offers (1) only investment advice, as defined in Regulation Section 2510.3-21, and executed through other brokers; or (2) ordinary brokerage services but not investment advice, as defined.

---

[195] 29 C.F.R. § 2510.3-21(d)(2); 26 C.F.R. § 54.4975-9(d)(2).
[196] ERISA § 408(a); I.R.C. § 4975(c)(2).

[a] Agency transactions

Exemption 75-1 protects not only pension managers purchasing supplementary services with commissions,[197] but also brokers supplying those services.[198] The Exemption expressly authorizes an executing broker acting as agent to provide supplementary services indefinitely and, until May 1, 1978, to offer management services to covered plans.[199]

---

[197] See ¶ 9.03[1] at note 79.

[198] See Prohibited Transaction Exemption 75-1, 40 Fed. Reg. 50,845, §§ I(b), I(c) (Oct. 31, 1975) (hereinafter cited as Exemption 75-1). See also note 197 *supra.*

[199] Sections 414(c)(4)(A) and 2003(c)(2)(D)(i) grandfather an exemption to the prohibited-transactions provisions, but in addition to not applying to all brokers, the statutory exemption expired June 30, 1977. Moreover, the statutory exemption does not apply to services rendered other than as part of a "binding contract" in existence on or before July 1, 1974.

Exemption 75-1, note 198 *supra,* § I reads:

"The restrictions of section 406 of the Employee Retirement Income Security Act of 1974 (the Act) and the taxes imposed by section 4975(a) and (b) of the Internal Revenue Code of 1954 (the Code), by reason of section 4975(c)(1) of the Code, shall not apply—

"(a) Until May 1, 1978, to the effecting of any securities transaction on behalf of an employee benefit plan by a person who is a fiduciary with respect to the plan, acting in such transaction as agent for the plan, and to the performance by such person of clearance, settlement, or custodial functions incidental to effecting such transactions, if such person ordinarily and customarily effected such securities transactions and performed such functions on May 1, 1975;

"(b) To the effecting of any securities transactions on behalf of an employee benefit plan by a person who is a party in interest or a disqualified person with respect to such plan (other than a person who is a fiduciary with respect to the plan), acting in such transaction as agent for the plan, and to the performance by such person of clearance, settlement, or custodial functions incidental to effecting such transaction; or

"(c) To the furnishing to an employee benefit plan by a person who is a party in interest or disqualified person with respect to such plan of any advice, either directly or through publications or writings, as to the value of securities or other property, the advisability of investing in, purchasing, or selling securities or other property, or the availability of securities or other property or of purchasers or sellers of securities or other property, or of any analyses or reports concerning issuers, industries, securities or other property, economic factors or trends, portfolio strategy, or the performance of accounts, under circumstances which do not make such party in interest or disqualified person a fiduciary with respect to such plan; Provided that, in each instance, such transactions

The Exemption also claims, as directed by Congress,[200] to bring the prohibited-transactions provisions of ERISA into conformity with Section 11(a) of the Securities Exchange Act. To an extent, this claim is true. The Exemption expressly permits a broker who is a fiduciary with respect to a plan (as a broker-manager would be by virtue of the regulatory definition of investment advice) to effect securities transactions on behalf of a plan and perform clearance, settlement, and custodial functions incidental thereto[201] until May 1, 1978, the date on which Section 11(a) takes full effect. But the Exemption does not correspond with Section 11(a) perfectly. For one thing, the Exemption had to be broader than Section 11(a) because the prohibited-transactions provisions of ERISA apply to all executions, whether or not effected on an exchange of which a broker-manager is a member as is required by the Exchange Act provision. Furthermore, unlike the statutory exemptions in Section 11(a), Exemption 75-1 is not absolute, but is contingent upon execution effected "on terms at least as favorable . . . as an arm's-length transaction with an unrelated party would be." [202] Though a reasonable interpretation of the quoted language would impose at least a standard of negligence on the failure to obtain such terms, it is also possible that Exemption 75-1 can be lost for any failure to obtain such terms. However that issue is resolved, the loss of Exemption 75-1 on those grounds automatically places a broker-manager in breach of the prohibited-transactions provision of the Act.

[b] Principal transactions

The section of Exemption 75-1 covering principal transactions, though indefinite in duration, is of limited value. Except in one context, it does not protect broker-managers. It permits a broker-dealer who is not a fiduciary to an employee benefit plan, or who is a party in interest

---

are effected on behalf of the plan, or such advice, analyses or reports are furnished to the plan, on terms at least as favorable to the plan as an arm's-length transaction with an unrelated party would be and were not, at the time such transactions were effected or at the time such advice, analyses or reports were furnished, prohibited transactions within the meaning of section 503(b) of the Code. For purposes of this exemption, the term 'person' shall include such person and any affiliates of such person, and the term 'affiliate' shall be defined in the same manner as that term is defined in 29 CFR 2510.3-21(e) and 26 CFR 54.4975-9 (e)."

200 See note 173 *supra*.
201 See Exemption 75-1, note 198 *supra*, § I(a).
202 *Id.* § I.

or disqualified person solely because he furnishes services to a plan, to purchase or sell securities to the plan for his own account.[203] But it does not extend to a broker-dealer fiduciary except to authorize the purchase and sale, as principal, of shares in a mutual fund if the broker-dealer is not a principal underwriter for the fund and is not otherwise

---

[203] Exemption 75-1, note 198 *supra*, § II reads:

"The restrictions of section 406(a) of the Employee Retirement Income Security Act of 1974 (the Act) and the taxes imposed by section 4975(a) and (b) of Internal Revenue Code of 1954 (the Code), by reason of section 4975(c)(1)(A) through (D) of the Code, shall not apply to any purchase or sale of a security between an employee benefit plan and a broker-dealer registered under the Securities Exchange Act of 1934 (15 U.S.C. 78a et seq.), a reporting dealer who makes primary markets in securities of the United States Government or of any agency of the United States Government ('Government securities') and reports daily to the Federal Reserve Bank of New York its positions with respect to Government securities and borrowings thereon, or a bank supervised by the United States or a State, if the following conditions are met:

"(a) In the case of such broker-dealer, it customarily purchases and sells securities for its own account in the ordinary course of its business as a broker-dealer.

"(b) In the case of such reporting dealer or bank, it customarily purchases and sells Government securities for its own account in the ordinary course of its business and such purchase or sale between the plan and such reporting dealer or bank is a purchase or sale of Government securities.

"(c) Such transaction is at least as favorable to the plan as an arm's length transaction with an unrelated party would be, and it was not, at the time of such transaction, a prohibited transaction within the meaning of section 503(b) of the Code.

"(d) Such broker-dealer, reporting dealer or bank is not a fiduciary with respect to the plan, and such broker-dealer, reporting dealer or bank is a party in interest or disqualified person with respect to the plan solely by reason of section 3(14)(B) of the Act or section 4975(e)(2) (B) of the Code or a relationship to a person described in such sections. For purposes of this paragraph, a broker-dealer, reporting dealer, or bank shall not be deemed to be a fiduciary with respect to a plan solely by reason of providing securities custodial services for a plan. Neither the restrictions of this paragraph nor (if the other conditions of this exemption are met) the restrictions of section 406(b) of the Act and the taxes imposed by section 4975(a) and (b) of the Code, by reason of section 4975(c)(1)(E) and (F) of the Code, shall apply to the purchase or sale by the plan of securities issued by an open-end investment company registered under the Investment Company Act of 1940 (15 U.S.C. 80a-1 et seq.), provided that a fiduciary with respect to the

affiliated with it.[204] This means, of course, that a broker-manager acting for his own account in executing transactions for the benefit of a covered plan must find some other source of protection, either in the underwritings or the market-making exemptions discussed below.

Furthermore, because of the limited availability of this section of Exemption 75-1, the construction of the regulatory definition of fiduciary takes on added importance with respect to services other than management. The decision not to regard the simple rendering of advice or the provision of custodial services as creating fiduciary status is an obvious aid to broker-dealers. But the treatment of specific services in differing factual contexts is yet to be determined (as, for example, the point at which advice becomes influence), and the Exemption is lost the instant a broker-dealer becomes a fiduciary.

---

plan is not a principal underwriter for, or affiliated with, such investment company within the meaning of sections 2(a)(29) and 2(a)(3) of the Investment Company Act of 1940 (15 U.S.C. 80a-2(a)(29) and 80a-2(a)(3)).

"(e) The plan maintains or causes to be maintained for a period of six years from the date of such transaction such records as are necessary to enable the persons described in paragraph (f) of this exemption to determine whether the conditions of this exemption have been met, except that—

"(1) Such broker-dealer, reporting dealer, or bank shall not be subject to the civil penalty which may be assessed under section 502(i) of the Act, or to the taxes imposed by section 4975(a) and (b) of the Code, if such records are not maintained, or are not available for examination as required by paragraph (f) below; and

"(2) A prohibited transaction will not be deemed to have occurred if, due to circumstances beyond the control of the plan fiduciaries, such record are lost or destroyed prior to the end of such six-year period.

"(f) Notwithstanding anything to the contrary in subsections (a)(2) and (b) of section 504 of the Act, the records referred to in paragraph (e) are unconditionally available for examination during normal business hours by duly authorized employees of (1) the Department of Labor, (2) the Internal Revenue Service, (3) plan participants and beneficiaries, (4) any employer of plan participants and beneficiaries, and (5) any employee organization any of whose members are covered by such plan. For purposes of this exemption, the terms 'broker-dealer,' 'reporting dealer' and 'bank' shall include such persons and any affiliates thereof, and the term 'affiliate' shall be defined in the same manner as that term is defined in 29 CFR 2510.3-21(e) and 26 CFR 54.4975-9(e)."

[204] The Exemption expressly adopts the statutory definitions in the Investment Company Act of principal underwriter (§ 2(a)(29), 15 U.S.C. § 80a-2(a)(29)), and affiliate (§ 2(a)(3), 15 U.S.C. § 80a-2(a)(3)). Exemption 75-1, note 198 *supra*, § II(d).

[c] Underwritings

Perhaps the most controversial problem in connection with Exemption 75-1 is how to deal with underwritings by a person who is classifiable as a party in interest or disqualified person because he provides some other service to a covered plan. The principal concern in the securities industry was that the Exemption as proposed would reach every member of an underwriting or selling syndicate and thereby make a prohibited transaction out of any participation in the underwriting by a plan. Based apparently on a fear (unsupported by the record) that a broad exemption would lead to excessive participation by covered plans in overvalued underwritings, the Department of Labor and the Internal Revenue Service initially intended to deny exemption to any underwriting for which a plan fiduciary was a member of the syndicate.

At the urging of the industry[205] and of the SEC,[206] the Department of Labor and the Service substantially modified their position to permit fiduciaries to be syndicate members and, until July 1, 1977, syndicate managers. Based on a finding that, during an underwriting, the public-offering price for securities will be more favorable than the net cost in the secondary market, the Department of Labor and the Service concluded that an employee benefit plan should be permitted to purchase securities from the underwriting syndicate.[207] The Exemption does not

---

[205] See, e.g., Wall Street Letter, Sept. 8, 1975, p. 5 (leading broker-dealers criticize proposed exemption as being overinclusive with respect to members of an underwriting syndicate). To similar effect, see Securities Week, Sept. 8, 1975, p. 2a (Secretary of Treasury); *id.* at 2b (Securities Industry Association); Securities Week, Aug. 11, 1975.

[206] The text of the SEC Comments is reproduced in 4 CCH Pension Plan Guide ¶ 25,037 (Aug. 29, 1975).

[207] Exemption 75-1, note 198 *supra*, § III reads:

"The restrictions of section 406 of the Employee Retirement Income Security Act of 1974 (the Act) and the taxes imposed by section 4975(a) and (b) of the Internal Revenue Code of 1954 (the Code), by reason of section 4975(c)(1) of the Code, shall not apply to the purchase or other acquisition of any securities by an employee benefit plan during the existence of an underwriting or selling syndicate with respect to such securities, from any person other than a fiduciary with respect to the plan, when such a fiduciary is a member of such syndicate, provided that the following conditions are met:

"(a) No fiduciary who is involved in any way in causing the plan to make the purchase is a manager of such underwriting or selling syndicate, except that this paragraph shall not apply until July 1, 1977. For purposes of this exemption, the term 'manager' means any member of an underwriting or selling syndicate who, either alone or together

extend, however, to the purchase of securities during an underwriting from a fiduciary. The effect of this limitation is to exclude ·broker-managers from selling shares out of their allotment to plans they manage. Furthermore, after July 1, 1977, a fiduciary who is a syndicate manager may not cause a plan to purchase any of the securities offered

---

with other members of the syndicate, is authorized to act on behalf of the members of the syndicate in connection with the sale and distribution of the securities being offered or who receives compensation from the members of the syndicate for its services as a manager of the syndicate.

"(b) The securities to be purchased or otherwise acquired are—

"(1) Part of an issue registered under the Securities Act of 1933 or, if exempt from such registration requirement, are (i) issued or guaranteed by the United States or by any person controlled or supervised by and acting as an instrumentality of the United States pursuant to authority granted by the Congress of the United States, (ii) issued by a bank, (iii) issued by a common or contract carrier, if such issuance is subject to the provisions of section 20a of the Interstate Commerce Act, as amended, (iv) exempt from such registration requirement pursuant to a Federal statute other than the Securities Act of 1933, or (v) are the subject of a distribution and are of a class which is required to be registered under section 12 of the Securities Exchange Act of 1934 (15 U.S.C. 781), and the issuer of which has been subject to the reporting requirements of section 13 of that Act (15 U.S.C. 78m) for a period of at least 90 days immediately preceding the sale of securities and has filed all reports required to be filed thereunder with the Securities and Exchange Commission during the preceding 12 months.

"(2) Purchased at not more than the public offering price prior to the end of the first full business day after the final terms of the securities have been fixed and announced to the public, except that—

"(i) If such securities are offered for subscription upon exercise of rights, they are purchased on or before the fourth day preceding the day on which the rights offering terminates; or

"(ii) If such securities are debt securities, they may be purchased at a public offering price on a day subsequent to the end of such first full business day, provided that the interest rates on comparable debt securities offered to the public subsequent to such first full business day and prior to the purchase are less than the interest rate of the debt securities being purchased.

"(3) Offered pursuant to an underwriting agreement under which the members of the syndicate are committed to purchase all of the securities being offered, except if—

"(i) Such securities are purchased by others pursuant to a rights offering; or

"(ii) Such securities are offered pursuant to an over-allotment option.

in the underwriting. Since "cause" is interpreted restrictively in the preamble to the underwritings section of the Exemption to mean either recommending the purchase to the plan or participating "in any other manner in the plan's decision to make the purchase," the practical effect of this qualification is to deny, for at least that portion of its as-

---

"(c) The issuer of such securities has been in continuous operation for not less than three years, including the operations of any predecessors, unless—

"(1) Such securities are non-convertible debt securities rated in one of the four highest rating categories by at least one nationally recognized statistical rating organization;

"(2) Such securities are issued or fully guaranteed by a person described in paragraph (b)(1)(i) of this exemption; or

"(3) Such securities are fully guaranteed by a person who has issued securities described in paragraph (b)(1)(ii), (iii), (iv) or (v) and this paragraph (c).

"(d) The amount of such securities to be purchased or otherwise acquired by the plan does not exceed three percent of the total amount of such securities being offered.

"(e) The consideration to be paid by the plan in purchasing or otherwise acquiring such securities does not exceed three percent of the fair market value of the total assets of the plan as of the last day of the most recent fiscal quarter of the plan prior to such transaction, provided that if such consideration exceeds $1 million, it does not exceed one percent of such fair market value of the total assets of the plan.

"(f) The plan maintains or causes to be maintained for a period of six years from the date of such transaction such records as are necessary to enable the persons described in paragraph (g) of this exemption to determine whether the conditions of this exemption have been met, except that a prohibited transaction will not be deemed to have occurred if, due to circumstances beyond the control of the plan fiduciaries, such records are lost or destroyed prior to the end of such six-year period.

"(g) Notwithstanding anything to the contrary in subsections (a)(2) and (b) of section 504 of the Act, the records referred to in paragraph (f) are unconditionally available for examination during normal business hours by duly authorized employees of (1) the Department of Labor, (2) the Internal Revenue Service, (3) plan participants and beneficiaries, (4) any employer of plan participants and beneficiaries, and (5) any employee organization any of whose members are covered by such plan.

"If such securities are purchased by the plan from a party in interest or disqualified person with respect to the plan, such party in interest or disqualified person shall not be subject to the civil penalty which may be assessed under section 502(i) of the Act, or to the taxes imposed by section 4975(a) and (b) of the Code, if the conditions of this exemption are not met. However, if such securities are purchased from a party in

sets for which a syndicate manager is a fiduciary, access to an underwriting managed by the fiduciary.[208]

In another significant change, Exemption 75-1 eliminated the condition previously proposed relating to the amount of the underwriting commission. The original proposal had closely followed the model of Investment Company Act Rule 10f-3,[209] but the industry[210] and even the SEC[211] opposed such a step on the grounds that it would be anticompetitive and might have the effect of setting underwriting rates by regulation rather than market action. The Department of Labor and the Service made the change "to provide necessary and appropriate

---

interest or disqualified person with respect to the plan, the restrictions of section 406(a) of the Act shall apply to any fiduciary with respect to the plan and the taxes imposed by section 4975(a) and (b) of the Code, by reason of section 4975(c)(1)(A) through (D) of the Code, shall apply to such party in interest or disqualified person, unless the conditions for exemption of Part II of this notice (relating to certain principal transactions) are met.

"For purposes of this exemption, the term 'fiduciary' shall include such fiduciary and any affiliates of such fiduciary, and the term 'affiliate' shall be defined in the same manner as that term is defined in 29 CFR 2510.3-21(e) and 26 CFR 54.4975-9(e)."

[208] The preamble to Exemption 75-1, note 198 *supra*, § III states that the Exemption applies to any purchase from a person who is not a fiduciary so long as the fiduciary does not cause the plan to make the purchase. Although this statement accurately describes the Exemption, it implies a much greater limitation on an underwriting syndicate than the Exemption actually imposes. The implication is that the Exemption is lost if a fiduciary causes the purchase. But except for purchases from a fiduciary during an underwriting, all participations by a plan in an underwriting were exempted before July 1, 1977, and thereafter, the Exemption is lost only if the plan fiduciary is also a syndicate manager, as defined in Section III(a). Beyond this technical analysis of the Exemption, there is the question of who, other than a syndicate-member investment manager with the power to recommend participation in an underwriting, would cause a fund to purchase securities in an underwriting. As a practical matter, if the investment manager, because he is a fiduciary, cannot do so, no one will, and the result would be effectively to deny the plan access, regardless of quality, to underwritings in which a fiduciary is interested.

[209] 17 C.F.R. § 270.10f-3. The rule is reprinted in ¶ 10.06[2] at note 305 *infra*.

[210] See Securities Week, Sept. 8, 1975, p. 6 (leading brokerage firm withdraws proposal for maximum spreads and recommends that levels set by competitive pricing be adopted).

[211] SEC Comments, note 206 *supra*, at 27,083 through 27,084.

flexibility." [212] But the Exemption remains subject to a number of other important restrictions:

(1) The securities purchased must be registered under the Securities Act of 1933 or exempt from registration by virtue of some other federal statute.[213] This qualification can restrict the access of a plan to private placements.

(2) Exemption 75-1 also does not apply to the securities of an issuer which has not been in continuous operation for at least three years.[214] This qualification can restrict a plan's access to new ventures.

(3) Exemption 75-1 limits the quantity of securities which can be purchased. A plan may not purchase more than 3 percent of the total amount of securities offered,[215] nor may it invest more than 3 percent of its assets (1 percent for large purchases) in an underwriting covered by ERISA's prohibited-transactions provisions.[216]

(4) Finally, Exemption 75-1 does not apply to underwritings purchased from a party-in-interest or disqualified-person member of an underwriting syndicate,[217] no distinction being made

---

[212] Preamble to Exemption 75-1, note 198 *supra*, § III. Regulatory limits on underwriting commissions are unnecessary where the amount of such commissions is permitted to be fixed by the syndicate. A more difficult problem presents itself where the fund can negotiate underwriting commissions or receive a rebate for excess underwriting commissions. Cf. Papilsky v. Brandt, [1976-1977 Transfer Binder] CCH Fed. Sec. L. Rep. ¶ 95,627 (S.D.N.Y. 1976). In that event, the issue is the same as with negotiated rates on ordinary securities transactions. See ¶¶ 9.02-9.04.

[213] Exemption 75-1, note 198 *supra*, §§ III(b)(1)(i), III(b)(1)(iv). The securities may also be issued by an instrumentality of the United States (§ III(b)(1)(i)), a bank (§ III(b)(1)(ii)), a common carrier under the provisions of Interstate Commerce Act § 20(a) (§ III(b)(1)(iii)), or an issuer pursuant to Securities Exchange Act of 1934 §§ 12 and 13 (§ III(b) (1)(iv)).

[214] Exemption 75-1, note 198 *supra*, § III(c). This restriction can be avoided if the securities are highly rated debt instruments or are guaranteed by persons described in Sections III(b)(1)(i)-III(b)(1)(v), note 213 *supra*.

[215] *Id.* § III(d).

[216] *Id.* § III(e). If the purchase price exceeds $1 million, the limit is one percent.

[217] *Id.* § 3 (Addendum) § III.

based on whether the selling member of the underwriting syndicate is acting as principal or agent.[218]

This last-listed restriction on Exemption 75-1 is a somewhat circuitous method of permitting broker-dealers who provide research and other ordinary brokerage services to an employee benefit plan to sell securities from their underwriting allotment to the plan. The Addendum to Section III of Exemption 75-1 subjects a broker-dealer who is a party in interest or disqualified person to excise taxes unless Section II of the Exemption applies. That section, which treats principal transactions, exempts purchases and sales of securities from a broker-dealer who is a party in interest or disqualified person solely because he provides other services to a plan.

[d] Market making

Strict application of ERISA's prohibited-transactions provisions to broker-dealers acting in a market-making capacity would cut a plan off from best net price in any case in which the broker-dealer was otherwise classifiable as a party in interest. Although the exemption for principal transactions permits a plan to purchase and sell securities from a brokerage firm which is a party in interest, that exemption explicitly does not apply to a firm acting as a fiduciary to the plan.[219] Recognizing that an absolute ban on transactions between a plan and a fiduciary acting in a market-making capacity can impose extra costs on the plan, the Department of Labor and the Internal Revenue Service decided to exempt such transactions, subject to some very important limitations.[220]

---

[218] The Department of Labor and the Internal Revenue Service did not discuss underwritings from this perspective and probably did not consider whether an agency/principal distinction would be appropriate as a matter of regulatory policy. The absence of a regulatory distinction is probably correct, however. Underwritings distributed on an agency basis should be no less tightly regulated than those distributed on a principal basis since firm-commitment underwritings are ordinarily a less risky investment than best-efforts underwritings. L. Loss, *Securities Regulation* 159-172 (1961).

[219] Exemption 75-1, note 198 *supra*, § II(d).

[220] Exemption 75-1, note 198 *supra*, § IV reads:

"The restrictions of section 406 of the Employee Retirement Income Security Act of 1974 (the Act) and the taxes imposed by section 4975(a) and (b) of the Internal Revenue Code of 1954 (the Code), by reason of section 4975(c)(1) of the Code, shall not apply to any purchase or sale of any securities by an employee benefit plan from or to a market-

First, the Exemption is conditioned on certain criteria of acceptability set for the issuer and the securities purchased. As with the underwriting Exemption, the issuer must have been in operation for at

---

maker with respect to such securities who is also a fiduciary with respect to such plan, provided that the following conditions are met:

"(a) The issuer of such securities has been in continuous operation for not less than three years, including the operations of any predecessors, unless—

"(1) Such securities are non-convertible debt securities rated in one of the four highest rating categories by at least one nationally recognized statistical rating organization;

"(2) Such securities are issued or guaranteed by the United States or by any person controlled or supervised by and acting as an instrumentality of the United States pursuant to authority granted by the Congress of the United States, or

"(3) Such securities are fully guaranteed by a person described in this paragraph (a).

"(b) As a result of purchasing such securities—

"(1) The fair market value of the aggregate amount of such securities owned, directly or indirectly, by the plan and with respect to which such fiduciary is a fiduciary, does not exceed three percent of the fair market value of the assets of the plan with respect to which such fiduciary is a fiduciary, as of the last day of the most recent fiscal quarter of the plan prior to such transaction, provided that if the fair market value of such securities exceeds $1 million, it does not exceed one percent of such fair market value of such assets of the plan, except that this paragraph shall not apply to securities described in paragraph (a)(2) of this exemption; and

"(2) The fair market value of the aggregate amount of all securities for which such fiduciary is a market-maker, which are owned, directly or indirectly, by the plan and with respect to which such fiduciary is a fiduciary, does not exceed 10 percent of the fair market value of the assets of the plan with respect to which such fiduciary is a fiduciary, as of the last day of the most recent fiscal quarter of the plan prior to such transaction, except that this paragraph shall not apply to securities described in paragraph (a)(2) of this exemption.

"(c) At least one person other than such fiduciary is a market-maker with respect to such securities.

"(d) The transaction is executed at a net price to the plan for the number of shares or other units to be purchased or sold in the transaction which is more favorable to the plan than that which such fiduciary, acting in good faith, reasonably believes to be available at the time of such transaction from all other market-makers with respect to such securities.

"(e) The plain maintains or causes to be maintained for a period of six years from the date of such transaction such records as are neces-

least three years.[221] Additionally, the Exemption places percentage limitations on the quantity of securities which may be bought from a fiduciary who is a market maker. The aggregate value of a single purchase may not exceed 3 percent of the asset value of the plan (1 percent for large purchases).[222] Also, the value of all plan securities for which the fiduciary is a market maker may not exceed 10 percent of the asset value of the plan.[223] Furthermore, this exemption is available only if at least one other person is also a market maker in the security to be purchased,[224] and the "transaction is executed at a net price . . . which is more favorable . . . than . . . [the] fiduciary, acting in good faith, reasonably believes to be available at the time . . . from all other marketmakers. . . ." [225] Note especially that the price cannot be equivalent, but must be more favorable than that available from other market makers.

---

sary to enable the persons described in paragraph (f) of this exemption to determine whether the conditions of this exemption have been met, except that a prohibited transaction will not be deemed to have occurred if, due to circumstances beyond the control of the plan fiduciaries, such records are lost or destroyed prior to the end of such six year period.

"(f) Notwithstanding anything to the contrary in subsections (a)(2) and (b) of sections 504 of the Act, the records referred to in paragraph (e) are unconditionally available for examination during normal business hours by duly authorized employees of (1) the Department of Labor, (2) the Internal Revenue Service, (3) plan participants and beneficiaries, (4) any employer of plan participants and beneficiaries, and (5) any employee organization any of whose members are covered by such plan.

"For purposes of this exemption—

"(1) The term 'market-maker' shall mean any specialist permitted to act as a dealer, and any dealer who, with respect to a security, holds himself out (by entering quotations in an interdealer communications system or otherwise) as being willing to buy and sell such security for his own account on a regular or continuous basis.

"(2) The term 'fiduciary' shall include such fiduciary and any affiliates of such fiduciary, and the term 'affiliate' shall be defined in the same manner as that term is defined in 29 CFR 2510.3-21(e) and 26 CFR 54.4975-9(e)."

[221] Exemption 75-1, note 198 *supra*, § IV(a). This restriction can be avoided if the securities are highly rated debt instruments or are adequately guaranteed. Compare Section III(c).

[222] *Id.* § IV(b)(1). If the purchase price exceeds $1 million, the limit is one percent. Compare Section III(e).

[223] *Id.* § IV(b)(2).

[224] *Id.* § IV(c).

[225] *Id.* § IV(d).

But the most significant limitation of the exemption for market makers is that it does not extend to block positioners. The Department of Labor and the Internal Revenue Service claimed in the preamble that they were adopting a definition of the term "market maker" which would conform more closely than originally proposed to the definition appearing in Section 3(a)(38) of the Securities Exchange Act.[226] The definition as adopted in the Exemption contains a significant omission, however. The Exemption omitted the phrase "any dealer acting in the capacity of block positioner" [227] on the grounds, according to the preamble, of a lack of "sufficient supportive data" to justify including block positioners.

While this action may insulate plans which are clients of block positioning houses from self-dealing by those houses, it also deprives those plans of some market liquidity, since relatively few houses are well enough capitalized to act as block positioners.[228] Furthermore, the implicit assumption of the Department of Labor and the Service that combined management and positioning is too hazardous to a plan to countenance an exemption from the prohibited-transactions provisions may well be flawed, particularly in the case of sales of blocks from a plan to its manager. According to the *Institutional Investor Study*, block-positioning houses do not like to retain positions in inventory but prefer to lay them off as soon as practicable.[229] This suggests that such houses will try vigorously to execute block trades on an agency basis and will position only as a last resort.[230] The practical effect of the denial of the market-making exemption to block positioning means that, if a plan's broker-manager cannot dispose of a block of securities as agent, the plan must forgo trading a number of shares that cannot be placed or must risk obtaining an unsatisfactory price by going directly to the floor of an exchange or to other market makers. It is also worthy of comment to contrast the attitude of Congress on this issue. It concluded that the value of the extra liquidity from block positioning out-

---

[226] 15 U.S.C. § 78c(a)(38).

[227] Exemption 75-1, note 198 *supra*, § IV (Addendum).

[228] The Department and the Service were not ignorant of this fact. On the contrary, they were expressly advised of it during the comment period. See, e.g., Wall Street Letter, Sept. 8, 1975, p. 5.

[229] See *Institutional Investor Study*, note 2 *supra*, at 1608-1614.

[230] The mechanics of block trading may make it difficult to avoid some positioning. Customers on the passive side frequently want assurances that the block trader will stabilize and, if others owning a block are aware of the initial trade, they can force the trader to position. *Id.* at 1610.

weighs the danger of the conflict of interest and fully exempted block positioning from application of the prohibition against combined brokerage and management in Section 11(a) of the Securities Exchange Act.[231]

[e] Extension of credit

To accommodate securities settlement procedures, including occasional failures to deliver, Prohibited Transaction Exemption 75-1 also covers the extension of credit in normal settlement proceedings.[232] The

---

[231] Securities Exchange Act § 11(a)(1)(A), 15 U.S.C. § 78k(a)(1)(A).
[232] Exemption 75-1, § V reads:

"The restrictions of section 406 of the Employee Retirement Income Security Act of 1974 (the Act) and the taxes imposed by section 4975(a) and (b) of the Internal Revenue Code of 1954 (the Code), by reason of section 4975(c)(1) of the Code, shall not apply to any extension of credit to an employee benefit plan by a party in interest or a disqualified person with respect to the plan, provided that the following conditions are met:

"(a) The party in interest or disqualified person—

"(1) Is a broker or dealer registered under the Securities Exchange Act of 1934; and

"(2) Is not a fiduciary with respect to any assets of such plan, unless no interest or other consideration is received by such fiduciary or any affiliate thereof in connection with such extension of credit.

"(b) Such extension of credit—

"(1) Is in connection with the purchase or sale of securities;

"(2) Is lawful under the Securities Exchange Act of 1934 and any rules and regulations promulgated thereunder; and

"(3) Is not a prohibited transaction within the meaning of section 503(b) of the Code.

"(c) The plan maintains or causes to be maintained for a period of six years from the date of such transaction such records as are necessary to enable the persons described in paragraph (d) of this exemption to determine whether the conditions of this exemption have been met, except that—

"(1) if such party in interest or disqualified person is not a fiduciary with respect to any assets of the plan, such party in interest or disqualified person shall not be subject to the civil penalty which may be assessed under section 502(i) of the Act, or to the taxes imposed by section 4975(a) and (b) of the Code, if such records are not maintained, or are not available for examination as required by paragraph (d) below; and

Exemption is available in connection with all securities purchases and sales from registered broker-dealers. If the broker-dealer extending credit to the plan is a fiduciary, he may not receive interest or other consideration for providing it,[233] and he is subject to certain record-keeping requirements.[234] Otherwise, however, fiduciaries may avail themselves of this section of Exemption 75-1. Perhaps the most significant feature of this section is the tie-in to Section 503(b) of the Internal Revenue Code,[235] according to which it is prohibited to participate in a transaction with certain interested parties for less than adequate consideration.

¶ 10.04. STRUCTURE OF THE ANALYSIS OF THE CONFLICTS OF INTEREST ASSOCIATED WITH SPECIAL RELATIONS BETWEEN MANAGER AND BROKER

Section 11(a) of the Securities Exchange Act and the prohibited-transactions provisions of the Employee Retirement Income Security Act establish circumstances under which certain relationships between brokers and investment managers are forbidden. They do not establish the contrary proposition—namely, when a special relationship between a manager and broker is lawful. There is always a conflict-of-interest problem whenever one of an investment manager's incentives for doing business with a particular broker is the service of his own interest. The

---

"(2) a prohibited transaction will not be deemed to have occurred if, due to circumstances beyond the control of the plan fiduciaries, such records are lost or destroyed prior to the end of such six-year period.

"(d) Notwithstanding anything to the contrary in subsections (a)(2) and (b) of section 504 of the Act, the records referred to in paragraph (c) are unconditionally available for examination during normal business hours by duly authorized employees of (1) the Department of Labor, (2) the Internal Revenue Service, (3) plan participants and beneficiaries, (4) any employer of plan participants nad beneficiaries, and (5) any employee organization any of whose members are covered by such plan. For purposes of this exemption, the terms 'party in interest' and 'disqualified person' shall include such party in interest or disqualified person and any affiliates thereof, and the term 'affiliate' shall be defined in the same manner as that term is defined in 29 CFR 2510.3-21 (e) and 26 CFR 54.4975-9(e)."

[233] Exemption 75-1, note 198 *supra*, § V(a)(2).

[234] *Id.* §§ V(c), V(d). Though the plan must keep the records, the fiduciary is liable for the plan's failure to keep them properly.

[235] See note 180 *supra*.

problem is especially severe where a broker and manager are closely enough affiliated that their combined revenues are a source of proprietary profit to a common party or related parties. But the conflict also exists in any case in which there is a mutual understanding that the manager will conduct business with the broker to their joint advantage. For example, an investment manager who relies on brokerage firms to refer accounts may be inclined to overtrade or to purchase overvalued securities or to sell undervalued securities in order to continue to receive referrals or to increase the rate of referrals.[236] For purposes of simplification, however, the discussions which follow in ¶¶ 10.05 and 10.06 treat the "worst" case, that of affiliation between brokers and managers, where a relationship between a broker and a manager is a factor relevant to the analysis. The principles developed there can be extended by analogy to mutual understanding between brokers and managers who are not formally affiliated. For purposes of clarity, the discussions in ¶¶ 10.05 and 10.06 also identify and examine conflicts of interest that arise out of portfolio executions but which are not necessarily restricted to managers connected with brokers. This ¶ 10.04 sets the framework for analysis.

The first step in the analysis of broker-manager conflict-of-interest problems is to recognize that, unlike paying excess commissions for research, the conduct which these conflicts can promote cannot be made lawful. Neither disclosure nor actual consent will insulate a broker-manager from liability for proven episodes of churning or dumping, for example.[237] No rational investor would agree to make a gift of part of his assets to his broker by trading for the purpose of generating commissions for the broker or by purchasing securities for the purpose of relieving the broker-manager of part of an overvalued inventory.[238] The question is how to resolve the conflict of interest so that, in cases in which a broker-manager does not deliberately engage in self-dealing by churning or dumping or paying higher commissions to himself than are obtainable elsewhere for the same services, he may protect himself from subsequent challenges to his execution practices on those grounds.

One way for a broker-manager to resolve these conflicts of interest,

---

[236] See ¶ 3.02[2][b].

[237] See Norris & Hirshberg, Inc., 21 S.E.C. 865 (1946), *aff'd* 177 F.2d 228 (D.C. Cir. 1949).

[238] See, e.g., Hughes v. SEC, 174 F.2d 969 (D.C. Cir. 1949) (clients could not give informed consent to broker-manager's dual role where they did not know best price of securities in open market or price of securities to broker-manager).

of course, is simply to avoid them. He can execute with other brokers and refuse to deal with his clients as principal or as agent for another. But although this approach, whether adopted voluntarily or imposed by law, may have the virtue of simplicity, it also can result in the client's forgoing best net price on some trades and losing attractive investment opportunities. The other way to resolve the conflict of interest is to adopt some mechanism which tests the fairness of a broker-manager's trading practices. It is in this context that issues of sufficiency of disclosure and quality of informed consent arise.

The second step in the analysis is to make a sharp distinction between those conflict-of-interest problems which are uniquely associated with combined brokerage and management and those which are not. It has been characteristic of the debate over whether there should be separation of brokerage and management imposed by law to lump conflict-of-interest problems together indiscriminately regardless of their pertinence to brokerage and management. Perhaps this phenomenon is merely another indicator of the secondary importance of the conflict-of-interest issue to the decision to separate brokerage and management, but whatever the explanation, the inclination to be overinclusive has appeared even at the most sophisticated levels.

Typical of the blunderbuss approach to the conflicts issue is the *House Securities Industry Study,* which lists seven "inherent conflicts of interest" associated with combined brokerage and management.[239] In addition to identifying as inherent conflicts the tendency to churn and to dump, and the difficulty of self-negotiation of commissions, the Study also argues that broker-managers are subject to incentives to "scalp" and to engage in various forms of preferential treatment of accounts, including selling from favored accounts while selling to less-favored accounts and vice versa, or, in like fashion, making research available earlier to favored managed accounts, or sacrificing best execution to support reciprocal arrangements. But close analysis reveals that, real as these latter conflicts of interest might be, they are not unique to broker-managers: They are unavoidable aspects of every management relationship in which a manager also invests for his own account or serves more than one client. Thus, the discussion of the various conflicts of interest ascribed to the existence of a broker-manager relationship is separated into two parts, one devoted to those conflicts which are not unique to the relationship (see ¶ 10.05), and the other devoted to those which are (see ¶ 10.06).

---

[239] *House Securities Industry Study,* note 4 *supra,* at 148-149.

¶ 10.05. RESOLVING CONFLICTS OF INTEREST THAT ARE NOT UNIQUE TO COMBINED BROKERAGE AND MANAGEMENT

[1] Management Manipulation of Short-Term Market Activity (Scalping)

Scalping, in its classic sense, is the practice of purchasing in advance of a recommendation to one's advisory clients to buy, or selling short in advance of a recommendation to sell. The adviser's purpose is to trade on anticipated short-run market activity. He hopes that investors who rely on him will force a market price rise in connection with a recommendation to buy and a price drop in connection with a recommendation to sell. If he buys or sells short early, he can make a quick profit on the price change produced by his clients' combined action. In *SEC v. Capital Gains Research Bureau, Inc.*, the Supreme Court held that, absent disclosure, purchasing or selling securities in advance of corresponding recommendations to clients violates Section 206 of the Investment Advisers Act of 1940.[240]

The *Capital Gains* case involved the purveyor of a market letter which had no authority or control over subscribers' investment decisions except to the extent they followed the recommendations in the text of the letter. There seems little doubt, therefore, that where an investment manager causes a client to purchase or sell a security solely for the purpose of inducing short-term price movement of which the manager can take advantage, either for his own account or for another more favored account, such a practice is unlawful—at least under the federal securities law antifraud provisions,[241] and probably under common-law fiduciary principles also. The more difficult questions are the extent to which an investment manager may invest for his own account based on the information he generates for use of his clients or to which he may cause clients to invest in issues in which he already is interested. As the Supreme Court stated, "an adviser who . . . secretly trades on the market effect of his own recommendation may be motivated—consciously or unconsciously—to recommend a given security not because of its potential for long-run price increase (which would profit the client), but because of its potential for short-run price increase in response to anticipated activity from the recommendation (which would

---

240 375 U.S. 180 (1963).

241 See Kidder, Peabody & Co., SEC Securities Exchange Act Release No. 8426 (Oct. 16, 1968), [1967-1969 Transfer Binder] CCH Fed. Sec. L. Rep. ¶ 77,618 (Rules 10b-5 and 15c1-2).

profit the adviser)." [242] Similarly, a manager who causes his clients to invest in securities in which he has holdings may be motivated more by his desire to protect his own interests than by a wish to promote the interests of his clients.[243]

One way to resolve these conflicts of interest, as the Supreme Court indicated, is for the manager to disclose to his clients in advance of every transaction his related trading and the nature of interests he has previously obtained or disposed of. Of some relevance in this regard, the SEC has adopted Investment Advisers Act Rule 204-2(a). Though not actually a disclosure rule, it requires, among other things, that statutory advisers keep records and reports of securities transactions consummated by all persons who obtain information about advisory recommendations prior to their dissemination.[244] But for managed accounts particularly, questions of adequacy and timing of disclosure and of independence of judgment in selecting securities for investment are troubling. Consequently, many in the industry have adopted as an ethical standard the practice of prohibiting personnel from using investment information generated to serve advisory clients until after the information has been effectively disseminated either to the clients themselves or to the portfolio managers responsible for their accounts.[245]

In any event, a significant feature of the scalping problem is its total irrelevance to the brokerage-and-management issue, unless one takes the position that brokers are more inclined than other types of investment managers to scalp their clients and that, since the separation of brokerage and management will result in less investment management by brokers, there will be less scalping. The opportunities for every investment manager to scalp his clients are identical, no matter who executes the transaction. Scalping raises only the question of the motivation behind an investment decision. Indeed, scalping has always been regarded as more of a problem connected with investment managers other than brokers. As *Capital Gains* suggests, scalping first came to the at-

---

[242] 375 U.S. at 196.

[243] See SEC v. Midwest Technical Development Corp., [1961-1964 Transfer Binder] CCH Fed. Sec. L. Rep. ¶ 91,252 (D. Minn. 1963).

[244] 17 C.F.R. §§ 275.204-2(a)(12) through 275.204-2(a)(13). The specific purpose of these provisions is to deal with the scalping problem. See SEC Investment Advisers Act Release No. 436 (Feb. 21, 1975), [1974-1975 Transfer Binder] CCH Fed. Sec. L. Rep. ¶ 80,113. While not providing for actual disclosure, the record-keeping requirement at least should have an inhibitory effect.

[245] See, e.g., *Special Study*, note 1 *supra*, Pt. 4, at 238, 251-252; *PPI Report*, note 15 *supra*, at 195-200.

tention of the SEC as a practice of registered investment advisers, and the *Special Study* confirms this point.[246] Furthermore, both the *Special Study* and the *PPI Report* expanded on the principles at issue by focusing on investment companies and investment advisers, not broker-dealers.[247] Eventually, the Investment Company Act (not the Securities Exchange Act) was amended to permit the SEC to prescribe ethical codes to control scalping and related abuses.[248]

Thereafter, emphasis shifted from type of manager to type of information. By analogy to the insider-trading cases, the Commission began developing the position that market information—nonpublic knowledge about the future market for a particular security, such as impending trades of substantial size and important research discoveries—imposes some form of disclosure duty.[249] In 1973, the SEC issued a release requesting comments on guidelines for inside information,[250] including one question on the proper regulatory posture for dealing with market information. Here again, there was no suggestion that a broker-manager's status as broker should have anything to do with the issue. The only place the SEC tried to draw a connection between scalping and combined brokerage and management was in the release accompanying adoption of Rule 19b-2.[251] In that instance, it was used only by analogy, to buttress the Commission's argument against institutional membership on exchanges and not for the purpose of attacking the combination of brokerage and management.

[2] Preferential Treatment

The more refined the inquiry into scalping becomes, the more one progresses ineluctably into the question of preferential treatment of ac-

---

246 See *Special Study,* note 1 *supra,* Pt. 1, at 382.

247 See *id.* Pt. 4, at 235-255; *PPI Report,* note 15 *supra,* at 195-200.

248 Pub. L. 91-547 § 9(c) (Dec. 14, 1970), *adding* Section 17(j) to the Investment Company Act, 15 U.S.C. § 80a-17(j). To implement this provision, the SEC proposed, but subsequently withdrew, Rule 17j-1. See SEC Investment Company Act Release No. 7581 (Dec. 26, 1972), [1972-1973 Transfer Binder] CCH Fed. Sec. L. Rep. ¶ 79,157.

249 See, e.g., Lipton, "Market Information," in R. Mundheim, A. Fleischer & J. Schupper, *Fifth Annual Institute on Securities Regulation* 287 (PLI 1974); Fleischer, Mundheim & Murphy, "An Initial Inquiry Into the Responsibility to Disclose Market Information," 121 U. Pa. L. Rev. 798 (1973).

250 SEC Securities Exchange Act Release No. 10316 (Aug. 1, 1973), [1973 Transfer Binder] CCH Fed. Sec. L. Rep. ¶ 79,446.

251 Adoption of Rule 19b-2, note 69 *supra,* at 113-114.

counts. If an investment manager is not deliberately trading to obtain short-term benefits for his own account or his favored accounts by taking advantage of price movements generated by the trading activities of his other accounts,[252] the focus of inquiry really becomes why, when facing an investment opportunity or executing a related group of trades, the manager takes action affecting one identifiable group of clients differently from another. But whether preferential treatment is intentional or inadvertent, inequitable or defensible, the problem, like that of scalping, has very little to do with the issue of whether brokerage and management should be separated. While a broker-manager may favor one set of managed accounts over another,[253] either in the application of

---

[252] See, e.g., Folk, "Restructuring the Securities Markets—The Martin Report: A Critique," 57 Va. L. Rev. 1315, 1362-1363 (1971). Professor Folk was describing a "subtle interest conflict" which may cause a broker-manager to buy an attractive stock for his managed accounts and then pass the word on to institutional customers whose buying power will cause the price to rise above what the managed accounts paid. Of course, this opportunity exists for any investment manager who services both managed accounts and informal advisees. The implication of Professor Folk's observation, however, is that brokers, by the nature of their business, are stronger candidates to engage in that practice because they service more clients in the informal advisee category. In this regard, he is quite right. Brokers are constantly soliciting customers to trade with them on the basis of the investment information they make available. Institutional salesmen try to interest institutions in a particular security, as do customer's men with respect to individual investors, because by doing so, they earn commission income.

But while it may well be true that broker-managers are likely to have far more extensive contacts with persons merely seeking investment information, the suggestion that the combination of brokerage and management exacerbates the inclination of broker-managers to trade for managed accounts before using investment information to stimulate interest with commission-only customers is flawed. Even assuming that fear of losing customers is no incentive to treat all parties evenhandedly, and that his registered representatives and institutional salesmen will sit still, a broker-manager who wants to promote a price change by acting for his managed accounts before making investment information otherwise available can just as easily execute for his managed accounts through other houses before he releases the information to straight-commission customers. The only difference is that he loses the commission income he otherwise would have received from his managed accounts. But that loss has little effect on his incentive to favor one group over the other since, by hypothesis, his unknowing customers will continue to execute through him.

[253] A manager may favor a more performance-conscious account over the account of a less sophisticated client, for example, because by doing so, he will preserve and possibly enhance his position with the former and others like him without seriously affecting his position with the latter. See, e.g., *Institutional Investor Study*, note 2 *supra*, at 348.

research to the investment decision-making process or in the execution
of investment decisions, this same opportunity also obtains for every
other type of investment manager, as the discussions in Chapter 9 on
allocating excess commission costs among multiple accounts amply
demonstrate.[254]

Actually, the real concern that brokers generate with respect to
preferential treatment is not that they, more than other types of investment managers, will make arbitrary distinctions among managed accounts. It is that public customers will suffer relative to brokers'
managed accounts. Broker-managers, far more than other investment
managers, serve two distinct clienteles whose interests are frequently
pitted against each other. Though not precisely articulated, the gist
of the concern is that brokers will use their trading capabilities and
their research resources for themselves and a closed private group of
clients ahead of public customers, both institutions and individuals, in
ways which will generate trading profits not because of superior investment acumen, but because of inside access to exchange facilities. This
state of affairs was perceived as being unfair to public customers and
subversive of an accessible and liquid securities market.[255] Indeed, the
specter of preferential treatment to the disadvantage of public customers
formed an essential part of the SEC's argument against institutional
membership in the release accompanying the issuance of Rule 19b-2.[256]

To be sure, the restrictions that should be placed on brokers in
dealing with their public customers to promote fairness in the marketplace is a complex matter.[257] But without gainsaying the seriousness
of the public-policy question of how extensively, in pursuing the goal
of a fair marketplace, brokers and persons having special relationships
with brokers should be excluded from investment management activities,
prohibiting brokers from carrying out in-house executions for their
managed accounts or otherwise limiting a broker-manager's place of
execution affects only a firm's commission revenues, not its incentives
or opportunities to disfavor public customers.

---

[254] See ¶¶ 9.05[2] and 9.06[4].

[255] See, e.g., *House 1974 Amendments Report*, note 118 *supra*, at 51.

[256] Adoption of Rule 19b-2, note 69 *supra*, at 109-129.

[257] One step Congress has taken in trying to strike a fair balance between
permitting a broker to act in his own interest and restricting his lawful
authority in the public interest, for example, is Securities Exchange Act
§ 11(a)(1)(G). It exempts from the restrictions on combined brokerage-
management executions for an exchange member's own account subject to
rules of the Commission which assure that such transactions yield "priority,
parity, and precedence" to orders of nonmembers. See note 126 *supra*.

To fully appreciate why preferential treatment is not a special problem of broker-managers, it is helpful to recognize that the preferential-treatment question is really an aspect of the market-information question. For a period, there seemed to be emerging under the antifraud provisions of the federal securities laws two contending duty standards reflecting the tension between the policy of enhancing fair dealing in the marketplace and the policy of permitting broker-entrepreneurs the opportunity to profit on proprietary information generated through investment of capital and superior insight. On one side was the parity-of-information test which, in its pure form, would require a broker to disclose to all his clients and customers any material market information about a security he was recommending, including such things as previous dissemination of research information, pending transactions sizable enough to effect the price of the security, and so forth.[258] On the other side was a special-relationship test which would require such disclosure only if there were a special relationship between the broker and customer.[259] The issue remains unresolved, though it seems safe to say as a general rule that the more important the market information and the more significant the involvement of the broker, the greater is the duty of disclosure to the public customer. Thus, for example, active solicitation by a broker would probably impose a correlative duty of disclosure.

But to the degree the parity-of-information test is rejected, the combination of brokerage and management can have no effect whatsoever on a broker-manager's incentives to favor his managed accounts over his public customers. Suppose, for example, a broker-manager concluded that U.S. Widget Co. was an attractive investment opportunity. A broker-manager might well purchase USW securities for his managed accounts before soliciting institutional and individual customers to make similar purchases. The authority of the broker to execute in-house for his managed accounts would be irrelevant, however, to his decision of whether or how much to favor his managed accounts by not disclosing to his other customers the use to which he has already put the research information about USW. If brokerage and management are not separated, he will execute in house (assuming his execution price is competitive). If brokerage and management are separated, he will execute through another firm (at a competitive execution price).

---

[258] See note 249 *supra*.
[259] *Id.* See Sec. Reg. & L. Rep. No. 352, May 12, 1976, p. A-7 (SEC Commissioner Loomis considers parity of information test too restrictive).

Rules regarding the place of execution affect only the commission revenues a broker-manager can realize through his managed accounts. They will not influence his decision of when to disseminate information beyond his managed accounts or in what order the information will be disseminated. If it is the judgment of public policy that present rules governing the treatment of public customers relative to managed accounts[260] are inadequate to prevent unfairness and that such rules cannot be amended to achieve sufficient fairness by refining market-information disclosure rules brokers should be precluded from all management activities, not simply from executing for their managed accounts.

[3] Reciprocal Dealing

The *House Securities Industry Study* also points to a perceived conflict of interest in combined brokerage and management whereby a broker-manager will tend to engage in reciprocal arrangements.[261] The *Study* does not expand on this perceived conflict, and it is difficult to see exactly what was meant. If anything, the separation of brokerage and management will promote reciprocal arrangements because they would become the only way by which broker-managers could benefit from the commissions their managed accounts would generate. Perhaps the Study was alluding to the reciprocal arrangements which had grown up under the fixed-rate commission system and was impliedly suggesting that comparable relationships would be likely for so long as fixed rates remained in effect. If that was the gist of the Study's point, it was entirely correct since, as the record shows, investors, particularly institutional investors, will find ways to use their economic power to force brokers to transfer excess commissions some place else so that either the institutions or their managers can obtain additional benefits. Furthermore, that may in fact be the reason the reciprocal arrangements argument was made, since at the time the House Study was published, it was not a sure bet that fixed commissions would be totally eliminated. That argument has no application under a fully negotiated rate system, however.

---

260 In addition to the controls imposed by the federal antifraud rules, the securities industry has its own set of guidelines. See, e.g., NYSE Member Firm Cir. No. 170 (Nov. 16, 1962); AMEX Info. Cir. No. 51-71 (April 20, 1971); AMEX Info. Cir. No. 79-69 (April 25, 1969); AMEX Info. Cir. No. 38-68 (Feb. 12, 1968).

261 *House Securities Industry Study*, note 4 *supra*, at 149.

¶ 10.06. RESOLVING CONFLICTS OF INTEREST THAT ARE UNIQUE TO COMBINED BROKERAGE AND MANAGEMENT

[1] Overtrading (Churning)

It is about as settled a proposition as there can be in securities law that churning is illegal. It has been held that churning violates Section 17(a) of the Securities Act of 1933,[262] Section 10(b) and Rule 10b-5,[263] Section 15(c)(1) and Rule 15c1-7,[264] and Section 20(a)[265] of the Securities Exchange Act of 1934. Under appropriate circumstances, it would presumably be held fraudulent under Section 206 of the Investment Advisers Act of 1940.[266] Indeed, churning is so well established as a fraudulent act that at least one court has awarded punitive damages for a churning offense.[267] Moreover, under the antifraud rules of the federal securities laws, it is not necessary to show specific intent to defraud to make out a case of churning. The gist of the action is excessive turnover of an account, and once excessive trading is estab-

---

[262] Lehman v. Merrill Lynch, Pierce, Fenner & Smith, Inc., Sec. Reg. L. Rep., March 10, 1976, at A-8 (N.Y. Sup. Ct., Feb. 23, 1976); Leonard v. Colton, [1967-1969 Transfer Binder] CCH Fed. Sec. L. Rep. ¶ 92,312 (E.D.N.Y. 1968); Newkirk v. Hayden, Stone & Co., [1964-1966 Transfer Binder] CCH Fed. Sec. L. Rep. ¶ 91,621 (S.D. Cal. 1965).

[263] E.g., Hecht v. Harris, Upham & Co., 430 F.2d 1202 (9th Cir. 1970); Jenny v. Shearson, Hammill & Co., [1974-1975 Transfer Binder] CCH Fed. Sec. L. Rep. ¶ 95,021 (S.D.N.Y. 1975); Stromillo v. Merrill Lynch, Pierce, Fenner & Smith, Inc., 54 F.R.D. 396 (E.D.N.Y. 1971).

[264] E.g., Newkirk v. Hayden, Stone & Co., [1964-1966 Transfer Binder] CCH Fed. Sec. L. Rep. ¶ 91,621 (S.D. Cal. 1965); *In re* Norris & Hirshberg, Inc., 21 S.E.C. 865 (1946), *aff'd* 177 F.2d 228 (D.C. Cir. 1949). In connection with discretionary accounts, Rule 15c1-7 expressly establishes as a "manipulative, deceptive or other fraudulent device" under Section 15(c)(1) (15 U.S.C. § 78o(c)(1)) "any transactions or purchase or sale which are excessive in size or frequency in view of the financial resources and character of such account."

[265] Hecht v. Harris, Upham & Co., 430 F.2d 1202 (9th Cir. 1970). But see Zweig v. Hearst Corp., 521 F.2d 1129 (9th Cir.), *cert. denied* 423 U.S. 1025 (1975).

[266] Cf. John C. Tead Co., [1973-1976 Transfer Binder] CCH Mutual Funds Guide ¶ 9896 (1973); Argus Sec. Management Corp., [1971-1972 Transfer Binder] CCH Fed. Sec. L. Rep. ¶ 78,366 (1971) (no-action letters denied referral arrangements between investment advisers and broker-dealers despite full disclosure).

[267] Lehman v. Merrill Lynch, Pierce, Fenner & Smith, Inc., Sec. Reg. L. Rep., March 10, 1976, at A-8 (N.Y. Sup. Ct., Feb. 23, 1976).

lished, liability depends on the purpose behind the trading activity.[268] Furthermore, proof of excessive turnover can be sufficient evidence of an intent to generate commissions as the broker's dominant purpose.

Implicit in a churning inquiry is the assumption that the higher the turnover rate, the greater the risk involved.[269] The various cases refer to such obvious suitability factors as the trading sophistication,[270] investment objectives,[271] and financial resources of the client.[272] Similarly, Rule 15c1-7 expressly requires that the churning determination be made "in view of the financial resources and character of such account." [273] A claim of churning, therefore, unavoidably brings into issue suitability considerations. This means that the first step in a churning inquiry is to determine, given a client's initial wealth position and attitude toward risk, whether the turnover rate and the client's investment objectives can be reconciled.[274] Ordinarily, however, the suitability issue is subsumed as a question of fact on the issue of whether the dominant purpose of the broker-manager was to generate commission income.

In *Hecht v. Harris, Upham & Co.*,[275] for example, the court specif-

---

[268] See Hecht v. Harris, Upham & Co., 430 F.2d 1202 (9th Cir. 1970). The necessity for proving "scienter" imposed in Ernst & Ernst v. Hochfelder, 425 U.S. 185 (1976) (discussed in ¶ 6.01 at note 5), would not seem to preclude an objective scienter test, based on an unjustifiable turnover rate in light of the client's investment objectives, tending to show the dominant purpose to be the generating of commissions. See Rolf v. Blyth Eastman Dillon & Co., [1976-1977 Transfer Binder] CCH Fed. Sec. L. Rep. ¶ 95,843 (S.D.N.Y. 1977). See generally Haimoff, "Holmes Looks at Hochfelder and 10b-5," 32 Bus. Law. 147 (1976).

[269] See ¶ 7.07 at note 111.

[270] Hecht v. Harris, Upham & Co., 430 F.2d 1202 (9th Cir. 1970); Fey v. Walston & Co., 493 F.2d 1036 (7th Cir. 1974).

[271] Fey v. Walston & Co., Inc., note 220 *supra*.

[272] E.H. Rollins & Sons, Inc., 18 S.E.C. 347 (1945).

[273] Rule 15c1-7 applies to discretionary accounts. The standard it announces would probably be incorporated under the general antifraud provisions, Sections 10(b) and 15(c)(1) of the Securities Exchange Act, and implemented through Rules 10b-5 and 15c1-2. Cf. Powers v. Francis I. DuPont & Co., 344 F. Supp. 429 (E.D. Pa. 1972) (churning claim dismissed in part on grounds of client's representation of ability to absorb financial losses). Furthermore, the definition of investment discretion in the Securities Exchange Act § 3(a)(35) (15 U.S.C. § 78c(a)(35)) gives Rule 15c1-7 a much broader scope than it would have had if restricted only to accounts in which a broker-manager has absolute power to invest without consulting the client.

[274] See, e.g., Landry v. Hemphill, Noyes & Co., [1972-1973 Transfer Binder] CCH Fed. Sec. L. Rep. ¶ 93,758 (1st Cir. 1973) (claim of churning dismissed because transactions for plaintiff's account held not excessive).

[275] 430 F.2d 1202 (9th Cir. 1970).

ically rejected a suitability claim at the same time it upheld a churning claim. This suggests that, even if a broker-manager could show that a high-turnover trading program was suitable for his client, proof of an intent to generate commissions would render a suitability defense immaterial. Damage awards in these cases tend to confirm this analysis. Although it has been argued that damages ought to be measured against a lost-profits standard,[276] damage awards are typically determined by reference to commission expenditures.[277] In short, although unsuitability can serve the same function as such other objective indicators of a broker's intent as turnover rate, in-and-out trading, and ratio of the client's investment to the broker's profits,[278] proof of unsuitability is not essential to the success of a churning claim.

But, though churning may be the worst example of a broker-manager's succumbing to the conflict of interest he faces when he has the responsibility for selecting sound investments for his clients as well as the opportunity to enhance his profits through commissions on executions, blatant churning is far from the only manifestation of this conflict. A broker-manager might induce a client to engage in a trading program which is unsuitable for the client. Or he might make a series of investments on the basis of investment analysis which reflects less than professional skill and care but which he rationalizes because of the opportunity to earn commissions. Finally, of course, both conditions can be present. The broker-manager's self-interest may cause him to induce a client to undertake a program of trading which is unsuitable for the client, and that same self-interest may encourage the broker-

---

[276] *Id.* (dissenting opinion). See Note, "Churning by Securities Dealers," 80 Harv. L. Rev. 869 (1967).

[277] In *Hecht,* for example, the district court's damage award included commissions and interest on margin transactions, lost dividends through sales of previously owned securities, and losses suffered in commodities trading. 283 F. Supp. 417 (N.D. Cal. 1968). But the court of appeals reduced the damages by the amount of dividends foregone and the commodities trading losses, 430 F.2d 1202 (9th Cir. 1970). See also Lehman v. Merrill Lynch, Pierce, Fenner & Smith, Inc., Sec. Reg. L. Rep., March 10, 1976, at A-8.

[278] See Jenny v. Shearson, Hammill & Co., Inc., [1974-1975 Transfer Binder] CCH Fed. Sec. L. Rep. ¶ 95,021 (S.D.N.Y. 1975); *In re* Charles E. Marland & Co., SEC Securities Exchange Act Release No. 11065 (Oct. 21, 1974), [1974-1975 Transfer Binder] CCH Fed. Sec. L. Rep. ¶ 80,002. See generally 3 L. Loss, *Securities Regulation* 1479-1480 (2d ed. 1961); *id.* Vol. 6, at 3674-3680 (Supp. 1969); Note, "Churning by Securities Dealers," 80 Harv. L. Rev. 869 (1967).

manager to purchase and sell securities on the basis of analyses which are professionally deficient.[279]

Thus, although in principle, a client may be suited for a high-turnover investment program, and although the mere fact the client suffers losses may not prove that the program was executed with less than professional skill and care,[280] the presence of the conflict of interest places a severe strain on a broker-manager's duty of loyalty. As with other duty of loyalty questions, the opportunity for self-dealing in this context either shifts the burden to the broker-manager to show that such losses were in fact the result of the vagaries of the marketplace and not a consequence of an attempt to enhance commission income, or requires him to resolve the conflict in advance so that the burden will remain with the client to prove that the broker-manager failed to act with professional skill and care.[281]

Unfortunately for broker-managers, the practical problems of proof in a case involving a claim of overtrading can be prodigious. Because suitability obligations increase as the risk associated with an investment program increases, a strategy of heavy trading not only requires a showing of suitability but also makes proof of suitability more difficult than is the case for less risky programs.[282] The problem of proof in relating trading-oriented investment programs to standards of professional skill and care is also severe,[283] since the evidence tends to show that heavy trading is not ordinarily an effective investment strategy. Furthermore, since retrospective evaluations of questions of fact can be unpredictable, it seems additionally hazardous for a broker-manager to rely on his ability to prove suitability and compliance with professional standards of care with respect to a high-turnover strategy.

A safer approach would be to resolve the conflict-of-interest problem to the extent practicable before undertaking any investment management relationship which includes executing for managed accounts. One way to resolve the conflict is to eliminate it. This can be done by taking a leaf from Section 11(a) of the Securities Exchange Act and Section 406 of ERISA and refusing to execute in house for managed accounts at all. This approach has in fact been adopted by some broker-managers

---

[279] See, e.g., Hecht v. Harris, Upham & Co., 430 F.2d 1202 (9th Cir. 1970).

[280] See ¶ 7.07.

[281] See ¶ 1.03.

[282] See Chapter 4 for an extensive discussion of the problems involved in proving suitability.

[283] See ¶ 7.07 at note 111.

on their own initiative,[284] but it has the disadvantage of depriving the client of in-house executions even when the broker-manager offers the best net price. To achieve the same result without depriving the client of the possibility of some advantageous executions, the broker-manager can, as the *Senate Securities Industry Study* notes,[285] simply credit commission income from in-house executions for a managed account against the advisory fee. Though not serious, there are problems with this solution also, however. If the entire commission is credited against the advisory fee, it becomes costly for a broker-manager to execute in house since he must pay the overhead and operating expenses associated with his brokerage activities. If the credit is restricted to commission profits, the problem then becomes one of determining and accounting for the extent of the profit margin on each trade. Furthermore, total elimination of brokerage profits can encourage inferior executions by inclining the brokerage arm to give greater attention and priority to paying customers or by inducing the management arm to execute with another house in the expectation of generating some reciprocal brokerage business.[286]

Since a broker-manager may not wish to forgo in-house executions which are advantageous to the client, and since trying to eliminate the conflict created by a broker-manager's interest in commissions by crediting commission profits against advisory fees unavoidably creates a different set of conflict-of-interest problems, a third option for resolving the conflict of interest which occurs when a broker-manager executes in-house and retains all or part of the commissions generated may be considered attractive. This option is the familiar approach to conflict resolution of disclosure and informed consent. Through appropriate disclosure and by obtaining an informed consent, a broker-manager, making an appropriate suitability determination and carrying out

---

[284] In Tannenbaum v. Zeller, 399 F. Supp. 945 (S.D.N.Y. 1975), *aff'd in part and rev'd in part* 522 F.2d 402 (2d Cir. 1977), for instance, the broker-manager of a mutual fund had a policy of not executing through its own facilities, a fact which seemed to influence the district court to hold in the broker-manager's favor in an action claiming breach of duty of recapture of commissions. The case is discussed extensively in ¶ 9.07[2]. See also Patocka, "Will Broker-Affiliates Still Manage Pension Money?" 9 Institutional Investor 67 (July 1975).

[285] *Senate Securities Industry Study,* note 1 *supra,* at 75.

[286] Some brokers charge a flat fee which includes management and all commissions. The fee is substantially higher than a straight management fee, of course, and it tends to reward undertrading rather than overtrading.

an investment program which comports with professional standards, ought to be able to shift the burden back to the client to show he has failed to meet these responsibilities with reasonable care. In this regard, disclosure and informed consent requires at least:

(1) That the client be told that the manager will execute through the facilities of an affiliated broker[287];

(2) That the client be sufficiently sophisticated to evaluate the hazards associated with combined brokerage and management[288]; and

(3) That the client be aware of the nature of the program the broker-manager proposes to undertake.[289]

Admittedly, the third factor is particularly imprecise, but there are ways to make it more objective. For example, if the broker-manager really does have experience in running a high-turnover investment program for purposes of investment return and not of generating commissions, he ought to be able to explain in advance the probable cost to the client and the range of risk to which he will be exposed. He should be able, for example, to describe within reasonable limits the rate of turnover the client can anticipate, the approximate cost of commissions generated by such a program, and the range of experience, both good and bad, of other clients with similar objectives.[290] With information

---

[287] See, e.g., Hartzmark & Co., [1973 Transfer Binder] CCH Fed. Sec. L. Rep. ¶ 79,563 (1973). See also Thomas L. Gordon, [1973-1974 Transfer Binder] CCH Fed. Sec. L. Rep. ¶ 79,757 (1974) (associations between investment advisers and broker-dealers permissible if there is full disclosure of the relationship).

[288] See, e.g., Hecht v. Harris, Upham & Co., 430 F.2d 1202 (9th Cir. 1970) (fact that client was aware of extent of trading because of confirmation slips did not make out estoppel defense to claim of churning). But cf. Greenfield v. D.H. Blair & Co., [1975-1976 Transfer Binder] CCH Fed. Sec. L. Rep. ¶ 95,239 (S.D.N.Y. 1975) (intelligent college-educated person sufficiently sophisticated to know whether account was being churned).

[289] See Jenny v. Shearson, Hammill & Co., [1974-1975 Transfer Binder] CCH Fed. Sec. L. Rep. ¶ 95,021 (S.D.N.Y. 1975) (transactions excessive in view of client's stated investment objectives).

[290] The purpose in describing the record of performance is to show the kind of variation possible in so risky an investment program as one involving heavy trading activity. If a discussion of performance record is also to induce a prospective client to enter a management arrangement, a broker-manager must take care to see that his marketing efforts satisfy legal requirements also. See ¶¶ 3.02[2][c], 3.02[2][d].

like this, the client can monitor the progress of his account against a practicable standard for determining whether the broker-manager is trading overly often. To rely, in contrast, on such vague terms as "aggressive growth" to describe the investment strategy hardly seems adequate to give the client a reasonable basis to satisfy himself of the purposes behind his manager's trading practices.

[2] Acting as Principal or Agent for Another (Dumping)

The everyday business of most brokerage firms frequently involves them in transactions in which they buy and sell to customers from their own account or act as brokerage agent for a buyer and a seller of securities on the same transaction. Their typical principal activities include underwriting, market making, and block positioning; dual agency operations typically include block trading and in-house cross-trading. These activities are all heavily regulated for brokers not performing significant management functions and the applicable regulatory requirements are effectively explored in a number of excellent authorities.[291] The purpose here is to examine the additional responsibilities that are imposed when a broker acting as manager transacts business as principal or agent for another. Plainly, the rules for broker-dealers acting as principal or agent for another in transacting business for ordinary customers set minimum standards for transactions with managed accounts. But, although a broker-manager must comply with these rules, compliance to that extent alone may not be sufficient to satisfy his fiduciary duty to his clients. Managed accounts imply greater reliance and trust in a broker than is normally the case in ordinary brokerage transactions. Thus, for example, disclosure of an adverse interest might suffice to put a brokerage customer on alert to assure himself of proper treatment. The same kind of disclosure might well be regarded as ineffective in a management relationship in which a broker-manager's influence over the investment decision-making process would remain essentially unaffected by disclosure.[292]

---

[291] E.g., R. Jennings & H. Marsh, *Securities Regulation* (1972); L. Loss, *Securities Regulation* (2d ed. 1961); SEC, Report of the Advisory Committee for the Broker-Dealer Model Compliance Program, "Guide to Broker-Dealer Compliance," announced in SEC Securities Exchange Act Release No. 11098 (Nov. 13, 1974) (hereinafter cited as *Compliance Report*).

[292] See, e.g., statement of (then) deputy director of SEC Division of Enforcement, in Rosenman, "Discretionary Accounts and Manipulative Trading Practices," in R. Mundheim, A. Fleischer & J. Schupper, *Fifth Annual Institute on Securities Regulation* 245, 251-253 (PLI 1974).

Conceptually, there are two related conflicts of interest when a broker-manager acts as a dual agent or as a principal. Acting as dual agent, he may sacrifice the interests of one of his principals to serve those of the other by selling overvalued securities in one account to the other or by buying undervalued securities from one and transferring them to the other.[293] Acting as principal, he may use his managed accounts to reduce his own unwanted inventory, to expand his position in an attractive security owned by those accounts, or to aid his trading activities. These conflicts may manifest themselves in deliberate perversions of fiduciary duty. For example, a broker-manager might use his managed accounts to help a strong client exit from an undesirable position[294]; he might trade back and forth to maintain an artificial market in a security[295]; he might purchase securities from a market maker and sell them to his clients at a large markup[296]; he might purchase securities from his clients at substantial markdowns[297]; he might use his managed accounts to dispose of overvalued underwritings and to manipulate the price of new issues[298]; and so forth.

But deliberate perversion of duty is not always the issue. The presence of these conflicts also complicates the management activities of brokers and those closely related to brokers whose intentions are not fraudulent but rather to serve the interests of all parties fairly. Consider,

---

[293] He may also disregard the interests of both principals by using his managed accounts to trade back and forth in order to generate commissions. See, e.g., Norris & Hirshberg, Inc., 21 S.E.C. 865 (1946), aff'd 177 F.2d 228 (D.C. Cir. 1949). This is only a refined version of churning, however, and requires no analysis beyond what has been discussed in ¶ 10.06[1] *supra*.

[294] See E. Herman, *Conflicts of Interest: Commercial Bank Trust Departments* 63 (Twentieth Century Fund 1975), in which the author describes an incident in which a bank performed such a chore for the pension fund of a large creditworthy customer by selling to the pension fund of a credit-dependent customer.

[295] See, e.g., Norris & Hirshberg, Inc., 21 S.E.C. 865 (1946), aff'd 177 F.2d 228 (D.C. Cir. 1949).

[296] See, e.g., Hughes v. SEC, 174 F.2d 969 (D.C. Cir. 1949).

[297] See, e.g., *In re* Thornton, SEC Securities Exchange Act Release No. 7693 (Aug. 31, 1965), [1964-1966 Transfer Binder] CCH Fed. Sec. L. Rep. ¶ 77,279.

[298] See SEC Securities Act Release No. 5398 (June 1, 1973), [1973 Transfer Binder] CCH Fed. Sec. L. Rep. ¶ 79,386, and SEC Securities Act Release No. 5395 (June 1, 1973), *id.* ¶ 79,383, both dealing with disclosure rules in connection with new issues. The SEC announced the new rules because of its findings that some broker-underwriters were using managed accounts to manipulate underwritings.

for example, the difficulties facing a broker-manager given the opportunity to purchase a stock in which his client has expressed interest and at a price which he knows is attractive to his client. Suppose the client has told the broker he would like a position in the stock at a price of $15 or less a share. Suppose a seller then approaches the broker and offers to sell for a price as low as $12 a share. To effect the transaction, the broker must resolve three unavoidably conflicting interests: the fairness of the price to his managed account; the fairness of the price to his selling customer; and the size of the commission he should charge.[299] Plainly, the pricing decision will depend on how he evaluates his commitment to each party.

Or consider the competing demands that might face a broker-manager who, acting as underwriter, can place part of a new issue in his managed accounts. In a best-efforts underwriting, the broker-manager must resolve the competing interests of the issuer who wants the entire issue placed, the interests of his clients who want their manager to use his best independent judgment with respect to all investment opportunities available at the time, and his own interests in receiving underwriting commissions, the amount of which depend on the number of shares he sells. In a firm-commitment underwriting, the broker-manager either must retain the stock in inventory, and thus at his own risk, or he must place it with his accounts and his customers. Even if he honestly believes in the soundness of the issue, and maintains part of the issue in inventory, his judgment as to whether that issue is better than other available investment opportunities may be affected by a desire to reduce at least a part of his exposure or by a desire to support the offering price through purchases by his managed accounts.

But the problems in resolving these conflicts of interest when a broker-manager acts as underwriter are fairly obvious. Others can be much more subtle. Suppose that a broker-manager's clients, though not participating in the new issue, own previously issued shares. It might be to their advantage to dispose of all or a part of those holdings while the syndicate is stabilizing. Yet it is almost inconceivable that a broker-manager would sell into a syndicate bid, much less one he was committed to stabilize, even if his clients' best interests suggested doing so.

---

[299] The commission decision depends, of course, on what he considers a reasonable profit for the firm. See M. Mayer, *Conflicts of Interest: Broker-Dealer Firms* 8-10 (Twentieth Century Fund 1975), in which a broker, acting purely as broker, executed the transaction described in the text in a stock he had previously underwritten and in which he was then making a market. The sales price was $13.50 on 60,000 shares, less an eighth of a point for commission. See note 329 *infra*.

Note especially the unique adversarial nature of the conflict-of-interest problem when a broker-manager acts as principal or as agent for another. With other conflict problems, a broker-manager's interest is, in a sense, parasitic to the investment program of the client. Churning, which focuses on a broker-manager's commission profits, and scalping and preferential treatment, which focus on how the total profits in any investment opportunity and the total costs in any trading sequence will be allocated, each permit a manager to reach the fundamental conclusion that a given security should be bought or should be sold irrespective of his own opportunities for profit. It is entirely possible in such cases, even where a manager thoroughly indulges his own interest in profit, for the client to enjoy a handsome return also if the manager is fortunate enough to select the right securities. The nature of the conflict is very different when a manager acts as principal or agent for another since the managed account is taking action exactly opposite to that taken by the manager for his own account or in behalf of another account he is representing. One is buying while another is selling, and the manager is in the position of claiming that his action works to the benefit of both.[300]

To be sure, it is possible for both buyer and seller to be better off, in fact, for the transaction. Indeed, that is the major premise supporting free exchange in trade generally. But the existence of a management relationship undercuts the justification for assuming that, in most cases, both parties to a trade will regard themselves as better off. An investment management client, by hypothesis, cannot fully identify his own interests, and is not as capable as his manager of determining whether a particular purchase or sale, or the amount to which he participates in a transaction, effectively serves his investment objectives. Furthermore, securities are a special kind of commodity distinguishable from most other goods and services in an important respect. Except where a seller must liquidate to meet current expenditures, securities are bought and sold because both parties disagree over their future value. Since each

---

[300] Mayer, adoping the language of game theory (see J. Von Neumann & O. Morgenstern, *Theory of Games and Economic Behavior* (1944)), distinguishes these two conflicts of interest as variable-sum and zero-sum conflicts. Variable-sum conflicts are those where "[managers], acting to maximize their own profits, may harm their [clients], although the clients may also win." Zero-sum conflicts are those where "each dollar gained by the [manager or third party] is a dollar the customer would have gained had the manager acted in the client's interest rather than its own [or the third party's]." M. Mayer, *Conflicts of Interest: Broker-Dealer Firms* (Twentieth Century Fund 1975).

cannot be correct,[301] there is an obvious strain on one who is a fiduciary to buy or sell for a client and be on the opposite side of the transaction at the same time.

Though the opportunity for fraud may be significant, bad faith is beside the point. A manager may believe in the utmost good faith that his client is making a good investment or wisely disposing of all or part of a holding. The fiduciary question, however, is whether the manager believes at the time that the action his client is taking is the *best* alternative known to the manager, given the client's investment objectives. And it is a rare case in which a manager, acting on both sides of a transaction, can honestly say that the judgment he reaches about what is fair and reasonable for both parties is the same one he would have reached if he were acting for one managed account alone, if only because it is impossible for him to know what his attitude would otherwise have been.

One way to resolve this conflict of interest, of course, is for the manager to act only as agent for a client as, for example, the Department of Labor and the Internal Revenue Service have insisted on with

---

[301] This is so even if both parties are in the marketplace merely to adjust the risk in their portfolios. Suppose the seller, a hedge fund, wants to raise the risk in its portfolio by liquidating its holdings in U.S. Widget (USW), a leading blue chip, and buying National Flyer Co., a speculative defense contractor. Suppose the buyer, a pension fund with cash to invest, wants USW in its portfolio to lower the risk. A trade between them appears plainly to benefit both parties, because each would better be able to pursue its investment objectives. But this analysis considers only the systematic return (i.e., market-determined return; see ¶ 7.03[1]) of USW, a figure on which both parties would agree. USW also has unsystematic return (i.e., idiosyncratic return; see ¶ 7.03[1]) which can be sizable, however low its systematic risk may be. It is this figure over which the seller and buyer disagree. If the seller thought that USW would show sharp gains because of the success of a new product line it was developing, an increase in demand for widgets, or for any other reason, it would dispose of some other low-volatility holding or not sell at all. Similarly, if the buyer feared labor unrest or a drop in demand for widgets or the rapid entry of foreign competition, it would buy a different low-volatility stock. The only context in which predictions about unsystematic risk are irrelevant is where *both* parties have adopted a passive strategy based on the capital asset pricing model or neither party has better information on the basis of which to predict unsystematic return (and their broker, if one is acting in behalf of both parties, has no firm convictions about the unsystematic return of USW one way or the other). In that event, both investors have concluded that the additional expense of better predicting unsystematic return does not warrant the effort and therefore treat it as irrelevant to their calculations.

regard to block positioning by fiduciaries to pension funds.[302] Such an approach has the advantage of making unnecessary those inquiries into subtle motives which, at least if good faith is unquestioned, can probably never be resolved entirely, even in the manager's own mind. Furthermore, except for assessment of damages, enforcement problems are relatively simple where acting as a dual agent or a principal is forbidden. But that approach forces investment management clients to forgo many useful investment opportunities and investment services. More important, an absolute ban has been rejected as a rule of law on so many occasions, including in the recent amendments to Section 11(a) of the Securities Exchange Act and in ERISA Prohibited Transaction Exemption 75-1, that one can safely say that, if such an approach is to be implied into an investment management relationship, it must be a contract which is the source.

Short of avoiding transactions as principal or agent for another, an investment manager can take steps to resolve the conflict-of-interest problem in three ways[303]:

(1) *Isolation.* The manager can isolate the performance of the different functions which place him in his principal or dual-agent status from each other. A portfolio manager, for example, can be separated from the trading department of the brokerage arm so that the manager, interested in his own performance record, will exercise his own judgment about the worth of participating in a block trade or an underwriting sponsored by the firm, or a solicited cross.

(2) *Disclosure.* The manager can disclose the material facts in advance of the transaction to obtain client consent or after the transaction to obtain client ratification of his action. Although this does not help the client in evaluating the investment decision the manager has reached, it at least alerts the client to the possibility that the investment judgment he has hired may not be disinterested with regard to a given transaction. He may reject the transaction on general principles, seek an outside opinion, or simply go along. But he, rather than the manager, is the one deciding how he should react.

---

[302] See ¶ 10.03[3][e] at notes 226-231 *supra.*

[303] See, e.g., Leiman, "Conflict of Interest and Related Problems of Broker-Dealers and Investment Advisers," in R. Mundheim, A. Fleischer & D. Glazer, *First Annual Institute on Securities Regulation* 323, 324 (PLI 1970).

(3) *Established procedures.* The manager can adopt a preset procedure according to which he will conduct himself whenever he acts in a principal or dual-agency capacity, unless he gets the express consent of the client to depart from that procedure. This method parallels the regulatory approach whereby conduct is controlled not so much to eliminate the conflict as to minimize the possibility of injury. The underwriting and market-making sections of ERISA Prohibited Transaction Exemption 75-1[304] and the underwriting exemption under Investment Company Act Rule 10f-3,[305] which place restrictions

---

[304] See notes 207 and 220 *supra.*

[305] 17 C.F.R. § 270.10f-3. Subject to an exemptive power reposed in the SEC, Act § 10(f) (15 U.S.C. § 80a-10(f)) prohibits participation by an investment company in underwritings sponsored by affiliated officers, directors and advisers. Rule 10f-3 provides the exemption permitted in the Act, and it was the model for Section III of Prohibited Transaction Exemption 75-1. See ¶ 10.03[3][c] *supra.* Rule 10f-3, "Exemption of Acquisition of Securities During the Existence of Underwriting Syndicate," reads:

"Any purchase of securities by a registered investment company prohibited by Section 10(f) of the Act shall be exempt from the provisions of such Section if the following conditions are met:

"(a) The securities to be purchased are (1) part of an issue effectively registered under the Securities Act of 1933 which is being offered to the public; (2) purchased at not more than the public offering price prior to the end of the first full business day after the first date on which the registered issue is offered to the public, if not offered for subscription upon exercise of rights or, if so offered, purchased on or before the 4th day preceding the day on which the rights' offering terminates; and (3) offered pursuant to an underwriting agreement under which the underwriters are committed to purchase all of the registered securities being offered, except those purchased by others pursuant to a rights' offering, if the underwriters purchase any thereof.

"(b) The gross commission, spread or profit to the principal underwriters (excluding, in the case of a rights' offering, any profits or losses resulting from purchases or sales by the underwriters of rights or securities during or after the rights period) shall not exceed: (1) 7.0 pecent of the public offering price if the security to be purchased is a common stock; (2) 3.50 percent of the public offering price if the security to be purchased is a preferred stock, whether or not convertible into common stock; (3) 2.50 percent of the public offering price if the security to be purchased is a subordinated debenture, or a bond or debenture convertible into common stock or having common stock purchase warrants attached; or (4) 1.50 percent of the public offering price in respect of any other security to be purchased.

"(c) The issuer of the securities to be purchased shall have been in

on the amount and proportion of participation as well as the quality of the issue, illustrate the method in its regulatory mode. But the principle applies equally well to privately established rules of conduct. They provide an objective standard against which a manager and client can satisfy themselves that the manager is acting responsibly if not absolutely independent of competing interests.

---

continuous operation for not less than 3 years, including the operations of any predecessors.

"(*d*) The amount of securities of any class of such registered issue to be purchased by the registered investment company or by two or more investment companies having the same investment adviser, shall not exceed 3 percent of the amount of the offering of such class.

"(*e*) The consideration to be paid by the registered investment company in purchasing the securities being offered shall not exceed 3 percent of the total assets of such registered investment company: *Provided,* That if such consideration shall exceed $1 million, it shall not exceed 1 percent of such company's total assets.

"(*f*) Such registered investment company does not purchase the securities being offered directly or indirectly from an officer, director, member of an advisory board, investment adviser or employee of such registered investment company or from a person of which any such officer, director, member of an advisory board, investment adviser or employee is an affiliated person. A purchase from a syndicate manager shall not be deemed to be a purchase from a specific underwriter so long as that underwriter does not benefit directly or indirectly from the transaction.

"(*g*) The purchase of the securities being offered shall have been authorized or approved by a resolution of the board of directors of the registered investment company, or of an executive, investment, or similar committee composed of at least three members of such board, or of a similar committee of the registered investment company's investment adviser provided that there is no affiliation direct or indirect between such investment adviser or any of its partners, employees, or stockholders and any principal underwriter of the issue being offered, which resolution shall state that in the judgment of the board or committee, the purchase of securities proposed will meet all the requirements of paragraphs (*a*) through (*f*) of this rule, and which authorization or approval shall have been supported by the vote (at a meeting or by written consent given without a meeting) of not less than a majority (consisting of at least three persons) of the members of the board of directors or of the committee who were not affiliated persons of any principal underwriter of the issue offered.

"(*h*) A statement of the transaction clearly indicating compliance with this rule shall be filed with the Commission within 30 days after consummation thereof."

It bears repeating that these methods of resolving the conflict of interest do not authorize a manager to give in to the conflict.[306] The fact of isolation means nothing if a portfolio manager acts with the purpose of enhancing brokerage profits or supporting prices of securities for which the firm makes markets. Disclosure is irrelevant if the manager realizes the client cannot appreciate what is disclosed. Preset procedures are not protection for the manager who deliberately pushes his own or another's interests to the limits allowable under the rules of conduct the manager has adopted and to which the client has agreed. The function these methods of conflict resolution serve is to shift the burden of proof, where a client subsequently challenges one or more transactions on conflict-of-interest grounds, back to the client to show that the manager acted intentionally in derogation of the client's interests. Assuming good faith,[307] then, let us consider these three methods of resolving the conflict of interest occurring when a manager acts as principal or agent for another.

[a] Isolation of activities

Reliance on isolation, or "Chinese walls," to insulate various departments or divisions from the pressures the activities of one can put on the fiduciary duty of the other have become an increasingly common practice, particularly in response to the inside information an investment banking department can obtain during an underwriting or the commercial side of a bank can obtain during financing negotiations with a

---

[306] See ¶ 9.07 at note 230.

[307] Good faith is necessarily a relative term. In any reasonably sized investment management operation which is only one division or department of an institution providing multiple financial services, it would be unreasonable and is probably impossible for a portfolio manager to pretend he is entirely independent of influence from the other branches or from the desires of the firm's largest customers. If the activities of investment managers who are unavoidably thrust frequently into principal and dual-agency roles by virtue of their multifaceted operations were as disrespectful of client interests as they could be (see, e.g., M. Mayer, *Conflicts of Interest: Broker-Dealer Firms* (Twentieth Century Fund 1975); and E. Herman, *Conflicts of Interest: Commercial Bank Trust Departments* (Twentieth Century Fund 1975)), the only practical alternatives would be to isolate investment management entirely from all other financial operations or to adopt caveat emptor and abandon fiduciary duty as a hopeless charade. But recognizing that investment managers will make small compromises and accepting that as a fact of life only emphasizes the importance to a manager of assuring that conflicts are resolved before proceeding to carry out an investment decision.

customer.[308] The idea is that through isolation, each department or division will remain ignorant of the operations of the other and therefore cannot be influenced by their organizational kinship.[309]

There is little doubt that isolation is useful in resolving the principal/dual-agency conflict. If a portfolio manager does not know that another customer of the firm is on the opposite side of a transaction he enters on behalf of a client, any danger from the fact the firm is acting in a dual-agency capacity is largely hypothetical. But the protective cover of isolation has its limits. As a practical matter, it only impedes the transmission of hard factual information revealing the extent of the firm's interest in a particular transaction. Isolation cannot make the manager ignorant of the fact of his firm's participation in an underwriting or a block trade in which he causes his accounts to take a position. It may well be that the manager bargains hardest with personnel in his own firm, but such behavior is not an automatic consequence of isolation.[310]

This point about the limited scope of protection available through isolation finds support in a line of development under the antifraud provisions of the federal securities laws concerning exposure to inside information and the combination of investment banking and brokerage functions. A brokerage firm in performing its underwriting duties will often uncover inside information. At the same time, the brokerage arm may be carrying out transactions in the securities of the issuer without being aware that the facts as they actually are differ markedly from the broker's reasonable beliefs about the condition of the issuer. For the firm to release the inside information to any of its customers would violate the antifraud prohibitions against insider trading.[311] But it also

---

[308] See, e.g., M. Mayer, note 307 *supra*, at 62-64; E. Herman, note 307 *supra,* Ch. III. See also Miller, "Chinese Walls," Rev. of Sec. Reg., Sept. 5, 1975, p. 865; Sec. Reg. & Trans. Rep., April 11, 1975, pp. 4-6; Lipton & Mazur, "The Chinese Wall Solution to the Conflict Problems of Securities Firms," 50 N.Y.U.L. Rev. 459 (1975); Chazen, "Reinforcing the Chinese Wall: A Response," 51 N.Y.U.L. Rev. 552 (1976); Lipton & Mazur, "The Chinese Wall: A Response to Chazen," 51 N.Y.U.L. Rev. 579 (1976).

[309] See, e.g., *Compliance Report,* note 291 *supra,* at 112.

[310] Compare Patocka, "Will Broker-Affiliates Still Manage Pension Money?" 9 Institutional Investor 67, 68-69 (July 1975) (portfolio trader claims his affiliation with brokerage firm makes him better able to achieve good prices on trades), with M. Mayer, note 307 *supra,* at 53 (pressure on manager to place clients in secondary distribution which firm was handling).

[311] Shapiro v. Merrill Lynch, Pierce, Fenner & Smith, 353 F. Supp. 264 (S.D.N.Y.), *aff'd* 495 F.2d 228 (2d Cir. 1974); Investors Management Co., SEC Securities Exchange Act Release No. 9267 (July 29, 1971), [1970-1971 Transfer Binder] CCH Fed. Sec. L. Rep. ¶ 78,163. See also Financial

has been held that, if the underwriting arm of a firm is in possession of material adverse information, the brokerage arm, even though ignorant, may not recommend the issuer's securities to its brokerage customers.[312] While this creates obvious problems for a broker-underwriter,[313] and presumably by analogy a bank with an active trust department following the securities of the customers of commercial side,[314] it also has implications for the utility of isolation as a means of resolving the conflict-of-interest problems arising from dealing with managed accounts as principal or as agent for another. To the extent market information—noninside but nonpublic information about the future market for a security[315]—is analogized to inside information, the line of development in the broker-underwriter cases throws into immediate question the effectiveness of isolation as a means of dealing with a broker-manager's market making, block trading and positioning, and underwriting activities. Since where there is a special relationship, the broker has a duty to disclose market information,[316] the rule would seem to require

Industrial Fund, Inc. v. McDonnell Douglas Corp., 315 F. Supp. 42 (D. Colo. 1971), rev'd 474 F.2d 514 (10th Cir.), cert. denied 414 U.S. 874 (1973); Merrill Lynch, Pierce, Fenner & Smith, Inc., SEC Securities Exchange Act Release No. 8459 (Nov. 25, 1968).

[312] See Slade v. Shearson, Hammill & Co., 356 F. Supp. 304 (S.D.N.Y.), aff'd sub nom. Odette v. Shearson Hammill & Co., 486 F.2d 1395 (2d Cir. 1973).

[313] A broker-underwriter must be careful not to create the impression it has discovered unusually adverse or positive inside information in its underwriting activities. Thus, a sudden change in a recommendation might be regarded as a signal of its findings as underwriter. Yet some change in recommendation may be necessary. Slade, note 312 supra, has been viewed as suggesting that a false recommendation is grounds for liability even though the source for a change in recommendation may be information uncovered by the underwriting arm (see Sec. Reg. & Trans, Rep., April 11, 1975, pp. 4-6), and a "no-recommendation" rule remains a matter of controversy. See Lipton & Mazur, "The Chinese Wall Solution to the Conflict Problems of Securities Firms," 50 N.Y.U.L. Rev. 159 (1975); Chazen, "Reinforcing the Chinese Wall: A Response," 51 N.Y.U.L. Rev. 552 (1976); Lipton & Mazur, "The Chinese Wall: A Reply to Chazen," id. at 579.

[314] See id. In its amicus brief in Slade, the SEC argued that it was not the Commission's intention to seek a rule preventing the commercial side of a bank from dealing with customers in the securities of which the trust department was investing.

[315] See note 249 supra.

[316] See In re Oppenheimer & Co., SEC Securities Exchange Act Release No. 12319 (April 2, 1976), in which an SEC administrative law judge censured a broker-manager for misuse of market information. An analyst for the broker-manager had been interviewed by a financial columnist for a

the firm's underwriting and trading departments not only to refuse to honor the wall between them and the management arm, but actually to breach it. Either that, or it seems that they must refuse to deal with the portfolio manager.

This analysis is not as paradoxical as it seems. Affiliated brokerage and management are not purely a conflict-of-interest risk to an investment advisory client. The brokerage arm's access to the marketplace can offer investment and execution advantages not available to managers less lose to trading and underwriting activities than broker-managers. If complete isolation were the rule, and the client were denied access to material market information, he would lose all benefit of the connection between the brokerage arm and the management arm while still risking the possibility the manager will favor the firm's interests anyway. At the same time, an approach which requires that market information be provided advisory clients—persons having a special relationship to the firm—does not affect the utility of isolation as a device for reducing conflict-of-interest risks. Market information consists of information which can have a substantial impact on an investment. Communication between departments at this level only would still keep a portfolio manager from learning the details of the firm's other operations, thereby making it more difficult for him to act boldly in furtherance of the firm's interests as principal or agent for another. Thus, even though isolation alone may not be sufficient to resolve the conflict of interest, it is clearly useful.

[b] Disclosure and informed consent

The second method for resolving the conflict is disclosure. There can be no doubt that some form of disclosure is mandatory when a

national newspaper and became convinced that the columnist would write negatively about a certain stock. The analyst revealed this information to a firm officer who in turn alerted relevant staff personnel. Customers of the firm avoided losses by selling and made profits by selling short. Because of the novelty of the case, the Commission reversed. But in reversing it said: "There is no question that the misuse of undisclosed 'market information' can be the basis of antifraud violations [citing cases]." The official report of the case contains few details of fact or reasoning. A fuller discussion of the record appears in [1975-1976 Transfer Binder] CCH Fed. Sec. L. Rep. ¶ 80,551, which includes a report of the decision of the administrative law judge. See also *Special Study*, note 1 *supra*, Pt. 2, at 239-240; SEC Securities Exchange Act Release No. 7290 (April 9, 1964), [1964-1966 Transfer Binder] CCH Fed. Sec. L. Rep. ¶ 76, 989; Lipton, "Market Information," in R. Mundheim, A. Fleischer & J. Schupper, *Fifth Annual Institute on Securities Regulation*, 288; ¶ 1.04.

manager acts as principal or agent for another. Section 206(3) of the Investment Advisers Act[317] makes it unlawful for any statutory investment adviser[318] knowingly to act as principal or as broker for another in a securities transaction with a client account "without disclosing to such client in writing before the completion of such transaction the capacity in which he is acting and obtaining the consent of the client to such transaction." Although the section excludes transactions with a broker or dealer "not acting as an investment adviser," the statutory definition of investment adviser is broad enough to deny the exclusion to any broker-dealer providing measurable investment management services for "special compensation." [319]

The SEC's interpretation of the exclusion confirms its limited availability to broker-dealers. When negotiated commission rates were introduced, broker-dealers became concerned that their support services, particularly those of an advisory nature, for ordinary customers might cause them to lose the exclusion in Section 206(3) if they charged separate fees which were deemed to be "special compensation" for those services. In response, the Commission adopted Rule 206(3)-1,[320] which

---

[317] 15 U.S.C. § 80b-6(3).

[318] Section 206 applies to all statutory advisers, not only those required to register under Section 203 (15 U.S.C. § 80b-3).

[319] Section 202(a)(11) (15 U.S.C. § 80b-2(a)(11)) defines investment adviser, exempting:

"(C) any broker or dealer whose performance of such services is solely incidental to the conduct of his business as a broker or dealer and who receives no special compensation therefor. . . ."

This exemption, when read against the "not acting as an investment adviser" exclusion in Section 206(3), strongly suggests that a broker-dealer will be regarded as a statutory investment adviser on any occasion he departs from providing the ordinary research and advice incident to the solicitation of business and the execution of customer orders. This point is discussed more extensively in ¶ 2.05[2][b]. See also Bines, "Regulating Discretionary Management: Broker-Dealers as Catalysts for Reform," 16 B.C. Ind. & Com. L. Rev. 347, 365-369 (1975).

[320] 17 C.F.R. § 275.206(3)-1. The Rule reads:

"(a) An investment adviser which is a broker or dealer registered pursuant to Section 15 of the Securities Exchange Act of 1934 shall be exempt from Section 206(3) in connection with any transaction in relation to which such broker or dealer is acting as an investment adviser solely (1) by means of publicly distributed written materials or publicly made oral statements; (2) by means of written materials or oral statements which do not purport to meet the objectives or needs of specific individuals or accounts; (3) through the issuance of statistical informa-

exempts broker-dealers from Section 206(3) if they would be deemed statutory investment advisers solely by virtue of publicly distributed written materials or oral statements or by virtue of responses to specific requests for statistical information involving no expression of opinion as to investment merits.[321] In that event, the Commission concluded, broker-dealers would be permitted to act as principal or agent for another if the materials provided contain a statement to that effect.

Complementing Rule 206(3)-1 is Rule 206A-1(T),[322] adopted under Section 206A of the Act, which grants general exemptive authority

---

tion containing no expressions of opinion as to the investment merits of a particular security; or (4) any combination of the foregoing services: *Provided,* however, that such materials and oral statements include a statement that if the purchaser of the advisory communication uses the services of the adviser in connection with a sale or purchase of a security which is a subject of such communication, the adviser may act as principal for its own account or as agent for another person.

"(b) For the purpose of this Rule, publicly distributed written materials are those which are distributed to 35 or more persons who pay for such materials, and publicly made oral statements are those made simultaneously to 35 or more persons who pay for access to such statements.

"NOTE: The requirement that the investment adviser disclose that it may act as principal or agent for another person in the sale or purchase of a security that is the subject of investment advice does not relieve the investment adviser of any disclosure obligation which, depending upon the nature of the relationship between the investment adviser and the client, may be imposed by subparagraphs (1) or (2) of Section 206 or the other provisions of the federal securities laws."

[321] See SEC Securities Exchange Act Release No. 11324 (April 2, 1975), [1974-1975 Transfer Binder] CCH Fed. Sec. L. Rep. ¶ 80,145. SEC Securities Exchange Act Release No. 11384 (April 30, 1975), *id.* ¶ 80,163, issued the rule temporarily as Rule 206(3)-1(T). It was finally adopted in SEC Securities Exchange Act Release No. 11606 (Aug. 20, 1976), [1975-1976 Transfer Binder] CCH Fed. Sec. L. Rep. ¶ 80,268.

[322] Rule 206A-1(T) (17 C.F.R. § 275.206A-IT)), "Temporary Exemption for Certain Broker-Dealers/Investment Advisers," reads:

"(a) Any person who was registered as a broker or dealer pursuant to Section 15 of the Securities Exchange Act of 1934 on May 1, 1975, and was not then registered as an investment adviser pursuant to Section 203 of the Investment Advisers Act of 1940 (or any successor, within the meaning of Rule 15b1-3 under the Securities Exchange Act of 1934, to such broker-dealer) shall be temporarily exempt from the provisions of the Act and the rules and regulations thereunder until April 30, 1978: *Provided, however,* that—

"(1) this exemption shall not be applicable to any such person (a) whose broker-dealer registration is withdrawn, suspended, cancelled or

to the SEC. Rule 206A-1(T) exempts from the Investment Advisers Act broker-dealers providing investment management services or investment supervisory services which are solely incidental to their business as broker-dealers and for which no special compensation is received. The careful drafting and limited scope of Rules 206(3)-1 and 206A-1(T) establish the duty of all other broker-managers providing advice "as to the value of securities or as to the advisability of investing in, purchasing, or selling securities . . ." [323] to make advance disclosure in writing to and obtain the consent of the client to a principal or dual-agency transaction.[324]

---

revoked, or (b) who acts as an investment adviser, as defined in Section 2(a)(20) of the Investment Company Act of 1940, to any investment company, registered or required to be registered under that Act; and (2) this exemption shall not be applicable after November 30, 1975, to any broker-dealer who, for special compensation or not solely incidental to his business as a broker-dealer, performs investment supervisory services as defined in Section 202(a)(13) of the Act or investment management services as defined in paragraph (b) of this rule.

"(b) For the purposes of this rule, a person performs 'investment management services' with respect to any account as to which such person, directly or indirectly.

"(1) is authorized to determine what securities shall be purchased or sold by or for the account; or

"(2) makes decisions as to what securities shall be purchased or sold by or for the account even though some other person may have responsibility for such investment decisions."

Rule 206A-1(T) has been amended from time to time to extend its effective date, the latest such extension appearing in SEC Securities Exchange Act Release No. 13454 (April 20, 1977), CCH Fed. Sec. L. Rep. ¶ 81,125. The extensions have been justified as necessary to assess, before a permanent rule can be adopted, the degree of unbundling of management and brokerage services occurring in a negotiated commission-rate environment.

[323] Section 202(a)(11), 15 U.S.C. § 80b-2(a)(11). The quoted language is part of the definition of an investment adviser.

[324] It is likely that Section 206(3) will set the standard for principal and dual-agency transactions for investment managers such as broker-dealers relying on Rule 206A-1(T) and banks that are exempt from the statutory definition of investment adviser. For one thing, it would be difficult to argue that, for identical transactions, banks and exempt broker-dealers should be subject to a less demanding standard than investment counselors, insurance companies, and other broker-managers. Particularly is this the case for exempt broker-dealers who obtained the benefit of Rule 206A-1(T) to ease the transition to negotiated rates and not to subject clients to lesser protection from self-dealing. In this regard, Section 10(b) and Rule 10b-5 could

Given the general consent and disclosure obligations of a manager,[325] the question is what must be disclosed and consented to. It goes almost without saying that if a broker-manager's markup or markdown is more costly to the client than that available elsewhere, the manager must disclose that fact as well as the price and the client must give his informed consent to the excess payment.[326] Similarly, riskless principal transactions also should have that fact disclosed.[327] In addition to

---

easily be the means for imposing a uniform federal standard. Furthermore, common-law agency and trust principles would seem to impose an obligation of comparable character to Section 206(3). See *Restatement (Second) of Agency* §§ 389-392 (1958); *Restatement (Second) of Trusts* §§ 170, 206 (1959).

[325] It has been argued that, for a broker-manager placing his underwritings in the accounts of his clients, a one-time letter of consent, pointing out the conflict of interest, would suffice (see Rosenman, "Discretionary Accounts and Manipulative Trading Practices," in R. Mundheim, A. Fleischer & J. Schupper, *Fifth Annual Institute on Securities Regulation* 245, 250-254, and 251 n.13 (PLI 1974)), and that similar principles would extend to the treatment of block transactions. (*Id.* at 255.) This argument was put forward as an interpretation of SEC Securities Exchange Act Releases Nos. 5395 and 5398 (June 1, 1973) [1973 Transfer Binder] CCH Fed. Sec. L. Rep. ¶¶ 79,383 and 79,386, respectively), issued in response to the SEC Investigation of Hot Issues Securities Markets, File No. 4-148, and concerning, among other things, the duty of an underwriter, acting as principal, with respect to his discretionary accounts. The releases require from such an underwriter "disclosure to and consent of its clients" when underwritings are placed in their discretionary accounts. Compare Chasins v. Smith, Barney & Co., 438 F.2d 1167 (2d Cir. 1971), in which a market maker was held to have violated Rule 10b-5 for disclosing only that it acted as principal. The case suggests that, at least with respect to certain facts highly material to the self-dealing question, separate disclosure must be made with respect to distinct transactions. See text at note 333 *infra*. Leiman, "Conflict of Interest and Related Problems of Broker-Dealers and Investment Advisers," R. Mundheim, A. Fleischer & D. Glazer, *First Institute on Securities Regulations* 323, 325-326 (PLI 1970). Whatever the merits of the argument at the time it was made (it depended on Investment Advisers Act § 206 being held not applicable to broker-dealers; see Rosenman, *supra*, at 254, and Bines, "Regulating Discretionary Management: Broker-Dealers as Catalysts for Reform," 16 B.C. Ind. & Com. L. Rev. 347, 365-374 (1975)), it is doubtful that broker-managers can avoid the requirements of Section 206(3) now that negotiated rates have been introduced. See text at notes 312-324 *supra*.

[326] See Hughes v. SEC, 174 F.2d 969 (D.C. Cir. 1949); *In re* Thornton, SEC Securities Exchange Act Release No. 7693 (Aug. 31, 1965), [1964-1966 Transfer Binder] CCH Fed. Sec. L. Rep. ¶ 77,279.

[327] See *In re* Norris & Hirshberg, Inc., 21 S.E.C. 865 (1946), *aff'd* 177 F.2d 228 (D.C. Cir. 1949).

these kinds of transactions, which virtually require affirmative justification to avoid the appearance of fraud, transactions in which the potential for self-dealing is high should be accompanied by extensive disclosure. For example, where the manager is sole market maker,[328] or
where the brokerage arm initiates contact by soliciting orders either as
principal or agent for another,[329] or where an underwriting promotes

---

[328] See *id.*; *In re* Palombi Securities Co., SEC Securities Exchange Act
Release No. 6961 (Nov. 30, 1962), [1961-1964 Transfer Binder] CCH Fed.
Sec. L. Rep. ¶ 76,866 (failure to disclose control of market). Compare
Exemption 75-1, § IV(c), note 220 *supra,* which denies the exemption if the
fiduciary is the sole market maker. See also Swift, Henke & Co., [1972-1973
Transfer Binder] CCH Fed. Sec. L. Rep. ¶ 78,962 (method of solicitation
by sole market maker raises serious antifraud issues). Cf. Securities Ex-
change Act Rule 15c1-8 (17 C.F.R. § 240.15c1-8).

[329] See Chasins v. Smith, Barney & Co., 438 F.2d 1167 (2d Cir. 1971)
(broker-dealer held to have violated Rule 10b-5 when it acted as market
maker without revealing that fact, even though it disclosed it acted as
principal as required by Rule 15c1-4). See also R. Jennings & H. Marsh,
Securities Regulations 863-864 (3d ed. 1972).

Securities Exchange Act Rule 15c1-4, which provides for disclosure of
principal or dual-agency status in ordinary brokerage transactions, should
be read in connection with Rule 15c1-6, which provides for disclosure in a
distribution. The fact that Rule 15c1-6 imposes a special disclosure obligation for a transaction that would be subject to Rule 15c1-4 suggests that
special facts known to a broker-manager, particularly where extra incentives
are involved, must be disclosed to a client. Both Rules 10b-5 and 15c1-2
would be effective tools for implementing such an obligation. Rule 15c-4
(17 C.F.R. § 240.15c1-4) provides:

"The term 'manipulative, deceptive, or other fraudulent device or
contrivance,' as used in section 15(c)(1) of the Act, is hereby defined
to include any act of any broker or dealer designed to effect with or
for the account of a customer any transaction in, or to induce the
purchase or sale by such customer of, any security (other than U.S. Tax
Savings Notes, U.S. Defense Savings Stamps, or U.S. Defense Savings
Bonds, Series E, F and G) unless such broker or dealer, at or before the
completion of each such transaction, gives or sends to such customer
written notification disclosing (1) whether he is acting as a broker for
such customer, as a dealer for his own account, as a broker for some
other person, or as a broker for both such customer and some other
person; and (2) in any case in which he is acting as a broker for such
customer or for both such customer and some other person, either the
name of the person from whom the security was purchased or to whom
it was sold for such customer and the date and time when such transaction took place or the fact that such information will be furnished
upon the request of such customer, and the source and amount of any
commission or other remuneration received or to be received by him in
connection with the transaction."

an untested company,[330] those facts should ordinarily be disclosed for the purpose of obtaining an informed consent.[331]

But, as in other contexts, it is difficult to generalize about disclosure obligations beyond observing that the extent of disclosure required is a function of the potential for harm to the client's interests, and that, given the references to disclosure *and* consent in Section 206(3) of the Investment Advisers Act and Commission releases under the other securities laws, disclosure obligations are, as a rule, stronger for principal and dual-agency transactions than is the case in other conflict-of-interest situations. A related problem is how often disclosure and consent for a particular type of transaction must be obtained. Is it possible for a client to give a blanket consent in advance of a number of transactions, or must the manager disclose the details of each transaction (in writing, when required) and obtain a separate consent each time?

As a matter of technical construction, Section 206(3) can be interpreted both ways. A narrow focus on the statutory language suggests individual disclosure and consent on the occasion of each transaction because the section refers to "such transaction" as the trigger for the disclosure and consent requirements. On the other hand, the section requires disclosure only of the capacity in which the adviser is acting, which can readily be disclosed in a general statement, particularly when

---

Rule 15c1-6 (17 C.F.R. § 240.15c1-6) provides:

"The term 'manipulative, deceptive, or other fraudulent device or contrivance,' as used in section 15(c)(1) of the Act, is hereby defined to include any act of any broker who is acting for a customer or for both such customer and some other person, or of any dealer who receives or has promise of receiving a fee from a customer for advising such customer with respect to securities, designed to effect with or for the account of such customer any transaction in, or to induce the purchase or sale by such customer of, any security in the primary or secondary distribution of which such broker or dealer is participating or is otherwise financially interested unless such broker or dealer at or before the completion of each such transaction, gives or sends to such customer written notification of the existence of such participation or interest."

[330] Compare Investment Company Act Rule 10f-3, note 305 *supra,* and Prohibited Transaction Exemption 75-1, § III(c), note 207 *supra.* In a similar vein, in a speech at the 1975 Mutual Funds and Investment Management Conference, March 11, 1975, the director of the Division of Investment Management Regulation of the SEC announced future consideration of a rule under the Investment Advisers Act to parallel Rule 10f-3. Remarks of A. Mostoff, "A Look Back: A Hopeful Look Ahead," [1974-1975 Transfer Binder] CCH Fed. Sec. L. Rep. ¶ 80,141, at 85,199.

[331] See also *Compliance Report,* note 291 *supra,* at 113.

each transaction is confirmed with a notation of the actual capacity in which the adviser acted. Moreover, the Commission staff has indicated that, at least for some kinds of principal and dual-agency transactions, a general advance consent would be acceptable.[332] Still, the case law makes clear that advanced generalized disclosure and consent will not always satisfy the disclosure obligations of a manager acting as principal or agent for another.

In *Chasins v. Smith, Barney & Co.*,[333] for example, the court held that the defendant's failure to disclose its market-maker status established liability under Rule 10b-5 even though there was disclosure that defendant had acted as principal. The plaintiff had received analysis of his existing securities holdings and had purchased the four stocks in question on the recommendation and advice of defendant. Damages in the case were held to be the difference between the purchase price to plaintiff and the price at which plaintiff sold them before discovering defendant's market-maker status. The sense of the case seems to be that the defendant was obliged to disclose its market-maker status for each separate transaction just as it must do with respect to its status as principal or agent for another under Rule 15c1-4. But even if *Chasins* can be interpreted as simply a case of inadequate disclosure which could have been remedied through a nonspecific advance statement that the defendant would act as market maker from time to time, the case would still stand for the proposition that unique facts in a transaction must be disclosed meaningfully.

In fact, *Chasins* probably suggests the most effective compromise between full disclosure and actual consent for each separate transaction

---

[332] In Madison & Burke Capital, [1973-1974 Transfer Binder] CCH Fed. Sec. L. Rep. ¶ 79,614 (1973), the staff answered a letter of inquiry by recommending that, to satisfy Section 206(3), "each of the investment adviser's advisory clients be given in advance a written statement . . . which makes all appropriate disclosures. Further, it would be advisable for the investment adviser to receive a written acknowledgement from each of his clients of their receipt of the disclosure statement. The disclosure statement should include the nature and extent of any adverse interest of the investment adviser, including the amount of compensation he would receive in connection with each transaction." Such a procedure would not be practicable on a transaction-by-transaction basis, and if the staff had intended the disclosure and consent to be repeated on each occasion, it could have said so directly.

[333] 438 F.2d 1167 (2d Cir. 1971). See also Albert Fried & Co. v. Seeburg Corp., [1974-1975 Transfer Binder] CCH Fed. Sec. L. Rep. ¶ 94,969 (S.D.N.Y. 1975) (undisclosed market making prior to settlement of lawsuit breaches fiduciary duty to selling stockholders).

with all its practical difficulties and a simple blanket license to execute transactions as principal or agent for another with its attendant opportunities for self-dealing. If a manager makes full and effective disclosure of the kinds of principal and dual-agency activities in which he expects to engage and obtains an informed consent to such transactions in advance, he ought to be able to satisfy his disclosure and consent obligations for each separate transaction by including reasonable notification to the client of the nature of the manager's involvement. In some circumstances, reasonable notification might mean actual notice because the activity presents unusual opportunities for self-dealing. In addition to compliance with the strict requirements of the series of rules under Section 15(c)(1) of the Securities Exchange Act, a manager might also alert his client to the existence of commission differentials on trade crosses[334]; notice of the fact that the manager is sole market maker whenever that is the case[335]; size of underwriting commission when the manager handles a secondary distribution[336]; whether the manager is also acting as positioner on a block, part of which the client is purchasing on an agency basis[337]; and so forth. In other circumstances, reasonable notification might simply mean periodic reports on principal

---

[334] The SEC's position on this under Rule 15c1-4 may be that such disclosure of actual differentials is required. In a letter to the NYSE, the staff said that brokers could say a "like" commission had been paid on the other side. There was no further guidance as to the language that could be used when the commission was not "like." See Sec. Reg. & Trans. Rep., May 30, 1975, p. 1.

[335] It is clear that there must be a real market in order for the transaction to be valid in the first place. See Rule 15c1-8. *In re* Norris & Hirshberg, Inc., 21 S.E.C. 865 (1946), *aff'd* 177 F.2d 228 (D.C. Cir. 1949). But there should be some objective proof that the market is not artificial, and for that reason, Prohibited Transaction Exemption 75-1 does not apply to fiduciaries making the sole market in a security. See *id.*, Section IV(c), note 220 *supra.*

[336] This seems particularly to be required in an exempt secondary distribution where the client would not receive the notification available through the prospectus issued in connection with registered offerings. Compare Rule 15c1-6, note 329 *supra.*

[337] See Statement of SEC Commissioner Loomis, in "Conflicts of Interest and the Regulation of Securities: A Panel Discussion," 28 Bus. Law. 545, 579 (1973), in which he noted that the advertising of firms seeking block-execution business tended heavily to emphasize their distribution systems and wondered aloud whether their customers were receiving adequate disclosure. See also M. Mayer, *Conflicts of Interest: Broker-Dealer Firms* 59-61 (Twentieth Century Fund 1975).

and dual-agency transactions.[338] But in either case, the technique of combining advance approval with reasonable notification has the practical advantage of permitting most ordinary principal and dual-agency tranactions to go on without the trouble and delay that would accompany individualized disclosure and informed consent for each separate transaction.[339]

Furthermore, this approach ties in neatly with the third technique of resolving the conflict of interest associated with principal and dual-agency transactions by a manager. If the initial disclosure is accompanied by a reasonably detailed set of procedures that the manager relies on when acting as principal or agent for another, the sense of sufficiency associated with advance general approval by a client increases measurably. If a client knows that his portfolio manager will execute on a principal or dual-agency basis only if the net price to him is more favorable than is available elsewhere,[340] he at least knows that he is getting the competitive market price, even though he may not be persuaded that his manager is exercising an entirely independent judgment on the investment merits. Or, if the client knows that an in-house cross is permissible on the sole discretion of the portfolio manager only in the event it meets an opposite order by coincidence at the trading desk, and that all solicited principal and dual-agency transactions require prior approval of an officer of the firm, he knows the financial responsibility of the officer as well as that the firm stands behind the decision to go forward. That may not protect him in a firm which is on the edge of desperation and about to go insolvent,[341] but there is a strong incentive in soundly run operations not to risk a lawsuit or enforcement proceeding.

---

[338] See, e.g., Dillon, Read & Co., [1975-1976 Transfer Binder] CCH Fed. Sec. L. Rep. ¶ 80,352 (1975), in which the staff approved an arrangement involving initial consent plus quarterly reports as satisfying Section 206(3) of the Investment Advisers Act, where a broker-dealer was providing a statistical service to subscribers. See also Securities Week, April 5, 1976, p. 2 (Connecticut bank commissioner modifies position and indicates approval of some form of general disclosure where broker-dealers act as principal).

[339] On the other hand, it is doubtful this kind of compromise would work where the potential for fraud is high to begin with. See notes 325-326, supra.

[340] Compare Prohibited Transaction Exemption 75-1, § IV(d), note 220 supra.

[341] See, e.g., In re Leo G. MacLaughlin Secs. Co., SEC Securities Exchange Act Release No. 7783 (Jan. 5, 1966), [1964-1966 Transfer Binder] CCH Fed. Sec. L. Rep. ¶ 77,317.

[c] Established procedures

To provide added reassurances to clients sufficient to resolve the conflict-of-interest problem, a firm may establish internal guidelines concerning the extent of client participation in principal and dual-agency transactions, both as to amount, percentage of client holdings, and percentage of the securities made available by the other side.[342] This is not to say that firms should not go beyond these limits when advisable. But at least by making transactions outside these limits subject to additional internal review and perhaps client consent, seemingly unusual activity in a client account in securities in which a firm is interested can be subjected to affirmative justification before a lawsuit or an enforcement action, and the informed consent of the client, if obtained, could dissipate the possibility of legal action at the outset.

[3] Negotiated Commissions and In-House Executions

One of the more perplexing conflict-of-interest problems associated with combined brokerage and management is the setting of commission rates on transactions executed in house. Ironically, this problem is perceived as largely a product of the negotiated-rate system.[343] With fixed rates, the commission charge on exchange transactions was preset by schedule, and, disregarding give-ups and reciprocals, a broker-manager could not get a better price no matter where he executed. With negotiated rates, there is always the possibility that a broker-manager will fail to represent his advisory clients as vigorously against his brokerage arm as he would if he were independent.

In many respects, the problem of a manager's negotiating commissions with a related broker has a strong analogue in the problem of overtrading. Although overtrading involves frequency of execution and self-negotiation involves amount of commission on a given trade, the self-dealing issue in both cases is the opportunity to increase commission revenues. Moreover, the client's investment return in either case suffers by precisely the same category of expenditure, namely, com-

---

342 Compare Investment Company Act Rule 10f-3, note 305 *supra,* and Prohibited Transaction Exemption 75-1, §§ III(b)-III(e), IV(b), notes 207, 220 *supra.*

343 See, e.g., *House Securities Industry Study*, note 4 *supra,* at 149; Folk "Restricting the Securities Markets—The Martin Report: A Critique," 57 Va. L. Rev. 1315, 1363 (1971); Welles, "Should Money Management and Brokerage Be Separated," 5 Institutional Investor 21 (June 1971).

mission costs. Nonetheless, perhaps because of its apparent newness,[344] the problem of self-negotiation is perceived as a unique issue.

It is true that, with negotiated rates, a broker-manager might execute in-house at higher commission rates than are available elsewhere, or a manager might interpose an affiliated broker in over-the-counter transactions to enhance commission income. But as a practical matter, most of the difficulty occurs only where the broker and manager are the same person and the client is so unsophisticated an individual or institution that he or it does not know how to compare commission rates. Indeed, it is far easier to determine whether a broker-manager is over-paying himself on commissions than it is to determine whether he is overtrading at competitive commission rates. To uncover overpayment, it is necessary for the client merely to learn the commission he is paying and to compare it to those generally available elsewhere. Determining overtrading, however, means that one must assess the broker-manager's investment strategy and determine whether he is carrying that strategy out properly. Furthermore, most institutional broker-managers separate their portfolio managers and traders from the trading desks which handle ordinary customer transactions. The portfolio managers are supposed to treat the affiliated brokerage arm like any other broker-dealer, executing with the firm which offers the best execution price. To the extent standard commission charges can be determined,[345] an institutional client's controls on a broker-manager's inclination to pay himself excess commissions are strong.

A different case pertains to individuals with limited knowledge of the securities industry. They are much more vulnerable to an unscrupulous broker's willingness to sacrifice best net price. As a consequence, an established practice which is in particular jeopardy is the management of an account for commissions only. It is almost certain that such broker-managers are not seeking competitive prices or passing on the economies of scale possible through the bunching of orders.[346]

---

[344] Self-negotiation of commissions is not as recent as first appears. At the institutional level, broker-managers have in effect been negotiating commission costs with themselves by crediting a part of commission charges against advisory fees and by providing supplementary services from custodianship to magazine subscriptions to their clients. At the institutional level at least, clients as well as brokers knew the equivalent value of those services and took full advantage of them. See generally ¶ 8.02.

[345] See ¶ 8.02[4].

[346] Cf. Kidder, Peabody & Co., SEC Securities Exchange Act Release No. 8426 (Oct. 16, 1968), [1967-1969 Transfer Binder] CCH Fed. Sec. L. Rep. ¶ 77,618 (broker must execute for advisory clients on agency rather than principal basis).

These excess commissions would be difficult to justify since they would represent, in effect, a variable management fee, with the degree of variance reflecting the broker-manager's assessment of the quality of his own services.[347] It is difficult to see how fiduciary principles could be construed to permit this, at least without full, precise, and continuing disclosure and informed consent.

Perhaps the most practical approach to the self-negotiation problem in the case of both individuals and institutions is to adopt a prophylactic rule similar to the rule respecting the authority afforded a market maker by Prohibited Transaction Exemption 75-1. The exemption permits pension fund fiduciaries making a market in a security being bought or sold by the fund to act as principal if the net execution price will be more favorable than is available elsewhere.[348] To the extent a broker-manager observes this approach, there can be no injury from self-negotiation to a client and the problem becomes simply one of enforcement. Anything short of this approach would seem to require extensive disclosure and consent, and could well be treated as equivalent to a riskless principal transaction.

---

[347] It might be possible to develop some kind of notification approach wherein a broker-manager discloses the actual execution price as well as best net price, thus permitting the client to determine how much he is paying for management services. Aside from the doubtful practicality of such an approach, it places strain on the obligations developed under the rules respecting disclosure of management fees.

[348] See Prohibited Transaction Exemption 75-1, § IV(d), note 220 *supra*.

BIBLIOGRAPHY

Chapter 1

THE FUNDAMENTAL PRINCIPLES OF INVESTMENT MANAGEMENT LAW

Articles

Arenson, "1965 Legislation Affecting Law of Trusts and Estates," 12 N.Y.L.F. 1 (1966).

Casey, " 'Finders Fee' Compensation to Brokers and Others," 31 Bus. Law. 707 (1976).

Committee on Trust Administration and Accounting, "The Trustee's Duty of Loyalty," 6 Real Prop., Prob. & Trust J. 528 (1971).

Committee Report, "Problems of Fiduciaries Under the Securities Laws," 9 Real Prop., Prob. & Trust J. 292 (1974).

Fleisher, Mundheim & Murphy, "An Initial Inquiry Into the Responsibility to Disclose Market Information," 121 U. Pa. L. Rev. 798 (1973).

Franklin, "Replacing the Negligence Lottery: Compensation and Selective Reimbursement," 53 Va. L. Rev. 774 (1967).

Friedman, "The Dynastic Trust," 73 Yale L.J. 547 (1964).

Hedberg, "Let's Regulate Investment Advice," 29 Fin. Anal. J. 24 (May-June 1973).

Herman, "Equity Funding, Inside Information, and the Regulators," 21 U.C.L.A.L. Rev. (1973).

Nelson, "Let's Make Investment Advisers Accountable," 29 Fin. Anal. J. 19 (Jan.-Feb. 1973).

Owens, "Investment Adviser Regulation: A Subject Too Long Neglected," 29 Fin. Anal. J. 12 (Jan.-Feb. 1973).

Schotland, "Bank Trust Departments and Public Policy Today," 4 Sec. Reg. L.J. 389 (1977).

Schuyler, "From Sulphur to Surcharge?—Corporate Trustee Exposure Under SEC Rule 10b-5," 67 Nw. U.L. Rev. 42 (1972).

Scott, "The Fiduciary Principle," 37 Calif. L. Rev. 539 (1949).

Shattuck, "The Development of the Prudent Man Rule for Fiduciary Investment in the United States in the Twentieth Century," 12 Ohio State L.J. 491 (1951).

———, "The Massachusetts Prudent Man Rule in Trust Investments," 25 B.U.L. Rev. 307 (1945).

Weinrib, "The Fiduciary Obligation," 25 U. Toronto L.J. 1 (1975).

Books

Advisory Committee on Endowment Management to the Ford Foundation, *Managing Educational Endowments* (Ford Foundation 1969).

American Law Institute, *Federal Securities Code* (Tentative Draft No. 2) (American Law Institute 1973).

Cary, W., & Bright, C., *The Law and the Lore of Endowment Funds* (Ford Foundation 1969).

Friedman, "Problems Involving Investment Advisers and Broker-Dealers Serving Individual Accounts," in Mundheim, R., Fleischer, A., & Schupper, J., *Fourth Annual Institute on Securities Regulation* (Practising Law Institute 1973).

Graham, B., Dodd, D., & Cottle, S., *Security Analysis* (McGraw-Hill Book Co., 4th ed., 1962).

Green, D., & Schuelke, M., *The Trust Activities of the Banking Industry* (Stanford Research Institute 1975).

Herman, E., *Conflicts of Interest: Commercial Bank Trust Departments* (The Twentieth Century Fund 1975).

Lipton, "Market Information," in Mundheim, R., Fleischer, A., & Schupper, J., *Fifth Annual Institute on Securities Regulation* (Practising Law Institute 1974).

Lipton & Katcher, "Liability of Buyers and Sellers in Market Transactions," in Bialkin, K., *The 10b Series of Rules* (Practising Law Institute 1974).

Restatement of Agency (American Law Institute 1933).

Restatement (Second) of Agency (American Law Institute 1958).

Restatement of Trusts (American Law Institute 1935).

Restatement (Second) of Trusts (American Law Institute 1959).

Scott, A., *The Law of Trusts* (Little, Brown & Co., 3d ed., 1967).

Seavey, W., *Handbook of the Law of Agency* (West Publishing Co. 1964).

U.S. Comptroller of the Currency, *Comptroller's Manual for Representatives in Trusts,* (U.S. Treasury 1963).

Williamson, J., *Performance Measurement and Investment Objectives for Educational Endowment Funds* (The Common Fund 1972).

Congressional and Regulatory References

H.R. 7597, 94th Cong., 1st Sess. (1975).

Hearings on S. 2849 Before the Subcomm. on Securities of the Senate Comm. on Banking, Housing and Urban Affairs, 94th Cong., 2d Sess. (1976).

Hearings Pursuant to S. Res. 71 Before a Subcomm. of the Senate Comm. on Banking and Currency, 71st Cong., 3d Sess. (1931).

Interim Report of the Subcomm. on Labor and Public Welfare, *Private Welfare and Pension Plan Study,* S. Rep. No. 634, 92d Cong., 2d Sess. (1972).

SEC, *Institutional Investor Study,* H.R. Doc. No. 64, 92d Cong., 1st Sess., Pt. 4 (1971).

———, *Report on Investment Trusts and Investment Companies,* H.R. Doc. No. 136, 77th Cong., 1st Sess. (1942).

Written Statements Submitted on H.R. 10474 (H.R. 2) to the House Comm. on Ways and Means, 93d Cong., 1st Sess. (1975).

Chapter 2

THE GOVERNING STATUTORY AND COMMON-LAW SYSTEMS

Articles

Blank, Keen, Payne & Miller, "Variable Life Insurance and the Federal Securities Laws," 60 Va. L. Rev. 71 (1974).

Callaghan, "The Comptroller of the Currency's Disclosure Regulation and a Banker's Right to Privacy," 92 Banking L.J. 119 (1975).

Cary & Bright, "The Delegation of Investment Responsibility for Endowment Funds," 74 Colum. L. Rev. 207 (1974).

———, "The Income of Endowment Funds," 69 Colum. L. Rev. 396 (1969).

Chadwick & Foster, "Federal Regulation of Retirement Plans: The Quest for Parity," 4 Vand. L. Rev. 641 (1975).

Comment, "Application of Section 17 of the Investment Company Act of 1940 to Portfolio Affiliates," 120 U. Pa. L. Rev. 983 (1972).

Gillis & Weld, "Securities Law and Regulation: Fiduciary Responsibility Under the 1974 Pension Act," 31 Fin. Anal. J. 10 (May-June 1975).

"Glass-Steagall Act—A History of Its Legislative Origins and Regulatory Construction," 92 Banking L.J. 38 (1975).

Heskell, "Some Problems with the Uniform Trustee's Powers Act," 32 Law & Contemp. Prob. 168 (1967).

Lovitch, "The Investment Advisers Act of 1940—Who Is An 'Investment Adviser'?" 24 Kan. L. Rev. 67 (1975).

Lund, Casey & Chamberlain, "A Financial Analysis of the ESOT," 32 Fin. Anal. J. 55 (Jan.-Feb. 1976).

Lybecker, "Regulation of Bank Trust Department Investment Activities: Seven Gaps, Eight Remedies," 90 Banking L.J. 912 (1973); 91 Banking L.J. 6 (1974).

Mace, "Standards of Care for Trustees," 54 Harv. Bus. Rev. 14 (Jan.-Feb. 1976).

Note, "Application of Section 17 of the Investment Company Act of 1940 to Portfolio Affiliates," 120 U. Pa. L. Rev. 983 (1972).

——, "Employee Stock Ownership Plans: A Step Toward Democratic Capitalism," 55 B.U.L. Rev. 195 (1975).

——, "The Legal Status of a National Bank's Automatic Stock Investment Service Under Sections 16 and 21 of the Glass-Steagall Act of 1933," 27 Vand. L. Rev. 1217 (1974).

——, "Procedures and Remedies in Limited Partners' Suits for Breach of the General Partner's Fiduciary Duty," 90 Harv. L. Rev. 763 (1977).

"Proceedings of Conference on Variable Annuities and Variable Life Insurance," 32 Bus. Law. 675 (1977).

Rosenblatt & Lybecker, "Some Thoughts on the Federal Securities Laws Regulating External Investment Management Arrangements and the ALI Federal Securities Code Project," 124 U. Pa. L. Rev. 587 (1976).

Books

Advisory Committee on Endowment Management to the Ford Foundation, *Managing Educational Endowments* (Ford Foundation 1969).

Cary, W., & Bright, C., *The Developing Law of Endowment Funds: "The Law and the Lore" Revisited* (Ford Foundation 1974).

——, *The Law and the Lore of Endowment Funds* (Ford Foundation 1969).

Green, D., & Schuelke, M., *The Trust Activities of the Banking Industry* (Stanford Research Institute 1975).

Herman, E., *Conflicts of Interest: Commercial Bank Trust Departments* (The Twentieth Century Fund 1975).

Restatement (Second) of Agency (American Law Institute 1958).

Restatement (Second) of Trusts (American Law Institute 1959).

Smith, W., & Chiechi, C., *Private Foundations Before and After the Tax Reform Act of 1969* (American Enterprise Institute for Public Policy Research 1976).

U.S. Comptroller of the Currency, *Comptroller's Manual for Representatives in Trusts* (U.S. Treasury 1963).

Williamson, J., *Performance Measurement and Investment Objectives for Educational Endowment Funds* (The Common Fund 1972).

Congressional and Regulatory References

Banking Circular 61 (Jan. 27, 1975), CCH Fed. Bank. L. Rep. ¶ 96,446.

77 Cong. Rec. 3491-3493 (1933).

86 Cong. Rec. 9809 (1940).

H.R. Rep. No. 2639, 76th Cong., 3d Sess. (1940).

Hearings on H.R. 10065 Before a Subcomm. of the House Comm. on Interstate and Foreign Commerce, 76th Cong., 3d Sess. (1940).

Hearings on S. 3580 Before a Subcomm. of the Senate Comm. on Banking and Currency, 76th Cong., 3d Sess. (1940).

Report on H.R. 10065 of the House Comm. on Interstate and Foreign Commerce, H.R. Rep. No. 2639, 76th Cong., 3d Sess. (June 18, 1940).

S. 3580, 76th Cong., 3d Sess., § 45(a)(16) (1940).

S. Rep. No. 1775, 76th Cong., 3d Sess. (1940).

SEC, *Report of the Advisory Comm. on Investment Management Services for Individual Investors, Small Account Investment Management Services,* CCH Fed. Sec. L. Rep. No. 465 (1973).

Study of the Securities Activities of Commercial Banks, Hearings Before the Subcomm. on Securities of the Senate Comm. on Banking, Housing and Urban Affairs, 94th Cong., 2d Sess. (1976).

T.I.R. 1334, Fed. Taxes (P-H) ¶ 54,974 (1975).

Chapter 3

DEVELOPING NEW BUSINESS

Articles

Bines, "Regulating Discretionary Management: Broker-Dealers as Catalysts for Reform," 16 B.C. Ind. & Com. L. Rev. 347 (1975).

Blank, Keen, Payne & Miller, "Variable Life Insurance and Securities Laws," 60 Va. L. Rev. 71 (1974).

Casey, " 'Finders Fee' Compensation to Brokers and Others," 31 Bus. Law. 707 (1976).

Church & Seidel, "The Entrance of Banks into the Field of Mutual Funds," 13 B.C. Ind. & Com. L. Rev. 1175 (1972).

Coffey, "The Economic Realities of a Security: Is There a More Meaningful Formula?" 18 W. Res. L. Rev. 367 (1967).

Cohen & Hatcher, "Applicability of the Investment Company Act of 1940 to Real Estate Syndications," 36 Ohio St. L.J. 482 (1975).

Comment, "National Banks and Mutual Funds: Where Can They Go After Investment Company Institute v. Camp?" 60 Ky. L.J. 757 (1972).

Hannan & Thomas, "The Importance of Economic Reality and Risk in Defining Federal Securities," 25 Hastings L.J. 219 (1974).

Jennings, "The New York Stock Exchange and the Commission Rate Struggle," 53 Calif. L. Rev. 1119 (1965).

Kerr, "The Inadvertent Investment Company: Section 3(a)(3) of the Investment Company Act," 12 Stan. L. Rev. 29 (1959).

Levy, "How to Measure Research Performance," 1 J. Portfolio Management 44 (Fall 1974).

Long, "An Attempt to Return 'Investment Contracts' to the Mainstream of Securities Regulation," 24 Okla. L. Rev. 135 (1971).

——, "Securities—Investment Advisers Act of 1940—Private Right of Action for Damages Allowed Against an Investment Adviser and His Accountant," 43 Fordham L. Rev. 493 (1974).

Overman, "Registration and Exemption From Registration of Employee Compensation Plans Under the Federal Securities Law," 28 Vand. L. Rev. 455 (1975).

Shapiro & Sachs, "Integration Under the Securities Act: Once an Exemption, Not Always?" 31 Md. L. Rev. 3 (1971).

Books

Cohen, J., Zinbarg, E., & Zeikel, A., *Investment Analysis and Portfolio Management* (R.D. Irwin., rev. ed., 1973).

Friedman, "Problems Involving Investment Advisers and Broker-Dealers Serving Individual Accounts," in Mundheim, R., Fleischer, A., & Schupper, J., *Fourth Annual Institute on Securities Regulation* (Practising Law Institute 1973).

Green, D., & Schuelke, M., *The Trust Activities of the Banking Industry* (Stanford Research Institute 1975).

Herman, E., *Conflicts of Interest: Commercial Bank Trust Departments* (The Twentieth Century Fund 1975).

Jennings, R., & Marsh, H., *Securities Regulation* (The Foundation Press, Inc., 3d ed., 1972).

Leinsdorf, D., & Etra, D., *CITIBANK; Ralph Nader's Study Group Report on First National City Bank* (Grossman Publishers 1973).

Lorie, J., & Hamilton, M., *The Stock Market: Theories and Evidence* (Richard D. Irwin, Inc. 1973).

Mayer, M., *The Bankers* (Weybright & Talley 1974).

Restatement (Second) of Agency (American Law Institute 1958).

Restatement of Contracts (American Law Institute 1932).

Restatement of Torts (American Law Institute 1938).

Restatement (Second) of Trusts (American Law Institute 1959).

Sprecher, C., *Introduction to Investment Management* (Houghton Mifflin 1975).

Whittlesey, C., Freedman, A., & Herman, E., *Money and Banking* (Macmillan; Oxford Clarendon Press 1968).

Congressional and Regulatory References

Administrator of National Banks, Letter to Presidents of All National Banks, "Statement of Policy on Advertising for Funds by National Banks," [1966-1967 Transfer Binder] CCH Fed. Sec. L. Rep. ¶ 77,421 (Dec. 16, 1966).

Am. Jur. 2d, "Brokers" § 173 (1964).

Conference Report, *Investment Company Amendments Act of 1970*, Conf. Rep. No. 1631, 91st Cong., 2d Sess. (1970).

"Fiduciary Powers," Banks Reminded of Prohibition Against Common Trust Fund Advertisement, Deputy Comptroller of the Currency, CCH Fed. Bank. L. Rep. ¶ 96,355 (Aug. 8, 1973).

Hearings on Mutual Fund Amendments Before the House Comm. on Interstate and Foreign Commerce, 91st Cong., 1st Sess. (1969).

Hearings on Mutual Fund Legislation of 1967 Before the Senate Comm. on Banking and Currency, 90th Cong., 1st Sess. (1967).

Munn, G., *Encyclopedia of Banking and Finance* (Bankers Publishing Co., 7th ed., rev. Garcia, F.L., 1973).

Report of the House Comm. on Interstate and Foreign Commerce, *Investment Company Amendments Act of 1970*, H.R. Rep. No. 1382, 91st Cong., 2d Sess. (1970).

Report of the Senate Comm. on Banking and Currency, *Investment Company Amendments Act of 1970,* S. Rep. No. 184, 91st Cong., 1st Sess. (1969).

SEC, *Institutional Investor Study,* H.R. Doc. No. 64, 92d Cong., 1st Sess. (1971).

———, *Report of the Advisory Comm. on Investment Management Services for Individual Investors, Small Account Investment Management Services,* CCH Fed. Sec. L. Rep. No. 465 (1973).

———, *Report on the Public Policy Implications of Investment Company Growth,* H.R. Rep. No. 2337, 89th Cong., 2d Sess. (1966).

SEC Commissioner Evans, Speech Before the Ninth Annual Banking Law Institute, [1973-1974 Transfer Binder] CCH Fed. Sec. L. Rep. ¶ 79,775 (1974).

SEC Commissioner Sommer, "The Emerging Responsibilities of the Securities Lawyer," [1973-1974 Transfer Binder] CCH Fed. Sec. L. Rep. ¶ 79,631 (1974).

"SEC—Commodity Futures Trading Commission Jurisdictional Correspondence," Letter of SEC Chairman Roderick M. Hills and CFTC Staff Response, [1975-1976 Transfer Binder] CCH Fed. Sec. L. Rep. ¶ 80,336 (1975).

Chapter 4

SETTING INVESTMENT OBJECTIVES

Articles

Bines, "Regulating Discretionary Management: Broker-Dealers as Catalysts for Reform," 16 B.C. Ind. & Com. L. Rev. 347 (1975).

Black, "The Investment Policy Spectrum: Individuals, Endowment Funds and Pension Funds," 32 Fin. Anal. J. 23 (Jan.-Feb. 1976).

Brody, "Options and Mathematics of Defense," 1 J. Portfolio Management 35 (Winter 1975).

Cary & Bright, "The Delegation of Investment Responsibility for Endowment Funds," 74 Colum. L. Rev. 207 (1974).

Casey, " 'Finders Fee' Compensation to Brokers and Others," 31 Bus. Law. 707 (1976).

Cohen, "The Suitability Rule and Economic Theory," 80 Yale L.J. 1604 (1971).

Comment, "Investor Suitability Standards in Real Estate Syndication: California's Procustean Bed Approach," 63 Calif. L. Rev. 471 (1975).

———, "A Symptomatic Approach to Securities Fraud: The SEC's Proposed Rule 15c2-6 and the Boiler Room," 72 Yale L.J. 1411 (1963).

Faust, "Suitability," 7 Rev. Sec. Reg. 899 (1974).

Friedman & Savage, "The Utility Analysis of Choices Involving Risk," 56 J. Pol. Econ. 279 (1948).

Green & Wittner, "Private Placements of Securities Under Rule 146," 21 Prac. Law. 9 (1975).

Kassouf, "Towards a Legal Framework for Efficiency and Equity in the Securities Markets," 25 Hastings L.J. 417 (1974).

Mundheim, "Professional Responsibilities of Broker-Dealers: The Suitability Doctrine," 1965 Duke L.J. 445.

Note, "Implication of Civil Liability Under the New York Stock Exchange Rules and Listing Agreement," 22 Vill. L. Rev. 130 (1976).

———, "The Regulation of Risky Investments," 83 Harv. L. Rev. 603 (1970).

———, "Securities—Investment Advisers Act of 1940—Private Right of Action for Damages Allowed Against an Investment Adviser and His Accountant," 43 Fordham L. Rev. 493 (1974).

Sharpe, "Likely Gains for Market Timing," 31 Fin. Anal. J. 60 (March-April 1975).

Wineberg & McManus, "The Private Placement Exemption under the Securities and Exchange Act of 1933 Revisited, and Rule 146," 27 Baylor L. Rev. 201 (1975).

Books

Bildersee, R., *Pension Regulation Manual: Analysis, Forms & Procedures* (Warren, Gorham & Lamont 1975).

Brooks, J., *Conflicts of Interest: Corporate Pension Fund Asset Management* (The Twentieth Century Fund 1975).

Butowsky, D., and Carlson, R., *Counselling the Investment Adviser* (Practising Law Institute 1975).

Lipton, "The Customer Suitability Doctrine," in Mundheim, R., Fleischer, A., & Schupper, J., *Fourth Annual Institute on Securities Regulation* (Practising Law Institute 1973).

Lorie, J., & Brealey, R., eds., *Modern Developments in Investment Management* (Praeger Publishers 1972).

Lorie, J., & Hamilton, M., *The Stock Market: Theories and Evidence* (Richard D. Irwin, Inc. 1973).

Loss, L., *Securities Regulation* (Little, Brown & Co., 2d ed., Supp., 1969).

Malkiel, B., & Quandt, R., *Strategies and Rational Decisions in the Securities Options Market* (MIT Press 1969).

Restatement (Second) of Agency (American Law Institute 1958).

Restatement (Second) of Trusts (American Law Institute 1959).

Scott, A., *The Law of Trusts* (Little, Brown & Co., 3d ed., 1967).

Sharpe, W., *Portfolio Theory and Capital Markets* (McGraw-Hill Book Co. 1970).

Congressional and Regulatory References

SEC, *Institutional Investor Study*, H.R. Doc. No. 64, 92d Cong., 1st Sess. (1971).

———, *Policy Statement on the Future Structure of the Securities Markets,* [Special Studies Transfer Binder] CCH Fed. Sec. L. Rep. ¶ 74,811 (Feb. 2, 1972).

———, *Report of Special Study of Securities Markets,* H.R. Doc. No. 95, 88th Cong., 1st Sess. (1963).

———, *Report of the Advisory Comm. on Investment Management Services for Individual Investors, Small Account Investment Management Services,* CCH Fed. Sec. L. Rep. No. 465 (1973).

Trust Banking Circular No. 2 (July 2, 1974), CCH Fed. Bank. L. Rep. ¶ 96,295.

Chapter 5

SPECIAL PROBLEMS IN STRUCTURING THE INVESTMENT MANAGEMENT AGREEMENT

Articles

Langbein & Posner, "Market Funds and Trust-Investment Law," 1976 Am. Bar Found. Research J. 1.

Manges, "The Investment Company Amendments Act of 1970," 26 Bus. Law. 1311 (1971).

Nash, "Pricing Policies in Government Contracts," 29 Law & Contemp. Prob. 361 (1964).

North, "A Brief History of Federal Investment Company Legislation," 44 Notre Dame Law. 677 (1969).

Note, "Directory Trusts and the Exculpatory Clause," 65 Colum. L. Rev. 138 (1965).

————, "The Mutual Fund Industry: A Legal Survey," 44 Notre Dame Law. 732 (1969).

Posner, "Liability of the Trustee Under the Corporate Indenture," 42 Harv. L. Rev. 198 (1928).

Shattuck, "The Legal Propriety of Investment by American Fiduciaries in the Shares of Boston-Type Open-End Investment Trusts," 25 B.U.L. Rev. 1 (1945).

Books

American Bar Foundation, *Model Debenture Indenture Provisions* (American Bar Foundation 1967).

American Law Institute, *Federal Securities Code* (Tentative Draft No. 4) (American Law Institute 1975).

Augenblick, "Compensation of Investment Managers," in Cohen, M., & Bialkin, K., *Institutional Investors in a Changing Economy* (Practising Law Institute 1970).

Bank Administration Institute, *Measuring the Investment Performance of Pension Funds* (Bank Administration Institute 1968).

Bernstein, "In-House Asset Management," in Cohen, M., & Bialkin, K., *Institutional Investors in a Changing Economy* (Practising Law Institute 1970).

Cohen, M., & Bialkin, K., *Institutional Investors in a Changing Economy* (Practising Law Institute 1970).

Corbin, A., *Corbin on Contracts* (West Publishing Co. 1952).

Farr, J., *An Estate Planner's Handbook* (Little, Brown & Co., 3d ed., 1966).

Friedman, "Problems Involving Investment Advisers and Broker-Dealers Serving Individual Accounts," in Mundheim, R., Fleischer, A., & Schupper, J., *Fourth Annual Institute on Securities Regulation* (Practising Law Institute 1973).

Lipper, "Fund Distribution," in Cohen, M., & Bialkin, K., *Institutional Investors in a Changing Economy* (Practising Law Institute 1970).

Lorie, J., & Hamilton, M., *The Stock Market: Theories and Evidence* (Richard D. Irwin, Inc. 1973).

Loring, A., *A Trustee's Handbook: Farr Revision* (Little, Brown & Co., 6th ed., rev. James F. Farr, 1962).

Restatement (Second) of Agency (American Law Institute 1958).

Restatement of Contracts (American Law Institute 1932).

Restatement (Second) of Trusts (American Law Institute 1959).

Scott, A., *The Law of Trusts* (Little, Brown & Co., 3d ed., 1967).

Williston, S., *A Treatise on the Law of Contracts* (Baker, Voorhis, 3d ed., 1957).

Congressional and Regulatory References

17 Am. Jur. 2d *Contracts* §§ 122, 343-354 (1964).

Annotation, "Limiting Effect in Contract, Will or Trust Instrument Taxing Trustee's or Executor's Fees," 19 A.L.R.3d 520 (1968).

——, "Validity and Effect of Provision of Contract of Trust Instrument Limiting Amount of Fees of Trustee," 161 A.L.R. 860 (1946).

H.R. 9510, 90th Cong., 1st Sess. (1967).

H.R. 10065, 76th Cong., 3d Sess. (1940).

H.R. 14742, 90th Cong., 2d Sess. (1968).

Hearings Before a Subcomm. of the Comm. on Banking and Currency, 76th Cong., 3d Sess. (1940).

Hearings on H.R. 9510 and H.R. 9511 Before the Subcomm. of Commerce and Finance of the House Comm. on Interstate and Foreign Commerce, 90th Cong., 1st Sess. (1967).

Hearings on H.R. 10065 Before a Subcomm. of the House Comm. on Interstate and Foreign Commerce, 76th Cong., 3d Sess. (1940).

Hearings on H.R. 11995, S. 2224, S. 13754 and S. 14737 Before the Subcomm. on Commerce and Finance of the House Comm. on Interstate and Foreign Commerce, 91st Cong., 1st Sess. (1969).

Hearings on S. 34 and S. 296 Before the Senate Comm. on Banking and Currency, 91st Cong., 1st Sess. (1969).

Hearings on S. 1659 Before the Senate Comm. on Banking and Currency, 90th Cong., 1st Sess. (1967).

Hearings on S. 3580 Before a Subcomm. of the Senate Comm. on Banking and Currency, 76th Cong., 3d Sess. (1940).

S. 34, 91st Cong., 1st Sess. (1969).

S. 1659, 90th Cong., 1st Sess. (1967).

S. 3580, 76th Cong., 3d Sess. (1940).

S. 3724, 90th Cong., 2d Sess. (1968).

S. Rep. No. 1775, 76th Cong., 3d Sess. (1940).

SEC, *Institutional Investor Study*, H.R. Doc. No. 64, 92d Cong., 1st Sess. (1971).

SEC, *Report of the Advisory Comm. on Investment Management Services for Individual Investors, Small Account Investment Management Services*, CCH Fed. Sec. L. Rep. No. 465 (1973).

———, *Report of the Wharton School of Finance and Commerce: A Study of Mutual Funds*, H.R. Rep. No. 2274, 87th Cong., 2d Sess. (1966).

———, *Report on Investment Trusts and Investment Companies* (1939-1942).

———, *Report on the Public Policy Implications of Investment Company Growth*, H.R. Rep. 2337, 98th Cong. 2d Sess. (1966).

———, *Supp. Report on Investment Counsel, Investment Management, Investment Supervisory, and Investment Advisory Services*, H.R. Doc. No. 477, 76th Cong., 2d Sess. (1939).

Chapter 6

PROFESSIONAL COMPETENCE IN PORTFOLIO SELECTION

Articles

Barack, "Book Review: B. Malkiel, *A Random Walk Down Wall Street*," 83 Yale L.J. 1516 (1974).

Cohen, "The Suitability Rule and Economic Theory," 80 Yale L.J. 1604 (1971).

Dyl, "Negative Betas: The Attractions of Selling Short," 1 J. Portfolio Management 74 (Spring 1975).

Friedman, "The Dynastic Trust," 73 Yale L.J. 547 (1964).

Graham, "The Future of Financial Analysis," 19 Fin. Anal. J. 65 (May-June 1963).

Haimoff, "Holmes Looks at Hochfelder and 10b-5," 32 Bus. Law. 147 (1976).

Hutchinson, "The Federal Prudent Man Rule Under ERISA," 22 Vill. L. Rev. 15 (1976).

Kassouf, "Towards a Legal Framework for Efficiency and Equity in the Securities Markets," 25 Hastings L.J. 417 (1974).

Langbein & Posner, "Market Funds and Trust-Investment Law," 1976 Am. Bar Found. Research J. 1.

———, "Market Funds and Trust-Investment Law: II," 1977 Am. Bar Found. Research J. 1.

MacDonald & Bacon, "Risk and Return on Short Positions in Common Stocks," 28 J. Fin. 97 (1973).

Markowitz, "Portfolio Selection," 7 J. Fin. 77 (1952).

Modigliani & Pogue, "An Introduction to Risk and Return," 30 Fin. Anal. J. 68 (March-April 1974).

Mundheim, "Responsibilities of Broker-Dealers: The Suitability Doctrine," 1965 Duke L. J. 445.

Note, "Fiduciary Standards and the Prudent Man Rule Under the Employment Retirement Income Security Act of 1974," 88 Harv. L. Rev. 960 (1975).

———, "Prudence in Trust Investment," U. Mich. J.L. Ref. 491 (1975).

———, "Regulating Risk Taking by Mutual Funds," 82 Yale L.J. 1305 (1973).

———, "The Regulation of Risky Investments," 83 Harv. L. Rev. 603 (1970).

———, "Trustee Investment Powers: Imprudent Application of the Prudent Man Rule," 50 Notre Dame Law. 519 (1975).

Pozen, "Money Managers and Securities Research," 51 N.Y.U.L. Rev. 923 (1976).

Rice, "Recommendations by a Broker-Dealer: The Requirement for a Reasonable Basis," 25 Mercer L. Rev. 537 (1974).

Shattuck, "The Massachusetts Prudent Man Rule in Trust Investments," 25 B.U.L. Rev. 307 (1945).

Sosnoff, "Hedge Fund Management," 22 Fin. Analy. J. 105 (July-Aug. 1966).

Books

Bank Administration Institute, *Measuring the Investment Performance of Pension Funds* (Bank Administration Institute 1968).

Engel, L., *How to Buy Stocks* (Bantam Books 1972).

Farr, J., *An Estate Planner's Handbook* (Little, Brown & Co., 3d ed., 1966).

Graham, B., Dodd, D., & Cottle, S., *Security Analysis* (McGraw-Hill Book Co., 4th ed., 1962).

Herman, E., *Conflicts of Interest: Commercial Bank Trust Departments* (The Twentieth Century Fund 1975).

Loeb, G., *The Battle for Investment Survival* (Simon & Schuster 1965).

Lorie, J., & Brealey, R., eds., *Modern Developments in Investment Management* (Praeger Publishers 1972).

Lorie, J., & Hamilton, M., *The Stock Market: Theories and Evidence* (Richard D. Irwin, Inc. 1973).

Loss, L., *Securities Regulation* (Little, Brown & Co., 2d ed., Supp., 1969).

Prosser, W., *Handbook of the Law of Torts* (West Publishing Co., 4th ed., 1971).

Scott, A., *The Law of Trusts* (Little, Brown & Co., 3d ed., 1967).

Sharpe, W., *Portfolio Theory and Capital Markets* (McGraw-Hill, Inc. 1970).

Tiffany, J., & Bullard, E., *The Law of Trusts and Trustees* (W.C. Little, Law Book Seller, 1862.

Congressional and Regulatory References

Annotation, "Charitable Trusts: Liability of Trustee for Permitting Trust Income to Accumulate in Non-Interest-Bearing Account," 51 A.L.R.3d 1293 (1973).

———, "Duty of Trustee to Diversify Investments and Liability for Failure To Do So," 24 A.L.R.3d 730 (1969).

S. 2849, 94th Cong., 2d Sess. (1976).

Chapter 7

THE APPLICATION OF MODERN PORTFOLIO THEORY TO LEGAL STANDARDS OF PROFESSIONAL COMPETENCE

Articles

Bines, "Regulating Discretionary Management: Broker-Dealers as Catalysts for Reform," 16 B.C. Ind. & Com. L. Rev. 347 (1975).

Black, "Fact or Fantasy in the Use of Options," 31 Fin. Anal. J. 36 (July-Aug. 1975).

———, "Implications of the Random Walk Hypothesis for Portfolio Management," 27 Fin. Anal. J. 16 (March-April 1971).

Black & Scholes, "From Theory to a New Financial Product," 29 J. Fin. 399 (1974).

Blume & Friend, "A New Look at the Capital Asset Pricing Model," 28 J. Fin. 19 (1973).

Brody, "Options and the Mathematics of Defense," 1 J. Portfolio Management 35 (Winter 1975).

Comment, "SEC and FRB Treatment of Options: An Experiment in Market Regulation," 53 Tex. L. Rev. 1243 (1975).

Comment, "Why the Beta Models Broke Down," 31 Fin. Anal. J. 6 (July-Aug. 1975).

Friedman & Savage, "The Utility Analysis of Choices Involving Risk," 41 J. Pol. Econ. 279 (1948).

Gillis, "Securities Law and Regulation: Professional Fiduciaries Under Fire," 28 Fin. Anal. J. 10 (Sept.-Oct. 1972).

Gillis & Weld, "The Money Manager as Fiduciary," 28 Fin. Anal. J. 10 (March-April 1972).

Graham, "The Future of Common Stocks," 30 Fin. Anal. J. 20 (Sept.-Oct. 1974).

Hedberg, "Let's Regulate Investment Advice," 29 Fin. Anal. J. 24 (May-June 1973).

Jorden, "Paying up for Research: A Regulatory and Legislative Analysis," 1975 Duke L.J. 1103.

Klein, "The Convertible Bond: A Peculiar Package," 123 U. Pa. L. Rev. 547 (1975).

Langbein & Posner, "Market Funds and Trust Investment Law," 1976 Am. Bar Found. Research J. 1.

Lorie, "Diversification: Old and New," 1 J. Portfolio Management 25 (Winter 1975).

Lorie & Halpern, "Conglomerates: The Rhetoric and the Evidence," 13 J. Law & Econ. 149 (1970).

Love, "The Use and Abuse of Leverage," 31 Fin. Anal. J. 51 (March-April 1975).

Markowitz, "Portfolio Selection," 7 J. Fin. 77 (1952).

Modigliani & Pogue, "An Introduction to Risk and Return," Pt. I, 30 Fin. Anal. J. 68 (March-April 1974); Pt. II, 30 Fin. Anal. J. 69 (May-June 1974).

Nelson, "Let's Make Investment Advisers Accountable," 29 Fin. Anal. J. 19 (Jan.-Feb. 1973).

Owens, "Investment Adviser Regulation: A Subject Too Long Neglected," 29 Fin. Anal. J. 12 (Jan.-Feb. 1973).

Reback, "Risk and Return in CBOE and AMEX Options Trading," 31 Fin. Anal. J. 42 (July-Aug. 1975).

Rozeff, "The Money Supply: The Demise of a Leading Indicator," 31 Fin. Anal. J. 18 (Sept.-Oct. 1975).

Schotland, "Bank Trust Departments and Public Policy Today," 4 Sec. Reg. L. J. 389 (1977).

Sharpe, "Likely Gains from Market Timing," 31 Fin. Anal. J. 60 (March-April 1975).

Shishko, "Why Gold?" 3 J. Portfolio Management 34 (Spring 1977).

Williams, "The Prudent Man Rule of ERISA," 31 Bus. Law. 99 (1975).

Books

Bernstein, L., *Financial Statement Analysis: Theory, Application and Interpretation* (R.D. Irwin 1974).

Brudney, "Origins and Limited Applicability of the 'Reasonable Basis' or 'Know Your Merchandise' Doctrine," in Mundheim, R., Fleischer, A., & Schupper, J., *Fourth Annual Institute on Securities Regulation* (Practising Law Institute 1973).

Cohen, "Analysis of Common Stock," in Levine, S., ed., *Financial Analyst's Handbook* (Dow Jones-Irwin, Inc. 1975).

Graham, B., Dodd, D., & Cottle, S., *Security Analysis* (McGraw-Hill Book Co. 1962).

Kavesh & Platt, "Economic Forecasting," in Levine, S., ed., *Financial Analyst's Handbook* (Dow Jones-Irwin, Inc. 1975).

Kuehner, "Efficient Markets and Random Walk," in Levine, S., ed., *Financial Analyst's Handbook* (Dow Jones-Irwin, Inc. 1975).

Lipton, "The Customer Suitability Doctrine," in Mundheim, R., Fleischer, A., & Schupper, J., *Fourth Annual Institute on Securities Regulation.* (Practising Law Institute 1973).

Lorie, J., & Brealey, R., eds., *Modern Developments in Investment Management* (Praeger Publishers 1972).

Lorie, J., & Hamilton, M., *The Stock Market: Theories and Evidence* (Richard D. Irwin, Inc. 1973).

Malkiel, B., & Quandt, R., *Strategies and Rational Decisions in the Securities Options Market* (MIT Press 1969).

Mennis, "An Integrated Approach to Portfolio Management," in Levine, S., ed., *Financial Analyst's Handbook* (Dow Jones-Irwin, Inc. 1975).

Milne, "Regression Analysis," in Levine, S., ed., *Financial Analyst's Handbook* (Dow Jones-Irwin, Inc. 1975).

Restatement (Second) of Agency (American Law Institute 1958).

Restatement (Second) of Trusts (American Law Institute 1959).

Scott, A., *The Law of Trusts* (Little, Brown & Co., 3d ed., 1967).

Shaw, "Technical Analysis," in Levine, S., ed., *Financial Analyst's Handbook* (Dow Jones-Irwin, Inc. 1975).

Stewart, "Corporate Forecasting," in Levine, S., ed., *Financial Analyst's Handbook* (Dow Jones-Irwin, Inc. 1975).

Tiffany, J., & Bullard, E., *The Law of Trusts and Trustees* (W.C. Little, Law Book Seller, 1862).

Train, J., *Dance of the Money Bees: A Professional Speaks Frankly on Investing* (Harper and Row 1974).

Transcript, "Managing Investment Funds," in Hawes, D., chmn., *Investment Partnerships and "Off-Shore" Investment Funds* (Practising Law Institute 1969).

Congressional and Regulatory References

Annotation, "Authorization by Trust Instrument of Investment of Trust Funds in Non-Legal Investments," 78 A.L.R.2d 7 (1961).

Hearings on S. 3580 Before a Subcomm. of the Senate Comm. on Banking and Currency, 76th Cong., 3d Sess. (1940).

S. 2849, 94th Cong., 2d Sess. (1976).

SEC, *Institutional Investor Study,* H.R. Doc. No. 64, 92d Cong., 1st Sess. (1971).

Trust Banking Circular No. 2 (July 2, 1974), CCH Fed. Bank. L. Rep. ¶ 96,295.

Trust Banking Circular No. 4 (Dec. 23, 1975), CCH Fed. Bank. L. Rep. ¶ 96,786.

Trust Banking Circular No. 4, revised (Sept. 29, 1976), CCH Fed. Bank. L. Rep. ¶ 96,941.

Chapter 8

EXECUTING INVESTMENT DECISIONS AS A LEGAL DUTY

Articles

Barnea & Logue, "The Effect of Risk on the Market Maker's Spread," 31 Fin. Anal. J. 45 (Nov.-Dec. 1975).

Cuneo & Wagner, "Reducing the Cost of Stock Trading," 31 Fin. Anal. J. 35 (Nov.-Dec. 1975).

Geyer, "A Primer on Institutional Trading," 25 Fin. Anal. J. 16 (March-April 1969).

Jennings, "The New York Stock Exchange and the Commission Rate Structure," 53 Calif. L. Rev. 1119 (1965).

Pozen, "Competition and Regulation in the Stock Markets," 73 Mich. L. Rev. 317 (1974).

Rowen, "The Securities Acts Amendments of 1975," 3 Sec. Reg. L.J. 329 (1976).

Books

Mennis, "An Integrated Approach to Portfolio Management," in Levine, S., ed., *Financial Analyst's Handbook* (Dow Jones-Irwin, Inc. 1975).

Restatement of Agency (American Law Institute 1933).

Congressional and Regulatory References

3 C.J.S. *Agency* §§ 503-507 (1973).

90 C.J.S. *Trusts* § 467 (1955).

H.R. 5050, 93d Cong., 1st Sess. (March 1, 1973).

Hearings on H.R. 5050 and H.R. 340 Before the Subcomm. on Commerce and Finance of the Comm. on Interstate and Foreign Commerce, 93d Cong., 1st Sess., Pt. 2 (1973).

The Mack Resolution, H.J. Res. 438, 87th Cong., 1st Sess., Pub. L. 87-196 (Sept. 5, 1961).

S. 470, 93d Cong., 1st Sess. (Jan. 18, 1973).

S. Res. 109, 92d Cong., 1st Sess. (June 21, 1971).

Report of the Senate Comm. on Banking, Housing and Urban Affairs, Containing a Report of the Subcomm. on Securities on S. Res, 109, *Securities Industry Study,* 92d Cong., 2d Sess. (1972).

Report of the Subcomm. on Commerce and Finance of the Committee on Interstate and Foreign Commerce, *Securities Industry Study,* H.R. Rep. No. 1519, 92d Cong., 2d Sess. (1972).

Report of the Subcomm. on Securities of the Senate Comm. on Banking, Housing and Urban Affairs, *Securities Industry Study,* S. Doc. No. 13, 93d Cong., 1st Sess. (1973).

SEC, *Annual Report* 5 (1974).

———, *Institutional Investor Study,* H.R. Doc. No. 64, 92d Cong., 1st Sess. (1971).

———, *Policy Statement on the Structure of a Central Market System,* CCH Fed. Sec. L. Rep. No. 473 (1973).

———, *Report of Special Study of Securities Markets,* H.R. Doc. No. 95, 88th Cong., 1st Sess. (1963).

——, *Report of the Wharton School of Finance and Commerce: A Study of Mutual Funds,* H.R. Rep. No. 2274, 87th Cong., 2d Sess. (1962).

——, *Report on the Public Policy Implications of Investment Company Growth,* H.R. Rep. No. 2337, 89th Cong., 2d Sess. (1966).

——, *Statement on the Future of the Securities Markets,* [Special Studies Transfer Binder] CCH Fed. Sec. L. Rep. ¶ 74,811 (Feb. 2, 1972).

——, *Statistical Bulletin* 13 (April 1962).

Summary of Principal Provisions of Securities Act Amendments of 1975, S. 249, for the Senate Comm. on Banking, Housing and Urban Affairs, 94th Cong., 1st Sess. (Jan. 1975).

Chapter 9

USE OF COMMISSIONS TO PURCHASE SUPPLEMENTARY SERVICES

Articles

Bines, "Regulating Discretionary Management: Broker-Dealers as Catalysts for Reform," 16 B.C. Ind. & Com. L. Rev. 347 (1975).

Butowsky, "Fiduciary Standards of Conduct Revisited—*Moses v. Burgin* and *Rosenfeld v. Black,*" 17 N.Y.L.F. 735 (1971).

Casey, " 'Finders Fee' Compensation to Brokers and Others," 31 Bus. Law. 707 (1976).

Comment, "Mutual Funds and Independent Directors: Can Moses Lead to Better Business Judgement," 1972 Duke L.J. 429.

Jorden, " 'Paying Up' for Research: A Regulatory and Legislative Analysis," 1975 Duke L.J. 1103.

Miller & Carlson, "Recapture of Brokerage Commissions by Mutual Funds," 46 N.Y.U.L. Rev. 35 (1971).

Note, "Conflict of Interest in the Allocation of Mutual Fund Brokerage Business," 180 Yale L.J. 372 (1970).

——, "Settlement Standards for Mutual Fund Shareholder Litigation Involving the Fiduciary Obligation to Recapture," 13 B.C. Ind. & Com. L. Rev. 1039 (1972).

Pozen, "Money Managers and Securities Research," 51 N.Y.U.L. Rev. 923 (1976).

Rowen, "The Securities Acts Amendments of 1975: A Legislative History," 3 Sec. Reg. L.J. 329 (1976).

Books

Bahn, "Two Current Broker-Dealer Problems," in Mundheim, R., & Fleischer, A., *First Annual Institute on Securities Regulation* (Practising Law Institute 1970).

Cohen, M., & Bialkin, K., *Institutional Investors in a Changing Economy* (Practising Law Institute 1970).

Herman, E., *Conflicts of Interest: Commercial Bank Trust Departments* (The Twentieth Century Fund 1975).

Mundheim, R., & Werner, W., *Mutual Funds* (Practising Law Institute 1970).

Restatement (Second) of Agency (American Law Institute 1958).

Restatement (Second) of Trusts (American Law Institute 1959).

Rotberg, "An Evaluation of Practices and Problems," in Mundheim, R., & Werner, W., *Mutual Funds,* (Practising Law Institute 1970).

Sommer, Jr., A., *New Trends and Special Problems under the Securities Laws* (Practising Law Institute 1970).

Stark, "Problems of Institutions Under Competitive Rates: 'Paying-Up' for Research," in Mundheim, R., Fleischer, A., & Vandegrift, B., *Seventh Annual Institute on Securities Regulation* (Practising Law Institute 1976).

Wells, "Negotiated Rates and the SEC's Institutional Investor Study," in *Proceedings of the Fourth Annual Institutional Investor Conference* (Practising Law Institute 1971).

Congressional and Regulatory References

Conference Report on H.R. 2, *ERISA,* 93d Cong., 2d Sess. (1974).

Conference Report on S. 249 of the House Comm. on Interstate and Foreign Commerce, *Securities Acts Amendments of 1975,* H.R. Rep. No. 229, 94th Cong., 1st Sess. (May 19, 1975).

H.R. 5050, 93d Cong., 1st Sess. (March 1, 1973).

H.R. 5050, 93d Cong., 2d Sess. (Nov. 19, 1974).

H.R. 5050, 94th Cong., 1st Sess. (Jan. 14, 1975).

Hearings Before the Subcomm. on Commerce and Finance of the House Comm. on Interstate and Foreign Commerce, Study of the Securities Industry, 92d Cong., 1st Sess., Ser. Nos. 37-37d, Pts. 1-5 (1971), 92d Cong., 2d Sess., Ser. Nos. 37e-37h, Pts. 6-9 (1972).

Hearings on H.R. 5050 and H.R. 340 Before the Subcomm. on Commerce and Finance of the House Comm. on Interstate and Foreign Commerce, 93d Cong., 1st Sess., Ser. No. 53 (1973).

Hearings on S. 249 Before the Subcomm. on Securities of the Senate Comm. on Banking, Housing and Urban Affairs, 94th Cong., 1st Sess. (1975).

Hearings on S. 470 and S. 488 Before the Subcomm. on Securities of the Senate Comm. on Banking, Housing and Urban Affairs, 93d Cong., 1st Sess. (1973).

Report of the Comm. on Banking, Housing and Urban Affairs to Accompany S. 470, *Regulation of Securities Trading by Members of National Securities Exchanges and the Sale by Investment Advisers of Registered Investment Companies,* S. Rep. No. 187, 93d Cong., 1st Sess. (1973).

Report of the Comm. on Interstate and Foreign Commerce on H.R. 5050, the Securities Acts Amendments of 1974, H.R. Rep. No. 1476, 93d Cong., 2d Sess. (1974).

Report of the Subcomm. on Commerce and Finance of the House Comm. on Interstate and Foreign Commerce, H.R. Rep. No. 1519, 92d Cong., 2d Sess. (1972).

Report on H.R. 4111 of the Committee on Interstate and Foreign Commerce, H.R. Rep. No. 123, 94th Cong., 1st Sess. (1975).

Report on S. 249 of the Senate Comm. on Banking, Housing and Urban Affairs, S. Rep. No. 75, 94th Cong., 1st Sess. (1975).

S. 249, 94th Cong., 1st Sess. (Jan. 17, 1975).

S. 249, 94th Cong., 1st Sess. (April 18, 1975).

S. 470, 93d Cong., 1st Sess. (Jan. 18, 1973).

SEC, *Institutional Investor Study,* H.R. Doc. No. 64, 92d Cong., 1st Sess. (1971).

——, *Report of Special Study of Securities Markets,* H.R. Doc. No. 95, 88th Cong., 1st Sess. (1963).

——, *Report of the Wharton School of Finance and Commerce: A Study of Mutual Funds,* H.R. Rep. No. 2274, 87th Cong., 2d Sess. (1962).

——, *Report on the Public Policy Implications of Investment Company Growth,* H.R. Rep. No. 2337, 89th Cong., 2d Sess. (1966).

Subcomm. on Securities of the Senate Comm. on Banking, Housing and Urban Affairs, *Securities Industry Study,* S. Doc. No. 13, 93d Cong., 1st Sess. (1973).

Chapter 10

SPECIAL RELATIONS BETWEEN MANAGER AND BROKER

Articles

Bines, "Regulating Discretionary Management: Broker-Dealers as Catalysts for Reform," 16 B.C. Ind. & Com. L. Rev. 347 (1975).

Chazen, "Reinforcing the Chinese Wall: A Response," 51 N.Y.U.L. Rev. 552 (1976).

"Conflicts of Interest and the Regulation of Securities: A Panel Discussion," 28 Bus. Law. 545 (1973).

Fleischer, Mundheim & Murphy, "An Initial Inquiry into the Responsibility to Disclose Market Information," 121 U. Pa. L. Rev. 795 (1973).

Folk, "Restructuring the Securities Markets—The Martin Report: A Critique," 57 Va. L. Rev. 1315 (1971).

Gerard & Schreiber, "ERISA," 9 Rev. Sec. Reg. 943 (1976).

Haimoff, "Holmes Looks at Hochfelder and 10b-5," 32 Bus. Law. 147 (1976).

Lipton & Mazur, "The Chinese Wall: A Reply to Chazen," 51 N.Y.U.L. Rev. 552 (1976).

———, "The Chinese Wall Solution to the Conflict Problems of Securities Firms," 50 N.Y.U.L. Rev. 159 (1975).

Lurie, "Prohibited Transactions," 31 Bus. Law. 131 (1975).

Miller, "Chinese Walls," 8 Rev. Sec. Reg. 865 (1975).

Note, "Churning by Securities Dealers," 80 Harv. L. Rev. 869 (1967).

Books

Brooks, J., *The Go-Go Years* (Weybright & Talley 1973).

Herman, E., *Conflicts of Interest: Commercial Bank Trust Departments* (The Twentieth Century Fund 1975).

Jennings, R., & Marsh, H., *Securities Regulation* (The Foundation Press, Inc., 3d ed., 1972).

Leiman, "Conflict of Interest and Related Problems of Broker-Dealers and Investment Advisers," in Mundheim, R., Fleischer, A., & Glazer, D., *First Annual Institute on Securities Regulation* (Practising Law Institute 1970).

Lipton, "Market Information," in Mundheim, R., Fleischer, A., &

Schupper, J., *Fifth Annual Institute on Securities Regulation* (Practising Law Institute 1974).

Loss, L., *Securities Regulation* (Little, Brown & Co., 2d ed., 1961).

Mayer, M., *Conflicts of Interest: Broker-Dealer Firms* (The Twentieth Century Fund 1975).

Restatement (Second) of Agency (American Law Institute 1958).

Restatement (Second) of Trusts (American Law Institute 1959).

Rosenman, "Discretionary Accounts and Manipulative Trading Practices," in Mundheim, R., Fleischer, A., & Schupper, J., *Fifth Annual Institute on Securities Regulation* (Practising Law Institute 1974).

Von Neumann, J., & Morgenstern, O., *Theory of Games and Economic Behavior* (Princeton University Press 1944).

Congressional and Regulatory References

AMEX Info. Cir. No. 38-68 (Feb. 12, 1968).

AMEX Info. Cir. No. 51-71 (April 20, 1971).

AMEX Info. Cir. No. 79-69 (April 25, 1969).

Conference Report, *ERISA,* H.R. Rep. No. 1280, 93d Cong., 2d Sess. (1974).

Conference Report, *Securities Acts Amendments of 1975,* H.R. Rep. No. 229, 94th Cong., 1st Sess. (1975).

H.R. 10, 94th Cong., 1st Sess. (Jan. 14, 1975).

H.R. 5050, 93d Cong., 1st Sess. (March 1, 1973).

H.R. 5050, 93d Cong., 2d Sess. (Nov. 19, 1974).

H.R. Rep. No. 138, 91st Cong., 2d Sess. (1970).

H.R. Rep. No. 1631, 91st Cong., 2d Sess. (1970).

Hearings on Brokerage and Related Commercial Bank Services Before the Subcomm. on Securities of the Senate Comm. on Banking, Housing and Urban Affairs, 94th Cong., 2d Sess. (1976).

Hearings on Fixed Rates and Institutional Membership Before the Subcomm. on Securities of the Senate Comm. on Banking, Housing and Urban Affairs, 93d Cong., 1st Sess. (1973).

Hearings on H.R. 5050 and H.R. 340 Before the Subcomm. on Commerce and Finance of the House Comm. on Interstate and Foreign Commerce, 92d Cong., 1st Sess. Ser. No. 52 (1973).

Hearings on H.R. 11995, 13754 and 14737 Before the Subcomm. on Commerce and Finance of the House Comm. on Interstate and Foreign Commerce, 91st Cong., 1st Sess. (1969).

Hearings on S. 34 and S. 296 Before the Senate Comm. on Banking and Currency, 91st Cong., 1st Sess. (1969).

Hearings on S. 1164 and S. 3347 Before the Subcomm. on Securities of the Senate Comm. on Banking, Housing and Urban Affairs, 92nd Cong., 2d Sess. (1972).

Hearings on S. 1659 Before the Senate Comm. on Banking and Currency, 90th Cong., 1st Sess. (1967).

Hearings on S. 2519 Before the Subcomm. on Securities of the Senate Comm. on Banking, Housing and Urban Affairs, 93d Cong., 1st Sess. (1973).

Hearings on the Study of the Securities Industry Before the Subcomm. on Commerce and Finance of the House Comm. on Interstate and Foreign Commerce, 92d Cong., 2d Sess., Ser. No. 37g, Pt. 8 (1972).

Interim Report of the Senate Subcomm. on Labor of the Comm. on Labor and Public Welfare, *Private Welfare and Pension Plan Study,* S. Rep. No. 634, 92d Cong., 2d Sess. (1972).

NYSE Member Firm Cir. No. 170 (Nov. 16, 1962).

Report of the House Comm. on Interstate and Foreign Commerce on H.R. 5050, *Securities Acts Amendments of 1974,* H.R. Rep. No. 1476, 93d Cong., 2d Sess. (1974).

Report of the House Comm. on Interstate and Foreign Commerce on H.R. 4111, *Securities Reform Act of 1975,* H.R. Rep. No. 123, 94th Cong., 1st Sess. (1975).

Report of the Senate Comm. on Banking, Housing and Urban Affairs, Containing a Report of the Subcomm. on Securities on S. Res. 109, *Securities Industry Study,* 92d Cong., 2d Sess. (1972).

Report of the Senate Comm. on Banking, Housing and Urban Affairs on S. 249, *Securities Acts Amendments of 1975,* S. Rep. No. 75, 94th Cong., 1st Sess. (1975).

Report of the Senate Comm. on Banking, Housing and Urban Affairs on S. 470, *Regulation of Securities Trading by Members of National Securities Exchanges,* S. Rep. No. 187, 93d Cong., 1st Sess. (1973).

Report of the Subcomm. on Commerce and Finance of the House Comm. on Interstate and Foreign Commerce, *House Securities Industry Study,* H.R. Rep. No. 1519, 92d Sess. (1972).

Report of the Subcomm. on Securities of the Senate Comm. on Banking, Housing and Urban Affairs, *Securities Industry Study,* S. Doc. No. 13, 93d Cong., 1st Sess. (1973).

S. 4, 93d Cong., 1st Sess. (Jan. 4, 1973).

S. 4, 93d Cong., 1st Sess. (April 18, 1973).

S. 249, 94th Cong., 1st Sess. (Jan. 17, 1975).

S. 470, 93d Cong., 1st Sess. (Jan. 18, 1973).

S. 470, 93d Cong., 1st Sess. (March 1, 1973).

S. 470, 93d Cong., 1st Sess. (June 19, 1973).

S. Rep. No. 184, 91st Cong., 1st Sess. (1969).

SEC, *Initial Report on Bank Securities Activities, Pursuant to Section 11 A(e) of the Securities Exchange Act of 1934* (Jan. 3, 1977).

——, *Institutional Investor Study,* H.R. Doc. No. 64, 92d Cong., 1st Sess. (1971).

——, *Policy Statement on the Future Structure of the Securities Markets,* [Special Studies Transfer Binder] CCH Fed. Sec. L. Rep. ¶ 74,811 (Feb. 2, 1972).

——, *Report of Special Study of Securities Markets,* H.R. Doc. No. 95, 88th Cong., 1st Sess. (1963).

——, *Report of the Wharton School of Finance and Commerce; A Study of Mutual Funds,* H.R. Rep. No. 2274, 87th Cong., 2d Sess. (1962).

——, *Report on the Public Policy Implications of Investment Company Growth,* H.R. Rep. No. 2337, 89th Cong., 2d Sess. (1966).

——, *Study of Unsafe and Unsound Practices of Brokers and Dealers,* H.R. Doc. No. 231, 92d Cong., 1st Sess. (1971).

Senate Comm. on Labor and Public Welfare, *Report on S. 4,* 93d Cong., 1st Sess. (1973).

Submission of the NYSE, in Hearings on S. 1164 and S. 3347 Before the Subcomm. on Securities of the Senate Comm. on Banking, Housing and Urban Affairs, 92d Cong., 2d Sess. 618 (1972).

Written Statements Submitted by Interested Organizations on H.R. 10470 to the House Comm. on Ways and Means, 93d Cong., 1st Sess. 564 (1973).

TABLE OF STATUTES

[References are to paragraphs (¶).]

GLASS-STEAGALL ACT

INTERNAL REVENUE CODE (I.R.C.)

[References are to paragraphs (¶).]

SECURITIES ACT OF 1933

SECTION

SECURITIES ACTS AMENDMENTS OF 1975

SECTION

[References are to paragraphs (¶).]

TABLE OF RULES AND REGULATIONS

[References are to paragraphs (¶).]

[References are to paragraphs (¶).]

TABLE OF RELEASES

[Matters that are the subject of combined releases appearing under the jurisdiction of more than one statute are ordinarily cited only by the first release number assigned.]

[References are to paragraphs (¶).]

INVESTMENT COMPANY ACT

RELEASE NO.

1932	7.05[2][b] n.92
5847	5.03 n.65
7113	5.03[2] n.114,
	5.03[2][c][iii] n.156,
	5.03[2][c][v] n.164,
	5.03[2][c][vi] ns.167, 168,
	5.03[2][c][vii] ns.172,
	173, 174, 175
7221	4.03[1][b][ii] ns.150, 152,
	7.05[2][b] n.92
7581	10.05[1] n.248
7644	2.04[1] n.49
8000	2.04[1] n.49,
	3.04 n.263
8646	2.04[1] n.45
8687	2.04[1] n.45
8690	2.04[1] n.49
8691	2.04[1] n.49
8826	2.04[1] n.49
8888	2.04[1] n.49

INVESTMENT ADVISERS ACT

RELEASE NO.

33	2.05[2][c] n.137
77	3.02[2][c] n.84,
	3.02[2][g] n.123
88	3.02[2][c] n.86,
	3.02[2][g] n.129
214	4.01[2][a] n.28
223	3.02[2][d] n.102,
	3.02[2][g] n.129
315	3.02[2][d] n.108,
	3.02[2][g] n.131
316	3.02[2][d] n.108
327	3.02[2][d] n.108
332	3.02[2][c] ns.84, 92,
	3.02[2][d] n.101,
	5.03[2][c][i] n.150

392	3.02[1] n.15
397	1.02[2][b] n.73
436	10.05[1] n.244
442	3.03[1][c] n.195,
	3.03[2][a] n.215,
	4.01[2][a] n.43,
	4.03[1][b] ns.129, 131,
	7.05 n.94,
	9.02[3] n.64,
	9.03[2][b] n.99
470	2.05[2][b] n.132
471	2.05[2][b] n.133
478	2.04[2] n.66
482	3.02[1] n.30
503	2.04[2] n.66,
	2.05[2][c] n.137
563	2.05[2][a] n.118

SECURITIES ACT OF 1933

RELEASE NO.

3942	6.02[1] n.22
4122	5.03 n.60
4716	6.02[1] n.21
4936	7.05 n.92
5115	5.03 ns.62, 64,
	9.02[2] n.25
5211	3.03[1][a] n.142
5275	4.01[2] n.24,
	4.03[1][a][i] n.92
5318	3.02[2][b] n.69,
	5.03 n.64
5336	3.03[2] n.206,
	4.03[1][a][i] ns.107, 108,
	4.03[2][b] ns.191, 192
5347	3.03[1][a] n.143,
	3.03[1][b] n.164
5395	10.06[2] n.298,
	10.06[2][b] n.325
5398	10.06[2] n.298,
	10.06[2][b] n.325

[Matters that are the subject of combined releases appearing under the jurisdiction of more than one statute are ordinarily cited only by the first release number assigned.]

[References are to paragraphs (¶).]

SECURITIES EXCHANGE ACT OF 1934

RELEASE No.

[Matters that are the subject of combined releases appearing under the jurisdiction of more than one statute are ordinarily cited only by the first release number assigned.]

[References are to paragraphs (¶).]

9387 .... 3.03[2][b] n.225	11314 .... 3.02[2][g] n.133
9478 .... 5.03 ns.58, 59,	11324 .... 10.06[2][b] n.321
6.01 n.5,	11384 .... 10.06[2][b] n.321
7.07[1] n.143	11496 .... 1.02[2][c] n.75,
9598 .... 9.02[2] ns.32, 33,	3.02[1] n.30,
34, 35, 36	7.07[1] n.139
9623 .... 10.02[1][c][i] n.76	11515 .... 4.01[2][a] n.29,
9716 .... 10.02[1][c][i] n.77	4.03[1][a] n.86,
9761 .... 10.02[3] n.145	4.03[1][a][i] n.102
9950 .... 10.02[1][c][i] ns.69, 73,	11569 .... 7.07[1] n.140
78, 79, 83, 84, 85, 86,	11606 .... 10.06[2][b] n.321
10.02[1][c][ii] n.91,	11773 .... 8.02[2][b] n.51
10.02[2] n.136,	12055 .... 10.01 n.7,
10.05[1] n.251,	10.02[3] ns.143, 150, 152,
10.05[2] n.256	10.03[1] n.159
10102 .... 9.07 n.230	12251 .... 9.03[2][c] n.111,
10246 .... 9.05[1] n.146	9.04[1] n.112,
10260 .... 4.01[1] n.14,	9.06[2] ns.168, 172,
4.01[2] n.25,	9.06[3][d] ns.202, 210,
4.03[1][a][i] n.93	9.07[2] n.244
10316 .... 10.05[1] n.250	12319 .... 1.01[3][c] n.59,
10383 .... 8.02[3] n.74	2.03 n.37,
10439 .... 9.05[1] n.146	10.02[1][a] n.37,
10550 ...... 4.03[1][a][ii] n.105	10.06[2][a] n.316
10560 .... 8.02[3] n.74	13454 .... 10.06[2][b] n.322
10634 .... 10.02[3] n.148	
10670 .... 8.02[3] n.74	
10751 .... 8.02[3] n.74	**LITIGATION RELEASES**
10986 .... 8.02[4] n.79	
11019 .... 8.02[4] n.79	RELEASE NO.
11065 .... 10.06[1] n.278	4534 .... 2.04[1] n.50,
11072 .... 9.02[2] ns.36, 37	2.05[1] n.115,
11073 .... 8.02[3] n.74,	3.03[1][c] ns.177, 181,
8.02[4] n.79	3.03[2][b] n.233,
11098 .... 10.06[2] n.291,	3.04 n.239
10.06[2][a] n.309,	6269 .... 4.03[1][b][i] n.136,
10.06[2][b] n.331	7.07[1] n.140
11203 .... 8.02[3] ns.74, 75,	6640 .... 3.03[1][c] n.183
9.04[1] n.116,	6645 .... 3.02[2][b] n.60,
9.04[2] n.124	3.03[1][c] n.189,
11312 .... 1.02[2][b] n.74,	3.03[2][b] n.231
3.02[2][g] n.123,	7044 .... 3.02[2][g] n.133
6.02[1] n.23,	7057 .... 3.03[1][c] n.189,
7.05 n.94,	3.03[2][b] n.231
7.07[1] n.139	

TABLE OF
NO-ACTION LETTERS

[References are to paragraphs (¶).]

[References are to paragraphs (¶).]

TABLE OF CASES

[References are to paragraphs (¶).]

[References are to paragraphs (¶).]

[References are to paragraphs (¶).]

[*References are to paragraphs (¶).*]

[References are to paragraphs (¶).]

[References are to paragraphs (¶).]

[References are to paragraphs (¶).]

[References are to paragraphs (¶).]

[References are to paragraphs (¶).]

[References are to paragraphs (¶).]

[References are to paragraphs (¶).]

[References are to paragraphs (¶).]

[References are to paragraphs (¶).]

INDEX

[References are to paragraphs (¶).]

A

Advertising

See also Marketing investment management services

formula management services, 3.02[2][f]

managed accounts as securities because of, 3.03[2][b]

past recommendations, 3.02[2][c]

performance, 3.02[2][d]

special services, 3.02[2][e]

testimonials, 3.02[2][a]

Advisory fees. *See* Compensation

Affiliate

See also Broker-dealers; Investment companies

antecedents to Section 11(a), defined in, 10.02[1][c][iii] ns.111-114

"managed account" defined in H.R. 5050, 10.2[1][c][i] n.89

Prohibited Transaction Exemption 75-1, 10.03[3][a] n.179, 10.03[3][b] n.203

Rule 19b-2, 10.02[1][c][i] n.79

Agency law

See also Diversification; Duty of loyalty; Duty of reasonable care; Exculpatory clauses; Speculation; Suitability; Trust Law; Valuation

agency relationship defined, 2.02[2] n.14

agents

compensation, 2.02[2] ns.16-17

who may act as, 2.02[2] n.15

agent for another, manager acting as, 10.06[2][b] n.324

allocation of benefits among accounts, 9.03[2][a] n.94

co-fiduciaries, responsibility for, 5.02[3][b] n.41

commingling, 9.05[2] n.149, 9.06[4] n.223

compensation, reasonableness of, 5.03[1] n.67

consent

incapacity, 9.07[1] n.240

informed, 1.01[2] n.25, 9.07[1], 9.07[2] n.255

controlling an investment management relationship, as, 2.02

diversification, 5.02[3][c] n.49, 6.01 n.11, 6.02[4] n.67

duty of reasonable care, 6.01

generally, 2.02[2]

investment management, as applied to, 2.02

middleman and agent compared, 3.02[2][b] n.55

multiple accounts, transactions among, 9.05[2] n.150

overvaluation of assets, 5.03 n.65

portfolio, duty to make productive, 6.01 n.10

principal, manager acting as, 10.06[2][b] n.324

prudent-man rule, 6.01 n.3, 6.02[3] n.58

remedies, 2.02[2] n.22

speculate, duty not to, 6.01 n.8

subagent's negligence, agent's liability for, 5.02[3][a] n.38

suitability, 4.01[2][a] n.35, 4.01[2][b] n.49

unsuitable investments, duty to dispose of, 6.01 n.9

Agents. *See* Agency law

Allocation of benefits. *See* Best execution; Preferential treatment

American Bankers Association, 1.01[3][a] n.30

Antifraud provisions. *See* Federal securities laws

Artificial market

client accounts used for purpose

[References are to paragraphs (¶).]

Artificial market *(cont'd)*
of maintaining, 10.06[2]
ns.295, 298
Automatic Investment Services. *See*
Banks

B

Banks
See also Glass-Steagall Act;
Marketing investment
management services;
Options
accounts holdings, disclosure of,
1.01[2], 1.04 n.130, 2.05[1]
n.112
ancillary services to employee
benefit plans, prohibited
transaction exemption,
9.03[1] n.75
automatic investment services,
2.05[1] n.115
brokerage activities, 2.05[i] n.115,
10.02[1][c][ii] ns.90-92
congressional investigations,
10.02[2][c][ii] n.92
brokerage distribution,
commercial deposits,
1.01[3][b] n.43
bunching executions, 8.02[4]
ns.101, 104
"Chinese walls," 10.06[2][a]
n.308
collective trust funds
investment companies, as,
2.04[1] n.48
participantions as securities,
3.03[1][a] n.149
commercial activities, segregation
from trust activities, SEC
position, 10.06[2][a] n.314
commingled agency accounts,
3.03[2][a] ns.217-224
Investment Company
Amendments Act of 1970,
3.03[2][a] n.224
Comptroller's regulations,
private rights of action,
3.02[2] n.43
deposits of managed accounts in

commercial department,
1.03 ns.109-110, 6.02[3]
n.56
employee benefit plans, ancillary
services, 9.03[1] n. 75,
10.03[1] ns.176-177
fiduciary powers, regulation of,
2.05[1]
foreign trust companies as
investment advisers
2.05[2][c] n.135
indemnity bond, securities law
violation as covered by,
3.02[1] n.15
investment services, nontrust,
2.05[1] n.115
IRAs nonfiduciary banks,
2.05[1] n.102
marketing investment management
services, anti-fraud
provisions, application to,
3.02[1] ns.25-31
nonfiduciary banks, IRAs,
acceptance of, 2.05[1]
n.102
nontrust investment services,
2.05[1] n.115
options
suitability determination,
4.01[2] n.17
trust accounts, as investments
for, 4.03[1][a][i] n.96,
4.03[1][a][iii] n.116
performance incentives,
3.03[2][a] ns.221-222
private right of action,
Comptroller's regulations,
3.02[2] n.43
research services
large banks providing to small,
9.06[3][f] n.221
payment for by deposits,
9.06[3][f] n.221
rebates, 9.06[3][f] n.221
SEC, regulatory authority of,
over, 2.05[1] n.115
securities activities
congressional investigation,
10.02[2][c][ii] n.92

[References are to paragraphs (¶).]

[References are to paragraphs (¶).]

[References are to paragraphs (¶).]

[References are to paragraphs (¶).]

Distributions
disclosure, 10.06[2][b] ns.329, 336

Diversification
See also Agency law; Exculpatory clauses, Trust law
capital asset pricing model
many-investor world of certain values, 7.03[3][d]
strategy based on, 7.08
concentration
investment policy, 7.08 n.195
reduction of, 7.02[2]
covariance
analysis, practical limitations, 7.08 n.189
beta coefficient as substitute for, 7.08 n.190
principle, as expression of diversification, 7.08
damages for failure of, 6.02[4] n.74
debt instruments, 7.08 n.190
duty, origins of, 6.02[4] n.64
failure of, 6.01 n.14
foreign securities, 7.08 n.190
full portfolio perspective, 7.04[3][a] ns.55-57, 62
gold, 7.08 n.190
high-volatility stocks, 7.08 n.184
how determined, 1.02[2][a], 7.08
industries, among, 7.08 n.183
legislative definitions, 6.02[4] ns.71-72
modern portfolio theory, diversification as precursor to 7.04[3][a] ns.55-57
number of holdings necessary, 7.08 ns.185-187
options, 7.08 n.190
perfect diversification defined, 7.02[4]
performance, relation to, 7.01 n.5
private placements, 7.08 n.190
professional practice as setting standard, 6.02[4]
real estate, 7.08 n.190
single-investor world, 7.02[4]

systematic and unsystematic risk, relation to, 7.03[1]
unsystematic return, 7.08 n.192
volatility of component securities, effect of, 7.05[1][a]

Dumping
See also Duty of loyalty
artificial market, maintaining, 1.06[2] ns.295, 298
broker-dealers, 10.04 n.236
churning, relation to, 10.06[2] n.293
congressional studies, 10.02[1][a]
defined, 10.01 n.2
disclosure, 10.04 ns.237, 238
favored client, aid to, 10.06[2] n.294
generally, 1.03, 10.06[2]
individual investor accounts, 10.02[1][c][iii] n.108
institutional accounts, 10.02[1][c][iii] n.107
investment companies, 3.04 n.255
markdowns, 10.06[2] n.297
markups, 10.06[2] n.296
underwritings, 10.06[2] n.298
unsystematic return, 10.06[2] n.301

Duty of loyalty
See also Banks; Broker-Dealers; Churning; Commissions; Dumping; Investment management; Referrals; Trust law
account/manager ratios, 9.06[4]
activism of the courts, 1.01[3][b]
agent for another, manager acting as
generally, 10.06[2]
unsystematic return, 10.06[2] n.301
bank brokerage practices, 1.01[3][b] n.43
best net price, deliberate departure from, 8.03
breach, remedies, 1.01[1]
client-directed brokerage, 1.03
confidence of client, 1.04 n.127
conflict-of-interest resolution

[References are to paragraphs (¶).]

[References are to paragraphs (¶).]

[References are to paragraphs (¶).]

[References are to paragraphs (¶).]

[References are to paragraphs (¶).]

[References are to paragraphs (¶).]

[References are to paragraphs (¶).]

[References are to paragraphs (¶).]

[References are to paragraphs (¶).]

[References are to paragraphs (¶).]

[References are to paragraphs (¶).]

[References are to paragraphs (¶).]

[References are to paragraphs (¶).]

[References are to paragraphs (¶).]

[References are to paragraphs (¶).]

[References are to paragraphs (¶).]

[References are to paragraphs (¶).]

[*References are to paragraphs (¶).*]

[References are to paragraphs (¶).]

[References are to paragraphs (¶).]

[References are to paragraphs (¶).]

[References are to paragraphs (¶).]

[References are to paragraphs (¶).]

[References are to paragraphs (¶).]